SERMONS

by the

REV. SAMUEL DAVIES, A.M.

President of the College of New Jersey

with a

FUNERAL SERMON BY THE REV. SAMUEL FINLEY, D.D.,
His Successor in that Office,

And some account of President Davies, by the
Rev. Thomas Gibbon, D.D., of London, and
the Rev. David Bostwick, M.A., of New York

———————

Containing also
AN INTRODUCTORY MEMOIR OF PRESIDENT DAVIES
by the
Rev. William B. Sprague, D.D.

———————

In three volumes

Vol. 1.

Soli Deo Gloria Publications
...for instruction in righteousness...

Soli Deo Gloria Publications
Suite 2311, The Clark Building
717 Liberty Avenue
Pittsburgh, PA 15222
(412) 232-0866/FAX (412) 232-0867

*

Sermons of the Rev. Samuel Davies, A.M.
was last reprinted in 1854 in 3 volumes
by the Presbyterian Board of Publication.
This copy is courtesy of the Speer Library
at Princeton Theological Seminary.

*

This Soli Deo Gloria Reprint is 1993.

*

Volume 1 of
Sermons of the Rev. Samuel Davies, A.M.
ISBN 1-877611-67-0

Introduction to The Sermons of the Rev. Samuel Davies

by Howard Griffith, Pastor
All Saints Reformed Presbyterian Church,
Richmond, Virginia

It is a privilege to introduce the first reprinting of Samuel Davies' sermons in over one hundred years. As previous generations of Christians recognized, they are a precious heritage, bequeathed to us from the soul of a blessed ambassador of Christ. Dr. Martyn Lloyd-Jones, for example, called Samuel Davies America's greatest preacher! In his own age, Jonathan Edwards admired Davies. When Edwards was dismissed from his Northampton church, Davies sought his help in the revival in Virginia. A generation later, the first professor at Princeton Seminary, Archibald Alexander, named a son for Davies.

Davies died at thirty-seven years of age. His public ministry lasted only fourteen years. What a ministry it was! These sermons were used of God in the powerful revival known as the Great Awakening. Samuel Davies had come in 1748, while only in his twenties, to Hanover County, Virginia as an evangelist. God had already begun a great work of conversion there, and had widely created a hunger for the preaching of His Word (see W.H. Foote, Sketches of Virginia, 1850, reprinted 1866). Davies' preaching was well-received; he travelled to seven meeting places in six counties and preached with great energy and solemnity. Virginia was in turmoil over the interest which was growing in true religion (what we would call experiential Calvinism) and its relation to the state-established church of England. God used Davies' tact and mildness of temper to further the cause of vital doctrinal-experiential Christianity and its free exercise in a hostile environment. Unsympathetic governmental authorities were persuaded by his respectful carriage and powerful reasoning. Connections have been drawn between Davies' case before the governor of Virginia, the later declarations of Hanover Presbytery (which Davies founded) on religious freedom, and Thomas Jefferson's still later and famed Statute of Religious Freedom in Virginia. Patrick Henry, who heard him as a child, paid tribute to Davies as his standard for eloquence. Many hundreds of people, high-born and slave, heard Davies gladly.

With Gilbert Tennent, Davies became an ambassador of the Great Awakening in Great Britain, travelling there on behalf of Princeton College. He died, successor to Edwards, as president of Princeton in 1761. (For other important and interesting facts about his life and ministry, see E.T. Thompson's Presbyterians in the South, 1963, V. 1, and the Rev. Thomas T. Ellis, "Samuel Davies: Apostle of Virginia", Banner of Truth Magazine, Issues 235-6.)

Samuel Davies was a missionary. His ministry was spent largely in itineration over a vast area on horseback. The bulk of his sermons are evangelistic, though he takes up other themes also. The question might be raised, "Why should the twentieth-century man read eighteenth-century evangelistic sermons?" The reasons are many.

I suppose no one who believes the Reformed faith will find fault when I write that, in America at least, the late twentieth century is not an era of great evangelism. Mass evangelists and televangelists are plentiful. But few of these are able or willing to preach the saving gospel of the sovereign, discriminating grace of God. There is confusion over the nature of conversion, over the relationship between justification and sanctification, and over Christ's Saviorhood and Lordship.

INTRODUCTION

Among ministers and churches who subscribe to a Reformed Confession, the work of evangelism is largely considered to be the sole province of the private Christian, so that evangelistic <u>preaching</u>, as such, is rare indeed. When it *is* heard, often the distinctive elements of Calvinism are curiously absent, having been judged to be "extras," or "fine points" not fit for general consumption; useful, perhaps, for the mature Christian, but of no practical worth to the unbeliever, if not actual hindrances to the gospel.

By contrast, among the more hearty adherents of the Reformed Confessions, the doctrines of fallen man's total inablility, and Christ's definite atonement, sometimes (though rejoiced in for their tendency to exalt the grace of God), are felt to hinder the Reformed pastor in offering Christ <u>freely</u> to the man dead in sin. This is a great mistake, but not an infrequent one. Samuel Davies' sermons, I submit, offer remedies for these ills.

First, here is real evangelistic <u>preaching</u>: the authoritative proclamations of a messenger of the Lord of Glory. *How shall they believe in Him whom they have not heard? How shall they hear without a preacher?* (Romans 10:14). No sterile lecturing can be found in these pages. Certainly, Davies reasoned with his hearers. He answered their objections. (See his answers to rationalistic unbelief in "The Divine Authority and Sufficiency of the Christian Religion".) But, always, he deals with souls that can never die. He speaks to people in every spiritual condition. He exhorts, he persuades, he warns, he invites. Tender concern for his hearers is found on every page. And, in all, he expounds the Scriptures. Consider Davies' tender appeal to African slaves (with whom he had an extensive ministry). After quoting John's vision of heaven, Revelation 7:9, *a great multitude...out of every kindred and tongue and nation,* he says:

...multitudes from Europe, Asia, Africa, and America; and <u>yet there is room</u>... There is room for you, poor Negroes! ... You may, with peculiar propriety, be represented by the poor, the blind, the halt, the maimed, in the highways and the hedges. To you, therefore, I am sent with the offer of all the rich blessings of the gospel: and, let me tell you, you are in extreme need of them, whether you feel your want or not; you need them more than libery, than food, than health, than life itself; and without them you must perish forever. Come then, let this feast be adorned with your sable countenances, and furnished with guests from the savage wilds of Africa. Do not mistake me, as if I was just not inviting you to sit down at the Lord's Table: alas! many have sat there who are now banished forever from that Saviour, whom they professed to commemorate; and shut up in the prison of hell. But I am inviting you to accept of the blessings of the gospel... A hearty consent to this, and nothing short of it, will save you. Come then, ye poor Africans, and add yourselves as guests at this divine entertainment; for yet there is room for you, and you are as welcome as kings and princes. ("The Gospel Invitation")

Second, here is Calvinistic evangelism at its best. Samuel Davies was God-centered in his message. (Much of his spare time was spent in composing sacred verse to God. See his moving <u>Collected Poems of Samuel Davies, 1723-1761</u>, Richard B. Davis, ed., 1968.) Davies was honest and careful with the truth he preached. We are reminded of Calvin's dictum that Scripture is to be treated with the same reverence as is God Himself. This evangelist was unashamed of the biblical doctrine of the inability of fallen man to believe. *Unless a man is born from above, he cannot see the kingdom of God.* (John 3:3). He did not hide this from the unconverted:

I well know, and it is fit you should know, that you are not able of yourselves to consent to these terms, but that it is the work of the power of God alone to reconcile you to himself, and that all my persuasions and entreaties will never make you either able or willing. You will ask me then, perhaps, "Why do you then propose terms to us, or use persuasives or entreaties with us?" I answer, because you never will be sensible of your inability until you make an honest trial; and because you will never look and pray for the aid of the blessed Spirit till you are deeply sensible of your own insufficiency; and further, because if the blessed Spirit should ever effectually work on you, it will be by enlightening your understanding to see the reasonableness of the terms ...sweetly constraining your obstinate will to yield yourselves to God. ("Sinners Entreated to be Reconciled to God")

This great pastor's candor is bracing medicine in our age of preachers' equivocations.

There is no false dilemma between sovereign grace and the means of grace, either. Samuel Davies both offered Christ to the lost and directed the unbelieving to seek sovereign grace with the natural (not spiritual) ability they had.

Third, Davies preached the marks of conversion clearly. He knew the ravages and deceit of sin in his own soul, as well as the holy workings of God's free Spirit there. See "The Divine Mercy to Mourning Penitents."

Fourth, while exalting the sovereignty of God in salvation, Davies also exalted the freeness of grace. Here, he can help us. For too frequently we set the mystery of the Spirit's freedom over against a free offer of Christ to sinners. Davies had no such antithesis. He presses the lost with their duty to come to Christ without delay.

INTRODUCTION

<u>The mercy of God endureth forever</u>. It is an inexhaustible ocean, sufficient to overwhelm and drown a world of the most mountainous sins, and supply the most numerous and desperate necessities... O my guilty brethren! Come, publicans and sinners, drunkards, harlots and thieves; come sinners of the vilest characters, <u>repent and believe the gospel</u>, you shall be admitted to the heavenly feast. Oh! Must it not break the heart of the hardest sinner among you, to hear that, after all your aggravated and long-continued provocations, and notwithstanding your enormous guilt, that great God whom you have offended, though he stands in no need of you, and might easily glorify himself by inflicting righteous punishment upon you, yet is ready to wash away all your sins... why should you not all comply? Why should any of you exclude yourselves? ("The Gospel Invitation")

It is no easy business to preach free and sovereign grace. Samuel Davies shows us how. Almighty God was pleased to glorify His grace and power by saving hundreds through these sermons. Should they not be a school for us? Perhaps God will teach a new generation of ministers to preach the gospel of His Son through this reprinting. May He soon give us another Awakening of hunger for that gospel and the glories of His Christ, whom Davies preached.

Great God of Wonders!
All Thy ways are matchless,
Godlike, and Divine...
Who is a pard'ning God, like Thee?
Or who has grace so rich and free?

CONTENTS

OF

VOLUME I.

SERMON I.

THE DIVINE AUTHORITY AND SUFFICIENCY OF THE CHRISTIAN RELIGION.

LUKE XVI. 27–31.—Then he said, I pray thee, therefore, father, that thou wouldest send him to my father's house: for I have five brethren; that he may testify unto them, lest they also come into this place of torment. Abraham saith unto him, They have Moses and the prophets; let them hear them. And he said, Nay, father Abraham: but if one went unto them from the dead, they will repent. And he said unto him, If they hear not Moses and the prophets, neither will they be persuaded though one rose from the dead. 71

SERMON II.

THE NATURE OF SALVATION THROUGH JESUS CHRIST EXPLAINED AND RECOMMENDED.

JOHN III. 16.—For God so loved the world, that he gave his only begotten Son, that whosoever believeth in him, should not perish, but have everlasting life. 109

4 CONTENTS.

CONTENTS.

PREFACE

TO THE

FIRST LONDON EDITION.

It is with real pleasure I now send into the world a collection of Sermons, by that eminent and amiable man, and my most esteemed and beloved friend, the Rev. Mr. Samuel Davies. I hope I may be the honoured instrument of promoting the great interests of vital evangelical godliness, by communicating to the public a number of Discourses, which appear to me admirably calculated to increase the knowledge and power of real religion in the minds and hearts of men.

Those who knew and heard Mr. Davies will need no further proof than the perusal of the discourses themselves, that they are the real productions of the author to whom they are ascribed. The sun shows himself to be the sun by the very beams with which he irradiates and enlivens mankind, and is easily distinguished from other luminaries by his surpassing lustre. 　　＊　　＊　　＊　　＊　　＊

I most sincerely wish that young ministers more especially would peruse these volumes with the deepest attention and seriousness, and endeavour, in conjunction with earnest prayer for divine illumination and assistance, to form their discourses according to the model of our author; in which, if I mistake not, are the following excellences, most worthy of imitation:

A calm and elaborate inquiry into the connection of those passages of Scripture which he chooses for his subjects, and a close investigation, when it appeared necessary, into the meaning of his text by researches into the original language, and fair and learned criticism; a careful attention to the portions of sacred writ upon which he proposes to treat, so that his discourse as naturally arises from his theme as the branch grows from the root, or the stream issues from the fountain. In every page, and almost every line of Mr. Davies' sermons, his readers may discover the subject he at first professed to handle ; and he is ever illustrating, proving, or enforcing some truth or another evidently contained in it; a reigning regard to the divine word by comparing and confirming Scripture by Scripture, by taking the sacred text in its easy and natural sense, and by apt and pertinent citations of passages from holy writ, both in the proof and amplification ; at the same time that our author by no means omits a regard to the dictates of natural conscience and reason, while he either makes his appeal to them, or introduces passages from Pagan antiquity on proper occasions, and to answer some valuable purposes; an observance of method and order, so as to proceed, like a wise builder, in laying the foundation, and regularly erecting the superstructure, and yet diversifying his method and order, by making them at some times open and express, and at other times indirect and implicit; a free, manly diction, without anything of a nice and affected accuracy, or a loud sounding torrent of almost unintelligible words on the one side, or a loose negligence, or mean and low-creeping phrases, unworthy an admission into the pulpit, on the other ; a rich vein of evangelical doctrine and promise, with a large infusion at proper seasons of practical duty, or awful denunciation of the divine wrath against impenitent and incorrigible sinners ; an impartial regard to the cases of all his hearers, like a good steward distributing to all their portion of meat in due season ; animated and pathetic application, in which our author collects and concentrates what he has been proving in his discourses, and urges it with all the powers of forcible address and melting persuasion to the heart.

Such appear to me to be the excellences of Mr. Davies' Sermons. May young ministers more particularly copy them with divine success, and be, like him, "burning and shining lights" in their several stations, till, having guided and animated their respective charges in the way to heaven, they and their people may at last "shine forth, like the sun, in the kingdom of their father."

Such are the sincere prayers of the editor,

THOMAS GIBBONS.

Hoxton-Square, October 21, 1770.

MEMOIR OF PRESIDENT DAVIES.

By the Rev. William B. Sprague, D.D.

SAMUEL DAVIES was born near Summit Ridge, in the county of Newcastle, Delaware, on the 3d of November, 1723. Both his parents were of Welsh extraction. His father was a farmer of very simple habits, of great integrity, and of well accredited Christian character. His mother was distinguished not only for fine intellectual endowments, but for deep spirituality and intense devotion to the cause of Christ; and this son is said to have been given her in answer to special prayer, in token of which she named him *Samuel*, as she solemnly devoted him to the Lord. The father died two years before the son; the mother survived him for a long period, and was an inmate of the family of the Rev. Dr. John Rodgers, of New York.

This child, thus dedicated in his infancy to the service of Christ and his Church, by parental faith, was early cared for, in all his intellectual, moral, and spiritual interests, in the best manner that the circumstances permitted. As there was no school in the neighbourhood, he received the rudiments of his education under the teaching of his mother; and though, during the years of his early boyhood, he evinced the usual vivacity and sprightliness incident to that period, he was, by no means, unaffected by his mother's pious counsels and instructions. At the age of ten, he was sent to an English school, at some distance from home, where he remained two years; and during this period made rapid progress in his studies, though at the expense of losing, in a measure, the religious impressions which a mother's watchful and devoted attentions had made upon him. He, however, still continued the habit of secret prayer, and cherished the purpose of

11

devoting himself to the Christian ministry. At the age of twelve, his impressions were greatly revived and strengthened, and there is reason to believe that, at this time, if not before, he became a subject of renewing grace. He did not, however, make a public profession of his faith until he had reached his fifteenth year. The subject of religion now became with him all-engrossing: while he enjoyed, in a high degree, the comforts of a good hope through grace, he scrutinized the motives and principles of his own conduct with the utmost care, and met the temptations of the world with an heroic resistance that would not have dishonoured the most advanced Christian.

Having the ministry now distinctly in his eye, he prosecuted his studies with renewed vigour, and made rapid progress in every department of knowledge to which he directed his attention. He commenced his classical course under the instruction of the Rev. Abel Morgan, a highly respectable Welsh minister, of the Baptist denomination; but when the Rev. Samuel Blair opened his famous school at Fagg's Manor, Chester county, Pa., he was transferred to that school, where he remained till both his classical and theological education was completed. The instruction here was most thorough, and the religious atmosphere most healthful; so that while young Davies was making rapid improvement in the various branches of human learning, as well as becoming a proficient in speculative theology, he was also steadily growing in grace, and rising into a nearer conformity to that Master to whom he had devoted himself. So intense was his application to study that, by the time his course in the institution was completed, his health, which was at best frail, had become quite seriously impaired. Having sustained his several preparatory trials in a most creditable manner, he was licensed to preach the Gospel, by the Presbytery of Newcastle, on the 30th of July, 1746. On the 23d of October following, he was married to Sarah Kirkpatrick.

On the 19th of February, 1747, he was ordained as an Evangelist, with a view to his visiting certain congregations in Hanover county, Va., whence he had received aid in his preparatory studies. His mission into that region was regarded as one of great delicacy and difficulty, especially in view of the fact that civil suits had already been instituted, and were then pending, against several clergymen, for holding religious worship in a manner not sanctioned by the laws of the Province; a matter in relation to which the public mind was then deeply agitated. Mr. Davies hesitated, partly on account of his inexperience in the ministry, and his want of familiarity with ecclesiastical rules and usages, and partly on account of his feeble health, to undertake the mission; but the remarkable powers he had developed, in connection with the very decidedly favourable impression which his preaching had made while he was a probationer, seemed to point him out as better fitted than any one else to occupy that difficult field.

In due time, Mr. Davies set out for Virginia, and, before going to his appointed field of labour, repaired to Williamsburg, to obtain from the General Court a license to officiate at four meeting-houses in and about Hanover. The Governor favoured the application, and, through his influence, the following license was obtained from the General Court, dated April 14, 1767 :—

"On the petition of Samuel Davies, a Dissenting minister, who, this day, in Court, took the usual oaths to His Majesty's person and government, and subscribed the Test, and likewise publicly declared his assent thereunto, he is allowed to assemble and meet any congregations of Dissenters at the several meeting-houses on the lands of Samuel Morris, David Rice, and Stephen Leacy, in Hanover County, and on the lands of Thomas Watkins, in Henrico County, without molestation, they behaving in a peaceable manner, and conforming themselves according to the directions of the Acts of Parliament in that behalf made."

While the trials of those who had been prosecuted for worshipping God contrary to law were still in progress, Mr. Davies proceeded to Hanover with his license in his pocket; and when the people knew under what circumstances he had come to them, they were ready to welcome him as an angel of mercy. His preaching was listened to on every side with profound attention and admiration; combining, as it did, the highest graces of rhetoric and elocution with the most luminous, simple, and forcible exhibition of divine truth. He laboured in Hanover and several adjacent counties not far from four months; and wherever he preached, a desire was expressed that his labours might be permanently secured. When the allotted time for his mission had expired, he returned to his friends at the North, but not till he had received the most importunate requests to come back and make Virginia his home. Indeed, he had no sooner taken his leave of them, than they made out a regular call for him, and sent it to the Presbytery.

Scarcely had he returned to Delaware, when he met with a sore affliction in the sudden death of his wife. The shock materially affected his health; his hectic tendencies, which had before developed themselves to some extent, now became more decided; and he was fully impressed with the conviction that the time of his departure was at hand. But this only seemed to quicken his zeal to labour to the utmost while the day should last; and hence, after preaching in the day-time, he would sometimes at night find himself with a burning fever which would bring on delirium, requiring one or more persons to sit up with him. Being unable to take charge of a congregation while in this feeble state, he travelled, as he was able, from one vacancy to another, preaching to the extent of his ability, and rendering himself everywhere an object of the highest interest. In the spring of 1748, there was considerable alleviation of his malady, though he himself regarded it as only temporary, and fully expected that the disease would have a fatal termination. Many earnest applications were made for his pastoral services; and the call from Virginia was renewed, signed by about one hundred and fifty heads of families, and urged with great importunity by the person who was appointed to present it. Of his own feelings in view of this call, he has left the following record :—" Upon the arrival of a messenger from Hanover, I put my life in my hand, and determined to accept their call, hoping I might live to prepare the way for some more useful successor, and willing to expire under the fatigues of duty, rather than in voluntary negligence." No man could have been better fitted than he to occupy the field to which he was now called. While the people were suffering manifold difficulties from the enforcement of the unrighteous laws of the Province, in the form of indictments, fines and costs of Court, the ears of many of them were open to receive the truth from his lips; and he, in turn, feeling that his time for active service was short, and that the demand for evangelical labour in the region around him was most urgent, addressed himself to his work with a strength of purpose and a simple dependence on Divine aid, that gave a mighty power to his ministrations.

On this, his second journey to Virginia, Mr. Davies was accompanied by his friend, the Rev. John Rodgers, (afterwards Dr. Rodgers, of New York,) who had been a fellow-student with him, under the Rev. Samuel Blair, at Fagg's Manor. They had become strongly attached to each other during the period of their education, and, under the same influences, had imbibed, in a high degree, the same spirit—both were glowing with love to the Saviour and the cause for which he died. It was at Mr. Davies' earnest request that the Presbytery appointed Mr. Rodgers to perform a few months' missionary labour in Virginia—that thus these two might become, for the time, not only companions, but fellow-helpers. They commenced their journey to Virginia, in April, 1748, and went directly to Hanover, when, after passing a Sabbath, and each of them preaching a sermon, they proceeded to Williamsburg, to procure for Mr. Rodgers a license to preach in the Province. In this, however, they were unsuccessful; for though the Governor (Gooch) strongly favoured the application, and did his utmost to have the license granted, the decision of the majority of the Council was adverse to it, and thus the young missionary was obliged to look out for another field of labour. Accordingly, before the close of May, he had taken leave of his friend Davies, crossed the Chesapeake Bay, and, after stopping for a while on the eastern shore of Maryland, finally settled as pastor of the church of St. George's, in Delaware.

The high motives which controlled Mr. Davies in the selection of his field of labour may be inferred from the following extract from a letter addressed by him to the Bishop of London, in whose diocese Virginia was reckoned, under date of January 10, 1752, nearly four years after his ministry in Hanover commenced:

"I solemnly assure your Lordship that it was not the secret thirst of filthy lucre, nor the prospect of any other personal advantage, that induced me to settle here in Virginia. For sundry congregations in Pennsylvania, my native country, and in other Northern colonies, most earnestly importuned me to settle among them; where I should have had at least an equal temporal maintenance, incomparably more ease, leisure, and peace, and the happiness of the frequent society of my brethren; and where I should never have made a great noise or bustle in the world, but concealed myself in the crowd of my superior brethren, and spent my life in some little service for God and his Church in some peaceful corner, which would have been most becoming so insignificant a creature, and more agreeable to my recluse natural temper. But all these strong inducements were overweighed by a sense of the necessities of the Dissenters, as they lay two or three hundred miles distant from the nearest minister of their own denomination, and laboured under peculiar embarrassments for the want of a settled ministry."

In the summer of 1748, Mr. Davies' preaching attracted great attention, and many more demands were made for his public services than he was able to meet. In order to avoid all collisions with the public authorities, who were resolutely determined to execute the laws in favour of the English Church, various petitions were presented to the General Court for an increased number of authorized houses of worship. Accordingly, three additional places of preaching were licensed, thus making seven in all, namely, three in Hanover, one in Henrico, one in Goochland, one in Louisa, and one in Caroline county. Of these he says in his letter to the Bishop of London :—"The nearest are twelve or fifteen miles apart, and many of the people have ten, fifteen, or twenty miles to the nearest, and thirty, forty, or sixty miles to the rest; nay, some of them have thirty or forty miles to the nearest."

On the 4th of October, 1748, Mr. Davies formed a second matrimonial connection with Miss Jane Holt, of Hanover. She was a lady of great excellence, became the mother of six children, and survived her husband many years. His residence at this time was about twelve miles from Richmond, in the neighbourhood of the meeting-house near what is known as "Morris' Reading House." The edifice, which accommodated about five hundred people, was quite too small for the multitude that thronged to hear him preach; the consequence of which was that they were obliged often to hold their services in an adjoining forest.

Though Mr. Davies had little difficulty in getting the sanction of the public authorities to his occupying so wide a field of labour, he was subsequently brought into collision with Peyton Randolph, the King's Attorney General, on the question whether the Act of Toleration which had been passed in England expressly for the relief of Protestant Dissenters, extended also to Virginia. That this was the design of the Act, he maintained, in the presence of the General Court, with such force of argument and eloquence, as to awaken the admiration even of those who were most hostile to the position he defended; and it was no small gratification to him, on his subsequent visit to England, to have his own views on this subject fully endorsed by the King in Council.

Mr. Davies, besides occupying seven different places for preaching, and taking frequent journeys to attend the judicatories of the Church, made many missionary excursions in the parts of the country now forming the counties of Cumberland, Powhatan, Prince Edward, Charlotte, Campbell, Nottoway, and Amelia. In performing these circuits, he was accustomed either to preach at the places where he lodged, or to address the family and servants in respect to their immortal interests, at evening worship. These services were often attended with a special blessing; and each successive tour that he made, brought some new requests for Presbyterian preaching. He was also deeply concerned for the spiritual interests of the coloured people labouring among them with the utmost condescension and faithfulness, and bringing not a few of them to the acknowledgment and obedience of the truth. And, to crown all, he not only laboured earnestly to supply the vacancies around him with ministers from the Northern Presbyteries, but inaugurated a system of measures for providing ministers for Virginia from among her own youth. He did not, however, desire that their education should be completed under his own direction, but encouraged them ultimately to seek the higher advantages which were furnished by the College of New Jersey.

As early as September, 1751, a petition was presented to the Synod of New York by the Trustees of the College of New Jersey, that the Rev. Ebenezer Pemberton, of New York, might be commissioned to visit Great Britain with a view to solicit donations in behalf of the then infant College. A committee was appointed to confer with Mr. Pemberton on the subject; but he persistently declined to listen to their proposals. The next year, by direction of Synod, collections were taken for the object in different congregations within their bounds, but the result was not, by any means, adequate to the exigency; in consequence of which, in the next following year, the plan of sending a commission abroad was resumed by the Synod, and Messrs. Gilbert Tennent and Samuel Davies were designated to this service.

The necessary preparations for the voyage having been made, these two brethren embarked in a vessel, bound to London, on the 7th of November, 1753, and were safely landed at the place of their destination on the 25th of December following. The two kept together until they had reached Edinburg; but there they parted,—Mr. Tennent to visit Glasgow, and then pass into Ireland;—Mr. Davies to visit the principal cities and towns in England. After having accomplished the object of their mission, they met again in London, in October, 1754. The next month Mr. Tennent sailed for Philadelphia, and Mr. Davies for York, in Virginia, where, after a protracted and unpleasant voyage, he arrived on the 13th of February, 1755.

This mission was probably the most successful and the most important ever made from the colonies to the mother country. A much larger sum of money was contributed than the most sanguine had ventured to hope for; in addition to which a large measure of public sympathy was awakened in behalf of the Dissenters in Virginia, as well as a greatly increased interest for the Christianizing of the American Indians. Mr. Davies every where commanded the highest respect, not only for his great powers of pulpit eloquence, in which he was justly considered as well nigh unrivalled, but for his fine social qualities and eminent Christian character. His manuscript journal, which he kept during this period, was preserved in two volumes, which, by some means, were separated from each other, the one having found its place of deposit in the library of the Union Theological Seminary, in Virginia, the other in the library of Princeton College,— both, however, have been published by Dr. Foot, in his "Sketches of Virginia." From this journal it appears that Mr. Davies made the acquaintance of a large part of the more distinguished of the English Dissenting clergy, and his observations upon them—of course the result of a brief acquaintance—are in remarkable harmony with the united testimony of tradition and history concerning them.

The following anecdote in connection with President Davies' visit to London has appeared in a memoir of his life, prefixed to one of the editions of his sermons, and has been republished in several newspapers:—

So great was his fame in London as an eloquent preacher, that certain noblemen who had heard him, spoke of him as one of the wonders of the day, in the presence of George II.; whereupon the King directed his chaplain to invite Davis to preach in his chapel. The invitation being given and accepted, the American minister, in due time appeared and preached before a splendid audience, consisting of the royal family and many of the nobility. While the sermon was being delivered, the preacher observed the King frequently whispering to those who sat near him, causing them to smile. Davies, by way of rebuking this irreverent behaviour, frowned and looked sternly towards the King, and then proceeded with his discourse. The offense was very soon repeated; whereupon the American Dissenter exclaimed,—" When the lion roars, all the beasts of the forest tremble : when King Jesus speaks, the kings of the earth should keep silent." The King bowed courteously, and remained silent till the service was closed. It afterwards appeared that the apparent disrespect of the King was the result of his high admiration of the eloquence to which he was listening;—that he was so much delighted that he could not avoid expressing his high gratification to those who were near him. The result was that the King sent for Davies to visit him; that they had several interesting interviews; and that His Majesty, as an evidence of his regard, made a liberal donation to the college.

The Rev. Dr. Carnahan, late President of the College of New Jersey, in a communication made to the New Jersey Historical Society, in 1848, proves conclusively that this story must be apocryphal; first, from the fact that in a most minute journal which Davies kept of this tour, descending to the details of each day's experience, (which is still extant,) there is no allusion to any one of the alleged facts which the anecdote includes; and secondly, from the fact that Dr. Gibbons and Dr. Finley, and Mr. Bostwick, and all the other of his contemporaries who have written concerning him, are entirely silent in respect to any such occurrence—an omission which can hardly be supposed if so striking an event had really taken place. The story is believed to have been originated by an agent employed in the Southern States, half a century ago, in selling an edition of Davies' sermons.

Mr. Davies, on his return to his people, found them and the whole country in the midst of the most violent agitation, occasioned by the French and Indian war. On the 10th of July, 1755, occurred Braddock's remarkable defeat, when the brave young Colonel Washington won for himself such imperishable laurels by saving the remnant of the army; and on the 20th of the same month, Mr. Davies preached a sermon in Hanover, on the words—" And in that day did the Lord God of hosts call to weeping, and to mourning, and to baldness, and to girding with sackcloth ; and behold joy and gladness, slaying oxen and killing sheep, eating flesh and drinking wine : let us eat and

drink, for to-morrow we shall die. (Isa. xxii. 12, 13, 14.)*   In this sermon he showed the highest type of patriotism in connection with the
most earnest and glowing piety, and called upon his hearers, in a strain
of fervid eloquence, from a regard to their interests as men, Britons,
and Christians, to make a noble stand against the cruel invasion.
Serious apprehensions were entertained that the negroes would become
the allies of the French and Indians, and Mr. Davies, whose influence
with the blacks was probably greater than that of any other person,
exerted himself to the utmost to prevent such a coalition.   On the
17th of August of the same year, he preached another thrilling sermon suited to the times, to the first volunteer company raised in Virginia, after Braddock's defeat, on 2 Samuel x. 12 : " Be of good
courage, and let us play the men for our people, and for the cities of our
God ; and the Lord do that which seemeth him good."†   In a note to
this eloquent discourse occurs this remarkable, and, as it proved, truly
prophetic sentence—"I may point out to the public that heroic youth,
Colonel Washington, whom I cannot but hope Providence has hitherto
preserved in so signal a manner, for some important service."   In
May, 1758, he preached another war sermon, on occasion of raising a
company of volunteers for Captain Meredith ; and the effect of the following passage is said to have been quite overwhelming :—" May I
not reasonably insist upon it that the company be made up this very
day before we leave this place.   Methinks your King, your country,
nay, your own interests, command me ; and therefore I insist upon it.
Oh, for the all-pervading force of Demosthenes' oratory—but I recall
my wish, that I may correct it—oh, for the influence of the Lord of
armies, the God of battles, the Author of true courage and every
heroic virtue, to fire you into patriots and true soldiers this moment !
Ye young and hardy men, whose very faces seem to speak that God
and nature formed you for soldiers, who are free from the incumbrance
of families depending upon you for subsistence, and who are perhaps
but of little service to society while at home, may I not speak for you
and declare at your mouth—here we are, all ready to abandon our
ease, and rush into the glorious dangers of the field, in defence of our
country ?   Ye that love your country, enlist; for honour will follow
you in life or death in such a cause.   You that love your religion,

* Sermon No. LXIX, in this edition of his works.
† Sermon No. LXI.

enlist ; for your religion is in danger. Can Protestant Christianity expect quarters from heathen savages and French papists ? Sure, in such an alliance the powers of hell make a third party. Ye that love your friends and relations, enlist; lest ye see them enslaved and butchered before your eyes." Such was the effect of the discourse that, within a few minutes after its delivery, the company was made up ; and even more offered their services than the captain was authorized to accept.*

But while Mr. Davies was so intensely interested for the cause of his country, and stood ready to identify himself with every effort for the vigorous prosecution of the war in defence of both their civil and Christian rights, his zeal for the spiritual welfare of his own flock never even seemed to wane—not only was he intent on preaching the Gospel within his own immediate sphere, which was very extended, but he was prompt to obey any summons that should carry him abroad, and had more to do with the formation of new churches and the settlement of ministers over them, than any other minister in the colony. Indeed he was, by universal consent, the master spirit of the Presbyterian Church throughout that region ; and probably in no part of the Church was there another minister who combined so many elements of a controlling and well-nigh irresistible influence.

But the time had now come when Mr. Davies was to be called to another, and in some respects a more prominent position. On the 16th of August, 1758, he was chosen to succeed Jonathan Edwards as President of the College of New Jersey. The question of his removal was immediately submitted to the Presbytery of Hanover, and was decided in the negative. A letter which he addressed to the Trustees of the College, dated October 17, 1758, contains a decided answer to a renewed request from Princeton, and shows an earnest wish to have

* It is impossible to tell how far the decisive action which was taken by the House of Burgesses of Virginia at the commencement of the Revolution, may have been brought about by the influence of Mr. Davies' opinions and eloquence in that colony. But it is well known that from the eleventh to the twenty-second year of his age, Patrick Henry heard the patriotic sermons of Davies delivered, and was his enthusiastic admirer. It has been asserted, and it was very probably true, that Davies afforded the model and kindled the fire of Henry's eloquence.

[EDITOR OF THE BOARD.]

the whole subject dismissed. Though the communication is some-what long, I think proper to introduce it in this connection, partly because I am not aware that it has ever been published, and partly because it brings out very impressively some of the prominent features in Mr. Davies' character. The letter is as follows :—

GENTLEMEN :—

I encouraged myself and my friends in Virginia, that my last answer, and the judgment of the Presbytery, would have been received as a final decision ; and that my perplexities would have no more been renewed by another application. And if, from my warm declaration of my zeal "to serve the college," my candid friend, Mr. Smith, inferred, and therefore reported to you, that I thought my way clear to serve it in the character of a President, either the incautious and vague form of expressing myself, or the generous partiality of his friendship for me, tempted him to put a construction upon my words that I by no means intended. I assure you, gentlemen, I do not desire the compliment of repeated entreaties to accept the honour the Trustees have been pleased to confer upon me ; but my hesitation, my delays and anxious inquiries, have been entirely owing to my sincere desire to discover my duty, and secure the approbation of my con-science in accepting or rejecting the proposal : and in this view, I hope the Trustees will excuse, or at least forgive me the trouble I have involuntarily occasioned them, which affords me more concern, I dare say, than to any of them.

Upon Mr. Halsey's unexpected arrival, I sent to consult those mem-bers of Presbytery who had formed the former judgment ; and I also made such inquiries of him, as I thought necessary to give me a fair and full view of the matter, and constrained him to be unreserved and open-hearted. I have already received the answer of two leading members of the Presbytery ; and as I expect that those of the rest will generally coincide with theirs ; and as I am called abroad and may not have leisure to write, when that comes to hand ; I venture to send you my final answer now, founded upon the best intelligence I can receive. And as I have honestly endeavoured to discover my duty, with all the impartiality and integrity I am capable of, I am encour-aged to hope, a gracious God will not suffer me to mistake it ; and therefore my former anxieties are subsided, and my mind has recovered that sacred calm which is the attendant of a full conviction.

My final answer then is, that in present circumstances, my way is not at all clear to accept the presidentship, or even to serve in that character *pro tempore* till the Synod ; and therefore I desire the Trustees would proceed to the choice of another, and have no more dependence upon me.

As this answer, gentlemen, may be somewhat unexpected, and as I give it in more decisive terms than I could safely use in my former, you may justly demand the reasons of it ; and they are such as these.

Though, to my great surprise, my reverend brethren and other friends in Virginia, have no objections to the offer upon the footing of my insufficiency, which is one of my chief objections ; yet, they apprehend I am of so much importance in my present situation, to the interests of religion, and the liberty and honour of the Dissenters of this colony, so exposed to the oppression of high-flyers, by the influence I have somehow acquired with the great men here, and my correspondence in Great Britain, that I can by no means be spared from Virginia ; and that the injury would be so great and irreparable here, that, if the College should even suffer by my non-compliance, it would be the lesser evil, and consequently rather to be chosen. It is with an ill grace these extravagant panegyrics upon myself come from my pen : but I transcribe them in the most modest language from their letters ; and I cannot avoid it if I would give you a full view of the case.

But here I must be so impartial as to add, that the Presbytery would acquiesce in my judgment, even if I should determine to remove, and have desired me to judge for myself. But I put more confidence in their judgment than my own, in so dubious a case ; and can by no means venture in opposition to it, though they give it with diffidence and hesitation.

Another reason of my refusal is, that the vote for me was not at all unanimous, and carried but by a very small majority ; that sundry of the Trustees, who are good judges of merit, and well acquainted with me, look upon me as unfit for the place ; and I am not capable of such gross self-flattery, as to dissent from them in this ; nor do I make the estimate they form of me, the standard of their worth or of my affection for them. I cannot bear the thought of thrusting myself in, though by a fair and honourable election, in opposition to gentlemen whom I do highly revere, and cannot bear to offend : and as I am a lover of peace, and never was formed to be a fire-brand of contention,

I cannot offer such violence to myself, nor do the college so great an injury, as to enter as an incendiary, to cast it into a conflagration, which could not be easily quenched, and which would soon melt away my tender, unmanly spirit. I have good authority, I think, for this, from speaking circumstances, or authentic information; but I beg you would not suspect Mr. Halsey has betrayed his trust; or that any one of the Trustees has wrote to dissuade me. Mr. Halsey has acquitted himself like an honest man; and the college is obliged to him for a faithful, artless representation. Not one of the Trustees that voted against me has either directly or indirectly, as far as I know, wrote to me, or any one in Virginia, to throw any obstacle in my way. But I have credible, well-informed correspondents, that do not belong to your honourable Board, in whom I can place the utmost confidence, and when the case is so intricate, that I have hardly any judgment of my own, I think it my duty even implicitly to act upon that of others.

But the principal reason of my refusal is, that as, from a very thorough and long acquaintance with my worthy rival, Mr. Finley, I believe, in my conscience, without the least ostentatious affectation of humility, he is incomparably better qualified for the place than I am, or ever expect to be, I cannot bear the thought of thrusting myself into the seat, to the exclusion of him who, I am persuaded, will fill it with dignity, and to the universal satisfaction of all candid judges of real worth, when fully tried and known. And whenever I have had any thought of accepting the invitation, it has always been upon the supposition that the Trustees to whom I have no right or inclination to prescribe, would not in general, think as I do; and, consequently that he would not be chosen, even if I should refuse. But as it now appears to me, there is at least a great probability that Mr. Finley will be chosen, I think myself bound in conscience to give up my election in his favour; and with all the force of persuasion and entreaty I can use to transfer to him whatever interest I may have obtained among the Trustees by the generous excess of their charity.

If my officiating in the college as Vice President for some months would be of any service to it, I would cheerfully comply, notwithstanding the mutual bereavement I and my helpless family would suffer by it. But since the way is not clear for my accepting the place as stated President; since the judgment of the Presbytery lies in my way; and it is not unlikely the Synod would confirm their judgment;

I apprehend it would answer no valuable end. But, on the other hand, it might be productive of sundry bad consequences; particularly, it would keep the college still longer in an unsettled state; and tempt some to suspect I have an eager ambition to accept the place; and I could give no umbrage for such a prodigious mistake.

I may venture to refer you to my honest and learned friend, Mr. Halsey, as well as to your former messenger, to attest the caution and impartiality with which I have proceeded in the whole matter. And could I communicate for a moment the sensations of my mind into yours, you would never impute my refusal to the want of affectionate zeal and concern for the College, or an ungrateful contempt or insensibility of the immerited honour the Trustees have done me.

I beg you would make my most dutiful compliments acceptable to His Excellency your Governor, for whom I have a very high veneration as a patron of virtue, liberty, and learning. I congratulate you and the College on the happiness of being under his administration, and pray God long to continue the blessing.

I present my affectionate compliments also to the whole Board of Trustees promiscuously, whether my electors or not. I am obliged to the former for their friendship for me: and I must value the latter for their better judgment in this instance, and the prevalence of public spirit over private friendship.

With a heart full of gratitude and love to you in particular, I am, gentlemen,

Your most obliged and most humble servant,

SAM'L DAVIES.

HANOVER, Oct. 18, 1758.

So deeply were the Trustees of the College impressed with the idea that Mr. Davies was the man for the place above any other within their reach, that notwithstanding the above letter, and the adverse decision of Presbytery already rendered, they brought the subject before the Synod of New York and Philadelphia, at its meeting in May, 1759, earnestly requesting that he might be liberated from his pastoral charge, with a view to being placed at the head of the College. Though this application met with a strong remonstrance from his congregation, so deeply was the Synod impressed with a sense of the importance of the institution, and of his rare qualifications for the presidential chair, that they reached the conclusion that the best inter-

ests of the church required that he should be transferred to Princeton; and, accordingly, his pastoral relation was dissolved.   He
deferred to the judgment of Synod in the matter, and preached his farewell sermon on the 1st of July following, from 2 Cor. xiii. 11. " Finally,
brethren, farewell," &c. *   In this sermon, while he expresses the
warmest regard for his people, and the deepest sorrow at the thought
of being separated from them, he details the circumstances which had
shut him up to the conviction that the providence of God favoured
his removal.

Mr. Davies immediately repaired to Princeton, and entered upon
his official duties on the 26th of July; though he was not formally
inaugurated as President of the College until the 26th of September.
From the commencement of his labours here, it was not easy to fix a
limit to his zeal, or his efforts for promoting the best interests of the
College.   And his success was what might have been expected from
his ability and his industry.   The friends of the College, in both
Europe and America, watched all his benevolent and efficient move-
ments in connection with the institution with the greatest interest; not
doubting that, under his mild, judicious, energetic control, it was destined to reach a much higher point of honourable usefulness than it
had done even under his illustrious predecessors.

But the bright hopes of his friends, of the College, and of the Church
at large, were destined to an early disappointment.   On the first of
January, 1761, he preached a New Year's sermon in the college
chapel, from the words,—" This year thou shalt die ;" and on the 4th
of February following, his text was verified in its application to himself.   He had taken a violent cold, for which he was bled on Satur-
day, though he was occupied during the day, in transcribing for the
press his sermon on the death of King George II.†   On the Sabbath
following, he preached twice in the College chapel.   On Monday morning, while sitting at the breakfast table, he was seized with chills, followed by an inflammatory fever, affecting his brain.   While his faculties were continued to him, his mind was composed, and the future
evidently opened upon him in a field of glory ; and during the wan-
derings incident to his disease, he was constantly occupied in endeavouring to devise plans for doing good.   His death was every way

* Sermon No. LXXXII. in these volumes.   † Sermon LX.

worthy of his life.   An affectionate tribute was paid to his memory by
Dr. Finley, his successor, in a sermon preached on occasion of his
death, from Rom xiv. 7, 8, and printed by request of the Trustees of
the College.*   The Rev. David Bostwick, of New York, one of Mr.
Davies' most intimate friends, had been intrusted by him with the
superintendence of the printing of the sermon on the death of George
II., and he accompanied it with a preface, not only commendatory of
the sermon, but highly eulogistic of the writer.†   Dr. Thomas Gibbons,
of London, who had been for several years his correspondent, and who
made the selection of his sermons for publication, preached a comme-
morative sermon, which he published in connection with that of Dr.
Finley, in the first volume of the sermons of his deceased friend.‡
    The following is a list of President Davies' publications :—A Ser-
mon on Man's Primitive State, 1748.   The State of Religion among
the Protestant Dissenters in Virginia, in a letter to the Rev. Joseph
Bellamy, 1751.   A Sermon preached at the Installation of the Rev.
John Todd, 1752.   Religion and Patriotism the Constituents of a
Good Soldier.   A Sermon preached before a Company of Volunteers,
1755.   Virginia's Danger and Remedy: two discourses occasioned by
the severe Drought, and the Defeat of General Braddock, 1756.
Letters showing the State of Religion in Virginia, particularly among
the Negroes, 1751–1757.   A Sermon on " Little Children invited to
Jesus Christ, 1757.   The Curse of Cowardice.   A Sermon before
the militia of Virginia, 1758.   A Valedictory Discourse to the Senior
Class in the College of New Jersey, 1760.   A Sermon on the Death
of George II., 1761.   He was also the author of several important
public documents, and of various hymns and other pieces of poetry,
some of which attracted great attention.   A selection of his sermons,
in three volumes, including most of those which had been published in
his life-time, was given to the world shortly after his death ; and it may
be doubted whether any sermons in the English language have been
more widely read or more universally approved and admired.
    President Davies, though his public life was all included within
the brief period of fourteen years, left a broader, deeper, more enduring mark than almost any of his contemporaries in the ministry on

* Inserted in this volume.
† Inserted in this volume.
‡ Also in part published in this volume.

either side of the ocean.   Of his personal appearance I find no authentic record beyond the fact that he was of a somewhat plethoric habit;
but his manners were highly graceful and polished, while yet they
were characterized by a beautiful simplicity.   He had great compre-
hensiveness and vigour of intellect; an exuberant but chaste imagination; a highly cultivated taste; and a memory from which hardly
any thing ever escaped that was lodged in it.   In his moral constitution also he was eminently favoured—he was naturally genial and
cordial; full of kindness, sympathy and charity.   And to crown all,
he was among the brightest models of Christian character—the work
of the Spirit in his heart had been most radical and thorough—his
religion, as it appeared in the outer life, was a most harmonious and
attractive development of all the Christian graces.   There was no
service which he was not ready to undertake, no cross which he
accounted it a hardship to bear for the honour of his Master.   While
he was steadfast to his own convictions of the truth, he was a fine
example of enlightened catholicism, and welcomed cordially in Christian fellowship all in whom he could recognize the Master's image.

Being thus richly endowed both by nature and by grace, it were
to be expected that he would adorn every relation, and that his life
would be one of eminent usefulness.   Accordingly, wherever he moved,
blessings seemed to hang upon his footsteps.   In his general intercourse with society, he was discreet and cautious, but was evidently
always upon the look-out for opportunities to benefit those with whom
he associated.   He never took on self-righteousness or consequential
airs, and yet every one saw and felt that his most ordinary actions
were performed under the influence of the powers of the world to
come.   In the pulpit, he possessed rare advantages in respect to the
style, the structure, and the delivery of his sermons.   Though his
style, as it appears in most of his printed sermons, might seem to an
exact taste to be somewhat verbose, and sometimes even declamatory,
yet it is to be borne in mind that these discourses, with few exceptions,
were not designed for publication; and being intended for the ear
rather than the eye, it may well be doubted whether the character-
istics alluded to should be considered as blemishes.   The power of
his manner consisted in the melody and compass of his voice, in the
naturalness, and gracefulness, and dignity of his attitudes, and in the
fervour of his spirit, brightening his countenance and animating his

whole form. The staple of his preaching was in the highest degree evangelical—he seemed always to dwell within sight of the cross; and every discourse was redolent at once of tenderness and sublimity. There are passages in some of his printed sermons, which for simple exhibition of divine truth, and fervent power of appeal, are perhaps unrivalled. Dr. John H. Livingston, the only man whom I ever heard speak of President Davies' preaching, who had personal recollections of it, assured me that he was the most impressive and powerful pulpit orator to whom he had ever listened; and this is in accordance with the recorded statements of others who have heard him, as well as with his traditionary reputation. But his labour for the spiritual interests of his fellow-men were far from being confined to the pulpit— he was a most devoted pastor. Though he had so many congregations to care for, and his charge was spread over so wide a territory, he had his eye, as far as possible, upon the spiritual needs of all; and none ever wanted for suitable counsel, or consolation, or help, whom his pastoral attentions could reach. And he never considered himself as stepping aside from his path of duty as a Christian minister, in enlisting vigorously in behalf of his country. In the day of her peril he came up to her help, not as a party-politician, but as a self-sacrificing Christian patriot; and it was through his eloquent tongue and pen that multitudes of the young men of Virginia were baptized with a spirit of invincible courage. And last of all, during the brief period that he had occupied the presidential chair at Princeton, he proved himself fully worthy of the place—his kindly spirit, his urbane manners, his inventive and comprehensive intellect, his overpowering eloquence, his untiring industry, all contributed to give him an influence not only with the students, but with the Trustees, and all the friends of the College, to which it was not easy to fix a limit. Through his whole active life, he moved in a glorious sphere, and the lapse of a century has left his memory as fragrant as ever.

DISINTERESTED AND DEVOTED CHRISTIAN.

A SERMON, PREACHED AT NASSAU-HALL, PRINCETON, MAY 28,
1761. OCCASIONED BY THE DEATH OF THE REV. SAMUEL DA-
VIES, A. M. LATE PRESIDENT OF THE COLLEGE OF NEW JERSEY.

By SAMUEL FINLEY, D. D.,

MR. DAVIES' SUCCESSOR AS PRESIDENT OF THE SAID COLLEGE.
TO WHICH ARE ADDED SOME MEMOIRS OF MR. DAVIES, BY
ANOTHER HAND.

ROMANS XIV. 7, 8.

*For none of us liveth to himself, and no man dieth to himself. For
whether we live, we live unto the Lord ; or whether we die, we die
unto the Lord : whether we live therefore, or die, we are the Lord's.*

As the very dear and reverend man, whose premature and unexpected death, we, amongst thousands, this day lament, expressed his
desire, that, upon this mournful event, a sermon should be preached
from these words, he plainly intimated his expectation, that the audience should be entertained, not with an ornamented funeral oration,
but with such an instructive discourse as the text itself naturally suggests. The subject being his own choice, I cannot doubt but this
friendly audience will the more closely and seriously attend, as con-
ceiving him, though dead, yet speaking to them the solemn truths it
contains. For having been admitted into the full knowledge of his
religious principles, I may presume on speaking many of the sentiments he intended from this text, though not in his more sublime and
oratorical manner.

When I reflect on the truly Christian, generous, yet strict Catholicism that distinguishes this whole chapter, and how deeply it was imprinted on Mr. Davies' own spirit, and influenced the course of his

31

life, I am ready to conclude, that perhaps no text could be more aptly chosen on the occasion. It expresses the very temper that should be predominant in all, and which actually is so in every pious breast.

That we may apprehend the scope and genuine sense of the words, it is necessary to observe, that warm debates at that time arose between the Jewish and Gentile converts, about the difference of meats and days established by the Mosaic law; and, so sharp was the contention, that they were mutually disposed to exclude each other from Christian communion. The Gentile being under no bias from the powerful prejudices of education and custom, was sooner and easier convinced of his freedom from that yoke of bondage, and despised the Jew as weak to admiration, and scrupulous to a fault. The Jew, on the other hand, persuaded that these ancient divine institutions were still obligatory, censured and condemned the Gentile as inconscientious, and profanely regardless of God's awful authority.

The Apostle, in order to quell the growing strife, maturely determines that, though the Gentile held the right side of the question, yet both parties were wrong as to their temper of mind, and the manner in which they managed the controversy; and that they laid an undue stress on the matters of difference, and carried their censures higher than the merits of the cause would at all justify. He therefore recommends moderation to both, and sets before them sufficient reasons why they should judge of each other more charitably, since they agreed in all those principal points that would justly denominate them " the servants of the Lord." For if they would reckon it a bold intrusion to call before their tribunal, condemn, and punish another man's servant, over whom they had no legal authority; how much more arrogant and presumptuous must it be so to treat a servant of the Lord; ver. 4.

Again, let them be so candid as to persuade themselves, that, unless the contrary be evident, they who differ from them, mistaken or not, are influenced by a conscientious regard to the divine glory, ver. 6. This admitted, their personal censures will necessarily be milder, even though their judgment of the points in debate continue unaltered; and this must be admitted, if they can charitably judge, that their respective opponents are real Christians: for in all such the governing principle is, " not to live to themselves, but to the Lord. For none of us liveth to himself, and no man dieth to himself. For whether we live, we live unto the Lord; or whether we die, we die unto the Lord: whether we live therefore, or die, we are the Lord's." Now, if no pious person lives merely to please himself, we ought not to judge that his aversion from, or attachment to certain meats and days, arises only from a selfish humour: but, on the contrary, since his whole life is governed by an honest regard to the will of God, it is altogether credible that, in his different conduct respecting meats and days, he acts from the same principle; for whatever is true of the general, is also true of all the particulars contained under it. Suppose a man to be a real Christian, you then suppose him to be of an upright heart, of a tender conscience, and one who dares not to neglect, nor live in contradiction to known duty. He makes it his main business to please God, and shall we be implacably disgusted because he does not rather endeavour to please us? God forbid.

Thus, while our text affords a convincing argument for moderation in judging of other Christians, who differ from us in circumstantials, it teaches us what should be the principle and end of our life, and that both negatively and positively. We may not live nor die to ourselves, but to the Lord.

I. "We may not live to ourselves."

This proposition supposes, what is a demonstrable truth, that we are not the absolute proprietors, and therefore have not the rightful disposal of our lives. For since we could exert no kind of efficiency in bringing ourselves from nothing into existence, we could not possibly design ourselves for any end or purpose of our own. Hence it is evident, that, whose property soever we are, we belong not to ourselves; consequently, it is the highest indecency to behave as though we were accountable to none other. As rationally may we claim self-existence and independence. It will, therefore, be an eternal solecism in action to aim chiefly at our own glory, seek only our own things, or pursue most eagerly our own pleasures. Right reason itself peremptorily denies that the dictates of our own minds are our supreme rule of conduct, or that our own will is our law; much less may we subject ourselves to the government of blind passions, or indulge irregular appetites.

We are not at liberty, nor have we any authority, to employ either the members of our bodies, or powers of our souls, at pleasure, as if we had originally designed their use. Hence it will appear criminal,

VOL. I.—5

on the one hand, to waste our time, or expend our strength in useless exercises; and, on the other, to allow an idle negligence in necessary business. Our tongues themselves, those unruly members, must be patient of restraint; for it is the language only of haughty rebels to say, "Our lips are our own, who is lord over us?" Psalm xii. 4. Our very thoughts are to be confined within prescribed limits, and all our rational powers statedly exercised, not in merely curious and amusing researches, but in matters the most useful and important.

It also follows, that the product of our activity, whatever is acquired by the exertion of these powers, ought not to terminate in ourselves. Are we in pursuit of learning, that ornament of human minds, it should not be with a view only to shine more conspicuous, but that we may serve our generation to better advantage. Has God blessed "the hand of the diligent" with abundant riches? We are not to consider them as the means of gratifying vanity, or "fulfilling the desires of the flesh, and of the mind;" for we must "honour the Lord with our substance." Prov. iii. 9. Has God clothed any of us with power? This is not a discharge from his service, nor a freedom from subjection to his laws, but a stronger obligation to duty, as it gives us an opportunity of more extensive usefulness.

Finally, since we were not the authors of our lives, we can have no right to take them away. We have no power to determine, either the time or kind of death, any more than we can ward off, or suspend its blow when commissioned to destroy. Therefore, amidst all the miseries that can make life itself an insupportable burden, and all the glorious prospects that can make us impatiently pant for dissolution, it must be our determinate purpose, that "all the days of our appointed time, we will wait till our change come." Job xiv. 14.

As these particulars, examined by the strictest reason, will all appear to be immediate consequences from self-evident principles, and must all be confessed by him, who acknowledges that "he is not his own lord and master;" it will follow as an evident truth, that the evangelical duty of self-denial is founded on the everlasting reason of things.

Reflecting farther on the preceding observations, they force upon us the disagreeable conviction, that our whole race has revolted from God, and risen up in rebellion against him. "The world evidently lies in wickedness;" for the allowed practice of men supposes principles, which, they themselves being judges, must confess to be palpably false and absurd. They act as if they believed they were made for themselves, and had no other business in life but the gratification of their respective humours. One exerts all his powers, and spends all his time in nothing else but endeavouring to amass heaps of worldly treasure : another, by riotous living, disperses what had been collected with anxious care and assiduous labour. Some live in malice and envy, whose favourite employ is calumny and wrathful contentions, as if they had been created for no other end but to be the pests of society : others blaspheme the name of God, despise his authority, mock at religion, and ridicule serious persons and things. One has no other purpose in life but sport and merriment : another eats to gluttony, and drinks to besottedness. Yet all these, and nameless ranks of other daring offenders, would be ashamed in a Christian country to profess it as their serious belief, that they were made by a most wise, holy, and righteous God, preserved, blessed, and loaded with benefits every day, on purpose that they " might work all these abominations," or, in order to live just as they do.

If, then, it is confessedly impious and unreasonable to live to ourselves, it necessarily follows that we are the property of another, for it will ever be " lawful for one to do what he will with his own." And whose can we be but his who gave us existence ? Or, if ties of gratitude can more powerfully influence ingenuous minds than even those of nature, who can so justly claim us as he, who, as we hope, " loved us and washed us from our sins in his own blood ?" Rev. i. 5. This leads me to observe,

II. That we should " live and die to the Lord." This can admit of no debate ; for if our Maker and Redeemer be our rightful owner, then whatever we are, or have, or can do, must be for him. Being his servants, we must " shew all good fidelity" in his business. The talents with which he has entrusted us, more or fewer, or of whatever kind, may not be returned without improvement; for, as is fit and proper, he " receives his own with usury." Matt. xxv. 27. He is our King, whose prerogative it is to direct our course of action, and propose the end at which we are to aim ; to " mete out the bounds of our habitation," and carve our portion ; and it becomes us to give the most ready and cheerful obedience to his commands, and submit to all his disposals.

Our living thus to the Lord plainly supposes our being sensible of
our entire dependence on him, and that we devote ourselves to his
service.   We must "present our bodies a living sacrifice," Rom. xii. 1,
without reserve or hesitation; and "avouch the Lord to be our God,
to walk in his ways, and to keep his statutes, and his commandments,
and his judgments, and to hearken to his voice." Deut. xxvi. 17.
We bind ourselves to him in a firm covenant, not for a limited term of
months and years, but for ever and ever, and acquiesce in Him as our
chief good.

The solemnity of such an infinitely important transaction between
the glorious majesty of heaven, and such mean creatures as we, who
are "but dust and ashes," cannot but strike us with reverential awe.
And what will make it yet more humbling is the consideration of our
guilt.   We not only as creatures take upon us to speak unto the Lord
our Maker, but as criminals approach to the seat of our offended and
most righteous Judge.   Dare we then trifle, and not rather be most
serious and deliberate?   Reflecting that we are in the presence of
the heart-searching God will naturally make us watchful over every
thought and motion of our spirits, and engage us to the greatest sincerity in surrendering to him our all.   We will give him our hearts
themselves; keep nothing back; nor except against any terms he shall
please to propose, but yield at discretion.

On this occasion a consciousness of our having revolted from him,
neglected his service, purloined his goods, and, in every respect, behaved most ungratefully and undutifully, will affect us with the most
genuine sorrow.   Therefore, when, repentant we return to him, we
shall, covered with shame, approach with the Prodigal's self-abasing
confession, "Father! I have sinned against heaven, and before thee,
and am no more worthy to be called thy son." Luke xv. 18, 19.   He
will "surely hear us bemoaning ourselves, like Ephraim," that we have
too long wrought the will of the flesh, and suffered other usurping
lords to have dominion over us; but now we humbly beg forgiveness,
his gracious acceptance of our persons, and admission into his family,
should it be only on trial, "as hired servants."

But though our sins have made us vile, and the view of their odious
nature makes us "loathe ourselves in our own sight," yet a conviction
of the free grace and mercy of God in Christ will comfort and encourage our dejected and diffident hearts.   The cords of love will

draw us nearer and nearer, until we shall assume an humble "boldness, to enter into the holiest by the blood of Jesus." Heb. x. 19. Sacred love, and a grateful sense of the unmerited favours of our God will now dispose us to, and animate us in the performance of every duty. Religion will be our chosen course, and the commandments of God will be so far from being burdensome to us, that we shall rejoice in them, and delight in doing the things that please him. Our whole time will be consecrated to his service : no part of it can be spared for fleshly indulgences, or sinful pleasures, but will be employed either in some positive duty, or in preparation for it in the proper season.

This religious bent of mind will manifest itself in all our conduct, and give even common actions a different direction. If we attend our ordinary callings, we shall be active and diligent, not in order to gratify an earthly temper, but from an obediential regard to supreme authority. When our spirits flag through intense application to business, and recreation becomes necessary, our very diversions will be considered as our duty, and so as a branch of our religion : and as they will always be innocent in their nature, so they will be no otherwise regarded than as means to fit us for the repetition of our work. If our friends or country demand our service, we shall not give way to selfishness and indolence, but, as lovers of God and men, generously exert ourselves for the common good. Thus will our whole life be religion, upon such a sincere, entire, and affectionate dedication of ourselves to the Lord. And such as is our course so will be its end. When the date of time is concluded we shall also " die to the Lord." This in general imports our living under the rational, affecting impression of our dissolution, and appearing before God, and our constant endeavours after actual preparation to enjoy him for ever. Then, upon the approach of death, we shall confidently " commit our spirits into his hands," recommend his ways to survivors, and glorify him with our dying breath.

But, on the other hand, if our lives are not thus consecrated to our God, we cannot be supposed to perform any duty in an acceptable manner, as the requisite principle and end are wanting. He, to whom the secret springs of action are all obvious, will not, cannot accept pretended services ; nor be pleased with the " blind and the lame for sacrifice," when the best are esteemed too good for him. To compliment him with our lips, when we refuse to give him our hearts, will be judged similar to the conduct of those, who " bowed the knee in

derision," and in derision said, " Hail! King of the Jews!" He,
" with whom we have to do," cannot be deceived, nor will be mocked.
He requires " Truth in the inward parts," which cannot subsist without an honest and upright design to serve him all the days of our
lives.

Now to live wholly to the Lord, will appear to be our reasonable
service, if we consider,

1. That "such a life is most worthy of rational and immortal
creatures." From the powers and faculties given us it may naturally be concluded that we are created for some very important
purpose ; but what can be so important, or bear so just a correspondence to our capacities, as to live to the glory of our great Creator?
This being our ultimate end, to which we refer all our actions, and
perform each of them in such a manner as may best answer it, will
influence our hearts, and frame our whole conversation agreeable to
the divine approving will.   And what can so ennoble the soul as conformity to the pattern of perfection ?   But to neglect this, and chiefly
regard our temporal affairs, would be infinitely unworthy of beings
capable of the highest pursuits, and formed for immortality.   Why
should we have been " wiser than the beasts of the field, or the fowls
of heaven," if we are to have no sublimer aims than they?   In a word,
we could never vindicate the wisdom of God in our formation, if he
intended us for meaner things than those for which we are qualified.
Therefore,

2. Such a life is most worthy of God our Maker. Nothing can
appear more decent and proper, than that he who is the beginning,
should also be the end ; that as all are of him, all should be to him.
And if his glory be the most excellent thing, and he the most perfect
being, it will necessarily follow, that he cannot ultimately design what
is less excellent.   Therefore the Scripture speaks agreeable to everlasting truth, when it asserts, that, " he made all things;" and,
that " for his pleasure they are, and were created." Rev. iv. 11.
And can it be rationally supposed, that he allows us, whom he made
for his own glory, to act for a different or opposite end?   It cannot.
We must therefore peremptorily affirm, that he cannot, in consistency
with his perfections, require less, than that " whether we eat or drink,
or whatsoever we do, we should do all to his glory." 1 Cor. x. 31.   And
this he does require, not because he needs our service, or can be

happier, or more glorious in himself by our praises, but because it is fit and right, and results as our duty from the eternal reason of things.

3. Such a life is our own happiness : for, acting as prescribed, we move in our proper sphere, and tend to our native centre. We live as near the fountain of blessedness as our present state can admit, and nothing can be so animating as the glorious and blissful prospects our course affords. Our hearts, being fixed on the chief good, are at rest, and no more tortured with anxious hesitation, and uneasy suspense, as to what we shall choose for our portion, nor do our desires wander in quest of a more suitable object. We can wish for no more but the full enjoyment of God, whom we " serve with our spirits ;" whose " peace, that passeth all understanding, rules in our hearts ;" and for whose glory we hope, secure from confounding disappointment in the day of our Lord.

Now methinks every attentive hearer prevents my improvement of the subject, being ready, of his own accord to make such reflections as these. How serene and placid is the life, and how triumphant must be the death, of a true Christian ! How reasonable a service do we perform, when we consecrate ourselves to the Lord, and receive him, freely offering himself to be our portion, our father, and our friend ! None can plausibly urge, that some things unfit, or detrimental, are required. None can pretend a conscientious scruple about complying with the proposal, nor dare any, however secretly reluctant, openly avow their dissent. Every mouth is stopped, and all acknowledge their obligation to this plain duty. What then should hinder the unanimous agreement, of this whole assembly to so advantageous an overture ? Why may we not join ourselves, this day, to the Lord in an everlasting covenant ? Would it not seem uncharitable to suppose, that any one in this Christian audience rejects a proposal so infinitely just and kind ? How pleasing is the very imagination of an universal concurrence ! Not only would each of our hearts who are here present exult, but unnumbered hosts of angels, and all " the spirits of just men made perfect" would rejoice.

Since therefore all things that pertain to our present or future happiness, conspire to urge this point, let us with one accord, in the most affectionate and reverent manner, approach the throne of our august Sovereign, and cheerfully resign ourselves to him for ever; spend our lives in his service, and expect his compensating approbation at our end.

In some such strain, but more diffusive and sublime, would our reverend and dear deceased friend have addressed us on such a subject. We may imagine how fervent his desire was of "living to the Lord" himself, and persuading others to the same course, when he fixed on this for the subject of his funeral sermon. Now, as it is generally agreed that example has the most powerful influence, perhaps a few sketches of his own life and character may best recommend the preceding discourse, as they will prove the life described to be practicable. And though he on whom this talk is devolved owns himself inferior to it, yet he is encouraged to undertake it, from a persuasion that a simple and unornamented narrative of what he knows, either personally or by certain information, concerning President Davies, will set him in a very agreeable point of light. He is now disinterested in all the praises and censures of mortals, and can neither receive benefit, or suffer detriment by them ; but his example may profit the living, as it tends to excite a laudable emulation ; and some brief hints of the dispensations of divine providence towards him may not be without very useful instruction.

He was an only son, and, which is more, was a son of prayers and vows ; was given in answer to fervent supplications, and, in gratitude, wholly devoted to God from the womb by his eminently pious mother, and named Samuel, on the like occasion as the ancient Prophet.* The event proved, that God accepted the consecrated boy, took him under his special care, furnished him for, and employed him in the service of his church, prospered his labours with remarkable success, and not only blessed him, but made him a blessing.

The first twelve years of his life were wasted in the most entire negligence of God and religion, which he often afterwards bitterly lamented, as having too "long wrought the will of the flesh." But

---

* The attachment always existing between Davies and his mother was a remarkably strong and holy one.

When his body was in the coffin, she gazed on it attentively and then exclaimed, " There is the son of my prayers and my hopes, my only son, my only earthly supporter, but *there is the will of God*, and I am satisfied !"

[EDITOR OF THE BOARD.]

about that time the God to whom he was dedicated by his word and Spirit awakened him to solemn thoughtfulness and anxious concern about his eternal state. He then saw sufficient reason to dread all the direful effects of divine displeasure against sin. And so deeply imprinted was the rational sense of his danger, as to make him habitually uneasy and restless, until he might obtain satisfying scriptural evidence of his interest in the forgiving love of God.

While thus exercised, he clearly saw the absolute necessity and certain reality of the gospel plan of salvation, and what abundant and suitable provision it makes for all the wants of a sinner. No other solid ground of hope, or unfailing source of comfort could he find, besides the merits and righteousness of him, " whom God hath set forth to be a propitiation for sin, through faith in his blood." Rom. iii. 25. On this righteousness he was enabled confidently to depend; by this blood his conscience was purged from guilt; and " believing, he rejoiced with joy unspeakable, and full of glory." 1 Pet. i. 8. Yet he was afterwards exercised with many perplexing doubts for a long season, but at length, after years of impartial repeated self-examination, he attained to a settled confidence of his interest in redeeming grace, which he retained to the end.

A diary, which he kept in the first years of his religious life, and continued to keep as long as his leisure would permit, clearly shows how intensely his mind was set on heavenly things; how observant he was of the temper of his heart; and how watchful over all his thoughts, words and actions. Did any censure his foibles, or juvenile indiscretions? They would have done it compassionately, had they known how severely he censured them himself. The tribunal daily erected in his own bosom was more critical in scrutinizing, and more impartial and severe in passing sentence, than either his friends or enemies could be.

His love to God, and tender concern for perishing sinners, excited his eager desire of being in a situation to serve mankind to the best advantage. With this view he engaged in the pursuit of learning, in which, amidst many obvious inconveniences, he made surprising progress, and, sooner than could have been expected, was found competently qualified for the ministerial office. He passed the usual previous trials with uncommon approbation; having exceeded the raised expectations of his most intimate friends and admirers.

When he was licensed to preach the gospel, he zealously declared the counsel of God, the truth and importance of which he knew by happy experience; and did it in such a manner as excited the earnest desires of every vacant congregation, where he was known, to obtain the happiness of his stated ministrations. But, far from gratifying his natural inclination to the society of his friends, or consulting his ease, moved by conscience of duty, he undertook the self-denying charge of a dissenting congregation in Virginia, separated from all his brethren, and exposed to the censure and resentment of many. But the more he was known in those parts, the more were prejudices removed; contempt was gradually turned into reverence; the number of his enemies daily diminished, and his friends increased.

Nor did he there labour in vain, or "spend his strength for nought." The "Lord, who counted him faithful, putting him into the ministry," succeeded his faithful endeavours, so that a great number, both of whites and blacks, were hopefully converted to the living God; for the proof of this, I must refer you to his own narrative, sent to the Rev. Mr. Bellamy, and by him published, and to his letters to some gentlemen of the Society in London, for propagating religion among the poor.

As to his natural genius, it was strong and masculine. His understanding was clear; his memory retentive; his invention quick; his imagination lively and florid; his thoughts sublime; and his language elegant, strong, and expressive.* And I cannot but presume that true and candid critics will readily discern a great degree of true poetic fire, style, and imagery, in his poetical compositions; and will grant that he was capable to have shone in that way, had his leisure permitted the due cultivation of his natural talent.

His appearance in company was manly and graceful; his behaviour genteel, not ceremonious; grave, yet pleasant; and solid, but sprightly too. In a word, he was an open, conversable, and entertaining companion, a polite gentleman, and devout Christian, at once.

* But with all his genius, Mr. Davies dreaded to preach without careful preparation. He declared that every discourse of his which he thought worthy of the name of a sermon, cost him four days of hard study in its preparation. When on one occasion urged to preach extemporaneously, he replied, " *It is a dreadful thing to talk nonsense in the name of the Lord.*"

[EDITOR OF THE BOARD.]

In the sacred desk, zeal for God, and love to men, animated his addresses, and made them tender, solemn, pungent, and persuasive; while at the same time they were ingenious, accurate, and oratorial. A certain dignity of sentiment and style, a venerable presence, a commanding voice, and emphatical delivery, concurred both to charm his audience, and overawe them into silence and attention.

Nor was his influence confined to the pulpit. His comprehensive mind could take under view the grand interests of his country and of religion at once; and these interests, as well as those of his friends, he was ever ready zealously to serve. It is known what an active instrument he was in stirring up a patriot spirit, a spirit of courage and resolution in Virginia, where he resided during the late barbarous French and Indian ravages.

His natural temper was remarkably sweet and dispassionate;* and his heart was one of the tenderest towards the distressed. His sympathetic soul could say, " Who is weak, and I am not weak ?" Accordingly his charitable disposition made him liberal to the poor, and that often beyond his ability. He was eminently obliging to all, and very sensible of favours conferred; which he could receive without servility, and manifest his grateful sense of them with proper dignity.

To his friend he was voluntarily transparent, and fully acted up to the poet's advice:

> Thy friend put in thy bosom: wear his eyes
> Still in thy heart, that he may see what's there.

And perhaps none better understood the ingenuities and delicacies of friendship, or had a higher relish for it, or was truer or more constant in it, than he. He was not easily disgusted: his knowledge of human nature in its present state, his candid heart, and enlarged soul, both disposing and enabling him to make allowances for indiscretions, which narrower and more selfish minds could not make. He readily and easily forgave offences against himself, whilst none could be more

---

* The Rev. Dr. John Rodgers, one of his most intimate friends, in a letter to me since his death, says, "I never saw him angry during several years of unbounded intimacy, though I have repeatedly known him to have been ungenerously treated."

careful to avoid offending others; which, if he at any time inadvert-
ently did, he was forward and desirous to make the most ample satisfaction.

He was amongst the first and brightest examples of filial piety, a
very indulgent parent, and humane master. As a husband he was
kind, tender, cordial, and respectful, with a fondness that was manly
and genuine. In a word, think what might rationally be expected, in
the present imperfect state, in a mature man, a Christian in minority,
a minister of Jesus of like passions with others, in a gentleman, companion, and cordial friend, and you conceive of President Davies.

It would hardly be expected, that one so rigid with respect to his
own faith and practice, could be so generous and catholic in his sentiments to those who differed from him in both, as he was. He was
strict, not bigoted; conscientious, not squeamishly scrupulous. His
clear and extensive knowledge of religion enabled him to discern
where the main stress should be laid, and to proportion his zeal to the
importance of things, too generous to be confined to the intersts of a
party as such. He considered the visible kingdom of Christ as extended beyond the boundaries of this or that particular denomination,
and never supposed that His declarative glory was wholly dependent
on the religious community which he most approved. Hence he
gloried more in being a Christian, than in being a Presbyterian,
though he was the latter from principle. His truly catholic address
to the established clergy of Virginia is a demonstration of the sincere
pleasure it would have given him, to have heard that " Christ was
preached," and substantial religion, common Christianity, promoted by
those who "walked not with him," and whom he judged in other
points to be mistaken. His benevolent heart could not be so soured,
nor his enlarged soul so contracted, as to value men from circumstantial distinctions, but according to their personal worth.

He sought truth for its own sake, and would profess his sentiments
with the undisguised openness of an honest Christian, and the inoffensive boldness of a manly spirit: yet, without the least apparent difficulty or hesitation, he would retract an opinion on full conviction of
its being a mistake. I have never known one, who appeared to lay
himself more fully open to the reception of truth, from whatever
quarter it came, than he; for he judged the knowledge of truth only,
to be real learning, and that endeavouring to defend an error was but

labouring to be more ignorant. But, until fully convinced, he was becomingly tenacious of his opinion.

The unavoidable consciousness of native power made him bold and enterprising. Yet the event proved that his boldness arose not from a partial, groundless self-conceit, but from true self-knowledge. Upon fair and candid trial, faithful and just to himself, he judged what he could do; and what he could, when called to it, he attempted; and what he attempted, he accomplished.

It may here be properly observed, that he was chosen by the Synod of New York, at the instance of the trustees of New Jersey College, as a fit person to accompany the Rev. Gilbert Tennent to Great Britain and Ireland, in order to solicit benefactions for the said college. As this manifested the high opinion which both the Synod and corporation entertained of his popular talents and superior abilities, so his ready compliance to undertake that service, hazardous and difficult in itself, and precarious in its consequences, which required him to overlook his domestic connections, however tender and endearing, manifested his resolution and self-denial. How well he was qualified as a solicitor, is witnessed by the numerous and large benefactions he received. His services, as was meet, were gratefully accepted by his constituents; and to the pious, generous, and public-spirited charity of the friends of religion and learning in Great Britain, received on that occasion, does the College of New Jersey, in a great degree, owe its present flourishing condition.

As his light shone, his ability to fill the president's chair in this college, then vacant, was not doubted by the honourable board of trustees. He was accordingly chosen, and earnestly invited to accept the charge of this society. Yet he once and again excused himself, not being convinced that he was called in duty to leave his then important province. But repeated application at length prevailed to make him apprehend that it was the will of God he should accept the call; yet, lest he should mistake in so important a case, he withheld his express consent, until the Reverend Synod of New York and Philadelphia gave their opinion in favour of the college. This determined his dubious mind. He came, and undertook the weighty charge.

And what were the consequences? Had his incessant labours in travelling and preaching the Gospel, his disadvantageous situation, and want of opportunity for improvement made some of his best friends diffident of his capacity and acquirements for moving with honour in this unaccustomed sphere? He agreeably disappointed their friendly fears, and convinced them that strength of genius, joined to industrious application, had surmounted all other disadvantages. Had any such raised expectations as seemed hard to answer? They were fully satisfied: so that from being highly approved he came to be admired.

His manner of conducting the college did honour to himself, and promoted its interests. Whatever alterations in the plans of education he introduced were confessedly improvements on those of his predecessors. Had I never had other means of intelligence, save only my knowledge of the man, I should naturally have expected that all his public appearances would have been conducted with spirit, elegance, and decorum; that his government would be mild and gentle, tempered with wisdom and authority, and calculated to command reverence while it attracted love, and that his manner of teaching would be agreeable and striking.

But I propose not these as mere conjectures. The learned tutors of the college, the partners of his counsels and deliberations for its good, and these young gentlemen, once his care and charge, who judged themselves happy under his tuition, all know more than I shall speak.

You know the tenderness and condescension with which he treated you; the paternal care with which he watched over you; the reluctance with which he at any time inflicted the prescribed punishment on a delinquent; and how pleased he was to succeed in reforming any abuse by private and easy methods. You felt yourselves voluntarily confined by the restraints of love, and obliged to subjection, not from slavish fear, but from principle and inclination. You have yet fresh in memory his instructive lectures, and can tell with what ease he communicated his sentiments, and impressed his ideas on your minds, and the entertaining manner in which he would represent even a common thought.

But his persuasive voice you will hear no more. He is removed far from mortals, has taken his aerial flight, and left us to lament, that "a great man has fallen in Israel!" He lived much in a little time; "he finished his course," performed sooner than many others his assigned task, and, in that view, might be said to have died mature. He shone like a light set in a high place, that burns out and expires.

He went through every stage of honour and usefulness, compatible with his character as a Dissenting clergyman : and, while we flattered our fond hopes of eminent services from him for many years to come, the fatal blow was struck ; our pleasing prospects are all at an end, and he is cut down like a tree that had yielded much fruit, and was loaded with blossoms even in its fall.

This dispensation, how mysterious ! how astonishing ! nay, how discouraging does it seem ! Why was he raised, by divine Providence, in the prime of life, to so important a station, and, amidst useful labours, whilst he was fast increasing in strength adapted to his business, quickly snatched away ? This is a perplexing case ; and the more so that it so soon succeeded the yet shorter continuance of the venerable Edwards. Were they set in so conspicuous a point of view, only that their imitable excellencies might be more observable ? or, was Nassau Hall erected by divine Providence for this, among other important purposes, that it might serve to adorn the latter end of some eminent servants of the living God, itself being adorned by them ? In this view, the short presidency of a Dickinson, a Burr, an Edwards, and a Davies, instead of arguing the displeasure of the Almighty, will evidence his peculiar favour to this institution ; which I know was planned, and has been carried ou with the most pious, benevolent, and generous designs. These designs God's goodness has hitherto amazingly prospered amidst apparent frowns ; and, if we may infer anything from what he has already done, it is an encouraging expectation that he will continue to bless this society, and make it an honour and happiness to this venerable Board to have been engaged in so noble and successful an undertaking.

Now one more shining orb is set on our world. Davies is departed, and with him all that love, zeal, activity, and benevolence, for which he was remarkable. This the church, and this the bereaved College mourns. For this we hang our once cheerful harps and indulge in plaintive strains. Yet we are not to lament as those who are hopeless, but rather with humble confidence to " pray the Lord of the harvest," with whom is " the residue of the Spirit," that he would send forth another Davies to assist our labour and forward his work.

Nor should the decease of useful labourers, the extinction of burning and shining lights, only send us to the throne of grace for supplies, but excite us to greater diligence and activity in our business, as we have for the present the more to do. And, instead of being dispirited by the loss of such eminent assistants, we should be animated by their example, and hope for the same divine aids that carried them through all the duties and dangers of life with safety, success, and honour.

Finally, this dispensation should lessen our esteem of this transitory disappointing world, and raise our affections to heaven, that place and state of permanent blessedness. Thither ascends, as to its native home, all the goodness that departs from earth; and the more of our pious friends go to glory, so many more secondary motives have we to excite our desires of " departing and being with Christ; which is far better" than any state under the sun : for there, in addition to superior felicity, we shall " come to the general assembly, and Church of the First born which are written in heaven,—and to the spirits of just men made perfect." Heb. xii. 23. Amen.

AN APPENDIX.

BY ANOTHER HAND.

The following facts, drawn up by a gentleman, who was Mr. Davies' intimate friend, and lived in the same town with him, while he was President of the College, were collected partly from Mr. Davies' private papers, and partly from the gentleman's personal knowledge, and, as they illustrate several things just hinted in the preceding discourse, and contain some anecdotes not before mentioned, may be properly subjoined to the narrative already given.

The Rev. Samuel Davies, late President of the College of New Jersey, was born on the 3rd day of November, A. D., 1724, in the county of Newcastle, in Delaware. His father was a planter, who lived with great plainness and simplicity, and supported the character of an honest and pious man to his death; which happened about two years ago. His mother, who was greatly distinguished for her eminent piety, some time before the conception of this favourite only son, earnestly desired such a blessing; and as she then had only borne a daughter, who was near five years old, she had special occasion for the exercise of her faith, in waiting for the divine answer to her petition. In this situation she took example from the mother of the prophet Samuel, and vowed a vow unto the Lord; that if he would indeed give her a man child, she would devote him to His service all the days of his life.

It may well be supposed that the parents received this child as from God, and that the mother especially, who had reason to look upon him as a token of the divine favour, and an express answer to her prayers, would, with the greatest tenderness, begin the rearing of this beloved plant. As there was no school in the neighbourhood, she herself taught him to read; and, although he was very young, he is said to have made such proficiency as surprised every person who heard it.

He continued at home with his parents till he was about ten years old; during which time he appears to have had no remarkable impressions of a religious kind; but behaving himself as is common for a sprightly, towardly child, under the influence of pious example and instruction. He was then sent to an English school, at some distance from his father's, where he continued two years, and made great progress in his learning; but, for want of the pious instruction with which he was favoured at home, he grew somewhat more careless of the things of religion.

It appears, that about this time of life, careless as he was, he made a practice of secret prayer, especially in the evening. The reasons (as he tells in his diary) why he was so punctual in the evening was, that "he feared lest he should perhaps die before morning." What is farther observable in his prayers at this time is, that " he was more ardent in his supplications for being introduced into the gospel ministry, than for any other thing."

[It is here presumed that Dr. Finley's sermon, preached on occasion of his death, by desire of the trustees, contains sufficient memorials of his life, from the time in which it pleased God more deeply to impress his mind with the important realities of another world, until he was elected President of the College.]

It may perhaps not be amiss to mention that when he returned home from his voyage to Great Britain, he entered again on his laborious and beloved task of preaching the gospel to his several congregations; and continued in this work until the year 1759, when he was elected President of the College of New Jersey, in the room of the Rev. Jonathan Edwards. The College, before he came, had been in an unhappy situation; partly owing to the length of that melancholy period between the death of President Burr and his accession, and partly to the evil dispositions and practices of a few members of the society. President Burr died in September, 1757; and although Mr. Edwards was elected a few days after, he did not take upon himself the government of the College till February, 1758; and about a fortnight after took the small-pox, of which he died in March following. Mr. Davies was not initiated in his office till the latter end of July, 1759. So that the College lay under the obvious disadvantages of a bereaved condition for almost two years. But the prudent measures taken by President Davies soon surmounted these disadvantages; so that in a few months a spirit of emulation in learning and morality, as had been usual, evidently characterized the students of Nassau Hall.

While he continued president his labours were great, and his application to study was necessarily more intense than that of his predecessors. For he came to this seat of the Muses, when its learning, by the eminent abilities of President Burr, was advanced to a very considerable degree; and he had just emerged from a sea of ministerial labour in various places, wherein a common genius would have been able to have made but little improvement in academical learning. Besides, the speedy passage he made through the course of his studies, previous to his entering into the ministry, made his after application the more necessary for so important and elevated a situation. He was determined not to degrade his office, but to be in reality what his station supposed him, and accordingly exerted himself to the utmost. The labours of the day seemed to him rather an incentive to study than to rest in the night; for he commonly sat up till twelve o'clock, and often later, although he rose by break of day. The success was proportionable; for by the mighty efforts of his great genius, and by dint of industry, he left the College of New Jersey, at his death, in as high a state of literary merit as it ever had been in since its first institution.

It is a piece of justice due to his memory to remark, that the few innovations he made in the academical exercises, were certainly improvements upon the plan of his predecessors. Among other things the monthly orations he instituted deserve particular notice. In order to give his pupils a taste for composition, and to form them for public speaking, he directed the members of the senior class each to choose his subject, and compose a popular harangue to be delivered publicly in the College Hall before the masters and students, and as many of the inhabitants of the town as chose to attend. When each had written his discourse, he brought it to the president, who made such observations and corrections as he judged proper; and, after their discourses were spoken, they severally attended him again for his remarks on their delivery. About six of the young gentlemen usually delivered their orations in the afternoon of the first Wednesday in every month, to crowded audiences; and it is hard to say, whether the entertainment of the hearers, or the improvement of the students, was the greater.

There is reason to believe, that the intense application with which Mr. Davies attended to the duties of his office was one great cause of his death. The habit of his body was plethoric: and it is not to be doubted but that his health for some years had very much depended upon the exercise of riding, to which he was necessarily obliged while he lived in Virginia, though even then he had several severe fevers, supposed to arise principally from his application to study in the intervals of riding abroad. When he came to the College he scarcely used any bodily exercise, save what was required in going from his own house to Nassau Hall, which is a space about ten rods, five or six times a day.

In the latter end of January, A. D. 1761, a bad cold seized him, and for his relief he was bled. The same day he transcribed for the press the sermon, which was soon after published, on the death of the late King, and the day after preached twice in the College Hall; by all which the arm, in which he was bled, became much inflamed, and increased his former indisposition. On the Monday morning after, at breakfast, he was seized with a violent chilly fit, which was succeeded by an inflammatory fever, and in ten days brought on the period of his important life.

Although premonitions of death in the present state of the world are seldom, if ever, given to mankind; and they who are disposed to interpret ordinary occurrences into such premonitions, when, by something similar in the event those occurrences would seem as if predictive, generally discover their weakness; yet the circumstances of the death of an eminent person are commonly very acceptable to the public, and for this reason it may not be amiss to mention an anecdote which Mr. Davies more than once took notice of in his last sickness.

An intimate friend of his, a few days before the beginning of the year in which he died, in conversation told him, that a sermon would be expected from him on the new year's day; and, among other things, happened to mention that the late President Burr, on the first day of the year wherein he died, preached a sermon on Jer. xxviii. 16. "Thus saith the Lord, This year thou shalt die;" and after his death, the people took occasion to say it was premonitory; upon which Mr. Davies observed, that "although it ought not to be viewed in that light, yet it was very remarkable." When new year's day came, he preached; and the congregation were not a little surprised at his taking the same text of Scripture. Upon his being taken with his last sickness, about three weeks after, he soon adverted to this circumstance, and mentioned it as remarkable that he had been undesignedly led to preach, as it were, his own funeral sermon.

It is much to be lamented that the violence of the disorder, of which this excellent man died, deprived him of the regular exercise of his reason the greater part of the time of his sickness, otherwise the public would undoubtedly have been gratified with his remarks on the views of an approaching eternity, and would have received another evidence of the superior excellency and power of that religion, which alone can support the soul, and make the otherwise gloomy prospect of death cheerful. For the issues of this decisive period his life had been eminently calculated from his youth. It abundantly appears, that from twelve or fourteen years of age, he had continually maintained the strictest watch over his thoughts and actions, and daily lived under a deep sense of his own unworthiness, of the transcendent excellency of the Christian religion, of the great importance of a public spirit, and the necessity of exerting it in promoting the general good. Even in his delirium his mind discovered the favourite object of his concern, the prosperity of Christ's Church, and the good of mankind. His bewildered brain was continually imagining, and his faltering tongue expressing some expedient for these important purposes. Alas! for us, that so great a light could no longer continue in this dark world!

TWO DISCOURSES,

PREACHED AT HABERDASHERS-HALL, LONDON, MARCH 29, A.D.
1761, OCCASIONED BY THE DECEASE OF THE

REV. SAMUEL DAVIES, A. M.,

LATE PRESIDENT OF THE COLLEGE OF NASSAU HALL, IN NEW
JERSEY.

BY THOMAS GIBBONS, D.D.

EPHESIANS I. 11.

Who worketh all things after the counsel of his own will.

THE last week gave me the awful assurance of the sudden and unexpected death of that most excellent and amiable man and minister
of Jesus Christ, the Rev. Samuel Davies, President of the College of
Nassau Hall, in New Jersey, by a most moving and melting letter
from a gentleman of Philadelphia, an acquaintance of Mr. Davies',
and who well knew his worth, to a correspondent of the gentleman's
here in London.

A greater loss, all things considered, could not perhaps befal the
Church of God in the death of a single person. The God of nature
had endowed Mr. Davies with extraordinary talents. Perhaps in sublimity and strength of genius there were very few, if any, who surpassed him. To the brightest and richest intellects Mr. Davies had
superadded the improvements of science, and a large acquaintance with

55

books, and possibly, had he lived, there would have been scarcely a
man in our world a more accomplished divine, or a more eminent
scholar. His character in life was wonderfully accommodated both to
his natural and acquired abilities. He was President of New Jersey
College, in the discharge of which office there would have been a demand for the exertion of his amazing talents, and the exhibition of
all his treasures of literature and knowledge. Thus, as he was a star
of the first magnitude, so he was placed in a situation where he might
have shone without any waste of his distinguished and supereminent
glories.

But what crowned all, or advanced his distinction as a man and a
scholar into the highest value and lustre, was, that his pious character
appeared not at all inferior to his great intellect and acquired accom-
plishments. Nay, (let me not be thought, for I intimately knew him,
to exceed the limits of truth in the ardour of my friendship) his pious
character as much surpassed all else that was remarkable in him, as
the sparkling eye in the countenance of a great genius does all the
other features of the face. If Mr. Davies' good sense and learning
were the pictures of silver, his graces and virtues were the apples of
gold.

Here let me stay awhile ; and, though I shall only give you a few
outlines of his piety and amiable disposition, yet let me be allowed to
present you with such a view of him as shall not only be sufficient to
demonstrate him to be the best of men and ministers, but as shall
leave room for you to conclude that great additions might be made to
his character by persons who had a longer acquaintance with him than
myself, and the collected testimonies of the friends who were favoured
with his intimate correspondence.

He informed me in one of his letters, for I was honoured with a
close intimacy with him several years, " That he was blessed with a
mother whom he might account, without filial vanity or partiality, one
of the most eminent saints he ever knew upon earth. And here,
says he, I cannot but mention to my friend an anecdote known but to
few, that is, that I am a son of prayer, like my name-sake Samuel the
prophet ; and my mother called me Samuel because, she said, I have
asked him of the Lord, 1 Sam. i. 20. This early dedication to God
has always been a strong inducement to me to devote myself to him
by my own personal act ; and the most important blessings of my life

I have looked upon as immediate answers to the prayers of a pious mother. But, alas! what a degenerate plant am I! How unworthy of such a parent, and such a birth!"

From the accounts Mr. Davies gave of himself in the conversation that passed between us when he was here in England, I learnt, as the inference from related fact, that he must have been very assiduous in his studies. When he was about entering the ministry, or had not long entered upon it, if I remember right, he was judged to be in a deep and irrecoverable consumption. Finding himself upon the borders of the grave, and without any hopes of recovery, he determined to spend the little remains of an almost exhausted life, as he apprehended it, in endeavouring to advance his Master's glory in the good of souls. Accordingly he removed from the place where he was, to another about an hundred miles distance, that was then in want of a minister. Here he laboured in season and out of season; and, as he told me, preached in the day, and had his hectic fever by night, and that to such a degree as to be sometimes delirious, and to stand in need of persons to sit up with him. Here God gave him some glorious first-fruits of his ministry, for two instances of the conversion of two gentlemen he related to me were very remarkable, and he had the satisfaction, as he informed me, to find in the after accounts of them, that there was good reason to believe that they were saints indeed; their goodness being by no means "as the grass upon the house tops, which withereth afore it groweth up, and wherewith the mower filleth not his hand," Psal. cxxix. 6, 7, but yielding the fruits meet for repentance, in an holy and well-ordered conversation.

Afterwards he settled in Virginia, a colony where profaneness and immorality called aloud for his sacred labours. His patience and perseverance, his magnanimity and piety, together with his powerful and evangelical ministrations, were not without success. The wilderness and the solitary places, in the course of his stay there, bloomed and blossomed before him. His tract of preaching, if I remember right, for some time was not less than sixty miles, and by what I have learnt, though not from himself, he had but little of this world's goods to repay his zealous and indefatigable labours; but his reward, as he well knew, was in heaven; and he felt, I doubt not, the animated joy that every negro slave, which under his ministration became the Lord's freeman, would furnish an additional jewel to his eternal crown.

Upon the decease of that excellent man, the Rev. Jonathan Edwards, President of the College of Nassau Hall, in New Jersey, Mr. Davies writes me word, that Mr. Lockwood, in New England, a gentleman of worthy character, was chosen to fill up the vacancy. " I have not yet heard, says Mr. Davies, whether he has accepted the place. The trustees were divided between him, another gentleman, and myself, but I happily escaped." But so it was ordered by Mr. Lockwood's not accepting the invitation, that Mr. Davies was afterwards elected President of the College ; and what concern, and indeed what consternation this choice gave him, his letters to me amply testify ; and I could particularly relate to you what views he had of things, and what steps he took to determine what was his duty. At last he accepted the call to his important office of presiding in the College ; and tells me in a letter, dated June 6, 1759, " That the evidence of his duty was so plain, that even his skeptical mind was satisfied ; and that his people saw the hand of Providence in it, and dared not to oppose."

Here he was settled for about eighteen months ; and as he could exercise his ministry as well as preside over the College, great things might have been expected from that rare and remarkable union there was in him of what was great and good ; and with pleasure I have received the information from his friends how well he supported and adorned his character, and what high expectations were formed as to the benefit and blessing he was likely to prove to that seminary of religion and learning. " His whole soul (says the letter that gives the news of his death) was engaged for the good of the youth under his care." And again, " Nassau Hall in tears, disconsolate, and refusing to be comforted."

But, alas ! in the midst of his days, (little more than thirty-six years of age) he was called away from this but opening scene of large and extraordinary usefulness to the invisible world, the world of glory and blessedness, never to sojourn in mortal clay, or to irradiate and bless the church militant more. He is dead, he is departed—America in groans proclaims her inexpressible loss, and we in Great Britain share the distress, and echo groan for groan.

Thus ended the days on earth of this truly great and good man ; having in his little circle of life shed more beams, and done more service than many a languid and less illuminated soul, even in a public sphere, in the revolution of sixty or fourscore years.

Truly great and good I may style him without the suspicion of flattery, and without the flight of hyperbole. Let me call to your remembrance, as proofs of what I say, the excellent discourses he has delivered in this pulpit, and the several sermons of his which have been published, strong in manly sense, loaded with full ideas, rich with evangelical truth, and animated with the most sacred fervour for the good of souls. And to these evidences of the admirable spirit that dwelt in him, let me add a few paragraphs from the many letters with which, in the course of about nine years' correspondence, he has favoured me.

Speaking in one of his letters concerning his children, he says, " I am solicitous for them when I consider what a contagious world they have entered into, and the innate infection of their natures. There is nothing that can wound a parent's heart so deep, as the thought that he should bring up children to dishonour his God here and be miserable hereafter. I beg your prayers for mine, and you may expect a retaliation in the same kind."

In another letter he says, " We have now three sons and two daughters; whose young minds as they open I am endeavouring to cultivate with my own hand, unwilling to trust them to a stranger; and I find the business of education much more difficult than I expected.—My dear little creatures sob and drop a tear now and then under my instructions, but I am not so happy as to see them under deep and lasting impressions of religion ; and this is the greatest grief they afford me. Grace cannot be communicated by natural descent, and, if it could, they would receive but little from me. I earnestly beg your prayers for them."

In another letter, " I desire seriously to devote to God and my dear country, all the labours of my head, my heart, my hand, and pen ; and if he pleases to bless any of them, I hope I shall be thankful, and wonder at his condescending grace. Oh, my dear brother ! could we spend and be spent all our lives in painful, disinterested, indefatigable service for God and the world, how serene and bright would it render the swift approaching eve of life ! I am labouring to do a little to save my country, and, which is of much more consequence, to save souls from death, from that tremendous kind of death, which a soul can die. I have but little success of late, but blessed be God, it surpasses my expectation, and much more my desert. Some of my brethren labour to better purpose. The pleasure of the Lord prospers in their hands."

Another epistle tells me, " As for myself, I am just striving not to live in vain. I entered the ministry with such a sense of my unfitness for it, that I had no sanguine expectations of success. And a condescending God (O, how condescending!) has made me much more serviceable than I could hope. But, alas! my brother, I have but little, very little true religion. My advancements in holiness are extremely small; I feel what I confess, and am sure it is true, and not the rant of excessive or affected humility. It is an easy thing to make a noise in the world, to flourish and harangue, to dazzle the crowd, and set them all agape, but deeply to imbibe the spirit of Christianity, to maintain a secret walk with God, to be holy as he is holy, this is the labour, this the work. I beg the assistance of your prayers in so grand and important an enterprise. The difficulty of the ministerial work seems to grow upon my hands. Perhaps once in three or four months I preach in some measure as I could wish; that is, I preach as in the sight of God, and as if I were to step from the pulpit to the supreme tribunal. I feel my subject. I melt into tears, or I shudder with horror, when I denounce the terrors of the Lord. I glow, I soar in sacred extacies, when the love of Jesus is my theme, and, as Mr. Baxter was wont to express it, in lines more striking to me than all the fine poetry in the world,

> " I preach as if I ne'er should preach again ;
> And as a dying man to dying men.

But, alas! my spirits soon flag, my devotions languish, and my zeal cools. It is really an afflictive thought that I serve so good a Master with so much inconstancy; but so it is, and my soul mourns upon that account."

In another letter he says, " I am labouring to do a little good in the world. But, alas! I find I am of little use or importance. I have many defects, but none gives me so much pain and mortification as my slow progress in personal holiness. This is the grand qualification of the office we sustain, as well as for that heaven we hope for, and I am shocked at myself when I see how little I have of it."

In another of his letters he acquaints me, "That he indeed feels an union of hearts which cannot bear without pain the intervention of the huge Atlantic, nor even the absence of a week. But our condescending Lord, adds he, calls his ministers stars, and he knows best in what part of the firmament of the church to fix them; and (O the delightful thought!) they can never be out of the reach of his beams, though they shine in different hemispheres with regard to each other. This leads me, undesignedly, to a criticism on Jude 13, on which perhaps an astronomer would be the best commentator. Wandering stars, to whom is reserved the blackness of darkness for ever. Perhaps an astronomical critic would observe that false teachers are represented as planetary or wandering stars, that in their eccentricities run out into an eternal aphelion from the Sun of Righteousness, beyond the system which he warms, illuminates, and beatifies, and are constantly receding from the Fountain of light, life, and bliss, and therefore must wander through the blackness of darkness for ever; a darkness unpierced by one ray from the great Sun and Centre of the moral world —blackness of darkness, an abstract predicated of an abstract. How gloomy and strong the expression!"

Let me give you another quotation from his letters. "I am very much pleased and affected, says he, with the subject of this week's study, and next Lord's day's entertainment, namely, "A bruised reed shall he not break, and the smoking flax shall he not quench." Such a bruised reed at best am I; a weak, oppressed, useless thing; a *stridens stipula* that can make no agreeable melody to entertain my great Shepherd. Yet this bruised reed I have reason to hope he will not break, but bind up and support. This shattered pipe of straw he will not cast away, but repair and tune to join in the angelic concert on high. I am at best but smoking flax; a dying snuff in the candlestick of his church; a wick just put out in the lamp of his sanctuary. The flame of divine love, sunk deep into the socket of a corrupt heart, quivers, and breaks, and catches, and seems just expiring at times. The devil and the world raise many storms to blow upon it. And yet this smoking flax, where the least spark of that sacred passion still remains which renders it more susceptive of his love, as a candle just put out but still smoking, is easily rekindled. This smoking flax he will not quench, but blow it to a flame, which shall shine brighter and brighter till it mingles, with its kindred flames in the pure element of love."

I shall conclude my extracts from his epistolary correspondence with a part of a letter, dated

HANOVER, *September*, 12, 1757.

" MY EVER DEAR FRIEND :—

" I am just beginning to creep back from the valley of the shadow of death, to which I made a very near approach a few days ago. I was seized with a most violent fever, which came to a crisis in a week, and now it is much abated, though I am still confined to my chamber. In this shattered state my trembling hand can write but little to you, and what I write will be languid and confused, like its author. But as the Virginia fleet is about to sail, and I know not when I shall have another opportunity, I cannot avoid writing something. I would sit down on the grave's mouth, and talk awhile with my favourite friend ; and from my situation you may foresee what subjects my conversation will turn upon—death—eternity—the supreme tribunal.

" Blessed be my Masters's name, this disorder found me employed in his service. It seized me in the pulpit, like a soldier wounded in the field. This has been a busy summer with me. In about two months I rode about five hundred miles, and preached about forty sermons. This affords me some pleasure in the review. But, alas ! the mixture of sin and of many nameless imperfections that run through and corrupt all my services, give me shame, sorrow, and mortification. My fever made unusual ravages upon my understanding, and rendered me frequently delirious, and always stupid. But, when I had any little sense of things, I generally felt pretty calm and serene, and death, that mighty terror, was disarmed. Indeed the thought of leaving my dear family destitute, and my flock shepherdless, made me often start back and cling to life ; but in other respects death appeared a kind of indifference to me. Formerly I have wished to live longer that I might be better prepared for heaven, but this consideration had but very little weight with me, and that for a very unusual reason, which was this. After long trial I found that this world is a place so unfriendly to the growth of every thing divine and heavenly, that I was afraid, if I should live longer, I should be no better fitted for heaven than I am. Indeed I have hardly any hopes of ever making any great attainments in holiness while in this world, though I should be doomed to stay in it as long as Methuselah. I see other Christians indeed around me make some progress, though they go on with but a snail-like motion : but when I consider that I set out about twelve years old, and what sanguine hopes I then had of my future progress, and yet that I have been almost at a stand ever since, I am quite discouraged. Oh, my good Master! if I may dare to call thee so, I am afraid I shall never serve thee much better on this side the region of perfection. The thought grieves me; it breaks my heart, but I can hardly hope better. But if I have the least spark of true piety in my breast, I shall not always labour under this complaint. No, my Lord, I shall yet serve thee—serve thee through an immortal duration—with the activity, the fervour, the perfection of the rapt seraph that adores and burns. I very much suspect this desponding view of the matter is wrong, and I do not mention it with approbation, but only relate it as an unusual reason for my willingness to die, which I never felt before, and which I could not suppress.

"In my sickness I found the unspeakable importance of a Mediator in a religion for sinners. Oh! I could have given you the word of a dying man for it, that that Jesus whom you preach is indeed a necessary, and an all-sufficient Saviour. Indeed he is the only support for a departing soul. None but Christ, none but Christ. Had I as many good works as Abraham or Paul, I would not have dared to build my hopes upon such a quicksand, but only on this firm, eternal Rock.

"I am rising up, my brother, with a desire to recommend him better to my fellow-sinners, than I have done. But, alas! I hardly hope to accomplish it. He has done a great deal more by me already than I ever expected, and infinitely more than I deserved. But he never intended me for great things. He has beings both of my own, and of superior orders, that can perform him more worthy service. Oh! if I might but untie the latchet of his shoes, or draw water for the service of his sanctuary, it is enough for me. I am no angel, nor would I murmur because I am not.

"My strength fails me, and I must give over. Pray for me—write to me—love me living and dying, on earth and in heaven."

Judge you from these passages, written in the freedom of friend-

ship, and to one to whom he scrupled not to lay open the secrets of
his bosom, what a loss the Church has sustained, and how much our
world is impoverished by the death of Mr. Davies, in the vigour of
his days, and in the meridian of his usefulness!

Such a blow, such an uncommon and distressing blow has been
given in the death of Mr Davies. And now what shall we do? to
what shall we recur, or to what quarter shall we look for help under
such an awful Providence?

CHARACTER

OF

THE REV. SAMUEL DAVIES.

BY THE REV. DAVID BOSTWICK, A. M.,

OF NEW YORK.

IT will doubtless be acknowledged on all hands, that a decent respect, and a proportionable tribute of honour are due to the memory
of those deceased, whom the God of nature and grace had furnished
with every valuable endowment, and in his providence had advanced
to an extensive sphere of usefulness while they lived; and that this
was eminently the case of my reverend friend and brother, no one,
who had the happiness of his personal acquaintance, or could rely on
the testimony of universal fame, will pretend to dispute.

I am, however, truly sensible that to exhibit a just portraiture of
President Davies, and draw the lineaments of his amiable character,
is a task too arduous for me, and would require a genius not inferior
to his own; but however, the friendship with which he was pleased
to honour me, the esteem and veneration I had for him while he lived,
with the just sense I still entertain of his uncommon worth, unitedly
demand the present exertion of my feeble attempts.

Mr. Davies was a man of such uncommon furniture, both of gifts
and grace, and adorned with such an assemblage of amiable and useful
qualities, and each shining with such distinguished lustre, that it is
truly hard to say in which he most excelled, and equally hard to mention one valuable or useful accomplishment in which he did not excel.

A large and capacious understanding — a solid, unbiassed, and well-regulated judgment — a quick apprehension — a genius truly penetrating — a fruitful invention — an elegant taste, — were all happily united in him, and constituted a real greatness of mind, which never failed to strike every observer with an agreeable surprise.

To this extraordinary natural capacity were added the improvements of a learned and polite education, which, though in the early years of his study it was embarrassed with many peculiar disadvantages, yet by the strength of his genius, and dint of indefatigable application, was cultivated to such a degree of elegance and refinement, as attracted the notice and admiration of all the friends of science wherever he was known.

And as the powers of his mind were enriched with every valuable human accomplishment, so they were eminently improved by the influence and efficacy of sanctifying grace; in consequence of which they were all sincerely devoted to the service of God, and the good of mankind. In the early stages of his life, it pleased a Sovereign God to call him effectually from his natural alienation to the knowledge and love of himself, to take a powerful possession of his heart, and seize all the faculties of his active and capacious soul for his service. Upon finishing, therefore, the course of his preparatory studies, he entered into the sacred employment of the gospel ministry, and solemnly dedicated himself with all his superior talents to the work of the sanctuary.

In the exercise of this sacred office, his fervent zeal and undissembled piety, his popular talents and engaging methods of address, soon acquired him a distinguished character, and general admiration. Scarce was he known as a public preacher but he was sent, on the earnest application of the people, to some of the distant settlements of Virginia, where many of the inhabitants, in respect of religion, were but a small remove from the darkness and ignorance of uncultivated heathenism, and where the religion of Jesus, which he endeavoured to propagate, had to encounter all the blindness, prejudice, and enmity that are natural to the heart of the most depraved sinner. Yet under all apparent disadvantages, his labours were attended with such remarkable success, that all opposition quitted the unequal combat, and gave way to the powerful energy of the divine Spirit, which was graciously pleased by his ministry to add many new subjects to the spiritual kingdom of our glorious Immanuel.

The work of the ministry was Mr. Davies' great delight; and for it he was admirably furnished with every valuable qualification of nature and grace. Divinity was a favourite study, in which he made a proficiency uncommon for his years, and yet he generally preferred the most necessary and practical branches of it to the dark mazes of endless controversy and intricate disputes; aiming chiefly at the conversion of sinners, and to change the hearts and lives of men by an affecting representation of the plain, but most important, interesting truths of the law and the gospel. His talent at composition, especially for the pulpit, was equaled by few, and perhaps exceeded by none. His taste was judicious, elegant, and polite, and yet his discourses were plain and pungent, peculiarly adapted to pierce the conscience and affect the heart. His diction was surpassingly beautiful and comprehensive, tending to make the most stupid hearer sensibly feel, as well as clearly understand. Sublimity and elegance, plainness and perspicuity, and all the force and energy that the language of mortals could convey, were the ingredients of almost every composition. His manner of delivery, as to pronunciation, gesture, and modulation of voice, seemed to be a perfect model of the most moving and striking oratory.

Whenever he ascended the sacred desk, he seemed to have not only the attention, but all the various passions of his auditory entirely at his command. And as his personal appearance was august and venerable, yet benevolent and mild, so he could speak with the most commanding authority, or melting tenderness, according to the variation of his subject. With what majesty and grandeur, with what energy and striking solemnity, with what powerful and almost irresistible eloquence would he illustrate the truths, and inculcate the duties of Christianity! Mount Sinai seemed to thunder from his lips, when he denounced the tremendous curses of the law, and sounded the dreadful alarm to guilty, secure, impenitent sinners. The solemn scenes of the last judgment seemed to rise in view, when he arraigned, tried, and convicted self-deceivers and formal hypocrites. And how did the balm of Gilead distil from his lips, when he exhibited a bleeding, dying Saviour to sinful mortals, as a sovereign remedy for the wounded heart, and anguished conscience! In a word, whatever subject he undertook, persuas've eloquence dwelt upon his tongue; and his audience was all attention. He spoke as on the borders of eternity, and as viewing the glories and terrors of an unseen world, and conveyed the most grand and affecting ideas of these important realities; realities which he then firmly believed, and which he now sees in the clearest light of intuitive demonstrations.

The unusual lustre with which he shone could not long be confined to that remote corner of the world, but soon attracted the notice and pleasing admiration of men of genius, learning, or piety, far and near; and therefore, on a vacancy at the College of New Jersey, occasioned by the decease of two former Presidents,* in a close and awful succession, he was elected to that important office in the year 1759.

Distressing as it was both to him and his people, united in the strongest bonds of mutual affection, to think of a separation, yet a conviction of absolute duty, resulting from the importance of the station, from the various concurring providences, and lastly, from the unanimous advice of his reverend brethren convened in synod, determined him to accept the proposal. Great and pleasing were the expectations with which we beheld him enter into that exalted sphere of service; yet I may boldly say that they were vastly exceeded in every respect by the reputable manner in which he discharged the arduous trust. The progress he made in all the branches of science, with his capacity and diligence to acquire new improvements, enabled him to conduct the youth with great advantage through the several stages of useful and polite literature. And, while he endeavoured to improve the minds, he was not less solicitous to reform the hearts and lives of his pupils, to make them good as well as great, and fit them for both worlds. He knew that religion was the brightest ornament of the human, and the fairest image of the divine nature, that all true benevolence to men must have its foundation laid in a supreme love to God, and that undissembled piety in the heart was the best security for usefulness in every character of life. It was therefore his constant endeavour to promote the eternal as well as the temporal good of the youth entrusted to his tuition, not only by his fervent preaching

---

* The Rev. Aaron Burr, in 1757, and the Rev. Jonathan Edwards, who succeeded him, and died the winter following.

and exemplary life, but by inculcating at the proper seasons the worth of their souls, and the vast, the inexpressible importance of their ever-lasting interests.

In the government of the College, he had the peculiar art of min-gling authority and lenity in such a due proportion, as seldom or never failed of the desired success. Hence he was revered and loved by every member of that collected family over which he presided. His performances at public anniversary Commencements, as they never failed to do honour to the institution, so they always surprised his friends themselves by exceeding, far exceeding their most sanguine expectations. His poetical compositions, and his elegant taste for cultivating the Muses, gave additional embellishments to those per-formances, and greatly heightened the pleasure of his crowded auditors.

His acquaintance with mankind, his easy and polite behaviour, his affability and condescension, his modesty and candour, his engag-ing manner of address, with his sprightly and entertaining conversa-tion, all the genuine fruits of a most benevolent heart, rendered him greatly beloved through the large circle of his acquaintance, and as greatly admired even by strangers, whose occasional excursions gave them only the opportunity of a transient interview.

His natural temper, amiable in itself, and sweetened with all the charms of divine grace, rendered him peculiarly dear in all the rela-tive characters of social life, whether as a husband, a father, a tutor, or a friend.

With this excellent man at the head of the College, what pleasing prospects did we form of the extensive usefulness of that infant seminary, both to the church and to the commonwealth! He was, in short, all we could wish or desire in a man, to promote the valuable interests of learning and piety, and render the College reputable and useful.

But, alas! all his ample furniture of gifts and graces, all the amiable qualities of the mind, with the advantages of the happiest constitution of body, could not secure him from the fate of mortals. He is gone; he has quitted this inferior world amidst the unfeigned sorrows of his family, his friends, the College, and our country; he has taken his flight to his native skies, and joined with kindred spirits in the regions of a glorious immortality, while his remains are gathered to those of his predecessors, in the dark and dreary repository of the grave.

Oh the unutterable and extensive loss to a distressed family, to a bereaved College, to the ministry, to the church, to the community, to the republic of letters, and in short to all the valuable interests of mankind !

SERMONS

ON

IMPORTANT SUBJECTS.

SERMON I.

THE DIVINE AUTHORITY AND SUFFICIENCY OF THE CHRISTIAN RELIGION.

LUKE xvi. 27–31: *Then he said, I pray thee therefore, father, that thou wouldst send him to my father's house : for I have five brethren ; that he may testify unto them, lest they also come into this place of torment. Abraham saith unto him, They have Moses and the prophets ; let them hear them. And he said, Nay, father Abraham : but if one went unto them from the dead they will repent. And he said unto him, If they hear not Moses and the prophets, neither will they be persuaded, though one rose from the dead.*

WHAT Micah said superstitiously, when he was robbed of his idols, *Ye have taken away my gods; and what have I more?* (Judg. xviii. 24) may be truly spoken with regard to the religion of Jesus. If that be taken from us, what have we more? *If the foundations be destroyed, what shall the righteous do?* Ps. xi. 3. The generality of you owe all your hopes of a glorious immortality to

71

this heaven-born religion, and you make it the rule of
your faith and practice; confident that in so doing you
please God.

But what if after all you should be mistaken? What
if the religion of Jesus should be an imposture?—I know
you are struck with horror at the thought, and perhaps,
alarmed at my making so shocking a supposition. But
this suspicion, horrid as it is, has probably been suggested
to you at times by infernal agency; this suspicion may at
times have arisen in your minds in their wanton and licentious excursions, or from the false alarms of a melancholy
and timorous imagination: and if this suspicion has never
been raised in you by the sophistical conversation of loose
wits and affected rationalists, it has been owing to your
happy retirement from the polite world, where infidelity
makes extensive conquests, under the specious name of
Deism. Since therefore you are subject to an assault from
such a suspicion, when you may not be armed ready to
repel it, let me this day start it from its ambush, that I
may try the force of a few arguments upon it, and furnish
you with weapons to conquer it.

Let me also tell you, that *that* faith in the Christian religion which proceeds from insufficient or bad principles,
is but little better than infidelity. If you believe the
Christian religion to be divine, because you hardly care
whether it be true or false, being utterly unconcerned
about religion in any shape, and therefore never examining the matter; if you believe it true, because you have
been educated in it; because your parents or ministers
have told you so; or because it is the religion of your
country; if these are the only grounds of your faith, it is
not such a faith as constitutes you true Christians; for
upon the very same grounds you would have been Mahometans in Turkey, disciples of Confucius in China, or

worshippers of the Devil among the Indians, if it had been your unhappy lot to be born in those countries; for a Mahometan, or a Chinese, or an Indian, can assign these grounds for his faith. Surely, I need not tell you, that the grounds of a mistaken belief in an imposture, are not a sufficient foundation for a saving faith in divine revelation. I am afraid there are many such implicit believers among us, who are in the right only by chance: and these lie a prey to every temptation, and may be turned out of the way of truth by every wind of doctrine. It is therefore necessary to teach them the grounds of the Christian religion, both to prevent their seduction, and to give them a rational and well-grounded faith, instead of that which is only blind and accidental.

Nay, such of us as have the clearest conviction of this important truth, have need to have it inculcated upon us, that we may be more and more impressed with it; for the influence of Christianity upon our hearts and lives will be proportioned to the realizing, affecting persuasion of its truth and certainty in our understandings.

If I can prove that Christianity answers all the ends of a religion from God; if I can prove that it is attended with sufficient attestation; if I can prove that no sufficient objections can be offered against it; and that men have no reason at all to desire another; but that if this proves ineffectual for their reformation and salvation, there is no ground to hope that any other would prove successful; I say, if I can prove these things, then the point in debate is carried, and we must all embrace the religion of Jesus as certainly true. These things are asserted or implied in my text, with respect to the Scriptures then extant, *Moses and the prophets*.

My text is a parabolical dialogue between Abraham and one of his wretched posterity, once rioting in the luxuries of high life, but now tormented in infernal flames.

We read of his brethren in his father's house. Among these probably his estate was divided upon his decease; from whence we may infer that he had no children: for had he had any, it would have been more natural to represent him as solicitous for their reformation by a messenger from the dead, than for that of his brothers. He seems, therefore, like some of our unhappy modern rakes, just to have come to his estate, and to have abandoned himself to such a course of debaucheries as soon shattered his constitution, and brought him down to the grave, and alas! to hell, in the bloom of life, when they were far from his thoughts. May this be a warning to all of his age and circumstances!

Whether, from some remaining affection to his brethren, or (which is more likely) from a fear that they who had shared with him in sin would increase his torment, should they descend to him in the infernal prison, he is solicitous that Lazarus might be sent as an apostle from the dead to warn them. His petition is to this purpose: "Since no request in my own favour can be granted; since I cannot obtain the poor favour of a drop of water to cool my flaming tongue, let me at least make one request in behalf of those that are as yet in the land of hope, and not beyond the reach of mercy. In my father's house I have five brethren, gay, thoughtless, young creatures, who are now rioting in those riches I was forced to leave; who interred my mouldering corpse in state, little apprehensive of the doom of my immortal part; who are now treading the same enchanting paths of pleasure I walked in: and will, unless reclaimed, soon descend, like me, thoughtless and unprepared, into these doleful regions: I therefore pray, that thou wouldest send Lazarus to alarm them in their wild career, with an account of my dreadful doom, and inform them of the reality and importance of everlasting happiness and misery, that they may reform, and so avoid this place of torment, whence I can never escape."

Abraham's answer may be thus paraphrased: " If thy brothers perish, it will not be for want of means; they enjoy the sacred Scriptures of the Old Testament, written by *Moses and the prophets ;* and these are sufficient to inform them of the necessary truths to regulate their practice, and particularly to warn them of everlasting punishment! Let them therefore hear and regard, study and obey, those writings: for they need no further means for their salvation."

To this the wretched creature replies, " Nay, father Abraham, these means will not avail; I enjoyed them all; and yet here I am, a lost soul; and I am afraid they will have as little effect upon them as they had upon me. These means are common and familiar, and therefore disregarded. But if one arose from the dead, if an apostle from the invisible world was sent to them, to declare as an eye-witness the great things he has seen, surely they would repent. The novelty and terror of the apparition would alarm them. Their senses would be struck with so unusual a messenger, and they would be convinced of the reality of eternal things; therefore I must renew my request; send Lazarus to them in all the pomp of heavenly splendour; Lazarus whom they once knew in so abject a condition, and whom they will therefore the more regard, when they see him appear in all his present glory."

Thus the miserable creature pleads, (and it is natural for us to wish for other means, when those we have enjoyed are ineffectual, though it should be through our own neglect;) but, alas! he pleads in vain.

Abraham continues inexorable, and gives a very good

reason for his denial: "If they pay no regard to the writings of *Moses and the prophets*, the standing revelation God has left in his church, it would be to no purpose to give them another: they would not be persuaded though one rose from the dead; the same disposition that renders them deaf to such messengers as *Moses and the prophets*, would also render them impersuasible by a messenger from the dead. Such an one might strike them with a panic, but it would soon be over, and then they would return to their usual round of pleasures; they would presently think the apparition was but the creature of their own imagination, or some unaccountable illusion of their senses. If one arose from the dead, he could but declare the same things substantially with *Moses and the prophets;* and he could not speak with greater authority, or give better credentials than they; and therefore they who are not benefited by these standing means must be given up as desperate; and God, for very good reasons, will not multiply new revelations to them."

This answer of Abraham was exemplified when another Lazarus was raised from the dead in the very sight of the Jews, and Christ burst the bands of death, and gave them incontestible evidences of his resurrection; and yet after all they were not persuaded, but persisted in invincible infidelity.

This parable was spoken before any part of the New Testament was written, and added to the sacred canon; and if it might be then asserted, that the standing revelation of God's will was sufficient, and that it was needless to demand farther, then much more may it be asserted now, when the canon of the Scriptures is completed, and we have received so much additional light from the New Testament. We have not only *Moses and the prophets*, but we have also Christ, who is a messenger from the dead, and his apostles; and therefore, surely, "if we do not hear them, neither will we be persuaded, though one rose from the dead." The Gospel is the last effort of the grace of God with a guilty world; and if this has no effect upon us, our disease is incurable that refuses to be healed.

I cannot insist upon all the important truths contained in this copious text, but only design,

I. To show the sufficiency of the standing revelation of God's will in the Scriptures, to bring men to repentance; and,

II. To expose the vanity and unreasonableness of the objections against this revelation, and of demanding another.

I. I am to show the sufficiency of the standing revelation in the Scriptures to bring men to repentance.

If the Scriptures give us sufficient instructions in matters of faith, and sufficient directions in matters of practice, if they are attended with sufficient evidences for our faith, and produce sufficient excitements to influence our practice, then they contain a sufficient revelation; for it is for these purposes we need a revelation, and a revelation that answers these purposes has the directest tendency to make us truly religious, and bring us to a happy immortality. But that the revelation in the Scriptures, (particularly in the New Testament, which I shall more immediately consider as being the immediate foundation of Christianity) is sufficient for all these purposes, will be evident from an induction of particulars.

1. The Scriptures give us sufficient instructions what we should believe, or are a sufficient rule of faith.

Religion cannot subsist without right notions of God and divine things; and entire ignorance or mistakes in its fundamental articles must be destructive of its nature; and therefore a divine revelation must be a collection of rays of light, a system of divine knowledge; and such we find the Christian revelation to be, as contained in the sacred writings.

In the Scriptures we find the faint discoveries of natural reason illustrated, its uncertain conjectures determined, and its mistakes corrected; so that Christianity includes natural religion in the greatest perfection. But it does not rest here; it brings to light things which *eye hath not seen, nor ear heard, neither have entered into the heart of man*, 1 Cor. ii. 9—things, which our feeble reason could never have discovered without the help of a supernatural revelation; and which yet are of the utmost importance for us to know.

In the Scriptures we have the clearest and most majestic account of the nature and perfections of the Deity, and of his being the Creator, Ruler, and Benefactor of the universe; to whom therefore all reasonable beings are under infinite obligations.

In the Scriptures we have an account of the present state of human nature, as degenerate, and a more rational and easy account of its apostacy, than could ever be given by the light of nature.

In the Scriptures too (which wound but to cure) we have the welcome account of a method of recovery from the ruins of our apostacy, through the mediation of the Son of God; there we have the assurance, which we could find no where else, that God is reconcilable, and willing to pardon penitents upon the account of the obedience and sufferings of Christ. There all our anxious inquiries, *Wherewith shall I come before the* LORD, *and bow myself before the high God? shall I come before him with burnt-offerings?* &c., Micah vi. 6, 7, are satisfactorily answered; and there the agonizing conscience can obtain relief, which might have sought it in vain among all the other religions in the world.

In the Scriptures also, eternity and the invisible worlds are laid open to our view; and "life and immortality are brought to light by the Gospel;" about which the heathen sages, after all their inquiries, laboured under uneasy suspicions. There we are assured of the state of future rewards and punishments, according to our conduct in this state of probation; and the nature, perfection, and duration of the happiness and misery, are described with as much accuracy as are necessary to engage us to seek the one and shun the other.

I particularize these doctrines of Christianity as a specimen, or as so many general heads, to which many others may be reduced; not intending a complete enumeration, which would lead me far beyond the bounds of one sermon; and for which my whole life is not sufficient. I therefore proceed to add,

2. The Holy Scriptures give us complete directions in matters of practice, or a sufficient rule of life.

A divine revelation must not be calculated merely to amuse us, and gratify our curiosity with sublime and refined notions and speculations, but adapted to direct and regulate our practice, and render us better as well as wiser.

Accordingly, the sacred writings give us a complete system of practical religion and morality. There, not only all the duties of natural religion are inculcated, but several important duties, as love to our enemies, humility, &c., are clearly discovered, which the feeble light of reason in the heathen moralists did either not perceive at all, or but very faintly. In short, there we are informed of our duties towards God, towards our neighbours, and towards ourselves. The Scriptures are full of particular injunctions and directions to particular duties, lest we should not be sagacious enough to infer them from general rules; and sometimes all these duties are summed up in some short maxim, or general rule; which we may easily remember, and always carry about with us. Such a noble summary is that which Christ has given us of the whole moral law; "Thou shalt love the Lord thy God, with all thy heart, &c., and thy neighbour as thyself." Or that all-comprehending rule of our conduct towards one another, "Whatsoever ye would that men should do unto you, do ye the same unto them."

What recommends these doctrinal instructions and practical directions is, that they are plain and obvious to common sense. It is as much the concern of the illiterate and vulgar to be religious, as of the few endowed with an exalted and philosophic genius; and consequently, whatever difficulties may be in a revelation to exercise the latter, yet all necessary matters of faith and practice must be delivered in a plain manner, level to the capacities of the former; otherwise it would be no revelation at all to them who stand in most need of it. Accordingly the religion of Jesus, though it has mysteries equal and infinitely superior to the largest capacity, yet in its necessary articles is intelligible to all ranks who apply themselves with proper diligence to the perusal of them; and I dare affirm, that a man of common sense, with the assistance of the sacred Scriptures, can form a better system of religion and morality than the wisest philosopher, with all his abilities and learning, can form without this help. This I dare affirm, because it has been put to trial, and attested by matter of fact; for whoever is acquainted with the writings of the ancient heathen philosophers, cannot but be convinced, that amidst all their learning and study, amidst all their shining thoughts and refined speculations, they had not such just notions of God and his perfections, of the most acceptable way of worshipping him, of the duties of morality, and of a future state, as any common Christian among us has learned from the Scriptures, without any uncommon natural parts, without extensive learning, and without such painful study and close application as the heathen moralists were forced to use to make their less perfect discoveries. In this sense the least in the kingdom of heaven, *i. e.*, any common Christian, is greater than all the Socrateses, the Platos, the Ciceros, and the Senecas of antiquity; as one that is of a weak sight can see more clearly by the help of day-light, than the clearest eye can without it.

And by whom was this vast treasure of knowledge laid up to enrich the world? by whom were these matchless writings composed, which furnish us with a system of religion and morality so much more plain, so much more perfect, than all the famous sages of antiquity could frame? Why, to our astonishment, they were composed by a company of fishermen, or persons not much superior; by persons generally without any liberal education; persons who had not devoted their lives to intellectual improvement; persons of no extraordinary natural parts, and who had not travelled, like the ancient philosophers, to gather up fragments of knowledge in different countries, but who lived in Judea, a country where learning was but little cultivated, in comparison of Greece and Rome. These were the most accomplished teachers of mankind that ever appeared in the world. And can this be accounted for, without acknowledging their inspiration from heaven? If human reason could have made such discoveries, surely it would have made them by those in whom it was improved to the greatest perfection, and not by a company of ignorant mechanics.

The persons themselves declare that they had not made these discoveries, but were taught them immediately from heaven, (which indeed we must have believed, though they had not told us so.)   Now we must believe their declaration, and own them inspired, or fall into this absurdity.   That a company of illiterate, wicked, and daring impostors, who were hardy enough to pretend themselves commissioned and inspired from God, have furnished us with an incomparably more excellent system of religion and virtue, than could be furnished by all the wisest and best of the sons of men beside; and he that can believe this may believe any thing; and should never more pretend that he cannot believe the Christian religion upon the account of the difficulties that attend it.

I have touched but superficially upon the sufficiency of the Scriptures as a rule of faith and practice; for to dwell long upon this, would be to fight without an antagonist. Our infidels reject the Christian religion, because they suppose it requires them to believe and practise too much, rather than too little.   Hence they are for lopping off a great part of its doctrines and precepts, as superfluities, or incumbrances, and forming a meagre skeleton of natural religion.   Their intellectual pride will not stoop to believe doctrines which they cannot comprehend; and they cannot bear such narrow bounds as the precepts of Christianity fix for them in their pursuits of pleasure, and therefore they would break these bands asunder.   That which they affect most to complain of, is the want of evidence to convince them of the truth of this ungrateful religion; it will therefore be necessary to prove more largely, that,

3. The Scriptures are attended with sufficient evidences of their truth and divinity.

It is certain that as God can accept no other worship

than rational from reasonable creatures, he cannot require us to believe a revelation to be divine without sufficient reason; and therefore, when he gives us a revelation, he will attest it with such evidences as will be a sufficient foundation of our belief.

Accordingly the Scriptures are attested with all the evidences intrinsic and extrinsic, which we can reasonably desire, and with all the evidences the nature of the thing will admit.

As for intrinsic evidences, many might be mentioned; but I must at present confine myself in proper limits. I shall resume the one I have already hinted at, namely, that the religion of the Bible has the directest tendency to promote true piety and solid virtue in the world; it is such a religion as becomes a God to reveal; such a religion as we might expect from him, in case he instituted any; a religion intended and adapted to regulate self-love, and to diffuse the love of God and man through the world, the only generous principles and vigorous springs of a suitable conduct towards God, towards one another, and towards ourselves; a religion productive of every humane, social, and divine virtue, and directly calculated to banish all sin out of the world; to transform impiety into devotion; injustice and oppression into equity and universal benevolence; and sensuality into sobriety: a religion infinitely preferable to any that has been contrived by the wisest and best of mortals. And whence do you think could this god-like religion proceed? Does not its nature prove its origin divine? Does it not evidently bear the lineaments of its heavenly Parent? Can you once imagine that such a pure, such a holy, such a perfect system, could be the contrivance of wicked, infernal spirits, of selfish, artful priests, or politicians, or of a parcel of daring impostors, or wild enthusiasts? Could these contrive a religion so contrary to their inclination, so destructive of their interest, and so directly conducing to promote the cause they abhor? If you can believe this, you may also believe that light is the product of darkness, virtue of vice, good of evil, &c. If such beings as these had contrived a religion, it would have borne the same appearance in the Bible as it does in Italy or Spain, where it is degenerated into a mere trade for the benefit of tyrannical and voracious priests; or it would have been such a religion as that of Mahomet, allowing its subjects to propagate it with the sword, that they might enrich themselves with the plunder of conquered nations; and indulging them in the gratification of their lusts, particularly in polygamy, or the unbounded enjoyment of women. This religion, I fear, would suit the taste of our licentious freethinkers much better than the holy religion of Jesus. Or if we should suppose Christianity to be the contrivance of visionary enthusiasts, then it would not be that rational system which it is, but a huddle of fanatical reveries and ridiculous whims. If, then, it could not be the contrivance of such authors as these, to whom shall we ascribe it? It must have had some author; for it could not come into being without a cause, no more than the system of the universe. Will you then ascribe it to good men? But these men were either inspired from heaven, or they were not; if they were not, then they could not be good men, but most audacious liars; for they plainly declared, they were divinely inspired, and stood in it to the last; which no good man would do if such a declaration was false. If they were inspired from heaven, then the point is gained; then Christianity is a religion from God; for to receive a religion from persons divinely inspired, and to receive it from God, is the same thing.

Another intrinsic evidence is that of prophecy.

Those future events which are contingent, or which shall be accomplished by causes that do not now exist or appear, cannot be certainly foreknown or foretold by man, as we find by our own experience. Such objects fall within the compass of Omniscience only; and therefore when short-sighted mortals are enabled to predict such events many years, and even ages before they happen, it is a certain evidence that they are let into the secrets of heaven, and that God communicates to them a knowledge which cannot be acquired by the most sagacious human mind; and this is an evidence that the persons thus divinely taught are the messengers of God, to declare his will to the world.

Now there are numberless instances of such prophecies in the sacred writings. Thus a prophet foretold the destruction of Jeroboam's altar by the good Josiah, many ages before, 1 Kings xiii. 2. Cyrus was foretold by name as the restorer of the Jews from Babylon, to rebuild their temple and city, about a hundred years before he was born, Isaiah xlv. 1, &c. Several of the prophets foretold the destruction of various kingdoms in a very punctual manner, as of Jerusalem, Babylon, Egypt, Ninevah, &c., which prediction was exactly fulfilled. But the most remarkable prophecies of the Old Testament are those relating to the Messiah; which are so numerous and full, that they might serve for materials for his history; they fix the time of his coming, viz., while the sceptre continued in Judah, Gen. xlix. 10, while the second temple was yet standing, Hag. ii. 7, Mal. iii. 1, and towards the close of Daniel's seventy weeks of years, i. e., four hundred and ninety years from the rebuilding of Jerusalem, Dan. ix. 24, &c. These prophecies also describe the lineage of the Messiah, the manner of his conception, his life and miracles, his death, and the various circumstances of it; his resurrection, ascension, and advancement to universal empire, and the spread of the gospel through the world.   In the New Testament also we meet with sundry remarkable prophecies.   There Christ foretells his own death, and the manner of it, and his triumphant resurrection; there, with surprising accuracy, he predicts the destruction of Jerusalem by the Romans.   We find various prophecies also in the apostolic epistles, particularly that of St. Paul, Rom. xi., concerning the conversion of the Jews; which, though it be not yet accomplished, yet we see a remarkable providence making way for it, in keeping the Jews, who are scattered over all the earth, distinct from all other nations for about one thousand seven hundred years, though they are hated of all nations, and consequently under the strongest temptation to coalesce with, and lose themselves among them; and though all other nations have in a much shorter time mixed in such a manner, that none of them can now trace their own original; e. g., who can now distinguish the posterity of the ancient Romans from the Goths and Vandals, and others that broke in upon their empire and settled among them; or of the ancient Angli from the Danes, &c., that mingled with them?

These and many other plain predictions are interspersed through the Scriptures, and prove their original to be from the Father of lights, who alone knows all his works from the beginning, and who declares such distant contingent futurities from ancient times. Isaiah xlv. 21.

I might, as another intrinsic evidence of the truth of Christianity, mention its glorious energy on the minds of men, in convincing them of sin, easing their consciences, inspiring them with unspeakable joy, subduing their lusts, and transforming them into its own likeness; which is attested by the daily experience of every true Christian. Every one that believeth hath this witness in himself: and this is an evidence level to the meanest capacity, which may be soon lost in the course of sublime reasoning. But as the deists declare, alas! with too much truth, that the gospel hath no such power upon them, it is not to my purpose to insist upon it.

I therefore proceed to mention some of the extrinsic evidences of the religion of Jesus, particularly the miracles with which it was confirmed, and its early propagation through the world.

Miracles of this case are events above or contrary to the established law of nature, done with a professed design to attest a revelation; and as they are obvious and striking to the senses of the most ignorant and unthinking, they are the most popular and convictive evidences, adapted to the generality of mankind, who are incapable of a long train of argumentation, or of perceiving the origin of a religion from its nature and tendency.

Now the religion of Jesus is abundantly attested with this kind of evidence. The history of the life of Jesus and his apostles is one continued series of miracles. Sight was restored to the blind, the deaf were enabled to hear, the lame to walk, the maimed furnished with new-created limbs, the sick healed, the rage of winds and seas controlled, yea, the dead were raised; and all this with an air of sovereignty, such as became a God; the apostles were also endowed with miraculous powers, enabled to speak with tongues, and to communicate the Holy Spirit to others. These miracles were done not in a corner, but in the most public places, before numerous spectators, friends and foes: and the persons that wrought them appealed to them as the evidences of their divine mission: and the account of them is conveyed down to us by the best medium, written tradition, in a history that bears all the evidences of credibility, of which any composition of that kind is capable.

Another extrinsic evidence of the truth of Christianity is its extensive propagation through the world in the most unpromising circumstances.

The only religion, besides the Christian, which has had any very considerable spread in the world, is that of Mahomet; but we may easily account for this, without supposing it divine, from its nature, as indulging the lusts of men; and especially from the manner of its propagation, not by the force of evidence, but by the force of arms. But the circumstances of the propagation of Christianity were quite otherwise, whether we consider its contrariety to the corruptions, prejudices, and interests of men; the easiness of detecting it, had it been false; the violent opposition it met with from all the powers of the earth; the instruments of its propagation; or the measures they took for that purpose.

Christianity is directly contrary to the corruptions, prejudices, and interests of mankind. It grants no indulgence to the corrupt propensities of a degenerate world; but requires that universal holiness of heart and life which, as we find by daily observation, is so ungrateful to them, and which is the principal reason that the religion of Jesus meets with so much contempt and opposition in every age.

When Christianity was first propagated, all nations had been educated in some other religion; the Jews were attached to Moses, and the Gentiles to their various systems of heathenism, and were all of them very zealous for their own religion; but Christianity proposed a new scheme, and could not take place without antiquating or exploding all other religions; and therefore it was contrary to the inveterate prejudices of all mankind, and could never have been so generally received, if it had not brought with it the most evident credentials; especially considering that some of its doctrines were such as seemed to the Jews a stumbling-block, and to the Greeks foolishness; particularly that one of obscure birth and low life, who was publicly executed as a slave and malefactor, should be worshipped and honoured as God, upon pain of everlasting damnation; and that there should be a resurrection of the dead: the last of which was an object of ridicule to all the wits and philosophers of the heathen world. Again, as some religion or other was established in all nations, there were many, like Demetrius and his craftsmen, whose temporal livings and interest depended upon the continuance of their religion; and if that was changed, they fell into poverty and disgrace. There was a powerful party in every nation, and they would exert themselves to prevent the spread of an innovation so dangerous to their interest, which we find by all histories of those times they actually did:—and yet the despised religion of Jesus triumphed over all their opposition, and maintained its credit in spite of all their endeavours to detect it as an imposture; and this proves it was not an imposture; for,

In the next place, it was easy to have detected Christianity as an imposture, nay, it was impossible it should not have been detected, if it had been such; for the great facts upon which the evidence of it rested, were said to be obvious and public, done before thousands and in all countries; for wherever the apostles travelled they carried their miraculous powers along with them. Thousands must know whether Christ had fed many thousands with provisions only sufficient for a few; whether Lazarus was raised from the dead before the admiring multitude; whether the apostles spoke with tongues to those various nations among whom they endeavoured to propagate their religion, (as indeed they must have done, otherwise they would not have been understood.) These things, and many others, upon which the evidence of Christianity depends, were public in their own nature; and therefore, if they had not been matters of fact, the cheat must have been unavoidably detected, especially when so many were concerned to detect it.

Farther: Christianity met with the most strenuous opposition from all the powers of the earth. The Jewish rulers and most of the populace were implacable enemies; and as they lived on the spot where its miraculous attestations were said to be given, it was in their power to crush it in its birth, and never have suffered it to spread farther, had it not been attended with invincible evidence. All the power of the Roman empire was also exerted for its extirpation; and its propagators and disciples could expect no profit or pleasure by it, but were assured, from the posture of affairs, from daily experience, and from the predictions of their Master, that they should meet with shame, persecution, and death itself, in its most tremendous shapes; and in the next world they could expect nothing, even according to their own doctrine, but everlasting damnation, if they were wilful impostors; and yet, in spite of all these discouragements, they courageously persisted in their testimony to the last, though they might have secured their lives, and helped their fortune (as Judas did) by retracting it; nay, their testimony prevailed, in defiance of all opposition; multitudes in all nations then known embraced the faith; though they expected tortures and death for it; and in a few centuries, the vast and mighty Roman empire submitted to the religion of a crucified Jesus. And who were those mighty heroes that thus triumphed over the world? Why, to our surprise,

The instruments of the propagation of Christianity were

a company of poor mechanics, publicans, tent-makers, and fishermen, from the despised nation of the Jews. And by what strange powers or arts did they make these extensive conquests?

The measures they took were a plain declaration of their religion; and they wrought miracles for its confirmation. They did not use the power of the sword, nor secular terrors, or bribery; they were without learning, without the arts of reasoning and persuasion; and without all the usual artifices of seducers to gain credit to their imposture.

Here I cannot but take particular notice of that matchless simplicity that appears in the history of Christ and his apostles. The evangelists write in that artless, calm, and unguarded manner, which is natural to persons confident of the undeniable truth of what they assert; they do not write with that scrupulous caution which would argue any fear that they might be confuted. They simply relate the naked facts, and leave them to stand upon their own evidence. They relate the most amazing, the most moving things, with the most cool serenity, without any passionate exclamations and warm reflections. For example, they relate the most astonishing miracles, as the resurrection of Lazarus, in the most simple, and, as it were, careless manner, without breaking out and celebrating the divine power of Christ. In the same manner they relate the most tragical circumstances of his condemnation and death, calmly mentioning matter of fact, without any invectives against the Jews, without any high eulogies upon Christ's innocence, without any rapturous celebrations of his grace in suffering all these things for sinners, and without any tender lamentations over their deceased Master. It is impossible for a heart so deeply impressed with such things, as theirs undoubtedly were, to

retain this dispassionate serenity, unless laid under supernatural restraints; and there appears very good reasons
for this restraint upon them, viz., that the gospel history
might carry intrinsic evidences of its simplicity and artless
impartiality; and that it might appear adapted to convince
the judgments of men, and not merely to raise their passions.   In this respect, the gospel-history is distinguished
from all histories in the world: and can we think so plain,
so undisguised, so artless a composure, the contrivance of
designing impostors?   Would not a consciousness that
they might be detected keep them more upon their guard,
and make them more ready to anticipate and confine objections, and take every artifice to recommend their cause,
and prepossess the reader in its favour?

It only remains under this head, that I should

4. Show that the religion of Jesus proposes sufficient
excitements to influence our faith and practice.

To enforce a system of doctrines and precepts, two
things are especially necessary; that they should be made
duty by competent authority, and matters of interest by
a sanction of rewards and punishments.   To which I may
add, that the excitements are still stronger, when we are
laid under the gentle obligations of gratitude.   In all these
respects the Christian religion has the most powerful en-
forcements.

The authority upon which we are required to receive
the doctrines, and observe the precepts of Christianity,
is no less than the authority of God, the supreme Lawgiver and infallible Teacher; whose wisdom to prescribe,
and right to command, are indisputable; and we may
safely submit our understandings to his instructions, however mysterious, and our wills to his injunctions, however
difficult they may seem to us.   This gives the religion of
Jesus a binding authority upon the consciences of men;

which is absolutely necessary to bring piety and virtue into practice in the world; for if men are left at liberty, they will follow their own inclinations, however wicked and pernicious. And in this respect, Christianity bears a glorious preference to all the systems of morality composed by the heathen philosophers; for though there were many good things in them, yet who gave authority to Socrates, Plato, or Seneca, to assume the province of lawgivers, and dictators to mankind, and prescribe to their consciences? All they could do was to teach, to advise, to persuade, to reason; but mankind were at liberty, after all, whether to take their advice or not. And this shows the necessity of supernatural revelation not merely to make known things beyond human apprehension, but to enforce with proper authority such duties as might be discovered by man; since without it they would not have the binding force of a law.

As to the sanction of rewards and punishments in Christianity, they are such as became a God to annex to his majestic law, such as are agreeable to creatures formed for immortality, and such as would have the most effectual tendency to encourage obedience, and prevent sin; they are no less than the most perfect happiness and misery, which human nature is capable of, and that through an endless duration. If these are not sufficient to allure rational creatures to obedience, then no considerations that can be proposed can have any effect. These tend to alarm our hopes and our fears, the most vigorous springs of human activity: and if these have no effect upon us, nothing that God can reveal, or our minds conceive, will have any effect. God, by adding the greatest sanctions possible to his law, has taken the best possible precautions to prevent disobedience; and since even these do not restrain men from it, we are sure that less would not suffice.

If men will go on in sin, though they believe the punishment due to it will be eternal, then much more would they persist in it, if it were not eternal; or, if they say they will indulge themselves in sin, because they believe it not eternal, then this proves from their own mouth, that it should be eternal in order to restrain them. The prevalence of sin in the world tends to render it miserable; and therefore, to prevent it, as well as to display God's eternal regard to moral goodness, it is fit that he should annex the highest degree of punishment to disobedience in every individual; for the indulgence of sin in one individual would be a temptation to the whole rational creation; and, on the other hand, the threatenings of everlasting punishment to all sinners indefinitely, is necessary to deter the whole rational world, and every particular person from disobedience. Thus in civil government, it is necessary that robbery should be threatened indefinitely with death, because though one robber may take from a man but what he can very well spare; yet, if every man might rob and plunder his neighbour, the consequence would be universal robbery and confusion. It is therefore necessary that the greatest punishment should be threatened to disobedience, both to prevent it, and to testify the divine displeasure against it; which is the primary design of the threatening; and since the penalty was annexed with this view, it follows, that it was primarily enacted with a view to the happiness of mankind, by preventing what would naturally make them miserable, and but secondarily with a view to be executed; for it is to be executed only upon condition of disobedience; which disobedience it was intended to prevent, and consequently it was not immediately intended to be executed, or enacted for the sake of the execution, as though God took a malignant pleasure in the misery of his creatures. But when the penalty has failed of its primary end, restraining from sin, then it is fit it should answer its secondary end, and be executed upon the offender, to keep the rest of reasonable creatures in their obedience, to illustrate the veracity and holiness of the lawgiver, and prevent his government from falling into contempt. There are the same reasons that threatenings should be executed when denounced, as for their being denounced at first; for threatenings never executed, are the same with no threatenings at all.

Let me add, that the gospel lays us under the strongest obligations from gratitude. It not only clearly informs us of our obligations to God, as the author of our being, and all our temporal blessings, which natural religion more faintly discovers, but superadds those more endearing ones derived from the scheme of man's redemption through the death of the eternal Son of God. Though the blessings of creation and providence are great in themselves, they are swallowed up, as it were, and lost in the love of God; which is commended to us by this matchless circumstance, "that while we were yet sinners, Christ died for us;" and while under the constraints of this love, we cannot but devote ourselves entirely to God, 2 Cor. v. 14, 15.

Thus I have hinted at a few things among the many that might be mentioned to prove the divinity of the religion of Jesus, and its sufficiency to bring men to repentance and salvation. And if it be so, why should it be rejected, or another sought? This reminds me that I promised,

II. To expose the vanity and unreasonableness of the objection against the Christian religion, or of demanding another, &c.

What can our ingenious infidels offer against what has been said? It must be something very weighty indeed to preponderate all this evidence. A laugh, or a sneer, a

pert witticism, declaiming against priestcraft and the prejudices of education, artful evasions, and shallow sophisms,
the usual arguments of our pretended free-thinkers, these
will not suffice to banter us out of our joyful confidence
of the divinity of the religion of Jesus; and I may add,
these will not suffice to indemnify them.   Nothing will be
sufficient for this but demonstration: it lies upon them to
prove the Christian religion to be certainly false: otherwise, unless they are hardened to a prodigy, they must be
racked with anxious fears lest they should find it true to
their cost; and lest that dismal threatening should stand
firm against them : " *He that believeth not, shall be damned.*"
What mighty objections, then, have they to offer?   Will
they say that the Christian religion contains mysterious
doctrines, which they cannot comprehend, which seem to
them unaccountable?   As that of the trinity, the incarnation, and satisfaction of Christ, &c.   But will they advance their understanding to be the universal standard of
truth?   Will they pretend to comprehend the infinite God,
in their finite minds? then let them go, and measure the
heavens with a span, and comprehend the ocean in the
hollow of their hand.   Will they pretend to understand
the divine nature, when they cannot understand their own?
when they cannot account for or explain the union betwixt
their own souls and bodies?   Will they reject mysteries
in Christianity, when they must own them in every thing
else ?   Let them first solve all the phenomena in nature; let
them give us a rational theory of the infinite divisibility
of a piece of finite matter; let them account for the seemingly magical operation of the loadstone; the circulation
of the blood upwards as well as downwards, contrary to all
the laws of motion; let them inform us of the causes of
the cohesion of the particles of matter; let them tell us,
how spirits can receive ideas from material organs; how

they hear and see, &c.: let them give us intelligible theories of these things, and then they may, with something of a better grace, set up for critics upon God and his ways; but, while they are mysteries to themselves, while every particle of matter baffles their understandings, it is the most impious intellectual pride to reject Christianity upon the account of its mysteries, and set up themselves as the supreme judges of truth.

Or will they object that there are a great many difficult and strange passages in Scripture, the meaning and propriety of which they do not see? And are there not many strange things in the book of nature, and the administration of Providence, the design and use of which they cannot see, many things that to them seem wrong and ill-contrived? Yet they own the world was created by God, and that his providence rules it: and why will they not allow that the Scriptures may be from God, notwithstanding these difficulties and seeming incongruities? When a learned man can easily raise his discourse above the capacity of common people, will they not condescend to grant that an infinite God can easily overshoot their little souls? Indeed a revelation which we could fully comprehend, would not appear the production of an infinite mind; it would bear no resemblance to its heavenly Father; and therefore we should have reason to suspect it spurious. It is necessary we should meet with difficulties in the Scriptures to mortify our pride. But farther, will they make no allowance for the different customs and practices of different ages? It is certain, that may be proper and graceful in one age which would be ridiculous and absurd in another; and since the Scriptures were written so many years ago, we may safely make this allowance for them, which will remove many seeming absurdities. There should also allowance be made for the Scriptures being rendered literally out of dead, difficult languages; for we know that many expressions may be beautiful and significant in one language, which would be ridiculous and nonsensical if literally translated into another. Were Homer or Virgil thus translated into English, without regard to the idiom of the language, instead of admiring their beauties, we should be apt to think (as Cowley expresses it) "that one madman had translated another madman."

Will they object the wicked lives of its professors against the holiness and good tendency of Christianity itself? But is it Christianity, as practised in the world, or Christianity as taught by Christ and his apostles, and continued in the Bible, that I am proving to be divine? You know it is the latter, and consequently the poor appearance it makes in the former sense, is no argument against its purity and divinity in this. Again, are the bad lives of professors taught and enjoined by genuine Christianity, and agreeable to it? No; they are quite contrary to it, and subversive of it; and it is so far from encouraging such professors, that it pronounces them miserable hypocrites; and their doom will be more severe than that of heathens. Again, are there not hypocritical professors of morality and natural religion, as well as of revealed? Are there not many who cry up morality and religion of nature, and yet boldly violate its plainest precepts? If therefore this be a sufficient objection against Christianity, it must be so too against all religion. Further: do men grow better by renouncing the religion of Jesus? Observation assures us quite the contrary. Finally, are there not some of the professors of Christianity who live habitually according to it? who give us the best patterns of piety and virtue that ever were exhibited to the world? This is sufficient to vindicate the religion they profess, and it is highly injurious to involve such promiscuously in the odium and contempt due to barefaced hypocrites. How would this reasoning please the Deists themselves in parallel cases? "Some that have no regard to Christianity have been murderers, thieves, &c., therefore all that disregard it are such." Or "some that pretended to be honest, have been found villains; therefore all that pretend to it are such; or therefore honesty is no virtue."

Or will they change the note, and instead of pleading that Christianity leads to licentiousness, object that it bears too hard upon the pleasures of mankind, and lays them under too severe restraints? Or that its penalties are excessive and cruel? But does it rob mankind of any pleasures worthy the rational nature, worthy the pursuit of creatures formed for immortality, and consistent with the good of the whole? It restrains them indeed; but it is only as a physician restrains his patient from poison or any improper regimen; it restrains men from living like beasts; it restrains them from those pleasures which will ruin their souls and bodies in the event; it restrains them from gratifying a private passion at the expense of the public; in short, it restrains them from making themselves and others miserable. Hard restraint indeed! and the Deists, to be sure, are generous patrons of human liberty, who would free us from such grievances as these! However, this objection lets us into the secret, and informs us of the reason why our pretended free-thinkers are such enemies to Christianity; it is because it checks their lusts, and will not permit them to act, as well as think freely, *i. e.*, as they please. If they would content themselves with manly and rational pleasures, they would not count the restraints of Christianity intolerable; nay, they would find in it a set of peculiarly noble and refined pleasures, which they might seek in vain elsewhere; for it is so far from being an enemy to the happiness of man, that it was designed to promote it; and then we make ourselves miserable when we reject it, or it becomes our interest that it should be false. As to the penalty of everlasting punishment annexed to sin, which is but a temporal evil, I would ask them whether they are competent judges in a matter in which they are parties? Are they capable to determine what degree of punishment should be inflicted upon disobedience to the infinite Majesty of heaven, when they are not only short-sighted creatures, but also concerned in the affair, and their judgments may be perverted by self-interest? Whether it is most fit that the Judge of all the earth should determine this point, or a company of malefactors, as they are? Is it allowed to criminals in civil courts to determine their own doom, or pronounce their own sentence? If it were, few of them would be punished at all, and government would fall into contempt. Again, let me remind them, that the penalty was annexed to prevent disobedience, and so to render the execution needless; and consequently it was primarily intended for their good. Why then will they frustrate this design, and, when they have rendered the execution necessary, complain of its severity? If they think the penalty so terrible, let them watch against sin, let them accept the salvation the gospel offers, and so avoid it instead of quarreling with its severity, and yet rushing upon it. Or, if they say they will persist in sin because they do not believe the punishment is eternal; this gives me room to appeal to themselves whether a less penalty than everlasting misery would be sufficient to restrain them from sin; and whether God would have taken all proper precautions to prevent sin, if he had annexed a less punishment to his law, since by their own confession, nothing less could deter them from it. I shall only add, that as the human soul must always exist, and as by indulgence in sin in the present state it contracts such habits as render it incapable of happiness in the holy enjoyment of the heavenly world, it must by a natural necessity be for ever miserable, though God should not exert any positive act for its punishment. And if the Deists say, that punishment for some time would reclaim offenders from sin and bring them to repentance, the difficulty is not removed, unless they can prove that misery will bring men to love that God who inflicts it, which they can never do; and it is evident, that that repentance which proceeds merely from self-love, without any regard to God at all, can never be pleasing to him, nor prepare them for happiness in the enjoyment of him. Punishment would produce a repentance like that of a sick-bed, forced, servile, and transitory.

Will they object, that miracles are not a sufficient evidence of the truth and divinity of a revelation, because infernal spirits may also work miracles, as in the case of the magicians of Egypt, to confirm an imposture? But it is known that our free-thinkers explode and laugh at the existence and power of evil spirits in other cases, and therefore must not be allowed to admit them here to serve a turn. However, we grant there are infernal spirits, and that they can perform many things above human power, which may appear to us miraculous, and yet the evidence in favour of Christianity taken from miracles, stands unshaken: for, (1.) Can we suppose that these malignant and wicked spirits, whose business it is to reduce men to sin and ruin, would be willing to exert their power to work miracles to confirm so holy a religion; a religion so contrary to their design, and so subversive of their kingdom and interest? This would be wretched policy indeed. Or if we should suppose them willing, yet (2.) Can we think that God, who has them all at his control, would suffer them to counterfeit the great seal of heaven, and annex it to an imposture? that is, to work such miracles as could not be distinguished from those wrought by him to attest an imposture? Would he permit them to impose upon mankind in a manner that could not be detected? This would be to deliver the world to their management, and suffer them to lead them blindfold to hell in unavoidable delusion: for miracles are such dazzling and pompous evidences, that the general run of mankind could not resist them, even though they were wrought to attest a religion that might be demonstrated, by a long train of sublime reasoning, to be false. God may indeed suffer the devil to mimic the miracles wrought by his immediate hand, as in the case of Jannes and Jambres; but then, as in that case too, he will take care to excel them, and give some distinguishing marks of his almighty agency, which all mankind may easily discriminate from the utmost exertion of infernal power. But though Satan should be willing, and God should permit him to work miracles, yet, (3.) Can we suppose that all the united powers of hell are able to work such astonishing miracles as were wrought for the confirmation of the Christian religion? Can we suppose that they can control the laws of nature at pleasure, and that with an air of sovereignty, and professing themselves the lords of the universe, as we know Christ did? If we can believe this, then we deny them, and may as well ascribe the creation and preservation of the world to them. If they could exert a creating power to form new limbs for the maimed, or to multiply five loaves and two fishes into a sufficient quantity of food for five thousand, and leave a greater quantity of fragments when that were done than the whole provision at first, then they might create the world, and support all the creatures in it. If they could animate the dead and remand the separate soul back to its former habitation, and reunite it with the body, then I see not why they might not have given us life at first. But to suppose this, would be to dethrone the King of heaven, and renounce his providence entirely. We therefore rest assured that the miracles related in the Scriptures were wrought by the finger of God.

But our free-thinkers will urge, how do we, at this distance, know that such miracles were actually wrought? they are only related in Scripture history; but to prove the truth of Scripture from arguments that suppose the Scripture true, is a ridiculous method of reasoning, and only a begging of the question. But, (1.) the reality of those miracles was granted by the enemies of Christianity in their writings against it; and they had no answer to make, but this sorry one, that they were wrought by the power of magic. They never durst deny that they were wrought; for they knew all the world could prove it. Indeed, an honorable testimony concerning them could not be expected from infidels; for it would be utterly inconsistent that they should own these miracles sufficient attestations of Christianity, and yet continue infidels. And this may answer an unreasonable demand of the Deists, that we should produce some honourable testimony concerning these attestations from Jews and Heathens, as well as from Christians, who were parties. We should have much more reason to suspect the testimony of the former as not convictive, when it did not convince the persons themselves. But,

(2.) As these miracles were of so public a nature, and as so many were concerned to detect them, that they would unavoidably have been detected when related in words, if they had not been done; so, for the same reasons, they could not but have been detected when related in writing; and this we know they never were. If these miracles had not been matters of undoubted fact, they could not have been inserted at first in the gospel history; for then, many thousands, in various countries were alive to confute them; and they could not have been introduced into it afterwards, for all the world would see that it was then too late, and that if there had been such things they should have heard of them before: for they were much more necessary for the propagation of Christianity than for its support when received.

But it may be objected, How can we at this distance know that these histories are genuine? May they not have been corrupted, and many additions made to them by designing men in ages since? And why is it not also asked, How do we know that there were such men as Alexander, Julius Cæsar or King William the Third? How do we know but their histories are all romance and fable? How do we know that there were any generations of mankind before ourselves? How do we know but all the acts of Parliament of former reigns are corrupted and we are ruled by impositions? In short, how can we know anything, but what we have seen with our eyes? We may as well make difficulties of all these things, and so destroy all human testimony, as scruple the genuineness of the sacred writings; for never were any writings conveyed down with so good evidence of their being genuine and uncorrupted as these. Upon their first publication they were put into all hands, they were scattered into all nations, translated into various languages, and all perused them; either to be taught by them, or to cavil at them. And ever since, they have been quoted by thousands of authors, appealed to by all parties of Christians, as the supreme judge of controversies; and not only the enemies of Christianity have carefully watched them to detect any alterations which pious fraud might attempt to make, but one sect of Christians has kept a watchful eye over the other, lest they should alter anything in favour of their own cause. And it is matter of astonishment as well as conviction, that all the various copies and translations of the Scriptures in different nations and libraries are substantially the same, and differ only in matters of small moment; so that from the worst copy of translation in the world, one might easily learn the substance of Christianity.

Or will our infidels insist to be eye-witnesses of these facts? Must one arise from the dead, or new miracles be wrought to convince them by ocular demonstration? This is a most unreasonable demand, for (1.) The continuance of miracles in every age would be attended with numerous inconveniences. For example, Multitudes must be born blind, deaf, or dumb; multitudes must be afflicted with incurable diseases, and possessed by evil spirits; multitudes must be disturbed in the sleep of death; and all the laws of nature must be made precarious and fickle, in order to leave room for miraculous operations; and all this to humour a company of obstinate infidels, who would not believe upon less striking though entirely sufficient evidence. (2.) The continuance of miracles from age to age would destroy their very nature, to which it is essential, that they be rare and extraordinary; for what is ordinary and frequent, we are apt to ascribe to the established laws of nature, however wonderful it be in itself. For example, if we saw dead bodies rise from their graves, as often as we see vegetables spring from seed rotten in the earth, we should be no more surprised at the one phenomenon than we are at the other, and our *virtuosi* would be equally busy to assign some natural cause for both.

And had we never seen the sun rise until this morning,

we should justly have accounted it as great a miracle as
any recorded in the Scriptures; but because it is common,
we neglect it as a thing of course.   Indeed, it is not anything in the event itself, or in the degree of power necessary for its accomplishment, that renders it miraculous,
but its being uncommon, and out of the ordinary course
of things; for example, the generation of the human body
is not in itself less astonishing, nor does it require less
power than its resurrection : the revolution of the sun in
its regular course is as wonderful, and as much requires a
divine power, as its standing still in the days of Joshua.
But we acknowledge a miracle in the one case, but not in
the other, because the one is extraordinary, while the
other frequently occurs.   Hence it follows, that the frequent repetition of miracles, as often as men are pleased to
plead the want of evidence to excuse their infidelity, would
destroy their very nature : and consequently, to demand
their continuance is to demand an impossibility.   But (3.)
Suppose that men should be indulged in this request, it
would not probably bring them to believe.   If they are
unbelievers now, it is not for want of evidence, but through
wilful blindness and obstinacy ; and as they that will shut
their eyes can see no more in meridian light than in the
twilight, so they that reject a sufficiency of evidence would
also resist a superfluity of it.   Thus the Jews, who were
eye-witnesses of the miracles recorded in the Scriptures,
continued invincible infidels still.   They had always some
trifling cavil ready to object against the brightest evidence.
And thus our modern infidels would no doubt evade the
force of the most miraculous attestation by some wretched
hypothesis or other ; they would look upon miracles either
as magical productions, or illusions of their senses; or
rather, as natural and necessary events, which they would
indeed have some reason to conclude, if they were fre-

quently performed before their eyes. Some have pretended to doubt of the existence and perfections of God, notwithstanding the evidences thereof upon this magnificent structure of the universe; and must God be always creating new worlds before these obstinate creatures for their conviction? Such persons have as much reason to demand it in this case, as our Deists have to insist for new miracles in the other. I might add, that such glaring evidence, as, like the light of the sun, would force itself irresistibly upon the minds of the most reluctant, would not leave room for us to show our regard to God in believing, for we should then believe from extrinsic necessity, and not from choice. It is therefore most correspondent to our present state of probation, that there should be something in the evidence of a divine revelation to try us; something that might fully convince the teachable and yet not remove all umbrages for cavilling from the obstinate.

Thus I have answered as many objections as the bounds of a sermon would admit; and I think they are the principal ones which lie against my subject in the view I have considered it. And as I have not designedly selected the weakest, in order to an easy triumph, you may look upon the answers that have been given as a ground of rational presumption, that all other objections may be answered with equal ease. Indeed, if they could not, it would not invalidate the positive arguments in favour of Christianity; for when we have sufficient positive evidence for a thing, we do not reject it because it is attended with some difficulties which we cannot solve.

My time will allow me to make but two or three short reflections upon the whole.

1. If the religion of Jesus be attested with such full evidence, and be sufficient to conduct men to everlasting

felicity, then how helpless are they that have enjoyed it all their life without profit: who either reject it as false, or have not felt its power to reform their hearts and lives? It is the last remedy provided for a guilty world; and if this fails, their disease is incurable, and they are not to expect better means.

2. If the religion of Jesus be true, then woe unto the wicked of all sorts: woe to infidels, both practical and speculative, for all the curses of it are in full force against them, and I need not tell you how dreadful they are.

3. If the religion of Jesus be true, then I congratulate such of you, whose hearts and lives are habitually conformed to it, and who have ventured your everlasting all upon it. You build upon a sure foundation, and your hope shall never make you ashamed.

Finally, Let us all strive to become rational and practical believers of this heaven-born religion. Let our understandings be more rationally and thoroughly convinced of its truth; and our hearts and lives be more and more conformed to its purity; and ere long we shall receive those glorious rewards it insures to all its sincere disciples; which may God grant to us all for Jesus' sake; AMEN!

SERMON II.

THE METHOD OF SALVATION THROUGH JESUS CHRIST.

JOHN iii. 16.—*For God so loved the world, that he gave his only begotten Son, that whosoever believeth in him, should not perish, but have everlasting life.*

I HAVE been solicitously thinking in what way my life, redeemed from the grave, may be of most service to my dear people. And I would collect all the feeble remains of my strength into one vigorous effort this day, to promote this benevolent end. If I knew what subject has the most direct tendency to save your souls, that is the subject to which my heart would cling with peculiar endearment, and which I would make the matter of the present discourse.

And when I consider I am speaking to an assembly of sinners, guilty, depraved, helpless creatures, and that, if ever you be saved, it will be only through Jesus Christ, in that way which the gospel reveals; when I consider that your everlasting life and happiness turn upon this hinge, namely, the reception you give to this Saviour, and this way of salvation; I say, when I consider these things, I can think of no subject I can more properly choose than to recommend the Lord Jesus to your acceptance, and to explain and inculcate the method of salvation through his mediation; or, in other words, to preach the pure gospel to you; for the gospel, in the most proper sense, is nothing else but a revelation of a way of salvation for sinners of Adam's race.

My text furnishes me with proper materials for my purpose. Let heaven and earth hear it with wonder, joy, and raptures of praise! *God so loved the world, that he gave his only begotten Son, that whosoever,* or that every one that *believeth in him should not perish, but have everlasting life.*

This is a part of the most important evening conversation that ever was held; I mean, that between Christ and Nicodemus, a Pharisee and ruler of the Jews. Our Lord first instructs him in the doctrine of regeneration, that grand constituent of a Christian, and pre-requisite to our admission in the kingdom of heaven; and then he proceeds to inform him of the gospel-method of salvation, which contains these two grand articles, the death of Christ, as the great foundation of blessedness; and faith in him, as the great qualification upon the part of the sinner. He presents this important doctrine to us in various forms, with a very significant repetition. *As Moses lifted up the serpent in the wilderness, even so must the Son of Man be lifted up;* that is, hung on high on a cross, *that whosoever believeth in him should not perish but have everlasting life.* Then follows my text, which expresses the same doctrine with great force: *God so loved the world, that he gave his only begotten Son, gave him up to death, that whosoever believeth in him should not perish, but have everlasting life.* He goes on to mention a wonder. This earth is a rebellious province of Jehovah's dominions, and therefore if his Son should ever visit it, one would think it would be as an angry judge, or as the executioner of his Father's vengeance. But, O astonishing! *God sent not his Son into the world to condemn the world, but that the world through him might be saved.* Hence the terms of life and death are thus fixed. *He that believeth on him is not condemned: but he that believeth not is comdemned already, because he hath not believed in the name of the only begotten Son of God.* Sure the heavenly rivers of pleasure flow in these verses. Never, methinks, was there so much gospel expressed in so few words. Here, take the gospel in miniature, and bind it to your hearts for ever. These verses alone, methinks, are a sufficient remedy for a dying world.

The truths I would infer from the text for present improvement are these: that without Christ you are all in a perishing condition; that through Jesus Christ a way is opened for your salvation; that the grand pre-requisite to your being saved in this way, is faith in Jesus Christ; that every one, without exception, whatever his former character has been, that is enabled to comply with this prerequisite, shall certainly be saved; and that the constitution of this method of salvation, or the mission of Christ into our world, as the Saviour of sinners, is a most striking and astonishing instance and display of the love of God.

I. My text implies, that without Christ you are all in a perishing condition. This holds true of you in particular, because it holds true of the world universally; for the world was undoubtedly in a perishing condition without Christ, and none but he could relieve it, otherwise God would never have given his only begotten Son to save it. God is not ostentatious or prodigal of his gifts, especially of so inestimable a gift as his Son, whom he loves infinitely more than the whole creation. So great, so dear a person would not have been sent upon a mission which could have been discharged by any other being. Thousands of rams must bleed in sacrifice, or ten thousands of rivers of oil must flow; our first-born must die for our transgressions, and the fruit of our body for the sin of our souls; or Gabriel, or some of the upper ranks of angels, must leave their thrones, and hang upon a cross, if such methods of salvation had been sufficient. All this would have been nothing in comparison of the only begotten Son of God leaving his native heaven, and all its glories, assuming our degraded nature, spending thirty-three long and tedious years in poverty, disgrace, and persecution, dying as a malefactor and a slave in the midst of ignominy and torture, and lying a mangled breathless corpse in the grave. We may be sure there was the highest degree of necessity for it, otherwise God would not have given up his dear Son to such a horrid scene of sufferings.

This, then, was the true state of the world, and consequently yours without Christ; it was hopeless and desperate in every view. In that situation there would not have been so much goodness in the world as to try the efficacy of sacrifices, prayers, tears, reformation, and repentance, or they would have been tried in vain. It would have been inconsistent with the honour of the divine perfections and government, to admit sacrifices, prayers, tears, repentance, and reformation, as a sufficient atonement.

What a melancholy view of the world have we now before us! We know the state of mankind only under the gracious government of a Mediator; and we but seldom realize what our miserable condition would have been, had this gracious administration never been set up. But exclude a Saviour in your thoughts for a moment, and then take a view of the world—helpless! hopeless!—under the righteous displeasure of God; and despairing of relief!—the very suburbs of hell! the range of malignant devils! the region of guilt, misery, and despair!—the mouth of the infernal pit!—the gate of hell!— This would have been the condition of our world had it not been for that Jesus who redeemed it; and yet in this very world he is neglected and despised.

But you will ask me, " How it comes that the world was in such an undone, helpless, hopeless condition without Christ; or what are the reasons of all this ?"

The true account of this will appear from these two considerations, that all mankind are sinners; and that no other method but the mediation of Christ could render the salvation of sinners consistent with the honour of the divine perfections and government, with the public good, and even with the nature of things.

All mankind are sinners. This is too evident to need proof. They are sinners, rebels against the greatest and best of beings, against their Maker, their liberal Benefactor, and their rightful Sovereign, to whom they are under stronger and more endearing obligations than they can be under to any creature, or even to the entire system of creatures; sinners, rebels in every part of our guilty globe; none righteous, no, not one; all sinners, without exception : sinners from age to age for thousands of years : thousands, millions, innumerable multitudes of sinners. What an obnoxious race is this ! There appears no difficulty in the way of justice to punish such creatures. But what seeming insuperable difficulties appear in the way of their salvation ! Let me mention a few of them to recommend that blessed Saviour who has removed them all.

If such sinners be saved, how shall the holiness and justice of God be displayed ? How shall he give an honorable view of himself to all worlds as a being of perfect purity, and an enemy to all moral evil ?

If such sinners be saved, how shall the honor of the divine government and law be secured ? How will the dignity of the law appear, if a race of rebels may trifle with it with impunity ? What a sorry law must that be that has no sanctions, or whose sanctions may be dispensed with at pleasure? What a contemptible government, that may be insulted and rejected, and the offender admitted into favour without exemplary punishment? No government can subsist upon such principles of excessive indulgence.

How can such sinners be saved, and yet the good of the public secured, which is always the end of every wise and good ruler? By the public good I do not mean the happiness of mankind alone, but I mean the happiness of all worlds of reasonable creatures collectively, in comparison of which the happiness of mankind alone may be only a private interest, which should always give way to the public good. Now sin has a direct tendency, not only according to law, but according to the nature of things, to scatter misery and ruin wherever its infection reaches. Therefore the public good cannot properly be consulted without giving a loud and effectual warning against all sin, and dealing with offenders in such a manner as to deter others from offending. But how can this be done? How can the sinner be saved, and yet the evil of sin displayed, and all other beings be deterred from it for ever? How can sin be discouraged by pardoning it? its evil displayed by letting the criminal escape punishment? These are such difficulties, that nothing but divine wisdom could ever surmount them.

These difficulties lie in the way of a mere pardon, and exemption from punishment: but salvation includes more than this. When sinners are saved, they are not only pardoned, but received into high favour, made the children, the friends, the courtiers of the King of heaven. They are not only delivered from punishment, but also advanced to a state of perfect positive happiness, and nothing short of this can render such creatures as we happy. Now, in this view, the difficulties rise still higher, and it is the more worthy of observation, as this is not generally the case in human governments; and as men are apt to form their notions of the divine government by human, they are less sensible of these difficulties. But this is indeed the true state of the case here; how can the sinner be not only delivered from punishment but also advanced to a state of perfect happiness? not only escape the displeasure of his offended Sovereign, but be received into full favour, and advanced to the highest honour and dignity; how can this be done without casting a cloud over the purity and justice of the Lord of all; without sinking his law and government into contempt; without diminishing the evil of sin, and emboldening others to venture upon it, and so at once injuring the character of the supreme Ruler, and the public good? How can sinners, I say, be saved without the salvation being attended with these bad consequences?

And here you must remember, that these consequences must be provided against. To save men at random, without considering the consequences, to distribute happiness to private persons with an undistinguishing hand, this would be at once inconsistent with the character of the supreme Magistrate of the universe, and with the public good. Private persons are at liberty to forgive private offences; nay, it is their duty to forgive; and they can hardly offend by way of excess in the generous virtues of mercy and compassion. But the case is otherwise with a magistrate; he is obliged to consult the dignity of his government and the interest of the public; and he may easily carry his lenity to a very dangerous extreme, and by his tenderness to criminals do an extensive injury to the state. This is particularly the case with regard to the great God, the universal supreme Magistrate of all worlds. And this ought to be seriously considered by those men of loose principles among us, who look upon God only under the fond character of a father, or a being of infinite mercy; and thence conclude, they have little to fear from him for all their audacious iniquities. There is no absolute necessity that sinners should be saved: justice may be suffered to take place upon them. But there is the most absolute necessity that the Ruler of the world should both be, and appear to be holy and just. There is the most absolute necessity that he should support the dignity of his government, and guard it from contempt, that he should strike all worlds with a proper horror of sin, and represent it in its genuine infernal colours, and so consult the good of the whole, rather than a part. There is, I say, the highest and most absolute necessity for these things; and they cannot be dispensed with as matters of arbitrary pleasure. And unless these ends can be answered in the salvation of men, they cannot be saved at all. No, they must all perish, rather than God should act out of character, as the supreme Magistrate of the universe, or bestow private favours to criminals, to the detriment of the public.

And in this lay the difficulty. Call a council of all the sages and wise men of the world, and they can never get over this difficulty, without borrowing assistance from the gospel. Nay, this, no doubt, puzzled all the angelic intelligences, who pry so deep into the mysteries of heaven, before the gospel was fully revealed.—Methinks the angels, when they saw the fall of man, gave him up as desperate. "Alas! (they cried) the poor creature is gone! he and all his numerous race are lost for ever." This, they knew, had been the doom of their fellow-angels that sinned: and could they hope better for man? Then they had not seen any of the wonders of pardoning love and mercy, and could they have once thought that the glorious person, who filled the middle throne, and was their Creator and Lord, would ever become a man, and die, like a criminal, to redeem an inferior rank of creatures? No, this thought they would probably have shuddered at as blasphemy.

And must we then give up ourselves and all our race as lost beyond recovery? There are huge and seemingly insuperable difficulties in the way; and we have seen that neither men nor angels can prescribe any relief. But, *sing, O ye heavens, for the* LORD *hath done it : shout, ye lower parts of the earth : break forth into singing, ye mountains, O forest, and every tree therein ; for the* LORD *hath redeemed Jacob, and glorified himself in Israel,* Isaiah xliv. 23. Which leads me to add,

II. My text implies, that through Jesus Christ a way is opened for your salvation. He, and he only was found equal to the undertaking; and before him all these mountains became a plain; all these difficulties vanish; and now God can be just, can secure the dignity of his character, as the Ruler of the world, and answer all the ends of government, and yet justify and save the sinner that believeth in Jesus.

This is plainly implied in this glorious epitome of the gospel: *God so loved the world, that he gave his only begotten Son, that whoever believeth in him should not perish, but have everlasting life.* Without this gift all was lost: but now, whosoever believeth in him may be saved; saved in a most honourable way. This will appear more particularly, if we consider the tendency the mediation of Christ had to remove the difficulties mentioned. But I would premise two general remarks.

The first is, That God being considered in this affair in his public character, as Supreme Magistrate, or Governor of the world, all the punishment which he is concerned to see inflicted upon sin is only such as answers the ends of government. Private revenge must vent itself on the very person of the offender, or be disappointed. But to a ruler, as such, it may in some cases be indifferent, whether the punishment be sustained by the very person that offended, or by a substitute suffering in his stead. It may also be indifferent whether the very same punishment, as to kind and degree, threatened in the law, be inflicted, or a punishment equivalent to it. If the honour of the ruler and his government be maintained, if all disobedience be properly discountenanced; if, in short, all the ends of government can be answered, such things as these are indifferences. Consequently, if these ends should be answered by Christ's suffering in the stead of sinners, there would be no objection against it. This remark introduces another, namely, (2.) That Jesus Christ was such a person that his suffering as the substitute or surety of sinners, answered all the ends of government which could be answered by the execution of the punishment upon the sinners themselves. To impose suffering upon the innocent, when uuwilling, is unjust; but Jesus was willing to undertake the dreadful task. And besides, he was a person (*sui juris*) at his own disposal, his own property, and therefore he had a right to dispose of his life as he pleased; and there was a merit in his consenting to that which he was not obliged to previous to his consent. He was also a person of infinite dignity, and infinitely beloved by his Father; and these considerations rendered the merit of his sufferings for a short time, and another kind of punishment than that of hell, equal, more than equal to the everlasting sufferings of sinners themselves. Jesus Christ was also above law; that is, not obliged to be subject to that law which he had made for his creatures, and consequently his obedience to the law, not being necessary for himself, might be imputed to others: whereas creatures are incapable of works of supererogation, or of doing more than they are bound to do, being obliged to obey their divine law-giver for themselves to the utmost extent of their abilities, and consequently their obedience, however perfect, can be sufficient only for themselves, but cannot be imputed to others. Thus it appears, in general, that the ends of government are as effectually answered by the sufferings of Christ in the room of sinners, as they could be by the everlasting punishment of the sinners themselves; nay, we shall presently find they are answered in a more striking and illustrious manner. To mention particulars:

Was it necessary that the holiness and justice of God should be displayed in the salvation of sinners? See how bright they shine in a suffering Saviour! Now it appears that such is the holiness and justice of God, that he will not let even his own Son escape unpunished, when he stands in the law-place of sinners, though guilty only by the slight stain (may I so speak) of imputation. Could the execution of everlasting punishment upon the hateful criminals themselves ever give so bright a display of these attributes? It were impossible. Again,

Was it a difficulty to save sinners, and yet maintain the rights of the divine government, and the honour of the law? See how this difficulty is removed by the obedience and death of Christ! Now it appears, that the rights of the divine government are so sacred and inviolable, that they must be maintained, though the darling Son of God should fall a sacrifice to justice; and that not one offence against this government can be pardoned, without his making a full atonement. Now it appears, that the Supreme Ruler is not to be trifled with, but that his injured honour must be repaired, though at the expense of his Son's blood and life.   Now, the precept of the law is perfectly obeyed in every part, and a full equivalent to its penalty endured, by a person of infinite dignity; and it is only upon this footing, that is, of complete satisfaction to all the demands of the law, that any of the rebellious sons of men can be restored into favour.   This is a satisfaction which Christ alone could give: to sinners it is utterly impossible, either by doing or suffering.   They cannot do all the things that are written in the law; nor can they endure its penalty, without being for ever miserable: and therefore the law has received a more complete satisfaction in Christ than it would ever receive from the offenders themselves.   Further,

Was it a difficulty how sinners might be saved, and yet the evil of sin be displayed in all its horrors?   Go to the cross of Christ; there, ye fools, that make a mock of sin, there learn its malignity, and its hatefulness to the great God.   There you may see it is so great an evil, that when it is but imputed to the man, that is God's fellow, as the surety of sinners, it cannot escape punishment.   No, when that dreadful stain lay upon him, immediately the commission was given to divine justice, *Awake, O sword, against my Shepherd, and against the man that is my fellow, saith the* LORD *of hosts; smite the Shepherd.* Zech. xiii. 7.—When Christ stood in the room of sinners, even the Father spared not his own Son, but gave him up to death.   That the criminals themselves, who are an inferior race of creatures, should not escape would not be strange : but what an enormous evil must that be, which cannot be connived at even in the favourite of heaven, the only begotten Son of God!   Surely nothing besides could give so striking a display of its malignity!

Was it a difficulty how to reconcile the salvation of sinners, and the public good? that is, how to forgive sins, and yet give an effectual warning against it? How to receive the sinner into favour, and advance him to the highest honour and happiness, and in the mean time deter all other beings from offending? All this is provided for in the sufferings of Christ as a surety. Let all worlds look to his cross, and receive the warning which his wounds, and groans, and blood, and dying agonies proclaim aloud; and sure they can never dare to offend after the example of man. Now they may see that the only instance of pardon to be found in the universe was brought about by such means as are not likely to be repeated; by the incarnation and death of the Lord of glory. And can they flatter themselves that he will leave his throne and hang upon a cross, as often as any of his creatures wantonly dare to offend him? No; such a miracle as this, the utmost effort of divine grace, is not often to be renewed; and therefore, if they dare to sin, it is at their peril. They have no reason to flatter themselves they shall be favoured like fallen man; but rather to expect they shall share in the doom of the fallen angels.

Or if they should think sin may escape with but a slight punishment, here they may be convinced of the contrary. If the Darling of heaven, the Lord of glory, though personally innocent, suffers so much when sin is but imputed to him, what shall the sinners themselves feel, who can claim no favour upon the footing of their own importance, or personal innocence? If these things be done " in the green tree, what shall be done in the dry ?"

Thus, my brethren, you may see how a way is opened through Jesus Christ for our salvation. All the ends of government may be answered, and yet you pardoned, and made happy. Those attributes of the divine nature, such as mercy and justice, which seemed to clash, are now reconciled; now they mingle their beams, and both shine with a brighter glory in the salvation of sinners, than either of them could apart. And must you not acknowledge this divine God-like scheme? Can you look round you over the works of the creation, and see the divine wisdom in every object, and can you not perceive the divine agency in this still more glorious work of redemption? Redemption, which gives a full view of the Deity, not as the sun in eclipse, half dark, half bright, but as

> A God all o'er consummate, absolute,
> Full orb'd, in his whole round of rays complete.—YOUNG.

And shall not men and angels join in wonder and praise at the survey of this amazing scheme? Angels are wrapt in wonder and praise, and will be so to all eternity. See! how they pry into this mystery! hark! how they sing! " Glory to God in the highest;" and celebrate the Lamb that was slain! and shall not men, who are personally interested in the affair, join with them? Oh! are there none to join with them in this assembly? Surely, none can refuse!

Now, since all obstructions are removed on God's part, that lay in the way of our salvation, why should we not all be saved together? What is there to hinder our crowding into heaven promiscuously? Or what is there requisite on our part, in order to make us partakers of this salvation? Here it is proper to pass on to the next truth inferred from the text, namely:

III. That the grand pre-requisite to your being saved in this way, is faith in Jesus Christ. Though the obstructions on God's part are removed by the death of Christ, yet there is one remaining in the sinner, which cannot be removed without his consent; and which, while it remains, renders his salvation impossible in the nature of things; that is, the depravity and corruption of his nature. Till this is cured, he cannot relish those fruitions and employments in which the happiness of heaven consists, and consequently he cannot be happy there. Therefore there is a necessity, in the very nature of things, that he should be made holy, in order to be saved; nay, his salvation itself consists in holiness. Now, faith is the root of all holiness in a sinner. Without a firm realizing belief of the great truths of the gospel, it is impossible a sinner should be sanctified by their influence : and without a particular faith in Jesus Christ he cannot derive from him those sanctifying influences by which alone he can be made holy, and which are conveyed through Jesus Christ, and through him alone.

Further : It would be highly incongruous, and indeed impossible, to save a sinner against his will, or in a way he dislikes. Now faith, as you shall see presently, principally consists in a hearty consent to and approbation of the way of salvation through Jesus Christ, the only way in which a sinner can be saved consistently with the divine honour : so that the constitution of the gospel is not only just, but as merciful as it can be, when it ordains that only *he that believeth shall be saved ; but that he that believeth not, shall be damned.*

Again : We cannot be saved through Jesus Christ, till his righteousness be so far made ours as that it will answer the demands of the laws for us, and procure the favour of God to us; but his righteousness cannot be thus imputed to us, or accounted ours in law, till we are so united to him as to be one in law, or one legal person with him. Now faith is the bond of union ; faith is that which interests us in Christ; and therefore without faith we cannot receive any benefit from his righteousness.

Here then a most interesting inquiry presents itself: " What is it to believe in Jesus Christ? or what is that faith which is the grand pre-requisite to salvation ?" If you are capable of attention to the most interesting affair in all the world, attend to this with the utmost seriousness and solemnity.

Faith in Christ includes something speculative in it; that is, it includes a speculative rational belief, upon the testimony of God, that Jesus Christ is the only Saviour of men. But yet it is not entirely a speculation, like the faith of multitudes among us: it is a more practical, experimental thing; and that you may understand its nature, you must take notice of the following particulars.

(1.) Faith pre-supposes a deep sense of our undone, helpless condition. I told you before, this is the condition of the world without Christ; and you must be sensible at heart that this is your condition in particular, before you can believe in him as your Saviour. He came to be a Saviour in a desperate case, when no relief could possibly be had from any other quarter, and you cannot receive him under that character till you feel yourselves in such a case; therefore, in order to your believing, all your pleas and excuses for your sins must be silenced, all your high conceit of your own goodness must be mortified, all your dependence upon your own righteousness, upon the merit of your prayers, your repentance, and good works, must be cast down, and you must feel that indeed you lie at mercy, that God may justly reject you for ever, and that all you can do can bring him under no obligation to save you. These things you must be deeply sensible of, otherwise you can never receive the Lord Jesus Christ in that view in which he is proposed to you, namely, as a Saviour in a desperate case.

I wish and pray you may this day see yourselves in this true, though mortifying light. It is the want of this sense of things that keeps such crowds of persons unbelievers among us. It is the want of this that causes the Lord

Jesus to be so little esteemed, so little sought for, so little desired among us. In short, it is the want of this that is the great occasion of so many perishing from under the gospel, and, as it were, from between the hands of a Saviour. It is this, alas! that causes them to perish, like the impenitent thief on the cross, with a Saviour by their side. O that you once rightly knew yourselves, you would then soon know Jesus Christ, and receive salvation from his hand.

(2.) Faith implies the enlightening of the understanding to discover the suitableness of Jesus Christ as a Saviour, and the excellency of the way of salvation through him. While the sinner lies undone and helpless in himself, and looking about in vain for some relief, it pleases a gracious God to shine into his heart, and enables him to see his glory in the face of Jesus Christ. Now this once neglected Saviour appears not only absolutely necessary, but also all-glorious and lovely, and the sinner's heart is wrapt away, and for ever captivated with his beauty: now the neglected gospel appears in a new light, as different from all his former apprehensions as if it were quite another thing. I have not time at present to enlarge upon this discovery of Christ and the gospel which faith includes; and indeed should I dwell upon it ever so long, I could not convey just ideas of it to such of you as have never had the happy experience of it. In short, the Lord Jesus, and the way of salvation through him, appear perfectly suitable, all-sufficient, and all-glorious: and in consequence of this,

(3.) The sinner is enabled to embrace this Saviour with all his heart, and to give a voluntary, cheerful consent to this glorious scheme of salvation. Now all his former unwillingness and reluctance are subdued, and his heart no more draws back from the terms of the gospel, but he complies with them, and that not merely out of constraint and necessity, but out of free choice, and with the greatest pleasure and' delight. How does his heart now cling to the blessed Jesus with the most affectionate endearment! How is he lost in wonder, joy, and gratitude, at the survey of the divine perfections, as displayed in this method of redemption! How does he rejoice in it, as not only bringing happiness to him, but glory to God; as making his salvation not only consistent with, but a bright illustration of, the divine perfections, and the dignity of his government! While he had no other but the low and selfish principles of corrupt nature, he had no concern about the honour of God; if he might be but saved, it was all he was solicitous about: but now he has a noble, generous heart; now he is concerned that God should be honoured in his salvation, and this method of salvation is recommended and endeared to him by the thought that it secures to God the supremacy, and makes his salvation subservient to the divine glory.

(4.) Faith in Jesus Christ implies an humble trust or dependence upon him alone for the pardon of sin, acceptance with God, and every blessing. As I told you before, the sinner's self-confidence is mortified; he gives up all hopes of acceptance upon the footing of his own righteousness; he is filled with self-despair, and yet he does not despair absolutely; he does not give up himself as lost, but has cheerful hopes of becoming a child of God, and being for ever happy, guilty and unworthy as he is; and what are these hopes founded upon? Why, upon the mere free grace and mercy of God, through the righteousness of Jesus Christ. On this he ventures a guilty, unworthy, helpless soul, and finds it a firm, immovable foundation, while every other ground of dependence proves but a quicksand. There are many that flatter themselves they put their trust in God; but their trust wants sundry qualifications essential to a true faith. It is not the trust of an humble helpless soul that draws all its encouragement from the mere mercy of God, and the free indefinite offer of the gospel; but it is the presumptuous trust of a proud self-confident sinner, who draws his encouragement in part at least from his imaginary goodness and importance. It is not a trust in the mercy of God through Jesus Christ, as the only medium through which it can be honourably conveyed; but either in the absolute mercy of God, without a proper reference to a Mediator, or in his mercy, as in some measure deserved or moved by something in the sinner. Examine whether your trust in God will stand this test.

I have now given you a brief answer to that grand question, What is it to believe in Jesus Christ? and I hope you understand it, though I have not enlarged so much upon it as I willingly would. I shall only add, that this faith may also be known by its inseparable effects; which are such as follow. Faith purifies the heart, and is a lively principle of inward holiness. Faith is always productive of good works, and leads us to universal obedience: faith overcomes the world and all its temptations: faith realizes eternal things, and brings them near; and hence it is defined by the apostle, *The substance of things hoped for, the evidence of things not seen.* Heb. xi. 1. Here I have a very important question to propose to you: Who among you can say, " Well, notwithstanding all my imperfections, and all my doubts and fears, I cannot but humbly hope, after the best examination I can make, that such a faith has been produced in this heart of mine?" And can you say so indeed? Then I bring you glad tidings of great joy; you shall be saved: yes, saved you shall be, in spite of earth and hell; saved, however great your past sins

have been. Which thought introduces the glorious truth
that comes next in order, namely :—

IV. My text implies, that every one, without exception,
whatever his former character has been, that is enabled to
believe in Jesus Christ, shall certainly be saved.

The number or aggravations of sins do not alter the
case; and the reason is, the sinner is not received into
favour, in whole or in part, upon the account of any thing
personal, but solely and entirely upon the account of the
righteousness of Jesus Christ. Now, this righteousness is
perfectly equal to all the demands of the law; and therefore, when this righteousness is made over to the sinner as
his by imputation, the law has no more demands upon him
for great sins than for small, for many than for few; because all demands are fully satisfied by the obedience of
Jesus Christ to the law. You see that sinners of all characters who believe in him are put upon an equality in this
respect: they are all admitted upon one common footing,
the righteousness of Christ; and that is as sufficient for one
as another.

This encouraging truth has the most abundant support
from the Holy Scriptures. Observe the agreeable indefinite *whosoever* so often repeated. " Whosoever believeth
in him, shall not perish, but have everlasting life." Whosoever he be, however vile, however guilty, however unworthy, if he does but believe, he shall not perish, but
have everlasting life. What an agreeable assurance is this
from the lips of him who has the final states of men at his
disposal! The same blessed lips have also declared, *Him
that cometh unto me, I will in no wise cast out.* John vi. 37.
And *Whosoever will, let him take the water of life freely.*
Rev. xxii. 17. He has given you more than bare words
to establish you in the belief of this truth; upon this principle he has acted, choosing some of the most abandoned

sinners to make them examples, not of his justice, as we might expect, but of his mercy, for the encouragement of others. In the days of his flesh he was reproached by his enemies for his friendship to publicans and sinners; but sure it is, instead of reproaching, we must love him on this account. When he rose from the dead, he did not rise with angry resentment against his murderers; no, but he singles them out from a world of sinners, to make them the first offers of pardon through the blood which they had just shed. He orders *that repentance and remission of sins should be preached in his name among all nations, beginning at Jerusalem.* Luke xxiv. 47. At Jerusalem, where he had been crucified a few days before, there he orders the first publication of pardon and life to be made. You may see what monsters of sin he chose to make the monuments of his grace in Corinth. *Neither fornicators, nor idolaters, nor adulterers, nor effeminate, nor abusers of themselves with mankind, nor thieves, nor covetous, nor drunkards, nor revilers, nor extortioners, shall inherit the kingdom of God.* What a dismal catalogue is this! It is no wonder such a crew should not inherit the kingdom of heaven; they are fit only for the infernal prison; and yet astonishing! it follows, *such were some of you; but ye are washed, but ye are sanctified, but ye are justified, in the name of the Lord Jesus, and by the Spirit of our God.* 1 Cor. vi. 9–11. What sinner after this can despair of mercy upon his believing in Jesus! St. Paul was another instance of the same kind: "This," says he, "is a faithful saying," a saying that may be depended on as true, "and worthy of all acceptation," from a guilty world, *that Christ Jesus came into the world to save sinners; of whom I am chief. Howbeit, for this cause I obtained mercy, that in me first Jesus Christ might show forth all long suffering, for a pattern to them which should hereafter believe in him to life everlasting.* 1 Tim. i. 15, 16. A sinner of less size would not have answered this end so well; but if Saul the persecutor obtains mercy upon his believing, who can despair?

You see upon the whole, my brethren, you are not excluded from Christ and life by the greatness of your sins; but if you perish it must be from another cause: it must be on account of your wilful unbelief in not accepting of Jesus Christ as your Saviour. If you reject him, then indeed you must perish, however small your sins have been; for it is only his death that can make atonement for the slightest guilt; and if you have no interest in that, the guilt of the smallest sin will sink you into ruin.

Here is a door wide enough for you all, if you will but enter in by faith. Come, then, enter in, you that have hitherto claimed a horrid precedence in sin, that have been ringleaders in vice, come now take the lead, and show others the way to Jesus Christ; harlots, publicans, thieves, and murderers, if such be among you, there is salvation even for you, if you will but believe. Oh! how astonishing is the love of God discovered in this way: a consideration which introduces the last inference from my text, namely,

V. That the constitution of this method of salvation, or the mission of a Saviour into our world, is a most striking and astonishing display of the love of God:—*God so loved the world as to give his only begotten Son,* &c.

View the scheme all through, and you will discover love, infinite love, in every part of it. Consider the great God as self-happy and independent upon all his creatures, and what but love, self-moved love, could excite him to make such provision for an inferior part of them! Consider the world sunk in sin, not only without merit, but most deserving of everlasting punishment, and what but love could move him to have mercy upon such a world? Consider the Saviour provided, not an angel, not the highest creature, but his Son, his only begotten Son; and what but love could move him to appoint such a Saviour? Consider the manner in which he was sent, as a gift, a free unmerited gift; "God gave his only begotten Son:" And what but infinite love could give such an unspeakable gift? Consider the blessings conferred through this Saviour, deliverance from perdition and the enjoyment of everlasting life, and what but the love of God could confer such blessings? Consider the condition upon which these blessings are offered, faith, that humble, self-emptied grace, so suitable to the circumstances of a poor sinner, that brings nothing, but receives all, and what but divine love could make such a gracious appointment? *It is of faith, that it might be by grace.* Rom. iv. 16. Consider the indefinite extent or the universality of the offer, which takes in sinners of the vilest character, and excepts against none: *Whosoever believeth shall not perish,* &c. Oh what love is this! But I must leave it as the theme of your meditations, not only in the house of your pilgrimage, but through all eternity: eternity will be short enough to pry into this mystery, and it will employ the understandings of men and angels through the revolutions of eternal ages.

And now, my brethren, to draw towards a conclusion, I would hold a treaty with you this day about the reconciliation to God through Jesus Christ. I have this day set life and death before you: I have opened to you the method of salvation through Jesus Christ: the only method in which you can be saved; the only method that could afford a gleam of hope to such a sinner as I in my late approach to the eternal world.* And now I would bring

---

* This sermon was preached a little after recovery from a severe fit of sickness, and is dated Hanover, October 2, 1757.

the matter home, and propose it to you all to consent to be saved in this method, or, in other words, to believe in the only begotten Son of God; this proposal I seriously make to you: and let heaven and earth, and your own consciences, witness that it is made to you: I also insist for a determinate answer this day; the matter will not admit of a delay, and the duty is so plain, that there is no need of time to deliberate. A Roman ambassador, treating about peace with the ambassador of a neighbouring state, if I remember rightly, and finding him desirous to gain time by shuffling and tedious negotiations, drew a circle about him, and said, " I demand an answer before you go out of this circle." Such a circle let the walls of this house, or the extent of my voice, be to you: before you leave this house, or go out of hearing, I insist on a full, decisive answer of this proposal, Whether you will believe in Jesus Christ this day, or not?

But before I proceed any farther, I would remove one stumbling-block out of your way. You are apt to object, "You teach us that faith is the gift of God, and that we cannot believe of ourselves; why then do you exhort us to it? Or how can we be concerned to endeavour that which it is impossible for us to do?"

In answer to this I grant the premises are true; and God forbid I should so much as intimate that faith is the spontaneous growth of corrupt nature, or that you can come to Christ without the Father's drawing you: but the conclusions you draw from these premises are very erroneous. I exhort and persuade you to believe in Jesus Christ, because it is while such means are used with sinners, and by the use of them, that it pleases God to enable them to comply, or to work faith in them. I would therefore use those means which God is pleased to bless for this end. I exhort you to believe in order to set you upon the trial; for it is putting it to trial, and that only, which can fully convince you of your own inability to believe; and till you are convinced of this, you can never expect strength from God. I exhort you to believe, because, sinful and enfeebled as you are, you are capable of using various preparatives to faith. You may attend upon prayer, hearing, and all the outward means of grace with natural seriousness; you may endeavour to get acquainted with your own helpless condition, and, as it were, put yourselves in the way of divine mercy; and though all these means cannot of themselves produce faith in you, yet it is only in the use of these means you are to expect divine grace to work it in you: never was it yet produced in one soul, while lying supine, lazy, and inactive.

I hope you now see good reasons why I should exhort you to believe, and also perceive my design in it; I therefore renew the proposal to you, that you should this day, as guilty, unworthy, self-despairing sinners, accept of the only begotten Son of God as your Saviour, and fall in with the gospel-method of salvation; and I once more demand your answer. I would by no means, if possible, leave the pulpit this day till I have effectually recommended the blessed Jesus, my Lord and Master, to your acceptance. I am strongly bound by the vows and resolutions of a sick bed to recommend him to you; and now I would endeavour to perform my vows. I would have us all this day, before we part, consent to God's covenant, that we may go away justified to our houses.

To this I persuade and exhort you, in the name and by the authority of the great God, by the death of Jesus Christ for sinners, by your own most urgent and absolute necessity, by the immense blessings proposed in the gospel, and by the heavy curse denounced against unbelievers.

All the blessings of the gospel, pardon of sin, sanctifying grace, eternal life, and whatever you can want, shall become yours this day, if you but believe in the Son of God; then let desolation overrun our land, let public and private calamities crowd upon you, and make you so many Jobs for poverty and affliction, still your main interest is secure; the storms and waves of trouble can only bear you to heaven, and hasten your passage to the harbour of eternal rest. Let devils accuse you before God, let conscience indict you and bring you in guilty, let the fiery law make its demands upon you, you have a righteousness in Jesus Christ that is sufficient to answer all demands, and having received it by faith, you may plead it as your own in law. Happy souls! rejoice in hope of the glory of God, for your hope will never make you ashamed!

But I expect, as usual, some of you will refuse to comply with this proposal. This, alas! has been the usual fate of the blessed gospel in all ages and in all countries; as some have received it, so some have rejected it. That old complaint of Isaiah has been justly repeated thousands of times; *Who hath believed our report? and to whom is the arm of the* LORD *revealed?* Isa. liii. 1. And is there no reason to pour it out from a broken heart over some of you, my dear people? Are you all this day determined to believe? If so, I pronounce you blessed in the name of the Lord; but if not, I must denounce your doom.

Be it known to you then from the living God, that if you thus continue in unbelief, you shut the door of mercy against yourselves, and exclude yourselves from eternal life. Whatever splendid appearances of virtue, whatever amiable qualities, whatever seeming good works you have, the express sentence of the gospel lies in full

force against you, *He that believeth not shall be damned.*
Mark xvi. 16. *He that believeth not is condemned already, because he hath not believed in the name of the only
begotten Son of God.* John iii. 18. *He that believeth not
the Son, shall not see life; but the wrath of God abideth
upon him.* John iii. 36. This is your doom repeatedly
pronounced by him whom you must own to be the best
friend of human nature; and if he condemn, who can
justify you?

Be it also known to you, that you will not only perish,
but you will perish with peculiar aggravations; you will
fall with no common ruin; you will envy the lot of
heathens who perished without the law; for oh! you incur
the peculiarly enormous guilt of rejecting the gospel, and
putting contempt upon the Son of God. This is a horrid
exploit of wickedness, and this God resents above all the
other crimes of which human nature is capable. Hence
Christ is come for judgment as well as for mercy into this
world, and he is set for the fall as well as the rising again
of many in Israel. You now enjoy the light of the gospel,
which has conducted many through this dark world to
eternal day; but remember also, *this is the condemnation;*
that is, it is the occasion of the most aggravated condemnation, *that light is come into the world, and men love darkness rather than light.* On this principle Jesus pronounced the doom of Chorazin and Bethsaida more intolerable than that of Sodom and Gomorrah. Matt. xi. 21, 22.
And would it not be hard to find a place in Virginia where
the doom of unbelievers is likely to be so terrible as
among us?

And now does not all this move you? Are you not
alarmed at the thought of perishing; of perishing by the
hand of a Saviour rejected and despised; perishing under
the stain of his profaned blood; perishing not only under

the curse of the law, but under that of the gospel, which is vastly heavier? Oh! are you hardy enough to venture upon such a doom? This doom is unavoidable if you refuse to comply with the proposal now made to you.

I must now conclude the treaty; but for my own acquittance, I must take witness that I have endeavoured to discharge my commission, whatever reception you give it. I call heaven and earth, and your own consciences to witness, that life and salvation, through Jesus Christ, have been offered to you on this day; and if you reject it, remember it; remember it whenever you see this place; remember it whenever you see my face, or one another; remember it, that you may witness for me at the supreme tribunal, that I am clear of your blood. Alas! you will remember it among a thousand painful reflections millions of ages hence, when the remembrance of it will rend your hearts like a vulture. Many sermons forgotten upon earth are remembered in hell, and haunt the guilty mind for ever. Oh that you would believe, and so prevent this dreadful effect from the present sermon!

SERMON III.

SINNERS ENTREATED TO BE RECONCILED TO GOD.

2 Cor. v. 20.—*Now then we are ambassadors for Christ, as though God did beseech you by us : we pray you in Christ's stead, be ye reconciled to God.*

To preside in the solemnities of public worship, to direct your thoughts, and choose for you the subjects of your meditation on those sacred hours which you spend in the house of God, and upon the right improvement of which your everlasting happiness so much depends, this is a province of the most tremendous importance that can be devolved upon a mortal; and every man of the sacred character who knows what he is about, must tremble at the thought, and be often anxiously perplexed what subject he shall choose, what he shall say upon it, and in what manner he shall deliver his message. His success in a great measure depends upon his choice, for though the blessed Spirit is the proper agent, and though the best means, without his efficacious concurrence, are altogether fruitless, yet he is wont to bless those means that are best adapted to do good; and after a long course of languid and fruitless efforts, which seem to have been unusually disowned by my divine Master, what text shall I choose out of the inexhaustible treasure of God's word? In what new method shall I speak upon it? What new untried experiments shall I make? Blessed Jesus! my heavenly Master! direct thy poor perplexed servant who is at a loss, and knows not what to do; direct him that has tried, and tried again, all the expedients he could think of, but almost in vain, and now scarcely knows what it is to hope for success! Divine direction, my brethren, has been sought; and may I hope it is that which has turned my mind to address you this day on the important subject of your reconciliation to God, and to become an humble imitator of the great St. Paul, whose affecting words I have read to you. *Now then we are ambassadors for Christ, as though God did beseech you by us; we pray you in Christ's stead, be ye reconciled to God.*

The introduction to this passage you find in the foregoing verses, *God hath given to us* (the apostles) *the ministry of reconciliation;* the sum and substance of which is, namely, "That God was in Christ reconciling the world unto himself, not imputing their trespasses unto them." As if he had said, "The great Sovereign of the universe, though highly provoked, and justly displeased with our rebellious world, has been so gracious as to contrive a plan of reconciliation whereby they may not only escape the punishment they deserve, but also be restored to the favour of God, and all the privileges of his favourite subjects. This plan was laid in Christ; that is, it was he who was appointed, and undertook to remove all obstacles out of the way of their reconciliation, so that it might be consistent with the honour and dignity of God and his government. This he performed by a life of perfect obedience, and an atoning death, instead of rebellious man. Though "he knew no sin" of his own: yet "he was made sin," that is, a sin-offering, or a sinner by imputation "for us," that we might "be made the righteousness of God in him." Thus all hindrances are removed on God's part. The plan of a treaty of reconciliation is formed, approved and ratified in the court of heaven; but then it must be published, all the terms made known, and the consent of the rebels solicited and gained. It is not enough that all impediments to peace are removed on God's part; they must also be removed on the part of man; the reconciliation must be mutual; both the parties must agree. Hence arises the necessity of the ministry of reconciliation which was committed to the apostles, those prime ministers of the kingdom of Christ, and in a lower sphere to the ordinary ministers of the gospel in every age. The great business of their office is to publish the treaty of peace; that is, the articles of reconciliation, and to use every motive to gain the consent of mankind to these articles. It is this office St. Paul is discharging, when he says, *We are ambassadors for Christ, as though God did beseech you by us; we pray you in Christ's stead, be ye reconciled to God.*

We are ambassadors for Christ. The proper notion of an ambassador, is that of a person sent by a king to transact affairs in his name, and according to his instructions, with foreign states, or part of his subjects, to whom he does not think proper to go himself and treat with them in his own person. Thus a peace is generally concluded between contending nations, not by their kings in person, but by their plenipotentiaries, acting in their name, and by their authority; and, while they keep to their instructions, their negotiations and agreements are as valid and authentic as if they were carried on and concluded by their masters in person. Thus the Lord Jesus Christ is not personally present in our world to manage the treaty of peace himself, but he has appointed first his apostles, and then the ministers of the gospel through every age, to carry it on in his name. This is their proper character; they are ambassadors for Christ, his plenipotentiaries, furnished with a commission and instructions to make overtures of reconciliation to a rebel world, and treat with them to gain their consent.

Indeed, aspiring ecclesiastics have assumed high sounding titles merely to produce extravagant honours to themselves. They have called themselves the ambassadors of Christ, messengers from God, the plenipotentiaries and viceroys of heaven, and I know not what, not with a design to do honour to their Master, but to keep the world in a superstitious awe of themselves. This priestly pride and insolence I utterly abhor; and yet I humbly adventure to assume the title of an ambassador of the great King of heaven, and require you to regard me in this high character: but then you must know, that while I am making this claim, I own myself obliged inviolably to adhere to the instructions of my divine Master contained in the Bible. I have no power over your faith, no power to dictate or prescribe; but my work is only just to publish the articles of peace as my Master has established and revealed them in his word, without the least addition, diminution, or alteration. I pretend to no higher power than this, and this power I must claim, unless I would renounce my office; for who can consistently profess himself a minister of Christ, without asserting his right and power to publish what his Lord has taught, and communicate his royal instructions?

Therefore without usurping an equality with St. Paul, or his fellow apostles, I must tell you in his language, I appear among you this day as the ambassador of the most high God; I am discharging an embassy for Christ;* and I tell you this with no other design than to procure your most serious regard to what I say. If you consider it only as my declaration, whatever regard you pay to it, the end of my ministry will not be answered upon you. The end of my office is not to make myself the object of your love and veneration, but to reconcile you to God; but

---

* This is the most literal translation of 'Υπερ Χριστου ουν πρεσβευομεν.

you cannot be reconciled to God while you consider the
proposal as made to you only by your fellow mortal.   You
must regard it as made to you by the Lord Jesus Christ, the
great Mediator between God and man.   I not only allow,
but even invite and charge you to inquire and judge whether what I say be agreeable to my divine instructions,
which are as open to your inspection as mine, and to regard it no farther than it is so : but if I follow these instructions, and propose the treaty of peace to you just as
it is concluded in heaven, then I charge you to regard
it as proposed by the Lord of heaven and earth, the King
of kings, and Lord of lords, though through my unworthy lips.   Consider yourselves this day as the hearers not
of a preacher formed out of the clay like yourselves, but
of the Lord Jesus Christ.   Suppose him here in person
treating with you about your reconciliation to God, and
what regard you would pay to a proposal made by him in
person, with all his divine royalties about him, that you
should now show to the treaty I am to negotiate with you
in his name and stead.

The next sentence in my text binds you still more
strongly to this; *as though God did beseech you by us.*
As if he had said, "God the Father also concurs in this
treaty of peace, as well as Christ the great Peace-maker ;
and as we discharge an embassy for Christ, so we do also
for God; and you are to regard our beseeching and exhorting,* as though the great God did in person beseech
and exhort you by us."   What astonishing condescension
is here intimated! not that the ministers of Christ should
beseech you; this would be no mighty condescension :
but that the supreme Jehovah should beseech you; that
he should not only command you with a stern air of authority as your Sovereign, but as a friend, nay, as a peti-

---

* παρακαλοῦντος signifies *exhorting* as well as *beseeching.*

tioner, should affectionately beseech you, you despicable,
guilty worms, obnoxious rebels! How astonishing, how
God-like, how unprecedented and inimitable is this condescension! Let heaven and earth admire and adore! It
is by us, indeed, by us your poor fellow mortals, that he
beseeches: but oh! let not this tempt you to disregard him
or his entreaty; though he employs such mean ambassadors, yet consider his dignity who sends us, and then you
cannot disregard his message even from our mouth.

The apostle, having thus prepared the way, proceeds to
the actual exercise of his office as an ambassador for
Christ: *We pray you*, says he, *in Christ's stead, be ye reconciled unto God.* As if he had said, "If Christ were now
present in person among you, this is what he would propose to you, and urge upon you, that you would be reconciled to God: but him the heavens must receive till the
time of the restitution of all things; but he has left us his
poor servants to officiate in his place as well as we can,
and we would prosecute the same design, we would urge
upon you what he would urge, were he to speak; therefore we pray you, in his stead, be ye reconciled to God:
we earnestly pray you to be reconciled; that is the utmost
which such feeble worms as we can do; we can only pray
and beg, but your compliance is not within the command
of our power; the compliance belongs to you; and remember, if you refuse, you must take it upon yourselves,
and answer the consequence."

Having thus explained the text, I proceed in my poor
manner to exemplify it by negotiating the treaty with you
for your reconciliation to God; and you see my business
lies directly with such of you as are yet enemies to God:
you are the only persons that stand in need of reconciliation. As for such of you (and I doubt not but there are
such among you) whose innate enmity has been subdued,

and who are become the friends and subjects of the King of heaven after your guilty revolt, I must desire you, as it were, to stand by yourselves for the present hour, and help me by your prayers, while I am speaking to your poor brethren, who still continue in that state of hostility and rebellion against God, in which you once were, and the miseries of which you well know, and still lament and deplore.

But by this proposal I am afraid I have deprived myself of hearers on this subject; for have you not already placed yourselves among the lovers of God, who consequently do not need to be reconciled to him? Is not every one of you ready to say to me, " If your business only lies with the enemies of God, you have no concern with me in this discourse; for, God forbid that I should be an enemy to him. I have indeed been guilty of a great many sins, but I had no bad design in them, and never had the least enmity against my Maker; so far from it that I shudder at the very thought!" This is the first obstacle that I meet with in discharging my embassy; the embassy itself is looked upon as needless by the persons concerned, like an attempt to reconcile those that are good friends already. This obstacle must be removed before we can proceed any farther.

I am far from charging any of you with so horrid a crime as enmity and rebellion against God, who can produce satisfactory evidences to your own conscience that you are his friends. I only desire that you would not flatter yourselves, nor draw a rash and groundless conclusion in an affair of such infinite moment, but that you would put the matter to a fair trial, according to evidence, and then let your conscience pass an impartial sentence as your judge, under the supreme Judge of the world.

You plead " not guilty" to the charge, and allege that you have always loved God; but if this be the case,

whence is it that you have afforded him so few of your
affectionate and warm thoughts? Do not your tenderest
thoughts dwell upon the objects of your love? But has
not your mind been shy of him who gave you your power
of thinking? Have you not lived stupidly thoughtless of
him for days and weeks together? Nay, have not serious
thoughts of him been unwelcome, and made you uneasy?
and have you not turned every way to avoid them? Have
you not often prayed to him, and concurred in other acts
of religious worship, and yet had but very few or no devout thoughts of him, even at the very time? And is
that mind well affected towards him that is so averse to
him, and turns every way to shun a glance of him? Alas!
is this your friendship for the God that made you, whose
you are, and whom you ought to serve!

Would you not have indulged the fool's wish, that there
were no God, had not the horror and impossibility of the
thing restrained you? But, notwithstanding this restraint,
has not this blasphemy shed its malignant poison at times
in your hearts? If there was no God, then you would
sin without control, and without dread of punishment;
and how sweet was this! Then you would have nothing
to do with that melancholy thing, religion; and what an
agreeable exemption would this be? But is this your love
for him, to wish the Parent of all beings out of being?
Alas! can the rankest enmity rise higher?

Again, if you are reconciled to God, whence is it that
you are secretly, or perhaps openly, disaffected to his image, I mean the purity and strictness of his law, and the
lineaments of holiness that appear upon the unfashionable
religious few? If you loved God, you would of course
love every thing that bears any resemblance to him. But
are you not conscious that it is otherwise with you; that
you murmur and cavil at the restraints of God's law, and

would much rather abjure it, be free from it, and live as
you list? Are you not conscious that nothing exposes a
man more to your secret disgust and contempt, and perhaps to your public mockery and ridicule, than a strict
and holy walk, and a conscientious observance of the
duties of devotion? And if you catch your neighbour in
any of these offences, do not your hearts rise against him?
and what is this but the effect of your enmity against
God? Do you thus disgust a man for wearing the genuine
image and resemblance of your friend? No; the effect
of love is quite the reverse.

Again, If you do but reflect upon the daily sensations
of your own minds, must you not be conscious that you
love other persons and things more than God? that you
love pleasure, honour, riches, your relations and friends,
more than the glorious and ever blessed God? Look
into your own hearts, and you will find it so; you will find
that this, and that, and a thousand things in this world,
engross more of your thoughts, your cares, desires, joys,
sorrows, hopes, and fears, than God, or any of his concerns. Now it is essential to the love of God that it be
supreme. You do not love him truly at all, in the least degree, if you do not love him above all; above all persons
and things in the whole universe. He is a jealous God,
and will not suffer a rival. A lower degree of love for
supreme excellence is an affront and indignity. Is it not
therefore evident, even to your own conviction, that you
do not love God at all? and what is this but to be his
enemy? To be indifferent towards him, as though he
were an insignificant being, neither good nor evil, a mere
cipher; to feel neither love nor hatred towards him, but to
neglect him, as if you had no concern with him one way
or other; what a horrible disposition is this towards him,
who is supremely and infinitely glorious and amiable, your

Creator, your Sovereign, and Benefactor; who therefore deserves and demands your highest love; or, in the words of his own law, *that you should love him with all your heart, with all your soul, with all your mind, and with all your strength*. Mark xii. 30. From what can such indifferency towards him proceed but from disaffection and enmity? It is in this way that the enmity of men towards God most generally discovers itself. They feel, perhaps, no positive workings of hatred towards him, unless when their innate corruption, like an exasperated serpent, is irritated by conviction from his law; but they feel an apathy, a listlessness, an indifferency towards him; and because they feel no more, they flatter themselves they are far from hating him; especially as they may have very honourable speculative thoughts of him floating on the surface of their minds. But alas! this very thing, this indifferency, or listless neutrality, is the very core of their enmity; and if they are thus indifferent to him now, while enjoying so many blessings from his hand, and while he delays their punishment, how will their enmity swell and rise to all the rage of a devil against him, when he puts forth his vindictive hand and touches them, and so gives occasion to it to discover its venom? My soul shudders to think what horrid insurrections and direct rebellion this temper will produce when once irritated, and all restraints are taken off; which will be the doom of sinners in the eternal world; and then they will have no more of the love of God in them than the most malignant devil in hell! If, therefore, you generally feel such an indifferency towards God, be assured you are not reconciled to him, but are his enemies in your hearts.

Again, All moral evil, or sin, is contrary to God; it is the only thing upon earth, or in hell, that is most opposite to his holy nature; and the object of his implacable and eternal indignation. He is of purer eyes than to behold it or endure it. It is his hatred to sin that has turned his heart against any of his creatures, and is the cause of all the vengeance that he has inflicted upon the guilty inhabitants of our world, or the spirits of hell. There is no object in the whole compass of the universe so odious to you as every sin is to a pure and all-holy God: now it is impossible you should at once love two things so opposite, so eternally irreconcilable. As much love as you have for any unlawful pleasure, just so much enmity there is in your hearts towards God. Hence, says St. Paul, *you were enemies in your mind, by wicked works.* Col. i. 21. Intimating that the love and practice of our wicked works is a plain evidence of inward enmity of mind towards God. The works of the flesh are sinful: hence, says the same apostle, *the carnal mind, or the minding of the flesh,* φρονῆμα τῆς σαρχος, Rom. viii. 7, *is enmity against God; it is not subject to the law of God, neither indeed can be: so then they that are in the flesh,* or under the power of a carnal mind, *cannot please God.* Rom. viii. 8. Because, what ever seeming acts of obedience they perform, and whatever appearances of friendship they put on, they are at heart enemies to God, and therefore cannot please him, who searches their heart, and sees the secret principle of their actions. Hence also St. James tells us, *that whosoever will be a friend of the world, is the enemy of God, because the friendship of the world is enmity against God.* James iv. 4. For the world inflames the lusts of men, and occasions much sin; and if we love the tempter, we love the sin to which it would allure us; and if we love the sin, we are the enemies of God; and therefore the friendship of the world is enmity against God. This then is an established maxim, without straining the matter too far, that as far as you love any sin, so far are you enemies to God. The love, as well as the service of such opposite masters, is utterly inconsistent. Now, do not your own consciences witness against you, that you have indulged, and still do habitually indulge the love of some sin or other? Whether it be covetousness or sensual pleasure, or ambition, or some angry passion, or whatever sin it be, as far as you love it, so far you are enemies to God: and if you take a view of your temper and practice, must you not unavoidably be convicted of this dreadful guilt? Horrible as the crime is, is it not an undeniable matter of fact, that you do really love some sin, and consequently hate the infinitely amiable and ever blessed God? and therefore you are the persons I have to deal with, as needing reconciliation with God.

Farther, take a view of your general manner of serving God in the duties of religion: your manner of praying, meditation, hearing the word of God, and other acts of devotion, and then inquire, Do you perform this service as the willing servants of a master you love? Do you not enter upon such service with reluctance or listlessness, and perform it with langour and indifferency as a business to which you have no heart? But is this your manner of performing a labour of love to a friend? Will your own reason suffer you to think you would be so luke-warm and heartless in the worship of God if you sincerely loved him? No; love is an active principle, a vigorous spring of action; and if this were the principle of your religious services, you would infuse more spirit and life into them, you would exert all your powers, and be *fervent in spirit, serving the Lord.* Rom. xii. 11.

But when you have performed offices of devotion with some degree of earnestness, which no doubt you have sometimes done, what was the principle or spring of your exertion? Was it the love of God? or was it purely the low principle of self-love? Why did you pray with such eager importunity, and attend upon the other means of grace with so much seriousness, but because you apprehended your dear selves were in danger, and you were not willing to be miserable for ever? This servile, mercenary kind of religious earnestness will not prove that you love God, but only that you love yourselves; and this you may do, and yet have no more true goodness, or genuine love to God than an infernal spirit; for there is not a spirit in hell but what loves himself. Indeed, self-love is so far from being an evidence of the love of God, that the extravagant excess of it is the source of that wickedness that abounds among men and devils. I do not mean by this utterly to exclude self-love out of genuine religion; it must have its place in the most excellent and best beings, but then it must be kept in a proper subordination, and not advance the creature above the Creator, and dethrone the supreme King of the universe. His love must be uppermost in the heart, and when that has the highest place, the indulgence of self-love in pursuing our own happiness is lawful, and an important duty. Now, do you not find from this view of the case, that you are not reconciled to God, even in your most devout and zealous hours, much less in the languid, inactive tenor of your lives? If so, place yourselves among those that I have to do with to-day; that is, the enemies of God.

So also, when you perform good offices to mankind; when you are harmless, obliging neighbours; when you are charitable to the poor, or strictly just in trade ; is the love of God, and a regard to his authority, the reason and principle of your actions? That is, do you do these things because God commands them, and because you delight to do what he commands? or rather, do you not do them merely because it is your nature to perform humane and honourable actions in such instances; or because you may acquire honour, or some selfish advantage by them? Alas! that God should be neglected, forgotten, and left out of the question, as of no importance even in those actions that are materially good! that even what he commands should be done, not because he commands it, but for some other sordid, selfish reason! Oh! if you did really love God, would you thus disregard him, and do nothing for his sake, not only when you are doing what he forbids, but even when you are performing what he has made your duty! Would he be such a cipher, a mere nothing in your practical esteem, if your hearts were reconciled to him as your God? No; such of you must look upon yourselves as the very persons whom I am to pray, in Christ's stead, to be reconciled to God.

I might thus, from obvious facts, lay before you many more evidences of your disaffection to the great God; but I must leave some room for the other part of my address to you, in which I am to persuade you to accept of the proposal of reconciliation; and therefore I shall add only one more test of your pretended friendship, a test which is established by the great Founder of our religion, as infallibly decisive in this case; and that is, obedience, or the keeping of the commandments of God. This, I say, is established in the strongest terms by Jesus Christ himself, as a decisive test of love, *If you love me, keep my commandments.* John xiv. 15. *Ye are my friends, if ye do whatsoever I command you.* John xv. 14. *If a man love me, he will keep my words. He that loveth me not, keepeth not my sayings.* John xiv. 23, 24. *This is the love of God,* says St. John, *that we keep his commandments; and his commandments are not grievous.* 1 John v. 3. That is, they are not grievous when love is the principle of obedience. The service of love is always willing

and pleasing. Now, my brethren bring your hearts and lives
to this standard, and let conscience declare, Are there not
some demands and restraints of the divine law so disagreable
to you, that you labour to keep yourselves ignorant of them,
and turn every way to avoid the painful light of conviction? Are there not several duties which you know in
your consciences to be such, which you do not so much
as honestly endeavour to perform, but knowingly and wilfully neglect? And are there not some favourite sins
which your consciences tell you God has forbidden, which
yet are so pleasing to you, that you knowingly and allow-
edly indulge and practise them? If this be your case,
you need not pretend to plead anything in your own
defence, or hesitate any longer; the case is plain, you are,
beyond all doubt, enemies to God; you are undeniably
convicted of it this day by irresistible evidence. You perhaps glory in the profession of Christians, but you are,
notwithstanding, enemies to God. You attend on public
worship, you pray, you read, you communicate, you are
perhaps a zealous churchman or dissenter, but you are
enemies of God. You have perhaps had many fits of religious affection, and serious concern about your everlasting
happiness, but notwithstanding you are enemies of God.
You may have reformed in many things, but you are still
enemies of God. Men may esteem you Christians, but
the God of heaven accounts you his enemies. In vain do
you insist upon it, that you have never hated your Maker
all your life, but even tremble at the thought, for undeniable facts are against you; and the reason why you have
not seen your enmity was, because you were blind, and
judged upon wrong principles; but if you this day feel
the force of conviction from the law, and have your eyes
opened, you will see and be shocked at your horrid enmity
against God, before yonder sun sets.

And now, when I have singled out from the rest those
I am now to beseech to reconciliation with God, have I
not got the majority of you to treat with? Where are
the sincere lovers of God? Alas! how few are they! and
how imperfect even in their love, so that they hardly
dare call themselves lovers of God, but tremble lest they
should still belong to the wretched crowd that are still
unreconciled to him!

Ye rebels against the King of heaven! ye enemies
against my Lord and Master Jesus Christ! (I cannot
flatter you with a softer name) hear me; attend to the
proposal I make to you, not in my own name, but in the
name and stead of your rightful Sovereign; and that is,
that you will this day be reconciled to God. "I pray you
in his stead (that is all I can do) be ye reconciled to God."
That you may know what I mean, I will more particularly explain this overture to you.

If you would be reconciled to God you must be deeply
sensible of the guilt, the wickedness, the baseness, the
inexpressible malignity of your enmity and rebellion against
him. You must return to your rightful Sovereign as convicted, self-condemned, penitent, broken-hearted rebels,
confounded and ashamed of your conduct, loathing yourselves because you have loathed the supreme Excellence,
mourning over your unnatural disaffection, your base
ingratitude, your horrid rebellion against so good a King,
And what do you say to this article of the treaty of peace?
Is it a hard thing for such causeless enemies to fall upon
the knee, and to mourn and weep as prostrate penitents at
the feet of their injured Maker? Is it a hard thing for one
that has all his life been guilty of the blackest crimes upon
earth, or even in hell, I mean enmity against God, to
confess "I have sinned," and to feel his own confession? to feel it, I say; for if he does not feel it, his

confession is but an empty compliment, that increases his guilt.

Again, if you would be reconciled to God, you must heartily consent to be reconciled to him in Christ; that is, you must come in upon the footing of that act of grace which is published in the gospel through Christ, and expecting no favour at all upon the footing of your own goodness. The merit of what you call your good actions, of your repentance, your prayers, your acts of charity and justice must all pass for nothing in this respect: you must depend only and entirely upon the merit of Christ's obedience and sufferings as the ground of your acceptance with God; and hope for forgiveness and favour from his mere mercy bestowed upon you, only for the sake of Christ, or on account of what he has done and suffered in the stead of sinners. The context informs you, that it is only in Christ that God is reconciling the world to himself; and consequently it is only in Christ that the world must accept of reconciliation and pardon. It does not consist with the dignity and perfections of the King of heaven to receive rebels into favour upon any other footing. I would have you consent to every article of the overture as I go along; and therefore here again I make a pause to ask you, what do you think of this article? Are you willing to comply with it, willing to come into favour with God, as convicted self-condemned rebels, upon an act of grace procured by the righteousness of Christ alone? Is it a mortification to creatures that never have done one action truly good in all their lives, because they have never loved God in one moment of their lives; creatures that have always, even in what they accounted their best dispositions, and best actions, been hateful to God, because even in their best dispositions, and best actions they were utterly destitute of his love? Is it a mortification to such creatures to renounce all their own merit, and consent to be saved only through grace, on account of the righteousness of another, even of Jesus Christ the great Peacemaker? Can it be a mortification to you to renounce what you have not, and to own yourselves guilty, and utterly unworthy, when you are really such? Oh! may I not expect your compliance with this term of reconciliation?

Again, If you would be reconciled to God, you must engage yourselves in his service for the future, and devote yourselves to do his will. His law must be the rule of your temper and practice: whatever he commands you must honestly endeavour to perform, without exception of any one duty as disagreeable and laborious; and whatever he forbids, you must for that reason, abstain from, however pleasing, advantageous, or fashionable. You must no longer look upon yourself as your own, but as bought with a price, and therefore bound to glorify God with your souls and your bodies, which are his. And can you make any difficulty of complying with this term; of obeying Him, whom the happy angels in heaven obey; of observing that law which always unites your duty and your happiness, and forbids nothing but what is itself injurious to you in the nature of things; of doing the will of the wisest and best of beings rather than your own, who are ignorant and depraved creatures? Oh! can you make any difficulty of this? If not, you will return home this day reconciled to God; a happiness you have never yet enjoyed for one moment.

Finally, if you would be reconciled to God, you must break off all friendship with his enemies; your friendship with the world, I mean your attachment to its wicked fashions and customs, and your fondness for its rebellious inhabitants, who continue enemies to God; your love of guilty pleasures, and every form of sin, however pleasing or gainful you might imagine it to be; your old habits and practices, while enemies to God; all these you must break off for ever; for your friendship with these is utterly inconsistent with the love of God. As long as you are resolved to love the world, to keep up your society with your old companions in sin, to retain your old pleasures and evil practices; as long, I say, as you are resolved upon this course, farewell all hope of your reconciliation to God: it is absolutely impossible. And do any of you hesitate at this article? Is sin so noble a thing in itself, and so happy in its consequences, as that you should be so loth to part with it? Is it so sweet a thing to you to sin against God, that you know not how to forbear? Alas! will you rather be an implacable enemy to the God that made you, than break your league with his enemies and your own! Do you love your sins so well, and are you so obliged to them, that you will lay down your life, your eternal life, for their sakes.

I might multiply particulars, but these are the principal articles of that treaty of peace, I am negotiating with you; and a consent to these includes a compliance with all the rest. And are you determined to comply? Does the heaven-born purpose now rise in your minds, " I am determined I will be an enemy of God no longer; but this very day I will be reconciled to God upon his own terms!" Is this your fixed purpose? or is there any occasion to pray and persuade you?

I well know, and it is fit you should know, that you are not able of yourselves to consent to these terms, but that it is the work of the power of God alone to reconcile you to himself; and that all my persuasions and entreaties will never make you either able or willing. You will then ask me, perhaps, " Why do I propose the terms to you, or use any persuasives or entreaties with you?" I answer, because you never will be sensible of your inability till you make an honest trial, and because you never will look and pray for the aid of the blessed Spirit till you are deeply sensible of your own insufficiency; and further, because, if the blessed Spirit should ever effectually work upon you, it will be by enlightening your understandings to see the reasonableness of the terms, and the force of the persuasives; aud in this way, agreeably to your reasonable natures, sweetly constraining your obstinate wills to yield yourselves to God; therefore the terms must be proposed to you, and persuasives used, if I would be subservient to this divine agent, and furnish him with materials with which to work; and I have some little hope that he will, as it were, catch my feeble words from my lips before they vanish into air, and bear them home to your hearts with a power which you will not be able to resist. Finally, a conviction of the true state of your case may constrain you from self-love and the low principles of nature to use the means of reconciliation with zeal and earnestness; this you are capable of, even with the mere strength of degenerate nature; and it is only in this way of earnest endeavours that you have any encouragement to hope for divine aid; therefore, notwithstanding your utter impotence, I must pray, entreat, and persuade you to be reconciled to God.

I pray you, in the name of the great God your heavenly Father, and of Jesus Christ your Redeemer. If God should once more renew the thunder and lightning, and darkness and tempest of Sinai, and speak to you as he once did to the trembling Israelites; or if he should appear to you in all the amiable and alluring glories of a sin-pardoning reconcilable God, and pray you to be reconciled to him, would you not then regard the proposal? or if Jesus, who once prayed for you from the cross, should now pray to you from his throne in heaven, and beg you with his own gracious voice to be reconciled, oh! could you disregard the entreaty? Surely no. Now the overture of peace is as really made to you by the blessed God and his Son Jesus Christ, as if it were expressly proposed to you by an immediate voice from heaven. For I beseech you, *as though God did beseech you* by me, and it is *in Christ's stead*, that I pray you be *reconciled to God*. Therefore, however lightly you may make of a mere proposal of mine, can you disregard an overture from the God that made you, and the Saviour that bought you with his blood! in which I am but the faint echo of their voice from heaven.

In the name of God I pray you; the name of the greatest and best of beings; that name which angels love and adore, and which strikes terror through the hardiest devil in the infernal regions; the name of your Father; the immediate Father of your spirits, and the Author of your mortal frames; the name of your Preserver and Benefactor, in whom you live, and move, and have your being; and who gives you life, and breath, and all things; the name of your rightful Sovereign and Lawgiver, who has a right to demand your love and obedience; the name of your supreme Judge, who will ascend the tribunal, and acquit or condemn you, as he finds you friends or foes; the name of that God, rich in goodness, who has replenished heaven with an infinite plenitude of happiness in which he will allow you to share after all your hostility and rebellion, if you consent to overtures of reconciliation; in the name of that God of terrible majesty and justice, who has prepared the dungeon of hell as a prison for his enemies, where he holds in chains the mighty powers of darkness, and thousands of your own race, who persisted in that enmity to him of which you are now guilty, and with whom you must have your everlasting portion, if, like them, you continue hardened and incorrigible in your rebellion; in the name of that compassionate God, who sent his dear Son (oh the transporting thought!) to satisfy divine justice for you by his death, and the precepts of the law by his life, and thus to remove all obstructions, out of the way of your reconciliation on the part of God; in this great, this endearing and tremendous name, I pray you be reconciled to God. I pray you for his sake; and has his name no weight with you? Will you do nothing for his sake? what, not so reasonable and advantageous a thing as dropping your unnatural rebellion, and being reconciled to him? Is your contempt of God risen to that pitch that you will not do the most reasonable and profitable thing in the world, if he entreat you to do it? Be astonished, O ye heavens! at this.

I pray you both in the name and for the sake of Jesus Christ, the true friend of publicans and sinners, in his name and for his sake, who assumed your degraded nature, that he might dignify and save it; who lived a life of labour, poverty, and persecution on earth, that you might enjoy a life of everlasting happiness and glory in heaven; who died upon a torturing cross, that you might sit upon heavenly thrones; who was imprisoned in the gloomy grave, that you might enjoy a glorious resurrection; who fell a victim to divine justice, that you might be set free from its dreadful arrest; who felt trouble and agony of soul, that you might enjoy the smiles, the pleasures of divine love; who, in short, has discovered more ardent and extensive love for you than all the friends in the world can do: in his name, and for his sake, I pray you to be reconciled to God. And is his dear name a trifle in your esteem? Will you not do any thing so reasonable and so necessary, and conducive to your happiness for his sake; for his sake who has done and suffered so much for you? Alas! has the name of Jesus no more influence among the creatures he bought with his blood! It is hard, indeed, if I beg in vain, when I beg for the sake of Christ, the Friend, the Saviour of perishing souls.

But if you have no regard for him, you certainly have for yourselves; therefore, for your own sakes, for the sake of your precious immortals souls, for the sake of your own everlasting happiness, I pray you to be reconciled to God. If you refuse, you degrade the honour of your nature, and commence incarnate devils. For what is the grand constituent of a devil, but enmity against God? You become the refuse of the creation, fit for no apartment of the universe but the prison of hell. While you are un-reconciled to God you can do nothing at all to please him. He that searches the heart knows that even your good actions do not proceed from love to him and therefore he abhors them. Ten thousand prayers and acts of devotion and morality, as you have no principles of real holiness, are so many provocations to a righteous God. While you refuse to be reconciled, you are accessary to, and patronize all the rebellion of men and devils; for if you have a right to continue in your rebellion, why may not others? why may not every man upon earth? why may not every mise-rable ghost in the infernal regions? And are you for raising a universal mutiny and rebellion against the throne of the Most High! Oh the inexpressible horror of the thought! If you refuse to be reconciled, you will soon weary out the mercy and patience of God towards you, and he will come forth against you in all the terrors of an almighty enemy. He will give death a commission to seize you, and drag you to his flaming tribunal. He will break off the treaty, and never make you one offer of re-conciliation more: he will strip you of all the enjoyments

he was pleased to lend you, while you were under a reprieve, and the treaty was not come to a final issue; and
will leave you nothing but bare being, and an extensive
capacity of misery, which will be filled up to the uttermost
from the vials of his indignation. He will treat you as his
implacable enemy, and you shall be to him as Amalek,
Exod. xvii. 16, with whom he will make war for ever and
ever. He will reprove you, and set your sins in order before you, and tear you in pieces, and there shall be none to
deliver. He will meet you as a lion, "and as a bear bereaved of her whelps, and will rend the caul of your hearts."
Hos. xiii. 8. He hath for a long time held his peace, and
endured your rebellion; but ere long he will go forth as a
mighty man: he shall stir up jealousy like a man of war;
he shall cry, yea, roar; he shall prevail against his enemies.
Ah! he will ease him of his adversaries, and avenge him
of his enemies. He will give orders to the executioners
of his justice: *Those mine enemies, that would not that I
should reign over them, bring them hither, and slay them
before me.* Luke xix. 27. And now, if you will not submit to peace, prepare to meet your God, oh sinners! gird
up your loins like men; put on all the terror of your rage,
and go forth to meet your almighty adversary, who will
soon meet you in the field, and try your strength. Call
the legions of hell to your aid, and strengthen the con-
federacy with all your fellow-sinners upon earth; put
briers and thorns around you to enclose from his reach.
Prepare the dry stubble to oppose devouring flame.
Associate yourselves, but ye shall be broken in pieces:
gird yourselves; but alas! ye shall be broken to
pieces.

But oh! I must drop this ironical challenge, and seriously pray you to make peace with him whom you cannot resist: then all your past rebellion will be forgiven;

you shall be the favourites of your sovereign, and happy
for ever; and earth and heaven will rejoice at the conclusion of this blessed peace; and my now sad heart will
share in the joy. Therefore, for your own sakes I pray
you to be reconciled to God.

SERMON IV.

THE NATURE AND UNIVERSALITY OF SPIRITUAL DEATH.

EPHES. ii. 1 *and* 5.—*Who were dead in trespasses and sins.—Even when we were dead in sins.*

THERE is a kind of death which we all expect to feel, that carries terror in the very sound, and all its circumstances are shocking to nature. The ghastly countenance, the convulsive agonies, the expiring groan, the coffin, the grave, the devouring worm, the stupor, the insensibility, the universal inactivity, these strike a damp to the spirit, and we turn pale at the thought. With such objects as these in view, courage fails, levity looks serious, presumption is dashed, the cheerful passions sink, and all is solemn, all is melancholy. The most stupid and hardy sinner cannot but be moved to see these things exemplified in others; and when he cannot avoid the prospect, he is shocked to think that he himself must feel them.

But there is another kind of death little regarded indeed, little feared, little lamented, which is infinitely more terrible—the death, not of the body, but of the soul; a death which does not stupify the limbs, but the faculties of the mind; a death which does not separate the soul and body, and consign the latter to the grave, but that separates the soul from God, excludes it from all the joys of his presence, and delivers it over to everlasting misery; a tremendous death indeed! "A death unto death." The expression of St. Paul is prodigiously strong and striking: Θανάτος εἰς θάνατον. Death unto death, death after death, in all dreadful succession, and the last more terrible than the first, 2 Cor. ii. 16, and this is the death meant in my text, *dead in trespasses and sins.*

To explain the context and show you the connection I shall make two short remarks.

The one is, That the apostle had observed in the nineteenth and twentieth verses of the foregoing chapter that the same almighty power of God, which raised Christ from the dead, is exerted to enable a sinner to believe.— *We believe,* says he, *according to the working* or energy Ενεργειαν *of his mighty power which he wrought in Christ, when he raised him from the dead.* The one, as well as the other, is an exploit of omnipotence. The exceeding greatness of his mighty power is exerted towards us that believe, as well as it was upon the dead body of Christ to restore it to life, after it had been torn and mangled upon the cross, and lain three days and three nights in the grave. What strong language is this! what a forcible illustration! Methinks this passage alone is sufficient to confound all the vanity and self-sufficiency of mortals, and entirely destroy the proud fiction of a self-sprung faith produced by the efforts of degenerate nature. In my text the apostle assigns the reason of this. The same exertion of the same power is necessary in the one case and the other; because, as the body of Christ was dead, and had no principle of life in it, so says he, *ye were dead in trespasses and sins;* and therefore could no more quicken yourselves than a dead body can restore itself to life. *But God,* verse 4th, *who is rich in mercy, for his great love wherewith he loved us;* that God, who raised the entombed Redeemer to life again, that same almighty God, by a like exertion of the same power, *hath quickened us,* verse 5th, *even when we were dead in sins;* dead, senseless, inactive, and incapable of animating ourselves. Let any man carefully read these verses, and consider their most natural meaning, and I cannot but think common sense will direct him thus to understand them. The Scriptures were written with a design to be understood; and therefore that sense which is most natural to a plain unprejudiced understanding is most likely to be true.

The other remark is, That the apostle having pronounced the Ephesians dead in sin, while unconverted, in the first verse, passes the same sentence upon himself and the whole body of the Jews, notwithstanding their high privileges, in the fifth verse. The sense and connection may be discovered in the following paraphrase: " You Ephesians were very lately heathens, and, while you were in that state, you were spiritually dead, and all your actions were dead works. In time past ye walked in trespasses and sins, nor were you singular in your course; though it be infinitely pernicious, yet it is the common course of this world, and it is also agreeable to the temper and instigation of that gloomy prince, who has a peculiar power in the region of the air; that malignant spirit who works with dreadful efficacy in the numerous children of disobedience; but this was not the case of you heathens alone: we also who are Jews, notwithstanding our many religious advantages, and even I myself, notwithstanding my high privileges and unblemishable life as a Pharisee, we also, I say, had our conversation in times past among the children of disobedience; we all, as well as they, walked in the lusts of the flesh, fulfilling the desires and inclinations ($\theta\epsilon\lambda\acute{\eta}\mu\alpha\tau\alpha$) of our sensual flesh, and of our depraved minds; for these were tainted with spiritual wickedness, independent upon our animal passions and appetites; and we are all, even by nature, children of wrath even as others; in this respect we Jews were just like the rest of mankind, corrupt from our very birth, transgressors from the womb, and liable to the wrath of God. Our external relation and privileges as the peculiar people of God, distinguished with a religion from heaven, make no distinction between us and others in this matter. As we are all children of disobedience by our lives, so we are all, without exception, children of wrath by nature; but when we were all dead in sins, when Jews and Gentiles were equally dead to God, then, even then, God who is rich in mercy, had pity upon us; *he quickened us;* "he inspired us with a new and spiritual life by his own almighty power, which raised the dead body of Christ from the grave." *He quickened us together with Christ:* "We received our life by virtue of our union with him as our vital head, who was raised to an immortal life, that he might quicken dead souls by those influences of his spirit which he purchased by his death; and therefore by grace are ye saved." It is the purest, richest, freest grace, that such dead souls as we were made alive to God, and not suffered to remain dead for ever.

This is the obvious meaning and connection of these verses; and we now proceed to consider the text, *dead in trespasses and sins;* you dead, we dead, Jews and Gentiles all dead together *in trespasses and sins.* A dismal, mortifying character! "This one place," says Beza, "like a thunder-bolt, dashes all mankind down to the dust, great and proud as they are; for it pronounces their nature not only hurt but dead by sin, and therefore liable to wrath.*

Death is a state of insensibility and inactivity, and a dead man is incapable of restoring himself to life; therefore the condition of an unconverted sinner must have

---

* "Hoc uno loco, quasi fulmine, totus homo, quantus quantus est prosternitur. Neque enim naturam, dicit læsam, sed mortuam, per peccatum; ideoque iræ obnoxiam."

some resemblance to such a state, in order to support the bold metaphor here used by the apostle. To understand it aright we must take care, on the one hand, that we do not explain it away in flattery to ourselves, or in compliment to the pride of human nature; and, on the other hand, that we do not carry the similitude too far, so as to lead into absurdities, and contradict matter of fact.

The metaphor must be understood with several limitations or exceptions; for it is certain there is a wide difference between the spiritual death of the soul, and the natural death of the body, particularly in this respect, that death puts an entire end to all the powers, actions, and sensations of our animal nature universally, with regard to all objects of every kind: but a soul dead in sin is one partially dead; that is, it is dead only with regard to a certain kind of sensations and exercises, but in the mean time it may be all life and activity about other things. It is alive, sensible, and vigorous about earthly objects and pursuits; these raise its passions and engage its thoughts. It has also a dreadful power and faculty of sinning, this is not its life but its disease, its death, like the tendency of a dead body to corruption. It can likewise exercise its intellectual powers, and make considerable improvements in science. A sinner dead in trespasses and sins may be a living treasury of knowledge, an universal scholar, a profound philosopher, and even a great divine, as far as mere speculative knowledge can render him such; nay, he is capable of many sensations and impressions from religious objects, and of performing all the external duties of religion. He is able to read, to hear, to pray, to meditate upon divine things; nay, he may be an instructor of others, and preach perhaps with extensive popularity; he may have a form of godliness, and obtain a name to live among men; he is in some measure able, and it is his duty to attend upon the means God has instituted for quickening him with spiritual life, and God deals with him as with a rational creature, by laws, sanctions, promises, expostulations, and invitations: these concessions I make not only to give you the sense of the text, but also to prevent the abuse of the doctrine, and anticipate some objections against it, as though it were an encouragement to continue idle, and use no means to obtain spiritual life: or as though it rendered all the means of grace needless and absurd, like arguments to the dead, to restore themselves to life. But, notwithstanding all these concessions, it is a melancholy truth that an unregenerate sinner is dead. Though he can commit sin with greediness, though he is capable of animal actions and secular pursuits, nay, though he can employ his mind even about intellectual and spiritual things, and is capable of performing the external duties of religion, yet there is something in religion with regard to which he is entirely dead: there is a kind of spiritual life of which he is entirely destitute: he is habitually insensible with regard to things divine and eternal: he has no activity, no vigour in the pure, spiritual and vital exercises of religion: he has no prevailing bent of mind towards them: he has not those views and apprehensions of things which a soul spiritually alive would necessarily receive and entertain: he is destitute of those sacred affections, that joy, that love, that desire, that hope, that fear, that sorrow, which are, as it were, the innate passions of the new man. In short, he is so inactive, so listless, so insensible in these respects, that death, which puts an end to all action and sensation, is a proper emblem of his state; and this is the meaning of the apostle in my text. He is also utterly unable to quicken himself. He may indeed use means in some sort; but to implant a vital principle in his soul, but to give himself vivid sensations of divine things, and make himself alive towards God, this is entirely beyond his utmost ability; this is as peculiarly the work of almighty power as the resurrection of a dead body from the grave. As to this death it is brought upon him by, and consists in, *trespasses and sins.* The innate depravity and corruption of the heart, and the habits of sin contracted and confirmed by repeated indulgences of inbred corruption, these are the poisonous, deadly things that have slain the soul; these have entirely indisposed and disabled it for living religion. *Trespasses and sins* are the grave, the corrupt effluvia, the malignant damps, the rottenness of a dead soul: it lies dead, senseless, inactive, buried *in trespasses and sins.* *Trespasses and sins* render it ghastly, odious, abominable, a noisome putrefaction before a holy God, like a rotten carcass, or a mere mass of corruption; the vilest lusts, like worms, riot upon and devour it, but it feels them not, nor can it lift a hand to drive the venom off. Such mortifying ideas as these may be contained in the striking metaphor, *dead in trespasses and sins;* and I hope you now understand its general meaning.

If you would know what has turned my thoughts to this subject, I will candidly tell you, though with a sorrowful heart. I am sure, if any objects within the compass of human knowledge have a tendency to make the deepest impressions upon our minds, they are those things which Christianity teaches us concerning God, concerning ourselves, and a future state; and if there be any exercises which should call forth all the life and powers of our souls into action, they are those of a religious nature: but alas! I often find a strange, astonishing stupour and listlessness about these things. In this I am not singular; the best among us complain of the same thing; the most lively Christians feel this unaccountable languor and insensibility; and the generality are evidently destitute of all habitual concern about them: they are all alive in the pursuit of pleasure, riches, or honours; their thoughts are easily engaged, and their affections raised by such things as these: but the concerns of religion, which above all other things are adapted to make impressions upon them, and stir up all the life within them, seem to have little or no effect. When I have made this observation with respect to others, and felt the melancholy confirmation of it in my own breast, I have really been struck with amazement, and ready to cry out, "Lord, what is this that has befallen me, and the rest of my fellow-mortals? what can be the cause of such conduct in rational nature, to be active and eager about trifles, and stupid and careless about matters of infinite importance? Oh, whence is this strange infatuation!" Thus I have been shocked at this astonishing fact, and I could account for it in no other way but by reflecting that we have all been *dead in trespasses and sins*. In such a solemn hour the apostle's expression does not seem at all too strong. I have no scruple at all to pronounce, not only from the authority of an apostle, but from the evidence of the thing, that I, and all around me, yea, and all the sons of men, have been dead; in the spiritual sense, utterly dead. Multitudes among us, yea, the generality are dead still; hence the stillness about religion among us; hence the stupor, the carelessness about eternal things, the thoughtless neglect of God, the insensibility under his providential dispensations, the impenitence, the presumption that so much prevail. God has indeed, out of the great love wherewith he loved us, quickened some of us, even when we were dead in sins; and we have a little life, some vital sensations and impressions at times, but oh! how little, how superficial, how much of a deadly stupor yet remains! how little life in prayer, in hearing,

or in the nearest approach to the living God! The reflection is shocking, but alas! it is too true; consult your
own hearts and you will find it even so. Animal life
seems to be a gradual thing; it gradually grows in an infant, it is perfect in mature age, and in old age it gradually
decays till all is gone; but how small is the degree of life
when the fœtus is just animated, or the infant born into
the world! but little superior to that of a plant or an
oyster. What faint sensations, what obscure and languid
perceptions, what feeble motions ! Such are the children
of grace in the present state. Spiritual life is gradual; it
is infused in regeneration; but oh! how far from perfection
while on this side heaven! Alas! the best of us are like
the poor traveller that fell among thieves, and was left
half dead; however, it is an unspeakable mercy to have
the least principle of spiritual life; and we should prize it
more than crowns and empires.

If you would know my design in choosing this subject,
it is partly for the conviction of sinners, that they may be
alarmed with their deplorable condition, which is the first
step towards their being quickened; partly to rouse the
children of grace to seek more life from their vital head;
and partly to display the rich grace of God in quickening
such dead sinners, and bestowing upon them a spiritual
and immortal life; and surely nothing can inflame our
gratitude and raise our wonder more than the consideration that we were dead in trespasses and sins! If I may
but answer these ends, it will be an unspeakable blessing
to us all. And oh, that divine grace may honour this
humble attempt of a poor creature, at best but half alive,
with success! I hope, my brethren, you will hear seriously
for it is really a most serious subject.

You have seen that the metaphorical expression in my
text is intended to represent the stupidity, inactivity, and

impotence of unregenerate sinners about divine things. This truth I might confirm by argument and Scripture authority; but I think it may be a better method for popular conviction to prove and illustrate it from plain instances of the temper and conduct of sinners about the concerns of religion, as this may force the conviction upon them from undoubted matters of fact and their own experience.

This, therefore, is the method I intend to pursue; and my time will allow me to particularize only the following instances.

I. Consider the excellency of the divine Being, the sum total, the great original of all perfections. How infinitely worthy is he of the adoration of all his creatures! how deserving of their most intense thoughts and most ardent affections! If majesty and glory can strike us with awe and veneration, does not Jehovah demand them, who is clothed with majesty and glory as with a garment, and before whom all the inhabitants of the earth are as grasshoppers, as nothing, as less than nothing, and vanity? If wisdom excites our pleasing wonder, here is an unfathomable depth. Oh the depth of the riches of the wisdom and knowledge of God! If goodness, grace, and mercy attract our love and gratitude, here these amiable perfections shine in their most alluring glories. If justice strikes a damp to the guilty, here is justice in all its tremendous majesty. If veracity, if candor, if any, or all of the moral virtues engage our esteem, here they all centre in their highest perfection. If the presence of a king strikes a reverence; if the eye of his judge awes the criminal, and restrains him from offending, certainly we should fear before the Lord all the day, for we are surrounded with his omnipresence, and he is the inspector and judge of all our thoughts and actions. If riches excite desire, here are unsearchable riches : if happiness has charms that draw all the world after it, here is an unbounded ocean of happiness; here is the only complete portion for an immortal mind.   Men are affected with these things in one another, though found in a very imperfect degree.   Power awes and commands; virtue and goodness please; beauty charms; justice strikes with solemnity and terror; a bright genius is admired; a benevolent, merciful temper is loved : thus men are affected with created excellences. Whence is it, then, they are so stupidly unaffected with the supreme excellences of Jehovah ?

Here, my brethren, turn your eyes inward upon yourselves, and inquire, are not several of you conscious that, though you have passions for such objects as these, and you are easily moved by them, yet, with regard to the perfections of the supreme and best of beings, your hearts are habitually senseless and unaffected ?   It is not an easy thing to make impressions upon you by them; and what increases the wonder, and aggravates your guilt, is, that you are thus senseless and unaffected, when you believe and profess that these perfections are really in God, and that in the highest degree possible.   In other cases you can love what appears amiable, you revere what is great and majestic, you eagerly desire and pursue what is valuable and tends to your happiness; and all this you do freely, spontaneously, vigorously, by the innate inclination and tendency of your nature, without reluctance, without compulsation, nay, without persuasion; but as to God and all his perfections, you are strangely insensible, backward, and averse.   Where is there one being that has any confessed excellency in the compass of human knowledge, that does not engage more of the thoughts and affections of mankind than the glorious and ever blessed God ?   The sun, moon, and stars have had more worshippers than the uncreated fountain of light from which they derive their lustre. Kings and ministers of state have more punctual homage and more frequent applications made to them than the King of kings and Lord of lords. Created enjoyments are more eagerly pursued than the supreme good. Search all the world over, and you will find but very little motions of heart towards God; little love, little desire, little searching after him. You will often, indeed, see him honoured with the compliment of a bended knee, and a few heartless words, under the name of a prayer; but where is the heart, or where are the thoughts, where the affections? These run wild through the world, and are scattered among a thousand other objects. The heart has no prevailing tendency toward God, the thoughts are shy of him, the affections have no innate propensity to him. In short, in this respect, the whole man is out of order: here he does not at all act like himself; here are no affectionate thoughts, no delightful meditations, no ardent desires, no eager pursuits and vigorous endeavours; but all is listless, stupid, indisposed, inactive, and averse: and what is the matter?—"Lord! what is this that has seized the souls of thine own offspring, that they are thus utterly disordered towards thee?" The reason is, they are dead, *dead in tresspasses and sins.* It is impossible a living soul should be so stupid and unaffected with such an object; it must be a dead soul that has no feeling. Yes, sinners, this is the melancholy reason why you are so thoughtless, so unconcerned, so senseless about the God that made you: you are dead. And what is the reason that you, who have been begotten again to a spiritual life, and who are united to Christ as your vital head, what is the reason that you so often feel such languishments; that the pulse of spiritual life beats so faint and irregular, and that its motions are so feeble and slow? All this you feel and lament, but how comes it to pass? what can be the cause that you, who have indeed tasted that the Lord is gracious, and are sensible that he is all-glorious and lovely, and your only happiness—Oh! what can be the cause, that you, of all men in the world, should be so little engaged to him? Alas! the cause is, you have been dead, and the deadly stupor has not yet left you: you have (blessed be the quickening Spirit of Christ!) you have received a little life; but, alas! it is a feeble spark; it finds the principles of death still strong in your constitution; these it must struggle with, and by them it is often borne down, suppressed, and just expiring. Walk humbly, then, and remember your shame, that you were once dead, and children of wrath, even as others. The carelessness and indisposition of the soul towards the supreme excellence will appear yet more evident and astonishing, if we consider,

II. The august and endearing relations the great and blessed God sustains to us, and the many ways he has taken to make dutiful and grateful impressions upon our hearts. What tender endearments are there contained in the relation of a Father! This he bears to us: *he made us, and not we ourselves.* Our bodies, indeed, are produced in a succession from Adam by generation, but who was it that began the series? It was the Almighty, who formed the first man of the dust: it was he who first put the succession of causes in motion; and, therefore, he is the grand original cause, and the whole chain depends upon him. Who was it that first established the laws of generation, and still continues them in force? It is the all-creating parent of nature: and without him men would have been no more able to produce one another than stones or clods of earth. As to our souls, the principal part of our persons, God is their immediate author, with-

out the least concurrence of secondary causes.   Hence he
is called the Father of your spirits in a peculiar sense,
Heb. xii. 9 ; and he assumes the endearing name of " the
God of the spirits of all flesh."   Numb. xvi. 22.   Now
the name of a father is wont to carry some endearment
and authority.   Children, especially in their young and
helpless years, are fond of their father; their little hearts
beat with a thousand grateful passions towards him; they
love to be dandled on his knees, and fondled in his arms;
and they fly to him upon every appearance of danger : but
if God be a father, where is his honour ? here, alas ! the
filial passions are senseless and immoveable.   It is but a
little time since we came from his creating hand, and yet
we have forgotten him.   It seems unnatural for his own
offspring to inquire, " Where is God my Maker ?"   They
show no fondness for him, no affectionate veneration, and
no humble confidence ; their hearts are dead towards him,
as though there were no such being, or no such near relation subsisting between them.   In childhood, a rattle or
a straw, or any trifle, is more thought of than their heavenly Father : in riper years, their vain pleasures and
secular pursuits command more of their affections than
their divine original and only happiness.

Compare your natural temper towards your heavenly
Father, and towards your earthly parents, and how wide
is the difference !   Nature works strong in your hearts
towards them, but towards him all the filial passions are
dull and dead; and why ? alas ! the reason is, you *are dead
in trespasses and sins*.   But this relation of a Father is
not the only relation our God sustains to you; he is your
supreme King, to whom you owe allegiance; your Lawgiver, whose will is the rule of your conduct; and your
Judge, who will call you to an account, and reward or
punish you according to your works; but how unnatural

is it to men to revere the most high God under these august characters! Where is there a king upon earth, however weak or tyrannical, but is more regarded by his subjects than the King of heaven by the generality of men? Were ever such excellent laws contemned and violated? Did ever criminals treat their judge with so much neglect and contempt? And are these souls alive to God who thus treat him? No. Alas! "they are dead in trespasses and sins;" however lively they are towards other things, yet in this respect they are seized with a deadly stupor. God is also our Guardian and Deliverer; and from how many dangers has he preserved us! from how many calamities has he delivered us! Dangers, distresses and deaths crowd upon us, and surround us in every age and every place: the air, the earth, the sea, and every element, are pregnant with numberless principles of pain and death ready to seize and destroy us: sickness and death swarm around us: nay, they lie in ambush in our own constitution, and are perpetually undermining our lives, and yet our divine Guardian preserves us for months and years unhurt, untouched; or if he suffers the calamity to fall, or death to threaten, he flies to our deliverance; and how many salvations of this kind has he wrought for us; salvations from accidents, from sicknesses, from pain, from sorrows, from death; salvations from dangers seen and unseen; salvations in infancy, in youth, and in maturer years! These things we cannot deny without the most stupid ignorance, and an atheistical disbelief of divine Providence. Now, such repeated, such long-continued, such unmerited favours as these would not pass for nothing between man and man. We have hearts to feel such obligations; nay, the ten thousandth, the millionth part of such gracious care and goodness would be gratefully received, and thankfully acknowledged. Indeed it is impossible we should receive even this small, this very small proportion of favours from men in comparison of what we receive from God; and even when they are the instruments of our deliverance, he is the original Author. But after all, is there a natural aptitude in the hearts of men to think of their gracious Guardian and Saviour? Does the principle of gratitude naturally lead them to love him, and to make thankful acknowledgments to him? Alas! no. They may indeed feel some transient, superficial workings of gratitude when under the fresh sense of some remarkable deliverance; but these impressions soon wear off, and they become as thoughtless and stupid as ever. But let a man, like yourselves, save you from some great distress, you will always gratefully remember him, think of him often with pleasure, and take all opportunities of returning his kindness, especially if your deliverer was much your superior, and independent upon you; if you had forfeited his favour, provoked him, and incurred his displeasure: great favours from such an one would make impressions upon the most obdurate heart.

But though God be infinitely superior to us, and it is nothing to him what becomes of us, though we have rebelled against him, and deserve his vengeance, yet ten thousand deliverances from his hands have little or no effect upon the hearts of men: all these cannot bring them to think of him, or love him as much as they do a friend, or a common benefactor of their own species; and does such stupid ingratitude discover any spiritual life in them? No: they are dead in this respect, though they are all alive to those passions that terminate upon created objects. Further, God is the Benefactor of mankind, not only in delivering them from dangers and calamities, but in bestowing unnumbered positive blessings upon them. Here I cannot pretend to be particular, for the list of blessings is endless; and it will be the happy employment of an eternity to recollect and enumerate them. What an extensive and well-furnished world has our God formed for our accommodation! For us he has enriched the sun with light and heat, and the earth with fruitfulness. The numerous inhabitants of every element, the plants, minerals, and beasts of the earth, the fishes of the sea, the fowls of the air, are all rendering their service to man; some afford him food, and others work for him: the wind and seas, fire and water, stones and trees, all conspire to be useful to him. Our divine Benefactor crowns us with the blessings of liberty, of society, of friendship, and the most endearing relations : he preserves our health, gives us " rain from heaven, and fruitful seasons, and fills our hearts with food and gladness." In short, he gives us life, and breath, and all things ; every day, every hour, every moment has arrived to us richly freighted with blessings ; blessings have resided with us at home, and attended us abroad; blessings presented themselves ready for our enjoyment as soon as we entered into the world; then God provided hands to receive us, knees to support us, breasts to suckle us, and parents to guard and cherish us ; blessings have grown up with us, and given such constant attendance, that they are become familiar to us, and are the inseparable companions of our lives. It is no new or useful thing to us to see an illustrious sun rising to give us the day, to enjoy repose in the night, to rise refreshed and vigourous in the morning, to see our tables spread with plenty, the trees covered with fruit, the fields with grain and various forms of animals growing up for our support or service. These are such familiar blessings to us, that they too often seem things of course, or necessary appendages of our being. What a crowd of blessings have crowned the present morning! You and yours are alive

and well, you have not come hither ghastly and pining
with hunger, or agonizing with pain. How many refreshing draughts of air have you drawn this morning! how
many sprightly and regular pulses have beat through your
frame! how many easy motions have you performed with
hands, feet, eyes, tongues, and other members of your
body! and are not all these favours from God? Yes, undoubtedly; and thus has he gone on blessing you all your
days, without any interruption at all in many of these particulars of kindness, and with but very little in the rest.
Sinful and miserable as this world is, it is a treasury rich
in blessings, a storehouse full of provisions, a dwelling well
furnished for the accommodation of mortals, and all by the
care, and at the expense of that gracious God who first
made and still preserves it what it is. " Lord, whence is
it then that the inhabitants forget and neglect thee, as
though they were not at all obliged to thee? Oh!
whence is it that they love thy gifts, and yet disregard the
Giver? that they think less of thee than an earthly father
or friend, or a human benefactor; that there should be so
little gratitude towards thee, that of all benefactors thou
shouldst be the least acknowledged; that the benefactors
of nations, and even of private persons, in instances unworthy to be mentioned with those of thy goodness, should
be celebrated, and even adored, while thou art neglected,
thine agency overlooked, and thy goodness forgotten?
Oh! whence is this strange phenomenon, this unaccountable, unprecedented stupidity and ingratitude in reasonable
creatures? Surely, if they had any life, any sensation in
this respect, they would not be capable of such a conduct;
but they are dead, dead to all the generous sensations of
gratitude to God; and as a dead corpse feels no gratitude to those that perform the last friendly office and
cover it with earth, so a dead soul stands unmoved

under all the profusion of blessings which heaven pours upon it.

The blessings I have mentioned, which are confined to the present state, are great, and deserve our wonder and thanksgiving; especially, considering that they are bestowed upon a race of rebellious, ungrateful creatures, who deserve the severest vengeance; but there is a set of blessings yet unmentioned, of infinitely greater importance, in which all others are swallowed up, by the glory of which they are obscured, like the stars of night by the rising sun. To some of our race God has given crowns and kingdoms. For Israel Jehovah wrought the most astonishing miracles; seas and rivers opened to make way for them; rocks burst into springs of water to quench their thirst; the clouds poured down manna, and fed them with bread from heaven; their God delivered Daniel from the jaws of hungry lions, and his three companions from the burning fiery furnace. He has restored health to the sick, sight to the blind, and life to the dead. These blessings and deliverances have something majestic and striking in them: and had we been the subjects of them, we could not but have regarded them as great and singular; but what are these in comparison of God's gift of his Son, and the blessings he has purchased! his Son, who is of greater value, and dearer to him than ten thousand worlds; his beloved Son, in whom he is well pleased; him has he given for us, given up to three-and-thirty years of the most mortifying abasement, and an incessant conflict with the severest trials; given up to death, and all the ignominy and agonies of crucifixion. Thus has God loved our world! and never was there such a display of love in heaven or on earth. You can no more find love equal to this among creatures, than you can find among them the infinite power that formed the universe out of nothing.

This will stand upon record to all eternity, as the unprecedented, unparalleled, inimitable love of God. And it appears the more illustrious when we consider that this unspeakable gift was given to sinners, to rebels, to enemies,
that were so far from deserving it, that, on the other hand,
it is a miracle of mercy that they are not all groaning for
ever under the tremendous weight of his justice. Oh!
that I could say something becoming this love; something
that might do honour to it! but, alas! the language of
mortals was formed for lower subjects. This love passes
all description and all knowledge. Consider also what rich
blessings Christ has purchased for us; purchased not with
such corruptible things as silver and gold, but with his own
precious blood; the price recommends and endears the
blessings, though they are so great in themselves, as to
need no such recommendation! What can be greater or
more suitable blessings to persons in our circumstances,
than pardon for the guilty, redemption for slaves, righteousness and justification for the condemned, sanctification for
the unholy, rest for the weary, comfort for mourners, the
favour of God for rebels and exiles, strength for the impotent, protection for the helpless, everlasting happiness for the
heirs of hell, and, to sum up all, grace and glory, and every
good thing, and all the unsearchable riches of Christ for
the wretched and miserable, the poor, the blind, and naked!
These are blessings indeed, and, in comparison of them,
all the riches of the world are impoverished, and vanish
to nothing; and all these blessings are published, offered
freely, indefinitely offered to you, to me, to the greatest
sinner on earth, in the gospel; and we are allowed—
allowed, did I say? we are invited with the utmost importunity, entreated with the most compassionate tenderness and condescension, and commanded by the highest
authority, upon pain of eternal damnation, to accept the

blessings presented to us! And what reception does all this love meet with in our world? I tremble to think of it.

It is plain, these things are proposed to a world dead in sin; for they are all still, all unmoved, all senseless under such a revelation of infinite grace; mankind know not what it is to be moved, melted, transported with the love of a crucified Saviour, till divine grace visits their hearts, and forms them into new creatures; they feel no longer solicitude, nay, not so much as willingness to receive these blessings, till they become willing by almighty power: and judge ye, my brethren, whether they are not dead souls that are proof even against the love of God in Christ, that are not moved and melted by the agonies of his cross, that are careless about such inestimable blessings as these? Has that soul any spiritual life in it, that can sit senseless under the cross of Jesus, that can forget him, neglect him, dishonour him, after all his love and all his sufferings: that feels a prevailing indifference and languor towards him; that loves him less than an earthly friend, and seeks him with less eagerness than gold and silver? Is not every generous passion, every principle of gratitude quite extinct in such a spirit? It may be alive to other objects, but towards this it is dead, and alas! is not this the common case? Oh look round the world, and what do you see but a general neglect of the blessed Jesus, and all the blessings of his gospel? How cold, how untoward, how reluctant, how averse are the hearts of men towards him! how hard to persuade them to think of him and love him! Try to persuade men to give over their sins which grieve him, dishonour him, and were the cause of his death; try to engage them to devote themselves entirely to him, and live to his glory, alas! you try in vain; their hearts still continue cold and hard as a stone; try to persuade them to murder or robbery, and you are more likely to prevail. Suffer me, in my astonishment, to repeat this most melancholy truth again; the generality of mankind are habitually careless about the blessed Jesus; they will not seek him, nor give their hearts and affections, though they must perish for ever by their neglect of him! Astonishing, and most lamentable, that ever such perverseness and stupidity should seize the soul of man! Methinks I could here take up a lamentation over human nature, and fall on my knees with this prayer for my fellow men, " Father of spirits, and Lord of life, quicken, oh quicken these dead souls!" Oh, Sirs, while we see death all around us, and feel it benumbing our own souls, who can help the most bitter wailing and lamentation? who can restrain himself from crying to the great Author of life for a happy resurrection? While the valley of dry bones lies before me, while the carnage, the charnel-house of immortal souls strikes my sight all around me far and wide, how can I forbear crying, *Come from the four winds, oh breath, and breathe upon these slain, that they may live!* But to turn from this digression, into which I was unavoidably hurried by the horror of the subject, I would observe farther, that kind usage and pleasing treatment may not always be best for such creatures as we are: fatherly severities and chastisements, though not agreeable to us, yet may be necessary and conducive to our greatest good. Accordingly, God has tried the force of chastisements to make impressions on our hearts: these indeed have been but few in comparison of his more agreeable dispensations; yet recollect whether you have not frequently felt his rod. Have you not languished under sickness and pain, and been brought within a near view of the king of terrors? Have you not suffered the bereavement of friends and relations, and met with losses, adversity, and disappointments? Others have felt still greater calamities in a closer succession, and with fewer mercies intermixed. These things, one would think, would immediately bring men to regard the hand that smites them, and make them sensible of their undutiful conduct, which has procured the correction; these are like the application of fire to one in a lethargy, to awaken him to life; but alas! under all these afflictions the stupor and insensibility still remain. Sinners groan by reason of oppression, but it is not natural for them to inquire, *Where is God my Maker, that giveth songs in the night?* It is not natural for them to repent of their undutiful conduct and amend; or if they are awakened to some little sense, while the painful rod of the Almighty is yet upon them, as soon as it is removed they become as hardened and senseless as ever. And is not a state of death a very proper representation of such sullen, incorrigible stupidity? Living souls have very tender sensations,; one touch of their heavenly Father's hand makes deep impressions upon them; they tremble at his frown, they fall and weep at his feet, they confess their offences, and mourn over them; they fly to the arms of mercy to escape the impending blow; and thus would all do were they not quite destitute of spiritual life.

I have materials sufficient for a discourse of some hours; but at present I must abruptly drop the subject: however, I cannot dismiss you without making a few reflections. And,

1. What a strange, affecting view does this subject give us of this assembly! I doubt not but I may accommodate the text to some of you with this agreeable addition, "You hath he quickened, though you were once dead in trespasses and sins." Though the vital pulse beats faint and irregular, and your spiritual life is but very low, yet,

blessed be God, you are not entirely dead: you have some living sensations, some lively and vigorous exercises in religion. On the other hand, I doubt not but some of you not only were, but still are, *dead in trespasses and sins.* It is not to be expected in our world, at least not before the millennium, that we shall see such a mixed company together, and all living souls. Here then is the difference between you; some of you are spiritually alive, and some of you are spiritually dead; here the living and the dead are blended together in the same assembly, on the same seat, and united in the nearest relations: here sits a dead soul, there another, and there another, and a few living souls scattered here and there among them; here is a dead parent and a living child, or a dead child and a living parent; here life and death (oh, shocking!) are united in the bonds of conjugal love, and dwell under the same roof: here is a dead servant and a living master: and there a dead master (oh, terrible!) commands a living servant. Should I trace the distinction beyond this assembly into the world, we shall find a family here and there that have a little life; perhaps one, perhaps two, discover some vital symptoms; but oh, what crowds of dead families! all dead together, and no endeavours used to bring one another to life; a death-like silence about eternal things; a deadly stupor and insensibility reign among them; they breathe out no desires and prayers after God, nor does the vital pulse of love beat in their hearts towards him; but, on the contrary, their souls are putrefying in sin, which is very emphatically called *corruption* by the sacred writers; they are overrun and devoured by their lusts, and worms insult and destroy the dead body. Call to them, they will not awake; thunder the terrors of the Lord in their ears, they will not hear; offer them all the blessings of the gospel, they will not stretch out the hand of faith to receive them;

lay the word of God, the bread of life, before them, they have no appetite for it. In short, the plain symptoms of death are upon them: the animal is alive, but alas! the spirit is dead towards God. And what an affecting, melancholy view does this give of this assembly, and of the world in general! *Oh, that my head were waters, and mine eyes a fountain of tears, that I might weep day and night for the slain of the daughter of my people!* Weep not for the afflicted, weep not over ghastly corpses dissolving into their original dust, but oh! weep for dead souls. Should God now strike all those persons dead in this assembly, whose souls are *dead in trespasses and sins,* should he lay them all in pale corpses before us, like Ananias and Sapphira at the apostles' feet, what numbers of you would never return from this house more, and what lamentations would there be among the surviving few! One would lose a husband or a wife, another a son or a daughter, another a father or a mother; alas! would not some whole families be swept off together, all blended in one promiscuous death? Such a sight as this would strike terror into the hardiest heart among you. But what is this to a company of rational spirits slain and dead in trespasses and sins? How deplorable and inexpressibly melancholy a sight this! Therefore,

2. *Awake thou that sleepest, and arise from the dead, and Christ shall give thee light.* This call is directed to you, dead sinners; which is a sufficient warrant for me to exhort and persuade you. The principle of reason is still alive in you; you are also sensible of your own interest, and feel the workings of self-love. It is God alone that can quicken you, but he effects this by a power that does not exclude, but attends rational instructions and persuasions to your understanding. Therefore, though I am sure you will continue dead still if left to yourselves, yet

with some trembling hopes that his power may accompany my feeble words, and impregnate them with life, I call upon, I entreat, I charge you sinners to rouse yourselves out of your dead sleep, and seek to obtain spiritual life! Now, while my voice sounds in your ears, now, this moment, waft up this prayer, "Lord, pity a dead soul, a soul that has been dead for ten, twenty, thirty, forty years or more, and lain corrupting in sin, and say unto me, Live : from this moment let me live unto thee." Let this prayer be still upon your hearts : keep your souls always in a supplicating posture, and who knows but that he, who raised Lazarus from the grave, may give you a spiritual resurrection to a more important life? But if you wilfully continue your security, expect in a little time to suffer the second death; the mortification will become incurable; and then, though you will be still dead to God, yet you will be "tremblingly alive all over" to the sensation of pain and torture. Oh that I could gain but this one request of you, which your own interest so strongly enforces ! but alas ! it has been so often refused, that to expect to prevail is to hope against hope.

3. Let the children of God be sensible of their great happiness in being made spiritually alive. Life is a principle, a capacity necessary for enjoyments of any kind. Without animal life you would be as incapable of animal pleasures as a stone or a clod; and without spiritual life you can no more enjoy the happiness of heaven than a beast or a devil. This therefore is a preparative, a previous qualification, and a sure pledge and earnest of everlasting life. How highly then are you distinguished, and what cause have you for gratitude and praise!

4. Let us all be sensible of this important truth, that it is entirely by grace we are saved. This is the inference the apostle expressly makes from this doctrine; and he is

so full of it, that he throws it into a parenthesis, (verse the 5th,) though it breaks the connection of his discourse ; and as soon as he has room he resumes it again, (verse 8th,) and repeats it over and over, in various forms, in the compass of a few verses. *By grace ye are saved. By grace are you saved through faith. It is the gift of God ; —not of yourselves—not of works.* (verse 9th.)   This, you see, is an inference that seemed of great importance to the apostle ; and what can more naturally follow from the premises ?   If we were once dead in sin, certainly it is owing to the freest grace that we have been quickened; therefore, when we survey the change, let us cry, " Grace, grace unto it !"

SERMON V.

THE NATURE AND PROCESS OF SPIRITUAL LIFE.

EPHES. ii. 4, 5.—*But God, who is rich in mercy, for his great love wherewith he loved us, even when we were dead in sins, hath quickened us together with Christ.*

IT is not my usual method to weary your attention by a long confinement to one subject; and our religion furnishes us with such a boundless variety of important topics, that a minister who makes them his study will find no temptation to cloy you with repetitions, but rather finds it difficult to speak so concisely on one subject, as to leave room for others of equal importance; however, the subject of my last discourse was so copious and interesting, that I cannot dismiss it without a supplement. I there showed you some of the symptoms of spiritual death; but I would not leave you dead as I found you; and therefore I intend now to consider the counterpart of that subject, and show you the nature and symptoms of spiritual life.

I doubt not but a number of you have been made alive to God by his quickening spirit; but many, I fear, still continue *dead in trespasses and sins;* and, while such are around me, I cannot help imagining my situation something like that of the prophet Ezekiel (chap. xxxvii.) in the midst of the valley full of dry bones, spread far and wide around him; and should I be asked, *Can these dry bones,* can these dead souls *live?* I must answer with him,—*Oh, Lord God, thou knowest.* Lord, I see no symptoms of life in them, no tendency towards it. I know nothing is impossible to thee; I firmly believe thou canst inspire them with life, dry and dead as they are; and what thy designs are towards them, whether thou intendest to exert thy all-quickening power upon them, thou only knowest, and I would not presume to determine; but this I know, that, if they are left to themselves, they will continue dead to all eternity; for, oh Lord, the experiment has been repeatedly tried; thy servant has over and over made those quickening applications to them, which thy word, that sacred dispensary, prescribes; but all in vain: they still continue dead towards thee, and lie putrefying more and more in trespasses and sins; however, at thy command, I would attempt the most unpromising undertaking; I would proclaim even unto dry bones and dead souls, *Oh ye dry bones*, oh ye dead souls, *hear the word of the Lord!* Ezek. xxxvii. 4.   I would also cry aloud for the animating breath of the Holy Spirit, *Come from the four winds, oh breath, and breathe upon these slain, that they may live*, v. 9.

Ye dead sinners, I would make one attempt more in the name of the Lord to bring you to life; and if I have the least hope of success, it is entirely owing to the encouraging peradventure that the quickening spirit of Christ may work upon your hearts while I am addressing myself to your ears.   And, oh sirs, let us all keep our souls in a praying posture, throughout this discourse.   If one of you should fall into a swoon or an apoplexy, how would all about you bestir themselves to bring you to life again! And alas! shall dead souls lie so thick among us, in every assembly, in every family; and shall no means be used for their recovery?   Did Martha and Mary apply to Jesus with all the arts of importunity in behalf of their sick and deceased brother, and are there not some of you that have dead relations, dear friends and neighbours, I mean dead in the worst sense, "dead in trespasses and sins?" and will you not apply to Jesus, the Lord of life, and follow him with your importunate cries, till he come and call them to life? Now let parents turn intercessors for their children, children for their parents, friend for friend, neighbour for neighbour, yea, enemy for enemy. Oh! should we all take this method, we might soon expect to see the valley of dry bones full of living souls, *an exceeding great army*. Ezek. xxxvii. 10.

In praying for this great and glorious event, you do not pray for an impossibility. Thousands as dead as they, have obtained a joyful resurrection by the power of God. Here in my text you have an instance of a promiscuous crowd of Jews and Gentiles that had lain dead in sin together, and even St. Paul among them, who were recovered to life, and are now enjoying an immortal life in the heavenly regions; and, blessed be God, this spiritual life is not entirely extinct among us. Among the multitudes of dead souls that we every where meet with, we find here and there a soul that has very different symptoms: once indeed it was like the rest; but now, while they are quite senseless of divine things, and have no vital aspirations after God, this soul cannot be content with the richest affluence of created enjoyment; it pants and breathes after God; it feeds upon his word, it feels an almighty energy in eternal things, and receives vital sensations from them. It discovers life and vigour in devotion, and serves the living God with pleasure, though it is also subject to fits of languishment, and at times seems just expiring, and to lose all sensation. And whence is this vast difference? Why is this soul so different from what it once was, and what thousands around still are? Why can it not, like them, and like itself formerly, lie dead and

senseless in sin, without any vital impressions or experiences from God or divine things ? The reason is, the
happy reason, my brethren, is, this is a living soul : " God,
out of the great love wherewith he loved it, hath quickened it together with Christ," and hence it is alive to him.

My present design is to explain the nature and properties of this divine life, and to show you the manner in
which it is usually begun in the soul : I shall open with
the consideration of the last particular.

Here you must observe, that, though spiritual life is instantaneously infused, yet God prepares the soul for its
reception by a course of previous operations. He spent
six days in the creation of the world, though he might
have spoken it into being in an instant. Thus he usually
creates the soul anew after a gradual process of preparatory actions. In forming the first man, he first created
chaos out of nothing, then he digested it into earth ; on
the sixth day he formed and organized the earth into a
body, with all its endless variety of members, juices, mus-
cles, fibres, veins, and arteries ; and then, after this process, he inspired it with a living soul ; and what was but
a lump of clay, sprung up a perfect man. Thus also the
fœtus in the womb is for some months in formation before
the soul, or the principle of life, is infused. In like manner the Almighty proceeds in quickening us with spiritual
life ; we all pass through a course of preparation, though
some through a longer, and some shorter. And as one
reason why the great Creator took up so much time in
the creation of the world, probably was, that he might
allow the angels time for leisurely surveys of the astonishing process, so he may advance thus gradually in the new
creation, that we may observe the various steps of the
operation, and make proper reflections upon it in future
life. My present design is to trace these steps to their

grand result, that you may know whether ever divine grace has carried you through this gracious process.

And that you may not fall into needless perplexities, it may be necessary for me to premise farther, that there is a great variety in these preparatory operations, and in the degrees of spiritual life. Indeed the difference is only circumstantial, for the work is substantially the same, and spiritual life is substantially the same in all; but then, in such circumstances as the length of time, the particular external means, the degree of previous terror, and of subsequent joy and vitality, &c., God exercises a sovereign freedom, and shows that he has a variety of ways by which to accomplish his end; and it is no matter how we obtain it, if we have but spiritual life. I shall therefore endeavour to confine myself to the substance of this work, without its peculiarities, in different subjects; and, when I cannot avoid descending to particulars, I shall endeavour so to diversify them, as that they may be easily adapted to the various cases of different Christians. To draw their common lineaments, whereby they may be distinguished from all others, is sufficient to my present purpose: whereas, to draw the particular lineaments, or peculiar features, whereby they may be distinguished from one another, is a very difficult task, and cannot be of any great service to what I have now in design.

I have only one thing more to premise, and that is, that the way by which divine grace prepares a sinner for spiritual life, is by working upon all the principles of the rational life, and exciting him to exert them to the utmost to obtain it. Here it is proper for you to recollect what I observed in my last discourse, that even a sinner dead in trespasses and sins, is alive and capable of action in other respects: he can not only perform the actions and feel the sensations of animal life, but he can also exercise his intellectual powers about intellectual objects, and even about divine things : he is capable of thinking of these, and of receiving some impressions from them : he is also capable of attending upon the ordinances of the gospel, and performing the external duties of religion.   These things a sinner may do, and yet be dead in sin.   Indeed he will not exercise his natural powers about these things while left to himself: he has the power, but then he has no disposition to employ it: he is indeed capable of meditating upon spiritual things, but what does this avail when he will not turn his mind to such objects? or if he does, he considers them as mere speculations, and not as the most interesting and important realities.   How few, or how superficial and unaffecting are a sinner's thoughts of them!   Heaven and hell are objects that may strike the passions, and raise the joys and fears of a natural man, but in general he is little or nothing impressed with them.   He is capable of prayer, hearing, and using the means of grace; but I believe, if you make observations upon the conduct of mankind, that you will find they are but seldom employed in these duties, or that they perform them in such a careless manner, that that they have no tendency to answer the end of their institution.   In short, the more I know of mankind, I have the lower opinion of what they will do in religion when left to themselves.   They have a natural power, and we have seen all possible means used with them to excite them to put it forth; but alas! all is in vain, and nothing will be done to purpose till God stir them up to exert their natural abilities; and this he performs as a preparative for spiritual life.   He brings the sinner to exert all his active powers in seeking this divine principle : nature does her utmost, and all outward means are tried before a supernatural principle is implanted.

The evangelist John has given us the history of the re-

surrection of the dead body of Lazarus after it had been
four days in the grave; and I would now give you the
history of a more glorious resurrection, the resurrection of
a soul that had lain dead for months and years, yet is at
last quickened by the same almighty power with a divine
and immortal life.

Should I exemplify it by a particular instance, I might
fix upon this or that person in this assembly, and remind
you, and inform others, of the process of this work in your
souls. And oh! how happy are such of you, that you
may be produced as instances in this case!

You lay for ten, twenty, thirty years, or more, dead in
traspasses and sins; you did not breathe and pant like a
living soul after God and holiness; you had little more
sense of the burden of sin than a corpse of the pressure
of a mountain; you had no appetite for the living bread
that came down from heaven; the vital pulse of sacred
passions did not beat in your hearts towards God and
divine things, but you lay putrefying in sin; filthy lusts
preyed upon you like worms on the bodies of the dead;
you spread the contagion of sin around you by your conversation and example, like the stench and corrupt effluvia
of a rotten carcass; you were odious and abominable to
God, fit to be shut up in the infernal pit, out of his sight:
and you were objects of horror and lamentation to all that
knew and daily considered your case, your deplorable
case. During this time many quickening applications
were made to you; you had friends that used all means to
bring you to life again; but alas! all in vain; conscience
proved your friend, and pierced and chafed you, to bring
you to some feeling, but you remained still senseless, or
the symptoms of life soon vanished. God did not cast
you away as irrecoverably dead, but stirred and agitated
you within, and struggled long with the principles of

death to subdue them: and if it was your happy lot to live under a faithful ministry, the living oracles that contain the seeds of the divine life were applied to you with care and solicitude. The terrors of the Lord were thundered in your ears to awaken you. The experiment of a Saviour's dying love, and the rich grace of the gospel, were repeatedly tried upon you: now you were carried within hearing of the heavenly music, and within sight of the glories of Paradise, to try if these would charm you; now you were, as it were, held over the flames of hell, that they might by their pungent pains scorch and startle you into life. Providence also concurred with these applications, and tried to recover you by mercies and judgments, sickness and health, losses and possessions, disappointments and successes, threatenings and deliverances. If it was your unhappy lot to lie among dead souls like yourself, you had indeed but little pity from them, nay, they and Satan were plying you with their opiates and poison to confirm the deadly sleep. And oh! how astonishing is it that you should be quickened in a charnel-house, in the mansions of the dead, with dead souls lying all around you! But if it was your happiness to be in the society of the living, they pitied you, they stirred and agitated you with their warnings and persuasions, they, like Martha and Mary in behalf of their deceased brother, went to Jesus with their cries and importunities, "Lord, my child, my parent, my servant, my neighbour is dead, oh come and restore him to life! Lord, if thou hadst been here, he would not have died; but even now I know it is not too late for thee to raise him." Thus, when one.is dead in our heavenly Father's family, the whole house should be alarmed, and all the domestics be busy in trying to bring him to life again. But, oh! reflect with shame and sorrow how long all these quickening applications were in vain; you still lay in a dead sleep, or, if at times you seemed to move, and gave us hopes you were coming to life again, you soon relapsed, and grew as senseless as ever. And alas! are there not some of you in this condition to this very moment? Oh deplorable sight! May the hour come, and oh that this may be the hour, in which such dead souls *shall hear the voice of the Son of God, and live.* John v. 25.

But as to such of you in whom I would exemplify this history of a spiritual resurrection, when your case was thus deplorable, and seemingly helpless, the happy hour, the time of love came, when you must live. When all these applications had been unsuccessful, the all-quickening Spirit of God had determined to exert more of his energy, and work more effectually upon you. Perhaps a verse in your Bible, a sentence in a sermon, an alarming Providence, the conversation of a pious friend, or something that unexpectedly occurred to your own thoughts, first struck your minds with unusual force; you found you could not harden yourselves against it as you were wont to do; it was attended with a power you never before had felt, and which you could not resist; this made you thoughtful and pensive, and turned your minds to objects that you were wont to neglect; this made you stand and pause, and think of the state of your neglected souls; you began to fear matters were wrong with you; "What will become of me, when I leave this world? Where shall I reside for ever? Am I prepared for the eternal world? How have I spent my life?" These, and the like inquiries, put you to a stand, and you could not pass over them so superficially as you were wont to do; your sins now appeared to you in a new light; you were shocked and surprised at their malignant nature, their number, their aggravations, and their dreadful consequences. The great God, whom you were wont to neglect, appeared to you as a Being that demanded your regard; you saw he was indeed a venerable, awful, majestic Being, with whom you had the most important concern : in short, you saw that such a life as you had led would never bring you to heaven: you saw you must make religion more your business than you had ever done, and hereupon you altered your former course : you broke off from several of your vices, you deserted your extravagant company, and you began to frequent the throne of grace, to study religion, and to attend upon its institutions: and this you did with some degree of earnestness and solicitude.

When you were thus reformed, you began to flatter yourself that you had escaped out of your dangerous condition, and secured the divine favour: now you began to view yourselves with secret self-applause as true Christians; but all this time the reformation was only outward, and there was no new principle of a divine supernatural life implanted in your hearts: you had not the generous passions and sensations of living souls towards God, but acted entirely from natural, selfish principles: you had no clear heart-affecting views of the intrinsic evil, and odious nature of sin, considered in itself, nor of the entire universal corruption of your nature, and the necessity not only of adorning your outer man by an external reformation, but of an inward change of heart by the almighty power of God: you were not deeply sensible of the extent and spirituality of the divine law, nor of the infinite purity and inexorable justice of the Deity: you had no love for religion and virtue for their own sakes, but only on account of their happy consequences. Indeed your love of novelty and a regard to your own happiness might so work upon you, for a time, that you might have very raised and delightful passions in religious duties; but all your religion at that time was a mere system of selfishness, and you had no generous disinterested delight in holiness for its own excellency, nor did you heartily relish the strictness of pure, living religion : you were also under the government of a self-righteous spirit: your own good works were the ground of your hopes, and you had no relish for the mortifying doctrine of salvation through the mere mercy of God and the righteousness of Jesus Christ: though your education taught you to acknowledge Christ as the only Saviour, and ascribe all your hopes to his death, yet in reality he was of very little importance in your religion ; he had but little place in your heart and affections, even when you urged his name as your only plea at the throne of grace : in short you had not the spirit of the gospel, nor any spiritual life within you. And this is all the religion with which multitudes are contented: with this they obtain a name that they live; but in the sight of God, and in reality, they are dead ; and had you been suffered to rest here, according to your own desire, you would have been dead still.

But God, who is rich (oh how inconceivably rich!) in mercy, for the great love wherewith he loved you, resolved to carry on his works in you; and therefore, while you were flattering yourselves, and elated with a proud conceit of a happy change in your condition, he surprised you with a very different view of your case; he opened your eyes farther, and then you saw, you felt those things of which, till then, you had but little sense or apprehension; such as the corruption of your hearts, the awful strictness of the divine law, your utter inability to yield perfect obedience, and the necessity of an inward change of the inclinations and relishes of your soul. These, and a great many other things of a like nature, broke in upon your minds with striking evidence and a kind of almighty energy;

and now you saw you were still " dead in sin," weak, indisposed, averse towards spiritual things, and " dead in law,"
condemned to everlasting death and misery by its righteous
sentence : now you set about the duties of religion with
more earnestness than ever; now you prayed, you heard,
and used the other means of grace as for your life, for you
saw that your eternal life was indeed at stake; and now,
when you put the matter to a thorough trial, you were
more sensible than ever of your own weakness, and the
difficulties in your way.   " Oh! who would have thought
my heart had been so depraved that it should thus fly off
from God, and struggle, and reluctate against returning to
him ?"   Such was then your language.   Alas! you found
yourselves quite helpless, and all your efforts feeble and
ineffectual: then you perceived yourselves really dead in
sin, and that you must continue so to all eternity, unless
quickened by a power infinitely superior to your own;
not that you lay slothful and inactive at this time; no,
never did you exert yourselves so vigorously in all
your life, never did you besiege the throne of grace
with such earnest importunity, never did you hear and
read with such eager attention, or make such a vigorous
resistance against sin and temptation: all your natural
powers were exerted to the highest pitch, for now you
saw your case required it: but you found all your most
vigourous endeavours insufficient, and you were sensible
that, without the assistance of a superior power, the work
of religion could never be effected.

Now you were reduced very low indeed.   While you
imagined you could render yourselves safe by a reformation
in your own power, you were not much alarmed at your
condition, though you saw it bad.   But oh! to feel yourselves dead in sin, and that you cannot help yourselves; to
see yourselves in a state of condemnation, liable to execu-

tion every moment, and yet to find all your own endeavours utterly insufficient to relieve you; to be obliged, after all you had done, to lie at mercy, and confess that you were as deserving of everlasting punishment as ever the most notorious criminal was of the stroke of public justice; this was a state of extreme dejection, terror, and anxiety indeed. The proud, self-confident creature was never thoroughly mortified and humbled till now, when he is slain by the law, and entirely cut off from all hopes from himself.

And now, finding you could not save yourselves, you began to cast about you, and look out for another to save you: now you were more sensible than ever of the absolute need of Jesus; and you cried and reached after him, and stirred up yourselves to take hold of him. The gospel brought the free offer of him to your ears, and you would fain have accepted of him; but here new difficulties arose. Alas! you did not think yourselves good enough to accept of him, and hence you took a great deal of fruitless pains to make yourselves better: you also found your hearts strangely averse to the gospel-method of salvation, and, though a sense of your necessity made you try to work up yourselves to an approbation of it, yet you could not affectionately acquiesce in it, and cordially relish it.

And now, how melancholy was your situation! You were "shut up unto the faith;" Gal. iii. 23; there was no other possible way of escape, and yet, alas! you could not take this way: now you were ready to cry, "I am cut off my strength and my hope are perished from the Lord;" but, blessed be God, he did not leave you in this condition. Man's extremity of distress is God's opportunity for relief and salvation; and so you found it.

Now the process of preparatory operations is just come to a result. Now it is time for God to work, for nature has done her utmost, and has been found utterly insufficient; now it is proper a divine, supernatural principle should be infused, for all the principles of nature have failed, and the proud sinner is obliged to own it, and stand still, and see the salvation of God. In this situation you wanted nothing but such a divine principle to make you living Christians indeed. These preparatives were like the taking away the stone from the sepulchre of Lazarus, which was a prelude of that almighty voice which called him from the dead. Now you appear to me like the dry bones in Ezekiel's vision in one stage of the operation. After there had been a noise, and a shaking among them, and the bones had come together, bone to his bone; *I beheld*, says he, *and lo, the sinews and the flesh came up upon them, and the skin covered them above; but there was no breath in them;* Ezek. xxxvii. 8; this was all that was wanting to making them living men. In like manner you, at this time, had the external appearance of Christians, but you had no divine supernatural life in you; you were but the fair carcasses of Christians; your religion had a body completely formed, but it had no soul in it; and had the holy Spirit now given over his work, you would have continued dead still.

But now the important crisis is come, when he who stood over the grave of Lazarus, and pronounced the life-restoring mandate, *Lazarus, come forth!* when he who breathed into Adam the breath of life, and made him a living soul; I say, now the crisis is come, when he will implant the principles of life in your souls; suddenly you feel the amazing change, and find you are acting from principles entirely new to you; for now your hearts that were wont to reluctate, and start back from God, rise to him with the strongest aspirations: now the way of salvation through Christ, which you could never relish before, appears all amiable and glorious, and captivates your whole souls. Holiness has lovely and powerful charms, which captivate you to the most willing obedience, notwithstanding your former disgust to it; and though once you were enamoured with sin, and disliked it only because you could not indulge it with impunity, it now appears to you a mere mass of corruption and deformity, an abominable thing, which you hate above all other things on earth or in hell. At this juncture you were animated with a new life in every faculty of your souls, and hereupon you felt the instincts, the appetites, the sympathies and antipathies of a new life, a divine life, justly styled by the apostle *the life of God;* the life of God in the soul of man. The pulse of sacred passions began to beat towards spirtual objects; the vital warmth of love spread itself through your whole frame; you breathed out your desires and prayers before God; like a new-born infant you began to cry after him, and at times you have learned to lisp his name with filial endearment, and cry *Abba Father*; you hungered and thirsted after righteousness, and as every kind of life must have its proper nourishment, so your spiritual life fed upon Christ, the living bread, and the sincere milk of his word. You also felt a new set of sensations; divine things now made deep and tender impressions upon you; the great realities of religion and eternity now affected you in a manner unknown before; you likewise found your souls actuated with life and vigour in the service of God, and in the duties you owed to mankind. This strange alteration no doubt filled you with surprise and amazement, something like that of Adam when he found himself start into life out of his eternal non-existence. With these new sensations everything appeared to you in a quite different light, and you could not but wonder that you had never perceived them in that manner before.

Thus, my dear brethren, when you were even dead in sin, God quickened you together with Christ. It is true, the principle of life might be very weak at first, like the life of a new-born infant, or a fœtus just animated in the womb; nay, it may be but very weak still, and at times may languish, and seem just expiring in the agonies of death; but, blessed be the quickening Spirit of Christ, since the happy hour of your resurrection you have never been, and you never will be to all eternity, what you once were, "dead in trespasses and sins." Should I give you your own history since that time, it would be to this purpose, and you will discern many symptoms of life in it. You have often known what sickness of soul is, as well as of body; and sometimes it has risen to such a height as to endanger your spiritual life. The seeds of sin, that still lurk in your constitution, like the principles of death, or a deadly poison circulating through your veins, have often struggled for the mastery, and cast you into languishing or violent disorders: then was the divine life oppressed, and you could not freely draw the breath of prayer and pious desires; you lost the appetite for the word of God, and what you received did not digest well and turn to kindly nourishment; the pulse of sacred passions beat faint and irregular, the vital heat decayed, and you felt a death-like cold creeping upon you and benumbing you. Sometimes you have been afflicted, perhaps, with convulsions of violent and outrageous passions, with the dropsy of insatiable desires after things below, with the lethargy of carnal security, or the fever of lust: at other times you have felt an universal disorder through your whole frame, and you hardly knew what ailed you, only you were sure your souls were not well; but perhaps your most common disorder that seizes you is a kind of consumption, a lowness of spirits, a languor and weakness, the want of appetite for your spiritual food, or perhaps a nausea and disgust towards it; you also live in a country very unwholesome to living souls; you dwell among the dead, and catch contagion from the conversation of those around you, and this heightens the disorder: and further, that old serpent the devil labours to infect you with his deadly poison, and increase the peccant humours by his temptations: at such times you can hardly feel any workings of spiritual life in you, and you fear you are entirely dead; but examine strictly, and you will discover some vital symptoms even in this bad habit of soul; for does not your new nature exert itself to work off the disorder? Are not your spirits in a ferment, and do you not feel yourselves in exquisite pain, or at least greatly uneasy? Give all the world to a sick man, and he despises it all: "Oh, give me my health," says he, "or you give me nothing." So it is with you; nothing can content you while your souls are thus out of order. Do you not long for their recovery, that you may go about your business again; I mean that you may engage in the service of God with all the vigour of health? and do you not apply to Christ as your only physician in this condition? And oh! what an healing balm is his blood! what a reviving cordial is his love! and how kindly does his Spirit purge off the corrupt humours, and subdue the principles of sin and death! Has not experience taught you the meaning of the apostle, when he says, *Christ is our life:* and *I live, yet not I, but Christ liveth in me,* Gal. ii. 20. Do you not perceive that Christ is your vital head, and that you revive or languish just as he communicates or withholds his influence? And have you not been taught in the same way what is the meaning of that expression so often repeated, *The just shall live by faith?* Hab. ii. 4. Do you not find that faith is, as it were, the grand artery by which you derive life from

Christ, and by which it is circulated through your whole frame; and that when faith languishes, then you weaken, pine away, and perhaps fall into a swoon, as though you were quite dead? Are you not careful of the health of your souls? You endeavour to keep them warm with the love of God; you shun those sickly regions as far as you can, where the example and conversation of the wicked spread their deadly infection, and you love to dwell among living souls, and breathe in their wholesome air. Upon the whole, it is evident, notwithstanding your frequent indispositions, you have some life within you; life takes occasion to show itself even from your disorders. It is a plain symptom of it, that you have something within you, that makes such a vigorous resistance against the principles of sin and death, and throws your whole frame into a ferment, till it has wrought off the distemper. In short, you have the sensations, the sympathies and antipathies, the pleasures and pains of living souls.

And is it so indeed? Then from this moment begin to rejoice and bless the Lord, who raised you to spiritual life. Oh, let the hearts he has quickened beat with his love; let the lips he has opened, when quivering in death, speak his praise, and devote that life to him which he has given you, and which he still supports!

Consider what a divine and noble kind of life he has given you. It is a capacity and aptitude for the most exalted and divine services and enjoyments. Now you have a relish for the Supreme Good as your happiness, the only proper food for your immortal souls, and he will not suffer you to hunger and thirst in vain, but will satisfy the appetites he has implanted in your nature. You have some spirit and life in his service, and are not like the dead souls around you, that are all alive toward other objects, but absolutely dead towards him: you have also noble and exalted sensations; you are capable of a set of pleasures of a more refined and sublime nature than what are relished by grovelling sinners. From your inmost souls you detest and nauseate whatever is mean, base, and abominable, and you can feast on what is pure, amiable, excellent, and worthy of your love. Your vitiated taste for trash and poison is cured, and you feed upon heavenly bread, upon food agreeable to the constitution of your spiritual nature; and hence you may infer your meetness for the heavenly world, that region of perfect vitality. You have a disposition for its enjoyments and services; and this is the grand preparative. God will not encumber the heaven of his glory with dead souls, nor infect the pure salubrious air of paradise with the poison of their corruption: but the everlasting doors are always open for living souls, and not one of them shall ever be excluded; nay, the life of heaven is already within you; the life that reigns with immortal health and vigour above, is the very same with that which works in your breasts; only there it is arrived to maturity and perfection, and here it is in its rudiments and weakness. Your animal life, which was hardly perceivable in the womb, was the very same with that which now possesses you, only now it is come to perfection. Thus you are now angels in embryo, the fœtus (might I be allowed the expression) of glorified immortals; and when you are born out of the womb of time into the eternal world, this feeble spark of spiritual life will kindle and blaze, and render you as active and vigorous as " the rapt seraph that adores and burns." Then you will fear no more weakness, no more languors, no more qualms of indisposition; the poison of temptation, and the contagion of bad example cannot reach you there; and the inward seeds of sickness and death will be purged entirely out of your soul: you will be got quite out of the sickly country, and breathe a

pure reviving air, the natural element of your souls.
There you will find the fountain, yea, whole rivers of the
waters of life, of which you will drink in large draughts
for ever and ever, and which will inspire you with immortal life and vigour.   Oh, how happy are you in this
single gift of spiritual life! this is a life that cannot perish,
even in the ruins of the world.   What though you must
ere long yield your mortal bodies and animal life to death
and rottenness? your most important life is immortal, and
subject to no such dissolution; and therefore be courageous
in the name of the Lord, and bid defiance to all the
calamities of life, and all the terrors of death; for *your life
is hid with Christ in God; and when Christ, who is our
life, shall appear, then shall ye also appear with him in
glory.* Col. iii. 3, 4.

I would willingly go on in this strain, and leave the
pulpit with a relish of these delightful truths upon my
spirit; but, alas! I must turn my address to another set
of persons in this assembly; but " where is the Lord God
of Elijah," who restored the Shunamite's son to life by
means of that prophet?   I am going to call to the dead,
and I know they will not hear, unless he attend my feeble
voice with his almighty power.   I would pray over you
like Elijah over the dead child, *Oh* Lord *my God, I pray
thee, let this* sinner's life *come into him again.* 1 Kings
xvii. 21.   Are not the living and the dead promiscuously
blended in this assembly?   Here is a dead soul, there another, and there another all over the house; and here and
there a few living souls thinly scattered among them.
Have you ever been carried through such a preparatory
process as I have described? or if you are uncertain about
this, as some may be who are animated with spiritual life,
inquire, have you the feelings, the appetites and aversions,
the pleasing and the painful sensations of living souls?

Methinks conscience breaks its silence in some of you, whether you will or not, and cries, "Oh no; there is not a spark of life in this breast."

Well, my poor deceased friends, (for so I may call you,) I hope you will seriously attend to what I am going seriously to say to you. I have no bad design upon you, but only to restore you to life. And though your case is really discouraging, yet I hope it is not quite desperate. The principles of nature, reason, self-love, joy, and fear, are still alive in you, and you are capable of some application to divine things. And, as I told you, it is upon the principles of nature that God is wont to work, to prepare the soul for the infusion of a supernatural life. And these I would now work upon, in hopes you are not proof against considerations of the greatest weight and energy; I earnestly beg you would lay to heart such things as these.

Can you content yourselves with an animal life, the life of beasts, with that superfluity, reason, just to render you a more ingenious and self-tormenting kind of brutes; more artful in gratifying your sordid appetites, and yet still uneasy for want of an unknown something; a care that the brutal world, being destitute of reason, are unmolested with? Oh! have you no ambition to be animated with a divine immortal life, the life of God?

Can you be contented with a mere temporal life, when your souls must exist for ever? That infinite world beyond the grave is replenished with nothing but the terrors of death to you, if you are destitute of spiritual life. And oh! can you bear the thought of residing among its grim and ghastly terrors for ever?

Are you contented to be cut off from God, as a mortified member from the body, and to be banished for ever from all the joys of his presence? You cannot be ad-

mitted to heaven without spiritual life. Hell is the sepulchre for dead souls, and thither you must be sent, if you
still continue dead. And does not this thought affect you?

Consider, also, now is the only time in which you can
be restored to life. And oh! will you let it pass by without improvement?

Shall all the means that have been used for your revival
be in vain? Or the strivings of the Spirit, the alarms of
your own consciences, the blessings and chastisements of
Providence, the persuasions, tears, and lamentations of
your living friends; Oh! shall all these be in vain? Can
you bear the thought? Surely, no. Therefore, oh heave
and struggle to burst the chains of death! Cry mightily
to God to quicken you. Use all the means of vivification,
and avoid every deadly and contagious thing.

I know not, my brethren, how this thought will affect
us at parting to-day, that we have left behind us many a
dead soul. But suppose we should leave as many bodies
here behind us as there are dead souls among us; suppose
every sinner destitute of spiritual life should now be struck
dead before us, oh how would this floor be overlaid with
dead corpses! How few of us would escape! What
bitter lamentations and tears would be among us! One
would lose a husband or a wife, another a friend or a
neighbour. And have we hearts to mourn, and tears to
shed over such an event as this, and have we no compassion for dead souls? Is there none to mourn over them?
Sinners, if you will still continue dead, there are some
here to-day who part with you with this wish, *Oh that my
head were waters, and mine eyes a fountain of tears, that
I might weep day and night for the slain of the daughter
of my people!* And oh that our mournings may reach
the Lord of life, and that you might be quickened from
your death in trespasses and sins! Amen and amen.

SERMON VI.

POOR AND CONTRITE SPIRITS THE OBJECTS OF THE DIVINE FAVOUR.

Isaiah lxvi. 2.—*To this man will I look, even to him that is poor and of a contrite spirit, and trembleth at my word.*

As we consist of animal bodies as well as immortal souls, and are endowed with corporeal senses as well as rational powers, God, who has wisely adapted our religion to our make, requires bodily as well as spiritual worship; and commands us not only to exercise the inward powers of our minds in proper acts of devotion, but also to express our inward devotion by suitable external actions, and to attend upon him in the sensible outward ordinances which he has appointed. Thus it is under the gospel; but it was more remarkably so under the law, which, compared with the pure and spiritual worship of the gospel, was a system of carnal ordinances, and required a great deal of external pomp and grandeur, and bodily services. Thus a costly and magnificent structure was erected, by divine direction, in the wilderness, called the tabernacle, because built in the form of a tent, and movable from place to place; and afterwards a most stately temple was built by Solomon, with immense cost, where the divine worship should be statedly celebrated, and where all the males of Israel should solemnly meet for that purpose three times in a year.

These externals were not intended to exclude the in-

ternal worship of the Spirit, but to express and assist it.
And these ceremonials were not to be put into the place
of morals, but observed as helps to the practice of them,
and to prefigure the great Messiah: even under the Mosaic dispensation, God had the greatest regard to holiness
of heart and a good life; and the strictest observer of
ceremonies could not be accepted without them.

But it is natural to degenerate mankind to invert the
order of things, to place a part, the easiest and meanest
part of religion, for the whole of it, to rest in the externals of religion as sufficient, without regarding the heart,
and to depend upon pharisaical strictness in ceremonial
observances, as an excuse or atonement for neglecting
the weightier matters of the law, judgment, mercy, and faith.

This was the unhappy error of the Jews in Isaiah's
time; and this the Lord would correct in the first verses
of this chapter.

The Jews gloried in their having the house of God
among them, and were ever trusting in vain words, saying,
The temple of the LORD, *the temple of the* LORD, *the temple of the* LORD *are these.* Jer. vii. 4. They filled his al-
tars with costly sacrifices; and in these they trusted to
make atonement for sin, and secure the divine favour.

As to their sacrifices God lets them know, that while
they had no regard to their morals, but chose their own
ways, and their souls delighted in their abominations,
while they presented them in a formal manner without
the fire of divine love, their sacrifices were so far from
procuring his acceptance, that they were odious to him.
He abhors their most expensive offerings as abominable
and profane. He *that killeth an ox for sacrifice* is as far
from being accepted *as if he* unjustly *slew a man ; he that
sacrificeth a lamb, as if he cut off a dog's neck, &c.* Isaiah
lxvi. 3.

To remove this superstitious confidence in the temple, the Lord informs them that he had no need of it; that, large and magnificent as it was, it was not fit to contain him; and that, in consecrating it to him, they should not proudly think that they had given him anything to which he had no prior right. "Thus saith the Lord, the heaven is my throne, where I reign conspicuous in the visible majesty and grandeur of a God; and though the earth is not adorned with such illustrious displays of my immediate presence, though it does not shine in all the glory of my royal palace on high, yet it is a little province in my immense empire, and subject to my authority; it is my footstool. If, then, heaven is my throne, and earth is my footstool; if the whole creation is my kingdom, where is the house that ye build unto me? where is your temple which appears so stately in your eyes? it is vanished, it is sunk into nothing. Is it able to contain that infinite Being to whom the whole earth is but an humble footstool, and the vast heaven but a throne? Can you vainly imagine that my presence can be confined to you in the narrow bounds of a temple, when the heaven and the heaven of heavens cannot contain me? Where is the place of my rest? can you provide a place for my repose, as though I were weary? or can my presence be restrained to one place, incapable of acting beyond the prescribed limits? No; infinite space only can equal my being and perfections; infinite space only is a sufficient sphere for my operations.

"Can you imagine you can bribe my favour, and give me something I had no right to before, by all the stately buildings you can rear to my name? Is not universal nature mine? For all these things hath mine hand made out of nothing, and all these things have been or still subsist by the support of my all-preserving hand, and what

right can be more valid and inalienable than that founded
upon creation? Your silver and gold are mine and mine
the cattle upon a thousand hills: and therefore of mine
own do you give me, saith the Lord."

These are such majestic strains of language as are
worthy a God. Thus it becomes him to advance himself
above the whole creation, and to assert his absolute property in, and independency upon, the universe.

Had he only turned to us the bright side of his throne,
that dazzles us with insufferable splendor; had he only
displayed his majesty unallayed with grace and condescension in such language as this, it would have overwhelmed
us, and cast us into the most abject despondency, as the
outcasts of his providence, beneath his notice. We might
fear he would overlook us with majestic disdain, or careless neglect, like the little things that are called great by
mortals, or as the busy emmets of our species are apt to
do. In the hurry of business they are liable to neglect,
and in the power of pride and grandeur to overlook or
disdain their dependents. We should be ready, in hopeless anxiety, to say, "Is all this earth which to us appears
so vast, and which is parceled into a thousand mighty kingdoms, as we call them, is it all but the humble foot-stool of
God? hardly worthy to bear his feet? What then am I?
an atom of an atom-world, a trifling individual of a trifling
race. Can I expect he will take any notice of such an insignificant thing as I? The vast affairs of heaven and earth lie
upon his head, and he is employed in the concerns of the
wide universe, and can he find leisure to concern himself
with me, and my little interests? Will a king, deliber-
ating upon the concerns of nations, interest himself in
favour of the worm that crawls at his footstool? If the
magnificent temple of Solomon was unworthy of the divine
inhabitant, will he admit me into his presence, and give

me audience? how can I expect it? It seems daring and presumptuous to hope for such condescension. And shall I then despair of the gracious regard of my Maker."

No, desponding creature! mean and unworthy as thou art, hear the voice of divine condescension, as well as of majesty: *To this man will I look, even to him that is poor, and of a contrite spirit, and that trembleth at my word.* Though God dwelleth not in temples made with hands, though he pours contempt upon princes, and scorns them in all their haughty glory and affected majesty, yet there are persons whom his gracious eye will regard. The high and lofty One that inhabiteth eternity, and dwelleth in the high and holy place, he will look down through all the shining ranks of angels upon—whom? Not on the proud, the haughty and presumptuous, but upon him *that is poor and of a contrite spirit, and trembleth at* his *word.* To this man will he look from the throne of his majesty, however low, however mean he may be. This man is an object that can, as it were, attract his eyes from all the glories of the heavenly world, so as to regard an humble, self-abasing worm. This man can never be lost or overlooked among the multitudes of creatures, but the eyes of the Lord will discover him in the greatest crowd, his eyes will graciously fix upon this man, this particular man, though there were but one such in the compass of the creation, or though he were banished into the remotest corner of the universe, like a diamond in a heap of rubbish, or at the bottom of the ocean.

Do you hear this, you that are poor and contrite in spirit, and that tremble at his word? ye that, above all others, are most apt to fear you shall be disregarded by him, because you, of all others, are most deeply sensible how unworthy you are of his gracious notice: God, the great, the glorious, the terrible God, looks down upon you with eyes of love, and by so much the more affectionately, by how much the lower you are in your own esteem. Does not your heart spring within you at the sound? Are you not lost in pleasing wonder and gratitude, and crying out, " Can it be? can it be? is it indeed possible? is it true?" Yes, you have his own word for it, and do you not think it too good news to be true, but believe, and rejoice, and give glory to his name; and fear not what men or devils can do unto you.

This, my brethren, is a matter of universal concern. It is the interest of each of us to know whether we are thus graciously regarded by that God on whom our very being and all our happiness entirely depend. And how shall we know this? In no other way than by discovering whether we have the characters of that happy man to whom he condescends to look. These are not pompous and high characters, they are not formed by earthly riches, learning, glory, and power: But *to this man will I look,* saith the Lord, *even to him that is poor and of a contrite spirit, and that trembleth at my word.* Let us inquire into the import of each of the characters.

I. It is the poor man to whom the Majesty of heaven condescends to look.

This does not principally refer to those that are poor in this world; for, though it be very common that " the poor of this world are chosen to be rich in faith and heirs of the kingdom;" James ii. 5; yet this is not a universal rule; for many, alas! that are poor in this world are not rich towards God, nor rich in good works, and therefore shall famish through eternity in remediless want and wretchedness. But the poor here signifies such as Christ characterizes more fully by the *poor in spirit;* Matt. v. 3. And this character implies the following ingredients:

1. The poor man, to whom Jehovah looks, is deeply

sensible of his own insufficiency, and that nothing but the enjoyment of God can make him happy.

The poor man feels that he is not formed self-sufficient, but a dependent upon God. He is sensible of the weakness and poverty of his nature, and that he was not endowed with a sufficient stock of riches in his creation to support him through the endless duration for which he was formed, or even for a single day. The feeble vine does not more closely adhere to the elm than he does to his God. He is not more sensible of the insufficiency of his body to subsist without air, or the productions of the earth, than of that of his soul without his God, and the enjoyment of his love. In short, he is reduced into his proper place in the system of the universe, low and mean in comparison with superior beings of the angelic order, and especially in comparison with the great Parent and support of nature. He feels himself to be, what he really is, a poor, impotent, dependent creature, that can neither live, nor move, nor exist without God. He is sensible that his *sufficiency is of God*, 2 Cor. iii. 5, " and that all the springs of his happiness are in him."

This sense of his dependence upon God is attended with a sense of the inability of all earthly enjoyments to make him happy, and fill the vast capacities of his soul, which were formed for the enjoyment of an infinite good. He has a relish for the blessings of this life, but it is attended with a sense of their insufficiency, and does not exclude a stronger relish for the superior pleasures of religion. He is not a precise hermit, or a sour ascetic, on the one hand; and, on the other, he is not a *lover of pleasure more than a lover of God.*

If he enjoys no great share of the comforts of this life, he does not labour, nor so much as wish for them as his supreme happiness: he is well assured they can never answer this end in their greatest affluence.   It is for God, it is for the living God, that his soul most eagerly thirsts. In the greatest extremity he is sensible that the enjoyment of his love is more necessary to his felicity than the possession of earthly blessings; nay, he is sensible that if he is miserable in the absence of these, the principal cause is the absence of his God.   Oh! if he were blest with the perfect enjoyment of God, he could say, with Habakkuk, *Although the fig-tree shall not blossom, neither shall fruit be in the vine; the labour of the olive shall fail, and the fields shall yield no meat; the flock shall be cut off from the fold, and there shall be no herd in the stall;* though universal famine should strip me of all my earthly blessings, *yet I will rejoice in the* LORD, as my complete happiness; *I will joy in the God of my salvation.* Hab. iii. 17, 18.

If he enjoys an affluence of earthly blessings, he still retains a sense of his need of the enjoyment of God.   To be discontented and dissatisfied is the common fate of the rich as well as the poor; they are still craving, craving an unknown something to complete their bliss.   The soul, being formed for the fruition of the Supreme Good, secretly languishes and pines away in the midst of other enjoyments, without knowing its cure.   It is the enjoyment of God only that can satisfy its unbounded desires; but, alas! it has no relish for him, no thirst after him; it is still crying, " More, more of the delights of the world;" like a man in a burning fever, that calls for cold water, that will but inflame his disease, and occasion a more painful return of thirst.   But the poor in spirit know where their cure lies.   They do not ask with uncertainty, *Who will show us* any sort of *good?* but their petitions centre in this as the grand constituent of their happiness, LORD, *lift thou up the light of thy countenance upon us;* and this puts more gladness into their hearts *than the abundance of corn and wine;* Psalm iv. 6, 7. This was the language of the Psalmist, *There is none upon earth that I desire besides thee. My flesh and my heart faileth; but God is the strength of my heart, and my portion for ever;* Psalm lxxiii. 25, 26. And as this disposition extends to all earthly things, so it does to all created enjoyments whatsoever, even to those of the heavenly world; the poor man is sensible that he could not be happy even there without the enjoyment of God. His language is, *Whom have I in heaven but thee?* It is *beholding thy face in righteousness, and awaking in thy likeness, that alone can satisfy me;* Psalm xvii. 15.

2. This spiritual poverty implies deep humility and self-abasement.

The poor man on whom the God of heaven condescends to look is mean in his own apprehensions; he accounts himself not a being of mighty importance. He has no high esteem of his own good qualities, but is little in his own eyes. He is not apt to give himself the preference to others, but is ready to give way to them as his superiors. He has a generous sagacity to behold their good qualities, and commendable blindness towards their imperfections: but he is not quick to discern his own excellencies, nor sparing to his own frailties.

Instead of being dazzled with the splendour of his own endowments or acquisitions, he is apt to overlook them with a noble neglect, and is sensible of the weakness and defects of his nature.

And as to his gracious qualities, they appear small, exceeding small to him: when he considers how much they fall short of what they should be, they as it were vanish and shrink into nothing. How cold does his love appear to him in its greatest fervour! How feeble his faith in its greatest confidence! How superficial his repentance in its greatest depth! How proud his lowest humility! And as for the good actions he has performed, alas! how few, how poorly done, how short of his duty do they appear! After he has done all, he counts himself an unprofitable servant. After he has done all, he is more apt to adopt the language of the publican than the pharisee, *God be merciful to me a sinner.* In his highest attainments he is not apt to admire himself; so far is he from it, that it is much more natural to him to fall into the opposite extreme, and to account himself the least, yea, less than the least of all other saints upon the face of the earth: and if he contends for any preference, it is for the lowest place in the list of Christians. This disposition was remarkably exemplified in St. Paul, who probably had made greater advancements in holiness than any other saint that was ever received to heaven from this guilty world.

He that is poor in spirit has also an humbling sense of his own sinfulness. His memory is quick to recollect his past sins, and he is very sharp-sighted to discover the remaining corruptions of his heart, and the imperfections of his best duties. He is not ingenious to excuse them, but views them impartially in all their deformity and aggravations. He sincerely doubts whether there be a saint upon earth so exceeding corrupt; and, though he may be convinced that the Lord has begun a work of grace in him, and consequently, that he is in a better state than such as are under the prevailing dominion of sin, yet he really questions whether there be such a depraved creature in the world as he sees he has been. He is apt to count himself the chief of sinners, and more indebted to free grace than any of the sons of men. He is intimately acquainted with himself; but he sees only the outside of others, and hence he concludes himself so much worse than others; hence he loathes himself in his own sight for all his abominations. Ezek. xxxvi. 31. Self-abasement is pleasing to him; his humility is not forced; he does not think it a great thing for him to sink thus low. He plainly sees himself to be a mean, sinful, exceeding sinful creature, and therefore is sure that it is no condescension, but the most reasonable thing in the world, for him to think meanly of himself, and to humble and abase himself. It is unnatural for one that esteems himself a being of great importance to stoop; but it is easy, and appears no self-denial for a poor mean creature to do so, who looks upon himself, and feels himself, to be such.

Finally, the poor man is deeply sensible of his own unworthiness. He sees that in himself he deserves no favour from God for all the good he has ever done, but that he may after all justly reject him. He makes no proud boasts of his good heart, or good life, but falls in the dust before God, and casts all his dependence upon his free grace:— which leads me to observe,

3. That he who is poor in spirit is sensible of his need of the influences of divine grace to sanctify him, and enrich him with the graces of the Spirit.

He is sensible of the want of holiness; this necessarily flows from his sense of his corruption, and the imperfection of all his graces. Holiness is the one thing needful with him, which he desires and longs for above all others; and he is deeply sensible that he cannot work it in his own heart by his own strength; he feels that without Christ he can do nothing, and that it is God who must work in him both to will and to do. Hence like a poor man that cannot subsist upon his stock, he depends entirely upon the grace of God to work all his works in him, and to enable him to work out his salvation with fear and trembling.

4. He is deeply sensible of the absolute necessity of the righteousness of Christ for his justification.

He does not think himself rich in good works to bribe his judge, and procure acquittance, but, like a poor criminal that, having nothing to purchase a pardon, nothing to plead in his own defence, casts himself upon the mercy of the court; he places his whole dependence upon the free grace of God through Jesus Christ. He pleads his righteousness only, and trusts in it alone. The rich scorn to be obliged; but the poor, that cannot subsist of themselves, will cheerfully receive it.

5. And lastly, the man that is poor in spirit is an importunate beggar at the throne of grace.

He lives upon charity; he lives upon the bounties of heaven; and, as these are not to be obtained without begging, he is frequently lifting up his cries to the Father of all his mercies for them. He attends upon the ordinances of God, as Bartimeus by the way-side, to ask the charity of passengers. Prayer is the natural language of spiritual poverty: *The poor*, saith Solomon, *useth entreaties*, Prov. xviii. 23; whereas they that are rich in their own conceit can live without prayer, or content themselves with the formal, careless performance of it.

This is the habitual character of that poor man to whom the Majesty of heaven vouchsafes the looks of his love. At times indeed he has but little sense of these things; but then he is uneasy, and he labours to re-obtain it, and sometimes is actually blessed with it.

And is there no such poor man or woman in this assembly? I hope there is. Where are ye, poor creatures? stand forth, and receive the blessings of your Redeemer, *Blessed are the poor in spirit*, &c. He who has his throne in the height of heaven, and to whom this vast earth is but a footstool, looks upon you with eyes of love.

This spiritual poverty is greater riches than the treasures of the universe. Be not ashamed, therefore, to own yourselves poor men, if such you are. May God thus impoverish us all; may he strip us of all our imaginary grandeur and riches, and reduce us to poor beggars at his door!

But it is time to consider the other character of the happy man upon whom the Lord of heaven will graciously look; and that is,

II. Contrition of spirit. *To this man will I look that is of a contrite spirit.*

The word *contrite* signifies one that is beaten or bruised with hard blows, or a heavy burden. And it belongs to the mourning penitent whose heart is broken and wounded for sin. Sin is an intolerable burden that crushes and bruises him, and he feels himself pained and sore under it. His stony heart, which could not be impressed, but rather repelled the blow, is taken away; and now he has a heart of flesh, easily bruised and wounded. His heart is not always hard and senseless, light and trifling; but it has tender sensations; he is easily susceptible of sorrow for sin, is humbled under a sense of his imperfections, and is really pained and distressed because he can serve his God no better, but daily sins against him. This character may also agree to the poor anxious soul that is broken with cruel fears of its state. The stout-hearted can venture their eternal all upon uncertainty; and indulge pleasing hopes without anxiously examining their foundation; but he that is of a contrite spirit is tenderly sensible of the importance of the matter, and cannot be easy without some good evidence of safety. Such shocking suppositions as these frequently startle him, and pierce his very heart; "What if I should be deceived at last? What if after all I should be banished from that God in whom lies all my happiness ?" &c. These are suppositions full of insupportable terror, when they appear but barely possible; and much more when there seems to be reason for them. Such an habitual pious jealousy as this, is a good symptom; and to your pleasing surprise, ye doubtful Christians, I may tell you that *that* Majesty, who you are afraid disregards you, looks down upon you with pity. Therefore lift up your eyes to him in wonder and joyful confidence. You are not such neglected things as you think. The Majesty of heaven thinks it not beneath him to look down through all the glorious orders of angels, and through interposing worlds, down, down even upon you in the depth of your self-abhorrence. Let us,

III. Consider the remaining character of the happy man to whom the Lord will look; *Him that trembleth at my word.*

This character implies a tender sense of the great things of the word, and a heart easily impressed with them as the most important realities. This was remarkably exemplified in tender-hearted Josiah. 2 Chron. xxxiv. 19, 20, 21, 27. To one that trembles at the divine word, the threatenings of it do not appear vain terrors, nor great swelling words of vanity, but the most tremendous realities. Such an one cannot bear up under them, but would tremble, and fall, and die away, if not relieved by some happy promise of deliverance. He that trembles at the word of God is not a stupid hearer or reader of it. It reaches and pierces his heart as a sharp two-edged sword; it carries power along with it, and he feels that it is the word of God, and not of men, even when it is spoken by feeble mortals. Thus he not only trembles at the terror, but at the authority of the word;—which leads me to observe farther, that he trembles with filial veneration of the majesty of God speaking in his word. He considers it as his voice who spake all things into being, and whose glory is such that a deep solemnity must seize those that are admitted to hear him speak.

How opposite is this to the temper of multitudes who regard the word of God no more than (with horror I express it) the word of a child or a fool. They will have their own way, let him say what he will. They persist in sin, in defiance of his threatenings. They sit as careless and stupid under his word, as though it were some old, dull, trifling story. It seldom makes any impressions upon their stony hearts. These are the brave, undaunted men of the world, who harden themselves against the fear of futurity. But, unhappy creatures! the God of heaven disdains to give them a gracious look, while he fixes his eyes upon the man that " is' contrite, and that trembles at his word."

And where is that happy man? Where in this assembly, where is the contrite spirit? Where the man that trembleth at the word? You are all ready to catch at the character, but be not presumptuous on the one hand, nor excessively timorous on the other. Inquire whether this be your prevailing character. If so, then claim it, and rejoice in it, though you have it not in perfection. But if you have it not prevailingly, do not seize it as your own. Though you have been at times distressed with a sense of sin and danger, and the word strikes a terror to your hearts, yet, unless you are habitually of a tender and a contrite spirit, you are not to claim the character.

But let such of you as are poor and contrite in spirit, and that tremble at the word of the Lord, enter deeply into the meaning of this expression, that the Lord looks to you. He does not look on you as a careless spectator, not concerning himself with you, or caring what will become of you, but he looks upon you as a father, a friend, a benefactor : his looks are efficacious for your good.

He looks upon you with acceptance. He is pleased with the sight. He loves to see you labouring towards him. He looks upon you as the objects of his everlasting love, and purchased by the blood of his Son, and he is well pleased with you for his righteousness' sake. Hence his looking upon him that is poor, &c., is opposed to his hating the wicked and their sacrifices, *ver.* 3. And is he whom you have so grievously offended, he whose wrath you fear above all other things, is he indeed reconciled to you, and does he delight in you? what cause of joy, and praise, and wonder is here!

Again, he looks to you so as to take particular notice of you. He sees all the workings of your hearts towards him. He sees and pities you in your honest, though feeble conflicts with indwelling sin. He observes all your faithful though weak endeavours to serve him. His eyes pierce your very hearts, and the least motion there cannot escape his notice. This indeed might make you tremble, if he looked upon you with the eyes of a judge, for oh, how many abominations must he see in you! But be of good cheer, he looks upon you with the eyes of a friend, and with that love which covers a multitude of sins. He looks upon you with the eyes of compassion in all your calamities. He looks upon you to see that you be not overborne and crushed. David, who passed through as many hardships and afflictions as any of you, could say from happy experience, *The eyes of the* LORD *are upon the righteous, and his ears are open to their cry.* Psal. xxxiv. 15.

Finally, he looks to you so as to look after you, as we do after the sick and weak. He looks to you so as to provide for you : and he will give you grace and glory,

and *no good thing will be withheld from you.* Psal. lxxxiv.
11.

And are you not safe and happy under the inspection
of a father and a friend? Let a little humble courage
then animate you amid your many dejections, and confide
in that care of which you feel yourself to be so unworthy.

Here it may not be amiss to observe, what must give
you no small pleasure, that those very persons who, according to the estimate of men, are the most likely to be
overlooked, are those whom God graciously regards.
The persons themselves are apt to cry, " Happy I, could
I believe that the God of heaven thus graciously regards
me; but, alas! I feel myself a poor unworthy creature; I
am a trembling, broken-hearted thing, beneath the notice
of so great a Majesty." And art thou so indeed? then I
may convert thy objection into an encouragement. Thou
art the very person upon whom God looks. His eyes
are running to and fro through the earth in quest of such
as thou art; and he will find thee out among the innumerable multitude of mankind. Wert thou surrounded with
crowds of kings and nobles, his eyes would pass by them
all to fix upon thee. What a glorious artifice, if I may
so speak, is this, to catch at and convert the person's dis-
couragment as a ground of courage! to make that the
character of the favourites of heaven, which they themselves look upon as marks of his neglect of them! " Alas!"
says the poor man, " if I was the object of divine notice,
he would not suffer me to continue thus poor and broken-
hearted." But you may reason directly the reverse; he
makes you thus poor in spirit, sensible of your sinfulness
and imperfections, because that he graciously regards you.
He will not suffer you to be puffed up with your imaginary
goodness, like the rest of the world, because he loves you
more than he loves them.

However unaccountable this procedure seems, there is very good reason for it. The poor are the only persons that would relish the enjoyment of God, and prize his love; they alone are capable of the happiness of heaven, which consists in the perfection of holiness.

To conclude, let us view the perfection and condescension of God as illustrated by this subject. Consider, ye poor in spirit, who he is that stoops to look upon such little things as you. It is he whose throne is in the highest heaven, surrounded with myriads of angels and archangels; it is he whose footstool is the earth, who supports every creature upon it; it is he who is exalted above the blessings and praise of all the celestial armies, and who cannot without condescension behold the things that are done in heaven: it is he that looks down upon such poor worms as you. And what a stoop is this!

It is he that looks upon you in particular, who looks after all the worlds he has made. He manages all the affairs of the universe; he takes care of every individual in his vast family; he provides for all his creatures, and yet he is at leisure to regard you. He takes as particular notice of you as if you were his only creatures. What perfection is this! what an infinite grasp of thought! what unbounded power! and what condescension too! Do but consider what a small figure you make in the universe of beings. You are not so much in comparison with the infinite multitude of creatures in the compass of nature, as a grain of sand to all the sands upon the sea shore, or as a mote to the vast globe of earth. And yet he, that has the care of the whole universe, takes particular notice of you—you who are but trifles compared with your fellow-creatures; and who, if you were annihilated, would hardly leave a blank in the creation. Consider this, and wonder at the condescension of God; consider this, and acknowledge your own meanness; you are but nothing, not only compared with God, but you are as nothing in the system of creation.

I shall add but this one natural reflection : If it be so great a happiness to have the great God for our patron, then what is it to be out of his favour ? to be disregarded by him ? methinks an universal tremor may seize this assembly at the very supposition. And is there a creature in the universe in this wretched condition ? methinks all the creation besides must pity him. Where is the wretched being to be found ? must we descend to hell to find him ; No, alas ! there are many such on this earth ! nay, I must come nearer you still, there are many such probably in this assembly : all among you are such who are not poor and contrite in spirit, and do not tremble at the word of the Lord. And art thou not one of the miserable number, oh man ? What ! disregarded by the God that made thee ! not favoured with one look of love by the author of all happiness ! He looks on thee indeed, but it is with eyes of indignation, marking thee out for vengeance ; and canst thou be easy in such a case ? wilt thou not labour to impoverish thyself, and have thy heart broken, that thou mayest become the object of his gracious regard ?

SERMON VII.

THE NATURE AND DANGER OF MAKING LIGHT OF CHRIST AND SALVATION.

MATT. xxii. 5.—*But they made light of it.*

THERE is not one of us in this assembly that has heard anything, but what has heard of Christ and salvation: there is not one of us but has had the rich blessings of the gospel freely and repeatedly offered to us: there is not one of us but stands in the most absolute need of these blessings, and must perish for ever without them; I wish I could add, there is not one of us but has cheerfully accepted them according to the offer of the gospel. But, alas! such an assembly is not to be expected on earth! Multitudes will make light of Christ and the invitations of the gospel, as the Jews did.

This parable represents the great God under the majestic idea of a king.

He is represented as making a marriage feast for his Son; that is, God in the gospel offers his Son Jesus Christ as a Saviour to the guilty sons of men, and, upon their acceptance of him, the most intimate and endearing union, and the tenderest mutual affection takes place between Christ and them; which may properly be represented by the marriage relation. And God has provided for them a rich variety of blessings, pardon, holiness, and everlasting felicity, which may be signified by a royal nuptial feast, *verse 2.*

These blessings were first offered to the Jews, who were bidden to the wedding by Moses and the prophets, whose great business it was to prepare them to receive the Messiah, *verse* 3.

The servants that were sent to call them, that were thus bidden, were the apostles and seventy disciples, whom Christ sent out to preach that the gospel kingdom was just at hand, *verse* 3.

When the Jews rejected this call, he sent forth other servants, namely, the apostles, after his ascension, who were to be more urgent in their invitations, and to tell them that, in consequence of Christ's death, all things were now ready, *verse* 4.

It is seldom that invitations to a royal feast are rejected; but alas! the Jews rejected the invitation of the gospel, and would not accept of its important blessings. They made light of Christ and his blessings: they were careless to them, and turned their attention to other things.

These things were not peculiar to the Jews, but belong to us sinners of the Gentiles in these ends of the earth. Christ is still proposed to us; to the same blessings we are invited; and I have the honour, my dear brethren, of appearing among you as a servant of the heavenly King, sent out to urge you to embrace the offer.

I doubt not but sundry of you have complied; and you are enriched and made for ever.

But alas! must I not entertain a godly jealousy over some of you? Have you not made light of Christ and salvation, to which you have been invited for so many years successively?

Your case is really lamentable, as I hope you will see before I have done; and I most sincerely compassionate you from my heart. I now rise up in this solemn place with the design to address you with the most awful seriousness, and the most compassionate concern: and did you know how much your happiness may depend upon it, and how anxious I am lest I should fail in the attempt, I am sure you could not but pray for me, and pity me.   If ever you regarded a man in the most serious temper and address, I beg you would now regard what I am going to say to you.

You cannot receive any benefit from this, or indeed any other subject, till you apply it to yourselves.   And therefore, in order to reform you of the sin of making light of Christ and the gospel, I must first inquire who are guilty of it.   For this purpose let us consider,

What is it to make light of Christ and the invitations of the gospel?

I can think of no plainer way to discover this, than to inquire how we treat those things that we highly esteem; and also by way of contrast, how we treat those things which we make light of; and hence we may discover whether Christ and the gospel may be ranked among the things we esteem, or those we disregard.

I. Men are apt to remember and affectionately think of the things that they highly esteem; but as for those which they disregard, they can easily forget them, and live from day to day without a single thought about them.

Now do you often affectionately remember the Lord Jesus Christ, and do your thoughts affectionately go after him? do they pay him early visits in the morning? do they make frequent excursions to him through the day? and do you lie down with him in your hearts at night?   Is not the contrary evident as to many of you?   Can you not live from day to day thoughtless of Jesus, and your everlasting salvation?   Recollect now, how many affectionate thoughts have you had of these things through the week past, or in this sacred morning.   And can you indeed highly esteem those things which you hardly ever think of? Follow your own hearts, sirs, observe which way they most naturally and freely run, and then judge whether you make light of the gospel or not. Alas! we cannot persuade men to one hour's serious consideration what they should do for an interest in Christ; we cannot persuade them so much as to afford him only their thoughts, which are such cheap things; and yet they will not be convinced that they make light of Christ. And here lies the infatuation of sin; it blinds and befools men, so that they do not know what they think of, what they love, or what they intend, much less do they know the habitual bent of their souls. They often imagine themselves free from those sins to which they are most enslaved, and particularly they think themselves innocent of the crime of making light of the gospel, when this is the very crime that is likely to destroy them for ever.

II. The things that men value, if of such a nature as to admit of publication, will be the frequent subjects of their discourse : the thoughts will command the tongue, and furnish materials for conversation. But those things that they forget and disregard they will not talk of.

Do not they therefore make light of Christ and salvation, who have no delight in conversing about them, and hardly ever mention the name of Christ but in a trifling or profane manner? They do not like the company where divine things are discoursed of, but think it precise and troublesome. They had much rather be entertained with humorous tales and idle stories, or talk about the affairs of the world. *They are of the world,* says St. John, *therefore speak they of the world, and the world heareth them.* 1 John iv. 5. They are in their element in such conversation. Or others may talk about religion; but it is only about the circumstances of it, as, "How such a man preached; it was a very good or a bad sermon," &c., but they care not to enter into the spirit and substance of divine things! and if they speak of Christ and experimental religion, it is in a heartless and insipid manner. And do not such make light of the gospel? and is not this the character of many of you?

III. Men make light of those things, if they are of a practical nature, which they only talk about, but do not reduce into practice.

Christianity was intended not to furnish matter for empty talkers, but to govern the heart and practice. But are there not some that only employ their tongues about it, especially when their spirits are raised with liquor, and then a torrent of noisy religion breaks from them. Watch their lives, and you will see little appearance of Christianity there. And do not these evidently make light of Christ, who make him the theme of their drunken conversation, or who seem to think that God sent his Son from heaven just to set the world a talking about him? There is nothing in nature that seems to me more abominable than this.

IV. We take the utmost pains and labour to secure the things we value, and cannot be easy while our property in them is uncertain; but those things that we think lightly of we care but little whether they be ours or not.

Therefore, have not such of you made light of Christ and salvation, who have lived twenty or thirty years uncertain whether you have interest in him, and yet have been easy and contented, and take no method to be resolved? Are all that hear me this day determined in this important question, "What shall become of me when I die?" Are you all certain upon good grounds, and after a thorough trial, that you shall be saved? Oh that you were! but, alas! you are not. And do you think you would bear this uncertainty about it, if you did not make light of salvation? No; you would carefully examine yourselves; you would diligently pursue the Scriptures to find out the marks of those that shall be saved; you would anxiously consult those that could direct you, and particularly pious ministers, who would think it the greatest favour you could do them to devolve such an office upon them. But now ministers may sit in their studies for a whole year, and not ten persons perhaps in five hundred agreeably intrude upon them on this important business.

Oh, sirs, if the gospel should pierce your hearts indeed, you would but cry out with the convicted Jews, *Men and brethren, what shall we do?* Acts ii. 37. Paul, when awakened, cries out, in a trembling consternation, *Lord! what wilt thou have me to do?* But when shall we hear such questions now-a-days?

V. The things that men highly esteem, deeply and tenderly affect them, and excite some motions in their hearts: but what they make light of, makes no impression upon them.

And if you did not make light of the gospel, what workings would there be in your hearts about it? what solemn, tender, and vigorous passion would it raise in you to hear such things about the world to come! what fear and astonishment would seize you at the consideration of your misery; what transports of joy and gratitude would you feel at the glad tidings of salvation by the blood of Christ! what strong efficacious purposes would be raised in you at the discovery of your duty! Oh what hearers should we have, were it not for this one sin, the making light of the gospel! whereas now we are in danger of wearying them, or preaching them asleep with our most solemn discourses about this momentous affair? We talk to them of Christ and salvation till they grow quite tired of this dull old tale, and this foolishness of preaching. Alas! little would one think from the air of carelessness, levity, and inattention that appears among them, that they were hearing such weighty truths, or have any concern in them.

VI. Our estimate of things may be discovered by the diligence and earnestness of our endeavours about them. Those things which we highly value, we think no pains too great to obtain; but what we think lightly of we use no endeavours about, or we use them in a languid, careless manner.

And do not they make light of Christ and salvation, who do not exert themselves in earnest to obtain them, and think a great deal of every little thing they do in religion? they are still ready to cry out, " What need of so much pains? we hope to be saved without so much trouble." And, though these may not be so honest as to speak it out, it is plain from their temper and practice, they grudge all the service they do for Christ as done to a master they do not love. They love and esteem the world, and therefore for the world they will labour and toil all day, and seem never to think they can do too much; but for the God that made them, for the Lord that bought them, and for their everlasting salvation, they seem afraid of taking too much pains. Let us preach to them as long as we will, we cannot bring them in earnest to desire and pursue after holiness. Follow them to their houses, and you will hardly ever find them reading a chapter in their Bibles, or calling upon God with their families, so much as once a day. Follow them into their retirements, and you will hear no penitent confessions of sin, no earnest cries for mercy. They will not allow to God that one day in seven which he has appropriated to his own immediate service, but they will steal and prostitute some even of those sacred hours for idleness, for worldly conversation, or business.

And many of them are so malignant in wickedness, that they will reproach and ridicule others that are not so made as themselves in these respects. And is not Christ worth seeking? Is not eternal salvation worth so much trouble? Does not that man make light of these things that thinks his ease or carnal pleasure of greater importance? Let common sense judge.

VII. That which we highly value we think we cannot buy too dear; and we are ready to part with every thing that comes in competition with it. The merchant that found one pearl of great price, sold all that he had to purchase it, Matt. xiii. 46, but those things that we make light of, we will not part with things of value for them.

Now, when Christ and the blessings of the gospel come in competition with the world and sinful pleasures, you may know which you most highly esteem, by considering which you are most ready to part with. You are called to part with every thing that is inconsistent with an interest in Christ, and yet many of you will not do it. You are called but to give God his own, to resign all to his will, to let go all those profits and pleasures which you must either part with, or part with Christ, and yet your hearts cling to these things; you grasp them eagerly, and nothing can tear them from you. You must have your pleasures, you must keep your credit in the world, you must look to your estates, whatever becomes of Christ and salvation; as if you could live and die better without Christ than without these things; or as if Christ could not make you happy without them. And does not this bring the matter to an issue, and plainly show that you make light of Christ in comparison with these things? Christ himself has assured you, over and over, that unless you are willing to part with all for his sake, you cannot be his disciples; and yet, while you have the quite contrary disposition, you will pretend to be his disciples; as if you knew better what it is that constituted his disciples than he.

VIII. Those things which we highly value, we shall be for helping our friends to obtain.

Do not those, then, make light of Christ, who do not take half so much pains to help their children to an interest in him, as to set them up in credit in the world, and leave them large fortunes? They supply the outward wants of their families, but they take little or no care about their everlasting salvation. Alas! Sirs, the neglected, ignorant, and vicious children and servants of such of you can witness against you, that you make very light of Christ and salvation, and their immortal souls.

IX. That which men highly esteem they will so diligently pursue, that you may see their regard for it in their endeavours after it, if it be a matter within their reach.

You may therefore see that many make light of the gospel by the little knowledge they have of it, after all the means of instruction with which they have been favoured. Alas! where is their improvement in holiness! how little do they know of their own hearts, of God and Christ, and the world to come, and what they must do to be saved! Ask them about these things, and you will find them stupidly ignorant; and yet they have so much conceited knowledge that they will not acknowledge it; or if they do, they have no better excuse than to say they are no scholars, or they have a poor memory; as if it required extensive learning, or a great genius to know the things that are necessary to salvation. Oh! if they had not made light of these things; if they had bestowed but half the pains upon them which they have taken to understand matters of trade and worldly business, they would not be so grossly ignorant as they are! When men can learn the hardest trade in a few years, when men of bright parts, and perhaps considerable learning, after living so many years, are still mere novices in matters of religion, and do not so much as know the terms of life according to the gospel, is it not plain that they care but little about these things, and that they make light of the Son of God, and all his inestimable, immortal blessings?

Thus I have offered you sufficient matter of conviction in this affair. And what is the result? Does not conscience smite some of you by this time, and say, " I am the man that have made light of Christ and his gospel?" If not, upon what evidence are you acquitted? Some of you, I doubt not, can say, in the integrity of your hearts, " Alas! I am too careless about this important affair, but God knows I am often deeply concerned about it; God knows that if ever I was in earnest about any thing in all my life, it has been about my everlasting state; and there is nothing in all the world that habitually lies so near my heart. But are there not some of you whom conscience does not accuse of this crime of too much carelessness about the gospel, not because you are innocent, but because you make so very light of it, that you will make no thorough search into it? and does not this alone prove you guilty? I beseech such to consider the folly of your conduct. Do you then think to excuse your crime, by being careless whether you are guilty of it or not? Can you avoid the precipice by shutting your eyes? If you discover your sin now, it may be of unspeakable service, but if you now shut your eyes you must see it hereafter, when it will be too late; when your conviction will be your punishment. I beseech you also to consider the dreadful evil of your conduct in making light of a Saviour. And here I shall offer such arguments to expose its aggravations as I am sure cannot fail to convince and astonish you, if you act like men of reason and understanding.

I. Consider you make light of him who did not make light of you, when you deserved his final neglect of you. You were worthy of nothing but contempt and abhorrence from him. As a man you are but a worm to God, and as a sinner you are viler than a toad or a serpent. Yet Christ was so far from making light of you that he left his native heaven, became a man of sorrows, and died in the most exquisite agonies, that a way might be opened for the salvation of your miserable soul: and can you make light of him after all his regard to you? What miracles of love and mercy has he shown towards you! and can you neglect him after all? Angels, who are less concerned in these things than we, cannot but pry into them with delightful wonder, 1 Peter i. 12, and shall sinners who have the most intimate personal concern in them, make light of them? This is a crime more than devilish; for the devils never had a Saviour offered to them, and consequently never could despise him. And can you live in a carelessness of Christ all your days, and yet feel no remorse?

II. Consider you make light of matters of the greatest excellency and importance in all the world. Oh, sirs, you know not what it is that you slight; had you known these things you would not have ventured to make light of them for ten thousand worlds. As Christ said to the woman of Samaria, *If thou knewest the gift of God, and who it is, that saith to thee, Give me to drink, thou wouldest have asked of him, and he would have given thee living water.* John iv. 13. *Had the Jews known, they would not have crucified the Lord of Glory:* 1 Cor. ii. 8. So, had you known what Jesus is, you would not have made light of him; he would have been to you the most important being in the universe.   Oh! had you been but one day in heaven, and seen and felt the happiness there! or had you been but one hour under the agonies of hell, you could never more have trifled with salvation.

Here I find my thoughts run so naturally into the same channel with those of the excellent Mr. Baxter, about a hundred years ago, that you will allow me to give a long quotation from him, that you may see in what light this great and good man viewed the neglected things which the gospel brings to your ears.   His words are these; and I am sure to me they have been very weighty:—

"Oh, sirs, they are no trifles or jesting matters that the gospel speaks of.   I must needs profess to you, that when I have the most serious thoughts of these things, I am ready to wonder that such amazing matters do not over-whelm the souls of men: that the greatness of the subject doth not so overmatch our understandings and affections, as even to drive men beside themselves, but that God hath always somewhat allayed it by distance; much more do I wonder that men should be so blockish as to make light of such things.   Oh, Lord, that men did but know what everlasting glory and everlasting torments are!   Would they then hear us as they do? would they read and think of these things as they do?   I profess I have been ready to wonder when I have heard such weighty things de-livered, how people can forbear crying out in the congre-gation, and much more do I wonder how they can rest, till they have gone to their ministers and learned what they shall do to be saved, that this great business should be put out of doubt.   Oh, that heaven and hell should work no more upon men!   Oh, that eternity should work no more!   Oh, how can you forbear when you are alone to think with yourselves what it is to be everlast-ingly in joy or torment.   I wonder that such thoughts do

not break your sleep, and that they do not crowd into
your minds when you are about your labour! I wonder
how you can almost do any thing else! How can you
have any quietness in your minds? how can you eat or
drink, or rest, till you have got some ground of everlasting
consolations? Is that a man, or a corpse, that is not affected with matters of this moment? that can be readier
to sleep than to tremble, when he hears how he must
stand at the bar of God? Is that a man, or a clod of clay,
that can rise up and lie down without being deeply affected
with his everlasting state? that can follow his worldly
business, and make nothing of the great business of salvation or damnation, and that when he knows it is so hard
at hand? Truly, sirs, when I think of the weight of the
matter, I wonder at the best saints upon earth, that they
are no better, and do no more in so weighty a case. I
wonder at those whom the world accounts more holy than
needs, and scorns for making too much ado, that they can
put off Christ and their souls with so little; that they do
not pour out their souls in every prayer; that they are not
more taken up with God; that their thoughts are not more
serious in preparation for their last account. I wonder
that they are not a thousand times more strict in their
lives, and more laborious and unwearied for the crown
than they are.   And for myself, (says that zealous,
flaming, and indefatigable preacher,) as I am ashamed of
my dull and careless heart, and of my slow and unprofitable course of life, so the Lord knows I am ashamed of
every sermon that I preach: when I think what I am, and
who sent me, and how much the salvation and damnation
of men is concerned in it, I am ready to tremble, lest God
should judge me as a slighter of his truth and the souls of
men, and lest, in my best sermon, I should be guilty of
their blood.   Methinks we should not speak a word to

men in matters of such consequence without tears, or the
greatest earnestness that possibly we can.   Were we not
too much guilty of the sin which we reprove, it would
be so.   Whether we are alone or in company, methinks
our end, and such an end, should still be in our mind,
and as before our eyes; and we should sooner forget any
thing, or set light by any thing, or by all things, than by
this."

And now, my brethren, if such a man as this viewed
these things in this light, oh what shall we, we languishing,
careless creatures, what shall we think of ourselves?   Into
what a dead sleep are we fallen!   Oh let the most active
and zealous among us awake, and be a thousand times
more earnest; and ye frozen-hearted, careless sinners,
for God's sake awake, and exert yourselves to good purpose in the pursuit of salvation, or you are lost to all
eternity.

III. Consider whose salvation it is you make light of.
It is your own.   And do you not care what becomes of
your own selves?   Is it nothing to you whether you are
saved or damned for ever?   Is the natural principle of
self-love extinct in you?   Have you no concern for your
own preservation?   Are you commenced your own enemies?   If you slight Christ and love sin, you virtually
love death, Prov. viii. 36.   You may as well say, " I will
live and yet neither eat nor drink," as say, " I will go to
heaven, and yet make light of Christ."   And you may as
well say this in words as by your practice.

IV. Consider, your sin is aggravated by professing to
believe that gospel which you make light of.   For a professed infidel that does not believe the Scripture revelation
concerning Christ and a future state of rewards and punishments, for such a one to be careless about these things
would not be so strange; but for you that make these

things your creed, and a part of your religion, for you that call yourselves Christians, and have been baptized into this faith; for you, I say, to make light of them, how astonishing! how utterly inexcusable! What! believe that you shall live for ever in the most perfect happiness or exquisite misery, and yet take no more pains to obtain the one, and escape the other? What! believe that the great and dreadful God will shortly be your judge, and yet make no more preparation for it? Either say plainly, " I am no Christian, I do not believe these things;" or else let your hearts be affected with your belief, and let it influence and govern your lives.

V. Consider what those things are which engross your affections, and which tempt you to neglect Christ and your salvation. Have you found out a better friend, or a more substantial and lasting happiness than his salvation? Oh! what trifles and vanities, what dreams and shadows are men pursuing, while they neglect the important realities of the eternal world! If crowns and kingdoms, if all the riches, glories, and pleasures of the world were ensured to you as a reward for making light of Christ, you would even then make the most foolish bargain possible; for what are these in the scale to eternal joy or eternal tempest? and *what is a man profited, if he shall gain* even *the whole world, and lose his own soul?* Matt. xvi. 26. But you cannot hope for the ten thousandth part; and will you cast away your souls for this? You that think it such a great thing to live in riches, pleasures, and honours, consider, is it such a mighty happiness to die rich? to die after a life of pleasure and honour? Will it be such a great happiness to give an account for the life of a rich sensualist, rather than of a poor mortified creature? Will Dives then be so much happier than Lazarus? Alas! what does the richest, the highest, the most voluptuous sinner, what does he do, but lay up treasures of wrath against the day of wrath? Oh how will the unhappy creatures torture themselves for ever with the most cutting reflections for selling their Saviour and their souls for such trifles! Let your sins and earthly enjoyments save you then, if they can; let them then do that for you which Christ would have done for you if you had chosen him. Then go and cry to the gods you have chosen; let them deliver you in the day of your tribulation.

VI. Your making light of Christ and salvation is a certain evidence that you have no interest in them.— Christ will not throw himself and his blessings away upon those who do not value them. "Those that honour him he will honour; but they that despise him shall be lightly esteemed," 1 Sam. ii. 30. There is a day coming, when you will feel you cannot do without him; when you will feel yourselves perishing for want of a Saviour; and then you may go and look for a Saviour where you will; then may you shift for yourselves as you can; he will have nothing to do with you; the Saviour of sinners will cast you off for ever. I tell you, sirs, whatever estimate you form of all these things, God thinks very highly of the blood of his Son, and the blessings of his purchase; and if ever you obtain them, he will have you think highly of them too. If you continue to make light of them, all the world cannot save you. And can you find fault with God for denying you that which was so little in your account?

VII. And lastly, the time is hastening when you will not think so slightly of Christ and salvation. Oh, sirs, when God shall commission death to tear your guilty souls out of your bodies, when devils shall drag you away to the place of torment, when you find yourselves condemned to everlasting fire by that Saviour whom you now neglect, what would you then give for a Saviour? when divine justice brings in its heavy charges against you, and you have nothing to answer, how will you then cry, "Oh if I had chosen Jesus for my Saviour, he would have answered all!" When you see that the world has deserted you, that your companions in sin have deceived themselves and you, and all your merry days are over for ever, would you not then give ten thousand worlds for Christ? And will you not now think him worthy of your esteem and earnest pursuit? Why will ye judge of things now quite the reverse of what you will do then when you will be more capable of judging rightly?

And now, dear immortal souls! I have discovered the nature and danger of this common but unsuspected and unlamented sin, making light of Christ. I have delivered my message, and now I must leave it with you, imploring the blessing of God upon it. I cannot follow you home to your houses to see what effect it has upon you, or to make application of it to each of you in particular; but oh, may your consciences undertake this office! Whenever you spend another prayerless, thoughtless day, whenever you give yourselves up to sinful pleasures, or an over-eager pursuit of the world, may your conscience become your preacher, and sting you with this expostulation: "Alas! is this the effect of all I have heard? Do I still make light of Christ and the concerns of religion? Oh what will be the end of such conduct!"

I cannot but fear, after all, that some of you, as usual, will continue careless and impenitent. Well, when you are suffering the punishment of this sin in hell, remember that you were warned, and acquit me from being accessary to your ruin. And when we all appear before the supreme Judge, and I am called to give an account of my ministry: when I am asked, "Did you warn these creatures of their danger? Did you lay before them their guilt in making light of these things?" you will allow me to answer, "Yes, Lord, I warned them in the best manner I could, but they would not believe me; they would not regard what I said, though enforced by the authority of thy awful name, and confirmed by thine own word." Oh sirs, must I give in this accusation against any of you? No, rather have mercy on yourselves, and have mercy upon me, that I may give an account of you with joy, and not with grief.

SERMON VIII.

THE COMPASSION OF CHRIST TO WEAK BELIEVERS.

MATT. XII. 20.—*A bruised reed shall he not break, and smoking flax shall he not quench.*

THE Lord Jesus possesses all those virtues in the highest perfection, which render him infinitely amiable, and qualify him for the administration of a just and gracious government over the world. The virtues of mortals, when carried to a high degree, very often run into those vices which have a kind of affinity to them. " Right, too rigid, hardens into wrong." Strict justice steels itself into excessive severity; and the man is lost in the judge. Goodness and mercy sometimes degenerate into softness and an irrational compassion inconsistent with government. But in Jesus Christ these seemingly opposite virtues centre and harmonize in the highest perfection, without running into extremes. Hence he is at once characterized as a Lamb, and as the Lion of the tribe of Judah: a lamb for gentleness towards humble penitents, and a lion to tear his enemies in pieces. Christ is said to *judge and make war*, Rev. xix. 11; and yet he is called *The Prince of Peace;* Isa. ix. 6. He will at length show himself terrible to the workers of iniquity; and the terrors of the Lord are a very proper topic whence to persuade men; but now he is patient towards all men, and he is all love and tenderness towards the meanest penitent. The meekness and gentleness of Christ is to be the pleasing entertainment of this day; and I enter upon it with a particular view to those mourning, desponding souls among us, whose weakness renders them in great need of strong consolation. To such, in particular, I address the words of my text, *A bruised reed shall he not break, and smoking flax shall he not quench.*

This is a part of the Redeemer's character, as delineated near three thousand years ago, by the evangelical prophet Isaiah; Isa. xlii. 1–4; and it is expressly applied to him by St. Mathew: *Behold,* says the Father, *my servant whom I have chosen* for the important undertaking of saving the guilty sons of men; "my Beloved, in whom my soul is well pleased;" my very soul is well pleased with his faithful discharge of the important office he has undertaken. I *will put my spirit upon him;* that is, I will completely furnish him by the gifts of my spirit for his high character; and *he shall show judgment to the Gentiles;* to the poor benighted Gentiles he shall show the light of salvation, by revealing the gospel to them; which, in the style of the Old Testament, may be called his judgments. Or, he will show and execute the judgment of this world by casting out its infernal prince, who had so long exercised an extensive cruel tyranny over it. *He shall not strive nor cry, neither shall any man hear his voice in the streets;* that is, though he enters the world as a mighty prince and conqueror, to establish a kingdom of righteousness, and overthrow the kingdom of darkness, yet he will not introduce it with the noisy terrors and thunders of war, but shall show himself mild and gentle as the prince of peace. Or the connection may lead us to understand these words in a different sense, namely, He shall do nothing with clamorous ostentation, nor proclaim his wonderful works, when it shall answer no valuable end. Accordingly the verse of our text stands thus connected: *Great multitudes*

*followed him; and he healed them all, and charged them
that they should not make him known.   That it might be
fulfilled which was spoken by Isaiah the prophet, saying,—
He shall not cry, neither shall any man hear his voice in
the streets;* that is, he shall not publish his miracles with
noisy triumphs in the streets and other public places.
And when it is said, *He shall not strive,* it may refer to his
inoffensive passive behaviour towards his enemies that
were plotting his death.   For thus we may connect this
quotation from Isaiah with the preceding history in the
chapter of our text: *Then the Pharisees went out, and held
a council against him, how they might destroy him.   But
when Jesus knew it,* instead of praying to his Father for a
guard of angels, or employing his own miraculous power
to destroy them, *he withdrew himself from thence ; that it
might be fulfilled which was spoken by the prophet Isaiah,
saying,—He shall not strive.*

The general meaning of my text seems to be contained
in this observation : " That the Lord Jesus has the tenderest and most compassionate regard to the feeblest penitents, however oppressed and desponding; and that he will
approve and cherish the least spark of true love towards
himself.

A bruised reed seems naturally to represent a soul at
once feeble in itself, and crushed with a burden; a soul
both weak and oppressed.   The reed is a slender, frail
vegetable in itself, and therefore a very proper image to
represent a soul that is feeble and weak.   A bruised reed
is still more frail, hangs its head, and is unable to stand
without some prop.   And what can be a more lively emblem of a poor soul, not only weak in itself, but bowed
down and broken under a load of sin and sorrow, that
droops and sinks, and is unable to stand without divine
support?   Strength may bear up under a burden, or

struggle with it, till it has thrown it off; but oppressed weakness, frailty under a burden, what can be more pitiable? and yet this is the case of many a poor penitent. He is weak in himself, and in the meantime crushed under a heavy weight of guilt and distress.

And what would become of such a frail oppressed creature, if, instead of raising him up and supporting him, Jesus should tread and crush him under the foot of his indignation? But though a reed, especially a bruised reed, is an insignificant thing, of little or no use, yet "a bruised reed he will not break," but he raises it up with a gentle hand, and enables it to stand, though weak in itself, and easily crushed in ruin.

Perhaps the imagery, when drawn at length, may be this: "The Lord Jesus is an Almighty Conqueror, marches in state through our world; and here and there a bruised reed lies in his way. But instead of disregarding it, or trampling it under foot, he takes care not to break it: he raises up the drooping straw, trifling as it is and supports it with his gentle hand." Thus, poor brokenhearted penitents, thus he takes care of you, and supports you, worthless and trifling as you are. Though you seem to lie in the way of his justice, and it might tread you with its heavy foot, yet he not only does not crush you, but takes you up, and inspires you with strength to bear your burden and flourish again.

Or perhaps the imagery may be derived from the practice of the ancient shepherds, who were wont to amuse themselves with the music of a pipe of reed or straw; and when it was bruised they broke it, or threw it away as useless. But the bruised reed shall not be broken by this divine Shepherd of souls. The music of broken sighs and groans is indeed all that the broken reed can afford him: the notes are but low, melancholy, and jarring: and yet he will not break the instrument, but he will repair and tune it, till it is fit to join in the concert of angels on high; and even now its humble strains are pleasing to his ears. Surely every broken heart among us must revive, while contemplating this tender and moving imagery.

The other emblem is equally significant and affecting. *The smoking flax shall he not quench.* It seems to be an allusion to the wick of a candle or lamp, the flame of which is put out, but it still smokes, and retains a little fire which may be again blown into a flame, or rekindled by the application of more fire. Many such dying snuffs or smoking wicks are to be found in the candlesticks of the churches, and in the lamps of the sanctuary. The flame of divine love is just expiring, it is sunk into the socket of a corrupt heart, and produces no clear, steady blaze, but only a smoke that is disagreeable, although it shows that a spark of the sacred fire yet remains; or it produces a faint quivering flame that dies away, then catches and revives, and seems unwilling to be quenched entirely. The devil and the world raise many storms of temptation to blow it out; and a corrupt heart, like a fountain, pours out water to quench it. But even this smoking flax, this dying snuff, Jesus will not quench, but he blows it up into a flame, and pours in the oil of his grace to recruit and nourish it. He walks among the golden candlesticks, and trims the lamps of his sanctuary. Where he finds empty vessels without oil or a spark of heavenly fire, like those of the foolish virgins, he breaks the vessels, or throws them out of his house. But where he finds the least spark of true grace, where he discovers but the glimpse of sincere love to him, where he sees the principle of true piety, which, though just expiring, yet renders the heart susceptive of divine love, as a candle just put out is easily rekindled, there he will strengthen the things which remain and are ready to die : he will blow up the dying snuff to a lively flame, and cause it to shine brighter and brighter to the perfect day. Where there is the least principle of true holiness he will cherish it. He will furnish the expiring lamp with fresh supplies of the oil of grace, and of heavenly fire ; and all the storms that beat upon it shall not be able to put it out, because sheltered by his hand.

I hope, my dear brethren, some of you begin already to feel the pleasing energy of this text. Are you not ready to say, " Blessed Jesus ! is this thy true character ? Then thou art just such a Saviour as I want, and I most willingly give up myself to thee." You are sensible you are at best but a bruised reed, a feeble, shattered, useless thing : an untunable, broken pipe of straw, that can make no proper music for the entertainment of your divine Shepherd. Your heart is at best but smoking flax, where the love of God often appears like a dying snuff; or an expiring flame that quivers and catches, and hovers over the lamp, just ready to go out. Such some of you probably feel yourselves to be. Well, and what think ye of Christ ? " He will not break the bruised reed, nor quench the smoking flax ;" and therefore, may not even your guilty eyes look to this gentle Saviour with encouraging hope ? May you not say to him, with the sweet singer of Israel, in his last moment, *He is all my salvation, and all my desire ?* 2 Sam. xxiii. 5.

In prosecuting this subject I intend to illustrate the character of a weak believer, as represented in my text, and then to illustrate the care and compassion of Jesus Christ even for such a poor weakling.

I. I am to illustrate the character of a weak believer, as represented in my text, by " a bruised reed, and smoking flax."

The metaphor of a bruised reed, as I observed, seems

most naturally to convey the idea of a state of weakness and oppression. And, therefore, in illustrating it I am naturally led to describe the various weaknesses which a believer sometimes painfully feels, and to point out the heavy burdens which he sometimes groans under; I say sometimes, for at other times even the weak believer finds himself strong, *strong in the Lord, and in the power of his might, and strengthened with might by the Spirit in the inner man.* The joy of the Lord is his strength: and he "can do all things through Christ strengthening him." Even the oppressed believer at times feels himself delivered from his burden, and he can lift up his drooping head, and walk upright. But, alas! the burden returns, and crushes him again. And under some burden or other many honest-hearted believers groan out the most part of their lives.

Let us now see what are those weaknesses which a believer feels and laments. He finds himself weak in knowledge; a simple child in the knowledge of God and divine things. He is weak in love; the sacred flame does not rise with a perpetual fervour, and diffuse itself through all his devotions, but at times it languishes and dies away into a smoking snuff. He is weak in faith; he cannot keep a strong hold of the Almighty, cannot suspend his all upon his promises with cheerful confidence, nor build a firm, immovable fabric of hope upon the rock Jesus Christ. He is weak in hope; his hope is dashed with rising billows of fears and jealousies, and sometimes just overset. He is weak in joy; he cannot extract the sweets of Christianity, nor taste the comforts of his religion. He is weak in zeal for God and the interests of his kingdom; he would wish himself always a flaming seraph, always glowing with zeal, always unwearied in serving his God, and promoting the designs of redeeming love in the world; but, alas! at times his zeal, with his love, languishes and dies away into a smoking snuff. He is weak in repentance; troubled with that plague of plagues, a hard heart. He is weak in the conflict with indwelling sin, that is perpetually making insurrections within him. He is weak in resisting temptations; which crowd upon him from without, and are often likely to overwhelm him. He is weak in courage to encounter the king of terrors, and venture through the valley of the shadow of death. He is weak in prayer, in importunity, in filial boldness, in approaching the mercyseat. He is weak in abilities to endeavour the conversion of sinners and save souls from death. In short, he is weak in every thing in which he should be strong. He has indeed, like the church of Philadelphia, a little strength, Rev. iii. 8, and at times he feels it; but oh! it seems to him much too little for the work he has to do. These weaknesses or defects the believer feels, painfully and tenderly feels, and bitterly laments. A sense of them keeps him upon his guard against temptations : he is not venturesome in rushing into the combat. He would not parley with temptation, but would keep out of its way; nor would he run the risk of a defeat by an ostentatious experiment of his strength. This sense of weakness also keeps him dependent upon divine strength. He clings to that support given to St. Paul in an hour of hard conflict, *My grace is sufficient for thee ; for my strength is made perfect in weakness ;* and when a sense of his weakness has this happy effect upon him, then with St. Paul he has reason to say, *When I am weak, then I am strong.* 2 Cor. xii. 9, 10.

I say the believer feels and laments these weaknesses; and this is the grand distinction in this case between him and the rest of the world. They are the weak too, much weaker than he; nay, they have, properly, no spiritual strength at all; but, alas! they do not feel their weakness, but the poor vain creatures boast of their strength, and think they can do great things when they are disposed for them. Or if their repeated falls and defeats by temptation extort them to a confession of their weakness, they plead it rather as an excuse, than lament it as at once a crime and a calamity. But the poor believer tries no such artifice to extenuate his guilt. He is senible that even his weakness itself has guilt in it, and therefore he laments it with ingenuous sorrow among his other sins.

Now, have I not delineated the very character of some of you; such weaklings, such frail reeds you feel yourselves to be? Well, hear this kind assurance, "Jesus will not break such a feeble reed, but he will support and strengthen it."

But you perhaps not only feel you are weak, but you are oppressed with some heavy burden or other. You are not only a reed for weakness, but you are a bruised reed, trodden under foot, crushed under a load. Even this is no unusual or discouraging case; for,

The weak believer often feels himself crushed under some heavy burden. The frail reed is often bruised; bruised under a due sense of guilt. Guilt lies heavy at times upon his conscience, and he cannot throw it off. Bruised with a sense of remaining sin, which he finds still strong within him, and which at times prevails, and treads him under foot. Bruised under a burden of wants, the want of tenderness of heart, of ardent love to God and mankind, the want of heavenly-mindedness and victory over the world; the want of conduct and resolution to direct his behaviour in a passage so intricate and difficult, and the want of nearer intercourse with the Father and his Spirit: in short, a thousand pressing wants crush and bruise him. He also feels his share of the calamities of life in common with other men. But these burdens I shall take no farther notice of, because they are not peculiar to him as a believer, nor do they lie heaviest upon his heart. He could easily bear up under the calamities of life if his spiritual wants were supplied, and the burden of guilt and sin were removed. Under these last he groans and sinks. Indeed these burdens lie with all their full weight upon the world around him; but they are dead in trespasses and sins, and feel them not: they do not groan under them, nor labour for deliverance from them. They lie contented under them, with more stupidity than beasts of burden, till they sink under the intolerable load into the depth of misery. But the poor believer is not so stupid, and his tender heart feels the burden and groans under it. *We that are in this tabernacle,* says St. Paul, *do groan, being burdened.* 2 Cor. v. 4. The believer understands feelingly that pathetic exclamation, *O wretched man that I am! Who shall deliver me from the body of this death?* Rom. vii. 24. He cannot be easy till his conscience is appeased by a well-attested pardon through the blood of Christ; and the sins he feels working within him are a real burden and uneasiness to him, though they should never break out into action, and publicly dishonour his holy profession.

And is not this the very character of some poor oppressed creatures among you? I hope it is. You may look upon your case to be very discouraging, but Jesus looks upon it in a more favourable light; he looks upon you as proper objects of his compassionate care. Bruised as you are, he will bind up, and support you.

II. But I proceed to take a view of the character of a weak Christian, as represented in the other metaphor in my text, namely, *smoking flax.* The idea most naturally conveyed by this metaphor is, that of grace true and sincere, but languishing and just expiring, like a candle just blown out, which still smokes and retains a feeble spark of fire.   It signifies a susceptibility of a farther grace, or a readiness to catch that sacred fire, as a candle just put out is easily re-kindled.   This metaphor therefore leads me to describe the reality of religion in a low degree, or to delineate the true Christian in his most languishing hours.   And in so doing I shall mention those disposi-tions and exercises which the weakest Christian feels, even in these melancholy seasons; for even in these he widely differs still from the most polished hypocrite in his highest improvements.   On this subject let me solicit your most serious attention; for, if you have the least spark of real religion within you, you are now likely to discover it, as I am not going to rise to the high attainments of Christians of the first rank, but to stoop to the character of the mean-est.   Now the peculiar dispositions and exercises of heart which such in some measure feel, you may discover from the following short history of their case.

The weak Christian in such languishing hours does in-deed sometimes fall into such a state of carelessness and insensibility, that he has very few and but superficial exer-cises of mind about divine things.   But generally he feels an uneasiness, an emptiness, an anxiety within, under which he droops and pines away, and all the world cannot heal the disease!   He has chosen the blessed God as his supreme happiness; and, when he cannot derive happiness from that source, all the sweets of created enjoyments be-come insipid to him, and cannot fill up the prodigious void which the absence of the Supreme Good leaves in his crav-ing soul.   Sometimes his anxiety is indistinct and con-fused, and he hardly knows what ails him; but at other times he feels it is for God, the living God, that his soul pants.   The evaporations of this smoking flax naturally ascend towards heaven. He knows that he never can be happy till he can enjoy the communications of divine love. Let him turn which way he will, he can find no solid ease, no rest, till he comes to this centre again.

Even at such times he cannot be thoroughly reconciled to his sins. He may be parleying with some of them in an unguarded hour, and seem to be negotiating a peace; but the truce is soon ended, and they are at variance again. The enmity of a renewed heart soon rises against this old enemy. And there is this circumstance remarkable in the believer's hatred and opposition to sin, that they do not proceed principally, much less entirely, from a fear of punishment, but from a generous sense to its instrinsic baseness and ingratitude, and its contrariety to the holy nature of God. This is the ground of his hatred to sin, and sorrow for it; and this shows that there is at least a spark of true grace in his heart, and that he does not act altogether from the low, interested, and mercenary principles of nature.

At such times he is very jealous of the sincerity of his religion, afraid that all his past experiences were delusive, and afraid that, if he should die in his present state, he would be for ever miserable. A very anxious state is this!

The stupid world can lie secure while this grand concern lies in the most dreadful suspense. But the tender-hearted believer is not capable of such fool-hardiness: he shudders at the thought of everlasting separation from that God and Saviour whom he loves. He loves him, and therefore the fear of separation from him, fills him with all the anxiety of bereaved love. This to him is the most painful ingredient of the punishment of hell. Hell would be a sevenfold hell to a lover of God, because it is a state of banishment from him whom he loves. He could for ever languish and pine away under the consuming distresses of widowed love, which those that love him cannot feel. And has God kindled the sacred flame in his heart in order to render him capable of the more exquisite pain? Will he exclude from his presence the poor creature that clings to him, and languishes for him? No, the flax that does but smoke with his love was never intended to be fuel for hell; but he will blow it up into a flame, and nourish it till it mingles with the seraphic ardours in the region of perfect love.

The weak believer seems sometimes driven by the tempest of lusts and temptation from off the rock of Jesus Christ. But he makes towards it on the stormy billows, and labours to lay hold upon it, and recover his station there; for he is sensible there is no other foundation of safety; but that without Christ he must perish for ever. It is the habitual disposition of the believer's soul to depend upon Jesus Christ alone. He retains a kind of direction or tendency towards him, like the needle touched with the load-stone towards the pole; and, if his heart is turned from its course, it trembles and quivers till it gains its favourite point again, and fixes there. Sometimes, indeed, a consciousness of guilt renders him shy of his God and Saviour; and after such base ingratitude he is ashamed to go to him: but at length necessity as well as inclination constrains him, and he is obliged to cry out, *Lord, to whom shall I go? thou hast the words of eternal life.* John vi. 68. "In thee alone I find rest to my soul; and therefore to thee I must fly, though I am ashamed and confounded to appear in thy presence."

In short, the weakest Christian upon earth sensibly feels that his comfort rises and falls, as he lives nearer to or farther from his God. The love of God has such an habitual predominancy even in his heart, that nothing in the world, nor even all the world together, can fill up his place. No, when he is gone, heaven and earth cannot replenish the mighty void. Even the weakest Christian upon earth longs to be delivered from sin, from all sin, without exception: and a body of death hanging about him is the burden of his life. Even the poor jealous languishing Christian has his hope, all the little hope that he has, built upon Jesus Christ. Even this smoking flax sends up some exhalations of love towards heaven. Even the poor creature that often fears he is altogether a slave to sin, honestly, though feebly, labours to be holy, to be holy as an angel, yea, to be holy as God is holy. He has a heart that feels the attractive charms of holiness, and he is so captivated by it, that sin can never recover its former place in his heart: no, the tyrant is for ever dethroned, and the believer would rather die than yield himself a tame slave to the usurped tyranny again.

Thus I have delineated to you, in the plainest manner I could, the character of a weak Christian. Some of you, I am afraid, cannot lay claim even to this low character. If so, you may be sure you are not true Christians, even of the lowest rank. You may be sure you have not the least spark of true religion in your hearts, but are utterly destitute of it.

But some of you, I hope, can say, " Well, after all my doubts and fears, if this be the character of a true, though weak Christian, then I may humbly hope that I am one. I am indeed confirmed in it, that I am less than the least of all other saints upon the face of the earth, but yet I see that I am a saint; for thus has my heart been exercised, even in my dark and languishing hours. This secret uneasiness and pining anxiety, this thirst for God, for the living God, this tendency of soul towards Jesus Christ, this implacable enmity to sin, this panting and struggling after holiness: these things have I often felt." And have you indeed? Then away with your doubts and jealousies;

away with your fears and despondencies! There is at least an immortal spark kindled in your hearts, which the united power of men and devils, of sin and temptation, shall never be able to quench. No, it shall yet rise into a flame, and burn with seraphic ardours for ever.

For your farther encouragement, I proceed,

II. To illustrate the care and compassion of Jesus Christ for such poor weaklings as you.

This may appear a needless task to some: for who is there that does not believe it? But to such would I say, it is no easy thing to establish a trembling soul in the full belief of this truth. It is easy for one that does not see his danger, and does not feel his extreme need of salvation, and the difficulty of the work, to believe that Christ is willing and able to save him. But oh! to a poor soul, deeply sensible of its condition, this is no easy matter. Besides, the heart may need be more deeply affected with this truth, though the understanding should need no farther arguments of the speculative kind for its conviction; and to impress this truth is my present design.

For this purpose I need but read and paraphrase to you a few of the many kind declarations and assurances which Jesus has given us in his word, and relate the happy experiences of some of his saints there recorded, who found him true and faithful to his word.

The Lord Jesus Christ seems to have a peculiar tenderness for the poor, the mourners, the broken-hearted; and these are peculiarly the objects of his mediatorial office. *The* Lord *hath anointed me,* says he, *to preach good tidings to the meek; he hath sent me* all the way from my native heaven down to earth, upon this compassionate errand, *to bind up the broken-hearted, to appoint unto them that mourn in Zion, to give unto them beauty for ashes, the oil of joy for mourning, the garment of praise for the spirit of heaviness.* Isa. lxi. 1–3. *Thus saith the* Lord, in strains of majesty that become him, *The heaven is my throne, and the earth is my footstool: where is the house that ye build unto me? and where is the place of my rest? For all those things hath my hand made, saith the* Lord. Had he spoken uniformly in this majestic language to us guilty worms, the declaration might have overwhelmed us with awe, but could not have inspired us with hope. But he advances himself thus high, on purpose to let us see how low he can stoop. Hear the encouraging sequel of this his majestic speech: *To this man will I look, even to him that is poor, and of a contrite spirit, and trembleth at my word.* Let heaven and earth wonder that he will look down through all the shining ranks of angels, and look by princes and nobles to fix his eye upon this man, this poor man, this contrite, broken-hearted, trembling creature. Isa. lxvi. 1, 2. He loves to dwell upon this subject, and therefore you hear it again in the same prophecy: "Thus saith the high and lofty One that inhabiteth eternity, whose name is holy,"—what does he say? *I dwell in the high and holy place.* Isa. lvii. 15. This is said in character. This is a dwelling in some measure worthy the inhabitant. But oh! will he stoop to dwell in a lower mansion, or pitch his tent among mortals? yes, he dwells not only in his *high and holy place,* but also, *with him that is of a contrite and humble spirit, to revive the spirit of the humble, and to revive the heart of the contrite ones.* He charges Peter to *feed his lambs* as well as his sheep; that is, to take the tenderest care even of the weakest in his flock. John xxi. 15. And he severely rebukes the shepherds of Israel, *Because,* says he, *ye have not strengthened the diseased, neither have ye healed that which was sick, neither have ye bound up that which was broken.* Ezek. xxxiv. 4. But what an amiable reverse is the character of the great Shepherd and Bishop of souls! *Behold*, says Isaiah, *the Lord God will come with strong hand, and his arm shall rule for him: behold his reward is with him, and his work before him.* How justly may we tremble at this proclamation of the approaching God! for who can stand when he appeareth? But how agreeably are our fears disappointed in what follows! If he comes to take vengeance on his enemies, he also comes to show mercy to the meanest of his people. *He shall feed his flock like a shepherd: he shall gather the lambs with his arm, and carry them in his bosom, and shall gently lead those that are with young:* Isa. xl. 10, 11, that is, he shall exercise the tenderest and most compassionate care towards the meanest and weakest of his flock. *He hath looked down,* says the Psalmist, *from the height of his sanctuary; from heaven did the Lord behold the earth;* not to view the grandeur and pride of courts and kings, nor the heroic exploits of conquerors, but *to hear the groaning of the prisoner, to loose those that are appointed to death. He will regard the prayer of the destitute, and not despise their prayer. This shall be written for the generation to come.* Psalm cii. 17–20. It was written for your encouragement, my brethren. Above three thousand years ago, this encouraging passage was entered into the sacred records for the support of poor desponding souls in Virginia, in the ends of the earth. Oh, what an early provident care does God show for his people! There are none of the seven churches of Asia so highly commended by Christ as that of Philadelphia; and yet in commending her, all he can say is, "Thou hast a little strength." *I know thy works; behold I have set before thee an open door, and no man can shut it: for thou hast a little strength.* Rev. iii. 8. Oh, how acceptable is a little strength to Jesus Christ, and how ready is he to improve it! *He giveth power to the faint,* says Isaiah, *and to them that have no might he increaseth strength.* Isa. xl. 29. Hear farther what words of grace and truth flowed from the lips of Jesus. *Come unto me, all ye that labour and are heavy laden, and I will give you rest: for I am meek and lowly in heart,* Matt. xi. 28, 29. *Him that cometh unto me, I will in no wise cast out.* John vi. 37. *If any man thirst, let him come unto me and drink.* John vii. 37. *Let him that is athirst come: and whosoever will, let him take of the water of life freely.* Rev. xxii. 17. Oh, what strong consolation is here! what exceeding great and precious promises are these! I might easily add to the catalogue, but these may suffice.

Let us now see how his people in every age have ever found these promises made good. Here David may be consulted *instar omnium,* and he will tell you, pointing to himself, *This poor man cried, and the* LORD *heard him, and saved him out of all his troubles.* Psalm xxxiv. 6. St. Paul, in the midst of affliction, calls God *the Father of mercies and the God of all comfort, who comforteth us in all our tribulation.* 2 Cor. i. 3, 4. *God,* says he *that comforteth those that are cast down, comforted us.* 2 Cor. vii. 6. What a sweetly emphatic declaration is this! "God, the comforter of the humble, comforted us."* He is not only the Lord of hosts, the King of kings, the Creator of the world, but among his more august characters he assumes this title, the Comforter of "the humble." Such St. Paul found him in an hour of temptation, when he had this supporting answer to his repeated prayer for deliverance, *My grace is sufficient for thee; for my strength is made perfect in weakness.* 2 Cor. xii. 9.

---

* This is the most literal translation of——ὅ παρακαλῶν τους ταπεινους παρεκάλεσεν ἡμᾶς ὁ θεός.

Since this was the case, since his weakness was more than supplied by the strength of Christ, and was a foil to set it off, St. Paul seems quite regardless what infirmities he laboured under. Nay, *most gladly*, says he, *will I rather glory in my infirmities, that the power of Christ may rest upon me. Therefore I take pleasure in infirmities—for when I am weak, then am I strong.* He could take no pleasure in feeling himself weak: but the mortification was made up by the pleasure he found in leaning upon this almighty support. His wounds were painful to him: but, oh! the pleasure he found in feeling the divine physician dressing his wounds, in some measure swallowed up the pain. It was probably experience, as well as inspiration, that dictated to the apostle that amiable character of Christ, that he is a "merciful and faithful High Priest, who, being himself tempted, knows how to succour them that are tempted." Heb. ii. 17, 18. And "we have not a high priest which cannot be touched with the feeling of our infirmities: but was in all points tempted like as we are, yet without sin." Heb iv. 15.

But why need I multiply arguments? Go to his cross, and there learn his love and compassion, from his groans and wounds, and blood, and death. Would he hang there in such agony for sinners if he were not willing to save them, and cherish every good principle in them? There you may have much the same evidence of his compassion as Thomas had of his resurrection; you may look into his hands, and see the print of the nails; and into his side, and see the scar of the spear; which loudly proclaims his readiness to pity and help you.

And now, poor, trembling, doubting souls, what hinders but you should raise up your drooping head, and take courage? May you not venture your souls into such compassionate and faithful hands? Why should the bruised reed shrink from him, when he comes not to tread it down, but raise it up?

As I am really solicitous that impenitent hearts among us should be pierced with the medicinal anguish and sorrow of conviction and repentance, and the most friendly heart cannot form a kinder wish for them, so I am truly solicitous that every honest soul, in which there is the least spark of true piety, should enjoy the pleasure of it. It is indeed to be lamented that they who have a title to so much happiness should enjoy so little of it; it is very incongruous that they should go bowing the head in their way towards heaven, as if they were hastening to the place of execution, and that they should serve so good a Master with such heavy hearts. Oh lift up the hands that hang down, and strengthen the feeble knees! "Comfort ye, comfort ye, my people, saith your God." " Be strong in the Lord, and in the power of his might." Trust in your all-sufficient Redeemer; trust in him though he should slay you.

And do not indulge causeless doubts and fears concerning your sincerity. When they arise in your minds, examine them, and search whether there be any sufficient reason for them; and if you discover there is not, then reject them and set them at defiance, and entertain your hopes in spite of them, and say with the Psalmist, "Why art thou cast down, oh my soul? and why art thou disquieted within me? Hope thou in God: for I shall yet praise him, who is the health of my countenance, and my God." Psalm xlii. 11.

SERMON IX.

THE CONNECTION BETWEEN PRESENT HOLINESS AND FUTURE FELICITY.

Heb. xii. 14.—*Follow holiness; without which no man shall see the Lord.*

As the human soul was originally designed for the enjoyment of no less a portion than the ever-blessed God, it was formed with a strong innate tendency towards happiness. It has not only an eager fondness for existence, but for some good to render its existence happy. And the privation of being itself is not more terrible than the privation of all its blessings. It is true, in the present degeneracy of human nature, this vehement desire is miserably perverted and misplaced; man seeks his supreme happiness in sinful, or at best in created enjoyments, forgetful of the uncreated fountain of bliss; but yet still he seeks happiness: still this innate *impetus* is predominant, and though he mistakes the means, yet he still retains a general aim at the end. Hence he ransacks this lower world in quest of felicity; climbs in search of it the slippery ascent of honour; hunts for it in the treasures of gold and silver; or plunges for it in the foul streams of sensual pleasures. But since all the sordid satisfaction resulting from these things is not adequate to the unbounded cravings of the mind, and since the satisfaction is transitory and perishing, or we may be wrenched from it by the inexorable hand of death, the mind breaks through the limits of the present enjoyments, and even of the lower creation, and ranges through the unknown scenes of futurity in quest of some untried good. Hope makes excursions into the dark duration between the present *now* and the grave, and forms to itself pleasing images of approaching blessings, which often vanish in the embrace, like delusive phantoms. Nay, it launches into the vast unknown world that lies beyond the grave, and roves through the regions of immensity after some complete felicity to supply the defects of sublunary enjoyments. Hence, though men, till their spirits are refined by regenerating grace, have no relish for celestial joys, but pant for the poor pleasures of time and sense, yet as they cannot avoid the unwelcome consciousness that death will ere long rend them from these sordid and momentary enjoyments, are constrained to indulge the hope of bliss in a future state : and they promise themselves happiness in another world when they can no longer enjoy any in this. And as reason and revelation unitedly assure them that this felicity cannot consist in sensual indulgences, they generally expect it will be of a more refined and spiritual nature, and flow more immediately from the great Father of spirits.

He must indeed be miserable that abandons all hope of this blessedness. The Christian religion affords him no other prospect but that of eternal, intolerable misery in the regions of darkness and despair; and if he flies to infidelity as a refuge, it can afford him no comfort but the shocking prospect of annihilation.

Now, if men were pressed into heaven by an unavoidable fatality, if happiness was promiscuously promised to them all without distinction of characters, then they might indulge a blind unexamined hope, and never perplex themselves with anxious inquiries about it. And he might justly be deemed a malignant disturber of the repose of mankind, that would attempt to shock their hope, and frighten them with causeless scruples.

But if the light of nature intimates, and the voice of Scripture proclaims aloud, that this eternal felicity is reserved only for persons of particular characters, and that multitudes, multitudes who entertained pleasing hopes of it, are confounded with an eternal disappointment, and shall suffer an endless duration in the most terrible miseries, we ought each of us to take the alarm, and examine the grounds of our hope, that, if they appear sufficient, we may allow ourselves a rational satisfaction in them; and if they are found delusive, we may abandon them, and seek for a hope which will bear the test now while it may be obtained. And however disagreeable the task be to give our fellow-creatures even profitable uneasiness, yet he must appear to the impartial a friend to the best interests of mankind, who points out the evidences and foundation of a rational and Scriptural hope, and exposes the various mistakes to which we are subject in so important a case.

And if, when we look around us, we find persons full of the hopes of heaven, who can give no Scriptural evidences of them to themselves or others; if we find many indulging this pleasing delusion, whose practices are mentioned by God himself as the certain marks of perishing sinners; and if persons are so tenacious of these hopes, that they will retain them to their everlasting ruin, unless the most convictive methods are taken to undeceive them; then it is high time for those to whom the care of souls (a weightier charge than that of kingdoms) is entrusted, to use the greatest plainness for this purpose.

This is my chief design at present, and to this my text naturally leads me. It contains these doctrines:

First, That without holiness here, it is impossible for us

to enjoy heavenly happiness in the future world. To see the Lord, is here put for enjoying him; see Rom. viii. 24. And the metaphor signifies the happiness of the future state in general; and more particularly intimates that the knowledge of God will be a special ingredient therein. See a parallel expression in Matt. v. 8.

Secondly, that this consideration should induce us to use the most earnest endeavours to obtain the heavenly happiness. Pursue holiness, because *without it no man can see the Lord.*

Hence I am naturally led,

I. To explain the nature of that *holiness, without which no man shall see the Lord.*

II. To show what endeavours should be used to obtain it. And,

III. To urge you to use them by the consideration of the absolute necessity of holiness.

I. I am to explain the nature of holiness. And I shall give you a brief definition of it, and then mention some of those dispositions and practices which naturally flow from it.

The most intelligible description of holiness, as it is inherent in us, may be this: "It is a conformity in heart and practice to the revealed will of God." As the Supreme Being is the standard of all perfection, his holiness in particular is the standard of ours. Then we are holy when his image is stamped upon our hearts and reflected in our lives; so the apostle defines it, *and that ye put on the new man, which after God is created in righteousness and true holiness.* Eph. iv. 24. *Whom he did predestinate to be conformed to the image of his Son.* Rom. viii. 29. Hence holiness may be defined, "A conformity to God in his moral perfections." But as we cannot have a distinct knowledge of these perfections but as they are manifested by the revealed will of God, I choose to define holiness, as above, "A conformity to his revealed will." Now his revealed will comprises both the law and the gospel; the law informs us of the duty which we as creatures owe to God as a being of supreme excellency, as our Creator and Benefactor, and to men as our fellow-creatures; and the gospel informs us of the duty which as sinners we owe to God as reconcilable through a Mediator. Our obedience to the former implies the whole of morality, and to the latter the whole of evangelical graces, as faith in a Mediator, repentance, &c.

From this definition of holiness it appears, on the one hand, that it is absolutely necessary, to see the Lord; for unless our dispositions are conformed to him, we cannot be happy in the enjoyment of him; and on the other hand, that they who are made thus holy, are prepared for the vision and fruition of his face, as they can relish the divine pleasure.

But as a concise definition of holiness may give an auditory but very imperfect ideas of it, I shall expatiate upon the dispositions and practices in which it consists, or which naturally result from it; and they are such as follow:

1. A delight in God for his holiness. Self-love may prompt us to love him for his goodness to us; and so, many unregenerate men may have a selfish love to God on this account. But to love God because he is infinitely holy, because he bears an infinite detestation to all sin, and will not indulge his creatures in the neglect of the least instance of holiness, but commands them to be holy as he is holy, this is a disposition connatural to a renewed soul only, and argues a conformity to his image. Every nature is most agreeable to itself, and a holy nature is most agreeable to a holy nature.

Here I would make a remark, which may God deeply

impress on your hearts, and which for that purpose I shall subjoin to each particular, that holiness in fallen man is supernatural; I mean we are not born with it, we give no discoveries of it, till we have experienced a great change. Thus we find it in the present case; we have no natural love to God because of his infinite purity and hatred to all sin; nay, we would love him more did he give us greater indulgences; and I am afraid the love of some persons is founded upon a mistake; they love him because they imagine he does not hate sin, nor them for it, so much as he really does; because they do not expect he is so inexorably just in his dealings with the sinner. It is no wonder they love such a soft, easy, passive being as this imaginary deity; but did they see the lustre of that holiness of God which dazzles the celestial armies; did they but know the terrors of his justice, and his implacable indignation against sin, their innate enmity would show its poison, and their hearts would rise against God in all those horrible blasphemies with which awakened sinners are so frequently shocked. Such love as this is so far from being acceptable, that it is the greatest affront to the Supreme Being; as, if a profligate loved you on the mistaken supposition that you were such a libertine as himself, it would rather inflame your indignation than procure your respect.

But to a regenerate mind how strong, how transporting are the charms of holiness! Such a mind joins the anthem of seraphs with the divinest complacency, Rev. iv. 8, and anticipates the song of glorified saints, *Who shall not fear thee, O Lord, and glorify thy name? for thou only art holy.* Rev. xv. 4. The perfections of God lose their lustre, or sink into objects of terror or contempt, if this glorious attribute be abstracted. Without holiness power becomes tyranny, omniscience craft, justice revenge and cruelty, and even the amiable attribute of goodness loses its charms, and degenerates into a blind promiscuous prodigality, or foolish undiscerning fondness : but when these perfections are clothed in the beauties of holiness, how Godlike, how majestic, how lovely and attractive do they appear! and with what complacence does a mind fashioned after the divine image acquiesce in them. It may appear amiable even to an unholy sinner that the exertions of almighty power should be regulated by the most consummate wisdom ; that justice should not without distinction punish the guilty and the innocent : but an holy soul only can rejoice that divine goodness will not communicate happiness to the disgrace of holiness; and that, rather than it should overflow in a blind promiscuous manner, the whole human race should be miserable. A selfish sinner has nothing in view but his own happiness; and if this be obtained, he has no anxiety about the illustration of the divine purity; but it recommends happiness itself to a sanctified soul, that it cannot be communicated in a way inconsistent with the beauties of holiness.

2. Holiness consists in a hearty complacence in the law of God, because of its purity. The law is the transcript of the moral perfections of God; and if we love the original, we shall love the copy. Accordingly it is natural to a renewed mind to love the divine law, because it is perfectly holy, because it makes no allowance for the least sin, and requires every duty that it becomes us to perform towards God. Psalm cxix. 140, and xix. 7–10, Romans vii. 12, compared with 22.

But is this our natural disposition ? Is this the disposition of the generality ? Do they not, on the contrary, secretly find fault with the law, because it is so strict ? And their common objection against that holiness of life which it enjoins is, that they cannot bear to be so precise.

Hence they are always for abating the rigour of the law, for bringing it down to some imaginary standard of their own, to their present ability, to sins of practice without regard to the sinful dispositions of the heart; or to the prevailing dispositions of the heart without regard to the first workings of concupiscence, those embryos of iniquity; and if they love the law at all, as they profess to do, it is upon the supposition that it is not so strict as it really is, but grants them greater indulgences. Rom. vii. 7.

Hence it appears that, if we are made holy at all, it must be by a supernatural change; and when that is effected, what a strange and happy alteration does the sinner perceive! with what pleasure does he resign himself a willing subject to that law to which he was once so averse! And when he fails, (as alas! he does in many things,) how is he humbled! He does not lay the fault upon the law as requiring impossibilities, but lays the whole fault upon himself as a corrupt sinner.

3. Holiness consists in a hearty complacence in the gospel method of salvation, because it tends to illustrate the moral perfections of the Deity, and to discover the beauties of holiness.

The gospel informs us of two grand pre-requisites to the salvation of the fallen sons of men, namely, the satisfaction of divine justice by the obedience and passion of Christ, that God might be reconciled to them consistently with his perfections; and the sanctification of sinners by the efficacy of the Holy Ghost, that they might be capable of enjoying God, and that he might maintain intimate communion with them without any stain to his holiness. These two grand articles contain the substance of the gospel; and our acquiescence in them is the substance of that evangelical obedience which it requires of us, and which is essential to holiness in a fallen creature.

Now, it is evident, that without either of these the moral perfections of the Deity, particularly his holiness, could not be illustrated, or even secured in the salvation of a sinner. Had he received an apostate race into favour, who had conspired in the most unnatural rebellion against him, without any satisfaction, his holiness would have been eclipsed; it would not have appeared that he had so invincible an abhorrence of sin, so zealous a regard for the vindication of his own holy law; or to his veracity, which had threatened condign punishment to offenders. But by the satisfaction of Christ, his holiness is illustrated in the most conspicuous manner: now it appears, that God would upon no terms save a sinner but that of adequate satisfaction, and that no other was sufficient but the suffering of his co-equal Son, otherwise he would not have appointed him to sustain the character of a Mediator; and now it appears that his hatred of sin is such that he would not let it pass unpunished even in his own Son, when only imputed to him. In like manner, if sinners, while unholy, were admitted into communion with God in heaven, it would obscure the glory of his holiness, and it would not then appear that such was the purity of his nature that he could have no fellowship with sin. But now it is evident, that even the blood of Immanuel cannot purchase heaven to be enjoyed by a sinner while unholy, but that every one that arrives at heaven must first be sanctified. An unholy sinner can no more be saved, while such, by the gospel than by the law; but here lies the difference, that the gospel makes provision for his sanctification, which is gradually carried on here, and perfected at death, before his admission into the heavenly glory.

Now it is the genius of true holiness to acquiesce in both these articles. A sanctified soul places all its dependence on the righteousness of Christ for acceptance.

It would be disagreeable to it to have the least concurrence in its own justification. It is not only willing, but delights to renounce all its own righteousness, and to glory in Christ alone. Phil. iii. 3. Free grace to such souls is a charming theme, and salvation is more acceptable, because conveyed in this way. It would render heaven itself disagreeable, and wither all its joys, were they brought thither in a way that degrades or does not illustrate the glory of God's holiness; but oh how agreeable the thought, that he that glorieth must glory in the Lord, and that the pride of all flesh shall be abased!

So a holy person rejoiceth that the way of holiness is the appointed way to heaven. He is not forced to be holy merely by the servile consideration that he must be so or perish, and so unwillingly submits to the necessity which he cannot avoid, when in the meantime, were it put to his choice, he would choose to reserve some sins, and neglect some painful duties. So far from this, that he delights in the gospel-constitution, because it requires universal holiness, and heaven would be less agreeable, were he to carry even the least sin there. He thinks it no hardship that he must deny himself in his sinful pleasures, and habituate himself to so much strictness in religion; no, but he blesses the Lord for obliging him to it, and where he fails he charges himself with it, and is self-abased upon the account.

This is solid rational religion, fit to be depended upon, in opposition to the antinomian licentiousness, the freaks of enthusiasm, and the irrational flights of passion and imagination on the one hand; and in opposition to formality, mere morality, and the self-sprung religion of nature on the other. And is it not evident we are destitute of this by nature? Men naturally are averse to this gospel method of salvation; they will not submit to the righteous-

ness of God, but fix their dependence, in part at least, upon
their own merit.   Their proud hearts cannot bear the
thought that all their performances must go for just nothing in their justification.   They are also averse to the way
of holiness; hence they will either abandon the expectation of heaven, and since they cannot obtain it in their sinful ways, desperately conclude to go on in sin, come what
will; or, with all the little sophistry they are capable of,
they will endeavour to widen the way to heaven, and persuade themselves they shall attain it, notwithstanding their
continuance in some known iniquity, and though their
hearts have never been thoroughly sanctified.   Alas! how
evident is this all around us!   How many either give up
their hopes of heaven rather than part with sin, or vainly
hold them, while their dispositions and practices prove
them groundless!   And must not such degenerate creatures be renewed ere they can be holy, or see the Lord?

4. Holiness consists in an habitual delight in all the
duties of holiness towards God and man, and an earnest
desire for communion with God in them.   This is the
natural result of all the foregoing particulars.   If we love
God for his holiness, we shall delight in that service in
which our conformity to him consists; if we love his law,
we shall delight in that obedience which it enjoins; and if
we take complacence in the evangelical method of salvation,
we shall take delight in that holiness, without which we cannot enjoy it.   The service of God is the element, the
pleasure of a holy soul; while others delight in the riches,
the honours, or the pleasures of this world, the holy soul
desires one thing of the Lord, that it may behold his
beauty while inquiring in his temple. Psalm xxvii. 4.
Such a person delights in retired converse with heaven, in
meditation and prayer. Psalm cxxxix. 17, and lxiii. 5, 6,
and lxxiii. 28.   He also takes pleasure in justice, benevo-

lence, and charity towards men, Psalm cxii. 5, 9, and in the strictest temperance and sobriety. 1 Cor. ix. 27.

Moreover, the mere formality of performing religious duties does not satisfy the true saint, unless he enjoys a divine friendship therein, receives communications of grace from heaven, and finds his graces quickened. Psalm xlii. 1, 2.

This consideration also shows us that holiness in us must be supernatural; for do we naturally thus delight in the service of God? or do you all now thus delight in it? is it not rather a weariness to you, and do you not find more pleasures in other things? Surely you must be changed, or you can have no relish for the enjoyments of heavenly happiness.

5. To constitute us saints indeed there must be universal holiness in practice. This naturally follows from the last, for as the body obeys the stronger volitions of the will, so when the heart is prevailingly disposed to the service of God, the man will habitually practice it. This is generally mentioned in Scripture as the grand characteristic of real religion, without which all our pretensions are vain. 1 John iii. 2–10, and v. 3; John xv. 15. True Christians are far from being perfect in practice, yet they are prevailingly holy in all manner of conversation; they do not live habitually in any one known sin, or wilfully neglect any one known duty. Psalm cxix. 6.

Without this practical holiness no man shall see the Lord; and if so, how great a change must be wrought on most before they can see him, for how few are thus adorned with a life of universal holiness! Many profess the name of Christ, but how few of them depart from iniquity? But to what purpose do they call him Master and Lord, while they do not the things which he commands them?

Thus I have, as plainly as I could, described the nature and properties of that holiness, without which no man shall see the Lord; and they who are possessed of it may lift up their heads with joy, assured that God has begun a good work in them, and that he will carry it on; and on the other hand, they that are destitute of it may be assured, that unless they are made new creatures they cannot see the Lord. I come,

II. To show you the endeavours we should use to obtain this holiness. And they are such as these:

1. Endeavour to know whether you are holy or not by close examination. It is hard indeed for some to know positively that they are holy, as they are perplexed with the appearances of realities, and the fears of counterfeits; but it is then easy for many to conclude negatively that they are not holy as they have not the likeness of it! To determine this point is of great use to our successful seeking after holiness. That an unregenerate sinner should attend on the means of grace with other aims than one that has reason to believe himself sanctified, is evident. The anxieties, sorrows, desires, and endeavours of the one should run in a very different channel from those of the other. The one should look upon himself as a guilty, condemned sinner; the other should allow himself the pleasures of a justified state; the one should pursue after the implantation; the other after the increase of holiness: the one should indulge in a seasonable concern about his lost condition; the other repose an humble confidence in God as reconciled to him; the one should look upon the threatenings of God as his doom; the other embrace the promises as his portion. Hence it follows, that while we are mistaken about our state, we cannot use endeavours after holiness in a proper manner. We act like a physician that applies medicines at random, without knowing the

disease. It is a certain conclusion that the most generous charity, under scriptural limitations, cannot avoid, that multitudes are destitute of holiness; and ought not we to inquire with proper anxiety whether we belong to that number? Let us be impartial, and proceed according to evidence. If we find those marks of holiness in heart and life which have been mentioned, let not an excessive scrupulosity frighten us from drawing the happy conclusion: and, if we find them not, let us exercise so much wholesome severity against ourselves, as honestly to conclude we are unholy sinners, and must be renewed before we can see the Lord. The conclusion, no doubt, will give you a painful anxiety : but if you was my dearest friend, I could not form a kinder wish for you than that you might be incessantly distressed with it till you are born again. This conclusion will not be always avoidable; the light of eternity will force you upon it; and whether is it better to give way to it now, when it may be to your advantage, or be forced to admit it then, when it will be only a torment?

2. Awake, arise, and betake yourselves in earnest to all the means of grace. Your life, your eternal life is concerned, and therefore it calls for all the ardour and earnestness you are capable of exerting. Accustom yourselves to meditation, converse with yourselves in retirement, and live no longer strangers at home. Read the word of God and other good books, with diligence, attention and self-application. Attend on the public administrations of the gospel, not as a trifler, but as one that sees his eternal all concerned. Shun the tents of sin, the rendezvous of sinners, and associate with those that have experienced the change you want, and can give you proper directions. Prostrate yourself before the God of heaven, confess your sin, implore his mercy, cry to him night and day, and give

him no rest, till the importunity prevail, and you take the kingdom of heaven by violence.

But, after all, acknowledge that it is God that must work in you both to will and to do, and that when you have done all these things you are but unprofitable servants. I do not prescribe these directions as though these means could effect holiness in you; no, they can no more do it than a pen can write without a hand. It is the holy Spirit's province alone to sanctify a degenerate sinner, but he is wont to do it while we are waiting upon him in the use of these means, though our best endeavours give us no title to his grace; but he may justly leave us after all in that state of condemnation and corruption into which we have voluntarily brought ourselves. I go on,

III. And lastly, to urge you to the use of these means, from the consideration mentioned in the text, the absolute necessity of holiness to the enjoyment of heavenly happiness.

Here I would show that holiness is absolutely necessary, and that the consideration of its necessity may strongly enforce the pursuit of it.

The necessity of holiness appears from the unchangeable appointment of heaven, and the nature of things.

1. The unchangeable appointment of God excludes all the unholy from the kingdom of heaven; see 2 Cor. ix. 6; Rev. xxi. 27; Psalm v. 4, 5; 2 Cor. v. 17; Gal. vi. 15. It is most astonishing that many who profess to believe the divine authority of the Scriptures, will yet indulge vain hopes of heaven in opposition to the plainest declarations of eternal truth. But though there were no positive constitution excluding the unholy from heaven, yet,

2. The very nature of things excludes sinners from heaven; that is, it is impossible, in the nature of things, that while they are unholy, they could receive happiness

from the employments and entertainments of the heavenly world. If these consisted in the affluence of those things which sinners delight in here; if its enjoyments were earthly riches, pleasures, and honours; if its employments were the amusements of the present life, then they might be happy there, as far as their sordid natures are capable of happiness. But these trifles have no place in heaven. The felicity of that state consists in the contemplation of the divine perfections, and their displays in the works of creation, providence, and redemption; hence it is described by seeing the Lord, Matt. v. 8, and as a state of knowledge, 1 Cor. xiii. 10–12, in the satisfaction resulting thence. Ps. xvii. 15, and a complacency in God as a portion, Ps. lxxiii. 25, 26, and is perpetual serving and praising the Lord; and hence adoration is generally mentioned as the employ of all the hosts of heaven. These are the entertainments of heaven, and they that cannot find supreme happiness in these, cannot find it in heaven. But it is evident these things could afford no satisfaction to an unholy person. He would pine away at the heavenly feast, for want of appetite for the entertainment; a holy God would be an object of horror rather than delight to him, and his service would be a weariness, as it is now. Hence it appears, that if we do not place our supreme delight in these things here, we cannot be happy hereafter; for there will be no change of dispositions in a future state, but only the perfection of those predominant in us here, whether good or evil. Either heaven must be changed, or the sinner, before he can be happy there. Hence also it appears, that God's excluding such from heaven is no more an act of cruelty than our not admitting a sick man to a feast, who has no relish for the entertainments; or not bringing a blind man into the light of the sun, or to view a beautiful prospect.

We see then that holiness is absolutely necessary; and what a great inducement should this consideration be to pursue it; if we do not see the Lord, we shall never see good. We are cut off at death from all earthly enjoyments, and can no longer make experiments to satisfy our unbounded desires with them; and we have no God to supply their room. We are banished from all the joys of heaven, and how vast, how inconceivably vast is the loss! We are doomed to the regions of darkness for ever, to bear the vengeance of eternal fire, to feel the lashes of a guilty conscience, and to spend an eternity in a horrid intimacy with infernal ghosts; and will we not then rather follow holiness, than incur so dreadful a doom? By the terrors of the Lord, then, be persuaded to break off your sins by righteousness, and follow holiness; *without which no man shall see the Lord.*

SERMON X.

THE MEDIATORIAL KINGDOM AND GLORIES OF JESUS CHRIST.

JOHN xviii. 37.—*Pilate therefore said unto him, Art thou a king then? Jesus answered, Thou sayest that I am a king. To this end was I born, and for this cause came I into the world, that I should bear witness unto the truth.*

KINGS and kingdoms are the most majestic sounds in the language of mortals, and have filled the world with noise, confusions, and blood, since mankind first left the state of nature, and formed themselves into societies. The disputes of kingdoms for superiority have set the world in arms from age to age, and destroyed or enslaved a considerable part of the human race; and the contest is not yet decided. Our country has been a region of peace and tranquility for a long time, but it has not been because the lust of power and riches is extinct in the world, but because we had no near neighbours whose interest might clash with ours, or who were able to disturb us. The absence of an enemy was our sole defence. But now, when the colonies of the sundry European nations on this continent begin to enlarge, and approach towards each other, the scene is changed; now encroachments, depredations, barbarities, and all the terrors of war begin to surround and alarm us. Now our country is invaded and ravaged, and bleeds in a thousand veins. We have already,* so early

* This sermon was preached in Hanover, Virginia, May 9, 1756.

in the year, received alarm upon alarm : and we may expect the alarms to grow louder and louder as the season advances.

These commotions and perturbations have had one good effect upon me, and that is, they have carried away my thoughts of late into a serene and peaceful region, a region beyond the reach of confusion and violence; I mean the kingdom of the Prince of Peace. And thither, my brethren, I would also transport your minds this day, as the best refuge from this boisterous world, and the most agreeable mansion for the lovers of peace and tranquillity. I find it advantageous both to you and myself, to entertain you with those subjects that have made the deepest impression upon my own mind : and this is the reason why I choose the present subject. In my text you hear one entering a claim to a kingdom, whom you would conclude, if you regarded only his outward appearance, to be the meanest and vilest of mankind. To hear a powerful prince, at the head of a victorious army, attended with all the royalties of his character, to hear such an one claim the kingdom he had acquired by force of arms, would not be strange. But here the despised Nazarene, rejected by his nation, forsaken by his followers, accused as the worst of criminals, standing defenceless at Pilate's bar, just about to be condemned and hung on a cross, like a malefactor and a slave; here he speaks in a royal style, even to his judge, *I am a King :* for this purpose *was I born, and for this cause came I into the world.* Strange language indeed to proceed from his lips in these circumstances! But the truth is, a great, a divine personage is concealed under this disguise; and his kingdom is of such a nature, that his abasement and crucifixion were so far from being a hinderance to it, that they were the only way to acquire it. These sufferings were meritorious; and by these he purchased his subjects, and a right to rule them.

The occasion of these words was this: the unbelieving Jews were determined to put Jesus to death as an impostor. The true reason of their opposition to him was, that he had severely exposed their hypocrisy, claimed the character of the Messiah, without answering their expectations as a temporal prince and mighty conqueror; and introduced a new religion, which superseded the law of Moses, in which they had been educated. But this reason they knew would have but little weight with Pilate the Roman governor, who was a heathen, and had no regard to their religion. They therefore bring a charge of another kind, which they knew would touch the governor very sensibly, and that was, that Christ had set himself up as the King of the Jews; which was treason against Cæsar the Roman emperor, under whose yoke they then were. This was all pretence and artifice. They would now seem to be very loyal to the emperor, and unable to bear with any claims inconsistent with his authority; whereas, in truth, they were impatient of a foreign government, and were watching for any opportunity to shake it off. And had Christ been really guilty of the charge they alleged against him, he would have been the more acceptable to them. Had he set himself up as a king of the Jews, in opposition to Cæsar, and employed his miraculous powers to make good his claim, the whole nation would have welcomed him as their deliverer, and flocked round his standard. But Jesus came not to work a deliverance of this kind, nor to erect such a kingdom as they desired, and therefore they rejected him as an impostor. This charge, however, they bring against him, in order to carry their point with the heathen governor. They knew he was zealous for the honour and interest of Cæsar his master; and Tiberius, the then Roman emperor, was so jealous a prince, and kept so many spies over his governors in all

the provinces, that they were obliged to be very circum-
spect, and show the strictest regard for his rights, in order
to escape degradation, or a severer punishment.   It was
this that determined Pilate, in the struggle with his conscience, to condemn the innocent Jesus.   He was afraid
the Jews would inform against him, as dismissing one that
set up as the rival of Cæsar; and the consequence of this
he well knew.   The Jews were sensible of this, and therefore they insist upon this charge, and at length plainly tell
him, *If thou let this man go, thou art not Cæsar's friend.*
Pilate, therefore, who cared but little what innovations
Christ should introduce into the Jewish religion, thought
proper to inquire into this matter, and asks him, " Art thou
the King of the Jews?" dost thou, indeed, claim such a
character, which may interfere with Cæsar's government?
Jesus replies, *My kingdom is not of this world ;* as much
as to say, " I do not deny that I claim a kingdom, but it is
of such a nature, that it need give no alarm to the kings
of the earth.   Their kingdoms are of this world, but
mine is spiritual and divine,* and therefore cannot interfere with theirs.   If my kingdom were of this world, like
theirs, I would take the same methods with them to obtain
and secure it; my servants would fight for me, that I should
not be delivered to the Jews; but now, you see, I use no
such means for my defence, or to raise me to my kingdom :
and therefore you may be assured my kingdom is not from
hence, and can give the Roman emperor no umbrage for
suspicion or uneasiness."   Pilate answers to this purpose :
Thou dost, however, speak of a kingdom; and *art thou a
king then ?* dost thou in any sense claim that character? The

* Domitian, the Roman emperor, being apprehensive that Christ's earthly
relations might claim a kingdom in his right, inquired of them concerning
the nature of his kingdom, and when and where it should be set up. They
replied, " It was not earthly, but heavenly and angelical, and to be set up
at the end of the world."

poor prisoner boldly replies, *Thou sayest that I am a king;*
that is, " Thou hast struck upon the truth : I am indeed a
king, in a certain sense, and nothing shall constrain me to
renounce the title. *To this end was I born, and for this*
cause came I into the world, that I should bear witness to
the truth; particularly to this truth, which now looks so
unlikely, namely, that I am really a king. I was born to a
kingdom and a crown, and came into the world to take possession of my right." This is that good confession which
St. Paul tells us, 1 Tim. vi. 13, our Lord witnessed before
Pontius Pilate. Neither the hopes of deliverance, nor the
terrors of death, could cause him to retract it, or renounce
his claim.

In prosecuting this subject I intend only to inquire into
the nature and properties of the kingdom of Christ. And
in order to render my discourse the more familiar, and to
adapt it to the present state of our country, I shall consider this kingdom in contrast with the kingdoms of the
earth, with which we are better acquainted.

The Scriptures represent the Lord Jesus under a great
variety of characters, which, though insufficient fully to
represent him, yet, in conjunction, assist us to form such
exalted ideas of this great personage as mortals can reach.
He is a Surety, that undertook and paid the dreadful debt
of obedience and suffering, which sinners owed to the
divine justice and law : He is a Priest, a great High Priest,
that once offered himself as a sacrifice for sin; and now
dwells in his native heaven, at his Father's right hand, as
the Advocate and Intercessor of his people : He is a
Prophet, who teaches his church, in all ages, by his word
and spirit : He is the supreme and universal Judge, to
whom men and angels are accountable; and his name is
Jesus, a Saviour, because he saves his people from their
sins. Under these august and endearing characters he is

often represented. But there is one character under which he is uniformly represented, both in the Old and New Testament, and that is, that of a King, a great King, invested with universal authority. And upon his appearance in the flesh, all nature, and especially the gospel-church, is represented as placed under him, as his kingdom. Under this idea the Jews were taught by their prophets to look for him; and it was their understanding these predictions of some illustrious king that should rise from the house of David, in a literal and carnal sense, that occasioned their unhappy prejudices concerning the Messiah as a secular prince and conqueror. Under this idea the Lord Jesus represented himself while upon earth, and under this idea he was published to the world by his apostles. The greatest kings of the Jewish nation, particularly David and Solomon, were types of him: and many things are primarily applied to them, which have their complete and final accomplishment in him alone. It is to him ultimately we are to apply the second psalm : " I have set my King," says Jehovah, " upon my holy hill of Zion. Ask of me, and I shall give thee the heathen for thine inheritance, and the utmost parts of the earth for thy possession :" Psalm ii. 6, 8. If we read the seventy-second Psalm we shall easily perceive that one greater than Solomon is there. " In his days shall the righteous flourish; and abundance of peace so long as the moon endureth. All kings shall fall down before him; all nations shall serve him. His name shall continue for ever; his name shall be continued as long as the sun: and men shall be blessed in him; and all nations shall call him blessed: Psalm lxxxii. 7, 11, 17.

The hundred and tenth Psalm is throughout a celebration of the kingly and priestly office of Christ united. *The Lord*, says David, *said unto my Lord*, unto that divine person who is my Lord, and will also be my son, *Sit thou at my right hand,* in the highest honour and authority, *until I make thine enemies thy footstool.* Rule thou in the midst of thine enemies. *Thy people shall be willing in the day of thy power,* and submit to thee in crowds as numerous as the drops of the morning dew. Ps. cx. 1–3. The evangelical prophet Isaiah is often transported with the foresight of this illustrious King, and the glorious kingdom of his grace:—"Unto us a child is born, unto us a son is given; and the government shall be upon his shoulder; and his name shall be called—the Prince of Peace. Of the increase of his government and peace there shall be no end, upon the throne of David and upon his kingdom, to order it, and to establish it with judgment and with justice from henceforth even for ever." Isa. ix. 6, 7. This is he who is described as another David in Ezekiel's prophecy, "Thus saith the Lord God; Behold, I will take the children of Israel from among the heathen. And I will make them one nation—and one king shall be king to them all, even David my servant shall be king over them." Ezek. xxxvii. 21, 22, 24. This is the kingdom represented to Nebuchadnezzar in his dream, as "a stone cut out without hands, which became a great mountain, and filled the whole earth." And Daniel, in expounding the dream, having described the Babylonian, the Persian, the Grecian, and Roman empires, subjoins, "In the days of these kings," that is, of the Roman emperors, "shall the God of heaven set up a kingdom, which shall never be destroyed; and the kingdom shall not," like the former, "be left to other people; but it shall break in pieces and consume all these kingdoms, and it shall stand for ever." Dan. ii. 34, 35, 44. There is no character which our Lord so often assumed in the days of his flesh as that of the Son of man; and he no doubt alludes to a majestic vision in Daniel, the only place where this character is given him in the Old Testament: "I saw in the night visions," says Daniel, "and behold one like the Son of man came to the Ancient of days, and there was given him dominion, and glory, and a kingdom, that all people, nations, and languages, should serve him; his dominion is an everlasting dominion, which shall not pass away, and his kingdom that which shall not be destroyed," Dan. vii. 13, 14, like the tottering kingdoms of the earth, which are perpetually rising and falling. This is the king that Zechariah refers to when, in prospect of his triumphant entrance into Jerusalem, he calls the inhabitants to give a proper reception to so great a Prince. "Rejoice greatly, O daughter of Zion; shout, O daughter of Jerusalem: behold thy king cometh unto thee," &c. Zech. ix. 9. Thus the prophets conspire to ascribe royal titles and a glorious kingdom to the Messiah. And these early and plain notices of him raised a general expectation of him under this royal character. It was from these prophecies concerning him as a king, that the Jews took occasion, as I observed, to look for the Messiah as a temporal prince; and it was a long time before the apostles themselves were delivered from these carnal prejudices. They were solicitous about posts of honour in that temporal kingdom which they expected he would set up: and even after his resurrection, they cannot forbear asking him, "Lord, wilt thou at this time restore again the kingdom to Israel?" Acts i. 6, that is, "Wilt thou now restore the Jews to their former liberty and independency, and deliver them from their present subjection to the Romans?" It was under this view that Herod was alarmed at his birth, and shed the blood of so many innocents, that he might not escape. He was afraid of him as the heir of David's family and crown, who might dispossess him of the government; nay, he was expected by other nations under the character of a mighty king; and they no doubt learned this notion of him from the Jewish prophecies, as well as their conversation with that people. Hence the Magi, or eastern wise men, when they came to pay homage to him upon his birth, inquired after him in this language,—"Where is he that is born King of the Jews?" Matt. ii. 2. And what is still more remarkable, we are told by two heathen historians, that about the time of his appearance a general expectation of him under this character prevailed through the world. " Many," says Tacitus, " had a persuasion that it was contained in the ancient writings of the priests, that at that very time the east should prevail, and that some descendant from Judah should obtain the universal government."* Suetonius speaks to the same purpose: "An old and constant opinion," says he, " commonly prevailed through all the east, that it was in the fates, that some should rise out of Judea, who should obtain the government of the world."† This royal character Christ himself assumed, even when he conversed among mortals in the humble form of a servant. "The Father," says he, " hath given me power over all flesh." John xvii. 2. Yea, " all power in heaven and earth is given to me," Matt. xxviii. 18. The gospel church which he erected is most commonly called the kingdom of heaven or of God, in the evangelists: when he was about to introduce it, this was the proclamation: "The kingdom of heaven is at hand."

---

* Pluribus persuasio inerat, antiquis sacerdotum literis contineri, eo ipso tempore fore, ut valesceret oriens profectique Judea rerum potirentur. Tacit. Hist. lib. v. cap. 13.

† Percrebuerat oriente toto vetus & constans opinio, esse in fatis, ut eo tempore Judea profecti rerum potirentur. Suet. in Vesp. c. 4.

The sameness of the expectation is remarkably evident, from the sameness of the words in which these two historians express it. *Judea profecti rerum potirentur.* It was not only a common expectation, but it was commonly expressed in the same language.

Under this character also his servants and disciples celebrated and preached him. Gabriel led the song in foretelling his birth to his mother. "He shall be great, and the Lord shall give unto him the throne of his father David; and he shall reign over the house of Jacob for ever: and of his kingdom there shall be no end." Luke i. 32, 33. St. Peter boldly tells the murderers of Christ, " God hath made that same Jesus whom ye have crucified, both Lord and Christ," Acts ii. 36; "and exalted him, with his right hand, to be a Prince and a Saviour." Acts v. 31. And St. Paul repeatedly represents him as advanced "far above principality, and power, and might, and dominion, and every name that is named, not only in this world, but also in that which is to come: and hath put all things under his feet, and gave him to be the head over all things to his church. Eph. i. 21, 22; Phil. ii. 9–11. Yea, to him all the hosts of heaven, and even the whole creation in concert, ascribe "power and strength, and honour, and glory," Rev. v. 12. Pilate the heathen was overruled to give a kind of accidental testimony to this truth, and to publish it to different nations, by the inscription upon the cross in the three languages then most in use, the Latin, Greek, and Hebrew: "This is Jesus of Nazareth, King of the Jews;" and all the remonstrances of the Jews could not prevail upon him to alter it. Finally, it is he that wears "on his vesture, and on his thigh, this name written, King of kings, and Lord of lords," Rev. xix. 16; and as his name is, so is he.

Thus you see, my brethren, by these instances, selected out of many, that the kingly character and dominion of our Lord Jesus runs through the whole Bible. That of a king is his favourite character. in which he glories, and which is the most expressive of his office. And this consideration alone may convince you that this character is of the greatest importance, and worthy of your most attentive regard.

It is the mediatorial kingdom of Christ that is here intended, not that which as God he exercises over all the works of his hand; it is that kingdom which is an empire of grace, and administration of mercy over our guilty world. It is the dispensation intended for the salvation of fallen sinners of our race by the gospel; and on this account the gospel is often called the kingdom of heaven; because its happy consequences are not confined to this earth, but appear in heaven in the highest perfection, and last through all eternity. Hence, not only the Church of Christ on earth, and the dispensation of the gospel, but all the saints in heaven, and that more finished economy under which they are placed, are all included in the kingdom of Christ. Here his kingdom is in its infancy, but in heaven is arrived to perfection; but it is substantially the same. Though the immediate design of this kingdom is the salvation of believers of the guilty race of man, and such are its subjects in a peculiar sense; yet it extends to all worlds, to heaven, and earth, and hell. The whole universe is put under a mediatorial head; but then, as the apostle observes, " he is made head over all things to his church," Eph. i. 22; that is, for the benefit and salvation of his Church. As Mediator he is carrying on a glorious scheme for the recovery of man, and all parts of the universe are interested or concern themselves in this grand event; and therefore they are all subjected to him, that he may so manage them as to promote this end, and baffle and overwhelm all opposition. The elect angels rejoice in so benevolent a design for peopling their mansions, left vacant by the fall of so many of their fellow-angels, with colonies transplanted from our world, from a race of creatures that they had given for lost. And therefore Christ as a Mediator, is made the head of all the heavenly armies, and he employs them as "his ministering spirits, to minister to them that are heirs of salvation." Heb. i. 14. These glorious creatures are always on the wing, ready to discharge his orders in any part of his vast empire, and delight to be employed in the services of his mediatorial kingdom.   This is also an event in which the fallen angels deeply interest themselves; they have united all their force and art for near six thousand years to disturb and subvert his kingdom, and blast the designs of redeeming love; they therefore are all subjected to the control of Christ, and he shortens and lengthens their chains as he pleases, and they cannot go a hair's breadth beyond his permission.   The Scriptures represent our world in its state of guilt and misery as the kingdom of Satan; sinners, while slaves to sin, are his subjects; and every act of disobedience against God is an act of homage to this infernal prince.   Hence Satan is called *the God of this world*, 2 Cor. iv. 4; *the prince of this world*, John xii. 31; *the power of darkness*, Luke xxii. 53; *the prince of the power of the air, the spirit that now worketh in the children of disobedience*. Eph. ii. 3.   And sinners are said *to be taken captive by him at his will*. 2 Tim. ii. 26.   Hence also the ministers of Christ, who are employed to recover sinners to a state of holiness and happiness, are represented as soldiers armed for war; not indeed with carnal weapons, but with those which are spiritual, plain truth arguments, and miracles; and "these are made mighty through God to the pulling down of strongholds, casting down imaginations, and every high thing that exalteth itself against the knowledge of God, and bringing into captivity every thought to the obedience of Christ." 2 Cor. x. 3, 4, 5.   And Christians in general are represented as "wrestling, not with flesh and blood, but against principalities, against powers, against the rulers of the darkness of this world, against spiritual wickedness in high places." Eph. vi. 12. Hence also in particular it is, that the death of Christ is represented not as a defeat, but as an illustrious conquest gained over the powers of hell; because, by this means, a way was opened for the deliverance of sinners from under their power, and restoring them unto liberty and the favour of God. By that strange, contemptible weapon, the cross, and by the glorious resurrection of Jesus, he "spoiled principalities and powers, and made a show of them openly, triumphing over them." Col. ii. 15. "Through death," says the apostle, "he destroyed him that had the power of death; that is, the devil." Heb. ii. 14. Had not Christ by his death offered a propitiatory sacrifice for the sins of men, they would have continued for ever under the tyranny of Satan; but he has purchased liberty, life, and salvation for them; and thus he hath destroyed the kingdom of darkness, and translated multitudes from it into his own gracious and glorious kingdom.

Hence, upon the right of redemption, his mediatorial authority extends to the infernal regions, and he controls and restrains those malignant, mighty, and turbulent potentates, according to his pleasure. Farther, the inanimate world is connected with our Lord's design to save sinners, and therefore is subjected to him as Mediator. He causes the sun to rise, the rain to fall, and the earth to yield her increase, to furnish provision for the subjects of his grace, and to raise, support, and accommodate heirs for his heavenly kingdom. As for the sons of men, who are more immediately concerned in this kingdom, and for whose sake it was erected, they are all its subjects; but then they are of different sorts, according to their characters. Multitudes are rebels against his government; that

is, they do not voluntarily submit to his authority, nor
choose they to do his service: they will not obey his laws.
But they are his subjects notwithstanding; that is, he rules
and manages them as he pleases, whether they will or not.
This power is necessary to carry on successfully his gracious design towards his people; for unless he had the
management of his enemies, they might baffle his under-
takings, and successfully counteract the purposes of his
love.   The kings of the earth, as well as vulgar rebels of
a private character, have often set themselves against his
kingdom, and sometimes they have flattered themselves
they had entirely demolished it.*   But Jesus reigns absolute and supreme over the kings of the earth, and over-
rules and controls them as he thinks proper; and he dis-
poses all the revolutions, the rises and falls of kingdoms
and empires, so as to be subservient to the great designs
of his mediation; and their united policies and powers
cannot frustrate the work which he has undertaken.   But
besides these rebellious, involuntary subjects, he has (bles·
sed be his name!) gained the consent of thousands, and
they have become his willing subjects by their own choice.
They regard his authority, they love his government, they
make it their study to please him, and to do his will.
Over these he exercises a government of special grace
here, and he will make them the happy subjects of the
kingdom of his glory hereafter.   And it is his government
over these that I intend more particularly to consider.
Once more, the kingdom of Jesus is not confined to this
world, but all the millions of mankind in the invisible
world are under his dominion, and will continue so to everlasting ages.   *He is the Lord of the dead and of the liv-*

---

* In the 10th and last Roman persecution, *Dioclesian* had a medal struck
with this inscription, " The Christian name demolished, and the worship
of the gods restored."

ing, Rom. xiv. 9, and has the keys of Hades, the vast invisible world, (including heaven as well as hell) and of death. Rev. i. 18. It is he that turns the key, and opens the door of death for mortals to pass from world to world; it is he that opens the gates of heaven, and welcomes and admits the nations that keep the commandments of God; and it is he that opens the prison of hell, and locks it fast upon the prisoners of divine justice. He will for ever exercise authority over the vast regions of the unseen world, and the unnumbered multitudes of spirits with which they are peopled. You hence see, my brethren, the universal extent of the Redeemer's kingdom; and in this respect how much does it differ from all the kingdoms of the earth? The kingdoms of Great Britain, France, China, Persia, are but little spots of the globe. Our world has indeed been oppressed in former times with what mortals call universal monarchies; such were the Babylonian, the Persian the Grecian, and especially the Roman. But in truth, these were so far from being strictly universal, that a considerable part of the habitable earth was not so much as known to them. But this is an empire strictly universal. It extends over land and sea; it reaches beyond the planetary worlds, and all the luminaries of heaven; nay, beyond the throne of the most exalted archangels, and downward to the lowest abyss of hell. An universal empire in the hands of a mortal is a huge, unwieldy thing; a heap of confusion; a burthen to mankind; and it has always rushed headlong from its glory, and fallen to pieces by its own weight. But Jesus is equal to the immense province of an empire strictly universal; his hand is able to hold the reins; and it is the blessing of our world to be under his administration. He will turn what appears to us scenes of confusion into perfect order, and convince all worlds that he has not taken one wrong step in the whole plan of his infinite government.

The kingdoms of the world have their laws and ordinances, and so has the kingdom of Christ. Look into your Bibles, and there you will find the laws of his kingdom from its first foundation immediately after the fall of man. The laws of human government are often defective or unrighteous ; but these are perfect, holy, just, and good. Human laws are enforced with sanctions : but the rewards and punishments can only affect our mortal bodies, and cannot reach beyond the present life : but the sanctions of these divine laws are eternal, and there shall never be an end to their execution. Everlasting happiness and everlasting misery, of the most exquisite kind and the highest degree, are the rewards and punishments which the immortal King distributes among his immortal subjects; and they become his character, and are adapted to their nature.

Human laws extend only to outward actions, but these laws reach the heart, and the principle of action within. Not a secret thought, not a motion of the soul, is exempted from them. If the subjects of earthly kings observe a decorum in their outward conduct, and give no visible evidence of disloyalty, they are treated as good subjects, though they should be enemies in their hearts. " But Jesus is the Lord of souls ;" he makes his subjects bow their hearts as well as the knee to him. He sweetly commands their thoughts and affections as well as their external practice, and makes himself inwardly beloved as well as outwardly obeyed. His subjects are such on whom he may depend : they are all ready to lay down their lives for him. Love, cordial, unfeigned, ardent love, is the principle of all their obedience : and hence it is, that his commandments are not grievous, but delightful to them.

Other kings have their ministers and officers of state. In like manner Jesus employs the armies of heaven as ministering spirits in his mediatorial kingdom : besides these he has ministers, of an humbler form, who negotiate more immediately in his name with mankind. These are intrusted with the ministry of reconciliation, to beseech men, in his stead, to be reconciled to God. These are appointed to preach his word, to administer his ordinances, and to manage the affairs of his kingdom. This view gives a peculiar dignity and importance to this office. These should be adorned, not like the ministers of earthly courts, with the trappings of gold and silver, but with the beauties of holiness, the ornament of a meek and quiet, zealous and faithful spirit, and a life becoming the gospel of Christ.

Other kings have their soldiers : so all the legions of the elect angels, the armies of heaven, are the soldiers of Jesus Christ, and under his command. This he asserted when he was in such defenceless circumstances, that he seemed to be abandoned by heaven and earth. " I could pray to my father," says he, " and he would send *me more than twelve legions of angels.*" Matt. xxvi. 53. I cannot forbear reading to you one of the most majestic descriptions of this all-conquering hero and his army, which the language of mortality is capable of. Rev. xix. 11. 16. " I saw heaven open, says St. John, "and behold a white horse," an emblem of victory and triumph, "and he that sat upon him was called Faithful and True." How different a character from that of mortal conquerors ! " And in righteousness he doth judge and make war." War is generally a scene of injustice and lawless violence; and those plagues of mankind, we call heroes and warriors, use their arms to gratify their own avarice or ambition, and make encroachments upon others. Jesus, the prince

of peace, makes war too, but it is in righteousness; it is
in the cause of righteousness he takes up arms. The
divine description proceeds: " His eyes were as a flame
of fire; and on his head were many crowns," emblems of
his manifold authority over the various kingdoms of the
world, and the various regions of the universe. "And he
was clothed with a vesture dipped in blood," in the blood of
his enemies; "and his name was called, The Word of
God; and the armies which were in heaven followed him
upon white horses, clothed in fine linen, white and clean :"
the whitest innocence and purity, and the beauties of holiness are, as it were, the uniform, the regimentals of these
celestial armies. "And out of his mouth goeth a sharp
sword, that with it he should smite the nations; and he
shall rule them with a rod of iron ; and he treadeth the
wine-press of the fierceness and wrath of Almighty God;
and he hath on his vesture and on his thigh a name written,
KING OF KINGS, AND LORD OF LORDS." In what manner
the war is carried on between the armies of heaven and
the powers of hell, we know not : but that there is really
something of this kind we may infer from Rev. xii. 7, 9.
" There was war in heaven; Michael and his angels
fought against the dragon; and the dragon fought and
his angels, and prevailed not, neither was their place
found any more in heaven. And the great dragon was
cast out, that old serpent, called the Devil and Satan."

Thus you see all the hosts of heaven are volunteers
under the Captain of our salvation. Nay, he marshals
the stars, and calls them by their names. *The stars in
their courses*, says the sublime Deborah, *fought against
Sisera*, the enemy of God's people. Judges v. 20. Every
part of the creation serves under him, and he can commission a gnat, or a fly, or the meanest insect, to be
the executioner of his enemies. Fire and water, hurri-

canes and earthquakes; earthquakes, which have so lately
shattered so great a part of our globe, now tottering with
age, and ready to fall to pieces, and bury the inhabitants
in its ruins; all these fight under him, and conspire to
avenge his quarrel with the guilty sons of men.   The subjects of his grace in particular are all so many soldiers;
their life is a constant warfare; and they are incessantly
engaged in hard conflict with temptations from without,
and the insurrection of sin from within.   Sometimes, alas!
they fall; but their General lifts them up again, and inspires
them with strength to renew the fight.   They fight most
successfully upon their knees.   This is the most advantageous posture for the soldiers of Jesus Christ; for prayer
brings down recruits from heaven in the hour of difficulty.
They are indeed but poor weaklings and invalids; and yet
they overcome, through the blood of the Lamb; and he
makes them conquerors, yea more than conquerors.   It is
the military character of Christians that gives the apostle
occasion to address them in the military style, like a general at the head of his army. Eph. vi. 10–18.   "Be strong
in the Lord, and in the power of his might.   Put on the
whole armour of God, that ye may be able to stand against
the wiles of the devil.   Stand, therefore, having your loins
girt about with truth, and having on the breastplate of
righteousness, and your feet shod with the preparation of
the gospel of peace; above all, taking the shield of faith,
wherewith ye shall be able to quench all the fiery darts of
the wicked.   And take the helmet of salvation, and the
sword of the Spirit, which is the word of God, praying
always with all prayer and supplication."   The ministers
of the gospel in particular, and especially the apostles, are
soldiers, or officers, in this spiritual army.   Hence St.
Paul speaks of his office in the military style; *I have*, says
he, *fought a good fight*. 2 Tim, iv. 7.   *We war*, says he,

though it be not after the flesh. The humble doctrines of
the cross are our weapons, and these *are mighty* through
God, *to demolish the strongholds of the prince of darkness,*
and to *bring every thought into* a joyful *captivity to the
obedience of faith.* 2 Cor. x. 3–5. *Fight the good fight,*
says he to Timothy. 1 Tim. vi. 12. And again, *thou
therefore endure hardness as a good soldier of Jesus Christ.*
2 Tim, ii. 3. The great design of the gospel ministry is
to rescue enslaved souls from the tyranny of sin and Satan,
and to recover them into a state of liberty and loyalty to
Jesus Christ; or, in the words of the apostle, "to turn
them from darkness to light, and from the power of Satan
unto God." Acts xxvi. 18. Mortals indeed, are very unequal for the conflict; but their success more conspicu-
ously shows that the excellency of the power is of God;"
and many have they subdued, through his strength, to the
obedience of faith, and made the willing captives of the
cross of our divine Immanuel. Other kingdoms are often
founded in blood, and many lives are lost on both sides in
acquiring them. The kingdom of Christ, too, was founded
in blood, but it was the blood of his own heart; life was
lost in the conflict ; but it was his own; his own life lost,
to purchase life for his people. Others have waded to
empire through the blood of mankind, and even of their
own subjects, but Christ shed only his own blood to spare
that of his soldiers. The general devotes his life as a
sacrifice to save his army. The Fabii and Decii of Rome,
who devoted themselves for their country, were but faint
shadows of this divine bravery. Oh! the generous patriotism, the ardent love of the Captain of our salvation!
How amiable does his character appear, in contrast with
that of the kings of the earth! They often sacrifice the
lives of their subjects, while they keep themselves out of
danger, or perhaps are rioting at ease in the pleasures and

luxuries of a court; but Jesus engaged in the conflict with death and hell alone. He stood a single champion in a field of blood. He conquered for his people by falling himself; he subdued his and their enemies by resigning himself to their power. Worthy is such a general to be Commander-in-Chief of the hosts of God, and to lead the armies of heaven and earth! Indeed much blood has been shed in carrying on this kingdom. The earth has been soaked with the blood of the saints; and millions have resisted even unto blood, striving against sin, and nobly laid down their lives for the sake of Christ and a good conscience. Rome has been remarkably the seat of persecution; both formerly under the heathen emperors, and in later times, under a succession of Popes, still more bloody and tyrannical. There were no less than ten general persecutions under the heathen Emperors, through the vast Roman empire, in a little more than two hundred years, which followed one another in a close succession ; in which innumerable multitudes of Christians lost their lives by an endless variety of tortures. And since the church of Rome has usurped her authority, the blood of the saints has hardly ever ceased running in some country or other; though, blessed be God, many kingdoms shook off the yoke at the ever-memorable period of the Reformation, above two hundred years ago : which has greatly weakened that persecuting power. This is that mystical Babylon which was represented to St. John as "drunken with the blood of the saints, and with the blood of the martyrs of Jesus." Rev. xvii. 6. In her was found the blood of prophets, and of saints, and of all that were slain upon the earth. Chap. xviii. 24. And these scenes of blood are still perpetrated in France, that plague of Europe, that has of late stretched her murderous arm across the wide ocean, to disturb us in these regions of peace. There the Pro-

testants are still plundered, chained to the galleys, broken
alive on the torturing wheel, denied the poor favour of
abandoning their country and their all, and flying naked
to beg their bread in other nations.   Thus the harmless
subjects of the Prince of Peace have ever been slaughtered
from age to age, and yet they are represented as triumphant conquerors.   Hear a poor persecuted Paul on this
head : " In tribulation, in distress, in persecution, in nakedness, in peril and sword, we are conquerors, we are more
than conquerors through him that loved us." Rom. viii.
36, 37.   " Thanks be to God, which always causeth us to
triumph in Christ." 2 Cor. ii. 14.   " Whatsoever is born
of God," says the evangelist, " overcometh the world."
1 John v. 4.   Whence came that glorious army which we
so often see in the Revelation ?   We are told " they came
out of great tribulation." Chap. vii. 14.   " And they overcame by the blood of the Lamb, and by the word of their
testimony; and they loved not their lives unto the death."
Chap. xii. 11.   They that suffered tortures and death
under the beast, are said *to have gotten the victory over
him.* Chap. xv., 2.   Victory and triumph sound strange
when thus ascribed;—but the gospel helps us to understand this mystery.   By these sufferings they obtained the
illustrious crown of martyrdom, and peculiar degrees of
glory and happiness through an endless duration.   Their
death was but a short transition from the lowest and more
remote regions of their Redeemer's Kingdom into his immediate presence and glorious court in heaven.   A temporal death is rewarded with an immortal life : and " their
light afflictions which were but for a moment, wrought out
for them a far more exceeding and eternal weight of glory."
2 Cor. iv. 17.   Even in the agonies of torture, their souls
were often filled with such delightful sensations of the
love of God, as swallowed up the sensations of bodily

pain; and a bed of flames was sweeter to them than a bed of roses. Their souls were beyond the reach of all the instruments of torment; and as to their bodies, they shall yet have a glorious resurrection to a blessed immortality. And now, I leave you to judge, whether they or their enemies got the victory in this conflict; and which had most cause to triumph. Like their Master, they rose by falling; they triumphed over their enemies by submitting, like lambs, to their power. If the soldiers of other generals die in the field, it is not in the power of their commanders to reward them. But the soldiers of Jesus Christ, by dying, are, as it were, carried in triumph from the field of blood into the presence of the Master, to receive his approbation, and a glorious crown. Death puts them into a capacity of receiving and enjoying greater rewards than they are capable of in the present state. And thus it appears, that his soldiers always win the day; or, as the apostle expresses it, he causes *them always to triumph;* and not one of them has ever been or ever shall be defeated, however weak and helpless in himself, and however terrible the power of his enemies. And oh! when all these warriors meet at length from every corner of the earth, and, as it were, pass in review before their General in the fields of heaven, with their robes washed in his blood, with palms of victory in their hands, and crowns of glory on their heads, all dressed in uniform with garments of salvation, what a glorious army will they make! and how will they cause heaven to ring with shouts of joy and triumph!

The founders of earthly kingdoms are famous for their heroic actions. They have braved the dangers of sea and land, routed powerful armies, and subjected nations to their will. They have shed rivers of blood, laid cities in ruins, and countries in desolation. These are the exploits which have rendered the Alexanders, the Cæsars, and other conquerors of this world, famous through all nations and ages. Jesus had his exploits too; but they were all of the gracious and beneficent kind. His conquests were so many deliverances, and his victories salvations. He subdued in order to set free; and made captives to deliver them from slavery. He conquered the legions of hell, that seemed let loose at that time, that he might have opportunity of displaying his power over them, and that mankind might be sensible how much they needed a deliverer from their tyranny. He triumphed over the temptations of Satan in the wilderness, by a quotation from his own word. He rescued wretched creatures from his power by an almighty command. He conquered the most inveterate and stubborn diseases, and restored health and vigour with a word of his mouth. He vanquished stubborn souls with the power of his love, and made them his willing people. He triumphed over death, the king of terrors, and delivered Lazarus from the prison of the grave, as an earnest and first-fruit of a general resurrection. Nay, by his own inherent powers he broke the bonds of death, and forced his way to his native heaven. He destroyed him that had the power of death, i. e., the devil, by his own death, and laid the foundation in his own blood for destroying his usurped kingdom, and forming a glorious kingdom of willing subjects redeemed from his tyranny.

The death of some great conquerors, particularly Julius Cæsar, is said to have been prognosticated or attended with prodigies: but none equal to those which solemnized the death of Jesus. The earth trembled, the rocks were burst to pieces, the vail of the temple was rent, the heavens were clothed in mourning, and the dead started into life: and no wonder, when the Lord of nature was expiring upon a cross. He subdued and calmed the stormy

wind, and the boisterous waves of the sea. In short, he
showed an absolute sovereignty over universal nature, and
managed the most unruly elements with a single word.
Other conquerors have gone from country to country, carrying desolation along with them; Jesus went about doing
good. His miraculous powers were but powers of miraculous mercy and beneficence. He could easily have advanced himself to a temporal kingdom, and routed all the
forces of the earth; but he had no ambition of this kind.
He that raised Lazarus from the grave could easily restore
his soldiers to vigour and life, after they had been wounded
or killed. He that fed five thousand with five loaves and
two fishes, could have supported his army with plenty of
provision in the greatest scarcity. He that walked upon the
boisterous ocean and enabled Peter to do the same, could
easily have transported his forces from country to country,
without the conveyance of ships. Nay, he was capable by
his own single power to have gained universal conquest.
What could all the armies of the earth have done against
Him, who struck an armed company down to the earth
with only a word of his mouth? But these were not the
victories he affected; Victories of grace, deliverances for
the oppressed, salvation for the lost; these were his heroic
actions. He glories in his being mighty to save. Isa.
lxiii. 1. When his warm disciples made a motion that he
should employ his miraculous powers to punish the Sama-
ritans who ungratefully refused him entertainment, he rebuked them, and answered like the Prince of Peace, *The
son of Man is not come to destroy men's lives, but to save.*
Luke ix. 56. *He came to seek and to save that which was
lost.* Luke xix. 10. Oh how amiable a character this!
How much more lovely the Saviour of sinners, the Deliverer of souls, than the enslavers and destroyers of mankind; which is the general character of the renowned he-

roes of our world. Who has ever performed such truly
heroic and brave actions as this almighty conqueror! He
has pardoned the most aggravated crimes, in a consistency
with the honours of the divine government: he has delivered an innumerable multitude of immortal souls from
the tyranny of sin and the powers of hell, set the prisoners
free, and brought them into the liberty of the Son of God;
he has peopled heaven with redeemed slaves, and advanced
them to royal dignity. "All his subjects are kings."
Rev. i. 6. "To him that overcometh," says he, "will I
grant to set with me in my throne, even as I also overcame,
and am sit down with my Father in his throne," Rev. iii.
21. They shall be adorned with royal robes and crowns
of unfading glory. They are advanced to empire over
their lusts and passions, and all their enemies. Who ever
gave such encouragement to his soldiers as this, *If we
suffer with him, we shall also reign with him?* 2 Tim. ii.
12. What mortal general could bestow immortality and
perfect happiness upon his favourites? But these boundless blessings Jesus has to bestow. In human governments merit is often neglected, and those who serve their
country best, are often rewarded with degradation. But
none have ever served the King of kings in vain. The
least good action, even the giving a cup of water to one
of his necessitous saints, shall not pass unrewarded in his
government.

Other kings have their arms, their swords, their cannon,
and other instruments of destruction; and with these they
acquire and defend their dominions. Jesus, our king, has
his arms too; but oh! of how different a kind! The
force of evidence and conviction in his doctrine, attested
with miracles, the energy of his dying love, the gentle, and
yet efficacious influence of his holy Spirit; these are the
weapons with which he conquered the world. His gospel

is the great magazine from whence his apostles, the first founders of his kingdom, drew their arms; and with these they subdued the nations to the obedience of faith. "The gospel," says St. Paul, "is the power of God unto salvation." Rom. i. 16. The humble doctrines of the cross became almighty, and, bore down all before them, and after a time subdued the vast Roman empire which had subdued the world. The holy Spirit gave edge and force to these weapons; and, blessed be God, though they are quite impotent without his assistance, yet when he concurs they are still successful. Many stubborn sinners have been unable to resist the preaching of Christ crucified: they have found him indeed the power of God. And is it not astonishing, that any one should be able to stand it out against his dying love, and continue the enemy of his cross? "I," says he, "if I be lifted up from the earth," *i. e.,* if I be suspended on the cross, "will draw all men unto me." John xii. 32. You see he expected his cross would be an irresistible weapon. And oh! blessed Jesus, who can see thee expiring there in agonies of torture and love; who can see thy blood gushing in streams from every vein; who can hear thee there, and not melt into submission at thy feet! Is there one heart in this assembly proof against the energy of this bleeding, agonizing, dying love? Methinks such a sight must kindle a correspondent affection in your hearts towards him, and it is an exploit of wickedness, it is the last desperate effort of an impenetrable heart, to be able to resist.

Other conquerors march at the head of their troops, with all the ensigns of power and grandeur, and their forces numerous, inured to war, and well armed; and from such appearances and preparations, who is there but what expects victory? But see the despised Nazarene, without riches, without arms, without forces, conflicting with the united powers of earth and hell; or see a company of poor fishermen and a tent-maker, with no other powers but those of doing good, with no other arms but those of reason, and the strange, unpopular doctrines of a crucified Christ! see the professed followers of a Master that was hung like a malefactor and a slave, see these men marching out to encounter the powers of darkness, the whole strength of the Roman empire, the lusts, prejudices, and interests of all nations, and travelling from country to country, without guards, without friends, exposed to insult and contempt, to the rage of persecution, to all manner of torture and tormented deaths which earth or hell could invent: see this little army marching into the wide world, in these circumstances, and can you expect they will have any success? Does this appear a promising expedition? No: human reason would forebode they will soon be cut in pieces, and the Christian cause buried with them. But these unpromising champions, with the aid of the Holy Spirit, conquered the world, and spread the religion of the crucified Jesus among all nations. It is true they lost their lives in the cause, like brave soldiers; but the cause did not die with them. Their blood proved the seed of the church. Their cause is immortal and invincible. Let devils in hell, let Heathens, Jews, and Mahometans, let Atheists, Freethinkers, Papists, and persecutors of every character do their worst; still this cause will live in spite of them. All the enemies of Christ will be obliged to confess at last, with Julian the apostate Roman emperor, who exerted all his art to abolish Christianity; but when mortally wounded in battle, outrageously sprinkled his blood towards heaven, and cried out, *Vicisti, O Galilæe!* "Thou hast conquered, O Galilean!" Yes, my brethren, Jesus, the Prophet of Galilee, will push his conquest from country to country, until all nations submit to him. And, blessed be his name, his victorious arm has reached to us in these ends of the earth : here he has subdued some obstinate rebels, and made their reluctant souls willingly bow in affectionate homage to him. And may I not produce some of you as the trophies of his victory? Has he not rooted out the enmity of your carnal minds, and sweetly constrained you to the most affectionate obedience? Thus, blessed Jesus! thus go on conquering and to conquer. *Gird thy sword upon thy thigh, O most mighty!* and in thy glory and majesty ride prosperously through our land, and make this country a dutiful province of the dominion of thy grace. My brethren, should we all become his willing subjects, he would no longer suffer the perfidious slaves of France, and their savage allies, to chastise and punish us for our rebellion against him; but *peace should again run down like a river, and righteousness like a mighty stream.*

The kingdoms of the world have their rise, their progress, perfection, declension, and ruin. And in these things, the kingdom of Christ bears some resemblance to them, excepting that it shall never have an end.

Its rise was small at first, and it has passed through many revolutions in various ages. It was first founded in the family of Adam, but in about 1,600 years, the space between the creation and the flood, it was almost demolished by the wickedness of the world; and at length confined to the little family of Noah. After the flood, the world soon fell into idolatry, but, that this kingdom of Christ might not be destroyed quite, it was erected in the family of Abraham ; and among the Jews it continued until the coming of Christ in the flesh. This was indeed but the infancy of his kingdom, and indeed is seldom called by that name. It is the gospel constitution that is represented as the kingdom of Christ, in a special sense.

This was but very small and unpromising at first. When its founder was dying upon Calvary, and all his followers had forsaken him and fled, who would have thought it would ever have come to any thing, ever have recovered? But it revived with him; and when he furnished his apostles with gifts and graces for their mission, and sent them forth to increase his kingdom, it made its progress through the world with amazing rapidity, notwithstanding it met with very early and powerful opposition. The Jews set themselves against it, and raised persecutions against its ministers, wherever they went. And presently the tyrant Nero employed all the power of the Roman empire to crush them. Peter, Paul, and thousands of the Christians fell a prey to his rage, like sheep for the slaughter. This persecution was continued under his successors with but little interruption, for about two hundred years.

But under all these pressures, the church bore up her head; yea, the more she was trodden, the more she spread and flourished; and at length she was delivered from oppression by Constantine the Great, about the year 420. But now she had a more dangerous enemy to encounter, I mean prosperity; and this did her much more injury than all the persecutions of her enemies. Now the kingdom of Christ began to be corrupted with heresies; the ministry of the gospel, formerly the most dangerous post in the world, now became a place of honour and profit, and men began to thrust themselves into it from principles of avarice and ambition; superstition and corruption of morals increased; and at length the Bishop of Rome set up for universal head of the church in the year 606; and gradually the whole monstrous system of popery was formed and established, and continued in force for near a thousand years. The kingdom of Christ was now at a low ebb; and tyranny and superstition reigned under that name over the greatest part of the Christian world. Nevertheless, our Lord still had his witnesses. The Waldenses and Albigenses, John Huss, and Jerome of Prague, and Wickliffe in England, opposed the torrent of corruption; until at length, Luther, Calvin, Zuinglius, and several others, were made the honoured instruments of introducing the Reformation from popery; when sundry whole kingdoms, which had given their power to the beast, and particularly our mother-country, shook off the papal authority, and admitted the pure light of the gospel. Since that time the kingdom of Christ has struggled hard, and it has lost ground in several countries; particularly in France, Poland, Bohemia, &c., where there once were many Protestant churches; but they are now in ruins. And, alas! those countries that still retain the reformed religion, have too generally reduced it into a mere formality: and it has but little influence upon the hearts and lives even of its professors. Thus we find the case remarkable among us. This gracious kingdom makes but little way in Virginia. The calamities of war and famine cannot, alas! draw subjects to it; but we seem generally determined to perish in our rebellion rather than submit. Thus it has been in this country from its first settlement; and how long it will continue in this situation is unknown to mortals: however, this we may know, it will not be so always. We have the strongest assurances that Jesus will yet take to him his strong power, and reign in a more extensive and illustrious manner than he has ever yet done; and that the kingdoms of the earth shall yet become the *kingdoms of our Lord and of his Christ.* There are various parts of the heathen world where the gospel has never yet been; and the Jews have never yet been converted as a nation; but both the calling of the Jews and the fulness of the Gentiles, you will find plainly foretold in the 11th chapter of the Romans; and it is, no doubt, to render the accomplishment of this event the more conspicuous, that the Jews, who are dispersed all over the world, have, by a strange, unprecedented, and singular providence, been kept a distinct people to this day, for 1,700 years; though all other nations have been so mixed and blended togther, who were not half so much dispersed into different countries, that their distinct original cannot be traced. Posterity shall see this glorious event in some happy future period. How far it is from us I will not determine; though, upon some grounds, I apprehend it is not very remote. I shall live and die in the unshaken belief that our guilty world shall yet see glorious days. Yes, my brethren, this despised gospel, that has so little effect in our age and country, shall yet shine like lightning, or like the sun, through all the dark regions of the earth. It shall triumph over Heathenism, Mahometanism, Judaism, Popery, and all those dangerous errors that have infected the Christian church. This gospel, poor negroes, shall yet reach your countrymen, whom you left behind you in Africa, in darkness and the shadow of death, and bless your eyes with the light of salvation : and the Indian savages, that are now ravaging our country, shall yet be transformed into lambs and doves by the gospel of peace. The scheme of Providence is not yet completed, and much remains to be accomplished of what God has spoken by his prophets, to ripen the world for the universal judgment; but when all these things are finished, then proclamation shall be made throughout all nature, " That time shall be no more:" then the Supreme Judge, the same Jesus that ascended the cross, will ascend the throne, and review the affairs of time : then will he put an end to the present course of nature, and the present form of administration. Then shall heaven and hell be filled with their respective inhabitants: then will time close, and eternity run on in one uniform tenor, without end. But the kingdom of Christ, though altered in its situation and form of government, will not then come to a conclusion. His kingdom is strictly the kingdom of heaven; and at the end of this world, his subjects will only be removed from these lower regions into a more glorious country, where they and their King shall live together for ever in the most endearing intimacy; where the noise and commotions of this restless world, the revolutions and perturbations of kingdoms, the terrors of war and persecution, shall no more reach them; but all will be perfect peace, love, and happiness, through immeasurable duration. This is the last and most illustrious state of the kingdom of Christ, now so small and weak in appearance: this is the final grand result of his administration: and it will appear to admiring worlds wisely planned, gloriously executed, and perfectly finished.

What conqueror ever erected such a kingdom? What subjects so completely, so lastingly happy, as those of the blessed Jesus?

SERMON XI.

THINGS UNSEEN TO BE PREFERRED TO THINGS SEEN.

2 Cor. iv. 18.—*While we look not at the things which are seen, but at the things which are not seen; for the things which are seen are temporal: but the things which are not seen are eternal.*

AMONG all the causes of the stupid unconcernedness of sinners about religion, and the feeble endeavours of saints to improve in it, there is none more common or more effectual, than their not forming a due estimate of the things of time, in comparison of those of eternity. Our present affairs engross all our thoughts, and exhaust all our activity, though they are but transitory trifles; while the awful realities of the future world are hid from our eyes by the veil of flesh and the clouds of ignorance. Did these break in upon our minds in all their almighty evidence and tremendous importance, they would annihilate the most majestic vanities of the present state, obscure the glare of earthly glory, render all its pleasures insipid, and give us a noble sensibility under all its sorrows. A realizing view of these would shock the libertine in his thoughtless career, tear off the hypocrite's mask, and inflame the devotion of the languishing saints. The concern of mankind would then be how they might make a safe exit out of this world, and not how they may live happy in it. Present pleasure and pain would be swallowed up in the prospect of everlasting happiness or misery hereafter.

Eternity, awful eternity, would then be our serious contemplation. The pleasures of sin would strike us with horror, if they issue in eternal pain, and our present afflictions, however tedious and severe, would appear but light and momentary, if they work out for us *a far more exceeding and eternal weight of glory.*

These were the views the apostle had of things, and these their effects upon him. He informs us in this chapter of his unwearied zeal to propagate the gospel amidst all the hardships and dangers that attend the painful discharge of his ministry. Though he bore about in his body the dying of the Lord Jesus, though he was always delivered unto death for Jesus' sake, yet he fainted not; and this was the prospect that animated him, that his "light affliction, which was but for a moment, would work out for him a far more exceeding and eternal weight of glory." When we view his sufferings absolutely, without any reference to eternity, they were very heavy and of many years' continuance; and when he represents them in this view, how moving is the relation! see 2 Cor. xi. 23–29. But when he views them in the light of eternity, and compared with their glorious issues, they sink into nothing; then scourging, stoning, imprisonment, and all the various deaths to which he was daily exposed, are but light, trifling afflictions, hardly worth naming; then a series of uninterrupted sufferings for many years are but afflictions that endure for a moment. And when he views a glorious futurity, human language cannot express the ideas he has of the happiness reserved for him; it is "a far more exceeding and eternal weight of glory;" a noble sentiment! and expressed in the sublimest manner the language of mortals can admit of.

It is glory, in opposition to affliction; a weight of glory, in opposition to light affliction; a massy, oppressive blessedness, which it requires all the powers of the soul, in their full exertion, to support: and in opposition to affliction for a moment, it is eternal glory: to finish all, it is a *far more exceeding glory.** What greater idea can be grasped by the human mind, or expressed in the feeble language of mortality! Nothing but feeling that weight of glory could enlarge his conception: and nothing but the dialect of heaven could better express it. No wonder that, with this view of things, " he should reckon that the sufferings of the present life are not worthy to be compared with the glory that shall be revealed." Rom. viii. 18.

The apostle observes, that he formed this estimate of things, while he looked not at the "things which are seen, but at those which are not seen." By the things that are seen, are meant the present life, and all the things of time; all the pleasures and pains, all the labours, pursuits, and amusements of the present state. By the things that are not seen, are intended all the invisible realities of the eternal world; all the beings, the enjoyments and sufferings that lie beyond the reach of human sight; as the great Father of spirits, the joys of paradise, and the punishment of hell. We look on these invisible things, and not on those that are seen. This seems like a contradiction; but is it easily solved by understanding this act, described by looking, to be the act not of the bodily eye, but of faith and enlightened reason. Faith is defined by this apostle to be "the substance of things hoped for, the evidence of things not seen." Heb. xi. 1. And it is the apostle's chief design in that chapter, to give instances of the surprising efficacy of such a realizing belief of eternal, invisible things; see particularly *ver.* 10, 13, 14, 16, 25, 26, 27.

---

* The original far surpasses the best translation. The adjective absolute [το ἐλαφρὸν τῆς θλίψεως] is very significant; and καθ᾽ ὑπερβολὴν εἰς ὑπερβολὴν is in imitable in any language.

Hence to look not at visible, but at invisible things, signifies that the apostle made the latter the chief objects of his contemplations, that he was governed in the whole of his conduct by the impression of eternal things, and not by the present; that he formed his maxims and schemes from a comprehensive survey of futurities, and not from a partial view of things present; and, in short, that he had acted as an expectant of eternity, and not as an everlasting inhabitant of this wretched world. This he elsewhere expresses in equivalent terms, "We walk by faith, and not by sight." 2 Cor. v. 7.

Further, he assigns a reason why he had a greater regard to invisible things than visible in the regulating of his conduct; "for the things which are seen, are temporal, but the things which are not seen," says he, "are eternal." An important reason indeed! Eternity annexed to a trifle would advance it into infinite importance, but when it is the attribute of the most perfect happiness, or of the most exquisite misery, then it transcends all comparison: then all temporal happiness and misery, however great and long-continued, shrink into nothing, are drowned and lost, like the small drop of a bucket in the boundless ocean.

My present design, and the contents of the text, prescribe to me the following method:

I. I shall give you a comparative view of visible and invisible things, that you may see the trifling nature of the one, and the importance of the other. This I choose to do under one head, because by placing these two classes of things in an immediate opposition, we may the more easily compare them, and see their infinite disparity. And,

II. I shall show you the great and happy influence a suitable impression of the superior importance of invisible to visible things would have upon us.

I. I shall give you a comparative view of visible and invisible things; and we may compare visible and invisible things, as to their intrinsic value, and as to their duration.

1. As to their intrinsic value, and in this respect the disparity is inconceivable.

This I shall illustrate in the two comprehensive instances of pleasure and pain. To shun the one, and obtain the other, is the natural effort of the human mind. This is its aim in all its endeavours and pursuits. The innate desire of happiness and aversion to misery are the two great springs of all human activity: and, were these springs relaxed or broken, all business would cease, all activity would stagnate, and universal torpor would seize the world. And these principles are co-existent with the soul itself, and will continue in full vigour in a future state. Nay, as the soul will then be matured, and all its powers arrived to their complete perfection, this eagerness after happiness, and aversion to misery, will be also more quick and vigorous. The soul in its present state of infancy, like a young child, or a man enfeebled and stupified by sickness, is incapable of very deep sensations of pleasure and pain; and hence an excess of joy, as well as sorrow, has sometimes dissolved its feeble union with the body. On this account we are incapable of such degrees of happiness or misery from the things of this world as beings of more lively sensations might receive from them; and much more are we incapable of the happiness or misery of the future world, until we have put on immortality. We cannot see God and live. Should the glory of heaven blaze upon us in all its insuperable splendour, it would overwhelm our feeble nature; we could not support such a weight of glory. And one twinge of the agonies of hell would dislodge the soul from its earthly mansion:

one pang would convulse and stupify it, were not its
powers strengthened by the separation from the body.
But in the future world all the powers of the soul will be
mature and strong, and the body will be clothed with immortality; the union between them after the resurrection
will be inseparable, and able to support the most oppressive weight of glory, or the most intolerable load of
torment.   Hence it follows that pleasure and pain include
all that we can desire or fear in the present or future
world; and therefore a comparative view of present and
future pleasure and pain is sufficient to enable us to form
a due estimate of visible and invisible things.   By present
pleasure I mean all the happiness we can receive from
present things, as from riches, honours, sensual gratifications, learning, and intellectual improvements, and all the
amusements and exercises of this life.   And by future
pleasure, or the pleasure which results from invisible
things, I mean all the fruitions and enjoyments in which
heavenly happiness consists.   By present pain, I intend
all the uneasiness which we can receive from the things
of the present life; as poverty, losses, disappointments,
bereavements, sickness, and bodily pains.   And by future
pain, I mean all the punishments of hell; as banishment
from God, and a privation of all created blessings, the
agonizing reflections of a guilty conscience, the horrid
company and exprobations of infernal ghosts, and the
torture of infernal flames.

Now let us put these in the balance, and the one will
sink into nothing, and the other rise into infinite importance.

Temporal things are of a contracted nature, and not
adequate to the capacities of the human soul; but eternal
things are great, and capable of communicating all the
happiness and misery which it can receive.   The soul in

its present state is not capable of such degrees of happiness and misery as it will be in the future, when it dwells among invisible realities. All that pleasure and pain which we receive from things that are seen, are intermingled with some ingredients of a contrary nature; but those proceeding from things that are not seen, are pure and unmingled.

1. Visible things are not equal to the capacities of the human soul. This little spark of being, the soul, which lies obscured in this prison of flesh, gives frequent discoveries of surprising powers; its desires in particular, have a kind of infinity. But all temporary objects are mean and contracted; they cannot afford it a happiness equal to its capacity, nor render it as miserable as its capacity of suffering will bear. Hence, in the greatest affluence of temporal enjoyments, in the midst of honours, pleasures, riches, friends, &c., it still feels a painful void within, and finds an unknown something wanting to complete its happiness. Kings have been unhappy upon their thrones, and all their grandeur has been but majestic misery. So Solomon found it, who had opportunity and curiosity to make the experiment; and this is his verdict upon all earthly enjoyments, after the most impartial trial: "Vanity of vanities," saith the Preacher, "vanity of vanities; all is vanity and vexation of spirit." On the other hand, the soul may possess some degree of happiness, under all the miseries it is capable of suffering from external and temporal things. Guilt indeed denies it this support; but if there be no intestine broils, no anguish resulting from its own reflections, not all the visible things can render it perfectly miserable; its capacity of suffering is not put to its utmost stretch. This has been attested by the experience of multitudes who have suffered for righteousness' sake. But oh, when we take a survey of

invisible things, we find them all great and majestic, not only equal but infinitely superior to the most enlarged powers of the human and even of the angelic nature. In the eternal world the great Invisible dwells, and there he acts with his own immediate hand. It is he that immediately communicates happiness through the heavenly regions; and it is his immediate breath that, like a stream of brimstone, kindles the flames of hell; whereas, in the present world, he rarely communicates happiness, and inflicts punishment, but by the instrumentality of creatures; and it is impossible the extremes of either should be communicated through this channel. This the infinite God alone can do, and, though in the future world he will use his creatures to heighten the happiness or misery of each other, yet he will have a more immediate agency in them himself. He will communicate happiness immediately from himself, the infinite fountain of it, into the vessels of mercy; and he will immediately show his wrath, and make his power known upon the vessels of wrath. I may add, that those creatures, angels and devils, which will be the instruments of happiness or misery to the human soul in the invisible world, are incomparably more powerful than any in this, and consequently capable of contributing more to our pleasure or pain. And let me also observe, that all the objects about which our faculties will be employed then, will be great and majestic; whereas, at present, we grovel among little sordid things. The objects of our contemplation will then be either the unveiled glories of the divine nature, and the naked wonders of creation, providence, and redemption; or the terrors of divine justice, the dreadful nature and aggravations of our sin, the horrors of everlasting punishment, &c. And since this is the case, how little should we regard the things that are seen, in comparison of them that are not seen? But though visible things were adequate to our present capacities, yet they are not to be compared with the things that are not seen; because,

2. The soul is at present in a state of infancy, and incapable of such degrees of pleasure or pain as it can bear in the future world. The enjoyments of this life are like the playthings of children; and none but childish souls would trifle with them, or fret and vex themselves or one another about them; but the invisible realities before us are manly and great, and such as an adult soul ought to concern itself with. The soul in another world can no more be happy or miserable from such toys, than men can be happy or wretched in the possession or loss of the baubles of children; it will then demand great things to give it pleasure or pain. The apostle illustrates this matter in this manner: 1 Cor. xiii. 9, 10, 11. How foolish is it then to be chiefly governed by these puerilities, while we neglect the manly concern of eternity, that can make our souls perfectly happy or miserable, when their powers are come to perfection!

3. And lastly, All the happiness and misery of the present state, resulting from things that are seen, are intermingled with contrary ingredients. We are never so happy in this world as to have no uneasiness; in the greatest affluence we languish for want of some absent good, or grieve under some incumbent evil. On the other hand, we are never so miserable as to have no ingredient of happiness. When we labour under a thousand calamities, we may still see ourselves surrounded with, perhaps, an equal number of blessings. And where is there a wretch so miserable as to endure simple, unmingled misery, without one comfortable ingredient? But in the invisible world there is an eternal separation made between good and evil, pleasure and pain; and they shall never mingle

more. In heaven, the rivers of pleasure flow untroubled with a drop of sorrow; in hell, there is not a drop of water to mitigate the fury of the flame. And who then would not prefer the things that are not seen to those that are seen? Especially if we consider,

4. The infinite disparity between them as to duration. This is the difference particularly intended in the text; *the things that are seen are temporal; but the things that are not seen are eternal.*

The transitoriness of visible things implies, both that the things themselves are perishable, and they may soon leave us; and that our residence among them is temporary, and we must soon leave them.

And the eternity of invisible things implies quite the contrary, that the things themselves are of endless duration; and that we shall always exist to receive happiness or misery from them.

Before we illustrate these instances of disparity, let us take a view of time and eternity in themselves, and as compared to one another.

Time is the duration of creatures in the present state. It commenced at the creation, and near six thousand years of it are since elapsed; and how much of it yet remains we know not. But this we know, that the duration of the world itself is as nothing in comparison of eternity. But what is our duration compared with the duration even of this world? It is but a span, a hair's-breadth; sixty, seventy, or eighty years, is generally the highest standard of human life, and it is by far the smallest number of mankind that arrives to these periods. The most of them die like a flower blasted in the morning, or at noon; and we have more reason to expect it will be our fate than to hope the contrary. Now the span of time we enjoy in life is all our time; we have no more property in the rest

of it than in the years before the flood. All beside is
eternity. "Eternity!" We are alarmed at the sound!
Lost in the prospect! Eternity with respect to God, is a
duration without beginning as well as without end. Eternity, as it is the attribute of human nature, is a duration
that had a beginning but shall never have an end. This
is inalienably entailed upon us poor, dying worms: and let
us survey our inheritance. Eternity! it is a duration that
excludes all number and computation; days, and months,
and years, yea, and ages, are lost in it, like drops in the
ocean. Millions of millions of years, as many years as
there are sands on the sea-shore, or particles of dust in
the globe of the earth, and these multiplied to the highest
reach of number, all these are nothing to eternity. They
do not bear the least imaginable proportion to it; for these
will come to an end, as certain as day; but eternity will
never, never come to an end. It is a line without end;
it is an ocean without a shore. Alas! what shall I
say of it! It is an infinite, unknown something, that
neither human thought can grasp, nor human language
describe.

Now place time in comparison with eternity, and what
is it? It shrinks into nothing, and less than nothing.
What then is that little span of time in which we have
any property? Alas! it is too diminutive a point to be
conceived. Indeed, properly speaking, we can call no
part of time our own but the present moment, this fleeting
now: future time is uncertain, and we may never enjoy it;
the breath we now respire may be our last; and as to our
past time, it is gone, and will never be ours again. Our
past days are dead and buried, though perhaps guilt, their
ghost, may haunt us still. And what is a moment to eternity? The disparity is too great to admit of comparison.

Let me now resume the former particulars, implied

in the transitoriness of visible and the eternity of invisible things.

Visible things are perishable and may soon leave us. When we think they are ours, they often fly from our embrace. Riches may vanish into smoke and ashes by an accidental fire. We may be thrown down from the pinnacle of honour, and sink the lower into disgrace. Sensual pleasures often end in satiety and disgust, or in sickness and death. Our friends are torn from our bleeding hearts by the inexorable hand of death. Our liberty and property may be wrested from us by the hand of tyranny, oppression, or fraud. In a word, what do we enjoy but we may lose? On the other hand, our miseries here are temporary; the heart receives many a wound, but it heals again. Poverty may end in riches; a clouded character may clear up, and from disgrace we may rise to honour; we may recover from sickness; and if we lose one comfort, we may obtain another. But in eternity every thing is everlasting and unchangeable. Happiness and misery are both of them without end; and the subjects of both well know that this is the case. It is this perpetuity that finishes the happiness of the inhabitants of heaven; the least suspicion of an end would intermingle itself with all their enjoyments, and embitter them: and the greater the happiness, the greater the anxiety at the expectation of losing it. But oh, how transporting for the saints on high to look forward through the succession of eternal ages, with an assurance that they shall be happy through them all, and that they shall feel no change but from glory to glory! On the other hand, this is the bitterest ingredient in the cup of divine displeasure in the future state, that the misery is eternal. Oh, with what horror does that despairing cry, For ever, for ever, for ever! echo through the vaults of hell? Eternity is such an important attribute, that it gives infinite weight to things that would be insignificant, were they temporary. A small degree of happiness, if it be eternal, exceeds the greatest degree that is transitory; and a small degree of misery that is everlasting, is of greater importance than the greatest degree that soon comes to an end. Would you rather endure the most painful tortures that nature can bear for a moment, than an eternal toothache or headache? Again, should we consider all the ingredients and causes of future happiness and misery, we should find them all everlasting. The blessed God is an inexhaustible, perennial fountain of bliss; his image can never be erased from the hearts of glorified spirits; the great contemplation will always be obvious to them; and they will always exist as the partakers and promoters of mutual bliss. On the other hand, in hell the worm of conscience dieth not, and the fire is not quenched; divine justice is immortal; malignant spirits will always exist as mutual tormentors, and their wicked habits will never be extirpated.

And now, need I offer any thing farther to convince you of the superior importance of invisible and eternal to visible and temporary things? Can a rational creature be at a loss to choose in so plain a case? Can you need any arguments to convince you that an eternity of the most perfect happiness is rather to be chosen than a few years of sordid, unsatisfying delight? Or that the former should not be forfeited for the sake of the latter? Have you any remaining scruples, whether the little anxieties and mortifications of a pious life are more intolerable than everlasting punishment? Oh! it is a plain case: what then mean an infatuated world, who lay out all their concern on temporal things, and neglect the important affairs of eternity? Let us illustrate this matter by supposition. Suppose a bird were to pick up and carry away a grain of sand or dust from the globe of this earth once in a thousand years, till it should be at length wholly carried away; the duration which this would take up appears a kind of eternity to us. Now suppose it were put to our choice, either to be happy during this time, and miserable ever after, or to be miserable during this time, and happy ever after, which would you choose? Why, though this duration seems endless, yet he would be a fool that would not make the latter choice; for, oh, oh! behind this vast duration, there lies an eternity, which exceeds it infinitely more than this duration exceeds a moment. But we have no such seemingly puzzling choice as this; the matter with us stands thus—Will you choose the little sordid pleasures of sin that may perhaps not last an hour, at most, not many years, rather than everlasting pleasure of the sublimest kind? Will you rather endure intolerable torment for ever, than painfully endeavour to be holy? What does your conduct, my brethren, answer to these questions? If your tongues reply, they will perhaps for your credit give a right answer; but what say your prevailing disposition and common practice? are you not more thoughtful for time than eternity? more concerned about visible vanities than invisible realities? If so, you make a fool's choice indeed.

But let it be further considered, that the transitoriness of visible things may imply that we must ere long be removed from them. Though they were immortal it would be nothing to us, since we are not so in our present state. Within a few years at most, we shall be beyond the reach of all happiness and misery from temporal things.

But when we pass out of this transitory state, we enter upon an everlasting state. Our souls will always exist, exist in a state of unchangeable, boundless happiness or

misery. It is but a little while since we came into being
out of a state of eternal non-existence; but we shall never
relapse into that state again. These little sparks of being
shall never be extinguished! they will survive the ruins
of the world, and kindle into immortality. When millions
of millions of ages are past, we shall still be in existence:
and oh! in what unknown region? In that of endless
bliss or of interminable misery? Be this the most anxious
inquiry of our lives.

Seeing then we must soon leave this world, and all its
joys and sorrows, and seeing we must enter on an unchangeable, everlasting state of happiness or misery, be it
our chief concern to end our present pilgrimage well. It
matters but little whether we lie easy or not during this
night of existence, if so be we awake in eternal day. It
is but a trifle, hardly worth a thought, whether we be
happy or miserable here, if we be happy for ever hereafter.
What then mean the bustle and noise of mankind about the
things of time? Oh, sirs, eternity! awful, all important
eternity! is the only thing that deserves a thought. I come,

II. To show the great and happy influence a suitable
impression of the superior importance of invisible to visible
things would have upon us. This I might exemplify in a
variety of instances with respect to saints and sinners.

When we are tempted to any unlawful pleasures, how
would we shrink away with horror from the pursuit, had
we a due sense of the misery incurred, and the happiness
forfeited by it!

When we find our hearts excessively eager after things
below, had we a suitable view of eternal things, all these
things would shrink into trifles hardly worth a thought,
much less our principal concern.

When the sinner, for the sake of a little present ease,
and to avoid a little present uneasiness stifles his conscience,

refuses to examine his condition, casts the thoughts of eternity out of his mind, and thinks it too hard to attend painfully on all the means of grace, has he then a due estimate of eternal things? Alas! no; he only looks at the things that are seen. Were the mouth of hell open before him, that he might behold its torments, and had he a sight of the joys of paradise, they would harden him into a generous insensibility of all the sorrows and anxieties of this life, and his inquiry would not be, whether these things required of him are easy; but, whether they are necessary to obtain eternal happiness, and avoid everlasting misery.

When we suffer any reproach or contempt on a religious account, how would a due estimate of eternal things fortify us with undaunted courage and make us willing to climb to heaven through disgrace, rather than sink to hell with general applause!

How would a realizing view of eternal things animate us in our devotions? Were this thought impressed on our hearts when in the secret or social duties of religion, " I am now acting for eternity," do you think we should pray, read, or hear with so much indifferency and langour? Oh no; it would rouse us out of our dead frames, and call forth all the vigour of our souls. With what unwearied importunity should we cry to God! with what eagerness hear the word of salvation!

How powerful an influence would a view of futurity have to alarm the secure sinner that has thought little of eternity all his life, though it be the only thing worth thinking of!

How would it hasten the determination of the lingering, wavering sinner, and shock him at the thought of living one day unprepared on the very brink of eternity!

In a word, a suitable impression of this would quite alter the aspect of things in the world, and would turn the concern and activity of the world into another channel. Eternity then would be the principal concern. Our inquiries would not be, Who will show us any temporal good? What shall we eat, or what shall we drink? But, What shall we do to be saved? How shall we escape the wrath to come? Let us then endeavour to impress our hearts with invisible things, and for that purpose consider, that

We shall, ere long, be ingulfed in this awful eternity, whether we think of it or not. A few days or years will launch us there; and oh, the surprising scenes that will then open to us!

Without deep impressions of eternity on our hearts, and frequent thoughtfulness about it, we cannot be prepared for it.

And if we are not prepared for it, oh, how inconceiveably miserable our case! But if prepared, how inconceiveably happy!

Look not then at the things which are seen, but at the things which are not seen ; for the things which are seen are temporal ; but the things which are not seen are eternal.

SERMON XII.

THE SACRED IMPORT OF THE CHRISTIAN NAME.

Acts xi. 26.—*The Disciples were called Christians first in Antioch.*

Mere names are empty sounds, and but of little consequence: and yet it must be owned there are names of honour and significancy; and, when they are attended with the things signified by them, they are of great and sacred importance.

Such is the Christian name; a name about seventeen hundred years old. And now when the name is almost lost in party-distinctions, and the thing is almost lost in ignorance, error, vice, hypocrisy, and formality, it may be worth our while to consider the original import of that sacred name, as a proper expedient to recover both name and thing.

The name of Christian was not the first by which the followers of Christ were distinguished. Their enemies called them Galileans, Nazarenes, and other names of contempt: and among themselves they were called Saints, from their holiness; Disciples, from their learning their religion from Christ as their teacher; Believers, from their believing in him as the Messiah; and Brethren, from their mutual love and their relation to God and each other. But after some time they were distinguished by the name of Christians. This they first received in Antioch, a heathen city, a city infamous for all manner of vice and de-

bauchery: a city that had its name from Antiochus Epi-
phanes, the bitterest enemy the church of the Jews ever
had. A city very rich and powerful, from whence the
Christian name would have an extensive circulation; but
it is long since laid in ruins, unprotected by that sacred
name: in such a city was Christ pleased to confer his name
upon his followers; and you cannot but see that the very
choice of the place discovers his wisdom, grace, and justice.

The original word, which is here rendered *called*, seems
to intimate that they were called Christians by divine appointment, for it generally signifies an oracular nomination
or a declaration from God; and to this purpose it is generally translated.* Hence it follows that the very name
Christian, as well as the thing, was of a divine original;
assumed not by a private agreement of the disciples among
themselves, but by the appointment of God. And in this
view it is a remarkable accomplishment of an old prophecy
of Isaiah, chap. lxii. 2. *The Gentiles shall see thy righteousness, and all kings thy glory : and thou shalt be called
by a new name, which the mouth of the* LORD *shall name.*
So Isaiah lxv. 15. *The Lord shall call his servants by another name.*

This name was at first confined to a few; but it soon
had a surprisingly extensive propagation through the
world. In many countries, indeed, it was lost, and mise-

---

* "It is this word that is used, Matt. ii. 12. Καὶ χρηματισθέντες, being
warned of God, and the like in Matt. ii. 22. So in Rom. xi. 4, χρηματισμός,
is rendered the answer of God. Rom. vii. 3, χρηματίσει, she shall be called,
viz. by the divine law,) an adultress. Luke ii. 26, κεχρηματισμένον, it was revealed to him by the Holy Ghost. Acts x. 22, εχρηματίσθε, was warned from
God. Heb. viii. 5, Κεχρημάτισται Μωσῆς, Moses was admonished of God.
Heb. xi. 7: Noah being warned of God, χρηματισθείς, Heb. xii. 25. If they
escaped not, who refused him that spake on earth; viz. by divine inspiration. These are all the places perhaps in which the word is used in the
New Testament: and in all these it seems to mean a revelation from God,
or something oracular. And this is a strong presumption that the word
is to be so understood in the text."

rably exchanged for that of Heathen, Mahometan, or Mus-
selman. Yet the European nations still retain the honour
of wearing it. A few scattered Christians are also still to
be found here and there in Asia and Africa, though crushed
under the oppressions of Mahometans and Pagans. This
name has likewise crossed the wide ocean to the wilderness of America, and is worn by the sundry European
colonies on this continent. We, in particular, call ourselves Christians, and should take it ill to be denied the
honour of that distinction. But do we not know the
meaning and sacred import of that name? Do we not
know what it is to be Christians indeed? That is, to be
in reality what we are in name: certainly it is time for us
to consider the matter; and it is my present design that
we should do so.

Now we may consider this name in various views; particularly as a name of distinction from the rest of the
world, who know not the Lord Jesus, or reject him as an
impostor;—as a patronymic name, pointing out the Father
and Founder of our holy religion and the Christian church;
—as a badge of our relation to Christ as his servants, his
children, his bride;—as intimating our unction by the holy
Spirit, or our being the subjects of his influences; as Christ
was anointed by the holy Spirit, or replenished with his
gifts above measure, (for you are to observe that anointed
is the English of the Greek name Christ, and of the Hebrew, Messiah*) and as a name of approbation, signifying
that we are the property of Christ, and his peculiar people. Each of these particulars might be properly illustrated.† But my present design confines me to consider

---

* Psalm cv. 15.   Touch not my Christs; that is, my anointed people.
So the Seventy.

† See a fine illustration of them in Dr. Grosvenor's excellent essay on the
Christian name ; from whom I am not ashamed to borrow several amiable
sentiments.

the Christian name only in two views; namely, as a catholic name, intended to bury all party denominations; and as a name of obligation upon all that wear it to be Christians indeed, or to form their temper and practice upon the sacred model of Christianity.

1. Let us consider the Christian name as a catholic name, intended to bury all party denominations.

The name Gentile was odious to the Jews, and the name Jew was odious to the Gentiles. The name Christian swallows up both in one common and agreeable appellation. He that hath taken down the partition-wall, has taken away partition names, and united all his followers in his own name, as a common denomination. For now, says Paul, "there is neither Greek nor Jew, circumcision nor uncircumcision, Barbarian, Scythian, bond nor free; but Christ is all and in all." Col. iii. 11. "And ye are all one in Christ Jesus." Gal. iii. 28. According to a prophecy of Zechariah, *The* LORD *shall be king over all the earth; and in that day there shall be one* LORD, *and his name one.* Zech. xiv. 9.

It is but a due honour to Jesus Christ, the founder of Christianity, that all who profess his religion should wear his name; and they pay an extravagant and even idolatrous compliment to his subordinate officers and ministers, when they take their denomination from them. Had this humour prevailed in the primitive church, instead of the common name Christians, there would have been as many party-names as there were apostles or eminent ministers. There would have been Paulites from Paul; Peterites from Peter; Johnites from John; Barnabites from Barnabas, &c. Paul took pains to crush the first risings of this party spirit in those churches which he planted; particularly in Corinth, where it most prevailed. While they were saying, *I am of Paul; and I of Apollos; and I of*

Cephas; and I of Christ; he puts this pungent question to them: "Is Christ divided?" Are his servants the ring-leaders of so many parties? Was Paul crucified for you? or were ye baptized in or into the name of Paul, that ye should be so fond to take your name from him? He counted it a happiness that Providence had directed him to such a conduct as gave no umbrage of encouragement to such a humour. *I thank God,* says he, *that I baptized none of you, but Crispus and Gaius: lest any should say, that I baptized in my own name,* and was gathering a party for myself. 1 Cor. i. 12–15.

But alas! how little has this convictive reasoning of the apostle been regarded in the future ages of the church? What an endless variety of denominations taken from some men of character, or from some little peculiarities, has prevailed in the Christian world, and crumbled it to pieces, while the Christian name is hardly regarded? Not to take notice of Jesuits, Jansenites, Dominicans, Franciscans, and other denominations and orders in the popish church, where having corrupted the thing, they act very consistently to lay aside the name, what party names have been adopted by the Protestant churches, whose religion is substantially the same common Christianity, and who agree in much more important articles than in those they differ; and who therefore might peaceably unite under the common name of Christians? We have Lutherans, Calvinists, Arminians, Zuinglians, Churchmen, Presbyterians, Independents, Baptists, and a long list of names which I cannot now enumerate. To be a Christian is not enough now-a-days, but a man must also be something more and better; that is, he must be a strenuous bigot to this or that particular church. But where is the reason or propriety of this? I may indeed believe the same things which Luther or Calvin believed: but I do not believe them on

the authority of Luther or Calvin, but upon the sole
authority of Jesus Christ, and therefore I should not call
myself by their name, as one of their disciples, but by the
name of Christ, whom alone I acknowledge as the Author
of my religion, and my only Master and Lord.   If I learn
my religion from one of these great men, it is indeed
proper I should assume their name.   If I learn it from a
parliament or convocation, and make their acts and canons
the rule and ground of my faith, then it is enough for me
to be of the established religion, be that what it will: I
may with propriety be called a mere conformist; that is
my highest character: but I cannot be properly called ˈa
Christian: for a Christian learns his religion, not from acts
of parliament or from the determinations of councils, but
from Jesus Christ and his gospel.

To guard against mistakes on this head, I would observe
that every man has a natural and legal right to judge and
choose for himself in matters of religion; and that is a
mean, supple soul indeed, and utterly careless about all religion, that makes a compliment of this right to any man,
or body of men upon earth, whether pope, king, parliament, convocation, or synod.   In the exercise of this right
and searching for himself, he will find that he agrees more
fully in lesser as well as more important articles with some
particular church than others; and thereupon it is his duty
to join in stated communion with that church; and he
may, if he pleases, assume the name which that church
wears, by way of distinction from others; this is not what
I condemn.   But for me to glory in the denomination of
any particular church as my highest character; to lay
more stress upon the name of a presbyterian or a churchman, than on the sacred name of Christian; to make a
punctilious agreement with my sentiments in the little peculiarities of a party the test of all religion; to make it the

object of my zeal to gain proselytes to some other than the Christian name; to connive at the faults of those of my own party, and to be blind to the good qualities of others, or invidiously to misrepresent or diminish them; these are the things which deserve universal condemnation from God and man; these proceed from a spirit of bigotry and faction, directly opposite to the generous catholic spirit of Christianity, and subversive of it. And yet how common is this spirit among all denominations! and what mischief has it done in the world! Hence proceed contentions and animosities, uncharitable suspicions and censures, slander and detraction, partiality and unreasonable prejudices, and a hideous group of evils, which I cannot now describe. This spirit also hinders the progress of serious practical religion, by turning the attention of men from the great concerns of eternity, and the essentials of Christianity, to vain jangling and contest about circumstances and trifles. Thus the Christian is swallowed up in the partisan and fundamentals lost in extra-essentials.

My brethren, I would now warn you against this wretched, mischievous spirit of party. I would not have you entirely sceptical and undetermined even about the smaller points of religion, the modes and forms, which are the matters of contention between different churches; nor would I have you quite indifferent what particular church to join with in stated communion. Endeavour to find out the truth even in these circumstantials, at least so far as is necessary for the direction of your own conduct. But do not make these the whole or the principal part of your religion; do not be excessively zealous about them, nor break the peace of the church by magisterially imposing them upon others. " Hast thou faith in these little disputables?" it is well; "but have it to thyself before God," and do not disturb others with it. You may, if you please, call yourselves Presbyterians and Dissenters, and you shall bear without shame or resentment all the names of reproach and contempt which the world may brand you with. But as you should not be mortified on the one side, so neither should you glory on the other. A Christian! a Christian! let that be your highest distinction; let that be the name which you labour to deserve. God forbid that my ministry should be the occasion of diverting your attention to any thing else. But I am so happy that I can appeal to yourselves, whether I have during several years of my ministry among you, laboured to instil into you the principles of bigotry, and make you warm proselytes to a party: or whether it has not been the great object of my zeal to inculcate upon you the grand essentials of our holy religion, and make you sincere, practical Christians. Alas! my dear people, unless I succeed in this, I labour to very little purpose, though I should presbyterianize the whole colony.

Calumny and slander, it is hoped, have by this time talked themselves out of breath; and the lying spirit may be at a loss for materials to form a popular, plausible falsehood, which is likely to be credited where the dissenters are known. But you have heard formerly, and some of you may still hear strange and uncommon surmises, wild conjectures, and most dismal insinuations. But if you would know the truth at once, if you would be fully informed by one that best knows what religion I am of, I will tell you (with Mr. Baxter,) " I am a Christian, a mere Christian; of no other religion: my church is the Christian church." The Bible! the Bible! is my religion; and if I am a dissenter, I dissent only from modes and forms of religion which I cannot find in my Bible; and which therefore I conclude have nothing to do with religion, much less should they be made terms of Christian communion, since Christ, the only lawgiver of his church, has not made them such. Let this congregation be that of a Christian society, and I little care what other name it wears. Let it be a little Antioch, where the followers of Christ shall be distinguished by their old Catholic name, Christians. To bear and deserve this character, let this be our ambition, this our labour. Let popes pronounce, and councils decree what they please; let statesmen and ecclesiastics prescribe what to believe; as for us, let us study our Bibles: let us learn of Christ; and if we are not dignified with the smiles, or enriched with the emoluments of an establishment, we shall have his approbation, who is the only Lord and Sovereign of the realm of conscience, and by whose judgment we must stand or fall for ever.

But it is time for me to proceed to consider the other view of the Christian name, on which I intend principally to insist; and that is,

II. As a name of obligation upon all that bear it to be Christians indeed, or to form their temper and practice upon the sacred model of Christianity. The prosecution of this subject will lead me to answer this important inquiry, What is it to be a Christian?

To be a Christian, in the popular and fashionable sense, is no difficult or excellent thing. It is to be baptized, to profess the Christian religion, to believe, like our neighbours, that Christ is the Messiah, and to attend upon public worship once a week, in some church or other that bears only the Christian name. In this sense a man may be a Christian, and yet be habitually careless about eternal things; a Christian, and yet fall short of the morality of many of the heathens; a Christian, and yet a drunkard, a swearer, or a slave to some vice or other; a Christian, and yet a wilful, impenitent offender against God and man. To be a Christian in this sense is no high character; and, if this be the whole of Christianity, it is very little matter whether the world be Christianized or not. But is this to be a Christian in the original and proper sense of the word? No; that is something of a very different and superior kind. To be a Christian indeed, is the highest character and dignity of which the human nature is capable: it is the most excellent thing that ever adorned our world: it is a thing that heaven itself beholds with approbation and delight.

To be a Christian is to be like to Christ, from whom the name is taken: it is to be a follower and imitator of him; to be possessed of his spirit and temper; and to live as he lived in the world: it is to have those just, exalted, and divine notions of God and divine things, and that just and full view of our duty to God and man, which Christ taught: in short it is to have our sentiments, our temper, and practice, formed upon the sacred model of the gospel. Let me expatiate a little upon this amiable character.

1. To be a Christian, is to depart from iniquity. To this the name obliges us; and without this we have no title to the name. "Let every one that nameth the name of Christ depart from iniquity," 2 Tim. ii 19; that is, let him depart from iniquity, or not dare to touch that sacred name. Christ was perfectly free from sin: he was "holy, harmless, undefiled, and separate from sinners." His followers also shall be perfectly free from sin in a little time; ere long they will enter into the pure regions of perfect holiness, and will drop all their sins, with their mortal bodies, into the grave. But this, alas! is not their character in the present state, but the remains of sin still cleave to them. Yet even in the present state, they are labouring after perfection in holiness. Nothing can satisfy them until they are conformed to the image of God's dear Son.

They are hourly conflicting with every temptation, and vigorously resisting every iniquity in its most alluring forms. And, though sin is perpetually struggling for the mastery, and sometimes, in an inadvertent hour, gets an advantage over them, yet, as they are not under the law, but under grace, they are assisted with recruits of grace, so that no sin has any habitual dominion over them. Rom. vi. 14. Hence they are free from the gross vices of the age, and are men of good morals. This is their habitual, universal character; and to pretend to be Christians without this requisite, is the greatest absurdity.

What then shall we think of the drunken, swearing, debauched, defrauding, rakish, profligate, profane Christians, that have overrun the Christian world? Can there be a greater contradiction? A loyal subject in arms against his sovereign, an ignorant scholar, a sober drunkard, a charitable miser, an honest thief, is not a greater absurdity, or a more direct contradiction. To depart from iniquity is essential to Christianity, and without it there can be no such thing. There was nothing that Christ was so remote from as sin: and therefore for those that indulge themselves in it to wear his name, is just as absurd and ridiculous as for a coward to denominate himself from Alexander the Great, or an illiterate dunce to call himself a Newtonian philosopher. Therefore, if you will not renounce iniquity, renounce the Christian name: for you cannot consistently retain both. Alexander had a fellow in his army that was of his own name, but a mere coward. "Either be like me," says Alexander, "or lay aside my name." Ye servants of sin, it is in vain for you to wear the name of Christ; it renders you the more ridiculous, and aggravates your guilt: you may with as much propriety call yourselves lords, or dukes, or kings, as Christians, while you are so unlike to Christ. His name is a sarcasm, a reproach to you, and you are a scandal to his name. His name is blasphemed among the Gentiles through you.

2. To be a Christian is to deny yourselves and take up the cross and follow Christ. These are the terms of discipleship fixed by Christ himself. *He said to them all, If any man will come after me, let him deny himself, and take up his cross daily, and follow me.* Luke ix. 23. To deny ourselves is to abstain from the pleasures of sin, to moderate our sensual appetites, to deny our own interest for the sake of Christ, and in short, to sacrifice every thing inconsistent with our duty to him, when these come in competition. To take up our cross, is to bear sufferings, to encounter difficulties, and break through them all in imitation of Jesus Christ, and for his sake. To follow him, is to trace his steps, and imitate his example, whatever it cost us. But this observation will coincide with the next head, and therefore I now dismiss it. These, sirs, and these only, are the terms, if you would be Christians, or the disciples of Christ. These he honestly warned mankind of when he first called them to be his disciples. He did not take an advantage of them, but let them know beforehand upon what terms they were admitted. He makes this declaration in the midst of a great crowd, in Luke xiv. 25, &c. *There went great multitudes with him,* fond of becoming his followers: *and he turned, and said unto them, If any man come to me, and hate not his father, and mother, and wife, and children, and brethren, and sisters, yea, and his own life also, he cannot be my disciple.* By hating, is here meant a smaller degree of love, or a comparative hatred; that is, if we would be Christ's disciples. we must be willing to part with our dearest relations, and even our lives, when we cannot retain them consistently with our duty to him. He goes on: *Whosoever doth not*

bear his cross, and encounter the greatest sufferings after my example, *cannot be my disciple*. The love of Christ is the ruling passion of every true Christian, and for his sake he is ready to give up all, and to suffer all that earth or hell can inflict. He must run all risks, and cleave to his cause at all adventures. This is the essential character of every true Christian.

What then shall we think of those crowds among us who retain the Christian name, and yet will not deny themselves of their sensual pleasures, nor part with their temporal interest for the sake of Christ? Who are so far from being willing to lay down their lives, that they cannot stand the force of a laugh or a sneer in the cause of religion, but immediately stumble and fall away? or, are they Christians, whom the commands of Christ cannot restrain from what their depraved hearts desire? No; a Christian, without self-denial, mortification, and a supreme love to Jesus Christ, is as great a contradiction as fire without heat, or a sun without light, a hero without courage, or a friend without love. And does not this strip some of you of the Christian name, and prove that you have no title at all to it?

3. I have repeatedly observed, that a true Christian must be a follower or imitator of Christ. *Be ye followers of me*, says St. Paul, *as I also am of Christ*. 1 Cor. xi. 1. Christ is the model after whom every Christian is formed; for, says St. Peter, *he left us an example, that we should follow his steps*. 1 Pet. ii. 21. St. Paul tells us, that *we must be conformed to the image of God's dear Son*, Rom. vii. 29, and that *the same mind must be in us which was also in Christ Jesus*. Phil. ii. 5; unless we partake of his spirit, and resemble him in practice; unless we be as he was in the world, we have no right to partake of his name.

Here I would observe, that what was miraculous in

our Lord's conduct, and peculiar to him as the Son of God and Mediator, is not a pattern for our imitation, but only what was done in obedience to that law of God which was common to him and us. His heart glowed with love to his Father; he delighted in universal obedience to him; it was his meat and drink to do his will, even in the most painful and self-denying instances; he abounded in devotion, in prayer, meditation, fasting, and every religious duty. He was also full of every grace and virtue towards mankind; meek and lowly, kind and benevolent, just and charitable, merciful and compassionate; a dutiful son, a loyal subject, a faithful friend, a good master, and an active, useful, public-spirited member of society. He was patient and resigned, and yet undaunted and brave under sufferings; he had all his appetites and passions under proper government, he was heavenly-minded, above this world in heart while he dwelt in it. Beneficence to the souls and bodies of men was the business of his life; for *he went about doing good.* Acts x. 38. This is an imperfect sketch of his amiable character; and in these things every one that deserves to be called after his name, does in some measure resemble and imitate him. This is not only his earnest endeavour, but what he actually attains, though in a much inferior degree; and his imperfections are the grief of his heart. This resemblance and imitation of Christ is essential to the very being of a Christian, and without it, it is a vain pretence. And does your Christianity, my brethren, stand this test? may one know that you belong to Christ by your living like him, and discovering the same temper and spirit? Do the manners of the divine Master spread through all his family; and do you show that you belong to it by your temper and conduct? Alas! if you must be denominated from hence, would not some of you with more propriety be called

Epicureans from Epicurus, the sensual atheistic philosopher, or mammonites from Mammon, the imaginary God of riches, or Bacchanals from Bacchus, the god of wine, than Christians from Christ, the most perfect pattern of living holiness and virtue that ever was exhibited in the world?

If you claim the name of Christians, where is that ardent devotion, that affectionate love to God, that zeal for his glory, that alacrity in his service, that resignation to his will, that generous benevolence to mankind, that zeal to promote their best interests, that meekness and forbearance under ill usage, that unwearied activity in doing good to all, that self-denial and heavenly-mindedness which shone so conspicuous in Christ, whose holy name you bear? Alas! while you are destitute of those graces, and yet wear his name, you burlesque it, and turn it into a reproach both to him and yourselves.

I might add, that the Christian name is not hereditary to you by your natural birth, but you must be born anew of the Spirit to entitle you to this new name; that a Christian is a believer, believing in him after whom he is called as his only Saviour and Lord, and that he is a true penitent. Repentance was incompatible with Christ's character, who was perfectly righteous, and had no sin of which to repent; but it is a proper virtue in a sinner, without which he cannot be a Christian. On these and several other particulars I might enlarge, but my time will not allow; I shall therefore conclude with a few reflections.

First, You may hence see that the Christian character is the highest, the most excellent and sublime in the world; it includes everything truly great and amiable. The Christian has exalted sentiments of the Supreme Being, just notions of duty, and a proper temper and conduct towards God and man. A Christian is a devout worshipper of the God of heaven, a cheerful observer of his whole law, and a broken-hearted penitent for his imperfections. A Christian is a complication of all the amiable and useful graces and virtues; temperate and sober, just, liberal, compassionate, and benevolent, humble, meek, gentle, peaceable, and in all things conscientious. A Christian is a good parent, a good child, a good master, a good servant, a good husband, a good wife, a faithful friend, an obliging neighbour, a dutiful subject, a good ruler, a zealous patriot, and an honest statesman; and as far as he is such, so far, and no farther, he is a Christian. And can there be a more amiable and excellent character exhibited to your view? It is an angelic, a divine character. Let it be your glory and your ambition to wear it with a good grace, to wear it so as to adorn it.

To acquire the title of kings and lords, is not in your power; to spread your fame as scholars, philosophers, or heroes, may be beyond your reach; but here is a character more excellent, more amiable, more honourable than all these, which it is your business to deserve and maintain. And blessed be God, this is a dignity which the meanest among you, which beggars and slaves may attain. Let this therefore be an object of universal ambition and pursuit, and let every other name and title be despised in comparison of it. This is the way to rise to true honour in the estimate of God, angels, and good men. What though the anti-christian Christians of our age and country ridicule you? let them consider their own absurd conduct and be ashamed. They think it an honour to wear the Christian name, and yet persist in unchristian practices; and who but a fool, with such palpable contradiction, would think so? A beggar that fancies himself a king and trails his rags with the gait of majesty, as though

they were royal robes, is not so ridiculous as one that will
usurp the Christian name without a Christian practice;
and yet such Christians are the favourites of the world.
To renounce the profession of Christianity is barbarous
and profane; to live according to that profession, and
practice Christianity, is preciseness and fanaticism. Can
anything be more preposterous? This is as if one should
ridicule learning, and yet glory in the character of a
scholar; or laugh at bravery, and yet celebrate the praises
of heroes. And are they fit to judge of the wisdom and
propriety, or their censures to be regarded, who fall into
such an absurdity themselves?

Secondly, Hence you may see that, if all the professors
of Christianity should behave in character, the religion of
Christ would soon appear divine to all mankind, and spread
through all nations of the earth. Were Christianity exhibited to the life in all its native inherent glories, it would
be as needless to offer arguments to prove it divine, as to
prove that the sun is full of light; the conviction would
flash upon all mankind by its own intrinsic evidence. Did
Christians exemplify the religion they profess, all the
world would immediately see that *that* religion which rendered them so different a people from all the rest of mankind, is indeed divine, and every way worthy of universal
acceptance.   *   *   *   *   Then would
Heathenism, Mahometanism, and all the false religions in
the world, fall before the heaven-born religion of Jesus
Christ. Then it would be sufficient to convince an infidel
just to bring him into a Christian country, and let him observe the different face of things there from all the world
beside. But alas!

Thirdly, How different is the Christian world from the
Christian religion! Who would imagine that they who
take their name from Christ have any relation to him, if

we observe their spirit and practice? Should a stranger learn Christianity from what he sees in Popish countries, he would conclude it principally consisted in bodily austerities, in worshipping saints, images, relics, and a thousand trifles, in theatrical fopperies and insignificant ceremonies, in believing implicitly all the determinations of a fallible man as infallibly true, and in persecuting all that differ from them, and showing their love to their souls by burning their bodies. In Protestant countries, alas! the face of things is but little better as to good morals and practical religion. Let us take our own country for a sample. Suppose a Heathen or Mahometan should take a tour through Virginia to learn the religion of the inhabitants from their general conduct, what would he conclude? would he not conclude that all the religion of the generality consisted in a few Sunday formalities, and that the rest of the week they had nothing to do with God, or any religion, but were at liberty to live as they please? And were he told these were the followers of one Christ, and were of his religion, would he not conclude that he was certainly an impostor, and the minister of sin? But when he came to find that, notwithstanding all this licentiousness, they professed the pure and holy religion of the Bible, how would he be astonished, and pronounce them the most inconsistent, bare-faced hypocrites! My brethren, great and heavy is the guilt that lies upon our country upon this account. It is a scandal to the Christian name; it is guilty of confirming the neighbouring heathen in their prejudices, and hinders the propagation of Christianity through the world. Oh let not us be accessary to this dreadful guilt, but do all we can to recommend our religion to universal acceptance!—I add,

Fourthly, and lastly, Let us examine whether we have any just title to the Christian name; that is, whether we are Christians indeed; for if we have not the thing, to retain the name is the most inconsistent folly and hypocrisy, and will answer no end but to aggravate our condemnation. A lost Christian is the most shocking character in hell; and unless you be such Christians as I have described, it will ere long be your character. Therefore, be followers of Christ, imbibe his spirit, practise his precepts, and depart from iniquity. Otherwise he will sentence you from him at last as workers of iniquity. *And then will I profess unto them* (they are Christ's own words) *I never knew you; depart from me, ye that work iniquity.* Matt. vii. 23.

SERMON XIII.

THE DIVINE MERCY TO MOURNING PENITENTS.

JER. xxxi. 18, 19, 20.—*I have surely heard Ephraim be-moaning himself thus; Thou hast chastised me, and I was chastised, as a bullock unaccustomed to the yoke: turn thou me, and I shall be turned; for thou art the* LORD *my God. Surely after that I was turned, I repented; and after that I was instructed, I smote upon my thigh: I was ashamed, yea, even confounded, because I did bear the reproach of my youth. Is Ephraim my dear son? is he a pleasant child? for since I spake against him, I do earnestly remember him still: therefore my bowels are troubled for him: I will surely have mercy upon him, saith the* LORD.

IN these words the mourning language of a penitent child, sensible of ingratitude, and at once desirous and ashamed to return, and the tender language of a compassionate father, at once chastising, pitying, and pardoning, are sweetly blended: and the images are so lively and moving, that if they were regarded only as poetical descriptions founded upon fiction, they would be irresistibly striking. But when we consider them as the most important realities, as descriptive of that ingenuous repentance which we must all feel, and of that gracious acceptance we must all obtain from God before we can be happy, what almighty energy should they have upon us! how may our hearts dissolve within us at the sound of such pathetic complaints, and such gracious encouragements ! Hard indeed is that heart that can hear these penitential strains without being melted into the like tender relentings; and inveterate is that melancholy, incurable is that despondency, that can listen to such expressions of fatherly compassion and love, without being cheered and animated.

This whole chapter had a primary reference to the Jews, and such of the Israelites as might mingle with them in their return from the Babylonian captivity. As they were enslaved to foreigners, and removed from their native land for their sins, so they could not be restored but upon their repentance. Upon this condition only a restoration was promised them. Lev. xxvi. 40–43; Deut. xxx. 1–16.

In this chapter we have a prediction of their repentance under the heavy chastisement of seventy years' captivity, and of their return thereupon to their own land. In the text the whole body of penitents among them is called by the name of a single person, Ephraim. In the prophetic writings, the kingdom of the ten tribes, as distinguished from that of Judah, is frequently denominated by this name, because the Ephraimites were a principal family among them. And sometimes, as here, the name is given to the Jews, probably on account of the great number of Ephraimites mingled with them, especially on their return from captivity. All the penitent Jews are included under this single name, to intimate their unanimity in their repentance; their hearts consented, like the heart of one man, to turn to the Lord, from whom with horrid unanimity they had revolted. This single name Ephraim also renders this passage more easily applicable to particular penitents in all ages. Every one of such may insert his own name, instead of that of Ephraim, and claim the encouragement originally given to them. And indeed this whole passage is applicable to all true penitents. Repenting Ephraim did but speak the language of every one of you, my brethen, who is made sensible of the plague of his own heart, and turned to the Lord; and the tender language of forgiving grace to mourning Ephraim is addressed to each of you; and it is with a view to you that I intend to consider this scripture.

The text naturally resolves itself into three parts, as it consists of three verses. In the first verse we find the careless, resolute impenitent, reduced by chastisement to a sense of his danger, and the necessity of turning to God; and yet sensible of his utter inability, and therefore crying for the attractive influence of divine grace. You hear Ephraim bemoaning his wretched case, and pouring out importunate groans for relief, thus: *Thou hast chastised me, and I was chastised, like a bullock unaccustomed to the yoke,* that struggles and wearies himself in vain to get free from it, and must be broken and tamed with severe usage. "Thus stubborn and unmanageable have I been; and now, when I am convinced of the necessity of a return to thee, I feel my obstinate heart reluctate, like a wild ox, and I cannot come. I therefore cry to thee for the attractive influence of thy grace;" *Turn thou me, and I shall be turned ;* draw me, and I shall run after thee. "To whom but to thee should I return; and to whom but to thee should I apply for strength to return? For thou only art the Lord my God, who can help me, and whom I am under infinite obligations to serve." Thus the awakened sinner prayed; and mercy listened to his cries. The attractive influences of divine grace are granted, and he is enabled to return; which introduces the second branch of the text in the 19th verse, in which the new convert is represented as reflecting upon the efficacy of converting grace, and the glorious change wrought in him by it: *Surely after that I was turned I repented; and after that I was instructed, I smote upon my thigh: I was ashamed, yea, even confounded, because I did bear the reproach of my youth.*

While the returning prodigal is venting himself in these plaintive strains in some solitary corner, his heavenly Father's bowels are moving over him. The third part of the text represents the blessed God listening to the cries of his mourning child. *I have surely heard;* or, according to the emphasis of the original, hearing I have heard *Ephraim bemoaning himself:* and while Ephraim is going on in his passionate complaints, God, as it were, interrupts him, and surprises him with the soothing voice of mercy. *Is Ephraim my dear son? is he a pleasant child?** surely he is. Or we may understand the words thus, as if God should say, " Whose mourning voice is this I hear? Is this Ephraim, my dear son? Is this my pleasant child that bemoans himself as a helpless orphan, or one abandoned by his father? And can I bear to hear his complaints without mingling divine consolations with them, and assuring him of pardon? No; for since I spake against him in my threatenings, I do earnestly remember him still;" *therefore my bowels are troubled for him: I will surely have mercy upon him, saith the Lord.*

I shall endeavour to illustrate each of these parts of the text, and thus shall be led to describe the preparative exercise, the nature and concomitants of true repentance; and the tender compassions of Heaven towards mourning penitents.

I. Let us view the returning sinner under his first spiritual concern, which is generally preparatory to evangelical repentance.

---

* Though affirmative interrogations are generally to be understood as strong negations, yet sometimes they are to be understood affirmatively. See 1 Sam. ii. 27, 28 ; Job xx. 4.

And where shall we find him? And what is he doing? We shall not find him, as usual in a thoughtless hurry about earthly things, confining all his attention to these trifles, and unmindful of the important concerns of eternity. We shall not find him merry, inconsiderate, and vain, in a circle of jovial, careless companions; much less shall we find him intrepid and secure in a course of sin, gratifying his flesh, and indulging his lusts. In this enchanted road the crowd of hardy impenitents pass secure and cheerful down to the chambers of death, but the awakened sinner flies from it with horror; or, if his depraved heart would tempt him to walk in it, he cannot take many steps before he is shocked with the horrid apparition of impending danger. He finds the flattering paths of sin haunted with the terrible spectres of guilt; and the sword of divine vengeance gleams bright and dreadful before him, and seems lifted to give the fatal blow. You will, therefore, find the awakened sinner solitary and solemn in some retired corner, not deceiving himself with vain hopes of safety in his present state, but alarmed with apprehensions of danger: not planning schemes for his secular advantage, nor asking, with sordid anxiety, "Who will show me any temporal good?" but solicitous about his perishing soul, and anxiously inquiring, *What shall I do to be saved?* He is not congratulating himself upon the imaginary goodness of his heart or life, or priding himself with secret wonder in a rich conceit of his excellencies; but you will hear him, in his sorrowful retirement, bemoaning, or (as the original signifies) condoling himself. He sees his case to be really awful and sad, and he, as it were, takes up a lamentation over himself. He is no more senseless, hard-hearted, and self-applauding, as he was wont to be: but, like a mourning turtle, he bewails himself in such tragical strains as these: " Unhappy creature that I am! into what a deplorable state have I brought myself! and how long have I continued in it, with the insensibility of a rock and the stupidity of a brute? Now I may mourn over my past neglected and unimproved days, as so many deceased friends, sent indeed from heaven to do me good, but cruelly killed by my ungrateful neglect and continued delays as to return to God and holiness. Fly back, ye abused months and years; arise from the dead; restore me your precious moments again, that I may unravel the web of life, and form it anew; and that I may improve the opportunities I have squandered away. Vain and desperate wish! the wheels of time will not return, and what shall I do? Here I am, a guilty, obnoxious creature, uncertain of life and unfit to die; alienated from God, and incapable (alas! I may add unwilling to return) a slave to sin, and too feeble to break the fetters of inveterate habits; liable to the arrest of divine justice, and unable to deliver myself; exposed to the vengeance of heaven, yet can make no atonement; destitute of an interest in Christ, and uncertain, awfully uncertain, whether I shall ever obtain it. Unhappy creatures! How justly may I take up a lamentation over myself! Pity me, ye brute creation, that know not to sin, and therefore cannot know the misery of my case; and have pity upon me, have pity upon me, O ye my friends! and if these guilty lips may dare to pronounce thy injured name, O thou God of grace, have pity upon me! But, alas! I deserve no pity, for how long have I denied it to myself! Ah, infatuated wretch! why did not I sooner begin to secure my unhappy soul, that has lain all this time neglected, and unpitied, upon the brink of ruin! Why did I not sooner lay my condition to heart? Alas! I should have gone on thoughtless still, had I not been awakened by the kind severity, the gracious chastisements of my dishonoured Father!"

Thou hast chastised me. This, as spoken by Ephraim, had a particular reference to the Babylonish captivity; but we may naturally take occasion from it to speak of those calamities in general, whether outward or inward, that are made the means of alarming the secure sinner.

There are many ways which our heavenly Father takes to correct his undutiful children until they return to him. Sometimes he kindly takes away their health, the abused occasion of their wantonness and security, and restrains them from their lusts with fetters of affliction. This is beautifully described by Elihu. "He is chastened with pain upon his bed, and the multitude of his bones with strong pain; so that his life abhorreth bread, and his soul dainty meat. His flesh is consumed away, that it cannot be seen; and his bones, that were not seen, stick out. Yea, his soul draweth near unto the grave, and his life unto the destroyers. If there be a messenger with him, an interpreter, one among a thousand, to show unto man his uprightness; then he is gracious unto him, and saith, Deliver him from going down to the pit:—I have found a ransom." Job xxxiii. 19, &c. Sometimes God awakens the sinner to bethink himself, by stripping him of his earthly supports and comforts, his estate, or his relatives, which drew away his heart from eternal things, and thus brings him to see the necessity of turning to God, the fountain of bliss, upon the failure of the streams. Thus he dealt with profligate Manasseh. 2 Chron. xxxiii. 11, 12. He was taken in "thorns, and bound in fetters, and carried to Babylon; and when he was in affliction he sought the Lord, and humbled himself greatly before him, and prayed unto him," &c. Thus also God promises to do with his chosen: "I will cause you to pass under the rod, and I will bring you into the bond of my covenant." Ezek. xx. 37; Psl. lxxxix. 32; Prov. xxii. 15, xxix. 15.

But the principal means of correction which God uses for the end of return to him is that of conscience; and indeed without this, all the rest are in vain. Outward afflictions are of service only as they tend to awaken the conscience from its lethargy to a faithful discharge of its trust. It is conscience that makes the sinner sensible of his misery and scourges him till he return to his duty. This is a chastisement the most severe that human nature can endure. The lashes of a guilty conscience are intolerable; and some under them have chosen strangling and death rather than life. The spirit of a man may bear him up under outward infirmities; but when the spirit itself is wounded, *who can bear it?* Prov. xviii. 14. Conscience is a serpent in his breast, which bites and gnaws his heart; and he can no more avoid it, than he can fly from himself. Its force is so great and universal that even the heathen poet Juvenal, not famous for the delicacy of his morals, taught by experience, could speak feelingly of its secret blows, and of agonizing sweats under its tortures.*

Let not such of you as have never been tortured with its remorse, congratulate yourselves upon your happiness, for you are not innocents; and therefore conscience will not always sleep; it will not always lie torpid and inactive, like a snake benumbed with cold, in your breast. It will awaken you either to your conversion or condemnation. Either the fire of God's wrath flaming from his law will enliven it in this world to sting you with medicinal anguish; or the unquenchable fire of his vengeance in the

---

* —————— Frigida mens est
Criminibus, tacita sudant præcordia culpa.
Juven. Sat. I.

Cur tamen hos tu
Erasisse putes, quos diri conscia facti
Mens habet attonitos, et surdo verbere cædit,
Occultum quatiente animo tortore flagellum;
Id. Sat. XIII.

lake of fire and brimstone will thaw it into life, and then it will horribly rage in your breast, and diffuse its torment-ing poison through your whole frame: and then it will be-come a never-dying worm, and prey upon your hearts for ever. But if you now suffer it to pain you with salutary remorse, and awaken you to a tender sensibility of your danger, this intestine enemy will in the end become your bosom friend, will support you under every calamity, and be your faithful companion and guardian through the most dangerous paths of life. Therefore now submit to its wholesome severities, now yield to its chastisements. Such of you as have submitted to its authority, and obeyed its faithful admonitions, find it your best friend: and you may bless the day in which you complied with its demands, though before divine grace renewed your heart, your wills were stubborn and reluctant; and you might say with Ephraim:

I was chastised, as a bullock unaccustomed to the yoke; that is, "As a wild young ox, unbroken from the herd, is unman-ageable, refuses the yoke, becomes outrageous at the whip or goad, and wearies himself in ineffectual struggles to throw off the burden clapt upon him, and regain his savage liberty, and never will submit until wearied out, and unable to re-sist any longer; so has my stubborn heart, unaccustomed to obey, refused the yoke of thy law, O my God, and struggled with sullen obstinacy under thy chastisements. Instead of calmly submitting to thy rod, and immediately reforming under correction, instead of turning to thee, and flying to thy arms to avoid the falling blow, I was unyield-ing and outrageous, like *a wild bull in a net.* Isa. li. 20. I wearied myself in desperate struggles to free myself from thy chastising hand; or vainly tried to harden myself to bear it with obdurate insensibility. I tried to break the rod of conscience that I might no more groan under its lashes, and my heart reluctated and rebelled against the gracious design of thy correction, which was to bring me back to thee my heavenly Father. But now I am wearied out, now I am sensible I must submit, or perish, and that my conscience is too strong for me, and must prevail."

You see, my brethren, the obstinate reluctance of an awakened sinner to return to God. Like a wild young bullock, he would range at large, and is impatient of the yoke of the law, and the restraints of conscience. He loves his sin and cannot bear to part with it. He has no relish for the exercises of devotion and ascetic mortification; and therefore will not submit to them. The way of holiness is disagreeable to his depraved heart, and he will not turn his feet to it. He loves to be stupidly easy, and serene in mind, and cannot bear to be checked in his pursuit of business or pleasure by anxieties of heart, and therefore he is impatient of the honest warnings of his conscience, and uses a variety of wretched expedients to silence its clamorous remonstrances. In short, he will do any thing, he will turn to any thing rather than turn to God. If his conscience will be but satisfied, he will forsake many of his sins: he will, like Herod, Mark vi. 20, do many things, and walk in the whole round of outward duties. All this he will do, if his conscience will be but bribed by it. But if conscience enlarges its demands, and, after he has reformed his life, requires him to make him a new heart, requires him to turn not only from the outward practice of gross vices, but from the love of all sins; not only to turn to the observance of religious duties, but to turn to the Lord with all his heart, and surrender himself entirely to him, and make it the main business of life to serve him; if conscience, I say, carries its demands thus far, he cannot bear it, he struggles to throw off the yoke.

And some are cursed with horrid success in the attempt: they are permitted to rest content in a partial reformation, or external religion, as sufficient, and so go down to the grave *with a lie in their right hand.* But the happy soul, on whom divine grace is determined to finish its work in spite of all opposition, is suffered to weary itself out in a vain resistance of the chastisements of conscience, till it is obliged to yield, and submit to the yoke. And then with Ephraim it will cry:

Turn thou me, and I shall be turned. This is the mourning sinner's language, when convinced that he must submit and turn to God, and in the meantime finds himself utterly unable to turn. Many essays he makes to give himself to the Lord; but oh! his heart starts back and shrinks away as though he were rushing into flames, when he is but flying to the gracious embraces of his Father. He strives, and strives to drag it along, but all in vain. And what shall he do in this extremity, but cry, " Lord, turn thou me, and I shall be turned; draw me, and I shall run after thee. Work in me to will and to do, and then I shall work out my own salvation." Lord, though I am sensible of the necessity of turning to thee, though I exert my feeble strength in many a languid effort, to come, yet I cannot so much as creep towards thee, though I should die on the spot. Not only thy word, but my own experience now convinces me that I cannot come unto thee, unless thou draw me. John vi. 44. Others vainly boast of their imaginary power, as though, when they set themselves about it, they could perform some great achievements. Thus I once flattered myself, but now, when I am most capable of judging, that is, when I come to the trial, all my boasts are humbled. Here I lie, a helpless creature, unable to go to the physician, unable to accept of pardon and life on the easy terms of the gospel, and unable to free myself from the bondage of sin; and thus I must lie for ever, unless that God, from whom I have revolted, draws me back to himself. Turn me, oh thou that hast the hearts of all men in thy hands, and canst turn them whithersoever thou pleasest, turn me; and then weak, and reluctant as I am, I shall be turned; this backward heart will yield to the almighty attraction of thy grace.

" Here am I as passive clay in the hand of the potter; incapable to fashion myself into a vessel fit for thy house; but thou canst form me as thou pleasest. This hard and stubborn heart will be ductile and pliable to thine irresistible power." Thus you see the awakened sinner is driven to earnest prayer in his exigence. Never did a drowning man call for help, or a condemned malefactor plead for pardon with more sincerity and ardour. If the sinner had neglected prayer all his life before now, he flies to it as the only expedient left, or if he formerly ran it over in a careless, unthinking manner, as an insignificant form, now he exerts all the importunity of his soul; now he prays as for his life, and cannot rest till his desires are answered.

The sinner ventures to enforce his petition by pleading his relation to God; " Turn me,—for thou art the Lord my God." There is a sense in which a sinner in his unregenerate state cannot call God his God; that is, he cannot claim a special interest in him as his portion, nor cry " Abba, Father," with the spirit of adoption, as reconciled to God. But even an unregenerate sinner may call him my God in other senses; he is his God by right, that is, though he has idolatrously yielded himself to other gods, yet by right he should have acknowledged him only. He is his God, as that name denotes authority and power, to which he should be subject: his God, as he would now choose him to be his God, his portion, and his all, which

is implied in turning to him; he is his God by anticipa-
tion and hope, as upon his turning to him he will become
his reconciled God in covenant; and he is his God by
outward profession and visible relation.   The force of this
argument, to urge his petition for converting grace, may
be viewed in various lights.

It may be understood thus: " Turn thou me, for thou
only who art the Lord of the universe, and hast all the
creation at thy control; thou only, who art my God and
ruler, and in whose hand my heart is, art able to turn so
obstinate a creature.   In vain do I seek for help elsewhere.   Not all the means upon earth, not all the persuasions, exhortations, invitations, and terrors that can be
used with me, can turn this heart; it is a work becoming
the Lord God Almighty, and it is thou alone canst effect
it."

Or we may understand the plea thus: " Turn thou me,
and I shall turn to thee; to thee who art the Lord my
God, and to whom I am under the most sacred obligations
to return.   I would resign thine own right to thee; I would
submit to thee who alone hast a just claim to me as thy
servant."

Or the words may be understood as an abjuration of
all the idol-lusts to which the sinner was enslaved before,
" I will turn to thee; for to whom should I turn but to
the Lord my God: " What have I to do any more with
idols ?" Hosea xiv. 8. " Why should I any longer submit
to other lords, who have no right to me? I would renounce them all; I would throw off all subjection to
them, and avouch thee alone for the Lord my God."
Thus have the Jews renounced their false gods upon their
return from Babylon.

Or we may understand the words as an encouragement
to hope for converting grace, since it is asked from a God

of infinite power and goodness. "Though I have most grievously offended, and had I done the thousandth part so much against my fellow creatures, I could never expect a favourable admission into their presence; yet I dare ask so great a favour of thee, for thou art God, and not man: thy power and thy grace are all divine, such as become a God. I therefore dare to hope for that from thy hands, which I might despair of from all the universe of beings besides."

Or finally, the passage may be looked upon as a plea drawn from the sinner's external relation to God, as a member of his visible church, and as dedicated to him. " Turn me, and I will turn to thee, whose name I bear, and to whom I have been early devoted. I would now of my own choice acknowledge the God of my fathers, and return to the guide of my youth. And, since thou hast honoured me with a place in thy visible church, I humbly hope thou wilt not reject me now, when I would sincerely consecrate myself to thee, and become thy servant in reality, as well as in appearance." In this sense the plea might be used with peculiar propriety by the Jews, who had been nationally adopted as the peculiar people of God.

In whatever sense we understand the words, they convey to us this important truth, that the awakened sinner is obliged to take all his encouragement from God, and not from himself. All his trust is in the divine mercy, and he is brought to a happy self-despair.

Having viewed Ephraim under the preparatory work of legal conviction, and the dawn of evangelical repentance, let us view him,

II. As reflecting upon the suprising efficacy of grace he had sought, and which was bestowed upon him in answer to his prayer.

We left him just now crying, *Turn thou me, and I shall*

be turned; here we find him actually turned. *Surely after that I was turned, I repented.* When the Lord exerts his power to subdue the stubbornness of the sinner, and sweetly to allure him to himself, then the sinner repents ; then his heart dissolves in ingenuous, disinterested relentings. His sorrow and concern before conversion are forced and mercenary; they are occasioned only by a selfish fear of punishment, and he would willingly get rid of them, but now his grief is free and spontaneous ; it flows from his heart as freely as streams from a fountain; and he takes pleasure in tender relentings before the Lord for his sin; he delights to be humble, and to feel his heart dissolve within him. A heart of flesh, soft and susceptive of impression, is his choice, and a stony, insensible heart a great burden ; the more penitent the more happy, and the more senseless, the more miserable he finds himself. Now also his heart is actuated with a generous concern for the glory of God; and he sees the horrid evil of sin as contrary to the holiness of God, and an ungrateful requital of his uninterrupted beneficence.

We learn from this passage, that the true penitent is sensible of a mighty turn in his temper and inclinations. *Surely after that I was turned, I repented.* His whole soul is turned from what he formerly delighted in, and turned to what he had no relish for before. Particularly his thoughts, his will, and affections are turned to God; there is a heavenly bias communicated to them which draws them to holiness, like the law of gravitation in the material world. There is indeed a new turn given to his outward practice; the world may in some measure see that he is a new man; but this is not all; the first spring that turns all the wheels of the soul and actions of life is the heart, and this is first set right. The change within is as evident as that without, could our eyes penetrate the heart. In short, *If any man be in Christ, he is through-out a new creature; old things are passed away, and be-hold, all things are become new.*

Apply this touchstone to your hearts, my brethren, and see if they will stand the test.

The penitent proceeds, *After that I was instructed, I smote upon my thigh.* The same grace that turns him does also instruct him; nay, it is by discovering to him the beauty of holiness, and the glory of God in the face of Jesus Christ, that it draws him. He is brought out of darkness into marvellous and astonishing light, that sur-prises him with new discoveries of things: he is instructed particularly, as to the necessity of turning to God, as to the horrid ingratitude, vileness, and deformity of sin, and as to his folly and wickedness in continuing so long alien-ated from God. By the way, have you ever been let into these secrets, my hearers? And when instructed in these,

" He smites upon his thigh." This gesture denotes consternation and amazement; and nature directs us thus to express these passions. Ezekiel is enjoined to use this gesture as a prophetic action, signifying the horror and as-tonishment of his mind. Ezek. xxi. 12. This action, there-fore, of the penitent, intimates what consternation and amazement he is cast into, when these new discoveries flash upon his soul. He stands amazed at himself. He is struck with horror to think what an ungrateful, ignorant, stupid wretch he has been all his life till this happy mo-ment. " Alas! what have I been doing? abusing all my days in ruining my own soul, and dishonouring the God of all my mercies! contentedly estranged from him, and not seeking to return! Where were my eyes, that I never before saw the horrid evil of my conduct and the shocking deformity of sin, which now opens to me in all its hideous colours! Amazing! that divine vengeance has not broken out upon me before now? Can it be that I am yet alive! in the land of hope too! yea, alive, an humble pardoned penitent! Let heaven and earth wonder at this, for surely the sun never shone upon a wretch so undeserving! so great a monument of mercy!"

The pardoned penitent proceeds—*I was ashamed, yea, even confounded, because I did bear the reproach of my youth.* We are ashamed when we are caught in a mean, base and scandalous action; we blush, and are confounded, and know not where to look, or what to say. Thus the penitent is heartily ashamed of himself, when he reflects upon the sordid dispositions he has indulged, and the base and scandalous actions he has committed. He blushes at his own inspection; he is confounded at his own tribunal. He appears to himself, a mean, base, contemptible wretch; and, though the world may honour him, he loaths himself, as viler than the earth he treads on; and is secretly ashamed to see the face of man. And how then shall he appear before God? how shall he hold up his face in the presence of his injured Father? He comes to him ashamed, and covering his head. He knows not what to say to him; he knows not how to look him in the face, but he falls down abashed and confounded at his feet. Thus was penitent Ezra ashamed before God. He fell upon his knees, and lifted up his hands (his eyes, like the publican, he durst not lift up) unto the heavens, and he says, *O my God, I am ashamed, and blush to lift up my face to thee, my God! for our iniquities are increased over our heads, and our trespass is grown up unto the heavens. And now, O our God, what shall we say after this? for we have forsaken thy commandments.* Ezra ix. 5–10. Thus it was foretold concerning the repenting Jews. *Then thou shalt remember thy ways and be ashamed. Thou shalt be confounded and never open thy mouth any more, because of*

thy shame. Ezek. xvi. 61–63. There is good reason for
this conscious shame, and therefore it is enjoined as a duty :
*Not for your sakes do I this, saith the Lord God, be it
known unto you : be ashamed and confounded for your
own ways, O house of Israel.* Ezek. xxxvi. 32.

And what is the cause of this shame in the mourning
penitent? Oh, says he, it is *because I bear the reproach
of my youth.* " I carry upon me (as the original word
signifies) the brand of infamy. My youth, alas! was
spent in a thoughtless neglect of God and the duties I
owed him; my vigorous days were wasted in sensual ex-
travagances, and gratifying my criminal inclinations. My
prime of life, which should have been sacred to the author
of my existence, was spent in rebellion against him. Alas!
my first thoughts, my virgin love, did not aspire to him;
nor did my young desires, as soon as fledged, wing their
flight to heaven. In short, the temper of my heart, and
my course of my life, from the first exercises of reason to
this happy hour of my conversion, were a disgrace to my
rational nature; I have degraded myself beneath the beasts
that perish." *Behold, I am vile ; I loath and abhor myself for all my filthiness and abominations.* Ezek. xxxvi.
31. "And how amazing the grace of God to honour so
base a wretch with a place among the children of his
love !"

Thus I have delineated the heart of penitent Ephraim;
and let me ask you, my brethren, is this your picture?
Have you ever felt such ingenuous relentings, such just
consternation, such holy shame and confusion? There
can be no transition from nature to grace, without previous
concern, &c. You all bear the reproach of that youth,
you have all spent some unhappy days in the scandalous
ways of sin, and your consciences still bear the brand of
infamy. And have you ever been made deeply sensible

of it? Has God ever heard you bemoaning yourselves thus in some mournful solitude, "Thou hast chastised me, and I was chastised, as a bullock unaccustomed to the yoke." Is there any such mourner here this day? then listen to the gracious voice of your heavenly Father, while,

III. I am illustrating the last, the sweetest part of the text, which expresses the tender compassion of God towards mourning penitents.

While they are bemoaning their case, and conscious that they do not deserve one look of love from God, he is represented as attentively listening to catch the first pentitential groan that breaks from their hearts. Ephraim, in the depth of his despondency, probably did hardly hope that God took any notice of his secret sorrows, which he suppressed as much as possible from the public view: but God heard him, God was watching to hear the first mournful cry; and he repeats all his complaints, to let him know (after the manner of men) what particular notice he had taken of them. "*I have surely heard*, or hearing I have heard:" that is, "I have attentively heard Ephraim bemoaning himself thus."

What strong consolation may this give to desponding mourners, who think themselves neglected by that God to whom they are pouring out their weeping supplications! He hears your secret groans, he courts your sighs, and puts your tears into his bottle. His eyes penetrate all the secrets of your heart, and he observes all their feeble struggles to turn to himself; and he beholds you not as an unconcerned spectator, but with all the tender emotions of fatherly compassion: for,

While he is listening to Ephraim's mournful complaints, he abruptly breaks in upon him, and sweetly surprises him with the warmest declarations of pity and grace. " Is this Ephraim, my dear son, whose mourning voice I hear; Is this my pleasant child, or (as it might be rendered) the child of my delights, who thus wounds my ear with his heart-rending groans?" What strange language this to an ungrateful, unyielding rebel, that continued obstinate till he was wearied out; that would not turn till drawn; that deserved to fall a victim to justice! This is the language of compassion all divine, of grace that becomes a God.

This passage contains a most encouraging truth, that, however vile and abandoned a sinner has been, yet upon his repentance, he becomes God's dear son, his favourite child. He will, from that moment, regard him, provide for him, protect him, and bring him to his heavenly inheritance, as his son and heir; for "Neither death, nor life, nor angels, nor principalities, nor powers, nor things present, nor things to come," &c. Rom. viii. 38, &c., shall separate him from his father's love but "he shall inherit all things." Rev. xxi. 7. Yea, all things are his already in title, and he shall be made "greater than the kings of the earth;" he shall be made such as becomes so dignified a relation as that of a Son to the King of kings, and Lord of lords.

And is not this magnet sufficient to attract all this assembly to their Father's house? Can you resist the almighty energy of such compassion? Return, ye perishing prodigals! Return; though you have *sinned against Heaven, and before your Father, and are no more worthy to be called his sons*, yet return, and you shall be made his dear sons, his pleasant children.

Are none of you in need of such strong consolation as this? Do you want encouragement to return, and are you ready to spring up and run to your Father's arms upon the first assurance of acceptance? If this be what you want, you have an abundance for your supply. Are all your souls then in motion to return? Does that eye which darts through the whole creation at once, now behold your hearts moving towards God? Or am I wasting these gracious encouragements upon stupid creatures, void of sensation, that do not care for them, or that are so conceited of their own worth, as not to need them? If so, I retract these consolations, with respect to you, and shall presently tell you your doom. But let us further pursue these melting strains of paternal pity.

"For since I spake against him, I do earnestly remember him still." Many and dreadful were the threatenings denounced against the sinner, while impenitent; and, had he continued impenitent, they would certainly have been executed upon him. But the primary and immediate design of the threatenings are to make men happy, and not to make them miserable; they are designed to deter them from disobedience, which is naturally productive of misery, or to reclaim them from it, which is but to restrain them in their career to ruin. And consequently these threatenings proceed from love as well as the promises of our God, from love to the person, though from hatred to sin. So the same love which prompts a parent to promise a reward to his son for obedience, will prompt him also to threaten him, if he takes some dangerous weapon to play with: or, to choose a more pertinent illustration, for God is the moral ruler as well as the father of the rational world; the same regard to the public weal, which induces a lawgiver to annex a reward to obedience, will also prompt him to add penalties to his law to deter from disobedience; and his immediate design is not to make any of his subjects miserable, but to keep them from making themselves and others miserable by disobedience; though when the threatening is once denounced, it is necessary it should be executed, to vindicate the veracity of the law-

giver, and secure his government from insult and contempt.
Thus when the primary end of the divine threatenings,
namely, the deterring and reclaiming men from disobedience, is not obtained, then it becomes necessary that they
should be executed upon the impenitent in all their dreadful extent; but when the sinner is brought to repentance,
and to submit to the divine government, then all these
threatenings are repealed, and they shall not hurt one hair
of his head. And the sinner himself will acknowledge
that these threatenings proved necessary mercies to him,
and that the denunciation of everlasting punishment was
one means of bringing him to everlasting happiness, and
that divine vengeance in this sense conspired with divine
grace to save him.

Consider this, ye desponding penitents, and allay your
terrors. That God, who has written such bitter things
against you in his word, earnestly and affectionately remembers you still, and it was with a kind intent to you
that he thundered out these terrors at which you tremble.
These acids, this bitter physic, were necessary for your
recovery. These coals of fire were necessary to awaken
you out of your lethargy. Therefore read the love of
your Father, even in these solemn warnings. He affectionately remembers you still; he cannot put you out of
his thoughts.

Therefore my bowels (adds the all-gracious Jehovah) *are
troubled for him.* Astonishing beyond conception! how
can we bear up under such words as these? Surely they
must break our hearts, and overwhelm our spirits! Here
is the great God, who has millions of superior beings to
serve him, and who is absolutely independent upon them
all, troubled, his very bowels troubled, for a rebellious,
useless, trifling worm! Be astonished at this, ye angels of
light, who are the witnesses of such amazing, such un-

bounded compassion; and wonder at it, O ye sons of men, who are more intimately concerned in it, stand and adore, as it were, in statues of admiration! It is true these words are not to be taken literally, as though the Deity were capable of sorrow, or any of the human passions: but he here condescends to adapt himself to the language of mortals, and to borrow such images as will convey to us the most lively ideas of his grace and tenderness to mourning penitents; and no image can answer this end better than that of a father, whose bowels are yearning over his mourning child, prostrate at his feet, and who, with eager embraces, raises him up, assuring him of pardon and acceptance. If any of you now know what it is to receive a penitent child in this manner, while all the father is tenderly working within you, you may form some affecting ideas of the readiness of our heavenly Father to receive returning sinners from this tender illustration.

The Lord concludes this moving speech with a promise that includes in it more than we can ask or think, sealed with his own sacred name. *I will surely have mercy*, or, (according to the more emphatical original) *with mercy, I will have mercy upon him saith the Lord ;* this is, I will show abundant mercy to him, I will give him all the blessings that infinite mercy can bestow; and what can be needed more? This promise includes pardon, acceptance, sanctification, joy in the Holy Ghost, peace of conscience, and immortal life and glory in the future world. Oh sirs! what a God, what a Father is this! *Who is a God like unto thee, that pardoneth iniquity*, &c. Micah vii. 18.

And can you, ye mourners in Zion, can you fear a rejection from such a tender Father? Can you dread to venture upon such abundant mercies? Is there a mourning Ephraim in this assembly? I may call you, as God did Adam, *Ephraim, where art thou?* Let the word of God find you out, and force a little encouragement upon you; your heavenly Father, whose angry hand you fear, is listening to your groans, and will measure you out a mercy for every groan, a blessing for every sigh, a drop, a draught of consolation for every tear. His bowels are moving over you, and he addresses you in such language as this, "Is this my dear son? is this my pleasant child?"

And as to you, ye hardy impenitents, ye abandoned profligates, ye careless formalists, ye almost Christians, can you hear these things, and not begin now to relent? Do you not find your frozen hearts begin to thaw within you? Can you resist such alluring grace? Can you bear the thoughts of continuing enemies to so good, so forgiving a Father? Does not Ephraim's petition now rise to your hearts, *Turn thou me, and I shall be turned*? then I congratulate you upon this happy day; you are this day become God's dear sons, the children of his delights.

Is there a wretch so senseless, so wicked, so abandoned, as to refuse to return? Where art thou, hardy rebel? Stand forth and meet the terrors of thy doom. To thee I must change my voice, and instead of representing the tender compassions of a father, must denounce the terrors of an angry judge. Thy doom is declared and fixed by the same lips that speak to penitents in such encouraging strains; by those gracious lips that never uttered a harsh censure. *God is angry with thee every day.* Psal. vii. 11. *Except thou repentest, thou shalt surely perish.* Luke xiii. 3. The example of Christ authorizes me to repeat it again; "Except thou repentest, thou shalt surely perish," ver. 5. "The God that made thee will destroy thee; and he that formed thee will show thee no favour." Isa. xxvi. 11. "Thou art treasuring up wrath *in horrid affluence* against the day of wrath." Rom. ii. 5. "God is jealous,

and the LORD revengeth; the LORD revengeth, and is
furious; the LORD will take vengeance on his adversaries;
and he reserveth wrath for his enemies. The mountains
quake at him, and the hills melt, and the earth is burnt at
his presence: yea, the world, and they that dwell therein.
Who can stand before his indignation? Who can abide
in the fierceness of his anger? His fury is poured out
like fire, and the rocks are thrown down by him." Nahum
i. 2–6. These flaming thunderbolts, sinners, are aimed at
thy heart, and if thou canst harden thyself against their
terror, let me read thee thy doom before we part. You
have it pronounced by God himself in Deuteronomy, the
twenty-ninth chapter, at the nineteenth and the following
verses, " If it come to pass, when he heareth the words of
this curse, that he bless himself in his heart, saying, I shall
have peace, though I walk in the imagination of my heart,
The Lord will not spare him: but then the anger of the
Lord and his jealousy shall smoke against that man, and all
the curses that are written in this book shall lie upon him,
and the LORD shall blot out his name from under heaven.
And the LORD shall separate him unto evil out of all the
tribes of Israel, according to all the curses of the covenant
that are written in this book of the law." And now, sinner, if thou canst return home careless and senseless with
this heavy curse upon thee, expect not a word of comfort,
expect no blessing till thou art made truly penitent; for
" how shall I bless whom God has not blessed?" The
ministerial blessing falls upon one on thy right hand, and
one on thy left, but it lights not upon thee. The curse is
thy lot, and this must thou have at the hand of God, if
thou continuest hardened and insolent in sin. *Thou must
lie down in sorrow.* Isa. l. 11. *Consider this, ye that forget God, lest he tear you in pieces, and there be none to
deliver.* Psal. l. 22.

SERMON XIV.

CHRIST PRECIOUS TO ALL TRUE BELIEVERS.

1 PETER ii. 7.—*Unto you therefore which believe, He is
precious.**

YES; blessed be God; though a great part of the
creation is disaffected to Jesus Christ; though fallen spirits,
both in flesh and without flesh, both upon earth and in
hell, neglect him or profess themselves open enemies to
him, yet he is precious; precious not only in himself, not
only to his Father, not only to the choirs of heaven, who
behold his full glory without a veil, but precious to some
even in our guilty world; precious to a sort of persons of
our sinful race, who make no great figure in mortal eyes,
who have no idea of their own goodness; who are mean,
unworthy creatures, in their own view, and who are
generally despicable in the view of others; I mean he is
precious to all true believers. And though they are but
few comparatively in our world; though there are, I am
afraid, but few additions made to them from among us;
yet, blessed be God, there are some believers even upon
our guilty globe; and I doubt not but I am now speaking
to some such.

My believing brethren, (if I may venture to claim
kindred with you,) I am now entering upon a design,
which I know you have much at heart: and that is, to
make the blessed Jesus more precious to you, and if pos-

---

* *Or preciousness* in the abstract, τιμη.

sible, to recommend him to the affections of the crowd
that neglect him. You know, alas! you love him but
little; but very little, compared to his infinite excellency
and your obligations to him; and you know that multitudes
love him not at all. Whatever they profess, their practice
shows that their carnal minds are enmity against him.
This you often see, and the sight affects your hearts. It
deeply affects you to think so much excellency should be
neglected and despised, and so much love meet with such
base returns of ingratitude. And you cannot but pity
your poor fellow sinners, that they are so blind to the
brightest glory and their own highest interest, and that
they should perish, through wilful neglect of their deliverer;
perish, as it were, within reach of the hand stretched out
to save them. This is indeed a very affecting, very
lamentable, and alas! a very common sight. And will
you not then bid me God-speed this day in my attempt to
recommend this precious, though neglected, Jesus? Will
you not contribute your share towards my success in so
pious and benevolent a design by your earnest prayers?
Now, shall not the interceding sigh rise to heaven from
every heart, and every soul be cast into a praying posture?
I shall hope to discharge my duty with more comfort and
advantage, if you afford me this assistance. And surely
such of you cannot deny me this aid, who desire that Jesus
may become still more precious to your own hearts, and
that he may be the object of universal love from all the
sons of men, who are now disaffected to him.

To you that believe, he is precious—He? Who? Is it
mammon, the god of the world? Is it pleasure, or honour?
No; none of these is the darling of the believing heart.
But it is he who is the uppermost in every pious heart;
he, who is first in the thoughts and affections; he whom
every friend of his must know, even without a name; if it

be but said of him, he is precious, this is enough to distinguish him from all others. "If it be he the apostle means," may every believer say, "who is most precious to my soul, then I can easily point him out, though without a name. It must be Jesus, for oh! it is he that is most precious to me." The connection also of the text directs us to the same person. It is he the apostle means, whom he had just described as a living stone, chosen of God, and precious; the chief corner-stone, the great foundation of the church, that spiritual temple of God, so stately and glorious, and reaching from earth to heaven; it is this precious stone, this heavenly jewel, that is precious to believers.

"To you that *believe, he is precious*," i. e., he is highly valued by you. You esteem him one of infinite worth, and he has the highest place in your affections. He is dearer to your hearts than all other persons and things. The word $\tau\iota\mu\eta$ requires a still stronger translation : "To you that believe, he is *preciousness ;*" preciousness in the abstract; all preciousness, and nothing but preciousness; a precious stone without one blemish. Or it may be translated with a little variation, "To you that believe, he is honour." It confers the highest honour upon you to be related to him; and you esteem it your highest honour to sustain that relation. Though Jesus and his cross are names of reproach in the unbelieving world, you glory in them, and they reflect a real glory upon you. Or, "To you that believe, there is honour."* Honour is now conferred upon you in your being built as living stones in the temple of God upon this precious foundation; and honour is reserved for you in heaven, where the crown of righteousness awaits you.

---

* The pronoun he, is not in the original; but the passage reads thus : To you who believe, honour.

" To you which believe, he is precious ;" that is to say,
the value of this precious stone is, alas! unknown to the
crowd. It is so far from being precious, that it is a stone
of stumbling, and a rock of offence; a stone disallowed of
men, (v. 4,) rejected even by the builders, (v. 7,) but you
believers, ye happy few, have another estimate of it.
Faith enables you to see the glories of the blessed Jesus ;
and, when you know him through this medium, you cannot but love him. The blind world neglect the Lord of
glory, because they know him not: but you believers know
him, and therefore to you he is precious. Faith presents
him to your view in a just light, and directs you to form a
proper estimate of him. It is truly lamentable that such
real excellency should be despised; but so it will be with
the world till they believe. The mere speculative recommendation of their reason, the prepossessions of education
in his favour, and the best human means, are not sufficient
to render Jesus precious to them. Nothing but saving
faith can effect this.

To you therefore which believe he is precious. The
illative particle, therefore, shows this passage is an inference from what went before; and the reasoning seems
to be this : " This stone is precious to God, therefore it is
precious to you that believe. You have the same estimate
of Jesus Christ which God the Father has ; and for that
very reason he is precious to you, because he is precious
to him." That this is the connection will appear, if you
look back to the 4th and 6th verses; where you find Jesus
described as "a chief corner-stone, laid in Zion, elect or
chosen, and precious; disallowed, indeed, of men, but
chosen of God, and precious."* Men wickedly disapprove

---

* The word used in ver. 4 and 6 is a compound, rendered " precious" in
the text. And this is an intimation that the text is an inference from the
above verses.

this stone, and even many of the professed builders of his church reject him. This, says the apostle, must be granted. But this is no objection to his real worth. He is precious to God, who knows him best, and who is a perfect judge of real excellency; and for that very reason he is precious to you that believe. Faith teaches you to look upon persons and things in the same light in which God views them; it makes your sentiments conformed to his. Christ is the Father's beloved son, in whom he is well pleased; and he is your beloved Saviour, in whom you are well pleased.

Is it any wonder that Jesus should be precious to believers, when he is so precious in himself, and in his offices, so precious to the angelic hosts, and so precious to his Father?

1. He is precious in himself. He is Immanuel, God-man; and consequently, whatever excellencies belong either to the divine or human nature, centre in him. If wisdom, power, and goodness, divine or human, created or uncreated, can render him worthy of the highest affection, he has a just claim to it. Whatever excellencies, natural or moral, appear in any part of the vast universe, they are but faint shadows of his beauty and glory. *All things were created by him, and for him: and he is before all things, and by him all things consist;* Col. i. 16, 17. And whatever excellencies are in the effect must be eminently in the cause. You do not wonder nor censure, when you see men delighted with the glories of the sun, and the various luminaries of the sky; you do not wonder nor blame when they take pleasure in the beautiful prospects of nature, or in that rich variety of good things, which earth, and sea, and every element furnishes for the support of man, or the gratification of his senses: you do not wonder and blame, when they are struck with moral

beauty, when you see them admire and approve wisdom, benevolence, justice, veracity, meekness, and mercy; you never think it strange, much less censurable, that men should love these things, and count them precious; and can you be astonished, can you ridicule or find fault, that Jesus is precious to poor believers? If the copy be so fair and lovely, who would not love the original, that has eyes to behold it? Believers see so much of the worth of Christ as is sufficient to captivate their hearts, and to convince them of their guilt in loving him no more; and the clearer their views are of him, the more they are mortified at the criminal defects of their love; for oh, they see he deserves infinitely more!

2. The Lord Jesus is precious in his offices. His mediatorial office is generally subdivided into three parts, namely, that of a Prophet, of a Priest, and of a King: and how precious is Christ in each of these!

As a Prophet, how sweet are his instructions to a bewildered soul! How precious the words of his lips, which are the words of eternal life! How delightful to sit and hear him teach the way of duty and happiness, revealing the Father, and the wonders of the invisible state! How transporting to hear him declare upon what terms an offended God may be reconciled! a discovery beyond the searches of all the sages and philosophers of the heathen world! How reviving is it to listen to his gracious promises and invitations! promises and invitations to the poor, the weary, and heavy-laden, to the broken-hearted, and even to the chief of sinners! The word of Christ has been the treasure, the support, and the joy of believers in all ages. "I have esteemed the words of his mouth," says Job, "more than my necessary food," Job xxiii. 12. It is this precious word the Psalmist so often and so highly celebrates. He celebrates it as "more to be desired than gold; yea, than much fine gold; sweeter also than honey, and the honey-comb," Psalm xix. 10. "Oh how I love thy law!" says he: "it is my meditation all the day," Psalm cxix. 97. "How sweet are thy words unto my taste! yea sweeter than honey to my mouth," ver. 103. "The law of thy mouth is better unto me than thousands of gold and silver," ver. 72. "Behold, I have longed after thy precepts," ver. 40. "Thy statutes have been my songs in the house of my pilgrimage," ver. 54. "In my affliction, thy word hath quickened me," ver. 50. "Unless thy law had been my delights, I should then have perished in my affliction," ver. 92. This is the language of David, in honour of this divine Prophet, near three thousand years ago, when Christ had not revealed the full gospel to the world, but only some rays of it shone through the veil of the Mosaic dispensation. And must not believers now, who live under the more complete and clear instructions of the great Prophet, entertain the same sentiments of him? Yes, to such of you as believe, even in this age, he is most precious.

But this external objective instruction is not all that Christ as a Prophet communicates; and, indeed, did he do no more than this, it would answer no valuable end. The mind of man, in his present fallen state, like a disordered eye, is incapable of perceiving divine things in a proper light, however clearly they are revealed; and therefore, till the perceiving faculty be rectified, all external revelation is in vain, and is only like opening a fair prospect to a blind eye. Hence this great Prophet carries his instruction further, not only by proposing divine things in a clear objective light by his word, but inwardly enlightening the mind, and enabling it to perceive what is revealed by his Spirit. And how precious are these internal subjective instructions! How sweet to feel a disordered, dark mind opening to admit the shinings of heavenly day; to perceive the glory of God in the face of Jesus Christ, the beauties of holiness, and the majestic wonders of the eternal world! Speak, ye that know by happy experience, and tell how precious Jesus appears to you, when, by his own blessed Spirit, he scatters the cloud that benighted your understandings, and lets in the rays of his glory upon your admiring souls; when he opens your eyes to see the wonders contained in his law, and the glorious mysteries of his gospel. What a divine glory does then spread upon every page of the sacred volume! Then it indeed appears the book of God, God-like, and worthy its Author. Oh, precious Jesus! let us all this day feel thine enlightening influences, that experience may teach us how sweet they are! Come, great Prophet! come, and make thine own Spirit our teacher, and then shall we be divinely wise.

Again, the Lord Jesus is precious to believers as a great High Priest. As a High Priest, he made complete atonement for sin by his propitiatory sacrifice on the cross; and he still makes intercession for the transgressors on his throne in heaven. It was his sacrifice that satisfied the demands of the law and justice of God, and rendered him reconcilable to the guilty, upon terms consistent with his honour and the rights of his government. It was by virtue of this sacrifice that he procured pardon for sin, the favour of God, freedom from hell, and eternal life for condemned, obnoxious rebels. And such of you, who have ever felt the pangs of a guilty conscience, and obtained relief from Jesus Christ, can tell how precious is his atoning sacrifice. How did it ease your self-tormenting consciences, and heal your broken hearts! How did it change the frowns of an angry God into smiles of love, and your trembling apprehensions of vengeance into delightful hopes of mercy!

How precious did Jesus appear, with a pardon in his hand, with atoning blood gushing from his opened veins, and making his cross, as it were, the key to open the gates of heaven for your admission! Blessed Saviour! our great High Priest! thus appear to us with all thy robes, dyed in thine own blood, and cause us all to feel the efficacy of thy propitiation.

Let us next turn our eyes upwards, and view this great High Priest as our Intercessor in the presence of God. There he appears as a lamb that was slain, bearing the memorials of his sacrifice, and putting the Father in remembrance of the blessings purchased for his people. There he urges it as his pleasure, as his authoritative will, that these blessings should in due time be conferred upon those for whom they were purchased. In this authoritative manner he could intercede even in the days of his humiliation upon earth, because of the Father's covenant engagements with him, the accomplishment of which he has a right to demand, as well as humbly to petition: "Father, I will—I will, that they also whom thou hast given me, be with me where I am; that they may behold my glory," John xvii. 24. Now how precious must Christ appear in the character of Intercessor! That the friendless sinner should have an all-prevailing advocate in the court of heaven to undertake his cause! that the great High Priest should offer up the grateful incense of his own merit, with the prayers of the saints! that he should add the sanction of his authoritative will to the humble petition of faith! that he should urge the claims of his people, as his own claims, founded upon an unchangeable covenant with his Father, of which he has fully performed the conditions required! that he should not intercede occasionally, but always appear in the holy of holies as the constant ever-living Intercessor, and maintain the same interest, the

same importunity at all times, even when the petitions of
his people languish upon their lips! What delightful reflections are these! and how warmly may they recommend
the Lord Jesus to the hearts of believers! How just is
the apostle's inference, " Having an High Priest over the
house of God, let us draw near with a true heart, in full
assurance of faith; and let us hold fast the profession of
our faith without wavering." Heb. x. 21–23. " He is
able to save them to the uttermost that come unto God
by him;" for this reason, because "he ever liveth to make
intercession for them." IIeb. vii. 25. May each of us
intrust his cause to this all-prevailing Advocate, and we
shall certainly gain it! The unchangeable promise has
passed his lips, " that whatsoever we ask the Father in his
name, he will give it us." John xvi. 23.

Let me add, the kingly office of Christ is precious to
believers. As King he gives laws, laws perfectly wise
and good, and enforced with the most important sanctions, everlasting rewards and punishments. And how
delightful, how advantageous, to live under such a government! to have our duty discovered with so much clear-
ness and certainty which frees us from so many painful
anxieties, and to have such powerful motives to obedience,
which have a tendency to infuse vigour and spirit into our
endeavours! As King, he appoints ordinances of worship.
And how sweet to converse with him in these ordinances,
and to be freed from perplexity about that manner of
worship which God will accept, without being exposed to
that question, so confounding to will-worshippers, *Who hath
required this at your hands?* As King, he is head over
all things to his church, and manages the whole creation,
as is most subservient to her good. The various ranks of
creatures in heaven, earth and hell, are subject to his direction and control; and they must all co-operate for the

good of his people. He reclaims, confounds, subdues, or destroys their enemies, according to his pleasure. And how precious must he be in this august character to the feeble helpless believer! To have an almighty friend sitting at the helm of the universe, with the supreme management of all things in his hands; to be assured that even the most injurious enemy can do the believer no real or lasting injury, but shall at length concur to work his greatest good; and that, come what will, it shall go well with him, and he shall at last be made triumphant over all difficulty and opposition. Oh! what transporting considerations are here! But this is not the whole exercise of the royal power of Christ. He not only makes laws and ordinances, and restrains the enemies of his people, but he exercises his power inwardly .upon their hearts. He is the King of souls; he reigns in the hearts of his subjects; and how infinitely dear and precious is he in this view! To feel him subdue the rebellion within, sweetly bending the stubborn heart into willing obedience, and reducing every thought into a cheerful captivity to himself, writing his law upon the heart, making the dispositions of his subjects a transcript of his will, corresponding to it, like wax to the seal, how delightful is all this! Oh the pleasures of humble submission! How pleasant to lie as subjects at the feet of this mediatorial King without arrogating the sovereignty to ourselves, for which we are utterly insufficient! Blessed Jesus! thus reign in our hearts thus subdue the nations to the obedience of faith! " Gird thy sword upon thy thigh, O most Mighty! and ride prosperously, attend with majesty, truth, meekness, and righteousness." Psalm xlv. 3, 4. "Send the rod of thy strength out of Sion: rule thou in the midst of thine enemies," Psalm cx. 2, rule us, and subdue the rebel in our hearts.

Thus you see the Lord Jesus is precious to believers in

all the views of his mediatorial office. But he is not precious to them alone : he is beloved as far as known, and the more known the more beloved : which leads me to add,

3. He is precious to all the angels of heaven.

St. Peter tells us that the things now reported to us by the gospel are *things which the angels desire to look into*, 1 Pet. i. 12. Jesus is the wonder of angels now in heaven; and he was so even when he appeared in the form of a servant upon earth. St. Paul mentions it as one part of the great mystery of godliness, that *God manifested in the flesh was seen of angels.* 1 Tim. iii. 16. Angels saw him, and admired and loved him in the various stages of his life, from his birth to his return to his native heaven. Hear the manner in which angels celebrated his entrance into our world. One of them spread his wings and flew with joyful haste to a company of poor shepherds that kept their midnight watches in the field, and abruptly tells the news, of which his heart was full: " Behold, I bring you good tidings of great joy which shall be to all people; for to you is born this day, in the city of David, a Saviour, which is Christ the Lord: and suddenly there was with the angel a multitude of the heavenly host." Crowds of angels left their stations in the celestial court in that memorable hour, and hovered over the place where their incarnate God lay in a manger: Jesus, their darling, was gone down to earth, and they must follow him; for who would not be where Jesus is? Men, ungrateful men, were silent upon that occasion, but angels tuned their song of praise. The astonished shepherds heard them sing, " Glory to God in the highest, and on earth peace, goodwill to men." Luke ii. 10–14. When he bringeth his first born into the world, the Father saith, *Let all the angels of God worship him,* Heb. i. 6. This seems to intimate that all the angels crowded round the manger,

where the Infant-God lay, and paid him their humble
worship. We are told, that when the devil had finished
his long process of temptations, after forty days, and had
left him, the *angels came and ministered unto him.* Matt.
iv. 11. When this disagreeable companion had left him,
his old attendants were fond of renewing their service to
him. In every hour of difficulty they were ready to fly
to his aid. He was seen of angels, in his hard conflict, in
the garden of Gethsemane; and one of them "appeared
unto him from heaven, strengthening him." Luke xxii. 43.
With what wonder, sympathy and readiness, did this angelic assistant raise his prostrate Lord from the cold
ground, wipe off his bloody sweat, and support his sinking
spirit with divine encouragements! But oh! ye blessed
angels, ye usual spectators, and adorers of the divine glories of our Redeemer, with what astonishment and horror
were you struck, when you saw him expire on the cross!

> "Around the bloody tree
> Ye press'd with strong desire,
> That wondrous sight to see,
> The Lord of life expire!
> And could your eyes
> Have known a tear,
> Had dropt it there
> In sad surprise."*

Ye also hovered round his tomb, while he lay in the
prison of the grave. The weeping women and his other
friends found you stationed there in their early impatient
visits to the sepulchre! Oh what wonders then appeared
to your astonished minds! Could you, that pry so deep into
the secrets of heaven, you that know so well what divine
love can do, could you have thought that even divine love
could have gone so far? could have laid the Lord of glory
a pale, mangled, senseless corpse in the mansions of the

* Doddridge.

dead? Was not this a strange surprise even to you? And, when the appointed day began to dawn, with what eager and joyful haste did ye roll away the stone, and set open the prison doors, that the rising Conqueror might march forth!

> " And when arrayed in light,
> The shining conqueror rode,
> Ye hail'd his rapturous flight
> Up to the throne of God ;
>   And wav'd around
>   Your golden wings,
>   And struck your strings
>   Of sweetest sound.*

When he ascended on high, he was attended " with the chariots of God, which are twenty thousand, even thousands of angels." Psalm lxviii. 17, 18. And now, when he is returned tó dwell among them, Jesus is still the darling of angels. His name sounds from all their harps, and his love is the subject of their everlasting song. St. John once heard them, and I hope we shall ere long hear them, saying with a loud voice, "Worthy is the Lamb that was slain to receive power, and riches, and wisdom, and strength, and honour, and glory, and blessing." Rev. v. 11, 12. This is the song of angels, as well as of the redeemed from among men :

> "Jesus the Lord, their harps employs ;
>   Jesus, my love, they sing ;
> Jesus, the name of both our joys,
>   Sounds sweet from every string."†

Oh my brethren, could we see what is doing in heaven at this instant, how would it surprise, astonish, and confound us? Do you think the name of Jesus is of as lit-

---

* An excellent hymn of Dr. Doddridge's on 1 Tim. iii. 16.—Seen of Angels.

† Watts' Hor. Lyric.

tle importance there as in the world? Do you think
there is one lukewarm or disaffected heart there among
ten thousand times ten thousand of thousands of thousands?
Oh no! there his love is the ruling passion of every heart,
and the favourite theme of every song. And is he so precious to angels? to angels, who are less interested in him,
and less indebted to him? And must he not be precious
to poor believers bought with his blood, and entitled to
life by his death? Yes, you that believe have an angelic
spirit in this respect; you love Jesus, though unseen, as
well as they who see him as he is, though alas! in a far
less degree. But to bring his worth to the highest standard of all, I add,

4. He is infinitely precious to his Father, who thoroughly knows him, and is an infallible judge of real
worth. He proclaimed more than once from the excellent glory, " This is my beloved Son, in whom I am well
pleased; hear ye him. Behold," says he, " my servant
whom I uphold; mine elect, in whom my soul delighteth."
Isa. xlii. 1. He is called by the names of the tenderest
endearment; his Son, his own Son, his dear Son, the Son
of his love. He is a stone disallowed indeed of men; if
their approbation were the true standard of merit, he
must be looked upon as a very worthless, insignificant
being, unworthy of their thoughts and affections. But let
men form what estimate of him they please, he is *chosen
of God, and precious.* And shall not the love of the omniscient God have weight with believers to love him too?
Yes, the apostle expressly draws the consequence; he is
precious to God, therefore to you that believe, he is precious. It is the characteristic of even the meanest believer, that he is God-like. He is a partaker of the divine nature, and therefore views things, in some measure,
as God does; and is affected towards them as God is,

though there be an infinite difference as to the degree. He prevailingly loves what God loves, and that because God loves it.

And now, my hearers, what think you of Christ? Will you not think of him as believers do? If so, he will be precious to your hearts above all things for the future. Or if you disregard this standard of excellence, as being but the estimate of fallible creatures, will you not think of him as angels do; angels, those bright intelligences, to whom he reveals his unveiled glories, who are more capable of perceiving and judging of him, and who therefore must know him better than you; angels, who have had a long acquaintance with him at home, if I may so speak, for near six thousand years, as God, i. e. ever since their creation, and for near two thousand years as God-man? Since angels then, who know him so thoroughly, love him so highly, certainly you may safely venture to love him; you might safely venture to love him implicitly, upon their word. He died for you, which is more than ever he did for them, and will you not love him after all this love? It is not the mode to think much of him in our world, but it is the mode in heaven. Yes, blessed be God, if he be despised and rejected of men, he is not despised and rejected of angels. Angels, that know him best, love him above all, and as far as their capacity will allow, do justice to his merit; and this is a very comfortable thought to a heart broken with a sense of the neglect and contempt he meets with among men. Blessed Jesus! may not one congregation be got together, even upon our guilty earth, that shall in this respect be like the angels, all lovers of thee? Oh! why should this be impossible, while they are all so much in need of thee, all so much obliged to thee, and thou art so lovely in thyself! Why, my brethren, should not this congregation be made of such, and such only as are lovers of Jesus? Why should he not be precious to every one of you, rich and poor, old and young, white and black? What reason can any one of you give why you in particular should neglect him? I am sure you can give none. And will you, without any reason, dissent from all the angels in heaven, in a point of which they must be the most competent judges? Will you differ from them, and agree in your sentiments of Christ with the ghosts of hell, his implacable, but conquered and miserable enemies?

If all this has no weight with you, let me ask you farther, will you not agree to that estimate of Jesus which his Father has of him? Will you run counter to the supreme reason? Will you set up yourselves as wiser than Omniscience? How must Jehovah resent it to see a worm at his footstool daring to despise him, whom he loves so highly! Oh let him be precious to you, because he is so to God, who knows him best.

But I am shocked at my own attempt. Oh precious Jesus! are matters come to that pass in our world, that creatures bought with thy blood, creatures that owe all their hopes to thee, should stand in need of persuasions to love thee? What horrors attend the thought! However, blessed be God, there are some, even among men, to whom he is precious. This world is not entirely peopled with the despisers of Christ. To as many of you as believe, he is precious, though to none else.

Would you know the reason of this? I will tell you: None but believers have eyes to see his glory, none but they are sensible of their need of him, and none but they have learned from experience how precious he is.

1. None but believers have eyes to see the glory of Christ. As the knowledge of Christ is entirely from revelation, an avowed unbeliever who rejects that revelation,

can have no right knowledge of him, and therefore must be entirely indifferent towards him, as one unknown, or must despise and abhor him as an enthusiast or impostor. But one, who is not an unbeliever in profession or speculation, may yet be destitute of that faith which constitutes a true believer, and which renders Jesus precious to the soul. Even devils are very orthodox in speculation; devils believe and tremble; and they could cry out, " What have we to do with thee, thou Jesus of Nazareth? We know thee, who thou art, the holy one of God." Mark i. 24. And there are crowds among us who believe, after a fashion, that Christ is the true Messiah, who yet show by their practices that they neglect him in their hearts, and are not believers in the full import of the character. True faith includes not only a speculative knowledge and belief, but a clear, affecting, realizing view, and a hearty approbation of the things known and believed concerning Jesus Christ; and such a view, such an approbation, cannot be produced by any human means, but only by the enlightening influence of the holy Spirit shining into the heart. Without such a faith as this, the mind is all dark and blind as to the glory of Jesus Christ; it can see no beauty in him, that he should be desired. Honourable and sublime speculations concerning him may hover in the understanding, and the tongue may pronounce many pompous panegyrics in his praise, but the understanding has no realizing, affecting views of his excellency; nor does the heart delight in him and love him as infinitely precious and lovely. The god of this world, the prince of darkness, has blinded the minds of them that believe not, lest the light of the glorious gospel of Christ should shine into them. But as to the enlightened believer, God, who first commanded light to shine out of darkness, has shined into his heart, to give him the light of the knowledge of the glory of God in

the face of Jesus Christ. This divine illumination pierces
the cloud that obscured his understanding, and enables
him to view the Lord Jesus in a strong and striking light;
a light entirely different from that of the crowd around
him; a light, in which it is impossible to view this glorious
object without loving him. A believer and an unbeliever
may be equally orthodox in speculation, and have the same
notions in theory concerning Jesus Christ, and yet it is
certainly true, that their views of him are vastly different.
Believers, do you think that, if the Christ-despising multitude around you had the same views of his worth and
preciousness which you have, they could neglect him, as
they do? It is impossible. You could once neglect him,
as others do now; you were no more charmed with his
beauty than they. But oh! when you were brought out
of darkness into God's marvellous light, when the glories
of the neglected Saviour broke in upon your astonished
minds, then was it possible for you to withhold your love
from him? Were not your hearts captivated with delightful violence? You could no more resist. Did not your
hearts then as naturally and freely love him, whom they
had once disgusted, as ever they loved a dear child or a
friend, or the sweetest created enjoyment? The improving your reason into faith is setting the disordered eye of
the mind right, that it may be able to see this subject; and
when once you viewed it with this eye of reason restored
and improved, how did the precious stone sparkle before
you, and charm you with its brilliancy and excellence?
Christ is one of those things unseen and hoped for, of
which St. Paul says, *faith is the substance and evidence.*
Heb. xi. 1. Faith gives Christ a present subsistence in
the mind, not as a majestic phantom, but as the most glorious and important reality: and this faith is a clear, affecting demonstration, or conviction, of his existence, and

of his being in reality what his word represents him. It is by such a faith, that is, under its habitual influence, that the believer lives; and hence, while he lives, Jesus is still precious to him.

2. None but believers are properly sensible of their need of Christ. They are deeply sensible of their ignorance and the disorder of their understanding, and therefore they are sensible of their want of both the external and internal instructions of this divine prophet. But as to others, they are puffed up with intellectual pride, and apprehended themselves in very little need of religious instructions; and therefore they think but very slightly of him. Believers feel themselves guilty, destitute of all righteousness, and incapable of making atonement for their sins, or recommending themselves to God, and therefore the satisfaction and righteousness of Jesus Christ are most precious to them, and they rejoice in him as their all-prevailing Intercessor. But as to the unbelieving crowd, they have no such mortifying thoughts of themselves! they have so many excuses to make for their sins, that they bring down their guilt to a very trifling thing, hardly worthy of divine resentment: and they magnify their good works to such a height, that they imagine they will nearly balance their bad, and procure them some favour at least from God, and therefore they must look upon this High Priest as needless. They also love to be free from the restraints of religion, and to have the command of themselves. They would usurp the power of self-government, and make their own pleasure their rule; and therefore the Lord Jesus Christ, as a King, is so far from being precious, that he is very unacceptable to such obstinate, headstrong rebels. They choose to have no lawgiver, but their own wills; and therefore they trample upon his laws, and, as it were, form insurrections against

his government. But the poor believer, sensible of his incapacity for self-government, loves to be under direction, and delights to feel the dependent, submissive, pliant spirit of a subject. He counts it a mercy not to have the management of himself, and feels his need of this mediatorial King to rule him. He hates the rebel within, hates every insurrection of sin, and longs to have it entirely subdued, and every thought, every motion of his soul brought into captivity to the obedience of Christ; and therefore he feels the need of his royal power to make an entire conquest of his hostile spirit. His commands are not uneasy impositions, but most acceptable and friendly directions to him; and the prohibitions of his law are not painful restraints, but a kind of privileges in his esteem. The language of his heart is, "Precious Jesus! be thou my King. I love to live in humble subjection to thee. I would voluntarily submit myself to thy control and direction. Thy will, and not mine be done! Oh subdue every rebellious principle within, and make me all resignation and cheerful obedience to thee!" To such a soul it is no wonder Jesus should be exceedingly precious: but oh how different is this spirit from that which generally prevails in the world? Let me add but one reason more why Jesus is precious to believers, and them only; namely,

3. None but believers have known by experience how precious he is. They, and only they, can reflect upon the glorious views of him, which themselves have had, to captivate their hearts for ever to him. They, and only they, have known what it is to feel a bleeding heart healed by his gentle hand; and a clamorous languishing conscience pacified by his atoning blood. They, and only they, know by experience how sweet it is to feel his love shed abroad in their hearts, to feel a heart, ravished with his glory, pant, and long, and breathe after him, and ex-

erting the various acts of faith, desire, joy, and hope towards him. They, and only they, know by experience how pleasant it is to converse with him in his ordinances, and to spend an hour of devotion in some retirement, as it were, in his company. They, and only they, have experienced the exertions of his royal power, conquering their mightiest sins, and sweetly subduing them to himself. These are, in some measure, matters of experience with every true believer, and therefore it is no wonder Jesus should be precious to them. But as to the unbelieving multitude, poor creatures! they are entire strangers to these things. They may have some superficial notions of them floating in their heads, but they have never felt them in their hearts, and therefore the infinitely precious Lord Jesus is a worthless, insignificant being to them: and thus, alas! it will be with the unhappy creatures, until experience becomes their teacher; until they taste for themselves *that the Lord is gracious.* 1 Pet. ii. 3.

There is an interesting question, which, I doubt not, has risen in the minds of such of you as have heard what has been said with a particular application to yourselves, and keeps you in a painful suspense: with an answer to which I shall conclude: "Am I indeed a true believer?" may some of you say; "and is Christ precious to me? My satisfaction in this sweet subject is vastly abated, till this subject is solved. Sometimes, I humbly think, the evidence is in my favour, and I begin to hope that he is indeed precious to my soul; but alas, my love for him soon languishes, and then my doubts and fears return, and I know not what to do, nor what to think of myself." Do not some of you, my brethren, long to have this perplexing case cleared up? Oh, what would you not give, if you might return home this evening fully satisfied in this point? Well, I would willingly help you, for experience has taught me to sympathize with you under this difficulty. Oh my heart! how often hast thou been suspicious of thyself in this respect? The readiest way I can now take to clear up the matter is to answer another question, naturally resulting from my subject; and that is, "How does that high esteem which a believer has for Jesus Christ discover itself? Or how does he show that Christ is indeed precious to him?" I answer, he shows it in various ways; particularly by his affectionate thoughts of him, which often rise in his mind, and always find welcome there. He discovers that Jesus is precious to him by hating and resisting whatever is displeasing to him, and by parting with every thing that comes in competition with him. He will let all go rather than part with Christ. Honour, reputation, ease, riches, pleasure, and even life itself, are nothing to him in comparison of Christ, and he will run the risk of all; nay, will actually lose all, if he may but win Christ. He discovers his high esteem for him by the pleasure he takes in feeling his heart suitably affected towards him, and by his uneasiness when it is otherwise. Oh! when he can love Jesus, when his thoughts affectionately clasp around him, and when he has a heart to serve him, then he is happy, his soul is well, and he is lively and cheerful. But, alas! when it is otherwise with him, when his love languishes, when his heart hardens, when it becomes out of order for his service, then he grows uneasy and discontented, and cannot be at rest. When Jesus favours him with his gracious presence, and revives him with his influence, how does he rejoice? But when his beloved withdraws himself and is gone, how does he lament his absence, and long for his return! He weeps and cries like a bereaved, deserted orphan, and moans like a loving turtle in the absence of its mate. Because Christ is so precious to him, he cannot bear the thought of parting with him, and the least jealousy of his love pierces his very heart. Because he loves him, he longs for the full enjoyment of him, and is ravished with the prospect of him. Because Christ is precious to him, his interests are so too, and he longs to see his kingdom flourish, and all men fired with his love. Because he loves him, he loves his ordinances; loves to hear, because it is the word of Jesus; loves to pray, because it is maintaining intercourse with Jesus; loves to sit at his table, because it is a memorial of Jesus; and loves his people, because they love Jesus. Whatever has a relation to his precious Saviour is for that reason precious to him; and when he feels anything of a contrary disposition, alas! it grieves him, and makes him abhor himself. These things are sufficient to show that the Lord Jesus has his heart, and is indeed precious to him; and is not this the very picture of some trembling, doubting souls among you? If it be, take courage. After so many vain searches, you have at length discovered the welcome secret, that Christ is indeed precious to you: and if so, you may be sure that you are precious to him. " They shall be mine, saith the LORD, in that day when I make up my jewels." Mal. iii. 17. If you are now satisfied, after thorough trial of the case, retain your hope, and let not every discouraging appearance renew your jealousies again; labour to be steady and firm Christians, and do not stagger through unbelief.

But, alas! I fear that many of you know nothing experimentally of the exercises of a believing heart, which I have been describing, and consequently that Christ is not precious to you. If this is the case, you may be sure indeed you are hateful to him. He is angry with the wicked every day. "Them that honour him, he will honour; and them that despise him shall be lightly esteemed." 1 Sam. ii. 30. And what will you do if Christ should become your enemy and fight against you? If this precious stone should become a stone of stumbling and a rock of offence to you, over which you will fall into ruin, oh how dreadful must the fall be! What must you expect but to lie down in unutterable and everlasting sorrow!

SERMON XV.

THE DANGER OF LUKEWARMNESS IN RELIGION.

Rev. iii. 15, 16.—*I know thy works, that thou art neither cold nor hot; I would thou wert cold or hot. So then, because thou art lukewarm, and neither cold nor hot, I will spew thee out of my mouth.*

THE soul of man is endowed with such active powers, that it cannot be idle; and, if we look round the world, we see it all alive and busy in some pursuit or other. What vigorous action, what labour and toil, what hurry, noise, and commotion about the necessaries of life, about riches and honours! Here men are in earnest: here there is no dissimulation, no indifferency about the event. They sincerely desire, and eagerly strive for these transient delights, or vain embellishments of a mortal life.

And may we infer farther, that creatures, thus formed for action, and thus laborious and unwearied in these inferior pursuits, are proportionably vigorous and in earnest in matters of infinitely greater importance? May we conclude, that they proportion their labour and activity to the nature of things, and that they are most in earnest where they are most concerned? A stranger to our world, that could conclude nothing concerning the conduct of mankind but from the generous presumptions of his own charitable heart, might persuade himself that this is the case. But one that has been but a little while conversant with them, and taken the least notice of their temper and practice with regard to that most interesting thing, Religion, must know it is quite otherwise. For look round you, and what do you see? Here and there indeed you may see a few unfashionable creatures, who act as if they looked upon religion to be the most interesting concern; and who seem determined, let others do as they will, to make sure of salvation, whatever becomes of them in other respects; but as to the generality, they are very indifferent about it. They will not indeed renounce all religion entirely; they will make some little profession of the religion that happens to be most modish and reputable in their country, and they will conform to some of its institutions; but it is a matter of indifferency with them, and they are but little concerned about it; or in the language of my text, they are *lukewarm, and neither cold nor hot.*

This threatening, *I will spew thee out of my mouth,* has been long ago executed with a dreadful severity upon the Laodicean church; and it is now succeeded by a mongrel race of Pagans and Mahometans; and the name of Christ is not heard among them. But, though this church has been demolished for so many hundreds of years, that lukewarmness of spirit in religion which brought this judgment upon them, still lives, and possesses the Christians of our age; it may therefore be expedient for us to consider Christ's friendly warning to them, that we may escape their doom.

The epistles to the seven churches in Asia are introduced with this solemn and striking preface, " I know thy works:" that is to say, your character is drawn by one that thoroughly knows you; one who inspects all your conduct, and takes notice of you when you take no notice of yourselves; one that cannot be imposed upon by an empty profession and artifice, but searches the heart and the reins. Oh that this truth were deeply impressed upon our hearts: for

surely we could not trifle and offend while sensible that we
are under the eye of our Judge!

I know thy works, says he to the Laodicean church,
that thou art neither cold nor hot. This church was in a
very bad condition, and Christ reproves her with the grav-
est severity;* and yet we do not find her charged with the
practice or toleration of any gross immoralities, as some
of the other churches were. She is not censured for indulging fornication among her members, or communicating
with idolaters in eating things sacrificed to idols, like some
of the rest. She was free from the infection of the Nico-
laitans, which had spread among them. What then is her
charge? It is a subtle, latent wickedness, that has no
shocking appearance, that makes no gross blemish in the
outward character of a professor in the view of others, and
may escape his own notice; it is, *Thou art lukewarm, and
neither cold nor not :* as if our Lord had said, Thou dost
not entirely renounce and openly disregard the Christian
religion, and thou dost not make it a serious business, and
mind it as thy grand concern. Thou hast a form of godliness, but deniest the power. All thy religion is a dull
languid thing, a mere indifferency; thine heart is not in it;
it is not animated with the fervour of thy spirit. Thou
hast neither the coldness of the profligate sinner, nor the
sacred fire and life of the true Christian; but thou keep-
est a sort of medium between them. In some things thou
resemblest the one, in other things the other; as lukewarmness partakes of the nature both of heat and cold.

Now such a lukewarmness is an eternal solecism in religion; it is the most absurd and inconsistent thing imaginable: more so than avowed impiety, or a professed rejec-

---

* She was as loathsome to him as lukewarm water to the stomach, and he
characterizes her as "wretched, and miserable, and poor, and blind, and
naked." What condition can be more deplorable and dangerous?

tion of all religion : therefore, says Christ, *I would thou wert cold or hot*—*i. e.*, " You might be any thing more consistently than what you are.   If you looked upon religion as a cheat, and openly rejected the profession of it, it would not be strange that you should be careless about it, and disregard it in practice.   But to own it true, and make a profession of it, and yet be lukewarm and indifferent about it, this is the most absurd conduct that can be conceived; for, if it be true, it is certainly the most important and interesting truth in all the world, and requires the utmost exertion of all your powers."

When Christ expresses his abhorrence of lukewarmness in the form of a wish, *I would thou wert cold or hot*, we are not to suppose his meaning to be, that coldness or fervour in religion is equally acceptable, or that coldness is at all acceptable to him; for reason and revelation concur to assure us, that the open rejection and avowed contempt of religion is an aggravated wickedness, as well as an hypocritical profession.   But our Lord's design is to express, in the strongest manner possible, how odious and abominable their lukewarmness was to him; as if he should say, " Your state is so bad, that you cannot change for the worse; I would rather you were any thing than what you are."   You are ready to observe, that the lukewarm professor is in reality wicked and corrupt at heart, a slave to sin, and an enemy to God, as well as the avowed sinner; and therefore they are both hateful in the sight of God, and both in a state of condemnation.   But there are some aggravations peculiar to the lukewarm professor that render him peculiarly odious; as, 1. He adds the sin of a hypocritical profession to his other sins.   The wickedness of real irreligion, and the wickedness of falsely pretending to be religious, meet and centre in him at once.   2. To all this he adds the guilt of presumption, pride, and self-flattery, imagining he is in a safe state and in favour with God; whereas he that makes no pretensions to religion, has no such umbrage for this conceit and delusion. Thus the miserable Laodiceans "thought themselves rich, and increased in goods, and in need of nothing." 3. Hence it follows, that the lukewarm professor is in the most dangerous condition, as he is not liable to conviction, nor so likely to be brought to repentance. Thus publicans and harlots received the gospel more readily than the self-righteous Pharisees. 4. The honour of God and religion is more injured by the negligent, unconscientious behaviour of these Laodiceans, than by the vices of those who make no pretensions to religion; with whom therefore its honour has no connection. On these accounts you see lukewarmness is more aggravatedly sinful and dangerous than entire coldness about religion.

So then, says Christ, "Because thou art lukewarm, and neither cold nor hot, I will spew thee out of my mouth;" this is their doom; as if he should say, "As lukewarm water is more disagreeable to the stomach than either cold or hot, so you, of all others, are the most abominable to me. I am quite sick of such professors, and I will cast them out of my church, and reject them for ever."

My present design is to expose the peculiar absurdity and wickedness of lukewarmness or indifferency in religion; a disease that has spread its deadly contagion far and wide among us, and calls for a speedy cure. And let me previously observe to you, that if I do not offer you sufficient arguments to convince your own reason of the absurdity and wickedness of such a temper, then you may still indulge it; but that if my arguments are sufficient, then shake off your sloth, and be fervent in spirit; and if you neglect your duty, be it at your peril.

In illustrating this point I shall proceed upon this plain principle, "That religion is, of all things, the most important in itself, and the most interesting to us." This we cannot deny, without openly pronouncing it an imposture. If there be a God, as religion teaches us, he is the most glorious, the most venerable, and the most lovely Being; and nothing can be so important to us as his favour, and nothing so terrible as his displeasure. If he be our Maker, our Benefactor, our Lawgiver and Judge, it must be our greatest concern to serve him with all our might. If Jesus Christ be such a Saviour as our religion represents, and we profess to believe, he demands our warmest love and most lively service. If eternity, if heaven and hell, and the final judgment, are realities, they are certainly the most august, the most awful, important, and interesting realities: and, in comparison of them, the most weighty concerns of the present life are but trifles, dreams, and shadows. If prayer and other religious exercises are our duty, certainly they require all the vigour of our souls; and nothing can be more absurd or incongruous than to perform them in a languid, spiritless manner, as if we knew not what we were about. If there be any life within us, these are proper objects to call it forth: if our souls are endowed with active powers, here are objects that demand their utmost exertion. Here we can never be so much in earnest as the case requires. Trifle about anything, but oh do not trifle here! Be careless and indifferent about crowns and kingdoms, about health, life, and all the world, but oh be not careless and indifferent about such immense concerns as these!

But to be more particular: let us take a view of a lukewarm temper in various attitudes, or with respect to several objects, particularly towards God—towards Jesus Christ—a future state of happiness or misery—and in the duties of

religion; and in each of these views we cannot but be
shocked at so monstrous a temper, especially if we consider our difficulties and dangers in a religious life, and the
eagerness and activity of mankind in inferior pursuits.

1. Consider who and what God is.   He is the original
uncreated beauty, the sum total of all natural and moral
perfections, the origin of all the excellencies that are scattered through this glorious universe; he is the supreme good,
and the only proper portion for our immortal spirits.   He
also sustains the most majestic and endearing relations to us:
our Father, our Preserver and Benefactor, our Lawgiver and
our Judge. And is such a Being to be put off with heartless,
lukewarm services ?   What can be more absurd or impious than to dishonour supreme excellency and beauty with
a languid love and esteem ; to trifle in the presence of the
most venerable Majesty ; to treat the best of Beings with indifferency ; to be careless about our duty to such a Father;
to return such a Benefactor only insipid complimental expressions of gratitude ; to be dull and spiritless in obedience
to such a lawgiver ; and to be indifferent about the favour
or displeasure of such a Judge !   I appeal to heaven and
earth, if this be not the most shocking conduct imaginable.
Does not your reason pronounce it horrid and most dar-
ingly wicked ?   And yet thus is the great and blessed God
treated by the generality of mankind.   It is most astonishing that he should bear with such treatment so long, and
that mankind themselves are not shocked at it: but such the
case really is.   And are there not some lukewarm Laodiceans in this assembly ?   Jesus knows your works, that
you are neither cold nor hot ; and it is fit you should also
know them.   May you not be convinced upon a little
inquiry, that your hearts are habitually indifferent towards
God ?   You may indeed entertain a speculative esteem or
a good opinion of him, but are your souls alive towards

him? Do they burn with his love? and are you fervent
in spirit when you are serving him? Some of you, I
hope, amid all your infirmities, can give comfortable answers to these inquiries. But alas! how few! But yet
as to such of you as are lukewarm, and neither cold nor
hot, you are the most abominable creatures upon earth to
a holy God. *Be zealous,* be warm, *therefore, and repent.*
(ver. 19.)

2. Is lukewarmness a proper temper towards Jesus
Christ? Is this a suitable return for that love which
brought him down from his native paradise into our
wretched world? That love which kept his mind for
thirty-three painful and tedious years intent upon this one
object, the salvation of sinners? That love which rendered him cheerfully patient of the shame, the curse, the
tortures of crucifiction, and all the agonies of the most
painful death? That love which makes him the sinner's
friend still in the courts of heaven, where he appears as
our prevailing Advocate and Intercessor? Blessed Jesus!
is lukewarmness a proper return to thee for all this kindness? No; methinks devils cannot treat thee worse.
My fellow-mortals, my fellow-sinners, who are the objects
of all this love, can you put him off with languid devotions
and faint services? Then every grateful and generous
passion is extinct in your souls, and you are qualified to
venture upon every form of ingratitude and baseness. Oh
was Christ indifferent about your salvation? Was his love
lukewarm towards you? No: your salvation was the object of his most intense application night and day through
the whole course of his life, and it lay nearest his heart in
the agonies of death. For this he had *a baptism to be
baptized with,* a baptism, an immersion in tears and blood;
and how am I straitened, says he, *till it be accomplished!*
For this *with desire, he desired to eat his last passover,*

because it introduced the last scene of his sufferings.   His
love! what shall I say of it?   What language can describe
its strength and ardour?   "His love was strong as death:
the coals thereof were as coals of fire, which had a most
vehement flame: many waters could not quench it, nor the
floods drown it." Cant. viii. 6, 7.   Never did a tender
mother love her sucking child with a love equal to his.
Never was a father more anxious to rescue an only son
from the hands of a murderer, or to pluck him out of the
fire than Jesus was to save perishing sinners.   Now to
neglect him after all; to forget him; or to think of him
with indifferency, as though he were a being of but little
importance, and we but little obliged to him, what is all
this but the most unnatural, barbarous ingratitude, and the
most shocking wickedness?   Do you not expect everlasting happiness from him purchased at the expense of his
blood?   And can you hope for such an immense blessing
from him without feeling yourselves most sensibly obliged
to him?   Can you hope he will do so much for you, and
can you be content to do nothing for him, or to go through
his service with lukewarmness and languor, as if you cared
not how you hurried through it, or how little you had to
do with it?   Can anything be more absurd or impious
than this?   Methinks you may defy hell to show a worse
temper.   May not Christ justly wish you were either cold
or hot; wish you were anything rather than thus lukewarm
towards him under a profession of friendship?   Alas! my
brethren, if this be your habitual temper, instead of being
saved by him, you may expect he will reject you with the
most nauseating disgust and abhorrence.   But,

3. Is lukewarmness and indifference a suitable temper
with respect to a future state of happiness or misery?   Is
it a suitable temper with respect to a happiness far exceeding the utmost bounds of our present thoughts and wishes;

a happiness equal to the largest capacities of our souls in their most improved and perfect state; a happiness beyond the grave, when all the enjoyments of this transitory life have taken an eternal flight from us, and leave us hungry and famishing for ever, if these be our only portion; a happiness that will last as long as our immortal spirits, and never fade or fly from us? Or are lukewarmness and indifferency a suitable temper with respect to a misery beyond expression, beyond conception dreadful; a misery inflicted by a God of almighty power and inexorable justice upon a number of obstinate, incorrigible rebels for numberless, wilful and daring provocations, inflicted on purpose to show his wrath and make his power known; a misery proceeding from the united fury of divine indignation, of turbulent passions, of a guilty conscience, of malicious tormenting devils; a misery (who can bear up under the horror of the thought?) that shall last as long as the eternal God shall live to inflict it; as long as sin shall continue evil to deserve it; as long as an immortal spirit shall endure to bear it; a misery that shall never be mitigated, never intermitted, never, never, never see an end? And remember, that a state of happiness or misery is not far remote from us, but near us, just before us; the next year, the next hour, or the next moment, we may enter into it; is a state for which we are now candidates, now upon trial; now our eternal all lies at stake; and oh, sirs, does an inactive, careless posture become us in such a situation? Is a state of such happiness, or such misery, is such a state just—just before us, a matter of indifferency to us? Oh can you be lukewarm about such matters? Was ever such a prodigious stupidity seen under the canopy of heaven, or even in the regions of hell, which abound with monstrous and horrid dispositions? No; the hardiest ghost below cannot make light of these things. Mortals! can you trifle about them?

Well, trifle a little longer, and your trifling will be over, for ever. You may be indifferent about the improving of your time; but time is not indifferent whether to pass by or not: it is determined to continue its rapid course, and hurry you into the ocean of eternity, though you should continue sleeping and dreaming through all the passage. Therefore awake, arise; exert yourselves before your doom be unchangeably fixed. If you have any fire within you, here let it burn; if you have any active powers, here let them be exerted; here or nowhere, and on no occasion. Be active, be in earnest where you should be; or debase or sink yourselves into stocks and stones, and escape the curse of being reasonable and active creatures. Let the criminal, condemned to die to-morrow, be indifferent about a reprieve or a pardon; let a drowning man be careless about catching at the only plank that can save him: but oh do not you be careless and indifferent about eternity, and such amazing realities as heaven and hell. If you disbelieve these things you are infidels; if you believe these things, and yet are unaffected with them, you are worse than infidels: you are a sort of shocking singularities, and prodigies in nature. Not hell itself can find a precedent of such a conduct. The devils believe, and tremble; you believe, and trifle with things whose very name strikes solemnity and awe through heaven and hell. But,

4. Let us see how this lukewarm temper agrees with the duties of religion. And as I cannot particularize them all, I shall only mention an instance or two. View a lukewarm professor in prayer; he pays to an omniscient God the compliment of a bended knee, as though he could impose upon him with such an empty pretence. When he is addressing the Supreme Majesty of heaven and earth, he hardly ever recollects in whose presence he is, or whom

he is speaking to, but seems as if he were worshipping without an object, or pouring out empty words into the air : perhaps through the whole prayer he had not so much as one solemn, affecting thought of that God whose name he so often invoked. Here is a criminal petitioning for pardon so carelessly, that he scarcely knows what he is about. Here is a needy, famishing beggar pleading for such immense blessings as everlasting salvation, and all the joys of heaven, so lukewarmly and thoughtlessly, as if he cared not whether his requests were granted or not. Here is an obnoxious offender confessing his sins with a heart untouched with sorrow : worshipping the living God with a dead heart; making great requests, but he forgets them as soon as he rises from his knees, and is not at all inquisitive what becomes of them, and whether they were accepted or not. And can there be a more shocking, impious, and daring conduct than this? To trifle in the royal presence would not be such an audacious affront. For a criminal to catch flies, or sport with a feather, when pleading with his judge for his pardon, would be but a faint shadow of such religious trifling. What are such prayers but solemn mockeries and disguised insults? And yet, is not this the usual method in which many of you address the great God? The words proceed no further than from your tongue: you do not pour them out from the bottom of your hearts; they have no life or spirit in them, and you hardly ever reflect upon their meaning. And when you have talked away to God in this manner, you will have it to pass for a prayer. But surely such prayers must bring down a curse upon you instead of a blessing : such sacrifices must be *an abomination to the Lord :* Prov. xv. 8; and it is astonishing that he has not mingled your blood with your sacrifices, and sent you from your knees to hell; from thoughtless, unmeaning prayer, to real blasphemy and torture.

The next instance I shall mention is with regard to the word of God. You own it divine, you profess it the standard of your religion, and the most excellent book in the world. Now, if this be the case, it is God that speaks to you; it is God that sends you an epistle when you are reading or hearing his word. How impious and provoking then must it be to neglect it, to let it lie by you as an antiquated, useless book, or to read it in a careless, superficial manner, and hear it with an inattentive, wandering mind? How would you take it, if, when you spoke to your servant about his own interest, he should turn away from you, and not regard you? Or if you should write a letter to your son, and he should not so much as carefully read it, or labour to understand it? And do not some of you treat the sacred oracles in this manner? You make but little use of your Bible, but to teach your children to read: or if you read or hear its contents yourselves, are you not unaffected with them? One would think you would be all attention and reverence to every word; you would drink it in, and thirst for it as new-born babes for their mother's milk, you would feel its energy, and acquire the character of that happy man to whom the God of heaven vouchsafes to look; you would tremble at his word. It reveals the only method of your salvation: it contains the only charter of all your blessings. In short, you have the nearest personal interest in it, and can you be unconcerned hearers of it? I am sure your reason and conscience must condemn such stupidity and indifferency as incongruous, and outrageously wicked.

And now let me remind you of the observation I made when entering upon this subject, that if I should not offer sufficient matter of conviction, you might go on in your lukewarmness; but if your own reason should be fully convinced that such a temper is most wicked and unrea-

sonable, then you might indulge at your peril. What do
you say now is the issue? Ye modern Laodiceans, are
you not yet struck with horror at the thought of that insipid, formal, spiritless religion you have hitherto been contented with? And do you not see the necessity of following the advice of Christ to the Laodicean church, *be zealous*, be fervent for the future, *and repent*, bitterly repent
of what is past? To urge this the more, I have two considerations in reserve, of no small weight. 1. Consider
the difficulties and dangers in your way. Oh, sirs, if you
know the difficulty of the work of your salvation, and the
great danger of miscarrying in it, you could not be so indifferent about it, nor could you flatter yourselves such
languid endeavours will ever succeed. It is a labour, a
striving, a race, a warfare; so it is called in the sacred
writings: but would there be any propriety in these expressions, if it were a course of sloth and inactivity?
Consider, you have strong lusts to be subdued, a hard
heart to be broken, a variety of graces, which you are entirely destitute of, to be implanted and cherished, and that
in an unnatural soil, where they will not grow without
careful cultivation, and that you have many temptations to
be encountered and resisted. In short, you must be made
new men, quite other creatures than you now are. And
oh! can this work be successfully performed while you
make such faint and feeble efforts? Indeed God is the
Agent, and all your best endeavours can never effect the
blessed revolution without him. But his assistance is not
to be expected in the neglect, or careless use of means,
nor is it intended to encourage idleness, but activity and
labour: and when he comes to work, he will soon inflame
your hearts, and put an end to your lukewarmness. Again,
your dangers are also great and numerous; you are in
danger from presumption and from despondency; from

coldness, from lukewarmness, and from false fires and enthusiastic heats; in danger from self-righteousness, and
from open wickedness, from your own corrupt hearts,
from this ensnaring world, and from the temptations of
the devil: you are in great danger of sleeping on in security, without ever being thoroughly awakened; or, if you
should be awakened, you are in danger of resting short of
vital religion; and in either of these cases you are undone
for ever. In a word, dangers crowd thick around you
on every hand, from every quarter; dangers, into which
thousands, millions of your fellow-men have fallen and
never recovered. Indeed, all things considered, it is very
doubtful whether ever you will be saved, who are now
lukewarm and secure: I do not mean that your success is
uncertain if you be brought to use means with proper
earnestness; but alas! it is awfully uncertain whether ever
you will be brought to use them in this manner. And,
O sirs! can you continue secure and inactive when you
have such difficulties to encounter with in a work of absolute necessity, and when you are surrounded with so many
and so great dangers? Alas! are you capable of such destructive madness? Oh that you knew the true state of
the case! Such a knowledge would soon fire you with
the greatest ardour, and make you all life and vigour in
this important work.

2. Consider how earnest and active men are in other
pursuits. Should we form a judgment of the faculties of
human nature by the conduct of the generality in religion,
we should be apt to conclude that men are mere snails,
and that they have no active powers belonging to them.
But view them about other affairs, and you find they are
all life, fire, and hurry. What labour and toil! what
schemes and contrivances! what solicitude about success!
what fears of disappointment! hands, heads, hearts, all

busy. And all this to procure those enjoyments which at best they cannot long retain, and which the next hour may tear from them. To acquire a name or a diadem, to obtain riches or honours, what hardships are undergone! what dangers dared! what rivers of blood shed! how many millions of lives have been lost! and how many more endangered! In short the world is all alive, all in motion with business. On sea and land, at home and abroad, you will find men eagerly pursuing some temporal good. They grow grey-headed, and die in the attempt without reaching their end; but this disappointment does not discourage the survivors and successors; still they will continue, or renew the endeavour. Now here men act like themselves; and they show they are alive, and endowed with powers of great activity. And shall they be thus zealous and laborious in the pursuit of earthly vanities, and quite indifferent and sluggish in the infinitely more important concerns of eternity? What! solicitous about a mortal body, but careless about an immortal soul! Eager in pursuit of joys of a few years, but careless and remiss in seeking an immortality of perfect happiness! Anxious to avoid poverty, shame, sickness, pain, and all the evils, real or imaginary, of the present life; but indifferent about a whole eternity of the most intolerable misery! Oh, the destructive folly, the daring wickedness of such a conduct! My brethren, is religion the only thing which demands the utmost exertion of all your powers, and alas! is that the only thing in which you will be dull and inactive? Is everlasting happiness the only thing about which you will be remiss? Is eternal punishment the only misery which you are indifferent whether you escape or not? Is God the only good which you pursue with faint and lazy desires? How preposterous! how absurd is this! You can love the world, you can love a father, a child, or a friend;

nay, you can love that abominable, hateful thing, sin: these you can love with ardour, serve with pleasure, pursue with eagerness, and with all your might; but the ever-blessed God, and the Lord Jesus, your best friend, you put off with a lukewarm heart and spiritless services. Oh inexpressibly monstrous! Lord, what is this that has befallen thine own offspring, that they are so disaffected towards thee? Blessed Jesus, what hast thou done that thou shouldst be treated thus? Oh sinners! what will be the consequence of such a conduct? Will that God take you into the bosom of his love? Will that Jesus save you by his blood, whom you make so light of? No, you may go and seek a heaven where you can find it; for God will give you none. Go, shift for yourselves, or look out for a Saviour where you will; Jesus will have nothing to do with you, except to take care to inflict proper punishment upon you if you retain this lukewarm temper towards him. Hence, by way of improvement, learn,

1. The vanity and wickedness of a lukewarm religion. Though you should profess the best religion that ever came from heaven, it will not save you; nay, it will condemn you with peculiar aggravations if you are lukewarm in it. This spirit of indifferency diffused through it, turns it all into deadly poison. Your religious duties are all abominable to God while the vigour of your spirits is not exerted in them. Your prayers are insults, and he will answer them as such by terrible things in righteousness. And do any of you hope to be saved by such a religion? I tell you from the God of truth, it will be so far from saving you, that it will certainly ruin you for ever: continue as you are to the last, and you will be as certainly damned to all eternity, as Judas, or Beelzebub, or any ghost in hell. But alas!

2. How common, how fashionable is this lukewarm

religion! This is the prevailing, epidemical sin of our
age and country; and it is well if it has not the same fatal
effect upon us it had upon Laodicea; Laodicea lost its
liberty, its religion, and its all. Therefore let Virginia
hear and fear, and do no more so wickedly. We have
thousands of Christians, such as they are; as many Christians as white men; but alas! they are generally of the
Laodicean stamp; they are neither cold nor hot. But it
is our first concern to know how it is with ourselves;
therefore let this inquiry go round this congregation; are
you not such lukewarm Christians? Is there any fire and
life in your devotions? Or are not all your active powers
engrossed by other pursuits? Impartially make the inquiry, for infinitely more depends upon it than upon your
temporal life.

3. If you have hitherto been possessed with this Laodicean spirit, I beseech you indulge it no longer. You
have seen that it mars all your religion, and will end in
your eternal ruin: and I hope you are not so hardened as
to be proof against the energy of this consideration.
Why halt you so long between two opinions? *I would
you were cold or hot.* Either make thorough work of religion, or do not pretend to it. Why should you profess
a religion which is but an insipid indifferency with you?
Such a religion is good for nothing. Therefore awake,
arise, exert yourselves. Strive to enter in at the strait
gate; strive earnestly, or you are shut out for ever. Infuse heart and spirit into your religion. Whatever your
hand findeth to do, do it with your might. Now, this
moment, while my voice sounds in your ears, now begin
the vigorous enterprise. Now collect all the vigour of
your souls and breathe it out in such a prayer as this,
" Lord, fire this heart with thy love." Prayer is a proper
introduction: for let me remind you of what I should

never forget, that God is the only Author of this sacred fire; it is only he that can quicken you; therefore, ye poor careless creatures, fly to him in an agony of importunity, and never desist, never grow weary till you prevail.

4. And lastly: Let the best of us lament our lukewarmness, and earnestly seek more fervour of spirit. Some of you have a little life; you enjoy some warm and vigorous moments; and oh! they are divinely sweet. But reflect how soon your spirits flag, your devotion cools, and your zeal languishes. Think of this, and be humble: think of this, and apply for more life. You know where to apply. Christ is your life: therefore cry to him for the communication of it. "Lord Jesus! a little more life, a little more vital heat to a languishing soul." Take this method, and "you shall run and not be weary; you shall walk and not faint." Isaiah xl. 31.

SERMON XVI.

THE DIVINE GOVERNMENT THE JOY OF OUR WORLD.

PSALM xcvii. 1.—*The* LORD *reigneth; let the earth rejoice; let the multitude of isles be glad thereof.*

WISE and good rulers are justly accounted an extensive blessing to their subjects. In a government where wisdom sits at the helm; and justice, tempered with clemency, holds the balance of retribution, liberty and property are secured, encroaching ambition is checked, helpless innocence is protected, and universal order is established, and consequently peace and happiness diffuse their streams through the land. In such a situation every heart must rejoice, every countenance look cheerful, and every bosom glow with gratitude to the happy instruments of such extended beneficence.

But, on the other hand, "Wo to thee, oh land, when thy king is a child," Eccles. x. 16; weak, injudicious, humorsome, and peevish. This is the denunciation of Solomon, a sage philosopher, and an opulent king, whose station, capacity, and inclination, conspired to give him the deepest skill in politics: and this denunciation has been accomplished in every age. Empires have fallen, liberty has been fettered, property has been invaded, the lives of men have been arbitrarily taken away, and misery and desolation have broken in like a flood, when the government has been entrusted in the hands of tyranny, of luxury, or rashness; and the advantages of climate and soil, and all others which nature could bestow, have not been able to make the subjects happy under the baleful influence of such an administration.

It has frequently been the unhappy fate of nations to be enslaved to such rulers; but such is the unavoidable imperfection of all human governments, that when, like our own, they are managed by the best hands, they are attended with many calamities, and cannot answer several valuable ends; and from both these considerations we may infer the necessity of a divine government over the whole universe and particularly over the earth, in which we are more especially concerned. Without this supreme universal Monarch, the affairs of this world would fall into confusion; and the concerns of the next could not be managed at all. The capacities of the wisest of men are scanty, and not equal to all the purposes of government; and hence many affairs of importance will be unavoidably misconducted; and dangerous plots and aggravated crimes may be undiscovered for want of knowledge, or pass unpunished for want of power. A wise and good ruler may be diffusing among his subjects all that happiness which can result from the imperfect administration of mortals, but he may be tumbled from his throne, and his government thrown into the greatest disorder by a more powerful invader; so that the best ruler could not make his subjects lastingly happy, unless he were universal monarch of the globe (a province too great for any mortal) and above the reach of the ambitious power of others. Further, human dominion cannot extend to the souls and consciences of men: civil rulers can neither know nor govern them; and yet these must be governed and brought into subjection to the eternal laws of reason, otherwise tranquillity cannot subsist on earth; and especially the great purposes of religion, which regard a future state, cannot be answered.

Men are placed here to be formed by a proper education for another world, for another class, and other employments; but civil rulers cannot form them for these important ends, and therefore they must be under the government of one who has access to their spirits, and can manage them as he pleases.

Deeply impressed with these and other considerations, which shall be presently mentioned, the Psalmist is transported into this reflection, "The LORD reigneth; let the earth rejoice; let the multitude of isles be glad thereof."

The Psalmist seems to have the mediatorial empire of grace erected by Immanuel more immediately in view; and this indeed deserves our special notice; but no doubt he included the divine government in general, which is a just ground of universal joy; and in this latitude I shall consider the text.

Persons in a transport are apt to speak abruptly, and omit the particles of connection and inference usual in calm reasoning. Thus the Psalmist cries out, "The LORD reigneth; let the earth rejoice; let the multitude of isles be glad thereof!" but if we reduce the passage into an argumentative form, it will stand thus, "The Lord reigneth; therefore let the earth rejoice; and let the multitude of isles be glad upon this account."

The earth may here signify by an usual metonymy, the rational inhabitants of the earth, who are especially concerned in the divine government; or, by a beautiful poetical prosopopœia, it may signify the inanimate globe of the earth, and then it intimates that the divine government is so important a blessing, that even the inanimate and senseless creation would rejoice in it, were it capable of such passions.* The isles may likewise be taken figuratively for their inhabitants, particularly the Gentiles, who resided in them; or literally for tracts of land surrounded with water.

My present design is

To illustrate this glorious truth, that *Jehovah's supreme government is a just cause of universal joy.*

For that end I shall consider the divine government in various views, as legislative, providential, mediatorial, and judicial; and show that in each of these views the divine government is matter of universal joy.

I. The Lord reigneth upon a throne of legislation. " Let the earth rejoice; let the multitude of isles be glad thereof."

He is the one supreme Lawgiver, James iv, 12, and is perfectly qualified for that important trust. Nothing tends more to the advantage of civil society than to have good laws established, according to which mankind are to conduct themselves, and according to which their rulers will deal with them. Now the supreme and universal king has enacted and published the best laws for the government of the moral world, and of the human race in particular.

Let the earth then rejoice that God has clearly revealed his will to us, and not left us in inextricable perplexities about our duty to him and mankind. Human reason, or the light of nature, gives us some intimations of the duties of morality, even in our degenerate state, and for this information we should bless God; but alas! these discoveries are very imperfect, and we need supernatural revelation to make known to us the way of life. Accordingly, the Lord has favoured us with the sacred oracles as a supple-

---

* By the same figure the inanimate parts of the creation are called upon to praise the Lord, Psalm cxlviii., and are said to travail and groan under the sin of man.—Rom. viii. 22.

ment to the feeble light of nature; and in them we are
fully "taught what is good, and what the law requireth of
us." And what cause of joy is this! How painful are
the anxieties that attend uncertainty about matters of duty!
How distressing a doubtful, fluctuating mind, in an affair of
such tremendous importance! This, no doubt, some of
you that are conscientious have had the experience of, in
particular cases, when you were at a loss to apply to them
the general directions in sacred Scripture.

Again, "let the earth rejoice; let the multitude of
isles be glad," that these laws are suitably enforced with
proper sanctions. The sanctions are such as become a
God of infinite wisdom, almighty power, inexorable justice,
untainted holiness, and unbounded goodness and grace,
and such as are agreeable to the nature of reasonable creatures formed for an immortal duration. The rewards of
obedience in the divine legislation are not such toys as
posts of honour and profit, crowns and empires, which are
the highest rewards that civil rulers can promise or bestow;
but rational peace and serenity of mind, undaunted bravery
under the frowns of adversity, a cheerful confidence in
the divine guardianship under all the calamities of life, and
in the future world an entire exemption from all sorrow
and from sin, the fruitful source of all our afflictions; the
possession of every good, the enjoyment of the divine presence, of the society of angels and the spirits of just men
made perfect; in short, the fruition of a happiness above
our present wishes, and equal to our then mature faculties,
and all this for ever: these are the rewards of evangelical
obedience, not indeed for its own sake, but upon account
of the righteousness of the blessed Jesus; and if these fail
to allure men to obedience, what can prevail? And how
happy is it to live under a government, where virtue and
religion, which in their own nature tend to our happiness,

are enforced with such resistless arguments! On the other
hand, the penalty annexed by the divine Lawgiver to disobedience is proportionably dreadful. To pine and languish under the secret curse of angry Heaven, which, like
a contagious poison, diffuses itself through all the enjoyments of the wicked, Mal ii. 2; to sweat under the agonies of a guilty conscience in this world, and in the future
world to be banished from the beatific presence of God and
all the joys of heaven; to feel the anguish and remorse of
guilty reflections; to burn in unquenchable fire; to consume a miserable eternity in the horrid society of malignant ghosts; and all this without the least rational expectation, nay, without so much as a deluded hope of deliverance, or the mitigation of torture, through the revolutions
of endless ages, all this is a faint representation of the
penalty annexed to disobedience; and it is a penalty
worthy a God to inflict, and equal to the infinite malignity of sin. And "let the earth rejoice; let the multitude of isles be glad," on account not only of the pro-
missory sanction of the law, but also of this tremendous penalty; for it flows not only from justice, but from
goodness, as well as its promise. The penalty is not
annexed to the law, nor will it be executed from a malignant pleasure in the misery of the creature, but it is annexed from a regard to the happiness of mankind, and will
be executed upon individuals for the extensive good of the
whole as well as for the honourable display of the divine
purity and justice. A penalty is primarily intended to
deter men from disobedience. Now disobedience tends
in its own nature to make us miserable; it renders it impossible, in the nature of things, that we should be happy
in the enjoyment of God and the employments of heaven,
which are eternally and immutably contrary to sinful dispositions; and it fills us with those malignant and unruly

passions which cannot but make us uneasy. Hence it follows, that, since the penalty tends to deter us from sin, and since sin naturally tends to make us miserable, therefore the penalty is a kind of gracious enclosure round the pit of misery, to keep us from falling into it: it is a friendly admonition not to drink poison; it is, in a word, a kind restraint upon us in our career to ruin; and indeed it is a blessing we could not spare; for we find, that, notwithstanding the terror of the threatening, men will run on in sin; and with how much more horrid alacrity and infernal zeal would they continue their course, if there were no divine threatening to check and withhold them? The earth may also rejoice for the execution of the penalty of the divine law against sin; for the conspicious punishment of the disobedient may serve as a loud warning to all rational beings that now exist, or that may hereafter be created, not to offend against God; and thus it may be the means of preserving them in obedience, and so promote the general good; and it may be that the number of those that shall be punished of the human and angelic natures, when compared to the number of reasonable beings that shall be confirmed in holiness and happiness by observing their doom, may bear no more proportion than the number of criminals executed in a government as public example does to all the subjects of it; and consequently such punishment may be vindicated on the same principles.

Farther, Justice is an amiable attribute in itself, and it appears so to all rational beings but criminals, whose interest it is, that it should not be displayed; and therefore the infliction of just punishment should be matter of general joy, since it is amiable in itself. So it is in human governments; while we are innocent, we approve of the conduct of our magistrates in inflicting capital punishment

upon notorious malefactors, though the malefactors themselves view it with horror.   But to proceed:

"Let the earth rejoice; let the multitude of isles be
glad," that the divine laws rea h the inner man, and have
power upon the hearts and consciences of men.   Human
laws can only smooth our external conduct at best, but
the heart in the meantime may be disloyal and wicked.
Now this defect is supplied by the laws of the King of
heaven, which are spiritual.   They require a complete
uniformity and self-consistency in us, that heart and life
may agree: and therefore they are wisely framed to make
us entirely good.   They have also an inimitable power
upon the consciences of men.   Should all the world acquit
us, yet we cannot acquit ourselves when we violate them.
The consciousness of a crime has made many a hardy
offender sweat and agonize with remorse, though no human
eye could witness to his offence.   Now what cause of joy
is it that these laws are quick and powerful, and that they
are attended with almighty energy, which in some measure intimidates and restrains the most audacious, and inspires the conscientious with a pious fear of offending!

II. The Lord reigneth by his Providence. "Let the
earth therefore rejoice; and the multitude of isles be glad
thereof."

The Providence of God is well described in our shorter
Catechism: "It is his most holy, wise, and powerful preserving and governing all his creatures, and all their
actions."   To particularize all the instances of providential government which may be matter of joy to the earth
would be endless, therefore I shall only mention the following:

Let the earth rejoice; and *the multitude of isles be
glad,* that the Lord reigneth over the kingdoms of the
earth, and manages all their affairs according to his sove-

reign and wise pleasure. We sometimes hear of wars, and rumors of wars, of thrones tottering, and kingdoms falling, of the nations tumultuously raging and dashing in angry conflict, like the waves of the boisterous ocean. In such a juncture we may say, " The floods have lifted up, O LORD, the floods have lifted up their voice. The floods lift up their waves. But the Lord reigneth, therefore the world shall be established that it cannot be moved.—The LORD on high is mightier than the noise of many waters; yea, than the mighty waves of the sea." Psalm xciii. Sometimes the ambition of foreign power, or the encroachments of domestic tyranny, may threaten our liberties, and persecution may seem ready to discharge its artillery against the church of God, while every pious heart trembles for the ark, lest it should be carried into the land of its enemies. But the Lord reigneth! let the earth, let the church rejoice! " the eternal God is her refuge, and underneath her are the everlasting arms." Deut. xxxiii. 27. He will overrule the various revolutions of the world for her good; he will give kings for her ransom, Æthiopia and Seba for her; and the united powers of earth and hell shall not prevail against her. Though the frame of nature should be unhinged, we may find refuge in our God. Yet it must be owned, that the Lord for the chastisement of his people may suffer their enemies to break in upon them, and may cast them into the furnace of affliction. But let the earth rejoice, let the church be glad that the Lord reigneth over her most powerful enemies, and that they are but executing his will even when they have no regard to it, but are gratifying their own ambition. They are but a rod in the hand of a tender father, who corrects only to amend: and when he has used the rod for this gracious purpose, he will then lay it aside. In this language the Almighty speaks of the haughty As-

syrian monarch who had pushed his conquest so far and
wide. Isaiah x. 5, 6, 7.   "Oh Assyrian, the rod of mine
anger," &c.   "I will give him my commission, and send
him against the Jews, my favourite people; because they
are degenerated into an hypocritical nation, and he shall
execute my orders."   "Howbeit, he meaneth not so;" it
is far from his heart to obey my will in this expedition;
but his only design is to aggrandize himself, "and to destroy and cut off nations not a few."   And when this instrument of the divine vengeance arrogates to himself the
honour of his own successes, with what just insult and
disdain does the King of kings speak of him! ver. 12–15.
" Shall the axe boast itself against him that heweth there-
with ?   As if the rod should shake itself against them that
lift it up," &c.   The design of God in these chastisements is to purge away the iniquity of his people; and
this is all the fruit of them to take away their sin; and
when this gracious design is answered, they shall be removed ;   "The rod of the wicked shall not rest upon the
lot of the righteous."   Psalm cxxv. 3.   Now what cause
of universal joy is this, that one infinitely wise sits at the
helm, and can steer the feeble vessel of his church through
all the outrageous storms of this unfriendly climate and
tempestuous ocean!   He may seem at times to lie asleep,
but in the article of extreme danger he will awake and still
the winds and the sea with his sovereign mandate, *Peace,
be still*.   Men may form deep and politic schemes, and
purpose their accomplishment in defiance of Heaven, " but
God disappointeth the devices of the crafty, so that their
hands cannot perform their enterprise.   He taketh the
wise in their own craftines, and the counsel of the froward
is carried headlong."   Job v. 12, 13.   This was exemplified in the cause of Ahithophel, 2 Sam. xvii. 14.   The
hearts of men, yea of kings, " are in the hand of the LORD,

and he turneth them whithersoever he will." Prov. xxi. 1, (see also chap. xvi. 1, 9, and xix. 21.) And how joyful a thought this, that we are not at the arbitrary disposal of our fellow mortals, and that affairs are not managed according to their capricious pleasure, but that our God is in heaven, and doth whatsoever he pleaseth! Psalm cxv. 3.

Again, the church may be endangered by intestine divisions and offences. The professors of religion may stumble and fall, and so wound the hearts of the friends of Zion, and give matter of triumph and insult to its enemies. Some may apostatize, and return like the dog to his vomit. A general lukewarmness may diffuse itself through the church, and even those who retain their integrity in the main may feel the contagion. Divisions and animosities may be inflamed, mutual love may be extinguished, and a spirit of discord succeed in its place. A most melancholy case this, and too much like our own: and our hearts sink at times beneath the burden. But *the* LORD *reigneth ; let the earth be glad.* He can reduce this confusion into order, and make the wrath of man to praise him, and restrain the remainder of it: Psalm lxxvi. 10. It is the peculiarity of divine wisdom to educe good out of evil, and let us rejoice in it. God is supreme, and therefore can control all the wicked passions of the mind. He has the residue of the Spirit, and can rekindle the languishing flame of devotion. And oh let us apply to him with the most vigorous and unwearied importunity for so necessary a blessing!

Again, we are exposed to numberless accidental and unforseen dangers, which we cannot prevent nor encounter. Sickness and death may proceed from a thousand unsuspected causes. Our friends, our estates, and, in short, all our earthly enjoyments, may be torn from us by a variety of accidents. We walk, as it were, in the dark, and may

tread on remediless dangers ere we are aware. *But the*
LORD *reigneth : let the earth be glad !* contingent events are
at his disposal, and necessity at his control.   The smallest
things are not beneath the notice of his providence, and
the greatest are not above it.   Diseases and misfortunes
that seem to happen by chance, are commissioned by the
Lord of all; and they that result evidently from natural
causes are sent by his almighty will.   He says to one, Go,
and it goeth ; and to another, Come, and it cometh; he
orders the devastations that are made by the most outrageous elements.   If flames lay our houses in ashes, they
are kindled by his breath.   If hurricanes sweep through
our land, and carry desolation along with them, they perform his will, and can do nothing beyond it : his hand
hurls the thunder, and directs it where to strike.   An ar-
row or a bullet shot at a venture in the heat of battle is
carried to its mark by divine direction.   How wretched a
world would this be were it not under the wise management of divine Providence !   If chance or blind fate were
its rulers, what desolation would crowd upon us every moment! we should soon be crushed in the ruins of a fallen
world.   Every wind that blows might blast us with death,
and fire and water would mingle in a blended chaos, and
bury us in their destruction.   But so extensive is the care
of Providence, that even the sparrows may find safety in
it; and we cannot lose so much as a hair of our heads
without its permission : Matt. x. 29, 30, 31.   And how
much more then are our persons and our affairs of importance under its guardianship and direction !

Again we are in perpetual danger from the malignant
agency of infernal spirits, who watch all opportunities to
ruin the souls, bodies, and estates of men.   These subtle
spirits can inject ensnaring thoughts into our minds, and
present such images to the fancy as may allure the soul

to sin. This is repeatedly asserted in Scripture, and attested by the melancholy experience of multitudes in all ages. That they have power also in the material world to raise storms and tempests, and to ruin men's estates and inflict diseases on their bodies, is plain from the case of Job, and many in our Saviour's time, and from Satan's being called *the prince of the power of the air;* and his associates *spiritual wickedness in high places.* And what horrid devastations would these powerful and malicious beings spread through the world if they were not under the control of divine Providence! They would perpetually haunt our minds with ensnaring or terrifying images; would meet us with temptations at every turn, and lead us willing captives to hell. They would also strip us entirely of all temporal enjoyments, torture our bodies with grievous pains, or moulder them into dust with consuming and loathsome diseases. *But the* Lord *reigneth; let the earth be glad.* He keeps the infernal lions in chains, and restrains their rage. He sees all their subtle plots and machinations against his feeble sheep, and baffles them all. He will not suffer his people to be tempted above what they are able to bear; but with the temptation will also make a way to escape; 1. Cor. x. 13. And when he suffers them to be buffeted, his grace shall be sufficient for them, &c.: 2 Cor. xii. 7, 9. He hath also (as Satan himself confessed with regard to Job) made a hedge about us, about our houses, and about all that we have on every side; Job i. 10; and hence we live and enjoy the blessings of life. What cause of grateful joy is this! Who would not rather die than live in a world ungoverned by divine Providence? This earth would soon be turned into a hell, if the infernal armies were let loose upon it.

III. The Lord reigneth upon a **throne of grace!**

"Let the earth rejoice; let the multitude of isles be glad thereof."

It is the mediatorial government of the Messiah which the Psalmist had more immediately in view; and this is the principal cause of joy to the earth and its guilty inhabitants. This is a kind of government peculiar to the human race; the upright angels do not need it, and the fallen angels are not favoured with it. This is invested in the person of Immanuel, "who is made head over all things to his church," Eph. i. 22; "to whom all power in heaven and earth is given," Matt. xi. 27, and xxviii. 18. This is the kingdom described in such august language in Dan. ii. ver. 44, 45, and vii. 14. Luke i. 32, 33. Hence that Jesus who was mocked with a crown of thorns, and condemned as a criminal at Pilate's bar, wears on his vesture and on his thigh this majestic inscription, KING OF KINGS, AND LORD OF LORDS. Rev. xix. 16. And behold I bring you glad tidings; this kingdom of God is come unto you, and you are called to become its subjects, and share in its blessings. Wherever the gospel is preached, there Jehovah sits upon a mercy-seat in majesty tempered with condescending grace. From thence he invites rebels that had rejected his government to return to their allegiance, and passes an act of grace upon all that comply with the invitation. To his throne of grace he invites all to come, and offers them the richest blessings. From thence he publishes peace on earth, and good will towards men. From thence he offers pardon to all that will submit to his government, and renounce their sins, those weapons of rebellion. From thence he distributes the influences of his Spirit to subdue obstinate hearts into cheerful submission, to support his subjects under every burden, and furnish them with strength for the spiritual warfare. He subdues their rebellious corruptions, animates their languishing graces, and protects them from their spiritual enemies. He enacts laws for the regulation of his church, appoints ordinances for her edification, and qualifies ministers to dispense them. He hath *ascended up on high ;* he hath received gifts for men; and these he hath distributed, and given "some apostles; and some prophets; and some evangelists; and some pastors and teachers; for the perfecting of the saints, for the work of the ministry, for the edifying of the body of Christ," Eph. iv. 8, 11, 12. And it is by virtue of authority derived from him, that his ministers now officiate, and you receive his ordinances at their hands. Now how happy are we, that we live under the mediatorial administration! under the empire of grace! —*Let the earth rejoice ; let the multitude of isles be glad* upon this account. And let us pray that all nations may become the willing subjects of our gracious Sovereign. If this administration of grace had not yet been erected, in what a miserable situation should we have been! guilty, miserable, and hopeless! Let us rejoice that the King of heaven, from whom we had revolted, has not suffered us to perish without remedy in our unnatural rebellion, but holds out the sceptre of his grace to us, that we may touch it and live.

IV. And lastly, the Lord will reign ere long upon a throne of universal judgment, conspicuous to the assembled universe. " *Let the earth* therefore *rejoice,* and *the multitude of isles be glad.*"

Here I may borrow the inimitable language of the Psalmist, Ps. xcvi. 10, 13. "The Lord shall judge the people righteously. Let the heavens rejoice, and let the earth be glad: let the sea roar, and the fulness thereof; let the field be joyful, and all that is therein; then shall all

* See his reign most beautifully described under the type of *Solomon.* Psalm lxxii.

the trees of the wood rejoice before the LORD, for he cometh! for he cometh to judge the earth. He shall judge the world with righteousness and the people with his truth." This will indeed be a day of insupportable terror to his enemies, Rev. vi. 15, 16, but, on many accounts, it will prove a day of joy and triumph.

This day will unfold all the mysteries of divine Providence which are now unsearchable. There are many dispensations now for which we cannot account. Many blessings are bestowed, many calamities fall, and many events happen, of which mortals cannot see the reason. Prosperity is the lot of some who seem the peculiar objects of divine vengeance; and many groan under afflictions who seem more proper objects of providential beneficence. We are often led into ways the end of which we cannot see, and are bewildered in various perplexities about the designs of divine Providence towards us. Hence also impiety takes occasion to cavil at the ways of God as not equal, and to censure his government as weakly administered. But in that day all his ways will appear to be judgment. The clouds and darkness that now surround them will vanish, and the beams of wisdom, goodness, and justice, shall shine illustrious before the whole universe, and every creature shall join the plaudit, *He hath done all things well!* Now we can at best but see a few links in the chain of providence, but then we shall see it all entire and complete; then the whole system will be exposed to view at once, which will discover the strange symmetry, connections, dependencies, and references of all the parts, without which we can no more judge of the excellency of the procedure than a rustic could tell the use of the several parts of a watch, if he saw them scattered in various places. Let the earth therefore be glad in expectation of this glorious discovery.

Again, let the earth rejoice that in that day the present unequal distributions of Providence will be for ever adjusted, and regulated according to the strictest justice. This is not the place or season for retribution, and therefore we need not be surprised that the blessings and calamities of this life are not disposed according to men's real characters; but then every man shall be dealt with according to his works. Oppressed innocence will be redressed, and insolence for ever mortified; calumny will be confuted, and flattery exposed: Lazarus shall be comforted, Dives tormented: impious kings shall be driven into the infernal pit, while pious beggars shall be advanced to the heights of happiness. In short, all matters will then be set right, and therefore let the earth rejoice.

Again, let the earth rejoice that in that day the righteous shall be completely delivered from all sin and sorrow, and advanced to the perfection of heavenly happiness. Then they shall enter upon the full fruition of that bliss, which is now the object of all their anxious hopes and earnest labours.

But we must change the scene into tragedy, and take a view of the trembling criminals hearing their dreadful doom, and sinking to hell with horrible anguish. And must the earth rejoice in this too? Yes, but with a solemn tremendous joy. Even the condemnation and everlasting misery of these is right and just, is amiable and glorious; and God, angels and saints, will at the great day rejoice in it. The awful grandeur of justice will be illustrated in it; and this is matter of joy. The punishment of irreclaimable impenitents will be an effectual warning to all reasonable beings, and to all future creations, as has been observed; and by it they will be deterred from disobedience; and this is the cause of joy. These criminals will then be beyond repentance and re-

formation, and therefore it is impossible in the nature of
things they should be happy; and why then should heaven
be encumbered with them? Is it not cause of joy that
they should be confined in prison who have made themselves unfit for society? In the present state sinners are
objects of our compassion and sorrow, and the whole creation mourns for them. Rom. viii. 22. But God will then
rejoice in their ruin, and laugh at their calamity, Prov. i.
26; and all dutiful creatures will join in his joy.

Thus you see that the Lord reigneth. And who, poor
feeble saints, who is this that sustains this universal
government, and rules the whole creation according to his
pleasure? It is your Father, your Saviour, your Friend!
It is he that entertains a tenderer regard for you than
ever glowed in a human breast. And can you be so
foolish as to regard the surmises of unbelief? Can you
force yourselves to fear that he will ever leave or forsake
you? Can you suspect that he will suffer you to fall a
helpless prey to your enemies? No, your Lord reigneth,
therefore rejoice. *Rejoice in the Lord alway; and again
I say rejoice.* While he keeps the throne of the universe,
you shall be safe and happy. Your Father is greater
than all, and none can pluck you out of his hands. Remember, he sits upon a throne of grace, therefore come to
him with boldness. You may smile at calamity and confusion, and rejoice amid the ruins of the world; you
may borrow the language of David, Psalm xlv.; or of
Habakkuk, chap. iii. ver. 17, 18. Remember also, that,
as he is a king, he demands your cheerful obedience, and
therefore make his service the business of your life.

And, unhappy sinners! let me ask you, Who is this
that reigns King of the universe? Why, it is he whom
you have rejected from being King over you; it is he
against whom you have rebelled, and who is therefore

your just enemy. And are you able to make good your cause against him who has universal nature at his nod? How dreadful is your situation! That which may make the earth rejoice, may make you fear and tremble. The Lord reigneth, let sinners tremble. You must fall before him, if you will not cheerfully submit to his government. Let me therefore renew the usual neglected declaration, "He sits upon a throne of grace." Let me once more in his name proclaim reconciliation! reconciliation!! in your ears, and invite you to return to your allegiance. Lay down your arms, forsake your sins! Hasten, hasten to him! The sword of his justice now hangs over your heads, while I am managing the treaty with you; and therefore delay not. Yield; yield, or die! surrender, or perish! for you have no other alternative. Submit, and you may join the general joy at his government. You upon earth, and devils and damned ghosts in hell, are the only beings that are sorry for it; but upon your submission your sorrow shall be turned into joy, and you shall exult when the Lord of all comes to judge "the world with righteousness, and the people with his truth." Psalm xcvi. 13.

SERMON XVII.

THE NAME OF GOD PROCLAIMED BY HIMSELF.

Exod. xxxiii. 18, 19.—*And he said, I beseech thee, show me thy glory. And he said, I will make all my goodness pass before thee, and I will proclaim the name of the* Lord *before thee.—*

WITH

Chap. xxxiv. 6, 7.—*And the* Lord *passed by before him, and proclaimed, The* Lord, *the* Lord God, *merciful and gracious, long-suffering, and abundant in goodness and truth; keeping mercy for thousands, forgiving iniquity and transgression and sin, and that will by no means clear the guilty.*

It is a very natural and proper inquiry for a creature, "Where is God my Maker?" And a heart that loves him must long to know more of him, and is ever ready to join with Moses in his petition, *Show me, I pray thee, thy glory;* or, "Reveal thyself to me." That thou *art,* I infer from my own existence, and from thy numerous works all around me; and that thou art *glorious,* I learn from the display of thy perfections in thy vast creation, and in the government of the world thou hast made. But, alas! how small a portion of God is known in the earth! How faintly does thy glory shine in the feeble eyes of mortals. My knowledge of things in the present state of flesh and blood depends in a great measure upon the senses; but God is a Spirit invisible to eyes of flesh, and imperceptible through the gross medium of sensation. How and when shall I know thee as thou art, thou great, thou dear unknown? In what a strange situation am I! I am surrounded with thy Omnipresence, yet I cannot perceive thee: thou art as near to me as I am to myself; "thou knowest my down-sitting and mine up-rising, thou understandest my thoughts afar off;" thou penetratest my very essence, and knowest me altogether. Psalm cxxxix. 2, &c. But to me thou dwellest in impervious darkness, or which is the same, in light inaccessible. "Oh that I knew where I might find him! Behold, I go forward, but he is not there; and backward, but I cannot perceive him: on the left hand, where he doth work, but I cannot behold him: he hideth himself on the right hand, that I cannot see him." Job xxiii. 3, 8, 9. I see his perfections beaming upon me from all his works, and his providence ever-active, ruling the vast universe, and diffusing life, motion, and vigour through the whole: the virtue of his wisdom, power, and goodness,

> Warms in the sun, refreshes in the breeze;
> Glows in the stars, and blossoms in the trees;
> Lives in all life, extends through all extent;
> Spreads undivided, operates unspent;
> Inspires our soul, informs our vital part.—POPE.

But where is the great Agent himself? These are his works, and they are glorious: "in wisdom has he made them all," but where is the divine Artificer? From these displays of his glory, which strike my senses, I derive some ideas of him; but oh! how faint and glimmering! how unlike to the all-perfect Archetype and Original! I have also heard of him by the hearing of the ear; I read his own descriptions of himself in his word; I contemplate the representations he has given of himself in his ordinances; and these are truly glorious, but they are adapted to the dark and grovelling minds of mortals in this obscure region, and fall infinitely short of the original glory. I can think of him; I can love him; I can converse and carry on a spiritual intercourse with him; I feel him working in my heart; I receive sensible communications of love and grace from him; I dwell at times with unknown delight in the contemplation of his glory, and am transported with the survey: but, alas! I cannot fully know him; I cannot dive deep into this mystery of glory; my senses cannot perceive him; and my intellectual powers in the present state are not qualified to converse with spiritual objects, and form a full acquaintance with them. Oh! if it would please my God to show me his glory in its full lustre! Oh that he would reveal himself to me so that my senses may assist my mind; if such a manner of revelation be possible!

Such thoughts as these may naturally rise in our minds; and probably some such thoughts possessed the mind of Moses, and were the occasion of his request, *I beseech thee, show me thy glory*.

These chapters, whence we have taken our subject of discourse, present us with transactions that must seem very strange and incredible to a mind that knows nothing of communion with the Father of spirits, and that is furnished only with modern ideas.

Here is, not an angel, but a man; not a creature only, but a sinner, a sinner once depraved as ourselves, in intimate audience with the Deity. Jehovah speaks to him *face to face, as a man speaketh to his friend*. Moses uses his interest in favour of a rebellious people, and it was so great that he prevailed: nay, to show the force of his intercessions, and to give him an encouragement to use them, God condescends to represent himself as restrained by this importunate petitioner, and unable to punish the ungrateful

Israelites, while Moses pleaded for them. " Let me alone,"
says he, " that my wrath may wax hot against them, that I
may consume them." Exod. xxxii. 10. Moses urges petition upon petition; and he obtains blessing upon blessing,
as though God could deny nothing to such a favourite.
He first deprecates the divine wrath, that it might not immediately break out upon the Israelites, and cut them off,
verses 11–14. When he has gained this point, he advances farther, and pleads that God would be their Con-
ductor through the wilderness, as he had been till that
time, and lead them into the promised land. In this article God seems to put him off, and to devolve the work of
conducting them upon himself; but Moses, sensible that
he was not equal to it, insists upon the request, and with
a sacred dexterity urges the divine promises to enforce it.
Jehovah at length appears, as it were, partly prevailed
upon, and promises to send his angel before him as his
guide. Chap. xxxii. 34, and xxxiii. 2. But, alas! an angel
cannot fill up his place; and Moses renews his petition to
the Lord, and humbly tells him that he had rather stay, or
even die where they were in the wilderness, than to go up
to the promised land without him. *If thy presence go not*
with me, carry us not up hence, chap. xxxiii. 15. " Alas!
the company of an angel, and the possession of a land
flowing with milk and honey, will not satisfy us without
thyself." His prayers prevail for this blessing also, and
Jehovah will not deny him any thing. Oh the surprising
prevalency of faith! Oh the efficacy of the fervent prayer
of a righteous man!

And now, when his people are restored unto the divine
favour, and God has engaged to go with them, has Moses
any thing more to ask? Yes, he found he had indeed
great interest with God, and oh! he loved him, and longed,
and languished for a clearer knowledge of him; he found

that after all his friendly interviews and conferences he knew but little of his glory; and now, thought he, it is proper time to put in a petition for this manifestation; who knows but it may be granted! Accordingly he prays with a mixture of filial boldness and trembling modesty, *I beseech thee, show me thy glory;* that is to say, "Now I am in converse with thee, I perceive thou art the most glorious of all beings; but it is but little of thy glory I as yet know. Oh! is it possible for a guilty mortal to receive clearer discoveries of it? If so, I pray thee favour me with a more full and bright view." This petition is also granted, and the Lord promises him, "I will make all my goodness pass before thee, and I will proclaim the name of the Lord before thee."

That you may the better understand this strange history, I would have you observe a few things.

1st. In the earliest ages of the world, it was a very common thing for God to assume some visible form, and in it to converse freely with his servants. Of this you frequently read in the history of the patriarchs, particularly of Adam, Abraham, Jacob, &c. It is also a tradition almost universally received in all ages, and among all nations, that God has sometimes appeared in a sensible form to mortals. You can hardly meet with one heathen writer but that you will find in him some traces of this tradition. Upon this, in particular, are founded the many extravagant stories of the poets concerning the appearances of their gods. Had there been no original truth in some appearances of the true God to men, there would have been no colour for such fables; for they would have evidently appeared groundless and unnatural to every reader. This tradition therefore was no doubt originally derived from the appearances of the Deity, in a coporeal form, in early ages.* Sometimes

---

* These appearances were probably made in the person of the Son, and might be intended as a prelude or earnest of his assuming human nature in

God assumed a human shape, and appeared as a man. Thus he appeared to Abraham, in company with two angels, Gen. xviii., and that good patriarch entertained them with food as travellers; yet one of them is repeatedly styled the Lord, or Jehovah, the incommunicable name of God; see verses 13, 20, 22, 26, &c., and speaks in a language proper to him only, verses 14, 21, &c. Sometimes he appeared as a visible brightness, or a body of light, or in some other sensible form of majesty and glory. Thus he was seen by Moses in the bush as a burning fire; thus he attended the Israelites through the wilderness, in the symbol of fire by night, and a cloud by day; and thus he often appeared in the tabernacle, and at the dedication of Solomon's temple, in some sensible form of glorious brightness, which the Jews called the *Shechinah;* and looked upon as a certain symbol of the divine presence.

2dly. You are to observe that God, who is a spirit, cannot be perceived by the senses; nor were these sensible forms intended to represent the divine essence, which is wholly immaterial. You can no more see God than you can see your own soul; and a bodily form can no more represent his nature than shape or colour can represent a thought or the affection of love. Yet,

3dly. It must be allowed that majestic and glorious emblems, or representations of God exhibited to the senses, may help to raise our ideas of him. When the senses and the imagination assist the power of pure understanding, its ideas are more lively and impressive: and though no sen-

the fulness of time, and his dwelling among mortals. He was the immediate Agent in the creation of the world; and the Father devolved upon him the whole economy of Providence from the beginning; and hence he had frequent occasions to appear on some grand design. It cannot seem incredible that he should thus assume some visible form to such as believe that God was at length really *manifested in the flesh;* for this temporary apparent incarnation cannot be deemed more strange than his really being *made flesh, and dwelling among us.*

sible representations can bear any strict resemblance to the
divine nature, yet they may strike our minds deeply, and
fill them with images of grandeur and majesty. When I
see a magnificent palace, it naturally tends to give me a
great idea of the owner or builder. The retinue and
pomp of kings, their glittering crowns, sceptres, and other
regalia, tend to inspire us with ideas of majesty. In like
manner those sensible representations of Deity, especially
when attended with some rational descriptions of the divine
nature, may help us to form higher conceptions of the
glory of God; and the want of such representations may
occasion less reverence and awe. For instance, had the
description of the Deity, *The* LORD *God, merciful and
gracious*, &c., been only suggested to the mind of Moses
as an object of calm contemplation, it would not have
struck him with such profound reverence, nor given him
such clear or impressive ideas as when it was proclaimed
with a loud majestic voice, and attended with a visible
glory too bright for mortal eyes. Human nature is of
such a make, that it cannot but be affected with things of
this nature.

Consider the matter well in the light in which I have
set it, and you may see something of the propriety and
good tendency of these appearances, and at the same time
guard yourselves against mistakes. Let me now give you
what I apprehend the true history of this remarkable and
illustrious appearance of God to Moses.

Moses had enjoyed frequent interviews with God, and
seen many symbols of his presence and representations of
his glory; but he still finds his knowledge of him very defective, and apprehends that God might give him some representation of his glory more striking and illustrious than
any he had seen. Therefore, finding that now he was in
great favour with him, he humbly moves this petition,

I beseech thee show me thy glory; "give me some more full and majestic representations of thy glory than I have hitherto seen." The Lord answers him, "I will cause all my goodness," that is a glorious, visible representation of my goodness, which is, "my glory, to pass before thee," which may strike thy senses, and make them the medium of conveying to thy mind more illustrious and majestic ideas of my glory. And as no sensible forms can fully represent the spiritual essence and perfections of my nature, while I cause a visible representation of my glory to pass before thee, I will at the same time proclaim the name of the Lord,* and describe some of the principal perfections that constitute my glory and goodness. But so bright will be the lustre of that form which I shall assume, that thou art not able to see my face, or the most splendid part of the representation; the glory is too bright to be beheld by any mortal, ver. 20. But there is a place in a rock where thou mayest wait, and I will cast darkness over it till the brightest part of the form of glory in which I shall appear is passed by, and then I will open a medium of light, and thou shalt see my back parts; that is those parts of the representation which are less illustrious, and which pass by last: the glory of these thou shalt be enable to bear, but my face shall not be seen." ver. 2–23.

Thus God condescended to promise; and when matters were duly prepared, he performs his engagement. The Lord assumed a visible form of glory, *and passed by before him and proclaimed his name,* which includes his perfections. Things are known by their names, and God is

---

* The LXX render the passage, *I will call by my name, the* LORD *before thee.* And this is the most literal translation of the Hebrew: they are rendered *Inclamabo nominatim Jehovah ante faciem tuam,* by Junius and Tremellius. According to this version the sense seems to be, "when the symbol of my glory is passing by, I will give thee notice, and call by my name the Lord, that I may not pass by unobserved."

known by his attributes, therefore his name includes his attributes. The proclamation ran in this august style, " The LORD, the LORD God, merciful and gracious, long-suffering, and abundant in goodness and truth, keeping mercy for thousands, forgiving iniquity and transgression and sin." Moses was struck with reverence and admiration, and bowed and worshipped.

My present design is to explain the several names and perfections here ascribed to God, and show that they all concur to constitute his goodness. For you must observe this is the connection. Moses prays for a view of God's glory. God promises him a view of his goodness, which intimates that his goodness is his glory; and when he describes his goodness, what is the description? It is " the LORD, the LORD God, merciful and gracious, long-suffering, and abundant in goodness and truth, keeping* mercy for thousands, forgiving iniquity, transgression and sin." That these attributes belong to his goodness we easily and naturally conceive; but what shall we think of his punitive justice, that awful and tremendous attribute, the object of terror and aversion to sinners? Is that a part of his goodness too? Yes, when God causes his goodness to pass before Moses, he proclaims as one part of it, that " he will by no means clear the guilty; and that he visits the iniquities of the fathers upon the children to the third and fourth generation." This awful attribute is an important part of his goodness, and without it he could not be good, amiable, or glorious.

I am now about to enter upon a subject the most sublime, august, and important, that can come within the com-

---

* The Hebrews observe, that the first letter of the word translated *keeping*, is much larger than usual; which shows that a particular emphasis is to be laid upon it; as if he should say, " I most strictly and richly keep mercy for thousands; the treasure is immense, and can never be exhausted.

pass of human or angelic minds, the name and perfections of the infinite and ever-glorious God. I attempt it with trembling and reverence, and I foresee I shall finish it with shame and confusion : for who by searching can find out God ? who can find out the Almighty unto perfection ? Job xi. 7. The question of Agur mortifies the pride of human knowledge; " What is his name, and what is his Son's name, if thou canst tell ?" Prov. xxx. 4. " Such knowledge is too wonderful for me ; it is high, I cannot attain unto it." Psalm cxxxix. 6. " It is as high as heaven ; what canst thou do ? deeper than hell; what canst thou know ? the measure thereof is longer than the earth, and broader than the sea." Job xi. 8, 9. Lend me your skill, ye angels, who have seen his face without intermission from the first moment of your happy existence ; or ye saints above, that " see him as he is, and know even as you are known," inspire me with your exalted ideas, and teach me your celestial language, while I attempt to bring heaven down to earth, and reveal its glories to the eyes of mortals. In vain I ask ; their knowledge is incommunicable to the inhabitants of flesh, and none but immortals can learn the language of immortality. But why do I ask of them ? Oh thou Father of angels and of men, who " canst perfect thy praise even out of the mouths of babes and sucklings," and who canst open all the avenues of knowledge, and pour thy glory upon created minds, do thou shine into my heart; to me give the light of the knowledge of thy glory ; *I beseech thee, show me thy glory :* cause it to shine upon my understanding, while I try to display it to thy people, that they may behold, adore, and love.

As to you my brethren, I solicit your most solemn and reverential attention, while I would lead you into the knowledge of the Lord your maker. One would think a kind of filial curiosity would inspire you with eager desires

to be acquainted with your divine Parent and original.
You would not be willing to worship you know not what,
or with the Athenians, adore an unknown God.   Do you
not long to know the greatest and best of beings, the glim-
merings of whose glory shine upon you from heaven and
earth ?   Would you not know him in whose presence you
hope to dwell and be happy for ever and for ever ?   Come
then, be all awe and attention, while I proclaim to you his
name and perfections, " The LORD, the LORD God, merciful and gracious, long-suffering, and abundant in goodness
and truth, keeping mercy for thousands, forgiving iniquity,
transgression and sin."

We may be sure God has assumed to himself such
names as are best adapted to describe his nature, as far as
mortal language can reach.   And everything belonging to
him is so dear and important, that his very name deserves
a particular consideration.   This is not to make empty
criticisms upon an arbitrary unmeaning sound, but to derive useful knowledge from a word of the greatest emphasis and significancy.

The first name in the order of the text, and in its own
dignity, is, *the* LORD, or Jehovah; a name here twice repeated, to show its importance, *the* LORD *the* LORD, or
Jehovah, Jehovah.   This is a name peculiar to God, and
incommunicable to the most exalted creature.   The Apostle tells us, *There are gods many and lords many.* 1 Cor.
viii. 5.   Magistrates in particular are so called, because
their authority is some shadow of the divine authority.
But the name Jehovah, which is rendered LORD in my
text, and in all those places in the Bible, where it is written in capitals, I say, this name Jehovah is appropriated to
the Supreme Being, and never applied to any other.   He
claims it to himself, as his peculiar glory.   Thus in Psalm
lxxxiii. ver. 18.   " Thou, whose name alone is Jehovah,

art the Most High over all the earth." And in Isaiah
xlii. ver. 8. *I am the* LORD, or (as it is in the original)
Jehovah ; that is my name, my proper incommunicable
name, *and my glory will I not give to another ;* that is, I
will not allow another to share with me in the glory of
wearing this name. Thus also in Amos iv. ver. 13. "Lo,
he that formeth the mountains, and createth the wind, that
declareth unto man what is in his thoughts, that maketh
the morning darkness, and treadeth upon the high places
of the earth, the LORD, the God of hosts, is his name," his
distinguishing, appropriated name. There must therefore
be something peculiarly sacred and significant in this name,
since it is thus incommunicably appropriated to the only
one God.

The Jews had such a prodigious veneration for this
name as amounted to a superstitious excess. They call it
"that name," by way of distinction, "The great name, the
glorious name, the appropriated name, the unutterable
name, the expounded name,"* because they never pronounced it, except in one instance, which I shall mention
presently, but always expounded it by some other: thus
when the name Jehovah occurred in the Old Testament,
they always read it *Adonai* or *Elohim*, the usual and less
sacred names, which we translate *Lord God*. It was
never pronounced by the Jews in reading, prayer, or the
most solemn act of worship, much less in common conversation, except once a year, on the great day of atonement,
and then only by the high priest in the sanctuary, in pronouncing the benediction: but at all other times, places,
and occasions, and to all other persons, the pronunciation
was deemed unlawful. The benediction was that which

---

* They also distinguish it by the name of the four letters that composed it,
jodh, he, vau, he ; and hence the Greeks called it *the four-lettered name.* See
Buxtorf.

you read in Numbers vi. verses 24, 25, 26, where the name Jehovah is thrice repeated in the Hebrew, "Jehovah bless thee, and keep thee : Jehovah make his face to shine upon thee, and be gracious unto thee : Jehovah lift up his countenance upon thee, and give thee peace." When this venerable name was pronounced upon this occasion, we are told by the Jewish rabbies, " that all the vast congregation then present bowed the knee, and fell down in the humblest prostration, crying out, *Blessed be his glorious name for ever and ever.*" They supposed this name had a miraculous virtue in it, and that by it Moses and others wrought such wonders : nay, so great was their superstition that they thought it a kind of charm or magical word, and that he that had it about him, and knew its true-pronunciation and virtue, could perform the most surprising things, and even shake heaven and earth.*

I do not mention these things with approbation, but only to show that there is something peculiarly significant, important, und sacred in this name, from whence the Jews took occasion for such extravagant notions; and this will appear from its etymology. You know it is not my usual method to carry a great quantity of learned disquisition with me into the pulpit, or to spend your time in trifling, pedantic criticisms upon words, which may indeed have a show of literature, and amuse those who admire what they do not understand, but can answer no valuable end in a popular audience. However, at present I must take the liberty of showing you the original meaning of the name *Jehovah*, that I may thoroughly explain my text, and that

---

* This name seems not to have been unknown among other nations. Hence probably is derived the name *Jovis, Jove*, the Latin name for the Supreme God. And it is probably in allusion to this that Varro says, "Deum Judæorum esse Jovem." The Moors also called God *Jubah*, and the Mahometans *Hou ;* which in their language signifies the same with Jehovah, namely, *He who is.* See Univ. Hist Vol. III. p. 357, note T.

you may know the import of a name that will occur so
often to you in reading your Bibles ; for, as I told you, wherever you meet with the word LORD in large letters, it is
always *Jehovah* in the original.

The name Jehovah is derived from the Hebrew verb,
to be ; and therefore the meaning of the word Jehovah is,
The existent, the being, or, *He that is.* Thus it seems explained in Exodus iii. ver. 14. I AM THAT I AM, or, " I
am because I am ;" that is, I exist, and have being in and
of myself without dependence upon any cause; and my
existence or being is always the same, unchangeable and
eternal. St. John well explains this name by the *Who is,
who was, and who is to come ;* or, as the passage might be
rendered, " The present Being, the past Being, and the
future Being;" or, The Being that is, the Being that was,
and the Being that will be; that is, the perpetual, the
eternal, and unchangeable Being. I shall only observe
farther, that Jehovah is not a relative, but an absolute
name : there is no pronoun or relative word that is ever
joined with it; we can say, My Lord, our Lord, our God,
&c., but the Hebrews never say or write, My Jehovah,
our Jehovah, &c. ; so that this name represents him as he
is in himself, without any relation to his creatures, as he
would have been if they had never existed. He would
still have been the Being, the absolute, independent existent, in which view he has nothing to do with his creatures, and can sustain no relation to them.

From this name, thus explained, we learn the following
glorious, incommunicable perfections of God; that he is
self-existent and independent; that his being is necessary;
that he is eternal ; and that he is unchangeable.

While I am about to enter upon these subjects, I seem
to stand upon the brink of an unbounded, fathomless ocean,
and tremble to launch into it; but, under the conduct of

Scripture and humble reason, let us make the adventure; for it is a happiness to be lost and swallowed in such an ocean of perfection.

1. The name Jehovah implies that God is *self-existent* and independent. I do not mean by this that he produced himself, for that would be a direct contradiction, and suppose him to exist, and not to exist at the same time: but I mean that the reason and ground of his existence is in his own nature, and does not at all depend upon anything besides. Being is essential to him. He contains an infinite fulness of being in himself, and no other being has contributed in the least towards his existence; and hence with great propriety he assumes that strange name, *I Am*. He is Being throughout, perfectly and universally vital; and the reason of this is entirely within his own nature.

How gloriously is he distinguished in this respect from all other beings, even the most illustrious and powerful! Time was, when they were nothing. Angels and archangels, men and beasts, sun, moon, and stars; in short, the whole universe besides, were once nothing, had no being at all: and what was the reason that they ever came into being? Certainly it was not in them: when they were nothing there was no reason at all in them why they should ever be something: for in not being, there can be no reason or ground for being. The mere pleasure of God, the fiat of this self-existing Jehovah, is the only reason and sole cause of their existence. If it had not been for him, they would have continued nothing as they were: their being therefore is entirely precarious, dependent, and wholly proceeds from a cause without themselves. But Jehovah glories in an unborrowed, underived, independent being. Whatever he is, it is his own: he owes it only to himself. What a glorious Being is this! how infinitely different from and superior to the whole system of creatures! Are you not already constrained to bow the knee before him, and wonder, adore, and love? But,

II. Hence it follows that his existence is necessary; that is, it is impossible for him not *to be*. His being does not depend upon any thing without him, nor does it depend upon his own arbitrary will, but it is essential to his nature. That he should not be is as great an impossibility as that two and two should not make four. It is impossible that any thing should be more closely connected with any thing than being is with his essence, and it is impossible any thing should be more opposite to any thing than he is to non-existence. Since he received his being from nothing without himself, and since the reason of his existence is not derived from any other, it follows, that unless he exists by the necessity of his own nature, he must exist without any necessity: that is, without any reason at all, which is the same as to say that nothing is the cause or ground of his existence; and what imagination can be more absurd! His being therefore must exist by an absolute, independent necessity.

What a glorious Being is this! how infinitely distant from nothing, or a possibility of not being! What an unbounded fund of existence, what an immense ocean of Being is here! Alas! what are we, what is the whole universe besides in this comparison? They *are nothing, less than nothing, and vanity.* Our Being is not only derived but arbitrary, depending entirely upon the mere pleasure of Jehovah. There was no necessity from our nature that we should *be* at all; and now there is no necessity that we should continue to *be*. If we exist, it is not owing to us. "He made us, and not we ourselves;" and if we shall continue to be for ever, it is not owing to a fund of being within ourselves, but to the same God who first formed us. It is but lately since we sprung from nothing, and how near are we still to the confines of no-thing! We hang over the dreadful gulf of annihilation by a slender thread of being, sustained by the self-originated Jehovah. Remove him, take away his agency, and uni-versal nature sinks into nothing at once. Take away the root, and the branches wither: dry up the fountain, and the streams cease. If any of you are such fools as to wish in your hearts there were no God, you imprecate annihila-tion upon the whole universe; you wish total destruction to yourself and every thing else; you wish the extinction of all being. All depend upon God, the uncaused cause, the only necessary Being. Suffer me here to make a digression. Is this the God whom the daring sons of men so much forget, dishonour, and disobey? Are they so entirely dependent upon him, and yet careless how they behave towards him, careless whether they love and please him? Do they owe their being and their all entirely to him? And are they wholly in his hand? What then do they mean by withholding their thoughts and affections from him, breaking his laws and neglecting his gospel? Can you find a name for such a conduct? Would it not be entirely incredible did we not see it with our eyes all around us? Sinners, what mean you by this conduct? Let the infant rend the womb that conceived it, or tear the breasts that cherish it; go, poison or destroy the bread that should feed you; dry up the streams that should allay your thirst; stop the breath that keeps you in life: do these things, or do any thing, but oh! do not for-get, disobey, and provoke the very Father of your being, to whom you owe it that you are not as much nothing now as you were ten thousand years ago, and on whom you depend, not only for this and that mercy, but for your very being, every moment of your existence, in time and eternity. He can do very well without you, but oh what are you without him! a stream without a fountain, a branch without a root, an effect without a cause, a mere blank, a nothing. He indeed is self-sufficient and self-existent. It is nothing to him, as to his existence, whether creation exists or not. Let men and angels and every creature sink to nothing, from whence they came, his being is still secure: he enjoys an unprecarious being of his own, necessarily, unchangeably, and eternally existent. Men and angels bow the knee, fall prostrate and adore before this Being of beings. How mean are you in his presence! what poor, arbitrary, dependent, perishing creatures! what shadows of existence! what mere nothings! And is it not fit you should humbly acknowledge it? Can there be any thing more unnatural, any thing more foolish, any thing more audaciously wicked, than to neglect or contemn such a Being, the Being of beings, the Being that includes all being? I can hardly bear up under the horror of the thought.

III. The name Jehovah implies that God is eternal that is, he always was, is, and ever will be. From *everlasting to everlasting he is God*. Psalm xc. 2. This is his grand peculiarity, *he only hath immortality*, 1 Tim. vi. 16, in a full and absolute sense. Men and angels indeed are immortal, but it is but a kind of half-eternity they enjoy. They once were nothing, and continued in that state through an eternal duration. But as Jehovah never will have an end, so he never had a beginning. This follows from his necessary self-existence. If the reason of his existence be in himself, then unless he always existed he never could exist, for nothing without himself could cause him to exist. And if he exists by absolute necessity, he must always exist, for absolute necessity is always the same, without any relation to time or place. Therefore he always was and ever will be.

And what a wonderful Being is this! a Being unbegun, and that can never have an end! a being possessed of a complete, entire eternity. Here, my brethren, let your thoughts take wing, and fly backward and forward, and see if you can trace his existence. Fly back in thought about six thousand years, and all nature, as far as appears to us, was a mere blank; no heaven nor earth, no men nor angels. But still the great Eternal lived—lived alone, self-sufficient and self-happy. Fly forward in thought as far as the conflagration, and you will see " the heavens dissolving, and the earth and the things that are therein burnt up;" but still Jehovah lives unchangeable, and absolutely independent. Exert all the powers of numbers, add centuries to centuries, thousands to thousands, millions to millions; fly back, back, back, as far as thought can possibly carry you, still Jehovah exists: nay, you are even then as far from the first moment of his existence as you are now, or ever can be. Take the same prospect before you, and you will find the King eternal and immortal still the same: he is then no nearer an end than at the creation, or millions of ages before it.

What a glorious being is this! Here, again, let men and angels, and all the offspring of time, bow the knee and adore. Let them lose themselves in this ocean, and spend their eternity in ecstatic admiration and love of this eternal Jehovah.

Oh! what a glorious portion is he to his people! Your earthly enjoyments may pass away like a shadow; your friends die, yourselves must die, and heaven and earth may vanish like a dream, but your God lives! he lives for ever, to give you a happiness equal to your immortal duration. Therefore, *blessed, blessed is the people whose God is the* LORD.

But oh! let sinners, let wicked men and devils tremble

before him, for how dreadful an enemy is an eternal God!
He lives for ever to punish you. He lives for ever to
hate your sin, to resent your rebellion, and to display his
justice; and while he lives you must be miserable. What
a dismal situation are you in, when the eternal existence
of Jehovah is an inexhaustible fund of terror to you! Oh
how have you inverted the order of things, when you have
made it your interest that the Fountain of being should
cease to be, and that with him yourselves and all other
creatures should vanish into nothing! What a malignant
thing is sin, that makes existence a curse, and universal
annihilation a blessing! What a strange region is hell,
where being, so sweet in itself, and the capacity of all enjoyments, is become the most intolerable burden, and
every wish is an imprecation of universal annihilation!
Sinners, you have now time to consider these miseries and
avoid them, and will you be so senseless and fool-hardy as
to rush headlong into them? Oh! if you were but sensible what will be the consequences of your conduct in a
few years, you would not need persuasions to reform it:
but oh the fatal blindness and stupidity of mortals, who
will not be convinced of these things till the conviction be
too late!

IV. The name of Jehovah implies that God is unchangeable, or always the same. If he exists necessarily,
he must always necessarily be what he is, and cannot be
any thing else. 'He is dependent upon none, and therefore he can be subject to no change from another; and
he is infinitely perfect, and therefore cannot desire to
change himself. So that he must be always the same
through all duration, from eternity to eternity: the same,
not only as to his being, but as to his perfections; the
same in power, wisdom, goodness, justice, and happiness.
Thus he represents himself in his word, as "the Father

of lights, with whom is no variableness, neither shadow of
turning:" James i. 17; "the same yesterday, and to-day,
and for ever;" Heb. xiii. 8. What a distinguished perfection is this! and indeed it is in Jehovah only that immutability can be a perfection. The most excellent
creature is capable of progressive improvements, and
seems intended for it; and to fix such a creature at first
in an immutable state, would be to limit and restrain it
from higher degrees of perfection, and keep it always in a
state of infancy. But Jehovah is absolutely, completely,
and infinitely perfect, at the highest summit of all possible
excellency, infinitely beyond any addition to his perfection,
and absolutely incapable of improvement; and consequently,
and as there is no room for, so there is no need of, a change
in him; and his immutability is a perpetual, invariable continuance in the highest degree of excellency, and therefore
the highest perfection. He is the cause and the spectator
of an endless variety of changes in the universe, without
the least change in himself. He sees worlds springing
into being, existing awhile, and then dissolving. He sees
kingdoms and empires forming, rising, and rushing headlong to ruin. He changes the times and the seasons; *he
removeth kings, and setteth up kings:* Dan. ii. 21; and he
sees the fickleness and vicissitudes of mortals; he sees
generations upon generations vanishing like successive
shadows; he sees them now wise, now foolish; now in
pursuit of one thing, now of another; now happy, now
miserable, and in a thousand different forms. He sees
the revolutions in nature, the successions of the seasons,
and of night and day. These and a thousand other
alterations he beholds, and they are all produced or permitted by his all-ruling providence; but all these make no
change in him; his being, his perfections, his counsels,
and his happiness, are invariably and eternally the same.

He is not wise, good, just, or happy, only at times, but he is equally, steadily, and immutably so through the whole of his infinite duration. Oh how unlike the fleeting offspring of time, and especially the changing race of man!

Since Jehovah is thus constant and unchangeable, how worthy is he to be chosen as our best friend! You that love him need fear no change in him. They are not small matters that will turn his heart from you: his love is fixed with judgment, and he never will see reason to reverse it: it is not a transient fit of fondness, but it is deliberate, calm, and steady. You may safely trust your all in his hands, for he cannot deceive you; and whatever or whoever fail you, he will not. You live in a fickle, uncertain world; your best friends may prove treacherous or cool towards you; all your earthly comforts may wither and die around you; yea, heaven and earth may pass away; but your God is still the same. He has assured you of it with his own mouth, and pointed out to you the happy consequences of it: " I am the LORD;" Jehovah, says he, " I change not; therefore ye sons of Jacob are not consumed:" Mal. iii. 6.

What a complete happiness is this Jehovah to those who have chosen him for their portion! If an infinite God is now sufficient to satisfy your utmost desires, he will be so to all eternity. He is an ocean of communicative happiness that never ebbs or flows, and therefore completely blessed will you ever be who have an interest in him.

But oh! how miserable are they who are the enemies of this Jehovah! Sinners, he is unchangeable, and can never lay aside his resentments against sin, or abate in the least degree in his love of virtue and holiness. He will never recede from his purpose to punish impenitent rebels, nor lose his power to accomplish it. His hatred of all moral evil is not a transient passion, but a fixed, invariable, deep-rooted hatred. Therefore, if ever you be happy, there must be a change in you. As you are so opposite to him, there must be an alteration in the one or the other; you see it cannot be in him, and therefore it must be in you; and this you ought to labour for above all other things. Let us then have grace, *whereby we may serve God acceptably, with reverence and godly fear; for our God is a consuming fire,* (Heb. xii. 28, 29,) to his impenitent and implacable enemies.*

* Our author has evidently not finished his subject, and I do not find it prosecuted in any of the discourses that have come to my hands; but yet I determined to publish the sermon, not only for its own (if I mistake not) substantial worth, but the rather as the sermon that next follows in order, may be considered as a prosecution, if not a completion of the great and glorious subject he has undertaken, particularly of his professed design in this sermon, "of explaining the several perfections here ascribed to God, and showing that they all concur to constitute his goodness. *The Editor.*

SERMON XVIII.

GOD IS LOVE.

1 JOHN iv. 8.—*God is love.*

LOVE is a gentle, pleasing theme, the noblest passion of the human breast, and the fairest ornament of the rational nature. Love is the cement of society, and the source of social happiness; and without it the great community of the rational universe would dissolve, and men and angels would turn savages, and roam apart in barbarous solitude. Love is the spring of every pleasure; for who could take pleasure in the possession of what he does not love! Love is the foundation of religion and morality; for what is more monstrous than religion without love to that God who is the object of it? Or who can perform social duties without feeling the endearments of those relations to which they belong? Love is the softener and polisher of human minds, and transforms barbarians into men; its pleasures are refined and delicate, and even its pains and anxieties have something in them soothing and pleasing. In a word, love is the brightest beam of divinity that has ever irradiated the creation; the nearest resemblance to the ever-blessed God; for *God is love.*

God is love. There is an unfathomable depth in this concise laconic sentence, which even the penetration of an angel's mind cannot reach; an ineffable excellence, which even celestial eloquence cannot fully represent. *God is love*; not only lovely and loving, but love itself; pure, unmixed love, nothing but love; love in his nature and in his operations; the object, source, and quintessence of all love.

My present design is to recommend the Deity to your affections under the amiable idea of love, and for that end to show that his other perfections are but various, modifications of love.

I. Love comprehends the various forms of divine beneficence. Goodness, that extends its bounties to innumerable ranks of creatures, and diffuses happiness through the various regions of the universe, except that which is set apart for the dreadful, but salutary and benevolent purpose of confining and punishing incorrigible malefactors; grace, which so richly showers its blessings upon the undeserving, without past merit or the prospect of future compensation; mercy, that commisserates and relieves the miserable as well as the undeserving; patience and long-suffering, which so long tolerate insolent and provoking offenders; what is all this beneficence in all these its different forms towards different objects, what but love under various names? It is gracious, merciful, patient and long-suffering love; love variegated, overflowing, and unbounded; what but love was the Creator of such a world as this, so well accommodated, so richly furnished for the sustenance and comfort of its inhabitants? and what but love has planted it so thick with an endless variety of beings, all capable of receiving some stream of happiness from that immense fountain of it, the divine goodness? Is it not love that preserves such an huge unwieldy world as this in order and harmony from age to age, and supplies all its numerous inhabitants with every good? and oh! was it not love, free, rich, unmerited love, that provided a Saviour for the guilty children of men? It was because God loved the world, that he gave his only begotten Son, that whosoever believeth in him should not perish, but have everlasting life. John iii. 16. Oh love, what hast thou done! what wonders hast thou wrought! It was thou, almighty love, that broughtest down the Lord of glory from his celestial throne, to die upon a cross an atoning sacrifice for the sins of the world. And what but love is it that peoples the heavenly world with colonies transplanted from this rebellious province of Jehovah's dominions; that forms such miracles of glory and happiness out of the dust, and the shattered, polluted fragments of human nature! and what but eternal love perpetuates their bliss through an eternal duration? but it is so evident, that these instances of divine goodness are only the effects of love, that it is needless to attempt any farther illustration.

II. What is divine wisdom but a modification of divine love, planning the best adapted schemes for communicating itself in the most advantageous, beneficent, and honourable manner, so as to promote the good of the great whole or collective system of creatures by the happiness of individuals; or to render the punishment and misery of individuals, which, for important reasons of state may be sometimes necessary in a good government, subservient to the same benevolent end? Whatever traces of divine wisdom we see in creation; as the order and harmony of the great system of nature, its rich and various furniture, and the conspiracy of all its parts to produce the good of each other and the whole; whatever divine wisdom appears in conducting the great scheme of providence through the various ages of time; or in the more astonishing and godlike work of redemption; in a word, whatever displays of divine wisdom appear in any part of the universe, they are only the signatures of divine love.

Why was yonder sun fixed where he is, and enriched with
such extensive vital influences, but because divine love saw
it was best and most conducive to the good of the system;
Why were our bodies so wonderfully and fearfully made,
and all their parts so well fitted for action and enjoyment,
but because divine love drew the plan, and stamped its
own amiable image upon them? Why was the manifold
wisdom of God displayed, not only to mortals, but also to
angelic *principalities and powers*, Eph. iii. 10, in the
scheme of redemption, which advances at once the honours
of the divine perfections and government, and the happiness of rebellious and ruined creatures, by an expedient
which nothing but infinite wisdom could ever devise, the
incarnation, the obedience, and passion of the co-equal
Son of God? Why, I say, but because divine love would
otherwise be under restraint, and incapable of giving full
scope to its kind propensions in a manner honourable to
itself and conducive to the public good? In short, divine
wisdom appears to be nothing else but the sagacity of love,
to discover ways and means to exercise itself to the greatest advantage; or, which is the same, divine wisdom always acts under the benign determination and conduct of
love; it is the counsellor of love to project schemes subservient to its gracious purposes; and in all its councils
love presides.

III. What is divine power but the omnipotence of love?
Why did omnipotence exert itself in the production of this
vast amazing world out of nothing? It was to open a
channel in which the overflowing ocean of love might extend itself, and diffuse its streams from creature to creature, upwards as high as the most exalted archangel, and
downwards as low as the meanest vital particle of being,
and extensive as the remotest limits of the universe, and
all the innumerable intermediate ranks of existence in the

endless chain of nature. And why does divine power still support this prodigious frame, but to keep the channel of love open from age to age? and for this purpose it will be exerted to all eternity. Perhaps I should assist your ideas of divine power, if I should call it the acting hand, the instrument, the servant of love, to perform its orders, and execute its gracious designs.

IV. What is the holiness of God but love—pure refined, and honourable love? What is it but the love of excellence, rectitude, and moral goodness? Holiness, in its own nature, has a tendency to promote the happiness of the universe; it is the health, the good constitution of a reasonable being; without which it has no capacity of relishing those enjoyments which are suitable to its nature. It is no arbitrary mandate of heaven that has established the inseparable connection between holiness and happiness, between vice and misery. The connection is as necessary, as immutable, and as much founded in the nature of things, as that between health of body and a capacity of animal enjoyments, or between sickness and a disrelish for the most agreeable food. Every creature in the universe, as far as he is holy, is happy; and as far as he is unholy, he is miserable. Therefore, by how much the more holy Jehovah is, by so much the more fit he is to communicate happiness to all that enjoy him; and consequently he is an infinite happiness, for he is infinitely holy. His taking so much care to promote holiness is but taking care of the public good. The strict exactions of his law, which contains every ingredient of the most perfect holiness, and admits of no dispensation, are but strict injunctions to his subjects to pursue that course which infallibly leads them to the most consummate happiness; and every abatement in his demands of obedience would be a license to them to deduct so much from their happiness, and render them-

selves so far miserable with his consent. That mitigation
of the rigour of his law, which some imagine he has made
to bring it down to a level with the abilities of degenerate
creatures, disabled by their voluntary wickedness, would
no more contribute to their felicity than the allowing a
sick man to gratify his vitiated taste by mixing a little
deadly poison in his food would contribute to the recovery
of his health, or the preservation of his life. The penal
sanctions of the divine law are but friendly warnings against
danger and misery, and honest admonitions of the destructive consequences of sin, according to the unchangeable
nature of things; they are threatenings which discover no
malignity or ill-nature, as sinners are apt to imagine, but
the infinite benevolence of the heart of God; threatenings
which are not primarily and unconditionally intended to
be executed, but to prevent all occasion of their being executed, by preventing sin, the natural source, as well as the
meritorious cause of every misery : threatenings which are
not executed, but as the only expedient left in a desperate
case, when all other means have been used in vain, and
no other method can secure the public good, or render a
worthless criminal *a vessel of wrath fitted for destruction*,
and fit for nothing else; of no other service to the great
community of rational beings. These are some of the
ingredients and displays of the holiness of God : and what
are these but so many exertions of pure love and benevolence? It is because he loves his creatures so much that
he requires them to be so holy : and that very thing, against
which there are so many cavils and objections, as too severe
and oppressive, and a rigid restraint from the pursuit of
pleasure, is the highest instance of the love of God for
them, and his regard for their happiness.

Let me therefore commence advocate for God with my
fellow-men, though it strikes me with horror to think there

should be any occasion for it. Ye children of the most tender Father, ye subjects of the most gracious and righteous Sovereign, ye beneficiaries of divine love, why do you harbour hard thoughts of him? Is it because his laws are so strict, and tolerate you in no guilty pleasure? This appointment is the kind restraint of love: the love of so good a being, will not allow him to dispense with your observance of any thing that may contribute to your improvement and advantage, nor indulge you in any thing that is in its own nature deadly and destructive, no more than a father will suffer a favourite child to play with a viper, or a good government permit a madman to run at large armed with weapons to destroy himself and others. Do you think hard of God because he hates all moral evil to such a degree, that he has annexed to it everlasting misery of the most exquisite kind? But what is this but an expression of his infinite hatred to every thing that is hurtful to his creatures, and his infinite regard to whatever tends to their benefit? Or has he been too rigid in exacting holiness as a necessary pre-requisite to the happiness of heaven? You may as well complain of the constitution of nature, that renders abstinence from poison necessary to the preservation of health, or that does not allow you to quench your thirst in a fever with cold water. Let me remind you once more, that holiness is essential to the happiness of heaven, and that without it you labour under a moral incapacity of enjoyment; and a moral incapacity will as inevitably deprive you of the pleasures of enjoyment, as if it were natural. While unholy you can no more be happy even in the region of happiness than a stone can enjoy the pleasure of animal life, or a mere animal those of reason. "But why," you will perhaps murmur and object, "why has God formed such a heaven as cannot be universally enjoyed? Why has he not provided a happiness for every taste?"　You may as well ask why he has not created a light that would be equally agreeable to every eye; to the mole and the owl, as well as to man and the eagle?　Or why has he not formed light with all the properties of darkness; that is, why has he not performed contradictions?　You may as well query, why has he not given us equal capacities of enjoyments in sickness and in health, and furnished us with equal pleasures in both?　I tell you that, in the nature of things, the low and impure pleasures which would suit the depraved taste of the wicked, would be nauseous and painful to pure minds refined and sanctified; and they cannot mingle, they cannot approach each other without being destroyed.　The element of water may as well be converted into a fit residence for the inhabitants of dry land, and yet retain all its properties that are suitable to its present natives; or the solid earth become a fit receptacle for fishes, and yet both it and the fishes retain their usual qualities.　In short, men, beasts, birds, fishes, insects, angels, devils, the inhabitants of every zone and climate, of every planet, or any other region of the universe, may as well form one society in one and the same place, and mingle their respective food and pleasures, as a heaven of happiness be prepared that would suit every taste.　God has prepared the only kind of heaven that is in its own nature possible; the only one that would be an expression of love, or afford real and extensive happiness to such of his creatures as are capable of it.　The heaven of sinners would be a nuisance to all other beings in the universe; a private good only to malefactors, at the expense of the public; an open reward of wickedness, and a public discountenancing of all moral goodness.　This would be the case upon the supposition that the heaven of sinners were possible.　But the supposition is infinitely absurd; it is as impossible as the pleasures of sickness, the

sensibility of a stone, or the meridian splendours of midnight.

Therefore acknowledge, admire, and love the beauty of
the Lord, his holiness. *Give thanks*, says the Psalmist,
at the remembrance of his holiness, Ps. xcvii. 12, of his
holiness, as well as of his goodness and love; for it is the
brightest modification of his love and goodness. An unholy being, in the character of supreme magistrate of the
universe, cannot all be love, or communicate nothing but
what is pleasing to all; nay, as far as he is unholy he
must have a malignant disposition towards the public happiness, and be essentially deficient in benevolence.

V. What is the justice, even the punitive justice of God,
but a modification of love and goodness!

As there is no divine perfection which appears so terrible to offenders as this, which therefore they toil and sweat
to disprove or explain away, I shall dwell the longer upon
it. And I hope to convince you that justice is not that
grim, stern, tremendous attribute which is delineated by
the guilty, partial imagination of sinners, who have made
it their interest that there should be no such attribute to
Deity, but that it is infinitely amiable and lovely, as well
as awful and majestic; nay, that it is love and benevolence
itself.

By the punitive justice of God, I mean that perfection
of his nature which executes the sentence of his law upon
offenders, or inflicts upon them the punishment he had threatened to disobedience, exactly according to his own denunciation. The present world, which is a state of trial and
discipline, and not of final rewards and punishments, is not
the proper theatre of vindictive justice, but of a promiscuous providence: *All things come alike to all*, and no man
can know the love or hatred of the Ruler of the world to
him, *by all that is before him*. Eccles. ix. 1, 2. Yet, some-

times, even in this life, justice arrests the guilty, and displays its illustrious terrors upon them, especially upon guilty nations that have no existence in a national capacity in the eternal world, and therefore can be punished in that capacity in this only. It was vindictive justice that deluged the whole world in a flood of vengeance; that kindled the flames of Sodom and Gomorrah; and that cut off the nations of Canaan when they *had filled up the measure of their iniquities*. It is justice that arms kingdoms from age to age, and makes them the executioners of divine wrath upon one another, while they are gratifying their own ambition, avarice, or revenge. The devastations of earthquakes, inundations, plagues, epidemical sicknesses, famines, and the various calamities in which mankind have been involved, are so many displays of divine justice; and their being brought on the world according to the course of nature, and by means of secondary causes, will by no means prove that they are not so, but only that the very make and constitution of this world are so planned and formed by divine wisdom as to admit of the execution of justice at proper periods, and that all its parts are the instruments of justice to accomplish its designs. But these and all the other judgments of heaven upon our world are only preludes and specimens of the most perfect administration of it in a future state. There the penalty of the law will be executed upon impenitent offenders with the utmost impartiality. And Revelation assures us that the punishment will be endless in duration, and of as exquisite a kind and high degree as the utmost capacity of the subject will admit; and consequently that it will not, like fatherly chastisements, have any tendency to their reformation or advantage, but to their entire and everlasting destruction. Now it is this display of punitive justice that appears so terrible and cruel to the guilty children of men; and therefore this is what I shall principally endeavour to vindidate and to clothe with all the gentle and amiable glories of love and public benevolence.

For this end I beg you would consider, that whatever has a tendency to prevent sin tends to prevent misery also, and to promote the happiness of the world and of all the individuals in it; that good laws are absolutely necessary for the prevention of sin; that penal sanctions are essential to good laws; and that the execution of the penal sanctions upon offenders is absolutely necessary to their efficacy and good tendency; and consequently the execution of them is a display of love and benevolence.

Consider also, that many are excited to seek everlasting happiness, and deterred from the ways that lead down to destruction, by means of the threatenings of the law: that even those on whom they are finally executed were once in a capacity of receiving immortal advantage from them, but defeated their good influence and tendency by their own wilful obstinacy : and that the righteous execution of these threatenings upon the incorrigible, may promote the common good of the universe.

Consider farther, that criminals are incompetent judges of vindictive justice, because they are parties; and therefore we should not form an estimate of it by their prejudices, but from the judgment of the disinterested and impartial part of the creation.

Finally consider, that proceedings similar to those of the divine government, are not only approved of as just in all human governments, but also loved and admired as amiable and praiseworthy, and essential to the goodness and benevolence of a ruler.

Let us briefly illustrate these several classes of propositions.

I. "Whatever has a tendency to prevent sin, tends to

prevent misery also, and to promote the happiness of the
universe and of all the individuals in it: good laws are
absolutely necessary for the prevention of sin: penal
sanctions are essential to good laws; and the seasonable execution of those sanctions is absolutely necessary
to their efficacy and good tendency; and consequently
the execution of them is a display of love and benevolence."

"Whatever has a tendency to prevent sin, tends to prevent misery also," and that for this reason, because sin is
necessarily productive of misery, and destructive of happiness. Can a rational creature be happy that is disaffected
to the Supreme Good, the only source of that kind of happiness which is adapted to a rational nature? This is as
impossible as that you should enjoy animal pleasures while
you abhor all animal enjoyments. Can a social creature
be happy in eternal solitude, or in a state of society, while
ill-affected towards the other members of society, or while
they are ill-affected towards him and he to them, *hateful,
and hating one another?* Can a creature, formed capable
of felicity superior to what any good can communicate,
be happy in the eager pursuit of bubbles; that is, of
its highest happiness in inferior enjoyments? All those
dispositions of heart, and the practices resulting from
them, in which sin consists, enmity to God, uneasy murmurings and insurrections against his perfections, and the
government of his law and providence; a churlish, malignant, envious temper towards mankind; an anxious, excessive eagerness of desire after vain, unsatisfactory enjoyments; a disrelish for the exalted pleasures of holiness and
benevolence; what are these and the like dispositions, but
so many ingredients of misery, and so many abatements
of happiness? and consequently all measures that are
taken for the prevention of sin are so many benevolent ex-

pedients for the prevention of misery and the increase of happiness.

I add, "good laws are absolutely necessary for the prevention of sin." Indeed those dispositions and actions which are sinful and forbidden by the divine law would be of a deadly nature to the soul, even if they were not forbidden, as a stab to the heart would prove mortal to the body, although there were no laws against it, and for that very reason laws have been made against it. Therefore the laws of God do not properly constitute the destructive nature of sin, but only point out and warn us against what is destructive in its own nature previous to all explicit law. And is it not absolutely necessary, and an act of the highest benevolence, that the supreme Lawgiver should warn us against this pernicious evil, and plainly inform us what it is? This is the design of his laws both natural and revealed. And without them, what sure instructor, what unerring guide, or what strong inducements to a proper conduct could we have in this most important case? Is it not necessary, is it not kind, that the supreme Legislator should interpose his authority, and lay us under the strongest obligations to avoid our own ruin? And if good laws are necessary, so are penal sanctions; for "penal sanctions are essential to good laws." Laws without penalties would be only the advices of an equal or an inferior, and not the obligatory commands of authority. They might be observed or not, according to pleasure, and consequently would answer no valuable purpose. They would also be infinitely absurd in their own nature; for if what the law enjoins be reasonable, necessary, and of good tendency, is it not necessary and fit that they who do not observe it should feel the bad effects of their omission? And what is this but a penalty? But on a point so plain I need not multiply words; I appeal to the com-

mon sense of mankind, I appeal to the universal practice
of all governments. Have there ever been, or can there
possibly be any laws without penal sanctions? Would
not such laws be exposed to perpetual insult and contempt,
and be destitute of all force and energy? The common
sense and universal practice of all the world, in all ages,
remonstrate against such an absurdity. But if penal sanctions are essential to good laws, then so is their execution;
for—

"The seasonable execution of penal sanctions is absolutely necessary to their efficacy and good tendency."
Penalties denounced can have no efficacy upon the subject
of the law; that is, they cannot excite fear, and by that
means deter them from disobedience, unless they are believed, and their execution expected. But they would
soon cease to be believed, and their execution would no
longer be expected, if in several instances they should be
dispensed with, and a succession of sinners should pass
with impunity. Other sinners, judging of future events
by past facts, would expect the same indulgence, and
therefore venture upon disobedience without any restraint
from the penalty of the law. Here again I shall bring
the matter to a quick decision, by appealing to the common reason and universal practice of mankind. Would
human laws have any force if the penalty was hung up as
an empty terror, and never executed? Would not such
laws be liable to perpetul violation and insult, and become
the sport of daring offenders? Would not the escapes of
former offenders encourage all future generations to give
themselves a-loose, in hopes of the same exemption? Is
it not necessary in all government that public justice should
make examples of some, to warn and deter others? Have
not all nations, especially the more civilized, made such
examples? And have not all the impartial world com-

mended their proceeding as necessary to the safety and happiness of society, and expressive of their regard to the public good?

View all these things together, and methinks I may bid defiance to common sense to draw any other conclusion than that the justice of God, in executing the penalties of his law upon impenitent offenders, is the heighth of goodness and love. If love requires that all proper expedients be used for the prevention of sin; if good laws are necessary for this end; if penalties are essential to good laws; and if the seasonable execution of penalties be absolutely necessary to give them their benevolent force and good tendency, does it not unavoidably follow, that love itself requires both the enacting of penal sanctions to the law of God, and the execution of them upon proper subjects? Without this wholesome severity, the divine laws would be less secure from contempt, and the divine government would be less favourable to the peace and happiness of the subjects than the laws and governments of mortals in all civilized nations.

"But why does the penalty rise so high? Why is the execution lengthened out through everlasting ages? Why might not a gentler punishment suffice?" This is the grand objection; and in such language as this the enmity of the rebellious heart against the justice of God generally expresses itself. But if the original design and natural tendency of the threatened penalty be to prevent sin, then by how much severer the penalty, by so much the more effectual tendency has it to answer this kind design. No punishment can rise higher than those which a righteous God has annexed to disobedience the natural source of every misery; and what is this but to say that no methods more effectual can be taken to prevent it than what he has actually taken? We may therefore infer the

ardor of the love of God from the terror of his threatenings. He has denounced the greatest misery against sin,
in order to restrain his creatures from running into that
very misery; and threatens the loss of heaven, in order to
prevent his creatures from losing it.

I must also here repeat the common argument, which
appears to me as valid as common; "that as the essence
of sin consists in the breach of an obligation, the evil of
sin must be exactly proportioned to the strength of the
obligation;" that as we are undoubtedly under infinite
obligations to a God of infinite excellency, our Maker,
Ruler, and Benefactor, the evil of sin, which violates those
obligations, must be infinite also; and that no punishment
short of what is infinite can be adequate to the demerit of
an infinite evil, and consequently sinners ought to suffer a
finite punishment through an infinite duration, because that
is the only way in which they are able to bear an infinite
punishment. But on this common topic a few hints may
suffice.

I proceed to the next set of propositions.

II. "That many are excited to the pursuit of everlasting happiness, and deterred from the ways of destruction,
by means of threatenings of the divine law; that even
those unhappy creatures on whom they are finally executed were once in a capacity of receiving immortal
advantage from them, but defeated their good influence
and tendency by their own wilful obstinacy: and that
the righteous execution of these threatenings upon the incorrigible may promote the common good of the universe."

"Many are excited to the pursuit of everlasting happiness, and deterred from the ways of destruction, by means
of the threatenings of the divine law." I appeal to experience and observation, whether the terrors of the Lord
are not the very first thing that gives a check to sinners in

their headlong career to ruin? It is *the law* that *worketh wrath*, Rom. iv. 15; that is, an alarming apprehension of the wrath of God against sin; and constrains them to use the instituted means of deliverance. Thus even the terrors of the law are made subservient to divine love, in " turning sinners from the error of their way, and saving souls from death." And could we consult the glorious assembly of the spirits of just men made perfect, they would all own that if their heavenly Father had not threatened them so severely, they would always have continued undutiful, and consequently rendered themselves miserable; and that they were saved from hell by being honestly warned of the danger of falling into it. It is true there are multitudes who do not receive this advantage by the penal sanctions of the divine law, but are made miserable for ever by the execution of them; yet it may be added,

" That even those unhappy creatures on whom they are executed, were once in a capacity of receiving infinite advantage from them, but defeated their good influence and tendency in their own wilful obstinacy." The threatenings of the divine law had the same good tendency in their own nature with respect to them, to deter them from disobedience, and urge their pursuit of happiness, as with respect to others; and these were some of the means of God appointed for their salvation. But they hardened themselves against them and thus defeated their good tendency, and obstinately ruined themselves in defiance of warning: they even forced a passage into the infernal pit through the strongest enclosures. But if they had not been thus warned, they not only would not have been saved in the event, but they would not have enjoyed the means of salvation. Now their enjoying these means was in itself an inexpressible blessing, though in the issue it only aggravates their misery; and consequently the enacting those penalties to the divine law was really an act of kindness even to them; and their abuse of the blessing does not alter its nature. The primary and direct end of a penalty is not the punishment of the subjects, but to restrain them from things injurious to themselves, and others, and urge them to pursue their own interest. But when this good end is not answered, by reason of their wilful folly and disobedience, then, and not till then, the execution is necessary for the good of others,* which leads me to add,

" That the righteous execution of the threatened penalty upon the incorrigible may promote the common good of the universe." This world of ours is a public theatre, surrounded with numerous spectators, who are interested in its affairs. Angels, in particular, are witnesses of the proceedings of Providence towards mankind and thence learn the perfections of God, and the maxims of his government. Hell is also a region dreadfully conspicuous to them ; and there, no doubt, the offended Judge intends to show his wrath, and make his power known to them as well as to mankind. Now they are held in obedience by rational motives, and not by any mechanical compulsion. And among other motives of a gentler kind, no doubt this is one of no small weight; namely, their observing the destructive consequences of sin upon men and angels, and

---

* Penalties, operate, like final causes, by a kind of retrospective influence ; that is, whilst they are only threatened. and the subject expects they will be executed, should he turn disobedient, they have a powerful tendency to deter him from disobedience. But they could not have this benevolent tendency, unless they be executed upon those, on whom their primary and chief design is not obtained : namely, the restraining of them from sin. It is enough that the offenders themselves once had an opportunity of taking warning, and reaping the advantage of the threatened penalty, while they were in a state of trial, and candidates for eternity. But it is absurd that they should receive any benefit from it, when, after sufficient trial, it appears they will take no warning, but are resolved to persist in sin, in defiance of the most tremendous penalties.

the terrible displeasure of God against it. It is not at all inconsistent with their dignity and purity to suppose them swayed by this motive in a proper connection with others of a more disinterested and generous nature. Therefore the confirmation of the elect angels in holiness, and their everlasting happiness is no doubt not a little secured and promoted by the execution of righteous punishment upon some notorious hardened malefactors, both of their own order and of the human race.

The same thing may be said of *the spirits of just men made perfect;* they are happily incapable of sinning, and consequently of becoming miserable; but their incapacity arises from the clear conviction of their understanding, which has the conduct of their will; and, while sin appears to them so deadly and destructive an evil, it is impossible, according to the make of a rational nature, that they should choose it. But the consequences of sin upon the wretched creatures on whom the penalty denounced against it is executed, is no doubt one thing that affords them this conviction; and so it contributes to their perseverance in obedience and happiness. Thus the joys of heaven are secured by the pains of hell, and even the most noxious criminals, the enemies of God and his creatures, are not useless in the universe, but answer the terrible but benevolent end of warning all other creatures against disobedience; which would involve them in the same misery, just as the execution of a few malefactors in human governments is of extensive service to the rest of the subjects.

But as the greater part of mankind perish, it may be queried, " How is it consistent with love and goodness, that the majority should be punished and made monuments of justice, for the benefit of the smaller number?" To this I reply, that though it be equally evident from Scripture and observation, that the greater part of mankind go down to destruction in the smooth, broad descending road of sin, in the ordinary ages of the world; and though revelation assures us that the number of the apostate angels is very great, yet I think we have no reason to conclude that the greater part of the rational creation shall be miserable; nay, it is possible the number of those on whom the penalty of the divine law is inflicted, may bear no more proportion to that of the innumerable ranks of creatures that may be retained in obedience and happiness by means of their conspicuous and exemplary punishment, than the number of criminals executed in our government, for the warning of others, bears to the rest of the subjects. If we consider that those who have been *redeemed from the earth,* even in the ordinary ages of the world, though comparatively but few, yet absolutely are a " multitude which no man can number, *of all nations, and kindreds, and people, and tongues,* Rev. vii. 9, and that the elect angels are *an innumerable company,*[*] Heb. xii. 22, perhaps much greater than the legions of hell; if to those we add the prodigious numbers that shall be converted in that long and blessed season when Satan shall be bound, when the prince of peace shall reign, and when " the kingdom and dominion, and the greatness of the kingdom under the whole heaven, shall be given to the people of the saints of the Most High," Dan. vii. 27, in which not only the greater number of the generations that shall live in that glorious millennium shall be saved, but perhaps a greater number than all that perished in former generations, which is very possible, if we consider the long continuance of that time, and that the world will then

---

[*] I do not forget that the original is *myriads of angels.* But the word is often, I think, generally used in the Greek classics, not for any definite number, but for a great and innumerable multitude. And so it is used here.

be under the peculiar blessing of heaven, and consequently mankind will multiply faster, and not be diminished as they now are by the calamities of war, plagues, epidemical sicknesses, and the other judgments of God upon those times of rebellion; if we also borrow a little light from the hypothesis of philosophy, and suppose that the other planets of our system are peopled like our earth with proper inhabitants, and particularly with reasonable creatures, (for he that made those vast bodies *made them not in vain, he made them to be inhabited ;*) if we further suppose that each of the innumerable fixed stars is a sun, the centre of habitable worlds, and that all these worlds, like our own, swarm with life, and particularly with various classes of reasonable beings, (which is not at all unlikely, if we argue from parity of cases, from things well known to things less known, or from the immense everflowing goodness, wisdom and power of the great Creator, who can replenish the infinite voids of space with being, life, and reason, and with equal ease produce and support ten thousand worlds as ten thousand grains;) if we suppose that his creative perfections will not lie inactive for ever, contented with one exertion for six days but that he still employs and will employ them for ever in causing new worlds, replenished with moral agents, to start into existence here and there in the endless vacancies of space; and finally, if we suppose that the flames of hell will blaze dreadfully bright and conspicuous in the view of all present and future creations; or that the destructive nature of sin will be some way or another made known to the rational inhabitants of all worlds by the punishment inflicted upon a number of men and angels, and that by this means they are effectually deterred from sin, and preserved from the misery inseparable from it; I say, if we admit these suppositions, some of which are undoubtedly true, and the rest I think not improbable, then it will follow that the number of holy and happy creatures in the universe will be incomparably greater than that of miserable criminals, and that the punishment of the latter is one principal mean of preserving this infinite number in obedience and happiness; and consequently is highly conducive to the public happiness, and expressive of the love and goodness of the universal Ruler to the immense community of his subjects. And thus *God is love*, even in the most terrible displays of his vindictive justice.

To illustrate this subject, consider farther:

III. "That criminals are incompetent judges of vindictive justice." They are parties, and it is their interest there should be no such attribute as justice in the Deity. It is natural for them to flatter themselves that their crimes are small; that their Judge will suffer them to escape with impunity, or with a gentle punishment, and that if he should do otherwise, he would be unmerciful, unjust, and cruel. The excess of self-love suggests to them a thousand excuses and extenuations of their guilt, and flatters them with a thousand favourable presumptions. An impenitent criminal is always an ungenerous, mean-spirited, selfish creature, and has nothing of that noble, disinterested self-denial and impartiality which would generously condemn himself and approve of that sentence by which he dies. A little acquaintance with the conduct of mankind will soon make us sensible of their partiality and wrong judgments in matters where self is concerned; and particularly how unfit they are to form an estimate of justice when themselves are to stand as criminals at its bar. Now this is the case of all mankind in the affair now under consideration. They are criminals at the bar of divine justice; they are the parties to be tried; they are under the dominion of a selfish spirit; it is natural to them to palliate their own crimes, and to form flattering expectations from the clemency of their Judge. And are they fit persons to prescribe to their Judge how he should deal with him, or what measure of punishment he ought to inflict upon them? Sinners! dare you usurp this high province! Dare you

> "Snatch from his hand the balance and the rod,
> Rejudge his justice, be the god of God!"*

Rather stand at the bar, ye criminals! that is your place. Do not dare to ascend the throne; that is the place of your Judge. Stand silent, and await his righteous sentence, which is always just, always best; or, if creatures must judge of the justice of their Sovereign, I appeal to the saints; I appeal to angels, those competent disinterested judges; I appeal to every upright, impartial being in the universe. They approve, they celebrate, they admire, and love all the displays of punitive justice, as necessary to the public good; and their judgment may be depended on; it is not misled by ignorance nor perverted by self-interest. To whom would you appeal as judges of the proceedings of courts of justice among men? To malefactors in a dungeon, who have made justice their enemy, and who are therefore enemies to it? No; but you would appeal to obedient subjects, who are not obnoxious to justice themselves, but enjoy protection under its guardianship, and are sensible of its beauty and public utility. They all approve it with one voice, and would look upon a supreme Magistrate without it as a very contemptible and odious character, and essentially deficient in goodness. Hence it follows that even the punitive justice of God not only is in reality, but to all impartial judges appears to be a most amiable, engaging, and beneficent

* Pope's Essay on Man.

perfection; majestic indeed, but not forbidding; awful, but
not sullen and hateful; terrible, but only to criminals; and
destructive only to what destroys the public good.   I have
so far anticipated myself that I need hardly add,

IV. " That proceedings similar to those of the divine
government are not only approved of as just in all human
governments, but also loved and admired as amiable and
praise-worthy, and highly essential to the goodness and
benevolence of a ruler."

Does the supreme Lawgiver annex severe penalties to
his laws, which render the disobedient miserable for ever?
So do human governments, with the unanimous approbation of their subjects; they inflict punishments that affect
life, and cut off the offender from civil society forever;
and this is the only kind of everlasting punishment that can
be endured or executed by mortals.   Does Jehovah maintain good order in his immense empire, protect his subjects, and deter them from offending by making examples
of the guilty ? and does he secure and advance the good
of the whole by the conspicuous punishment of obnoxious
individuals ?   This is done every day for the same ends in
human governments, and that with universal approbation.
Does he inflict punishments that are not at all intended for
the reformation and advantage of the guilty sufferer, but
only for the admonition and benefit of others?   This is
always the case in human governments when the punishments reaches to the life; for then the offender himself is
put out of all capacity of reformation or personal advantage by it, but he suffers entirely for the good of others.
Even criminals must be made useful to society; and this
is the only use they are fit to answer.   Would it not be
inexpedient and greatly injurious for a magistrate, in his
public character, to forgive crimes and suffer criminals to
escape, though to do so in a private character might be a

virtue? Just so God, who is the supreme Magistrate of the universe, and not at all to be considered, in this case, as a private person acting only in a private character; the great God, I say, is obliged, by his regard for his own honour and the benefit of his subjects, to inflict proper punishments and distribute his pardoning mercy to individuals consistently with the general good of the whole. What would be revenge in a private person, which is the ruling passion of devils, is justice, honour, and benevolence itself in the supreme ruler of the world; and a failure in this would render him not only less glorious and majestic, but less amiable, less beneficent to his creatures.

I know hardly any thing of so much importance to give us just sentiments of the proceedings of God, with his creatures, as that we should conceive of him as a moral Ruler, or the supreme Magistrate of the world. And it is owing to their not considering him in this character that sinners indulge such mistaken, dangerous presumptions concerning him. They choose to conceive of him under some fond and tender name, as a Being of infinite grace, the indulgent Father of his creatures, &c. All this is true; but it is equally true that he is their moral Ruler as well as their Father. His creatures are his subjects as well as his children: and he must act the wise and righteous Magistrate as well as the tender Father towards them. His goodness is that of a Ruler, and not of a private person; and his pardoning of sin and receiving offenders into favour, are not private kindnesses, but acts of government, and therefore they must be conducted with the utmost wisdom; for a wrong step in his infinite administration, which affects such innumerable multitudes of subjects, would be an infinite evil, and might admit of no reparation.

Though I have thus enlarged upon this subject, yet I

am far from exhausting my materials. But these things, I hope, are sufficient to convince your understandings that divine justice is not that unkind, cruel, and savage thing sinners are wont to imagine it; but that God is just, because *God is love;* and that he punishes, not because he is the enemy, but because he is the friend of his creatures, and because he loves the whole too well to let particular offenders do mischief with impunity.*

I shall only add, that this is the view Jehovah has given of himself in the clearest manifestation of his perfections that he ever made to mortals. He promises his favourite Moses, that he would *make all his goodness pass before him.* Observe, it is his goodness he intends to exhibit; and the proclamation runs thus: "The LORD, the LORD God, merciful and gracious, long-suffering, forgiving iniquity," &c. That these are acts or modifications of goodness, will be easily granted. But observe, it is added even in this proclamation of his goodness, *That he will by no means clear the guilty;* intimating, that to be just and punish sin is an act of goodness, as well as to be merciful and to forgive it.

And now when we have this copious subject in review, does it not suggest to us such conclusions as these:

---

* It may perhaps be objected, " That to represent justice under the notion of love is to affect singularity in language, to destroy the distinction of the divine attributes, and the essential difference of things."—To which I answer, 1. That a catachresis may be beautiful and emphatical, though it be always a seeming impropriety in language. Such is this representation, "Divine justice, divine love." 2. I do not deny that God's executing righteous punishment upon the guilty may be called justice; but then it is his love to the public that excites him to do this; and therefore his doing it may be properly denominated love, as well as justice, or love under the name of justice, which is love still. 3. I do not mean that the usual names of things should be changed, but that we should affix suitable ideas to them. We may retain the name of justice still, but let us not affix ideas to it that are inconsistent with divine love. Let us not look upon it as the attribute of a tyrant, but of a wise and good ruler.

I. May we not conclude that the case of impenitent sinners is desperate indeed, when it is not excessive rigour, not a malignity of temper, nor tyranny, or a savage delight in torture that condemns them, but goodness itself, love itself? Even the gentler perfections of the Deity, those from which they derive their presumptuous hopes, are conspired against them, and unite their forces to render them miserable, in order to prevent greater misery from spreading through the universe. Impenitent sinners! even the unbounded love of God to his creatures is your enemy. Love, under the name and form of justice, which is equally love still, demands your execution; and to suffer you to escape would not only be an act of injustice, but an act of malignity and hostility against the whole system of rational beings. Therefore repent and be holy, otherwise divine love will not suffer you to be happy. *God is love ;* therefore will he confine you in the infernal prison, as a regard to the public welfare in human governments shuts up criminals in a dungeon, and madmen in Bedlam.

II. May we not hence conclude that all the acts of the Deity may be resolved into the benevolent principle of love? *God is love ;* therefore he made this vast universe, and planted it so thick with variegated life. *God is love ;* therefore he still rules the world he has made, and inflicts chastisements and judgments upon it from every age. *God is love ;* therefore he spared not his own Son, but made him the victim of his justice. *God is love ;* therefore he requires perfect holiness, perfect obedience from all his subjects. *God is love ;* therefore he has enacted such tremendous sanctions to his law, and executes them in their full extent upon offenders. *God is love ;* therefore he has made the prison of hell, and there confines in chains of everlasting darkness those malevolent creatures, that would be a nuisance to society, and public mischiefs, if suffered to run at large In short, whatever he does, he does it because he is love. How amiable a view of him is this! Therefore,

III. We may certainly conclude that if God be love, then all his creatures ought to love him. Love him, O all ye inhabitants of heaven! But they need not my exhortation; they know him, and therefore cannot but love him. Love him, all ye inhabitants of the planetary worlds! if such there be. These also, I hope, need no exhortation, for we would willingly persuade ourselves that other territories of this immense empire have not rebelled against him as this earth has done. Love him, O ye children of men! To you I call: but oh! I fear I shall call in vain. To love him who is all love is the most hopeless proposal one can make to the world. But whatever others do, love the Lord, all ye his saints! You, I know, cannot resist the motion. Surely your love even now is all on fire. *Love the Lord, O my soul!* Amen.

SERMON XIX.

THE GENERAL RESURRECTION.

JOHN v. 28, 29.—*The hour is coming, in the which all
that are in the graves shall hear his voice, and shall come
forth ; they that have done good, unto the resurrection of
life ; and they that have done evil, unto the resurrection
of damnation.*

EVER since sin entered into the world, and death by sin,
this earth has been a vast grave-yard, or burying-place, for
her children.   In every age, and in every country, that
sentence has been executing, *Dust thou art, and unto dust
thou shalt return.*   The earth has been arched with graves,
the last lodgings of mortals, and the bottom of the ocean
paved with the bones of men.*   Human nature was at first
confined to one pair, but how soon and how wide did it
spread !   How inconceivably numerous are the sons of
Adam !   How many different nations on our globe contain
many millions of men even in one generation !   And how
many generations have succeeded one another in the long
run of near six thousand years !   Let imagination call up
this vast army : children that just light upon our globe, and
then wing their flight into an unknown world ; the gray-
headed that have had a long journey through life ; the bloom-
ing youth and the middle-aged, let them pass in review before us from all countries and from all ages ; and how vast

---

* No spot on earth but has supplied a grave ;
And human sculls the spacious ocean pave.—YOUNG.

and astonishing the multitude! If the posterity of one
man (Abraham) by one son was, according to the divine
promise, as the stars of heaven, or as the sand by the sea-
shore, innumerable, what numbers can compute the multitudes that have sprung from all the patriarchs, the sons
of Adam and Noah? But what is become of them all?
Alas! they are turned into earth, their original element;
they are all imprisoned in the grave, except the present generation, and we are dropping one after another in quick
succession into that *place appointed for all living*. There
has not been perhaps a moment of time for five thousand
years, but what some one or other has sunk into the mansions of the dead; and in some fatal hours, by the sword
of war or the devouring jaws of earthquakes, thousands
have been cut off and swept away at once, and left in
one huge promiscuous carnage. The greatest number of
mankind beyond comparison are sleeping under ground.
There lies beauty mouldering into dust, rotting into stench
and loathsomeness, and feeding the vilest worms. There
lies the head that once wore a crown, as low and contemptible as the meanest beggar. There lie the mighty giants,
the heroes and conquerors, the Samsons, the Ajaxes, the Alexanders, and the Cæsars of the world! there they lie stupid,
senseless, and inactive, and unable to drive off the worms
that riot on their marrow, and make their houses in those
sockets where the eyes sparkled with living lustre. There
lie the wise and the learned, as rotten, as helpless as the
fool. There lie some that we once conversed with, some
that were our friends, our companions; and there lie our
fathers and mothers, our brothers and sisters.

And shall they lie there always? Shall this body, this
curious workmanship of heaven, so wonderfully and fearfully made, always lie in ruins, and never be repaired?
Shall the wide-extended valleys of dry bones never more

live? This we know, that *it is not a thing impossible with God to raise the dead.* He that could first form our bodies out of nothing, is certainly able to form them anew, and repair the wastes of time and death. But what is his declared will in this case? On this the matter turns; and this is fully revealed in my text. "The hour is coming, when all that are in the graves," all that are dead, without exception, "shall hear the voice of the Son of God, and shall come forth."

And for what end shall they come forth? Oh! for very different purposes; "some to the resurrection of life; and some to the resurrection of damnation."

And what is the ground of this vast distinction? Or what is the difference in character between those that shall receive so different a doom? It is this, "They that have done good shall rise to life, and they that have done evil to damnation." It is this, and this only, that will then be the rule of distinction.

I would avoid all art in my method of handling this subject, and intend only to illustrate the several parts of the text. "All that are in the graves shall hear his voice, and shall come forth; they that have done well, to the resurrection of life; and they that have done evil, to the resurrection of damnation."

I. They that are in the graves shall hear his voice. The voice of the Son of God here probably means the sound of the archangel's trumpet, which is called his voice, because sounded by his orders and attended with his all-quickening power. This all-wakening call to the tenents of the grave we frequently find foretold in Scripture. I shall refer you to two plain passages. *Behold,* says St. Paul, *I show you a mystery,* an important and astonishing secret, *we shall not all sleep ;* that is mankind will not all be sleeping in death when that day comes; there will be a generation then alive upon the earth; and though they cannot have a proper resurrection, yet they shall pass through a change equivalent to it. " We shall all be changed," says he, " in a moment, in the twinkling of an eye, at the last trump: for the trumpet shall sound," it shall give the alarm; and no sooner is the awful clangor heard than all the living shall be transformed into immortals; *and the dead shall be raised incorruptible ; and we,* who are then alive, *shall be changed,* 1 Cor. xv. 51, 52; this is all the difference, *they shall be raised, and we shall be changed.* This awful prelude of the trumpet is also mentioned in 1 Thess. iv. 15, 16. " We which are alive and remain unto the coming of the Lord shall not prevent them which are asleep;" that is, we shall not be beforehand with them in meeting our descending Lord, " for the Lord himself shall descend from heaven with a shout, with the voice of the archangel, and with the trump of God;" that is, with a godlike trump, such as it becomes his majesty to sound, *and the dead in Christ shall rise first :* that is, before the living shall be caught up in the clouds to meet the Lord in the air: and when they are risen, and the living transformed, they shall ascend together to the place of judgment.

My brethren, realize the majesty and terror of this universal alarm. When the dead are sleeping in the silent grave; when the living are thoughtless and unapprehensive of the grand event, or intent on other pursuits; some of them asleep in the dead of night; some of them dissolved in sensual pleasures, eating and drinking, marrying and giving in marriage; some of them planning or executing schemes for riches or honours; some in the very act of sin; the generality stupid and careless about the concerns of eternity, and the dreadful day just at hand; and a few here and there conversing with their God, and "looking for the glorious appearance of their Lord and Saviour;" when the course of nature runs on uniform and regular as usual, and infidel scoffers are taking umbrage from thence to ask, " Where is the promise of his coming? for since the fathers fell asleep, all things continue as they were from the beginning of the creation." 2 Pet. iii. 4. In short, when there are no more visible appearances of this approaching day, than of the destruction of Sodom on that fine clear morning in which Lot fled away; or of the deluge, when Noah entered into the ark; then in that hour of unapprehensive security, then suddenly shall the heavens open over the astonished world; then shall the all-alarming clangor break over their heads like a clap of thunder in a clear sky. Immediately the living turn their gazing eyes upon the amazing phenomenon; a few hear the long-expected sound with rapture, and lift up their heads with joy, assured that *the day of their redemption is come*, while the thoughtless world are struck with the wildest horror and consternation. In the same instant the sound reaches all the mansions of the dead, and in a moment, in the twinkling of an eye, they are raised, and the living are changed. This call will be as animating to all the sons of men, as that call to a single person, *Lazarus, come forth*. Oh what a surprise will this be to a thoughtless world! Should this alarm burst over our heads this moment, into what a terror would it strike many in this assembly! Such will be the terror, such the consternation, when it actually comes to pass. Sinners will be the same timorous, self-condemned creatures then, as they are now. And then they will not be able to stop their ears, who are deaf to all the gentler calls of the gospel now. Then the trump of God will constrain them to hear and fear, to whom the ministers of Christ now preach in vain. Then they must all hear, for

II. My text tells you, *all that are in the graves,* all without exception, *shall hear his voice.* Now the voice of mercy calls, reason pleads, conscience warns, but multitudes will not hear. But this is a voice which shall, which must reach every one of the millions of mankind, and not one of them will be able to stop his ears. Infants and giants, kings and subjects, all ranks, all ages of mankind shall hear the call. The living shall start and be changed, and the dead rise at the sound. The dust that was once alive and formed a human body, whether it flies in the air, floats in ocean, or vegetates on earth, shall hear the new-creating fiat. Wherever the fragments of the human frame are scattered, this all-penetrating call shall reach and speak them into life. We may consider this voice as a summons not only to dead bodies to rise, but to the souls that once animated them, to appear and be re-united to them, whether in heaven or hell. To the grave, the call will be, *Arise, ye dead, and come to judgment;* to heaven, ye *spirits of just men made perfect;* "descend to the world whence you originally came; and assume your new-formed bodies:" to hell, " Come forth and appear, ye damned ghosts, ye prisoners of darkness, and be again united to the bodies in which you once sinned, that in them ye may now suffer." Thus will this summons spread through every corner of the universe; and heaven, earth, and hell, and all their inhabitants, shall hear and obey. Devils, as well as sinners of our race, will tremble at the sound; for now they know they can plead no more as they once did, *Torment us not before the time;* for the time is come, and they must mingle with the prisoners at the bar. And now when all that are in the graves hear this all-quickening voice,

III. *They shall come forth.* Now methinks I see, I hear the earth heaving, charnel-houses rattling, tombs bursting, graves opening. Now the nations under ground begin to stir. There is a noise and a shaking among the dry bones. The dust is all alive, and in motion, and the globe breaks and trembles, as with an earthquake, while this vast army is working its way through and bursting into life. The ruins of human bodies are scattered far and wide, and have passed through many and surprising transformations. A limb in one country, and another in another; here the head and there the trunk, and the ocean rolling between.* Multitudes have sunk in a watery grave, been swallowed up by the monsters of the deep, and transformed into a part of their flesh. Multitudes have been eaten by beasts and birds of prey, and incorporated with them; and some have been devoured by their fellow-men in the rage of a desperate hunger, or of unnatural cannibal appetite, and digested into a part of them. Multitudes have mouldered into dust, and this dust has been blown about by winds, and washed away with water, or it has petrified into stone, or been burnt into brick to form dwellings for their posterity; or it has grown up in grain, trees, plants, and other vegetables, which are the support of man and beast, and are transformed into their flesh and blood. But through all these various transformations and changes, not a particle that was essential to one human body has been lost, or incorporated with another human body, so as to become an essential part of it. And as to those particles that were not essential, they are not necessary to the identity of the body or of the person; and therefore we need not think they will be raised again. The omniscient God knows how to collect, distinguish, and compound all those scattered and mingled seeds of our mortal bodies. And now

---

* This was the fate of Pompey, who was slain on the African shore. His body was left there, and his head carried over the Mediterranean to Julius Cæsar.

at the sound of the trumpet, they shall all be collected, wherever they were scattered; all properly sorted and united, however they were confused; atom to its fellow-atom, bone to its fellow-bone. Now methinks you may see the air darkened with fragments of bodies flying from country to country, to meet and join their proper parts:

> " Scatter'd limbs, and all
> The various bones obsequious to the call,
> Self-mov'd, advance ; the neck perhaps to meet
> The distant head, the distant legs, the feet.
> Dreadful to view, see through the dusky sky
> Fragments of bodies in confusion fly,
> To distant regions journeying, there to claim
> Deserted members, and complete the frame—
> The sever'd head and trunk shall join once more,
> Tho' realms now rise between, and oceans roar,
> The trumpet's sound each vagrant mote shall hear,
> Or fixed in earth, or if afloat in air,
> Obey the signal, wafted in the wind,
> And not one sleeping atom lag behind."—*
> All hear : and now, in fairer prospect shown,
> Limb clings to limb, and bone rejoins its bone.—†

Then, my brethren, your dust and mine shall be reanimated and organized; " and though after our skin worms destroy these bodies, yet in our flesh shall we see God." Job xix. 16.

---

* Young's Last Day, Book II.

† These two last lines are taken from a poem, which is a lively imitation of Dr. Young, entitled, *The Day of Judgment,* ascribed to Mr. Ogilvie, a promising young genius of Aberdeen, in Scotland, not above nineteen years of age, as I was informed, when he composed this poem. The lines preceding these quoted are as follows :

> O'er boiling waves the severed members swim,
> Each breeze is loaded with a broken limb:
> The living atoms, with peculiar care,
> Drawn from their cells, come flying thro' the air.
> Where'er they lurk'd, thro' ages undecay'd,
> Deep in the rock, or cloth'd some smiling mead ;
> Or in the lily's snowy bosom grew,
> Or ting'd the sapphire with its lovely blue ;

And what a vast improvement will the frail nature of
man then receive? Our bodies will then be substantially
the same; but how different in qualities, in strength, in
agility, in capacities for pleasure or pain, in beauty or
deformity, in glory or terror, according to the moral
character of the person to whom they belong? Matter,
we know, is capable of prodigious alterations and refinements; and there it will appear in the highest perfection.
The bodies of the saints will be formed glorious, incorruptible, without the seeds of sickness and death. The
glorified body of Christ, which is undoubtedly carried to
the highest perfection that matter is capable of, will be the
pattern after which they shall be formed. *He will change
our vile body*, says St. Paul, *that it may be fashioned like
unto his glorious body*. Phil. iii. 21. "Flesh and blood,"
in their present state of grossness and frailty, "cannot
inherit the kingdom of God: neither doth corruption inherit incorruption. For this corruptible must put on incorruption, and this mortal must put on immortality."
1 Cor. xv. 50, 53. And how vast the change, how high
the improvement from this present state! "It is sown in
corruption, it is raised in incorruption; it is sown in dis-

> Or in some purling stream refresh'd the plains ;
> Or form'd the mountain's adamantine veins ;
> Or gaily sporting in the breathing spring,
> Perfum'd the whisp'ring zephyr's balmy wing—
> All hear, &c.

The thought seems to be borrowed from Mr. Addison's fine Latin poem
on the resurrection, in which are the following beautiful lines :

> Jam pulvis varias terræ dispersa per oras,
> Sive inter venas teneri concreta metalli,
> Sensim diriguit, seu sese immiscuit herbis,
> Explicita est; molem rursus coalescit in unam
> Divisum Funus, sparsos prior alligat artus
> Junctura, aptanturque ; iterum coeuntia membra.

honour, it is raised in glory; it is sown in weakness, it is raised in power," verses 42, 43, &c. Then will the body be able to bear up under the exceeding great and eternal weight of glory; it will no longer be a clog or an incumbrance to the soul, but a proper instrument and assistant in all the exalted services and enjoyments of the heavenly state.

The bodies of the wicked will also be improved, but their improvements will all be terrible and vindictive. Their capacities will be thoroughly enlarged, but then it will be that they may be made capable of greater misery : they will be strengthened, but it will be that they may bear the heavier load of torment. Their sensations will be more quick and strong, but it will be that they may feel the more exquisite pain. They will be raised immortal that they may not be consumed by everlasting fire, or escape punishment by dissolution or annihilation. In short, their augmented strength, their enlarged capacities, and their immortality, will be their eternal curse; and they would willingly exchange them for the fleeting duration of a fading flower, or the faint sensations of an infant. The only power they would rejoice in is that of self-annihilation.

And now when the bodies are completely formed and fit to be inhabited, the souls that once animated them, being collected from heaven and hell, re-enter and take possession of their old mansions. They are united in bonds which shall never more be dissolved: and the mouldering tabernacles are now become everlasting habitations.

And with what joy will the spirits of the righteous welcome their old companions from their long sleep in the dust, and congratulate their glorious resurrection! How will they rejoice to re-enter their old habitations,

now so completely repaired and highly improved! to find
those bodies which were once their incumbrance, once
frail and mortal, in which they were imprisoned, and
languished, once their temptation, tainted with the seeds
of sin, now their assistants and co-partners in the business
of heaven, now vigorous, incorruptible, and immortal,
now free from all corrupt mixtures, and shining in all the
beauties of perfect holiness! In these bodies they once
served their God with honest though feeble efforts, con-
flicted with sin and temptation, and passed through all
the united trials and hardships of mortality and the Christian life. But now they are united to them for more
exalted and blissful purposes. The lungs that were wont
to heave with penitential sighs and groans, shall now
shout forth their joys and the praises of their God and
Saviour. The heart that was once broken with sorrows
shall now be bound up for ever, and overflow with immortal pleasures. Those very eyes that were wont to
run down with tears, and to behold many a tragical sight,
shall now *behold the King in his beauty*, shall behold the
Saviour whom, though unseen, they loved, and all the
glories of heaven; and *God shall wipe away all their tears*.
All the senses, which were once avenues of pain, shall
now be inlets of the most exalted pleasure. In short,
every organ, every member shall be employed in the most
noble services and enjoyments, instead of the sordid and
laborious drudgery, and the painful sufferings of the present state. Blessed change indeed! Rejoice, ye children
of God, in the prospect of it.

But how shall I glance a thought upon the dreadful
case of the wicked in that tremendous day! While their
bodies burst from their graves, the miserable spectacles of
horror and deformity, see the millions of gloomy ghosts
that once animated them, rise like pillars of smoke from

the bottomless pit! and with what reluctance and anguish do they re-enter their old habitations! Oh what a dreadful meeting! What shocking salutations! "And must I be chained to thee again, (may the guilty soul say,) Oh thou accursed, polluted body, thou system of deformity and terror! In thee I once sinned, by thee I was once ensnared, debased, and ruined: to gratify thy vile lusts and appetites I neglected my own immortal interests, degraded my native dignity, and made myself miserable for ever. And hast thou now met me to torment me for ever? Oh that thou hadst still slept in the dust, and never been repaired again! Let me rather be condemned to animate a toad or serpent than that odious body once defiled with sin, and the instrument of my guilty pleasures, now made strong and immortal to torment me with strong and immortal pains. Once indeed I received sensations of pleasure from thee, but now thou art transformed into an engine of torture. No more shall I through thine eyes behold the cheerful light of the day, and the beautiful prospects of nature, but the thick glooms of hell, grim and ghastly ghosts, heaven at an impassable distance, and all the horrid sights of wo in the infernal regions. No more shall thine ears charm me with the harmony of sounds, but terrify and distress me with the echo of eternal groans, and the thunder of almighty vengeance! No more shall the gratification of thine appetites afford me pleasure, but thine appetites, for ever hungry, for ever unsatisfied, shall eternally torment me with their eager importunate cravings. No more shall thy tongue be employed in mirth, and jest, and song, but complain, and groan, and blaspheme, and roar for ever. Thy feet, that once walked in the flowery enchanted paths of sin, must now walk on the dismal burning soil of hell. Oh my wretched companion! I parted with thee with pain and reluctance in the struggles of death, but now I meet thee with greater terror and agony. Return to thy bed in the dust; there to sleep and rot, and let me never see thy shocking visage more." In vain the petition! the reluctant soul must enter its prison, from whence it shall never more be dismissed. And if we might indulge imagination so far, we might suppose the body begins to recriminate in such language as this: "Come, guilty soul, enter thy old mansion; if it be horrible and shocking, it is owing to thyself. Was not the animal frame, the brutal nature, subjected to thy government, who art a rational principle? instead of being debased by me, it became thee to have not only retained the dignity of thy nature, but to have exalted mine, by nobler employments and gratifications worthy an earthly body united to an immortal spirit.

Thou mightest have restrained my members from being the instruments of sin, and made them the instruments of righteousness. My knees would have bowed at the throne of grace, but thou didst not affect that posture. Mine eyes would have read, and mine ears heard the word of life; but thou wouldest not set them to that employ, or wouldst not attend to it. And now it is but just the body thou didst prostitute to sin should be the instrument of thy punishment. Indeed, fain would I relapse into senseless earth as I was, and continue in that insensibility for ever:—but didst thou not hear the all-rousing trumpet just now? did it not even shake the foundations of thy infernal prison? It was that call that awakened me, and summoned me to meet thee, and I could not resist it. Therefore, come, miserable soul, take possession of this frame, and let us prepare for everlasting burning. Oh that it were now possible to die! Oh that we could be again separated, and never be united more! Vain wish; the weight of mountains, the pangs of hell, the flames of unquenchable fire, can never dissolve these chains which now bind us together?"*

O sirs! what a shocking interview is this! Oh the glorious, dreadful morning of the resurrection! What scenes of unknown joy and terror will then open! Methinks we must always have it in prospect; it must even now engage our thoughts, and fill us with trembling solicitude, and make it the great object of our labour and pursuit to share in the resurrection of the just.

But for what ends do these sleeping multitudes rise? For what purposes do they come forth? My text will tell you.

IV. They shall come forth, "some to the resurrection of life, and some to the resurrection of damnation." They are summoned from their graves to stand at the bar, and brought out of prison by angelic guards to pass their last trial. And as in this impartial trial they will be found to be persons of very different characters, the righteous Judge of the earth will accordingly pronounce their different doom.

See a glorious *multitude, which none can number*, openly acquitted, pronounced blessed, and welcomed "into the

---

* The Rev. Mr. John Reynolds, in his poem entitled *Death's Vision*, introduces the soul speaking against the body, and afterwards checking its censures, and turning them upon itself, in a vein of thought not unlike that of Mr. Davies.

> Go, tempter, go, as thou hast been
>   A quick extinguisher of heav'nly fires!
> A source of black enormity and sin,
>   Thou cramp of sacred motions and desires!
> How brave and bless'd am I.
> Unfetter'd from the company,
> Thou enemy of my joys and me?
> But pardon that I thus
> Unconsciously accuse!
> How much more cruel have I been to thee!
> " 'Twas cruel that I oblig'd thee to obey,
> The wilful dictates of my guilty sway."

kingdom prepared for them from the foundation of the world." Now they enter upon a state which deserves the name of life. They are all vital, all active, all glorious, all happy. They " shine brighter than the stars in the firmament; like the sun for ever and ever." All their faculties overflow with happiness. They mingle with the glorious company of angels; they behold that Saviour whom unseen they loved; they dwell in eternal intimacy with the Father of their spirits; they are employed with ever-new and growing delight in the exalted services of the heavenly sanctuary. They shall never more fear, nor feel the least touch of sorrow, pain, or any kind of misery, but shall be as happy as their natures can admit through an immortal duration. What a glorious new creation is here! what illustrious creatures formed of the dust! And shall any of us join in this happy company? Oh shall any of us, feeble, dying, sinful creatures, share in their glory and happiness? This is a most interesting inquiry, and I would have you think of it with trembling anxiety; and I shall presently answer it in its place.

The prospect would be delightful, if our charity could hope that this will be the happy end of all the sons of men. But, alas! multitudes, and we have reason to fear the far greater number, shall come forth, not to the resurrection of life, but to the resurrection of damnation! what terror is in the sound! If audacious sinners in our world make light of it, and pray for it on every trifling occasion, their infernal brethren, that feel its tremendous import, are not so hardy, but tremble and groan, and can trifle with it no more.

Let us realize the miserable doom of this class of mankind. See them bursting into life from their subterranean dungeons, hideous shapes of deformity and terror, expressive of the vindictive design for which their bodies are repaired, and of the boisterous and malignant passions that ravage their souls. Horror throbs through every vein, and glares wild and furious in their eyes. Every joint trembles, and every countenance looks downcast and gloomy. Now they see that tremendous day of which they were warned in vain, and shudder at those terrors of which they once made light. They immediately know the grand business of the day, and the dreadful purpose for which they are roused from their slumbers in the grave; to be tried, to be convicted, to be condemned, and to be dragged away to execution. Conscience has been anticipating the trial in a separate state; and no sooner is the soul united to the body, than immediately conscience ascends its throne in the breast, and begins to accuse, to convict, to pass sentence, to upbraid, and to torment. The sinner is condemned, condemned at his own tribunal, before he arrives at the bar of his Judge. The first act of consciousness in his new state of existence is a conviction that he is condemned, an irrevocably condemned creature. He enters the court, knowing beforehand how it will go with him. When he finds himself ordered to the left hand of his Judge, when he hears the dreadful sentence thundered out against him, *Depart from me, accursed*, it was but what he expected. Now he can flatter himself with vain hopes, and shut his eyes against the light of conviction, but then he will not be able to hope better; then he must know the worst of his case. The formality of the judicial trial is necessary for the conviction of the world, but not for his; his own conscience has already determined his condition. However, to convince others of the justice of his doom, he is dragged and guarded from his grave to the judgment-seat by fierce, unrelenting devils, now his tempters, but then his tormentors. With what horror does he view the burning throne and the frowning face of his Judge, that Jesus whom he once disregarded, in spite of all his dying love and the salvation he offered! How does he wish for a covering of rocks and mountains to conceal him from his angry eye! but all in vain. Appear he must. He is ordered to the left among the trembling criminals; and now the trial comes on. All his evil deeds, and all his omissions of duty, are now produced against him. All the mercies he abused, all the chastisements he despised, all the means of grace he neglected or misimproved, every sinful, and even every idle word, nay, his most secret thoughts and dispositions, are all exposed, and brought into judgment against him. And when the Judge puts it to him, " Is it not so, sinner? Are not these charges true?" conscience obliges him to confess and cry out, Guilty! guilty! And now the trembling criminal being plainly convicted and left without all plea and all excuse, the supreme Judge, in stern majesty and inexorable justice, thunders out the dreadful sentence, " Depart from me, ye cursed, into everlasting fire, prepared for the devil and his angels." Matt. xxv. 41. Oh tremendous doom! every word is big with terror, and shoots a thunderbolt through the heart. " Depart: away from my presence; I cannot bear so loathsome a sight. I once invited thee to come to me, that thou mightest have life, but thou wouldst not regard the invitation; and now thou shalt never hear that inviting voice more. Depart from me; from me, the only Fountain of happiness, the only proper Good for an immortal mind." " But, Lord," (we may suppose the criminal to say,) " if I must depart, bless me before I go." " No," says the angry Judge, " depart accursed; depart with my eternal and heavy curse upon thee; the curse of that power that made thee; a curse dreadfully efficacious, that blasts whatever it falls upon like flashes of consuming, irresistible lightning." " But if I must go away under thy curse, (the criminal may be supposed to say,) let that be all my punishment; let me depart to some agreeable, or at least tolerable recess, where I may meet with something to mitigate the curse." "No, depart into fire; there burn in all the excruciating tortures of that outrageous element." "But, Lord, if I must make my bed in fire, oh let it be transient blaze, that will soon burn itself out, and put an end to my torment." "No, depart into everlasting fire; there burn without consuming, and be tormented without end." "But, Lord, grant me (cries the poor wretch) at least the mitigation of friendly, entertaining, and sympathizing company; or, if this cannot be granted, grant me this small, this almost no request, to be doomed to some solitary corner in hell, where I shall be punished only by my own conscience and thine immediate hand; but oh deliver me from these malicious, tormenting devils; banish me into some apartment in the infernal pit far from their society." "No, depart into everlasting fire prepared for the devil and his angels: thou must make one of their wretched crew for ever: thou didst join with them in sinning, and now must share in their punishment: thou didst submit to them as thy tempters, and now thou must submit to them as thy tormentors."

Sentence being pronounced, it is immediately executed. *These shall go away into everlasting punishment.* Matt. xxv. 46. Devils drag them away to the pit, and push them down headlong. There they are confined in chains of darkness, and in a lake burning with fire and brimstone, for ever, for ever! In that dreadful word lies the emphasis of torment; it is a hell in hell. If they might be but released from pain, though it were by annihilation after they have wept away ten thousand millions of ages in extremity of pain, it would be some mitigation, some encouragement; but, alas! when as many millions of ages are passed as the stars of heaven, or the sands on the sea-shore, or the atoms of dust in this huge globe of earth, their punishment is as far from an end as when the sentence was pronounced upon them. For ever! there is no exhausting of that word; and when it is affixed to the highest degree of misery, the terror of the sound is utterly insupportable. See, sirs, what depends upon time, that span of time we may enjoy in this fleeting life. Eternity! awful, all-important eternity! depends upon it.

All this while conscience tears the sinner's heart with the most tormenting reflections. "Oh what a fair opportunity I once had for salvation, had I improved it! I was warned of the consequences of a life of sin and carelessness; I was told of the necessity of faith, repentance, and universal holiness of heart and life; I enjoyed a sufficient space for repentance, and all the necessary means of salvation, but, fool that I was, I neglected all, I abused all; I refused to part with my sins; I refused to engage seriously in religion, and to seek God in earnest; and now I am lost for ever, without hope. Oh! for one of those months, one of those weeks, or even so much as one of those days or hours I once trifled away; with what earnestness, with what solicitude would I improve it! But all my opportunities are past, beyond recovery, and not a moment shall be given me for this purpose any more. Oh what a fool was I to sell my soul for such trifles! to set so light by heaven, and fall into hell through mere neglect and carelessness! Ye impenitent, unthinking sinners, though you may now be able to silence or drown the clamours of your consciences, yet the time, or rather the dread eternity is coming, when they will speak in spite of you; when they will speak home, and be felt by the most hardened and remorseless heart. Therefore now regard their warnings while they may be the means of your recovery.

You and I, my brethren, are concerned in the solemn transaction of the day I have been describing. You and I shall either be changed in a moment, in the twinkling of an eye, or while mouldering " in the grave, we shall hear the voice of the Son of God, and come forth, either to the resurrection of life, or to the resurrection of damnation." And which, my brethren, shall be our doom? Can we foreknow it at this distance of time? I proposed it to your inquiry already, whether you have any good reason to hope you shall be of that happy number who shall rise to life? and now I propose it again, with this counterpart, Have you any evidence to hope you shall not be of that wretched, numerous multitude who shall rise to damnation? If there be any inquiry within the compass of human knowledge that demands your solicitous thoughts, certainly it is this. Methinks you cannot enjoy one moment's ease or security while this is undetermined. And is it an answerable inquiry? Can we now know what are the present distinguishing characters of those who shall then receive so different a doom? Yes, my text determines the point; for,

V. " They that have done good shall come forth to the resurrection of life; and they that have done evil, to the resurrection of damnation." These are the grounds of the distinction that shall then be made in the final states of men, doing good and doing evil. And certainly this distinction is perceivable now; to do good and to do evil are not so much alike as that it should be impossible to distinguish between them. Let us then see what is implied in these characters, and to whom of us they respectively belong.

1. What is it to do good? This implies, (1.) An honest

endeavour to keep all God's commandments; I say, all his commandments, with regard to God, our neighbour, and ourselves, whether easy or difficult, whether fashionable or not, whether agreeable to our natural constitution or not, whether enjoining the performauce of duty or forbidding the commission of sin, whether regarding the heart or the outward practice. I say, an uniform, impartial regard to all God's commandments, of whatever kind, in all circumstances, and at all times, is implied in doing good; for if we do any thing because God commands it, we will endeavour to do everything that he commands, because where the reason of our conduct is the same, our conduct itself will be the same. I do not mean that good men, in the present state, perfectly keep the commandments of God in every thing, or indeed in any thing; but I mean that universal obedience is their honest endeavour. Their character is in some measure uniform and all of a piece; that is, they do not place all their religion in obedience to some commands which may be agreeable to them, as though that would make atonement for their neglect of others; but, like David, they are for having a respect, and indeed *have a respect to all God's commandments :* Psalm cxix. 6. My brethren, try yourselves by this test.

(2.) To do good in an acceptable manner pre-supposes a change of nature and a new principle. Our nature is so corrupted that nothing really and formally good can be performed by us till it be renewed. To confirm this I shall only refer you to Eph. ii. 10, and Ezek. xxxvi. 26, 27, where being created in Christ Jesus to good works, and receiving a new heart of flesh, are mentioned as pre-requisites to our walking in God's statutes. As for the principle of obedience, *it is the love of God :* 1 John v. 3, that is, we must obey God, because we love him; we must do good, because we delight to do good; otherwise it is all hypocrisy, constraint, or selfishness, and cannot be acceptable to God. Here, again, my brethren, look into your hearts, and examine what is the principle of your obedience, and whether ever you have been made new creatures.

(3.) I must add, especially as we live under the gospel, that your dependence for life must not be upon the good you do, but entirely upon the righteousness of Jesus Christ. After you have done all, you must acknowledge you are but unprofitable servants; and renounce all your works in point of merit, while you abound in them in point of practice; Phil. iii. 7, 8. This is an essential characteristic of evangelical obedience, and without it you cannot expect to have a resurrection to eternal life and blessedness.

I might enlarge upon this head, but time will not permit; and I hope these three characters may suffice to show you what is implied in doing good. Let us now proceed to the opposite character.

2. What is it to do evil? This implies such things as these; the habitual neglect of well-doing, or the performance of duties in a languid, formal manner, or without a right principle, and the wilful indulgence of any one sin; the secret love of sin, though not suffered to break forth into the outward practice. Here it is evident at first sight that profane sinners, drunkards, swearers, defrauders, avowed neglecters of religion, &c., have this dismal brand upon them, that they are such as do evil. Nay, all such who are in their natural state, without regeneration, whatever their outside be, must be ranked in this class; "for that which is born of the flesh is flesh," John iii. 6; and they that are in the flesh cannot please God, nor be rightly subject to his law. Rom. viii. 7, 8.

And now who is for life, and who for dammation among

you? These characters are intended to make the distinction among you, and I pray you apply them for that purpose.

As for such of you, who, amidst all your lamented infirmities, are endeavouring honestly to do good, and grieved at heart that you can do no more, you also must die; you must die, and feed the worms in the dust. But you shall rise gloriously improved, rise to an immortal life, and in all the terrors and consternation of that last day, you will be secure, serene, and undisturbed. The almighty Judge will be your friend, and that is enough. Let this thought disarm the king of terrors, and give you courage to look down into the grave, and forward to the great rising-day. Oh what a happy immortality opens its glorious prospects beyond the ken of sight before you! and after a few struggles more in this state of warfare, and resting awhile in the bed of death, at the regions of eternal blessedness you will arrive, and take up your residence there for ever.

But are there not some here who are conscious that these favourable characters do not belong to them? that know that well-doing is not the business of their life, but that they are workers of iniquity? I tell you plainly, and with all the authority the word of God can give, that if you continue such, you shall rise to damnation. That undoubtedly will be your doom, unless you are greatly changed and reformed in heart and life. And will this be no excitement to vigorous endeavours? Are you proof against the energy of such a consideration? Ye careless sinners, awake out of your security, and prepare for death and judgment! this fleeting life is all the time you have for preparation, and can you trifle it away? Your all, your eternal all is set upon the single cast of life, and you must stand the hazard of the die. You can make but one experiment, and if that fail, through your sloth or mismanagement, you are irrecoverably undone for ever. There-fore, by the dread authority of the great God, by the ter-rors of death, and the great rising-day, by the joys of heaven, and the torments of hell, and by the value of your immortal souls, I entreat, I charge, I adjure you to awake out of your security, and improve the precious moments of life. The world is dying all around you. And can you rest easy in such a world, while unprepared for eternity? Awake to righteousness now, at the gentle call of the gospel, before the last trumpet give you an alarm of another kind.

SERMON XX.

THE UNIVERSAL JUDGMENT.

ACTS XVII. 30, 31.—*And the times of this ignorance God winked at ; but now 'commandeth all men everywhere to repent : because he hath appointed a day, in the which he will judge the world in righteousness, by that man whom he hath ordained ; whereof he hath given assurance unto all men, in that he hath raised him from the dead.*

THE present state is the infancy of human nature; and all the events of time, even those that make such noise, and determine the fate of kingdoms, are but the little affairs of children. But if we look forward and trace human nature to maturity, we meet with events vast, interesting, and majestic; and such as nothing but divine authority can render credible to us who are so apt to judge of things by what we see. To one of those scenes I would direct your attention this day; I mean the solemn, tremendous, and glorious scene of the universal judgment.

You have sometimes seen a stately building in ruins; come now and view the ruins of a demolished world. You have often seen a feeble mortal struggling in the agonies of death, and his shattered frame dissolved; come now and view universal nature severely labouring and agonizing in her last convulsions and her well-compacted system dissolved. You have heard of earthquakes here and there that have laid Lisbon, Palermo, and a few other cities in ruins; come now and feel the tremors and convulsions of the whole globe, that blend cities and countries, oceans and continents, mountains, plains, and valleys, in one promiscuous heap. You have a thousand times beheld the moon walking in brightness, and the sun shining in his strength; now look and see the sun turned into darkness, and the moon into blood.

It is our lot to live in an age of confusion, blood, and slaughter; an age in which our attention is engaged by the clash of arms, the clangor of trumpets, the roar of artillery, and the dubious fate of kingdoms; but draw off your thoughts from these objects for an hour, and fix them on objects more solemn and interesting: come view

> " A scene that yields
> A louder trumpet, and more dreadful fields;
> The world alarmed, both earth and heaven o'erthrown,
> And gasping nature's last tremendous groan;
> Death's ancient sceptre broke, the teeming tomb,
> The Righteous Judge, and man's eternal doom."

Such a scene there certainly is before us; for St. Paul tells us that " God hath given assurance to all men that he will judge the world in righteousness by that man whom he hath ordained;" and that his resurrection, the resurrection of him who is God and man, is a demonstrative proof of it.

My text is the conclusion of St. Paul's defence or sermon before the famous court of Areopagus, in the learned and philosophical city of Athens. In this august and polite assembly he speaks with the boldness, and in the evangelical strain, of an apostle of Christ. He first inculcates upon them the great truths of natural religion, and labours faithfully, though in a very gentle and inoffensive manner, to reform them from that stupid idolatry and superstition into which even this learned philosophical city was sunk, though a Socrates, a Plato, and the most celebrated sages and moralists of pagan antiquity had lived and taught in it. Afterwards, in the close of his discourse, he introduces the glorious peculiarities of Christianity, particularly the great duty of repentance, from evangelical motives, the resurrection of the dead, and the final judgment. But no sooner has he entered upon this subject than he is interrupted, and seems to have broken off abruptly; for when he had just hinted at the then unpopular doctrine of the resurrection of the dead, we are told, *some mocked,* and others put it off to another hearing: *We will hear thee again of this matter.*

In these dark times of ignorance which preceded the publication of the gospel, God seemed to wink or connive at the idolatry and various forms of wickedness that had overspread the world; that is, he seemed to overlook* or to take no notice of them, so as either to punish them, or to give the nations explicit calls to repentance. But now, says St. Paul, the case is altered. Now the gospel is published through the world, and therefore God will no longer seem to connive at the wickedness and impenitence of mankind, but publishes his great mandate to a rebel world, explicitly and loudly, *commanding all men every where to repent;* and he now gives them particular motives and encouragements to this duty.

One motive of the greatest weight, which was never so clearly or extensively published before, is the doctrine of the universal judgment. This the connection implies: "He now commandeth all men to repent, because he hath appointed a day for judging all men." And surely the pros-

* ὑπεριδων.

pect of a judgment must be a strong motive to sinners to repent :—this, if anything, will rouse them from their thoughtless security, and bring them to repentance.　Repentance
should, and one would think must, be as extensive as this
reason for it.　This St. Paul intimates.　"He now commandeth all men to repent, because he hath given assurance
to all men" that he has "appointed a day to judge the
world."　Wherever the gospel publishes the doctrine of
future judgment, there it requires all men to repent; and
wherever it requires repentance, there it enforces the command of this alarming doctrine.

God has *given assurance to all men;* that is, to all that
hear the gospel, that he has appointed a day for this great
purpose, and that Jesus Christ, God-man, is to preside in
person in this majestic solemnity.　He has given assurance of this; that is, sufficient ground of faith; and the
assurance consists in this, that *he hath raised him from the
dead.*

The resurrection of Christ gives assurance of this in
several respects.　It is a specimen and a pledge of a
general resurrection, that grand preparative for the judgment: it is an incontestible proof of his divine mission; for
God will never work so unprecedented a miracle in favour
of an impostor: it is also an authentic attestation of all our
Lord's claims; and he expressly claimed the authority of
supreme Judge as delegated to him by the Father; "the
Father judgeth no man, but hath committed all judgment
to the Son." John v. 22.

There is a peculiar fitness and propriety in this constitution.　It is fit that a world placed under the administration of a Mediator should have a mediatorial Judge.
It is fit this high office should be conferred upon him as
an honourary reward for his important services and extreme abasement.　Because he humbled himself, therefore

God hath highly exalted him. Phil. ii. 8, 9. It is fit that
creatures clothed with bodies should be judged by a man
clothed in a body like themselves. Hence it is said that
" God hath given him authority to execute judgment, because he is the Son of man." John v. 27. This would
seem a strange reason, did we not understand it in this
light. Indeed, was Jesus Christ man only, he would be
infinitely unequal to the office of universal Judge; but he
is God and man, *Immanuel, God with us;* and is the fittest
person in the universe for the work. It is also fit that
Christ should be the supreme Judge, as it will be a great
encouragement to his people for their Mediator to execute
this office: and it may be added, that hereby the condemnation of the wicked will be rendered more con-
spicuously just; for, if a Mediator, a Saviour, the Friend
of sinners, condemns them, they must be worthy of condemnation indeed.

Let us now enter upon the majestic scene. But alas!
what images shall I use to represent it? Nothing that we
have seen, nothing that we have heard, nothing that has
ever happened on the stage of time, can furnish us with
proper illustrations. All is low and grovelling, all is faint
and obscure that ever the sun shone upon, when compared
with the grand phenomena of that day; and we are so
accustomed to low and little objects, that it is impossible
we should ever raise our thoughts to a suitable pitch of
elevation. Ere long we shall be amazed spectators of
these majestic wonders, and our eyes and our ears will be
our instructors. But now it is necessary we should have
such ideas of them as may affect our hearts, and prepare
us for them. Let us therefore present to our view those
representations which divine revelation, our only guide in
this case, gives us of the person of the Judge, and the
manner of his appearance; of the resurrection of the dead,

and the transformation of the living; of the universal convention of all the sons of men before the supreme tribunal;
of their separation to the right and left hand of the Judge,
according to their characters; of the judicial process itself;
of the decisive sentence; of its execution, and of the conflagration of the world.

As to the person of the Judge, the psalmist tells you,
God is Judge himself. Psalm l. 6. Yet Christ tells us,
"the Father judgeth no man, but hath committed all
judgment unto the Son; and hath given him authority to
execute judgment also, because he is the Son of man."
John v. 22, 27. It is therefore Christ Jesus, God-man,
as I observed, who shall sustain this high character; and
for the reasons already alleged, it is most fit it should be
devolved upon him. Being God and man, all the advantages of divinity and humanity centre in him, and render
him more fit for this office than if he were God only, or
man only. This is the august Judge before whom we
must stand; and the prospect may inspiré us with reverence, joy, and terror.

As for the manner of his appearance, it will be such as
becomes the dignity of his person and office. He will
shine in all the uncreated glories of the Godhead, and in
all the gentler glories of a perfect man. His attendants
will add a dignity to the grand appearance, and the sympathy of nature will increase the solemnity and terror of
the day. Let his own word describe him. "The Son
of man shall come in the glory of his Father, with his
angels." Matt. xvi. 27. "The Son of man shall come in
his glory, and all the holy angels with him; then shall he
sit upon the throne of his glory." Matt. xxv. 31: "The
Lord Jesus shall be revealed from heaven with his mighty
angels, in flaming fire taking vengeance on them that know
not God, and that obey not the gospel of our Lord Jesus

Christ." 2 Thess. i. 7, 8. And not only will the angels, those illustrious ministers of the court of heaven, attend upon that solemn occasion, but also all the saints who had left the world from Adam to that day; for *those that sleep in Jesus*, says St. Paul, *will God bring with him.* 1 Thess. iv. 14. The grand imagery in Daniel's vision is applicable to this day: and perhaps to this it primarily refers: " I beheld till the thrones were cast down," or rather set up,* " and the Ancient of days did sit, whose garment was white as snow, and the hair of his head like the pure wool: his throne was like the fiery flame, and his wheels as burning fire. A fiery stream issued and came forth from before him: thousand thousands ministered unto him, and ten thousand times ten thousand stood before him." Dan. vii. 9, 10. Perhaps our Lord may exhibit himself to the whole world upon this most grand occasion, in the same glorious form in which he was seen by his favourite John, " clothed with a garment down to the foot, and girt about the breasts with a golden girdle: his head and his hairs white like wool, as white as snow; his eyes as a flame of fire: his feet like unto fine brass, as if they burned in a furnace; his voice as the sound of many waters, and his countenance as the sun shining in his strength." Rev. i. 13, &c. Another image of inimitable majesty and terror the same writer gives us, when he says, " I saw a great white throne, and him that sat on it, from whose face the earth and the heaven fled away, and there was found no place for them." Astonishing! what an image is this! the stable earth and heaven cannot bear the majesty and terror of his look; they fly away affrighted, and seek a place to hide themselves, but no place is found to shelter them; every region

---

* This sense is more agreeable to the connection, and the original word will bear it ; which signifies *to pitch down* or *place*, as well as *to throw down* or *demolish*. And the LXX translate it, *the thrones were put up*, or *fixed*.

through the immensity of space lies open before him.*
Rev. xx. 11.

This is the Judge before whom we must stand; and this
is the manner of his appearance.   But is this the babe of
Bethlehem that lay and wept in the manger?   Is this the
supposed son of the carpenter, the despised Galilean?   Is
this the man of sorrows?   Is this he that was arrested,
was condemned, was buffeted, was spit upon, was crowned
with thorns, was executed as a slave and a criminal, upon
the cross?   Yes, it is he; the very same Jesus of Nazareth.
But oh how changed! how deservedly exalted!   Let
heaven and earth congratulate his advancement.   Now let
his enemies appear and show their usual contempt and
malignity.   Now, Pilate, condemn the King of the Jews
as an usurper.   Now, ye Jews, raise the clamour, *Crucify
him, crucify him !*

> " Now bow the knee in scorn, present the reed ;
> Now tell the scourg'd Impostor he must bleed."—YOUNG.

Now, ye Deists and Infidels, dispute his divinity and
the truth of his religion if you can.   Now, ye hypocritical

---

* This is the picture drawn by the pencil of inspiration.   We may now
contemplate the imagery of a fine human pen.

> ——————————From his great abode
> Full on a whirlwind rides the dreadful God :
> The tempest's rattling winds, the fiery car,
> Ten thousand hosts his ministers of war,
> The flaming Cherubim, attend his flight.
> And heaven's foundations groan beneath the weight.
> Thro' all the skies the forky lightnings play,
> And radiant splendours round his head display.
> From his bright eyes affrighted worlds retire :
> He speaks in thunder and he breathes in fire.
> Garments of heavenly light array the God ;
> His throne a bright consolidated cloud—
> Support me, heaven, I shudder with affright ;
> I quake, I sink with terror at the sight.
> *The Day of Judgment, a Poem, a little varied.*

Christians, try to impose upon him with your idle pre-
tences. Now despise his grace, laugh at his threatenings,
and make light of his displeasure if you are able. Ah!
now their courage fails, and terror surrounds them like
armed men. Now they hide themselves in the dens, and
in the rocks of the mountains; and say to the mountains
and rocks, Fall on us, and hide us from the face of him that
sitteth on the throne, and from the wrath of the Lamb;
for the Lamb that once bled as a sacrifice for sin now appears in all the terrors of a lion; and the great day of his
wrath is come, and who shall be able to stand? Rev. vi.
15. Oh! could they hide themselves in the bottom of the
ocean, or in some rock that bears the weight of the mountains, how happy would they think themselves. But, alas!

> " Seas cast the monsters forth to meet their doom,
> And rocks but prison up for wrath to come.—YOUNG.

While the Judge is descending, the parties to be judged
will be summoned to appear. But where are they?
They are all asleep in their dusty beds, except the then
generation. And how shall they be roused from their long
sleep of thousands of years? Why, "the Lord himself
shall descend from heaven with a shout, with the voice of
the archangel, and with the trump of God." 1 Thess. iv. 16.
The trumpet shall sound, and they that are then alive shall
not pass into eternity through the beaten road of death,
but *at the last trumpet they shall be changed,* changed into
immortals, *in a moment, in the twinkliug of an eye.* 1 Cor.
xv. 51, 52. Now all the millions of mankind, of whatever
country and nation, whether they expect this tremendous
day or not, all feel a shock through their whole frames,
while they are instantaneously metamorphosed in every
limb, and the pulse of immortality begins to beat strong in
every part. Now also the slumberers under ground begin

to stir, to rouse, and spring to life. Now see graves opening, tombs bursting, charnel-houses rattling, the earth heaving, and all alive, while these subterranean armies are bursting their way through. See clouds of human dust and broken bones darkening the air, and flying from country to country over intervening continents and oceans to meet their kindred fragments, and repair the shattered frame with pieces collected from a thousand different quarters, whither they were blown away by winds, or washed by waters. See what millions start up in company in the spots where Ninevah, Babylon, Jerusalem, Rome, and London once stood! Whole armies spring to life in fields where they once lost their lives in battle, and were left unburied; in fields which fattened with their blood, produced a thousand harvests, and now produce a crop of men. See a succession of thousands of years rising in crowds from grave-yards round the places where they once attended, in order to prepare for this decisive day. Nay, graves yawn, and swarms burst into life under palaces and buildings of pride and pleasure, in fields and forests, in thousands of places where graves were never suspected. How are the living surprised to find men starting into life under their feet, or just beside them; some begining to stir and heave the ground; others half-risen, and others quite disengaged from the incumbrance of earth, and standing upright before them! What vast multitudes that had slept in a watery grave, now emerge from rivers, and seas, and oceans, and throw them into a tumult! Now appear to the view of all the world the Goliahs, the Anakims, and the other giants of ancient times; and now the millions of infants, those little particles of life, start up at once, perhaps in full maturity, or perhaps in the lowest class of mankind, dwarfs of immortality. *The dead, small and great, will arise to stand before God; and the sea* shall *give up the dead which were in it.* Rev. xx. 12, 13. Now the *many that sleep in the dust of the earth shall awake, some to everlasting life, and some to shame and everlasting contempt.* Dan. xii. 2. *Now the hour is come when all that are in the grave shall hear the voice of the Son of God, and shall come forth; they that have done good, to the resurrection of life; and they that have done evil, to the resurrection of damnation.* John v. 28. *Though after our skin, worms destroy this body, yet in our flesh shall we see God, whom we shall see for ourselves; and* these *eyes shall behold him, and not another.* Job. xix. 26, 27. Then *this corruptible* [body] *shall put on incorruption, and this mortal shall put on immortality.* 1 Cor. xv. 23.

As the characters, and consequently the doom of mankind, will be very different, so we may reasonably suppose they will rise in very different forms of glory or dishonour, of beauty or deformity. Their bodies indeed will all be improved to the highest degree, and all made vigorous, capacious, and immortal. But here lies the difference: the bodies of the righteous will be strengthened to bear *an exceeding great and eternal weight of glory,* but those of the wicked will be strengthened to sustain a heavier load of misery; their strength will be but mere strength to suffer a horrid capacity of greater pain. The immortality of the righteous will be the duration of their happiness, but that of the wicked of their misery; their immortality, the highest privilege of their nature, will be their heaviest curse: and they would willingly exchange their duration with an insect of a day, or a fading flower. The bodies of the righteous will " shine as the sun, and as the stars in the firmament for ever and ever;" but those of the wicked will be grim, and shocking, and ugly, and hateful as hell. The bodies of the righteous will be fit mansions for their heavenly spirits to inhabit, and every feature will speak the delightful passions that agreeably work within; but the wicked will be but spirits of hell clothed in the material bodies; and malice, rage, despair, and all the infernal passions, will lower in their countenances, and cast a dismal gloom around them! Oh! they will then be nothing else but shapes of deformity and terror! they will look like the natives of hell, and spread horror around them with every look.*

With what reluctance may we suppose will the souls of the wicked enter again into a state of union with these shocking forms, that will be everlasting engines of torture to them, as they once were instruments of sin! But oh! with what joy will the souls of the righteous return to their old habitations, in which they once served their God with honest though feeble endeavours, now so gloriously repaired and improved! How will they congratulate the resurrection of their old companions from their long sleep in death, now made fit to share with them in the sublime employments and fruitions of heaven? Every organ will be an instrument of service and an inlet of pleasure, and the soul shall no longer be encumbered but assisted by this union to the body. Oh what surprising creatures can Omnipotence raise from the dust! To what a high degree of beauty can the Almighty refine the offspring of the earth! and into what miracles of glory and blessedness can he form them! †

---

* How weak, how pale, how haggard, how obscene,
  What more than death in every face and mien!
  With what distress, and glarings of affright
  They shock the heart, and turn away the sight!
  In gloomy orbs their trembling eye-balls roll,
  And tell the horrid secrets of the soul.
  Each gesture mourns, each look is black with care;
  And every groan is loaden with despair.—YOUNG.

† Mark, on the right, how amiable a grace!
  Their Maker's image fresh in every face!

Now the Judge is come, the Judgment-seat is erected, the dead are raised. And what follows? Why, the universal convention of all the sons of men before the Judgment-seat. The place of judgment will probably be the extensive region of the air, the most capacious for the reception of such a multitude; for St. Paul tells us the saint shall "be caught up together in the clouds to meet the Lord in the air." 1 Thess. iv. 17. And that the air will be the place of judicature, perhaps, may be intimated when our Lord is represented as coming in the clouds, and sitting upon a cloudy throne. These expressions can hardly be understood literally, for clouds which consisted of vapours and rarified particles of water, seem very improper materials for a chariot of state, or a throne of judgment but they may very properly intimate that Christ will make his appearance, and hold his court in the region of the clouds; that is, in the air; and perhaps that the rays of light and majestic darkness shall be so blended around him as to form the appearance of a cloud to the view of the wondering and gazing world.

To this upper region, from whence our globe will lie open to view far and wide, will all the sons of men be convened. And they will be gathered together by the ministry of angels, the officers of this grand court. The Son of man, when he comes in the clouds of heaven with power and great glory, "shall send forth his angels with a great sound of the trumpet, and they shall gather together his elect from the four winds, and from one end of heaven to the other." Matt. xxiv. 30, 31. Their ministry also extends to the wicked, whom they will drag away to

What purple bloom my ravish'd soul admires,
And their eyes sparkling with immortal fires!
Triumphant beauty! charms that rise above
This world, and in blest angels kindle love!—
Oh! the transcendent glories of the Just!—YOUNG.

judgment and execution, and separate from the righteous.
For " in the end of the world," says Christ, " the Son of
man shall send forth his angels, and they shall gather out
of his kingdom all things that offend, and them which do
iniquity: and shall cast them into a furnace of fire: there
shall be wailing and gnashing of teeth." Matt. xiii. 40,
41, 42.

What an august convocation, what a vast assembly is
this! See flights of angels darting round the globe from
east to west, from pole to pole, gathering up here and
there the scattered saints, choosing them out from among
the crowd of the ungodly, and bearing them aloft on their
wings *to meet the Lord in the air!* while the wretched
crowd look and gaze, and stretch their hands, and would
mount up along with them; but, alas! they must be left
behind, and wait for another kind of convoy; a convoy of
cruel, unrelenting devils, who shall snatch them up as their
prey with malignant joy, and place them before the flaming
tribunal.   Now all the sons of men meet in one immense
assembly.   Adam beholds the long line of his posterity,
and they behold their common father.   Now Europeans
and Asiatics, the swarthy sons of Africa and the savages
of America, mingle together.   Christians, Jews, Mahometans, and Pagans, the learned and the ignorant, kings and
subjects, rich and poor, free and bond, form one promiscuous crowd.   Now all the vast armies that conquered or
fell under Xerxes, Darius, Alexander, Cæsar, Scipio,
Tamerlane, Marlborough, and other illustrious warriors,
unite in one vast army.   There, in short, all the successive
inhabitants of the earth for thousands of years appear in
one assembly.   And how inconceivably great must the
number be!   When the inhabitants of but one county are
met together, you are struck with the survey.   Were all
the inhabitants of a kingdom convened in one place, how

much more striking would be the sight! Were all the inhabitants of the kingdoms of the earth convened in one general rendezvous, how astonishing and vast would be the multitude! But what is even this vast multitude compared with the long succession of generations that have peopled the globe, in all ages, and in all countries, from the first commencement of time to the last day! Here numbers fail, and our thoughts are lost in the immense survey. The extensive region of the air is very properly chosen as the place of judgment; for this globe would not be sufficient for such a multitude to stand upon. In that prodigious assembly, my brethren, you and I must mingle. And we shall not be lost in the crowd, nor escape the notice of our Judge; but his eye will be as particulary fixed on every one of us as though there were but one before him.

To increase the number, and add a majesty and terror to the assembly, the fallen angels also make their appearance at the bar. This they have long expected with horror, as the period when their consummate misery is to commence. When Christ, in the form of a servant, exercised a god-like power over them in the days of his residence upon earth, they almost mistook his first coming as a Saviour for his second coming as their Judge; and therefore they expostulated, *Art thou come to torment us before the time?* Matt. viii. 29. That is to say, We expect thou wilt at last appear to torment us, but we did not expect thy coming so soon. Agreeable to this, St. Peter tells us, " God spared not the angels that sinned, but cast them down to hell, and delivered them into chains of darkness, to be reserved unto judgment." 2 Peter ii. 4. To the same purpose St. Jude speaks : "The angels which kept not their first estate, but left their own habitation, he hath reserved in everlasting chains under darkness, unto the judgment of the great day." Jude 6. What horribly majestic figures will these be! and what a dreadful appearance will they make at the bar! angels and archangels, thrones, and dominions, and principalities, and powers blasted, stripped of their primeval glories, and lying in ruins; yet majestic even in ruins, gigantic forms of terror and deformity; great though degraded, horribly illustrious, angels fallen, gods undeified and deposed.*

Now the Judge is seated, and anxious millions stand before him waiting for their doom. As yet there is no separation made between them; but men and devils, saints and sinners, are promiscuously blended together. But see! at the order of the Judge, the crowd is all in motion! they part, they sort together according to their character, and divide to the right and left. When all nations are gathered before the Son of man, *himself has told us,* " He shall separate them one from another, as a shepherd divideth his sheep from the goats; and he shall set the sheep on his right hand, but the goats on the left." Matt. xxv. 32, 33. And, oh! what strange separations are now made! what multitudes that once ranked themselves among the saints, and were highly esteemed for their piety, by others as well as themselves, are now banished from among them, and placed with the trembling criminals on the left hand! and how many poor, honest-hearted, doubting, desponding souls, whose foreboding fears had often placed them there, now find themselves, to their agreeable sur-

---

*————————The foe of God and man
From his dark den, blaspheming, drags his chain,
And rears his blazing front, with thunder scarred;
Receives his sentence, and begins his hell.
All vengeance past, now seems abundant grace;
Like meteors in a stormy sky, how roll
His baleful eyes! he curses whom he dreads,
And deems it the first moment of his fall.—YOUNG.

prise, stationed on the right hand of their Judge, who smiles upon them! What connections are now broken! what hearts torn assunder! what intimate companions, what dear relations parted for ever! neighbour from neighbour, masters from servants, friend from friend, parents from children, husband from wife; those who were but one flesh, and who lay in one another's bosoms, must part for ever. Those that lived in the same country, who sustained the same denomination, who worshipped in the same place, who lived under one roof, who lay in the same womb, and sucked the same breasts, must now part for ever. And is there no separation likely to be made then in our families or in our congregation? Is it likely we shall all be placed in a body upon the right hand? Are all the members of our families prepared for that glorious station? Alas! are there not some families among us who, it is to be feared, shall all be sent off to the left hand, without so much as one exception? for who are those miserable multitudes on the left hand? There, through the medium of revelation, I see the drunkard, the swearer, the whoremonger, the liar, the defrauder, and the various classes of profane, profligate sinners. There I see the unbeliever, the impenitent, the lukewarm formalist, and the various classes of hypocrites, and half-Christians. There I see the *families that call not upon God's name*, and whole nations that forget him. And, oh! what vast multitudes, what millions of millions of millions do all these make! And do not some, alas! do not many of you belong to one or other of these classes of sinners whom God, and Christ, and Scripture, and conscience conspire to condemn? If so, to the left hand you must depart among devils and trembling criminals, whose guilty minds forbode their doom before the judicial process begins. But who are those glorious immortals upon the right hand? They

are those who have surrendered themselves entirely to
God, through Jesus Christ, who have heartily complied
with the method of salvation revealed in the gospel; who
have been formed new creatures by the almighty power
of God; who make it the most earnest, persevering endeavour of their lives to work out their own salvation, and
to live righteously, soberly, and godly in the world.   These
are some of the principal lineaments of their character
who shall have their safe and honourable station at the
right hand of the sovereign Judge.   And is not this the
prevailing character of some of you?   I hope and believe
it is.   Through the medium of Scripture revelation then
I see you in that blessed station.   And, oh! I would make
an appointment with you this day to meet you there.
Yes, let us this day appoint the time and place where we
shall meet after the separation and dispersion that death
will make among us; and let it be at the right hand of the
Judge at the last day.   If I be so happy as to obtain some
humble place there, I shall look out for you, my dear
people.   There I shall expect your company, that we may
ascend together to join in the more exalted services and
enjoyments of heaven, as we have frequently in the humbler forms of worship in the church on earth.   But, oh!
when I think what unexpected separations will then be
made, I tremble lest I should miss some of you there.
Are you not afraid lest you should miss some of your
friends, or some of your families there? or that you should
then see them move off to the left hand, and looking back
with eagerness upon you, as if they would say, " This is
my doom through your carelessness; had you but acted a
faithful part towards me, while conversant with you or
under your care, I might now have had my place among
the saints."   Oh! how could you bear such significant
piercing looks from a child, a servant, or a friend!   There-

fore now do all in your power to "convert sinners from
the error of their way, and to save their souls from
death."

When we entered upon this practical digression, we left
all things ready for the judicial process. And now the trial
begins. Now "God judges the secrets of men by Jesus
Christ." Rom. ii. 16. All the works of all the sons of
men will then be tried; "For," says St. Paul, "we must
all appear before the judgment-seat of Christ, that every
one may receive the things done in his body, according to
that he hath done, whether it be good or bad." 2 Cor. v.
10. St. John in his vision "saw the dead judged according to their works." Rev. xx. 12, 13. These works immediately refer to the actions of the life, but they may also
include the inward temper, and thoughts of the soul, and
the words of the lips; for all these shall be brought into
judgment. "God," says Solmon, "shall bring every work
into judgment, and every secret thing, whether it be good,
or whether it be evil." Eccl. xii. 14. And though we are
too apt to think our words are free, he that is to be our
Judge has told us that "for every idle word which men
speak, they shall give an account in the day of judgment;
for by thy words," as well as thy actions, "thou shalt be
justified; and by thy words thou shalt be condemned."
Matt. xii. 36, 37.

What strange discoveries will this trial make? what
noble dispositions that never shone in full beauty to mortal
eyes; what generous purposes crushed in embryo for
want of power to execute them; what pious and noble
actions concealed under the veil of modesty, or miscon-
strued by ignorance and prejudice; what affectionate
aspirations, what devout exercises of heart, which lay open
only to the eyes of Omniscience, are now brought to full
light, and receive the approbation of the Supreme Judge

before the assembled universe? But on the other hand, what works of shame and darkness, what hidden things of dishonesty, what dire secrets of treachery, hypocrisy, lewdness, and various forms of wickedness artfully and industriously concealed from human sight, what horrid exploits of sin now burst to light in all their hellish colours, to the confusion of the guilty, and the astonishment and horror of the universe! Sure the history of mankind must then appear like the annals of hell, or the biography of devils! Then the mask of dissimulation will be torn off. Clouded characters will clear up, and men as well as things will appear in their true light. Their hearts will be, as it were, turned outwards, and all their secrets exposed to full view. The design of the judicial inquiry will not be to inform the omniscient Judge, but to convince all worlds of the justice of his proceedings; and this design renders it necessary that all these things should be laid open to their sight, that they may see the grounds upon which he passes sentence. And may not the prospect of such a discovery fill some of you with horror? for many of your actions, and especially of your thoughts, will not bear the light. How would it confound you, if they were now all published, even in the small circle of your acquaintance? How then can you bear to have them all fully exposed before God, angels, and men! Will it not confound you with shame, and make you objects of everlasting contempt to all worlds?

These are the facts to be tried. But by what rule shall they be tried? From the goodness and justice of God we may conclude that men will be judged by some rule known to them, or which at least it was in their power to know. Now the light of reason, the law of nature, or conscience, is a universal rule, and universally known, or at least knowable by all the sons of men, heathens and

Mahometans, as well as Jews and Christians: and therefore all mankind shall be judged by this rule. This the consciences of all now forebodes; " for when the Gentiles which have not the law, do by nature the things contained in the law, these, not having the law, are a law unto themselves, which show the works of the law written in their hearts, their conscience also bearing witness, and their thoughts, the meanwhile, accusing or else excusing one another." Rom. ii. 14, 15. By this rule their consciences now acquit or condemn them, because they know that by this rule they shall then be judged: this seems to be a kind of innate presentiment of human nature. As the heathens were invincibly ignorant of every rule but this, they shall be judged by this only. But as to those parts of the world that enjoyed, or might enjoy the advantages of revelation, whether by tradition with the Anti-Mosaic world, or in the writings of Moses and the prophets with the Jews, or in the clearer dispensation of the gospel with the Christian world, they shall be judged by this revealed law. And by how much the more perfect the rule, by so much the stricter will their account be. That which would be an excusable infirmity in an African or an American Indian, may be an aggravated crime in us who enjoy such superior advantages. This is evident from the repeated declarations of sacred writ. " As many as have sinned without law, (that is, without the written law,) shall also perish without law ; and as many as have sinned in the law shall be judged by the law, in the day when God shall judge the secrets of men according to my gospel." Rom. ii. 12, 16. " If I had not come and spoken unto them," says the blessed Jesus, " they had not had sin ;" that is, they would not have had sin so aggravated, or they would not have had the particular sin of unbelief in rejecting the Messiah : *but now they have no cloak for their sin,*

John xv. 22; that is, now when they have had such abundant conviction, they are utterly inexcusable. "This," says he, "is the condemnation;" that is, this is the occasion of the most aggravated condemnation; "that light is come into the world, and men loved darkness rather than light, because their deeds were evil." John iii. 19. "That servant which knew his Lord's will, and prepared not himself, neither did according to his will, shall be beaten with many stripes; but he that knew not, and did commit things worthy of stripes, (observe, ignorance is no sufficient excuse, except when invincible,) shall be beaten with few stripes; for unto whomsoever much is given, of him shall be much required." Luke xii. 47, 48. Upon these maxims of eternal righteousness, the Judge will proceed in pronouncing the doom of the world; and it was upon these principles he declared, in the days of his flesh, "that it should be more tolerable in the day of judgment for Sodom and Gomorrah, for Tyre and Sidon," than for those places that enjoyed the advantages of his ministry, and misimproved it. Matt. xi. 21, 24. Whether upon these principles sinners among us have not reason to expect they will obtain a horrid precedence among the million of sinners in that day, I leave you to judge, and to tremble at the thought.

There is another representation of this proceeding, which we often meet with in the sacred writings, in allusion to the forms of proceedings in human courts. In courts of law, law-books are referred to, opened, and read for the direction of the judges, and sentence is passed according to them. In allusion to this custom, Daniel, in vision, saw *the judgment was set, and the books were opened:* Dan. vii. 10. And St. John had the same representation made to him: "I saw the dead," says he, "small and great, stand before God, and the books were opened; and another book was opened, which is the book of life; and the dead were judged out of the things which were written in the books, according to their works: Rev. xx. 12.

Should we pursue this significant allusion, we may say, then will be opened the book of the law of nature; and mankind will be tried according to its precepts, and doomed according to its sentence. This is a plain and vast volume, opened and legible now to all that can read their own hearts; that have eyes to look round upon the works of God, which show his glory and their duty; and who have ears to hear the lectures which the sun and moon, and all the works of creation, read to them night and day. Then, too, will be opened the book of Scripture-revelation, in all its parts, both the law of Moses and the gospel of Christ; and according to it will those be judged who lived under one or other of these dispensations. Then it will appear that *that* neglected, old-fashioned book called the Bible is not a romance, or a system of trifling truths, but the standard of life and death to all who had access to it. Then will also be opened the book of God's remembrance. In that are recorded all the thoughts, words, actions, both good and bad, of all the sons of men: and now the immense account shall be publicly read before the assembled universe. Then, likewise, as a counterpart to this, will be opened the book of conscience; conscience which, though unnoticed, writes our whole history as with an iron pen and the point of a diamond.*

* O treacherous Conscience! while she seems to sleep
   On rose and myrtle, lull'd with Syren song;
   While she seems, nodding o'er her charge, to drop
   On headlong appetite the slacken'd reign,
   And give us up to license unrecall'd,
   Unmark'd—as from behind her secret stand
   The sly informer minutes every fault,

Then, also, we are expressly told, will be opened the book of life : Rev. xx. 12, in which are contained all the names of all the heirs of heaven. This seems to be an allusion to those registers which are kept in cities or corporations, of the names of all the citizens or members who have a right to all the privileges of the society. And I know not what we can understand by it so properly as the perfect knowledge which the omniscient God has, and always had from eternity, of those on whom he purposed to bestow eternal life, and whom he has from eternity, as it were, registered as members of the general assembly and church of the first-born, who are written in heaven, or as denizens of that blessed city. These, having been all prepared by his grace in time, shall be admitted into the New Jerusalem in that day of the Lord.

Farther, the representation which the Scripture gives us of the proceedings of that day leads us to conceive of witnesses being produced to prove the facts. The omniscient Judge will be a witness against the guilty. " I will come near to you to judgment, and I will be a swift witness against the sorcerers, and against the adulterers, and against false swearers, and against those that oppress, and hear not me, saith the Lord of Hosts :" Mal. iii. 5. And he will, no doubt, be a witness for his people, and attest their sincere piety, their interest in Christ, and those good dispositions or actions which were known only to him.

> And her dread diary with horror fills—
> Unnoted notes each moment misapply'd,
> In leaves more durable than leaves of brass,
> Writes our whole history ; which Death shall read
> In every pale offender's private ear ;
> And Judgment publish, publish to more worlds
> Than this and endless age in groans resound.
> Such, sinner, is that sleeper in thy breast ;
> Such is her slumber ; and her vengeance such
> For slighted counsel.————————   YOUNG.

Angels, also, that ministered to the heirs of salvation, and no doubt inspected the affairs of mankind, will be witnesses. Devils too, who once tempted, will now become accusers. Conscience within will also be a witness! it shall acquit the righteous of many unjust imputations, and attest the sincerity of their hearts and their many good actions. But oh! it will be the most terrible witness against the ungodly! They will be witnesses against themselves, (Josh. xxiv. 22,) and this will render them self-tormentors. Conscience will re-echo to the voice of the Judge, and cry, Guilty, guilty, to all his accusations. And who can make the wicked happy when they torment themselves? Who can acquit them when they are self-condemned? Conscience, whose evidence is now so often suppressed will then have full scope, and shall be regarded. Whom conscience condemns the righteous Judge will also condemn; for, "if our hearts condemn us, God is greater than our hearts, and knoweth all things," 1 John iii. 20, knoweth many more grounds for condemning us than we, and therefore much more will he condemn us. In short, so full will be the evidence against the sinner, that the Scripture which is full of striking imagery to affect human nature, gives life to inanimated things upon this occasion, and represents them as speaking. Stones and dust shall witness against the ungodly. The dust under the feet of their ministers shall witness against them: Matt. x. 14. "The stone shall cry out of the wall, and the beam out of the timber shall answer it." Heb. ii. 11. The rust of their gold and silver shall be a witness against them, and shall eat their flesh as it were fire. James v. 3. Nay, the heavens shall reveal their iniquity, and the earth shall rise up against them. Job xx. 27. Heaven and earth were called to witness that life and death were set before them, Deut. xxx. 19, and now they will give in their evidence that they chose death. Thus God and all his creatures, heaven, earth, and hell, rise up against them, accuse and condemn them. And will not sinners accuse and witness against one another? Undoubtedly they will. They who lived or conversed together upon earth, and were spectators of each other's conduct, will then turn mutual witnesses against each other. Oh, tremendous thought! that friend should inform and witness against friend; parents against children, and children against parents; ministers against their people, and people against their ministers; alas! what a confounding testimony against each other must those give in who are now sinning together!

Thus the way is prepared for the passing sentence. The case was always clear to the omniscient Judge, but now it is so fully discussed and attested by so many evidences, that it is quite plain to the whole world of creatures, who can judge only by such evidence, and for whose conviction the formality of a judicial process is appointed. How long a time this grand court will sit, we cannot determine, nor has God thought fit to inform us; but when we consider how particular the trial will be, and the innumerable multitude to be tried, it seems reasonable to suppose it will be a long session. It is indeed often called a day; but it is evident a day in such cases does not signify a natural day, but the space of time allotted for transacting a business, though it be a hundred or even a thousand years. Creatures are incapable of viewing all things at once, and therefore, since the trial, as I observed, is intended to convince them of the equity of the divine proceedings, it is proper the proceedings should be particular and leisurely, that they may have time to observe them.

We are now come to the grand crisis, upon which the eternal states of all mankind turn; I mean the passing the great decisive sentence. Heaven and earth are all silence and attention, while the Judge, with smiles in his face, and a voice sweeter than heavenly music, turns to the glorious company on his right hand, and pours all the joys of heaven into their souls, in that transporting sentence, of which he has graciously left us a copy; *Come, ye blessed of my Father, inherit the kingdom prepared for you from the foundation of the world.* Every word is full of emphasis, full of heaven, and exactly agreeable to the desires of those to whom it is addressed. They desired, and longed, and languished to be near their Lord; and now their Lord invites them, Come near me, and dwell with me for ever. There was nothing they desired so much as the blessing of God, nothing they feared so much as his curse, and now their fears are entirely removed, and their designs fully accomplished, for the supreme Judge pronounces them blessed of his Father. They were all poor in spirit, most of them poor in this world, and all sensible of their unworthiness. How agreeably then are they surprised, to hear themselves invited to a kingdom, invited to inherit a kingdom, as princes of the blood-royal, born to thrones and crowns! How will they be lost in wonder, joy, and praise, to find that the great God entertained thoughts of love towards them, before they had a being, or the world in which they dwelt had its foundation laid, and that he was preparing a kingdom for them while they were nothing, unknown even in idea, except to himself? O brethren! dare any of us expect this sentence will be passed upon us? Methinks the very thought overwhelms us. Methinks our feeble frames must be unable to bear up under the extatic hope of so sweetly oppressive a blessedness. Oh! if this be our sentence in that day, it is no matter what we suffer in the intermediate space; that sentence would compensate for all, and annihilate the sufferings of ten thousand years.

But hark! another sentence breaks from the mouth of the angry Judge, like vengeful thunder. Nature gives a deep tremendous groan; the heavens lower and gather blackness, the earth trembles, and guilty millions sink with horror at the sound! And see, he whose words are works, whose fiat produces worlds out of nothing; he who could remand ten thousand worlds into nothing at a frown; he whose thunder quelled the insurrection of rebel angels in heaven, and hurled them headlong down, down, down, to the dungeon of hell; see, he turns to the guilty crowd on his left hand; his angry countenance discovers the righteous indignation that glows in his breast. His countenance bespeaks him inexorable, and that there is now no room for prayers and tears. Now, the sweet, mild, mediatorial hour is past, and nothing appears but the majesty and terror of the judge. Horror and darkness frown upon his brow, and vindictive lightnings flash from his eyes. And now, (Oh! who can bear the sound!) he speaks, " Depart from me, ye cursed, into everlasting fire prepared for the devil and his angels!" Oh! the cutting emphasis of every word! Depart! depart from me; from me, the Author of all good, the Fountain of all good, the Fountain of all happiness. Depart, with all my heavy, all-consuming curse upon you! Depart into fire, into everlasting, fire, prepared, furnished with fuel, and blown up into rage, prepared for the devil and his angels, once your companions in sin, and now the companions and executioners of your punishment!

Now the grand period is arrived in which the final, everlasting states of mankind are unchangeably settled. From this all-important era their happiness or misery runs on in one uniform, uninterrupted tenor; no change, no gradation, but from glory to glory, in the scale of perfection, or from gulf to gulf in hell. This is the day in which all the schemes of Providence, carried on for thousands of years, terminate.

> " Great day ! for which all other days were made :
> For which earth rose from chaos : man from earth :
> And an eternity, the date of gods,
> Descended on poor earth-created man !"—YOUNG.

Time was; but it is no more! Now all the sons of men enter upon a duration not to be measured by the revolutions of the sun, nor by days, and months, and years. Now eternity dawns, a day that shall never see an evening. And this terribly illustrious morning is solemnized with the execution of the sentence. No sooner is it passed than immediately the wicked "go away into everlasting pun ishment, but the righteous into life eternal." Matt. xxv. 46. See the astonished, thunder-struck multitude on the left hand, with sullen horror, and grief, and despair in their looks, writhing with agony, crying and wringing their hands, and glancing a wishful eye towards that heaven which they lost: dragged away by devils to the place of execution! See, hell expands her voracious jaws, and swallows them up! and now an eternal farewell to earth and all its enjoyments! Farewell to the cheerful light of heaven! Farewell to hope, that sweet relief of affliction !

> ———" Farewell, happy fields,
> Where joy for ever dwells ! Hail, horrors ! hail,
> Infernal world ! and thou, profoundest hell,
> Receive thy new possessors !"—MILTON.

Heaven frowns upon them from above, the horrors of hell spread far and wide around them, and conscience within preys upon their hearts. Conscience! O thou abused, exasperated power, that now sleepest in so many breasts! what severe ample revenge wilt thou then take upon those that now dare to do thee violence! Oh the dire reflections which memory will then suggest! the remembrance of mercies abused! of a Saviour slighted! of means and opportunities of salvation neglected and lost! this remembrance will sting the heart like a scorpion. But O eternity! eternity! with what horror will thy name circulate through the vaults of hell! eternity in misery! no end to pain! no hope of an end! Oh this is the hell of hell! this is the parent of despair! despair the direst ingredient of misery, the most tormenting passion which devils feel. But let us view a more delightful and illustrious scene.

See the bright and triumphant army marching up to their eternal home, under the conduct of the Captain of their salvation, where they *shall ever be with the Lord,* 1 Thess. iv. 17, as happy as their nature in its highest improvements is capable of being made. With what shouts of joy and triumph do they ascend! with what sublime hallelujahs do they crown their Deliverer! with what wonder and joy, with what pleasing horror, like one that has narrowly escaped some tremendous precipice, do they look back upon what they once were! once mean, guilty, depraved, condemned sinners! afterward imperfect, broken-hearted, sighing, weeping saints! but now innocent, holy, happy, glorious immortals!

> " Are these the forms that mouldered in the dust?
> Oh the transcendent glories of the just!"—YOUNG.

Now with what pleasure and rapture do they look forward through the long, long prospect of immortality, and call it their own! the duration not only of their existence, but of their happiness and glory! Oh shall any of us share in this immensely valuable privilege! how immensely transporting the thought!

"Shall we, who some few years ago were less
  Than worm, or mite, or shadow can express;
  Were nothing; shall we live, when every fire
  Of every star shall languish or expire?
  When earth's no more, shall we survive above,
  And through the shining ranks of angels move?
  Or, as before the throne of God we stand,
  See new worlds rolling from his mighty hand?—
  All that has being in full concert join,
  And celebrate the depths of love divine!"—YOUNG.

Oh what exploits, what miracles of power and grace, are these! But why do I darken such splendours with words without knowledge? the language of mortals was formed for lower descriptions. " Eye hath not seen, nor ear heard, neither have entered into the heart of man, the things which God hath prepared for them that love him." 1 Cor. ii. 9.

And now when the inhabitants of our world, for whose sake it was formed, are all removed to other regions, and it is left a wide extended desert, what remains, but that it also meet its fate? It is fit so guilty a globe, that had been the stage of sin for so many thousands of years, and which even supported the cross on which its Maker expired, should be made a monument of the divine displeasure, and either be laid in ruins, or refined by fire. And see! the universal blaze begins! the heavens pass away with a great noise; the elements melt with fervent heat; the earth also and the works that are therein are burnt up. 2 Pet. iii. 10. Now stars rush from their orbits; comets glare; the earth trembles with convulsions; the Alps, the Andes, and all the lofty peaks or long extended ridges of mountains burst out into so many burning Ætnas, or thunder, and lighten, and smoke, and flame, and quake like Sinai, when God descended upon it to publish his fiery law! Rocks melt and run down in torrents of flame; rivers, lakes, and oceans boil and evaporate. Sheets of fire and pillars of smoke, outrageous and insufferable thunders and lightnings burst, and bellow, and blaze, and involve the atmosphere from pole to pole.* The whole globe is now dissolved into a shoreless ocean of liquid fire. And where now shall we find the places where cities stood, where armies fought, where mountains stretched their ridges, and reared their heads on high? Alas! they are all lost, and have left no trace behind them where they once stood. Where art thou, oh my country? Sunk with the rest as a drop into the burning ocean. Where now are your houses, your lands, and those earthly possessions you were once so fond of? They are nowhere to be found. How sorry a portion for an immortal mind is such a dying world as this! And, oh!

> " How rich that God who can such charge defray,
> And bear to fling ten thousand worlds away !"—YOUNG.

Thus, my brethren, I have given you a view of the solemnities of the last day which our world shall see. The view has indeed been but very faint and obscure : and such will be all our views and descriptions of it, till our eyes and our ears teach us better. Through these avenues you will at length receive your instructions. Yes, brethren, those ears that now hear my voice shall hear the all-alarming clangor of the last trumpet, the decisive sentence from the mouth of the universal Judge, and the horrid crash of falling worlds. These very eyes with which you now see one another, shall yet see the descending Judge, the assembled multitudes, and all the majestic phenomena of that day. And we shall not see

---

* " See all the formidable sons of fire,
  Eruptions, earthquakes, comets, lightnings play
  Their various engines ; all at once discharge
  Their blazing magazines ; and take by storm
  This poor terrestrial citadel of man."—YOUNG.

them as indifferent spectators; no, we are as much concerned in this great transaction as any of the children of
men. We must all appear before the judgment-seat, and
receive our sentence according to the deeds done in the
body. And if so, what are we doing that we are not more
diligently preparing? Why does not the prospect affect
us more? Why does it not transport the righteous with
joy unspeakable, and full of glory? 1 ,Peter i. 8. And
why are not the *sinners in Zion afraid? Why does not
fearfulness surprise the hypocrites?* Isa. xxxiii. 14. Can
one of you be careless from this hour till you are in
readiness for that tremendous day?

What! do the sinners among you now think of repentance? Repentance is the grand preparative for this awful
day; and the apostle, as I observed, mentions the final
judgment in my text as a powerful motive to repentance.
And what will criminals think of repentance when they see
the Judge ascend his throne? Come, sinners, look forward and see the flaming tribunal erected, your crimes
exposed, your doom pronounced, and your hell begun; see
a whole world demolished, and ravaged by boundless conflagration for your sins! With these objects before you, I
call you to repent! I call you! I retract the words:
God, the great God, whom heaven and earth obey, commands you to repent. Whatever be your characters,
whether rich or poor, old or young, white or black,
wherever you sit or stand, this command reaches you;
for God now commandeth all men everywhere to repent.
You are this day firmly bound to this duty by his authority. And dare you disobey with the prospect of all the
awful solemnities of judgment before you in so near a
view? Oh! methinks I have now brought you into such
a situation, that the often-repeated but hitherto neglected
call to repentance will be regarded by you. Repent you

must, either upon earth or in hell. You must either spend your time or your eternity in repentance. It is absolutely unavoidable. Putting it off now does not remove the necessity, but will only render it the more bitter and severe hereafter. Which then do you choose? the tolerable, hopeful medicinal repentance of the present life, or the intolerable, unprofitable, despairing repentance of hell? Will you choose to spend time or eternity in this melancholy exercise? Oh! make the choice which God, which reason, which self-interest, which common sense recommend to you. Now repent at the command of God, *because he hath appointed a day in which he will judge the world in righteousness, by that Man whom he hath ordained, of which he hath given you all full assurance in that he raised him from the dead.* AMEN.

SERMON XXI.

THE ONE THING NEEDFUL.*

LUKE x. 41, 42.—*And Jesus answered, and said unto her, Martha, Martha, thou art careful, and troubled about many things : but one thing is needful ; and Mary hath chosen that good part, which shall not be taken away from her.*

FOR what are we placed in this world? Is it to dwell here always? You cannot think so, when the millions of mankind that have appeared upon the stage of time are so many instances of the contrary. The true notion therefore of the present state is, that it is a state of preparation and trial for the eternal world; a state of education for our adult age. As children are sent to school, and youth bound out to trades, to prepare them for business, and qualify them to live in the world, so we are placed here to prepare us for the grand business of immortality, the state of our maturity, and to qualify us to live for ever. And is there a heaven of the most perfect happiness, and a hell of the most exquisite misery, just before us, perhaps not a year or even a day distant from us? And is it the great design, the business and duty of the present state, to obtain

* A gentleman who heard this sermon delivered, told Dr. Archibald Alexander, many years afterward, that "the mere enunciation of the text produced a greater effect upon him than any sermon he had ever heard, so commanding was the personal appearance of Mr. Davies, and so solemn and impressive was his utterance "
[EDITOR OF THE BOARD OF PUBLICATION.]

the one and escape the other? Then what are we doing? What is the world doing all around us? Are they acting as it becomes candidates for eternity? Are they indeed making that the principal object of their most zealous endeavours, which is the grand design, business and duty of the present state? Are they minding this at all adventures, whatever else they neglect? This is what we might expect from them as reasonable creatures that love themselves, and have a strong innate desire of happiness. This a stranger to our world might charitably presume concerning them. But, alas! look upon the conduct of the world around you, or look nearer home, and where you are more nearly interested, upon your own conduct, and you will see this is not generally the case. No; instead of pursuing the one thing needful, the world is all in motion, all bustle and hurry, like ants upon a mole-hill, about other affairs. They are in a still higher degree than officious Martha, *careful and troubled about many things.* Now to recall you from this endless variety of vain pursuits, and direct your endeavours to the proper object, I can think of no better expedient than to explain and inculcate upon you the admonition of Christ to Martha, and his commendation of Mary upon this head.

Martha was the head of a little family, probably a widow in a village near Jerusalem, called Bethany. Her brother and sister, Lazarus and Mary, lived along with her. And what is remarkable concerning this little family is, that they were all lovers of Jesus: and their love was not without return on his side; for we are expressly told that *Jesus loved Martha, and her sister, and Lazarus.* What a happy family is this! but oh how rare in the world! This was a convenient place of retirement to Jesus, after the labours and fatigues of his ministry in the city, and here we often find him. Though spent and exhausted with his public services, yet when he gets into the circle of a few friends in a private house, he cannot be idle; he still instructs them with his heavenly discourse; and his conversation is a constant sermon. Mary, who was passionately devout, and eager for instruction, would not let such a rare opportunity slip, but sits down at the feet of this great Teacher, which was the posture of the Jewish pupils before their masters,* and eagerly catches every word from his lips; from which dropped knowledge sweeter than honey from the honey-comb. Though she is solicitous for the comfort of her heavenly guest, yet she makes no great stir to provide for him an elegant or sumptuous entertainment; for she knew his happiness did not consist in luxurious eating and drinking: it was his *meat and his drink to do the will of his Father ;* and as the sustenance of his body, plain food was most acceptable to him. He was not willing that any should lose their souls by losing opportunities of instruction, while they were making sumptuous provision for him. Mary was also so deeply engaged about her salvation, that she was nobly careless about the little decencies of entertainments. The body and all its supports and gratifications appeared of very small importance to her when compared with the immortal soul. Oh! if that be but fed with the words of eternal life, it is enough. All this she did with Christ's warm approbation, and therefore her conduct is an example worthy of our imitation: and if it were imitated, it would happily reform the pride, luxury, excessive delicacy, and multiform extravagance which have crept in upon us under the ingratiating names of politeness, decency, hospitality, good economy, and I know not what. These guilty superfluities and refinements render the life of some a course of idola-

---

* Hence St. Paul's expression, that he was brought up at the feet of Gamaliel.

try to so sordid a god as their bellies; and that of others a course of busy, laborious, and expensive trifling. But to return:

Martha, though a pious woman, yet, like too many among us, was too solicitous about these things. She seemed more concerned to maintain her reputation for good economy and hospitality, than to improve in divine knowledge at every opportunity; and to entertain her guest rather as a gentleman than as a divine teacher and the Saviour of souls. Hence, instead of sitting at his feet with her sister, in the posture of a humble disciple, she was busy in making preparations; and her mind was distracted with the cares of her family. As moderate labour and care about earthly things is lawful, and even a duty, persons are not readily suspicious or easily convinced of their guilty excesses in these labours and cares. Hence Martha is so far from condemning herself on this account, that she blames her devout sister for not following her example. Nay, she has the confidence to complain to Christ himself of her neglect, and that in language too that sounds somewhat rude and irreverent. "Carest thou not that my sister hath left me to serve alone?" Art thou so partial as to suffer her to devolve all the trouble upon me while she sits idle at thy feet?

Jesus turns upon her with just severity, and throws the blame where it should lie. *Martha, Martha!* There is a vehemence and pungency in the repetition, *Martha, Martha, thou art careful and troubled about many things.* "Thy worldly mind has many objects, and many objects excite many cares and troubles, fruitless troubles and useless cares. Thy restless mind is scattered among a thousand things, and tossed from one to another with an endless variety of anxieties. But let me collect thy thoughts and cares to one point, a point where they should

all terminate; *one thing is needful;* and therefore, dropping thy excessive care about many things, make this one
thing the great object of thy pursuit. This one thing is
what thy sister is now attending to, while thou art vainly
careful about many things; and therefore, instead of
blaming her conduct, I must approve it. She has made
the best choice, for she *hath chosen that good part which
shall not be taken away from her.* After all thy care
and labour, the things of this vain world must be given
up at last, and lost for ever. But Mary hath made a wiser
choice; the portion she hath chosen shall be her's for ever;
it shall never be taken away from her."

But what does Christ mean by this *one thing* which
alone is needful?

I answer, We may learn what he meant by the occasion and circumstances of his speaking. He mentions this
one thing in an admonition to Martha for excessive worldly
cares and the neglect of an opportunity for promoting her
salvation; and he expressly opposes this one thing to the
many things which engrossed her care; and therefore it
must mean something different from and superior to all the
pursuits of time. This one thing is that which Mary was
so much concerned about while attentively listening to his
instruction. And what can that be but salvation as the
end, and holiness as the means, or a proper care of the
soul? This is that which is opposite and superior to the
many cares of life;—this is that which Mary was attending to and pursuing: and I may add, this is that good part
which Mary had chosen, which should never be taken away
from her; for that good part which Mary had chosen seems
intended by Christ to explain what he meant by the one
thing needful. Therefore the one thing needful must mean
the salvation of the soul, and an earnest application to the
means necessary to obtain this end above all other things

in the world. To be holy in order to be happy; to pray, to hear, to meditate, and use all the means of grace appointed to produce or cherish holiness in us; to use these means with constancy, frequency, earnestness, and zeal; to use them diligently whatever else be neglected, or to make all other things give way in comparison of this; this I apprehend is the one thing needful which Christ here intends: this is that which is absolutely necessary, necessary above all other things, and necessary for ever. The end, namely, salvation, will be granted by all to be necessary, and the necessity of the end renders the means also necessary. If it be necessary you shall be for ever happy, and escape everlasting misery, it is necessary you should be holy; for you can no more be saved without holiness than you can be healthy without health, see without light, or live without food. And if holiness be necessary, then the earnest use of means appointed for the production and improvement of holiness in us must be necessary too; for you can no more expect to become holy without the use of these means, than to reap without sowing, or become truly virtuous and good by chance or fatality. To be holy in order to be happy, and to use all the means of grace in order to be holy, is therefore the one thing needful.

But why is this concern which is so complex called one thing?

I answer: Though salvation and holiness include various ingredients, and though the means of grace are various, yet they may be all taken collectively and called one thing; that is, one great business, one important object of pursuit, in which all our endeavours and aims should centre and terminate. It is also said to be one, in opposition to the many things that are the objects of a worldly mind. This world owes its variety in a great measure to contradiction and inconsistency. There is no harmony or unity in the earthly objects of men's pursuits, nor in the means they use to secure them. Riches, honours, and pleasures generally clash. If a man will be rich he must restrain himself in the pleasures of gratifying his eager appetites, and perhaps use some mean artifice that may stain his honour. If he would be honourable, he must often be prodigal of his riches, and abstain from some sordid pleasures. If he would have the full enjoyment of sensual pleasures, he must often squander away his riches, and injure his honour to procure them. The lusts of men as well as their objects, are also various and contradictory. Covetousness and sensuality, pride and tranquility, envy and the love of ease, and a thousand jarring passions, maintain a constant fight in the sinner's breast. The means for gratifying these lusts are likewise contrary; sometimes truth, sometimes falsehood, sometimes indolence, sometimes action and labour are necessary. In these things there is no unity of design, nor consistency of means; but the sinner is properly distracted, drawn this way and that, tossed from wave to wave; and there is no steadiness or uniformity in his pursuits. But the work of salvation is one, the means and the end correspond, and the means are consistent one with another; and therefore the whole, though consisting of many parts, may be said to be one.

It may also be called the one thing needful, to intimate that this is needful above all other things. It is a common form of speech to say of that which is necessary above all other things, that it is the one or only thing necessary: so we may understand this passage. There are what we call the real necessaries of life; such as food and raiment; there are also necessary callings and necessary labours. All these are necessary in a lower sense; necessary in their proper place. But in comparison of the great work of our salvation, they are all unnecessary; if we be but saved,

we may do very well without them all. This is so necessary, that nothing else deserves to be called necessary in
comparison of it.

This shows you also, not only why this is called one thing,
but why or in what sense it is said to be necessary. It is
of absolute and incomparable necessity. There is no absolute necessity to our happiness that we should be rich
or honourable; nay, there is no absolute necessity to our
happiness that we should live in this world at all, for we
may live infinitely more happy in another. And if life
itself be not absolutely necessary, then much less are food,
or raiment, or health, or any of those things which in a
lower sense we call the necessaries of life. In comparison
of this, they are all needless. I add farther, this one thing
may be said to be necessary, because it is necessary always,
or for ever. The necessaries of this life we cannot want
long, for we must soon remove into a world where there
is no room for them; but holiness and salvation we shall
find needful always: needful under the calamities of
life; needful in the agonies of death; needful in the
world of spirits; needful millions of ages hence; needful
to all eternity; and without it we are eternally undone.
This is a necessity indeed! a necessity, in comparison of
which all other necessaries are but superfluities.

I hope by this short explication I have cleared the way
through your understandings to your hearts, and to your
hearts I would now address myself. However solemnly
I may speak upon this interesting subject, you will have
more reason to blame me for the deficiency, than for the
excess of my zeal and solemnity. I hope I have entered
this sacred place to-day with a sincere desire to do some
service to your immortal souls before I leave it. And
may I not hope you have come here with a desire to receive some advantage? If not, you may number this seem-

ing act of religion among the sins of your life; you have come here to-day to sin away these sacred hours in hypocrisy and a profane mockery of the great God. But if you are willing to receive any benefit, hear attentively: hear, that your souls may live.

My first request to you is,* that you would make this passage the test of your characters, and seriously inquire whether you have lived in the world as those that really and practically believe that this is the one thing of absolute necessity. Are not all the joys of heaven and your immortal souls worth the little pains of seriously putting this short question to your consciences? Review your life, look into your hearts, and inquire, has this one thing lain more upon your hearts than all other things together? Has this been, above all other things, the object of your most vehement desires, your most earnest endeavours, and eager pursuit? I do not ask whether you have heard or read that this one thing is necessary, or whether you have sometimes talked about it. I do not ask whether you have paid to God the compliment of appearing in his house once a week, or of performing him a little lip-service morning and evening in your families, or in your closets, after you have served yourselves and the world all the rest of your time, without one affectionate thought of God. Nor do I inquire whether in a pang of horror after the commission of some gross sin, you have tried to make your conscience easy by a few prayers and tears, of which you form an opiate to cast you again into a dead sleep in sin; I do not ask whether you have performed many actions that are materially good, and abstained from many sins.

* Many of the following sentiments, as to the substance of them, are borrowed from Mr. Baxter's excellent discourse, entitled A SAINT OR A BRUTE; and I know no better pattern for a minister to follow in his address to sinners, than that flaming and successful preacher.

All this you may have done, and yet have neglected the one thing needful all your lives.

But I ask you, whether this one thing needful has been habitually uppermost in your hearts, the favourite object of your desires, the prize of your most vigorous endeavours, the supreme happiness of your souls, and the principal object of your concern above all things in the world? Sirs, you may now hear this question with stupid unconcern and indifferency; but I must tell you, you will find, another day, how much depends upon it. In that day it will be found, that the main difference between true Christians and the various classes of sinners is this;—God, Christ, holiness, and the concerns of eternity, are habitually uppermost in the hearts of the former; but, to the latter, they are generally but things by the by; and the world engrosses the vigour of their souls, and is the principal concern of their lives. To serve God, to obtain his favour, and to be happy for ever in his love, is the main business of the saint, to which all the concerns of the world and the flesh must give way; but to live in ease, in reputation, in pleasure, or riches, or to gratify himself in the pursuit and enjoyment of some created good, this is the main concern of the sinner. The one has made a hearty resignation of himself, and all that he is and has, to God, through Jesus Christ; he serves him with the best, and thinks nothing too good for him. But the other has his exceptions and reserves; he will serve God willingly, provided it may consist with his ease, and pleasure, and temporal interest; he will serve God with a bended knee, and the external forms of devotion; but, with the vigour of his spirit, he serves the world and his flesh. This is the grand difference between a true Christian and the various forms of half-Christians and hypocrites. And certainly this is a difference that may be discerned. The tenor of a man's practice, and the object of his love, especially of his highest love and practical esteem, must certainly be very distinguishable from a thing by the by, and from the object of a languid passion, or mere speculation. Therefore, if you make but an impartial trial, you have reason to hope you will make a just discovery of your true character; or if you cannot make the discovery yourselves, call in the assistance of others. Ask not your worldly and sensual neighbours, for they are but poor judges, and they will flatter you in self-defence; but ask your pious friends whether you have spoke and acted like persons that practically made this the one thing needful. They can tell you what subject you talked most seriously about, what pursuit seemed to lie most upon your hearts, and chiefly to exhaust your activity. Brethren, I beseech you, by one means or other, to bring this matter to an issue, and let it hang in suspense no longer. Why are you so indifferent how this matter stands with you? Is it because you imagine you may be true Christians, and obtain salvation, however this matter be with you? But be not deceived: no man can serve two masters, whose commands are contrary; and *ye cannot serve God and mammon*, with a service equally devoted to both. *If any man love the world*, with supreme affection, *the love of the Father is not in him*. 1 John ii. 15. *Be not deceived; God is not mocked: whatsoever a man soweth, that shall he also reap; he that soweth to his flesh, shall of the flesh reap corruption:* a miserable harvest indeed; *but he that soweth to the spirit, shall of the spirit reap everlasting life.* Gal. vi. 7, 8. Therefore you may be sure that *if you live after the flesh, you shall die;* and that you can never enjoy the one thing needful unless you mind and pursue it above all other things.

But I shall not urge you any farther to try yourselves

by this test. I take it for granted the consciences of some of you have determined the matter, and that you are plainly convicted of having hitherto neglected the one thing needful. Allow me then honestly to expose, your conduct in its proper colours, and tell you what you have been doing while you were busy about other things, and neglecting this one thing needful.

1. However well you have improved your time for other purposes, you have lost it all, unless you have improved it in securing the one thing needful. The proper notion of time is, that it is a space for repentance. Time is given us to prepare for eternity. If this is done, we have lived long enough, and the great end of time and life is answered, whatever else be undone. But if this be undone, you have lived in vain, and all your time is lost, however busily and successfully you have pursued other things. Though you have studied yourselves pale to furnish your minds with knowledge; though you have spent the night and the day in heaping up riches, or climbing up to the pinacle of honour, and not lost an hour that might be turned to your advantage, yet you have been most wretchedly fooling away your time, and lost it all, if you have not laid it out in securing the one thing needful. And, believe me, time is a precious thing. So it will appear in a dying hour, or in the eternal world, to the greatest spendthrift among you. Then, oh for a year, or even a week, or a day, to secure that one thing which you are now neglecting! And will you now waste your time, while you enjoy it? Shall so precious a blessing be lost? By this calculation, how many days, how many years, have you lost for ever! For, is not that lost which is spent in crossing the end for which it was given you? Time was given you to secure an eternity of happiness, but you have spent it in adding sin to sin, and consequently in treasuring

up wrath against the day of wrath. And is not your time
then a thousand times worse than lost? Let me tell you,
if you continue in this course to the end, you will wish
a thousand times, either that you had never had one
hour's time given you, or that you had made a better use
of it.

2. Whatever else you have been doing, you have lost
your labour with your time, if you have not laboured
above all things for this one thing needful. No doubt you
have been busy about something all your life; but you
might as well have been idle; you have been busy in
doing nothing. You have perhaps toiled through many
anxious and laborious days, and your nights have shared
in the anxieties and labours of your days. But if you
have not laboured for the one thing necessary, all your
labour and all the fruits of it are lost. Indeed God may
have made use of you for the good of his church, or of
your country, as we make use of thorns and briers to stop
a breach, or of useless wood for firing to warm our families;
but as to any lasting and solid advantage to yourselves, all
your labour has been lost.

But this is not all. Not only your secular labour is
lost, but all your toil and pains, if you have used any in
the duties of religion, they are lost likewise. Your reading, hearing, praying, and communicating; all your serious
thoughts of death and eternity, all your struggles with
particular lusts and temptations, all the kind offices you
have done to mankind, all are lost, since you have performed them by halves with a lukewarm heart, and have
not made the one thing needful your great business and
pursuit. All these things will not save you; and what is
that religion good for which will not save your souls?
What do those religious endeavours avail which will suffer
you to fall into hell after all? Certainly such religion is vain.

And now, my hearers, do you believe this, or do you not? If you do, will you, dare you still go on in the same course? If you do not believe it, let me reason the matter with you a little. You will not believe that all the labour and pains you have taken all your life have been quite lost: no, you now enjoy the fruits of them. But show me now, if you can, what you have gotten by all that stir you have made, that will follow one step beyond the grave, or that you can call your own to-morrow. Where is that sure immortal acquisition that you can carry with you into the eternal world? Were you to die this hour, would it afford you any pleasuse to reflect that you have lived a merry life, and had a satiety of sensual pleasures, or that you have laboured for riches and honours, and perhaps acquired them? Will this reflection afford you pleasure or pain? Will this abate the agony of eternal pain, or make up for the loss of heaven, which you wilfully incurred by an over-eager pursuit of these perishing vanities?

Do you not see the extravagant folly, the distracted frenzy of such a conduct? Alas! while you are neglecting the one thing needful, what are you doing but spending your time and labour in laborious idleness, honourably debasing yourselves, delightfully tormenting yourselves, wisely befooling yourselves, and frugally impoverishing and ruining yourselves for ever? A child or an idiot riding upon a staff, building their mimic houses, or playing with a feather, are not so foolish as you in your conduct, while you are so seriously pursuing the affairs of time, and neglecting those of eternity. But,

3. This is not all: all your labour and pains have not only been lost while you have neglected this one thing, but you have taken pains to ruin yourselves, and laboured hard all your lives for your own destruction. To this you will

immediately answer, "God forbid that we should do any thing to hurt ourselves; we were far from having any such design." But the question is not, what was your design? but, what is the unavoidable consequence of your conduct, according to the nature of things, and the unchangeable constitution of heaven? Whatever your design in going on in sin, *the wages of sin is death*, eternal death. You may indulge the carnal mind, and walk after the flesh, and yet hope no bad consequence will follow: but God has told you that *to be carnally minded is death*, and that if you live after the flesh you shall die. The robber on the highway has no design to be hanged; but this does not render him a jot safer. Therefore, design what you will, it is certain you are positively destroying yourselves while your labours about other things hinder you from pursuing the one thing needful. And does not this thought shock you, that you should be acting the part of enemies against yourselves, the most pernicious and deadly enemies to yourselves in the whole universe? No enemy in the whole universe could do you that injury without your consent which you are doing to yourselves. To tempt you to sin is all the devil can do; but the temptation alone can do you no injury; it is consenting to it that ruins you; and this consent is your own voluntary act. All the devils in hell could not force you to sin without your consent, and therefore all the devils in hell do not injure you as you do yourselves. God has not given them so much power over you as he has given you over yourselves; and this power you abuse to your own destruction.

Oh! in what a distracted state is the world of the ungodly! If any other man be their enemy, how do they resent it! But they are their own worst enemies, and yet never fall out with themselves. If another occasion them a disappointment in their pursuits, defraud them of an expected good, or lay schemes to make them miserable, what sullen grudge, what keen revenge, what flaming resentments immediately rise in their breasts against him! And yet they are all their lives disinheriting themselves of the heavenly inheritance, laying a train to blow up all their own hopes, and heaping a mountain of guilt upon themselves to sink them into the bottomless pit: and all this while they think they are the best friends to themselves, and consulting their own interest. As for the devil, the common enemy of mankind, they abhor him, and bless themselves from him; but they are worse to themselves than devils, and yet never fall out with themselves for it.

This, sinners, may seem a harsh representation of your conduct, but, alas! it is true. And if it be so shocking to you to hear it, what must it be to be guilty of it! And oh! think what must be the consequences of such a conduct, such unnatural suicide!

4. If you have hitherto neglected the one thing needful, you have unmanned yourselves, acted beneath and contrary to your own reason, and in plain terms behaved as if you had been out of your senses. If you have the use of your reason, it must certainly tell you for what it was given to you. And I beseech you to tell me what was it given you for but to serve the God that made you, to secure his favour, to prepare for your eternal state, and to enjoy the supreme good as your portion? Can you once think your reason, that *divinæ particula auræ*, was given you for such low purposes as the contrivances, labour, and pursuits of this vain life, and to make you a more ingenious sort of brutes? He was master of an unusual share of reason who said, "There is very little difference between having reason and having none, if we had nothing to do with it but cunningly to lay up for our food, and make provision for this corruptible flesh, and had not an-

other life to mind." Therefore I may safely affirm that
you have cast away your reason, and acted as if you were
out of your wits, if you have not employed your rational
powers in the pursuit of the one thing needful. Where
was your reason when your dying flesh was preferred to
your immortal spirits? Was reason your guide when you
chose the trash of this perishing world, and sought it more
than the favour of God and all the joys of heaven? Can
you pretend to common sense, when you might have had
the pardon of sin, sanctifying grace, and a title to heaven,
secured to you ere now? But you have neglected all, and
instead of having a sure title to heaven, or being prepared
for it, you are fitted for destruction, and nothing else; and
are only awaiting for a fever or a flux, or some other executioner of divine vengeance, to cut the thread of life, and
let you sink to hell by your own weight. Thither you
gravitate under the load of sin as naturally as a stone to
the centre; and you need no other weight to sink you
down. What have you done all your life to make a wise
man think you truly reasonable? Is that your reason, to
be wise to do evil, while to do good you have no knowledge; or to be ingenious and active about the trifles of
time, while you neglect that great work for which you
were created and redeemed? Can you be wise and yet
not consider your latter end? Nay, can you pretend to so
much as common sense, while you sell your eternal salvation for the sordid pleasures of a few flying years? Have
you common sense, when you will not keep yourselves out
of everlasting fire? What can a madman do worse than
wilfully destroy himself? And this you are doing every day.

And yet these very persons are proud of their madness,
and are apt to fling the charge of folly upon others, especially if they observe some poor weak creatures, though
it be but one in five hundred, fall into melancholy, or lose

their reason for a time, while they are groaning under a sense of sin, and anxious about their eternal state; then what a clamour against religion and preciseness, as the ready way to make people run mad! then they even dare to publish their resolution that they will not read and pore so much upon these things, lest it should drive them out of their senses.   O miserable mortals! is it possible they should be more dangerously mad than they are already? Do you lay out your reason, your strength, and time in pursuing vain shadows, and in feeding a mortal body for the grave, while the important realities of the eternal world, and the salvation of your immortal souls are forgotten or neglected?   Do you sell your Saviour with Judas for a little money, and change your part in God and heaven for the sordid pleasures of sin, which are but for a season? and are you afraid of seriously reflecting upon this course, that you may reform it, for fear such thoughts should make you mad?   What greater madness than this can you fear?   Will you run from God, from Christ, from mercy, from the saints, from heaven itself, for fear of being mad?   Alas! you are mad in the worst sense already. Will you run to hell to prove yourselves in your senses? He was a wise and good man who said, " Though the loss of a man's understanding is a grievous affliction, and such as I hope God will never lay upon me, yet I had a thousand times rather go distracted to Bedlam with the excessive care about my salvation, than to be one of you that cast away the care of your salvation for fear of being distracted, and will go among the infernal Bedlams into hell for fear of being mad."   Distraction in itself is not a moral evil, but a physical, like those disorders of the body from which it often proceeds, and therefore is no object for punishment; and had you no capacity of understanding you would have a cloak for your sin; but your madness is your crime, because it is voluntary, and therefore you must give an account for it to the Supreme Judge.

It would be easy to offer many more considerations to expose the absurdity and danger of your conduct in neglecting the one thing necessary; but these must suffice for the present hour. And I only desire you to consider farther, if this be a just view of the conduct of such as are guilty of this neglect, in what a miserable, pitiable condition is the world in general. I have so often tried the utmost energy of my words upon you with so little success as to many, that I am quite grown weary of them. Allow me therefore for once to borrow the more striking and pungent words of one now in heaven; of one who had more success than almost any of his contemporaries or successors in the important work of " converting sinners from the error of their way and saving souls from death :" I mean that incomparable preacher, Mr. Baxter, who sowed an immortal seed in his parish of Kidderminster, which grows and brings forth fruit to this day. His words have, through the divine blessing, been irresistible to thousands; and oh that such of you, my dear hearers, whose hearts may have been proof against mine, may not be so against his also!

" Look upon this text of Scripture," says he, " and look also upon the course of the earth, and consider of the disagreement; and whether it be not still as before the flood, that all the imaginations of man's heart are evil continually. Gen. vi. 5. Were it possible for a man to see the affections and motions of all the world at once, as God seeth them, what a pitiful sight it would be! What a stir do they make, alas, poor souls! for they know not what! while they forget, or slight, or hate the one thing needful. What a heap of gadding ants should we see, that do nothing but gather sticks and straws! Look among persons of

every rank, in city and country, and look into families
about you, and see what trade it is they are most busily
driving on, whether it be for heaven or earth! And
whether you can discern by their care and labours that
they understand what is the one thing necessary! They
are as busy as bees; but not for honey, but in spinning
such a spider's web as the besom of death will presently
sweep down. Job viii. 14. They labour hard, but for
what? *For the food that perisheth,* but not for that *which
endureth to everlasting life.* John vi. 27. They are diligent seekers; but for what? Not first for God, his kingdom and righteousness, but for that which they might have
had as an addition to their blessedness. Matt. vi. 33.
They are still doing; what are they doing? Even un-
doing themselves by running away from God, to hunt after
the perishing pleasures of the world. Instead of providing for the life to come, they are making *provision for the
flesh to fulfil its lusts.* Rom. xiii. 14. Some of them hear
the word of God, but presently choke it *by the deceitful-
ness of riches, and the cares of this life.* Luke viii. 14.
They *are careful and troubled about many things ;* but the
one thing that should be all to them is cast by as if it were
nothing. Providing for the flesh and minding the world
is the employment of their lives. They labour with a
canine appetite for their trash; but to holiness they have
no appetite, and are worse than indifferent to the things
that are indeed desirable. They have no covetousness for
the things which they are commanded *earnestly to covet.*
1 Cor. xii. 31. They have so little hunger and thirst
after righteousness, that a very little or none will satisfy
them. Here they are pleading always for moderation, and
against too much, and too earnest, and too long; and all
is too much with them that is above stark naught, or dead
hypocrisy; and all is too earnest and too long that would

make religion seem a business, or engage them to seem serious in their own profession, or put them past jest in the worship of God and the matters of their salvation. Let but their children or servants neglect their worldly business, (which I confess they should not do,) and they shall hear of it with both their ears; but if they sin against God, or neglect his word or worship, they shall meet with more patience than Eli's son did: a cold reproof is usually the most; and it is well if they be not encouraged in their sin; it is well if a child or servant that begins to be serious for salvation be not rebuked, derided, and hindered by them. If on their days of labour they oversleep themselves, they shall be sure to be called up to work, (and good reason,) but when do they call them up to prayer? when do they urge them to consider or converse upon the things that concern their everlasting life? The Lord's own day, which is appointed to be set apart for matters of this nature, is wasted in idleness or worldly talk. Come at any time into their company, and you may talk enough, and too much of news, or other men's matters, of their worldly business, sports, and pleasures, but about God and their salvation they have so little to say, and that so heartlessly, and by-the-by, as if they were things that belonged not to their care and duty, and no whit concerned them. Talk with them about the renovation of the soul, the nature of holiness, and the life to come, and you will find them almost as dumb as a fish. The most understand not matters of this nature, nor much desire or care to understand them. If one would teach them personally, they are too old to be catechized or to learn, though not too old to be ignorant of the matters they were made for and preserved for in the world. They are too wise to learn to be wise, and too good to be taught how to be good, though not too wise to follow the seducements of the devil and the world, nor too good to be the slaves of Satan and the despisers and enemies of goodness. If they do anything which they call serving God, it is some cold and heartless use of words to make themselves believe that for all their sins they shall be saved; so that God will call that a serving their sins and abominations, which they will call a serving of God. Some of them will confess that holiness is good, but they hope God will be merciful to them without it; and some do so hate it, that it is a displeasing irksome thing to them to hear any serious discourse of holiness; and they detest and deride those as fanatical, troublesome precisians that diligently seek the one thing necessary : so that if the belief of the most may be judged by their practices, we may confidently say, that they do not practically believe that ever they should be brought to judgment, or that there is any heaven or hell to be expected : and that their confession of the truth of the Scriptures and the articles of the Christian faith are no proofs that they heartily take them to be true. Who can be such a stranger to the world as not to see that this is the case of the greatest part of men? And, which is worst of all, they go on in this course against all that can be said to them, and will give no impartial, considerate hearing to the truth, which would recover them to their wits, but live as if it would be a felicity to them in hell to think that they came thither by wilful resolution, and in despite of the remedy."

This, sinners, is a true representation of your case, drawn by one that well knew it and lamented it. And what do you now think of it yourselves? What do you think will be the consequence of such a course? Is it safe to persist in it? or shall I be so happy as to bring you to a stand? Will you still go on, troubling yourselves with many things? or will you resolve for the future to

mind the one thing needful above all? I beseech you to
come to some resolution. Time is on the wing, and does
not allow you to hesitate in so plain and important an
affair. Do you need any farther excitements? Then I
shall try the force of one consideration more contained in
my text, and that is necessity.

Remember necessity, the most pressing, absolute necessity, enforces this care upon you. One thing is needful,
absolutely needful, and needful above all other things.
This, one would think, is such an argument as cannot but
prevail. What exploits has necessity performed in the
world! What arts has it discovered as the mother of invention! what labours, what fatigues, what sufferings has
it undergone! What dangers has it encountered! What
difficulties has it overcome! Necessity is a plea which
you think will warrant you to do anything and excuse
anything. Reasoning against necessity is but reasoning
against a hurricane; it bears all before it. To obtain the
necessaries of life, as they are called, how much will men
do and suffer! Nay, with what hardships and perils will
they not conflict for things that they imagine necessary,
not to their life but to their ease, their honour, or pleasure! But what is this necessity when compared to that
which I am now urging upon you? In comparison of
this, the most necessary of those things are but superfluities; for if your ease, or honour, or pleasure, or even your
life in this world be not absolutely necessary, as they cannot be to the heirs of immortality, then certainly those
things which you imagine necessary to your ease, your
honour, your pleasure, or mortal life, are still less necessary. But oh! to escape everlasting misery, and to secure
everlasting salvation, this is the grand necessity! This will
appear necessary in every point of your immortal duration;
necessary when you have done with this world for ever, and

must leave all its cares, enjoyments, and pursuits behind you. And shall not this grand necessity prevail upon you to work out your salvation, and make that your great business, when a far less necessity, a necessity that will last but a few years at most, set you and the world around you upon such hard labours and eager pursuits for perishing vanities? All the necessity in the world is nothing in comparison of that which lies upon you to work out your salvation; and shall this have no weight? If you do not labour or contrive for *the bread that perisheth*, you must beg or starve; but if you will not labour for the bread that endureth unto everlasting life, you must burn in hell for ever. You must lie in prison if your debts with men be not paid; but, oh! what is it to the prison of hell, where you must be confined for ever if your debts to the justice of God be not remitted, and you do not obtain an interest in the righteousness of Christ, which alone can make satisfaction for them! You must suffer hunger and nakedness unless you take care to provide food and raiment; but you must suffer eternal banishment from God and all the joys of his presence, if you do not labour to secure the one thing needful. Without the riches of this world you may be rich in faith, and heirs of the heavenly inheritance. Without earthly pleasures you may have joy unspeakable and full of glory in the love of God, and the expectation of the kingdom reserved in heaven for you. Without health of body you may have happiness of spirit; and even without this mortal life you may enjoy eternal life. Without the things of the world you may live in want for a little while, but then you will soon be upon an equality with the greatest princes. But without this one thing needful you are undone, absolutely undone. Though you were as rich as Crœsus, you "are wretched, and miserable, and poor, and blind, and naked." Your very being becomes a curse to you. It is your curse that you are a man, a reasonable creature. It had been infinitely better for you if you had been a toad or a snake, and so incapable of sin and of immortality, and consequently of punishment. Oh then let this grand necessity prevail with you!

I know you have other wants, which you should moderately labour to provide for, but oh how small and of how short continuance! If life and all should be lost, you may more than find all in heaven. But if you miss at this one thing, all the world cannot make up the loss.

Therefore to conclude with the awakening and resistless words of the author I before quoted, "Awake, you sluggish, careless souls! your house over your head is in a flame! the hand of God is lifted up! If you love yourselves, prevent the stroke. Vengeance is at your backs, the wrath of God pursues your sin, and wo to you if he finds it upon you when he overtaketh you. Away with it speedily! up and begone; return to God; make Christ and mercy your friends in time, if you love your lives! the Judge is coming! for all that you have heard of it so long, yet still you believe it not. You shall shortly see the majesty of his appearance and the dreadful glory of his face; and yet do you not begin to look about you, and make ready for such a day? Yea, before that day, your separated souls shall begin to reap as you have sowed here. Though now the partition that stands between you and the world to come do keep unbelievers strangers to the things that most concern them, yet death will quickly find a portal to let you in; and then, sinners, you will find such doings there as you little thought of, or did not sensibly regard upon earth. Before your friends will have time enough to wrap up your pale corpse in your winding-sheet, you will see and feel that which will tell you to the quick, that one thing was necessary. If you die without this one thing necessary, before your friends can have finished your funerals, your souls will have taken up their places among devils in endless torments and despair, and all the wealth, and honour, and pleasure that the world afforded you will not ease you. This is sad, but it is true, sirs; for God hath spoken it. Up, therefore, and bestir you for the life of your souls. Necessity will awake even the sluggard. Necessity, we say, will break through stone walls. The proudest will stoop to necessity: the most slothful will bestir themselves in necessity: the most careless will be industrious in necessity: necessity will make men do anything that is possible to be done. And is not necessity, the highest necessity, your own necessity, able to make you cast away your sins, and take up a holy and heavenly life? O poor souls! is there a greater necessity for your sin than of your salvation, and of pleasing your flesh for a little time than of pleasing the Lord and escaping everlasting misery? Oh that you would consider what I say! and the Lord give you understanding in all things. Amen.

SERMON XXII.

SAINTS SAVED WITH DIFFICULTY, AND THE CERTAIN PER-
DITION OF SINNERS.

1 Pet. iv. 18.—*And if the righteous scarcely be saved,
where shall the ungodly and the sinner appear.*

This text may sound in your ears like a message from
the dead; for it is at the request of our deceased friend*
that I now insist upon it. He knew so much from the
trials he made in life, that if he should be saved at all, it
would be with great difficulty, and if he should escape
destruction at all, it would be a very narrow escape; and
he also knew so much of this stupid, careless world, that
they stood in need of a solemn warning on this head; and
therefore desired that his death should give occasion to a
sermon on this alarming subject. But now the unknown
wonders of the invisible world lie open to his eyes; and
now also he can take a full review of his passage through
this mortal life; now he sees the many unsuspected
dangers he narrowly escaped, and the many fiery darts of
the devil which the shield of faith repelled; now, like a
ship arrived in port, he reviews the rocks and shoals he
passed through, many of which lay under water and out
of sight; and therefore now he is more fully acquainted
with the difficulty of salvation than ever. And should he
now rise and make his appearance in this assembly in the

* The person was Mr. James Hooper; and the sermon is dated August
21, 1756.

solemn and dread attire of an inhabitant of the world of spirits, and again direct me to a more proper subject, methinks he would still stand to his choice, and propose it to your serious thoughts, that " if the righteous scarcely be saved, where shall the ungodly and the sinner appear ?"

The apostle's principal design in the context seems to be to prepare the Christians for those sufferings which he saw coming upon them, on account of their religion. " Beloved," says he, " think it not strange concerning the fiery trial which is to try you, as though some strange thing happened unto you:" verse 12, " but rejoice inasmuch as ye are partakers of Christ's sufferings:" it is no strange thing that you should suffer on account of your religion in such a wicked world as this, for Christ the founder of your religion met with the same treatment; and it is enough that the servant be as his master, ver. 13, only he advises them, that if they must suffer, that they did not suffer as malefactors, but only for the name of Christ, ver. 14, 15. "Yet," says he, "if any man suffer as a Christian, let him not be ashamed;" ver. 16, "for the time is come that judgment must begin at the house of God." He seems to have a particular view to the cruel persecutions that a little after this was raised against the Christians by the tyrant Nero, and more directly to that which was raised against them everywhere by the seditious Jews, who were the most inveterate enemies of Christianity. The dreadful destruction of Jerusalem, which was plainly foretold by Christ in the hearing of St. Peter was now at hand. And from the sufferings which Christians, the favourites of heaven, endured, he infers how much more dreadful the vengeance would be which should fall upon their enemies, the infidel Jews. If judgment begin at the house of God, his church, what shall

be the doom of the camp of rebels? If it begin at us
Christians who obey the gospel, what shall be the end of
them that obey it not? Alas! what shall become of
them? *Them that obey not the gospel of God,* is a description of the unbelieving Jews, to whom it was peculiarly applicable; and the apostle may have a primary
reference to the dreadful destruction of their city and
nation which was much more severe than all the sufferings
the persecuted Christians had then endured. But I see
no reason for confining the apostle's view entirely to this
temporal destruction of the Jews; he seems to refer
farther to that still more terrible destruction that awaits all
that obey not the gospel in the eternal world: that is to
say, if the children are so severely chastised in this world,
what shall become of rebels in the world to come, the
proper state of retribution? How much more tremendous
must be their fate!

In the text he carries on the same reflection. *If the
righteous scarcely be saved, where shall the ungodly and
the sinner appear?* The righteous is the common character of all good men or true Christians; and the ungodly and sinner are characters which may include the
wicked of all nations and ages. Now, says he, if the
righteous be but scarcely saved, saved with great difficulty, just saved, and no more, where shall idolaters
and vicious sinners appear, whose characters are so
opposite?

The abrupt and pungent form of expression is very
emphatical. *Where shall the ungodly and the sinner appear?* I need not tell you, your own reason will inform
you: I appeal to yourselves for an answer, for you are all
capable of determining upon so plain a case. *Where shall
the ungodly and the sinner appear?* Alas! it strikes me
dumb with horror to think of it: it is so shocking and terri-

ble that I cannot bear to describe it. Now they are gay, merry, and rich; but when I look a little forward, I see them appear in very different circumstances, and the horror of the prospect is hardly supportable.

St. Peter here supposes that there is something in the condition and character of a righteous man that renders his salvation comparatively easy; something from whence we might expect that he will certainly be saved, and that without much difficulty: and on the other hand, that there is something in the opposite character and condition of the ungodly and the sinner, that gives us reason to conclude that there is no probability at all of their salvation while they continue as such. But he asserts that even the righteous, whose salvation seems so likely and comparatively easy, is not saved without great difficulty; he is just saved, and that is all: what then shall we conclude of the ungodly and the sinner, whose character gives no ground for favourable expectations at all? If our hopes are but just accomplished, with regard to the most promising, what shall become of those whose case is evidently hopeless? Alas! where shall they appear?

The method in which I intend to prosecute our subject is this:

I. I shall point out the principal difficulties, which even the righteous meet with in the way to salvation.

II. I shall mention those things in the condition and character of the righteous, which render his salvation so promising and seemingly easy, and then show you that, if with all these favourable and hopeful circumstances he is not saved but with great difficulty and danger, those who are of an opposite character, and whose condition is so evidently and apparently desperate, cannot be saved at all.

I. I am to point out the principal difficulties which even the righteous meet with in the way to salvation.

Here I would premise, that such who have become truly religious, and persevered in the way of holiness and virtue to the last, will meet with no difficulty at all to be admitted into the kingdom of heaven. The difficulty does not lie here, for the same apostle Peter assures us, that if we give all diligence *to make our calling and election sure*, we shall never fall; but so *an entrance shall be ministered unto us abundantly into the everlasting kingdom of our Lord and Saviour Jesus Christ.* 2 Peter i. 10, 11. But the difficulty lies in this, that, all things considered, it is a very difficult thing to obtain, and persevere in real religion in the present corrupt state of things, where we meet with so many temptations and such powerful opposition. Or in other words, it is difficult in such a world as this to prepare for salvation; and this renders it difficult to be saved, because we cannot be saved without preparation.

It must also be observed, that a religious life is attended with the most pure and solid pleasures even in this world; and they who choose it act the wisest part with respect to the present state: they are really the happiest people upon our globe. Yet, were it otherwise, the blessed consequences of a religious life in the eternal world would make amends for all, and recommend such a course, notwithstanding the greatest difficulties and the severest sufferings that might attend it.

But notwithstanding this concession, the Christian course is full of hardships, oppositions, trials, and discouragements. This we may learn from the metaphorical representations of it in the sacred writings, which strongly imply that it is attended with difficulties which require the utmost exertion of all our powers to surmount. It is called a warfare, 1 Tim i. 18; fighting, 2 Tim. iv. 7. The graces of the Christian, and the means of begetting and cherishing them, are called weapons of war: there is the shield of faith:

the hope of salvation, which is the helmet; the sword of the Spirit, which is the word of God, 2 Cor. x. 4; Eph. vi. 13, 17. The end of the Christian's course is victory after conflict, Rev. ii. 7. And Christians are soldiers; and such as must endure hardships, 2 Tim. ii. 3. Now a military life, you know, is a scene of labour, hardships and dangers; and therefore so is the Christian life, which is compared to it in these respects, it is compared to a race, Heb. xii. 1, 2, to wrestling and the other vigorous exercises of the Olympic games, Eph. vi. 12; Luke xiii. 24, to walking in a narrow way, Matt. vii. 14, and entering at the strait gate, Luke xiii. 24. This, my brethren, and this only, is the way to salvation. And is this the way in which you are walking? Or is it the smooth, easy downward road to destruction? You may slide along that without exertion or difficulty, like a dead fish swimming with the stream; but oh! look before you, and see whither it leads!

The enemies that oppose our religious progress are the devil, the world, and the flesh. These form a powerful alliance against our salvation, and leave no artifice untried to obstruct it.

The things of the world, though good in themselves, are temptations to such depraved hearts as ours. Riches, honours, pleasure, spread their charms, and tempt us to the pursuit of flying shadows to the neglect of the one thing needful. These engross the thoughts and concerns, the affections and labours of multitudes. They engage with such eagerness in an excessive hurry of business and anxious care, or so debauch and stupefy themselves with sensual pleasures, that the voice of God is not heard, the clamors of conscience are drowned, the state of their souls is not inquired into, the interests of eternity are forgotten, the eternal God, the joys of heaven, and the pains of hell, are cast out of the mind, and disregarded; and they care not for any or all of these important realities, if they can but gratify the lust of avarice, ambition, and sensuality. And are such likely to perform the arduous work of salvation? No; they do not so much as seriously attempt it. Now these things which are fatal to multitudes throw great difficulties in the way even of the righteous man. He finds it hard to keep his mind intent npon his great concern in the midst of such labours and cares as he is obliged to engage in; and frequently he feels his heart estranged from God and ensnared into the ways of sin, his devotion cooled, and his whole soul disordered by these allurements. In short, he finds it one of the hardest things in the world to maintain a heavenly mind in such an earthly region, a spiritual temper, among so many carnal objects.

The men of this world also increase his difficulties. Their vain, trifling, or wicked conversation, their ensnaring examples, their persuasions, false reasonings, reproaches, menaces, and all their arts of flattery and terror, have sometimes a very sensible effect upon him. These would draw him into some guilty compliances, damp his courage, and tempt him to apostatize, were he not always upon his guard; and sometimes in an inadvertent hour he feels their fatal influence upon him. As for the generality, they yield themselves up to these temptations, and make little or no resistance; and thus are carried down the stream into the infernal pit. Alas! how many ruin themselves through a base, unmanly complaisance, and servile conformity to the mode! Believe it, sirs, to be fashionably religious and no more, is to be really irreligious in the sight of God. The way of the multitude may seem easy, pleasant, and sociable; but, alas, my brethren! see where it ends; it leadeth down into destruction. Matt. vii. 14.

But in the next place, the greatest difficulty in our way

arises from the corruption and wickedness of our own
hearts.   This is an enemy within; and it is this that
betrays us into the hands of our enemies without.   When
we turn our eyes to this quarter, what vast difficulties rise
in our way! difficulties which are impossible to us, unless
the almighty Power enables us to surmount them.   Such
are a blind mind, ignorant of divine things, or that specu-
lates only upon them, but does not see their reality and
dread importance; a mind empty of God and full of the
lumber and vanities of this world.   Such are a hard heart,
insensible of sin, insensible of the glory of God, and the
beauties of holiness, and the infinite moment of eternal things.   Such are a heart disaffected to God and
his service, bent upon sin, and impatient of restraint.
Such are wild, unruly passions thrown into a ferment by every trifle, raised by vanities, erroneous
in the choice of objects, irregular in their motions,
and extravagant in the degree of attachment.   Such
difficulties are strong, ungovernable lusts and appetites
in animal nature, eager for gratification, and turbulent
under restraint.   And how strangely does this inward
corruption indispose men for religion!   Hence their ignorance, their security, carelessness, presumptuous hopes,
and impenitence.   Hence their unwillingness to admit
conviction, their resistance to the Holy Spirit, and their
contempt of the gospel, their disregard to all religious instructions, their neglect of the means of grace, and the
ordinances of Christ, or their careless, formal, lukewarm
attendance upon them.   Hence their earthly-mindedness,
their sensuality, and excessive love of animal pleasures.
Hence it is so difficult to awaken them to a just sense of
their spiritual condition, and to suitable earnestness in their
religious endeavours; and hence their fickleness and inconstancy, their relapses and backslidings, when they have

been a little alarmed. Hence it is so difficult to bring their religious impressions to a right issue, and to lead them to Jesus Christ as the Saviour. In short, hence it is that so many thousands perish amidst the means of salvation. These difficulties prove eventually insuperable to the generality: and they never surmount them. But even the righteous, who is daily conquering them by the aid of divine grace, and will at last be more than a conqueror, he still finds many hinderances and discouragements from this quarter. The remains of these innate corruptions still cleave to him in the present state, and these render his progress heavenward so slow and heavy. These render his life a constant warfare, and he is obliged to fight his way through. These frequently check the aspirations of his soul to God, cool his devotion, damp his courage, ensnare his thoughts and affections to things below, and expose him to the successful attacks of temptation. Alas! it is his innate corruption that involves him in darkness and jealousies, in tears and terrors, after hours of spiritual light, joy, and confidence. It is this that banishes him from the comfortable presence of his God, and causes him to go mourning without the light of his countenance. Were it not for this, he would glide along through life easy and unmolested; he would find the ways of religion to be ways of pleasantness, and all her paths peace. In short, it is this that lies upon his heart as the heaviest burden, and renders his course so rugged and dangerous. And such of you as do not know this by experience, know nothing at all of true experimental Christianity.

Finally, the devil and his angels are active, powerful, and artful enemies to our salvation: their agency is often unperceived, but it is insinuating, unsuspected, and therefore the more dangerous and successful. These malignant spirits present ensnaring images to the imagination, and no doubt blow the flame of passion and appetite. They labour to banish serious thoughts from the mind, and entertain it with trifles. They give force to the attacks of temptations from the world, and raise and foment insurrections of sin within. And if they cannot hinder the righteous man from entering upon a religious course, or divert him from it, they will at least render it as difficult, laborious, and uncomfortable to him as possible.

See, my brethren, see the way in which you must walk if you would enter into the kingdom of heaven. In this rugged road they have all walked who are now safe, arrived at their journey's end, the land of rest. They were saved, but it was with great difficulty: they escaped the fatal rocks and shoals, but it was a very narrow escape; and methinks it is with a kind of pleasing horror they now review the numerous dangers through which they passed, many of which they did not perhaps suspect till they were over.* And is this the way in which you are walking? Is your religion a course of watchfulness, labour, conflict, and vigorous exertions? Are you indeed in earnest in it above all things in this world? Or are not many of you lukewarm Laodiceans and indifferent Gallios about these things? If your religion (if it may be so called) is a course of security, carelessness, sloth, and formality—alas! if all the vigour and exertion of the righteous man be but just sufficient for his salvation, where, oh where shall you appear? Which leads me,

---

* There on a green and flowery mount,
  Their weary souls now sit;
And with transporting joys recount
  The labours of their feet.
Eternal glories to the King
  That brought them safely through
Their lips shall never cease to sing,
  And endless praise renew.

II. To mention those things in the character and condition of the righteous, which render his salvation so promising and seemingly easy, and then show, that if with all those hopeful circumstances he shall not be saved but with great difficulty, that they, whose character is directly opposite, and has nothing encouraging in it, cannot possibly be saved at all.   And this head I shall cast into such a form as to exemplify the text.

1. If those that abstain from immorality and vice be but scarcely saved, where shall the vicious, profligate sinner appear?

It is the habitual character of a righteous man to be temperate and sober, chaste, just, and charitable; to revere the name of God, and everything sacred, and religiously observe the holy hours devoted to the service of God.   This is always an essential part of his character, though not the whole of it.   Now such a man looks promising; he evidently appears so far prepared for the heavenly state, because he is so far conformed to the law of God, and free from those enormities which are never found in the region of happiness.   And if such shall scarcely be saved, where shall those of the opposite character appear?   Where shall the brute of a drunkard, the audacious swearer, the scoffer at religion, the unclean, lecherous wretch, the liar, the defrauder, the thief, the extortioner, the Sabbath-breaker, the reveller, where shall these appear?   Are these likely to stand in the congregation of the righteous, or to appear in the presence of God with joy?   Is there the least likelihood that such shall be saved?   If you will regard the authority of an inspired apostle in the case, I can direct you to those places where you may find his express determination. 1 Cor. vi. 9, 10. "Know ye not that the unrighteous shall not inherit the kingdom of God?   Be not deceived; neither fornicators, nor idolaters, nor adulterers, nor effeminate, nor abusers of themselves with mankind, nor thieves, nor covetous, nor drunkards, nor revilers, nor extortioners, shall inherit the kingdom of God." So Gal. v. 19–21. "The works of the flesh are manifest, which are these—adultery, fornication, uncleanness, lasciviousness, hatred, variance, emulations, wrath, strife, heresies, seditions, envyings, revellings, and such like, of the which I tell you before;" that is, I honestly forewarn you, as I have also told you in time past, that they who do such things shall not inherit the kingdom of God. Rev. xxi. 8. "The fearful, (that is, the cowardly in the cause of religion,) the unbelieving, and the abominable, and murderers, and whoremongers, and all liars, shall have their part in the lake which burneth with fire and brimstone." You see, my brethren, the declarations of the Scripture are express enough and repeated on this point. And are there not some of you here who indulge yourselves in one or other of these vices, and yet hope to be saved in that course? that is, you hope your Bible and your religion too are false; for it is only on that supposition that your hope of salvation can be accomplished. Alas! will you venture your eternal all upon the truth of such a blasphemous supposition as this? But,

2. If those that conscientiously perform the duties of religion be scarcely saved, where shall the neglecters of them appear?

The righteous are characterized as persons that honestly endeavour to perform all the duties they owe to God. They devoutly read and hear his word, and make divine things their study; they are no strangers to the throne of of grace; they live a life of prayer in their retirements, and in a social capacity. They make their families little churches, in which divine worship is solemnly performed.

Let others do as they will; as for them and their houses, like Joshua, *they will serve the Lord :* Josh. xxiv. 15. They gratefully commemorate the sufferings of Christ, and give themselves up to him at his table; and seriously improve all the ordinances of the gospel.   In short, like Zacharias and Elizabeth, they *walk in all the commandments and ordinances of God, blameless :* Luke i. 6.   This is their prevailing and habitual character.. And there is something in this character that gives reason to presume they will be saved; for they have now a relish for the service of God, in which the happiness of heaven consists; they are training up in the humble forms of devotion in the church below, for the more exalted employments of the church triumphant on high.   Now if persons of this character are but *scarcely saved, where shall the ungodly appear,* who persist in the wilful neglect of these known duties of religion?   Can they be saved who do not so much as use the means of salvation?   Can those who do not study their Bible, the only directory to eternal life, expect to find the way thither?   Can prayerless souls receive answers to prayer?   Will all the bliss of heaven be thrown away upon such as do not think it worth their while importunately to ask it?   Are they likely to be admitted into the general assembly and church of the Firstborn in heaven, who do not endeavour to make their families little circles of religion here upon earth?   In a word, are they likely to join for ever in the devotions of the heavenly state, who do not accustom themselves to these sacred exercises in this preparatory state?   Will you venture your souls upon it that you shall be saved, notwithstanding these improbabilities, or rather impossibilities?   Alas! are there any of you that have no better hopes of heaven than these?   Where, then, will you appear?

3. If they that are more than externally moral and re-

ligious in their conduct, that have been born again, created
in Christ Jesus to good works, as every man that is truly
righteous has been; if such, I say, be but scarcely saved,
where shall they appear who rest in their mere outward
morality, their proud self-righteous virtue, and their religious formalities, and have never been made new creatures,
never had the inward principles of action changed by the
power of God, and the inbred disorders of the heart
rectified? Where shall they appear who have nothing
but a self-sprung religion, the genuine offspring of degenerate nature, and never had a supernatural principle
of grace implanted in their souls? Has that solemn as-
severation of the Amen, the faithful and true witness, lost
all its force, and become falsehood in our age and country?
"Verily, verily, I say unto thee, except a man be born
again, he cannot see the kingdom of God:" John iii. 3.
Is there no weight in such apostolic declarations as these?
"If any man be in Christ he is a new creature; old things
are passed away; behold all things are become new.   And
all things are of God:" 2 Cor. v. 17.   "Neither circumcision availeth any thing nor uncircumcision:"   Gal. vi.
15 : that is to say, a conformity to the rituals of the Jewish
or Christian religion availeth nothing, but the new creature.
Can men flatter themselves they shall be saved by the
Christian religion, in opposition to these plain, strong,
and repeated declarations of the Christian revelation?
And yet, are there not many here who are entirely ignorant of this renovation of the temper of their mind, of this
inward, heaven-born religion?

4. If they that are striving to enter in at the strait gate
and pressing into the kingdom of heaven, do but just obtain admission; if they who forget the things that are behind, and reach after those that are before them, and press
with all their might towards the goal, do scarcely obtain

the prize, what shall become of those lukewarm, careless, formal, presumptuous professors of Christianity who are so numerous among us? Where shall they appear who have but *a form of godliness without the power*, 2 Tim. iii. 5; and have no spiritual life in their religion, *but only a name to live?* Rev. iii. 1. If those whose hearts are habitually solicitous about their eternal state, who labour in earnest for the immortal bread, who pray with unutterable groans, Rom. viii. 26; who, in short, make the care of their souls the principal business of their life, and in some measure proportion their industry and earnestness to the importance and difficulty of the work; if such are but scarcely saved, with all their labour and pains, where shall they appear who are at ease in Zion, Amos vi. 1, whose religion is but a mere indifferency, a thing by-the-by with them? If we cannot enter into the kingdom of heaven unless our righteousness exceed that of the Scribes and Pharisees, Matt. v. 20, where shall they appear whose righteousness is far short of theirs? And are there not many such in this assembly? Alas! my brethren, where do you expect to appear?

5. If they that have believed in Jesus Christ, which is the grand condition of salvation, be but scarcely saved, where shall the unbeliever appear?

Faith in Christ is an essential ingredient in the character of a righteous man; and faith cannot be implanted in our hearts till we have been made deeply sensible of our sins, of our condemnation by the law of God, and our utter inability to procure pardon and salvation by the merit of our repentance, reformation, or any thing we can do. And when we are reduced to this extremity, then we shall listen with eager ears to the proposal of a Saviour. And when we see his glory and sufficiency, and cast our guilty souls upon him; when we submit to his commands, depend entirely upon his atonement, and give up ourselves to God through him, then we believe. Now, if they who thus believe, to whom salvation is so often ensured, be not saved but with great difficulty, where shall those appear who never have experienced those exercises which are the antecedents or constituents of saving faith? who have never seen their own guilt and helplessness in an affecting light; who have never seen the glory of God in the face of Jesus Christ; who have never submitted to him as their Prophet, Priest, and King, and who do not live in the flesh by faith in the Son of God? Alas! are they likely to be saved who are destitute of the grand pre-requisite of salvation? And yet, is not this the melancholy case of some of you? You may not be avowed unbelievers; you may believe there is one God, and that Jesus is the true Messiah: in this you do well, but still it is no mighty attainment, for the devils also believe and tremble, and you may have this speculative faith, and yet be wholly destitute of the faith of the operation of God, the precious faith of God's elect; that faith which purifies the heart, produces good works, and unites the soul to Jesus Christ. Certainly the having or not having of such a faith, must make a great difference in a man's character, and must be followed by a proportionally different doom. And if they that have it be but scarcely saved, I appeal to yourselves, can they be saved at all who have it not?

6. If true penitents be scarcely saved, where shall the impenitent appear?

It is the character of the righteous that he is deeply affected with sorrow for his sins in heart and practice; that he hates them without exception with an implacable enmity; that he strives against them, and would resist them even unto blood; that his repentance is attended with reformation, and that he forsakes those things for the commission of which his heart is broken with sorrows. Now, repentance appears evidently to the common reason of mankind a hopeful preparative for acceptance with God and eternal happiness; and therefore if they who repent are saved with great difficulty, where shall they appear who persist impenitent in sin? Where shall they appear who have hard, unbroken hearts in their breasts, who are insensible of the evil of sin, who indulge themselves in it, and cannot be persuaded to forsake it? Can you be at any loss to know the doom of such, after Christ has told us with his own lips, which never pronounced a harsh censure? *Except ye repent, ye shall all likewise perish.* Luke xiii. 3, 5. And are there not some of this character in this assembly? Alas! there is not the least likelihood, or even possibility of your salvation in such a condition.

7. The righteous man has the love of God shed abroad in his heart, and it produces the usual sentiments and conduct of love towards him. God is dearer to him than all other things in heaven and earth: the *strength of his heart, and his portion for ever.* Psalm lxxiii. 25, 26. His affectionate thoughts fix upon him, Psalm lxiii. 6; he rejoices in the light of his countenance, Psalm iv. 7; and longs and languishes for him in his absence, Psalm xlii. 1, 2, and lxiii. 1; Cant. iii. 1. His love is a powerful principle of willing obedience, and carries him to keep his commandments. 1 John v. 3. He delights in the law and service of God, and in communion with him in his ordinances. Now, such a principle of love is a very hopeful preparative for heaven, the region of love, and for the enjoyment of God. Such a one would take pleasure in him and in his service, and therefore he certainly shall never be excluded. But if even such are but scarcely saved, where shall they appear who are destitute of the love of

God? There are few indeed but pretend to be lovers of
God, but their love has not the inseparable properties of
that sacred passion. Their pretence to it is an absurdity,
and if put into language, would be such jargon as this,
" Lord, I love thee above all things, though I hardly ever
affectionately think of thee; I love thee above all, though
I am not careful to please thee; I love thee above all,
though my conduct towards thee is quite the reverse of
what it is towards one I love." Will such an inconsistency as this pass for genuine supreme love to God, when
it will not pass for common friendship among men? No,
such have not the least spark of that heavenly fire in their
breasts, for their carnal mind is enmity against God. And
are these likely to be saved? likely to be admitted into
the region of love, where there is not one cold or disloyal
heart? likely to be happy in the presence and service of
that God to whom they are disaffected? Alas! no.
Where, then, shall they appear? Oh! in what forlorn,
remote region of eternal exile from the blessed God!

I shall now conclude with a few reflections. 1. You
may hence see the work of salvation is not that easy trifling
thing which many take it to be. They seem mighty cautious of laying out too much pains upon it; and they cannot
bear that people should make so much ado, and keep such
a stir and noise about it.* For their part, they hope to
go to heaven as well as the best of them, without all this
preciseness and upon these principles they act. They
think they can never be too much in earnest, or too laborious in the pursuit of earthly things; but religion is a
matter by-the-by with them; only the business of an hour
once a week. But have these learned their religion from
Christ the founder of it, or from his apostles whom he ap-

---

* I here affect this low style on purpose to represent more exactly the sentiments of such careless sinners in their own usual language.

pointed teachers of it? No; they have formed some easy system from their own imaginations suited to their depraved taste, indulgent to their sloth and carnality, and favourable to their lusts, and this they call Christianity. But you have seen this is not the religion of the Bible; this is not the way to life laid out by God, but it is the smooth downward road to destruction. Therefore,

2. Examine yourselves to which class you belong, whether to that of the righteous, who shall be saved, though with difficulty, or to that of the ungodly and the sinner, who must appear in a very different situation. To determine this important inquiry, recollect the sundry parts of the righteous man's character which I have briefly described, and see whether they belong to you. Do you carefully abstain from vice and immorality? Do you make conscience of every duty of religion. Have you ever been born again of God, and made more than externally religious? Are you sensible of the difficulties in your way from Satan, the world, and the flesh? And do you exert yourselves as in a field of battle or in a race? Do you work out your salvation with fear and trembling, and press into the kingdom of God? Are you true believers, penitents, and lovers of God? Are these or the contrary the constituents of your habitual character? I pray you, make an impartial trial, for much depends upon it.

3. If this be your habitual character, be of good cheer, for you shall be saved, though with difficulty. Be not discouraged when you fall into fiery trials, for they are no strange things in the present state. All that have walked in the same narrow road before you have met with them, but now they are safe arrived in their eternal home. Let your dependence be upon the aids of divine grace to bear you through, and you will overcome at last. But,

4. If your character be that of the ungodly and the

sinner, pause and think, where shall you appear at last?
When, like our deceased friend, you leave this mortal state,
and launch into regions unknown, where will you then appear? Must it not be in the region of sin, which is your
element now? in the society of the devils, whom you resemble in temper, and imitate in conduct? among the trembling criminals at the left hand of the Judge, where the
ungodly and sinners shall all be crowded? If you continue such as you now are, have you any reason at all to
hope for a more favourable doom?

I shall conclude with a reflection to exemplify the context in another view, that is, "If judgment begin at the
house of God, what shall be the end of them that obey
not the gospel? If the righteous, the favourites of heaven, suffer so much in this world, what shall sinners, with
whom God is angry every day, and who are vessels of
wrath fitted for destruction, what shall they suffer in the
eternal world, the proper place for rewards and punishments, and where an equitable Providence deals with every
man according to his works? If the children are chastised with various calamities, and even die in common with
the rest of mankind, what shall be the doom of enemies
and rebels? If those meet with so many difficulties in
the pursuit of salvation, what shall these suffer in enduring
damnation? If the infernal powers are permitted to worry
Christ's sheep, how will they rend and tear the wicked as
their proper prey? Oh that you may in this your day
know the things that belong to your peace, before they are
for ever hid from your eyes. Luke xix 42.

SERMON XXIII.

INDIFFERENCE TO LIFE URGED FROM ITS SHORTNESS AND VANITY.*

1 Cor. vii. 29, 30, 31.—*But this. I say, brethren, the time is short. It remaineth, that both they that have wives be as though they had none ; and they that weep, as though they wept not ; and they that rejoice, as though they rejoiced not; and they that buy, as though they possessed not; and they that use this world, as not abusing it. For the fashion of this world passeth away.*

A creature treading every moment upon the slippery brink of the grave, and ready every moment to shoot the gulf of eternity, and launch away to some unknown coast, ought to stand always in the posture of serious expectation; ought every day to be in his own mind taking leave of this world, breaking off the connections of his heart from it, and preparing for his last remove into that world in which he must reside, not for a few months or years as in this, but through a boundless everlasting duration. Such a situation requires habitual, constant thoughtfulness, abstraction from the world, and serious preparation for death and eternity. But when we are called, as we frequently are, to perform the last sad offices to our friends and neighbours who have taken their flight a little before us; when the solemn pomp and horrors of death strike our senses,

* This sermon is dated, at Mr. Thompson's funeral, February 16, 1759.

then certainly it becomes us to be unusually thoughtful
and serious.   Dying beds, the last struggles and groans of
dissolving nature, pale, cold, ghastly corpses:

"The knell, the shroud, the mattock, and the grave:
The deep damp vault, the darkness and the worm;"

these are very alarming monitors of our own mortality:
these out-preach the loudest preacher; and they must be
deep and senseless rocks, and not men, who do not hear
and feel their voice.   Among the numberless instances of
the divine skill in bringing good out of evil, this is one,
that past generations have sickened and died to warn their
successors.   One here and there also is singled out of our
neighbourhood or families, and made an example, a *me-
mento mori*, to us that survive, to rouse us out of our stupid
sleep, to give us the signal of the approach of the last
enemy, death, to constrain us to let go our eager grasp of
this vain world, and set us upon looking out and preparing
for another.   And may I hope my hearers are come here
to-day determined to make this improvement of this melancholy occasion, and to gain this great advantage from
our loss?   To this I call you as with a voice from the
grave; and therefore *he that hath ears to hear, let him hear.*

One great reason of men's excessive attachment to the
present state, and their stupid neglect of the concerns of
eternity, is their forming too high an estimate of the affairs
of time in comparison with those of eternity.   While the
important realities of the eternal world are out of view,
unthought of, and disregarded, as, alas! they generally
are by the most of mankind, what mighty things in their
esteem are the relations, the joys and sorrows, the possessions and bereavements, the acquisitions and pursuits of
this life?   What airs of importance do they put on in their
view?   How do they engross their anxious thoughts and

cares, and exhaust their strength and spirits! To be happy,
to be rich, to be great and honourable, to enjoy your fill
of pleasure in this world, is not this a great matter, the
main interest in many of you? is not this the object of
your ambition, your eager desire and laborious pursuit?
But to consume away your life in sickness and pain, in
poverty and disgrace, in abortive schemes and disappointed
pursuits, what a serious calamity, what a huge affliction is
this in your esteem? What is there in the compass of the
universe that you are so much afraid of, and so cautiously
shunning? Whether large profits or losses in trade be not
a mightier matter, ask the busy, anxious merchant. Whether poverty be not a most miserable state, ask the poor
that feel it, and the rich that fear it. Whether riches be
not a very important happiness, ask the possessors; or
rather ask the restless pursuers of them, who expect still
greater happiness from them than those that are taught by
experience can flatter themselves with. Whether the pleasures of the conjugal state are not great and delicate, consult the few happy pairs here and there who enjoy them.
Whether the loss of an affectionate husband and a tender
father be not a most afflictive bereavement, a torturing
separation of heart from heart, or rather a tearing of one's
heart in pieces, ask the mourning, weeping widow, and
fatherless children, when hovering round his dying-bed, or
conducting his dear remains to the cold grave. In short,
it is evident from a thousand instances, that the enjoyments,
pursuits, and sorrows of this life are mighty matters! nay,
are all in all in the esteem of the generality of mankind.
These are the things they most deeply feel, the things
about which they are chiefly concerned, and which are the
objects of their strongest passions.

But is this a just estimate of things? Are the affairs
of this world then indeed so interesting and all-important?

Yes, if eternity be a dream, and heaven and hell but majestic chimeras, or fairy lands; if we were always to live
in this world, and had no concern with anything beyond
it; if the joys of earth were the highest we could hope for,
or its miseries the most terrible we could fear, then indeed
we might take this world for our all, and regard its affairs
as the most important that our nature is capable of. *But
this I say, brethren,* (and I pronounce it as the echo of an
inspired apostle's voice,) this I say, *the time is short ;* the
time of life in which we have anything to do with these
affairs is a short, contracted span. Therefore *it remaineth,*
that is, this is the inference we should draw from the
shortness of time, *they that have wives, be as though they
had none ; and they that weep, as though they wept not ;
and they that rejoice, as though they rejoiced not ; and they
that buy, as though they possessed ·not ; and they that use
this world, as not abusing it,* or using it to excess; *for the
fashion of this world,* these tender relations, this weeping
and rejoicing, this buying, possessing, and using this world
passeth away. The phantom will soon vanish, the shadow
will soon fly off; and they that have wives or husbands in
this transitory life, will in reality be as though they had
none; and they that weep now, as though they wept not;
and they that now rejoice, as though they rejoiced not;
and they that now buy, possess and use this world, as
though they never had the least property in it. This is
the solemn, mortifying doctrine I am now to inculcate
upon you in the further illustration of the several parts of
my text; a doctrine justly alarming to the lovers of this
world, and the neglecters of that life which is to come.

When St. Paul pronounces anything with an unusual
air of solemnity and authority, and after the formality of
an introduction to gain attention, it must be a matter of
uncommon weight, and worthy of the most serious regard.

In this manner he introduces the funeral sentiments in my text. *This I say, brethren;* this I solemnly pronounce as the mouth of God: this I declare as a great truth but little regarded; and which therefore there is much need I should repeatedly declare: this I say with all the authority of an apostle, a messenger from heaven; and I demand your serious attention to what I am going to say.

And what is it he is introducing with all this solemn formality? Why, it is an old, plain, familiar truth universally known and confessed, namely, that the time of our continuance in this world is short. But why so much formality in introducing such a common plain truth, as this? Because, however generally it be known and confessed, it is very rarely regarded; and it requires more than even the most solemn address of an apostle to turn the attention of a thoughtless world to it. How many of you, my brethren, are convinced against your wills of this melancholy truth, and yet turn every way to avoid the mortifying thought, are always uneasy when it forces itself upon your minds, and do not suffer it to have a proper influence upon your temper and practice, but live as if you believed the time of life were long, and even everlasting? Oh! when will the happy hour come when you will think and act like those who believe that common, uncontroverted truth, that the time of life is short? Then you would no longer think of delays, nor contrive artifices to put off the work of your salvation; then you could not bear the thought of such negligent, or languid, feeble endeavours in a work that must be done, and that in so short a time.

This I say, my brethren, the time is short : the time of life is absolutely short; a span, an inch, a hair's breadth. How near the neighbourhood between the cradle and the grave! How short the journey from infancy to old age, through all the intermediate stages! Let the few among

you who bear the marks of old age upon you in gray hairs,
wrinkles, weakness, and pains, look back upon your tire-
some pilgrimage through life, and does it not appear to
you, as though you commenced men but yesterday? And
how little a way can you trace it back till you are lost in
the forgotten unconscious days of infancy, or in that eternal non-existence in which you lay before your creation!
But they are but a very few that drag on their lives
through seventy or eighty years. Old men can hardly
find contemporaries: a new race has started up, and they
are become almost strangers in their own neighbourhoods.
By the best calculations that have been made, at least one
half of mankind die under seven years old. They are
little particles of life, sparks of being just kindled and then
quenched, or rather dismissed from their suffocating confinement in clay, that they may aspire, blaze out, and
mingle with their kindred flames in the eternal world, the
proper region, the native element of spirits.

And how strongly does the shortness of this life prove
the certainty of another? Would it be worth while, would
it be consistent with the wisdom and goodness of the
Deity, to send so many infant millions of reasonable creatures into this world, to live the low life of a vegetable or
an animal for a few moments, or days, or years, if there
were no other world for these young immortals to remove
to, in which their powers might open, enlarge, and ripen?
Certainly men are not such insects of a day: certainly
this is not the last stage of human nature: certainly there
is an eternity; there is a heaven and a hell:—otherwise
we might expostulate with our Maker, as David once did
upon that supposition, *Wherefore hast thou made all men
in vain?* Psalm. lxxxix. 47.

In that awful eternity we must all be in a short time.
Yes, my brethren, I may venture to prophesy that, in less

than seventy or eighty years, the most, if not all this assembly, must be in some apartment of that strange untried world. The merry, unthinking, irreligious multitude in that doleful mansion which I must mention, grating as the sound is to their ears, and that is hell!* and the pious, penitent, believing few in the blissful seats of heaven. There we shall reside a long, long time indeed, or rather through a long, endless eternity. Which leads me to add,

That the time of life is short absolutely in itself, so especially it is short comparatively; that is, in comparison with eternity. In this comparison, even the long life of Methuselah and the antedeluvians shrink into a mere point, a nothing. Indeed no duration of time, however long, will bear the comparison. Millions of millions of years! as many years as the sands upon the sea-shore! as many years as the particles of dust in this huge globe of earth; as many years as the particles of matter in the vaster heavenly bodies that roll above us, and even in the whole material universe, all these years do not bear so much proportion to eternity as a moment, a pulse, or the twinkling of an eye, to ten thousand ages! not so much as a hair's breadth to the distance from the spot where we stand to the farthest star, or the remotest corner of creation. In short, they do not bear the least imaginable proportion at all; for all this length of years, though beyond the power of distinct enumeration to us, will as certainly come to an end as an hour or a moment; and when it comes to an end, it is entirely and irrecoverably past; but eternity (oh the solemn, tremendous sound!) eternity will never, never,

---

* Regions of sorrow! doleful shades! where peace
  And rest can never dwell! Hope never comes
  That comes to all! But torture without end
  Still urges, and a fiery deluge fed
  With ever-burning sulphur unconsum'd.—MILTON.

never come to an end! eternity will never, never, never be past!

And is this eternity, this awful, all-important eternity, entailed upon us? upon us, the offspring of the dust? the creatures of yesterday? upon us, who a little while ago were less than a gnat, less than a mote, were nothing? upon us who are every moment liable to the arrest of death, sinking into the grave, and mouldering into dust one after another in a thick succession? upon us whose thoughts and cares, and pursuits are so confined to time and earth, as if we had nothing to do with anything beyond?   Oh! is this immense inheritance unalienably ours? Yes, brethren, it is; reason and revelation prove our title beyond all dispute.   It is an inheritance entailed upon us, whether we will or not; whether we have made it our interest it should be ours or not.   To command ourselves into nothing is as much above our power as to bring ourselves into being. Sin may make our souls miserable, but it cannot make them mortal. Sin may forfeit a happy eternity, and render our immortality a curse; so that it would be better for us if we never had been born; but sin cannot put an end to our being, as it can to our happiness, nor procure for us the shocking relief of rest in the hideous gulf of annihilation.

And is a little time, a few months or years, a great matter to us? to us who are heirs of an eternal duration? How insignificant is a moment in seventy or eighty years! but how much more insignificant is even the longest life upon earth, when compared with eternity! How trifling are all the concerns of time to those of immortality! What is it to us who are to live for ever, whether we live happy or miserable for an hour? whether we have wives, or whether we have none; whether we rejoice, or whether we weep; whether we buy, possess, and use this world;

or whether we consume away our life in hunger, and nakedness, and the want of all things? it will be all one in a
little, little time.   Eternity will level all; and eternity is
at the door.

And how shall we spend this eternal duration that is
thus entailed upon us?   Shall we sleep it away in a stupid
insensibility or in a state of indifferency, neither happy
nor miserable?   No, no, my brethren; we must spend it
in the height of happiness or in the depth of misery.   The
happiness and misery of the world to come will not consist in such childish toys as those that give us pleasure and
pain in this infant state of our existence, but in the most
substantial realities suitable to an immortal spirit, capable
of vast improvements and arrived at its adult age.   Now,
as the apostle illustrates it, we are children, and we speak
like children, we understand like children; but then we
shall become men, and put away childish things. 1 Cor.
xiii. 11.   Then we shall be beyond receiving pleasure or
pain from such trifles as excite them in this puerile state.
This is not the place of rewards or punishments, and
therefore the great Ruler of the world does not exert his
perfections in the distribution of either; but eternity is
allotted for that very purpose, and therefore he will then
distribute rewards and punishments worthy himself, such
as will proclaim him God in acts of grace and vengeance,
as he has appeared in all his other works.   Then he will
show his wrath, and *make* his power *known on the vessels
of wrath who have made themselves fit for destruction* and
nothing else; *and he will show the riches of the glory of
his grace upon the vessels of mercy whom he prepared beforehand for glory.* Rom. ix. 22, 23.   Thus heaven and
hell will proclaim the God, will show him to be the Author
of their respective joys and pains, by their agreeable or
terrible magnificence and grandeur.   Oh eternity! with

what majestic wonders art thou replenished, where Jehovah acts with his own immediate hand, and displays himself God-like and unrivalled, in his exploits both of vengeance and of grace! In this present state, our good and evil are blended; our happiness has some bitter ingredients, and our miseries have some agreeable mitigations; but in the eternal world good and evil shall be entirely and for ever separated; all will be pure, unmingled happiness, or pure, unmingled misery. In the present state the best have not uninterrupted peace within; conscience has frequent cause to make them uneasy; some mote or other falls into its tender eye, and sets it a-weeping; and the worst also have their arts to keep conscience sometimes easy, and silence its clamors. But then conscience will have its full scope. It will never more pass a censure upon the righteous, and it will never more be a friend, or even an inactive enemy to the wicked for so much as one moment. And oh what a perennial fountain of bliss or pain will conscience then be! Society contributes much to our happiness or misery. But what misery can be felt or feared in the immediate presence and fellowship of the blessed God and Jesus (the friend of man); of angels and saints, and all the glorious natives of heaven! But, on the other hand, what happiness can be enjoyed or hoped for, what misery can be escaped in the horrid society of lost, abandoned ghosts of the angelic and human nature; dreadfully mighty and malignant, and rejoicing only in each other's misery; mutual enemies, and mutual tormentors, bound together inseparably in everlasting chains of darkness! Oh the horror of the thought! in short, even a heathen* could say,

* Non mihi si linguæ centum sint, oraque centum,
Ferrea vox, omnes scelerum comprendere formas,
Omnia pœnarum percurere nomina possum.
                                        VIRG. Æn. VI. I. 625.

" Had I a hundred tongues, a hundred mouths,
   An iron voice, I could not comprehend
   The various forms and punishments of vice."

The most terrible images which even the pencil of divine inspiration can draw, such as a lake of fire and
brimstone, utter darkness, the blackness of darkness, a
never-dying worm, unquenchable everlasting fire, and all
the most dreadful figures that can be drawn from all parts
of the universe, are not sufficient to represent the punishments of the eternal world.   And, on the other hand, *the
eye*, which has ranged through so many objects, *has not
seen : the ear*, which has had still more extensive intelligence, *has not heard ; neither have entered into the heart
of man*, which is even unbounded in its conceptions, *the
things that God hath laid up for them that love him.*
The enjoyments of time fall as much short of those of
eternity, as time itself falls short of eternity itself.

But what gives infinite importance to these joys and
sorrows is, that they are enjoyed or suffered in the eternal
world, they are themselves eternal.   Eternal joys! eternal
pains! joys and pains that will last as long as the King
eternal and immortal will live to distribute them! as long
as our immortal spirits will live to feel them!   Oh what
joys and pains are these !

And these, my brethren, are awaiting every one of us.
These pleasures, or these pains, are felt this moment by
such of our friends and acquaintance as have shot the
gulf before us; and in a little, little while, you and I must
feel them.

And what then have we to do with time and earth?
Are the pleasures and pains of this world worthy to be
compared with these?   " Vanity of vanities, all is vanity;"
the enjoyments and sufferings, the labours and pursuits,
the laughter and tears of the present state, are all nothing

in this comparison. What is the loss of an estate or of a dear relative to the loss of a happy immortality? But if our heavenly inheritance be secure, what though we should be reduced into Job's forlorn situation, we have enough left more than to fill up all deficiencies. What though we are poor, sickly, melancholy, racked with pains, and involved in every human misery, heaven will more than make amends for all. But if we have no evidences of our title to that, the sense of these transitory distresses may be swallowed up in the just fear of the miseries of eternity. Alas! what avails it that we play away a few years in mirth and gayety, in grandeur and pleasure, if when these few years are fled, we lift up our eyes in hell, tormented in flames! Oh what are all these things to a candidate for eternity! an heir of everlasting happiness, or everlasting misery!

It is from such convictive premises as these that St. Paul draws his inference in my text; " It remaineth therefore that they that have wives be as though they had none; and they that weep, as though they wept not; and they that rejoice, as though they rejoiced not; and they that buy, as though they possessed not; and they that use this world as not abusing it."

The first branch of the inference refers to the dear and tender relations that we sustain in this life. *It remaineth that those that have wives,* and by a parity of reason those that have husbands, parents, children, or friends dear as their own souls, *be as though they had none.* St. Paul is far from recommending a stoical neglect of these dear relations. That he tenderly felt the sensations, and warmly recommended the mutual duties of such relations, appears in the strongest light in other parts of his writings, where he is addressing himself to husbands and wives, parents and children. But his design here is to represent the insignificancy even of these dear relations, considering how short and vanishing they are, and comparing them with the infinite concerns of eternity. These dear creatures we shall be able to call our own for so short a time, that it is hardly worth while to esteem them ours now. The concerns of eternity are of so much greater moment, that it is very little matter whether we enjoy these comforts or not. In a few years at most, it will be all one. The dear ties that now unite the hearts of husband and wife, parent and child, friend and friend, will be broken for ever. In that world where we must all be in a little, little time, they neither marry nor are given in marriage; but are in this respect like the angels. And of how small consequence is it to creatures that are to exist for ever in the most perfect happiness or misery, and that must so soon break off all their tender connections with the dear creatures that were united to their hearts in the present transitory state! of how small consequence is it to such, whether they spend a few years of their existence in all the delights of the conjugal state and the social life, or are forlorn, bereaved, destitute, widowed, childless, fatherless, friendless! The grave and eternity will level all these little inequalities. The dust of Job has no more sense of his past calamities, than that of Solomon who felt so few; and their immortal parts are equally happy in heaven, if they were equally holy upon earth. And of how small consequence is it to Judas now, after he has been above seventeen hundred years in his own place, whether he died single or married, a parent or childless? This makes no distinction in heaven or hell, unless that, as relations increase, the duties belonging to them are multiplied, and the trust becomes the heavier; the discharge of which meets with a more glorious reward in heaven, and the neglect of which suffers a severer punishment in hell.

Farther, the apostle, in saying that *they who have wives should be as though they had none*, intends that we should not excessively set our hearts upon any of our dearest relatives so as to tempt us to neglect the superior concerns of the world to come, or draw off our affections from God. We should always remember who it was that said, " He that loveth father, or mother, or wife, or children, more than me, is not worthy of me." " He that is married," says St. Paul, in the context, " careth for the things of the world, how he may please his wife," verse 33. But we should beware lest this care should run to excess, and render us careless of the interests of our souls, and the concerns of immortality. To moderate excessive care and anxiety about the things of this world is the design the apostle has immediately in view in my text; for having taught " those that have wives to be as though they had none," &c., he immediately adds, " I would have you without carefulness ;" and this is the reason why I would have you form such an estimate of all the conditions of life, and count them as on a level. Those that have the agreeable weights of these relations ought no more to abandon themselves to the over-eager pursuit of this world, or place their happiness in it ; ought no more to neglect the concerns of religion and eternity, than if they did not bear these relations. The busy head of a numerous family is as much concerned to secure his everlasting interest as a single man. Whatever becomes of him and his in this vanishing world, he must by no means neglect to provide for his subsistence in the eternal world; and nothing in this world can at all excuse that neglect.

Oh that these thoughts may deeply affect the hearts of such of us as are agreeably connected in such relations ! and may they inspire us with a proper insensibility and indifference towards them when compared with the affairs of religion and eternity! May this consideration moderate the sorrows of the mourners on this melancholy occasion, and teach them to esteem the gain or loss of a happy eternity as that which should swallow up every other concern!

The next branch of the inference refers to the sorrows of life. "It remaineth that they that weep be as if they wept not." Whatever afflictions may befall us here, they will not last long, but will soon be swallowed up in the greater joys or sorrows of the eternal world. These tears will not always flow; these sighs will not always heave our breasts. We can sigh no longer than the vital breath inspires our lungs; and we can weep no longer than till death stops all the fountains of our tears; and that will be in a very little time. And when we enter into the eternal world, if we have been the dutiful children of God here, his own gentle hand shall wipe away every tear from our faces, and he will comfort the mourners. Then all the sorrows of life will cease for ever, and no more painful remembrance of them will remain than of the pains and sickness of our unconscious infancy. But if all the discipline of our heavenly Father fails to reduce us to our duty, if we still continue rebellious and incorrigible under his rod, and consequently the miseries of this life convey us to those of the future, the smaller will be swallowed up and lost in the greater as a drop in the ocean. Some desperate sinners have hardened themselves in sin with this cold comfort, "That since they must be miserable hereafter, they will at least take their fill of pleasure here, and take a merry journey to hell." But, alas! what a sorry mitigation will this be! how entirely will all this career of pleasure be forgotten at the first pang of infernal anguish! Oh! what poor relief to a soul lost for ever, to reflect that this eternity of pain followed upon and was procured by a few months or years of sordid guilty pleasure! Was that a relief or an aggravation which Abraham mentions to his lost son, when he puts him in mind, "Son, remember that thou in thy life time receivedst thy good things?" Luke xvi. 25. Thou hadst then all the share of good which thou ever shalt enjoy; thou hadst thy portion in that world where thou didst choose to have it, and therefore stand to the consequences of thine own choice, and look for no other portion. Oh! who can bear to be thus reminded and upbraided in the midst of remediless misery!

Upon the whole, whatever afflictions or bereavements we suffer in this world, let us moderate our sorrows and keep them within bounds. Let them not work up and ferment into murmurings and insurrections against God, who gives and takes away, and blessed be his name! Let them not sink us into a sullen dislike of the mercies still left into our possession. How unreasonable and ungrateful, that God's retaking one of his mercies should tempt us to despise all the rest! Take a view of the rich inventory of blessings still remaining, and you will find them much more numerous and important than those you have lost. Do not mistake me, as if I recommended or expected an utter insensibility under the calamities of life. I allow nature its moderate tears; but let them not rise to floods of inconsolable sorrows; I allow you to feel your afflictions like men and Christians, but then you must bear them like men and Christians too. May God grant that we may all exemplify this direction when we are put to the trial.

The third branch of the inference refers to the joys and pleasures of life. "The time is short; it remaineth therefore that they that rejoice be as if they rejoiced not;" that is, the joys of this life, from whatever earthly cause they spring, are so short and transitory, that they are as of no account to a creature that is to exist for ever; to exist for ever in joys or pains of an infinitely higher and more important kind. To such a creature it is an indifferency whether he laughs or weeps, whether he is joyful or sad, for only a few fleeting moments. These vanishing, uncertain joys should not engross our hearts as our chief happiness, nor cause us to neglect and forfeit the divine and everlasting joys above the skies. The pleasure we receive from any created enjoyment should not ensnare us to make it our idol, to forget that we must part with it, or to fret, and murmur, and repine, when the parting hour comes. When we are rejoicing in the abundance of earthly blessings, we should be as careful and laborious in securing the favour of God and everlasting happiness as if we rejoiced not. If our eternal All is secure, it is enough; and it will not at all be heightened or diminished by the reflection that we lived a joyful or a sad life in this pilgrimage. But if we spend our immortality in misery, what sorry comfort will it be that we laughed, and played, and frolicked away a few years upon earth? years that were given us for a serious purpose, as a space for repentance and preparation for eternity? Therefore, let " those that rejoice be as though they rejoiced not;" that is, be nobly indifferent to all the little amusements and pleasures of so short a life.

And let " those that buy be as if they possessed not." This is the fourth particular in the inference from the shortness of time, and it refers to the trade and business of life. It refers not only to the busy merchant, whose life is a vicissitude of buying and selling, but also to the planter, the tradesman, and indeed to every man among us; for we are all carrying on a commerce, more or less, for the purposes of this life. You all buy, and sell, and exchange, in some form or other; and the things of this

world are perpetually passing from hand to hand. Sometimes you have good bargains, and make large acquisitions.
But set not your hearts upon them; but in the midst of
all your possessions, live as if you possessed them not.
Alas! of what small account are all the things you call
your own upon earth, to you who are to stay here so
short a time; to you who must so soon bid an eternal farewell to them all, and go as naked out of the world as you
came into it; to you who must spend an everlasting duration far beyond the reach of all these enjoyments?   It is
not worth your while to call them your own, since you
must so soon resign them to other hands.   The melancholy occasion of this day may convince you, that success
in trade, and plentiful estate, procured and kept by industry and good management, is neither a security against
death, nor a comfort in it.   Alas! what service can
these houses and lands, and numerous domestics, perform
to the cold clay that moulders in yonder grave, or to
the immortal spirit that is fled we know not where?
Therefore buy, sensible that you can buy nothing upon a
sure and lasting title; nothing that you can certainly call
yours to-morrow.   Buy, but do not sell your hearts to the
trifles you buy, and let them not tempt you to act as if
this were your final home, or to neglect to lay up for yourselves treasures in heaven; treasures which you can call
your own when this world is laid in ashes, and which you
can enjoy and live upon in what I may call an angelic
state, when these bodies have nothing but a coffin, a shroud,
and a few feet of earth.

Finally, let " those that use this world use it as not abusing it."   This is the fifth branch of the inference from the
shortness of time; and it seems to have a particular reference to such as have had such success in their pursuit of
the world, that they have now retired from business, and

appear to themselves to have nothing to do but enjoy the world, for which they so long toiled. Or it may refer to those who are born heirs of plentiful estates, and therefore are not concerned to acquire the world, but to use and enjoy it. To such I say, "Use this world as not abusing it;" that is, use it, enjoy it, take moderate pleasure in it, but do not abuse it by prostituting it to sinful purposes, making provision for the flesh to fulfill the lusts thereof, indulging yourselves in debauchery and extravagance, placing your confidence in it, and singing a *requiem* to your souls: "Soul, take thine ease; eat, drink, and be merry; for thou hast much goods laid up in store for many years." Oh! presumptuous "fool, this night thy soul may be required of thee." Luke xii. 19, 20. Do not use this world to excess,* (so the word may be translated,) by placing your hearts excessively upon it as your favourite portion and principal happiness, and by suffering it to draw off your thoughts and affections from the superior blessedness of the world to come. Use the world, but let it not tempt you to excess in eating, drinking, dress, equipage, or in any article of the parade of riches. Religion by no means enjoins a sordid, niggardly, churlish manner of living; it allows you to enjoy the blessings of life, but then it forbids all excess, and requires you to keep within the bounds of moderation in your enjoyments. Thus "use this world as not abusing it."

The apostle's inference is not only drawn from strong premises, but also enforced with a very weighty reason; "for the fashion of this world passeth away." The whole scheme and system of worldly affairs, all this marrying, and rejoicing, and weeping, and buying, and enjoying, *passeth away*, passeth away this moment; it not only will pass away, but it is even now passing away. The stream

---

* καταχώμενοι. So it is rendered by Doddridge, and others.

of time, with all the trifles that float on it, and all the eager
pursuers of these bubbles, is in motion, in swift, incessant
motion to empty itself and all that sail upon it into the
shoreless ocean of eternity, where all will be absorbed and
lost for ever.   And shall we excessively doat upon things
that are perpetually flying from us, and in a little time will
be no more our property than the riches of the world before the flood?   " O ye sons of men, how long will ye
follow after vanity? why do you spend your money for
that which is not bread, and your labour for that which
profiteth not?"

Some critics apprehend this sentence, *the fashion of
this world passeth away*, contains a fine striking allusion to
the stage, and that it might be rendered, " the scene of this
world passeth away."   " You know," says a fine writer
upon this text, " that upon the stage the actors assume
imaginary characters, and appear in borrowed forms.   One
mimics the courage and triumph of the hero; another appears with a crown and a sceptre, and struts about with
all the solemnity and majesty of a prince; a third puts on
the fawning smile of a courtier, or the haughtiness of a
successful favourite; and the fourth is represented in the
dress of a scholar or a divine.   An hour or two they act
their several parts on the stage, and amuse the spectators;
but the scenes are constantly shifting; and when the play
is concluded, the feigned characters are laid aside, and the
imaginary kings and emperors are immediately divested of
their pretended authority and ensigns of royalty, and appear in their native meanness.

" Just so this world is a great stage that presents as va-
riable scenes, and as fantastical characters: princes, politicians, and warriors, the rich, the learned, and the wise;
and, on the other hand, the poor, weak, and despised part
of mankind possess their several places on the theatre;

some lurk absolutely in a corner, seldom come from behind the scenes, or creep along unnoticed; others make a splendid show and a loud noise, are adorned with the honours of a crown, or possessed of large estates and great powers; fill the world with the glory of their names and actions, conquer in the field, or are laboriously employed in the cabinet. Well, in a little time the scene is shifted, and all these vain phantoms disappear. The king of terrors clears the stage of the busy actors, strips them of all their fictitious ornaments, and ends the vain farce of life; and being brought all upon a level, they go down to the grave in their original nakedness, are jumbled together undistinguished, and pass away as a tale that is told."

Farther: " Upon the Greek or Roman theatres, to which the apostle alludes, the actors, if I mistake not, frequently, if not always, came upon the stage in a disguise, with a false face, which was adapted to the different person or character they designed to assume; so that no man was to be seen with his real face, but all put on borrowed visages. And in allusion to this, the text might be rendered, ' The masquerade of the world passeth away,' pointing out the fraud and disguises which mankind put on, and the flattering forms in which they generally appear, which will all pass away when the grave shall pull off the mask; and ' they go down to the other world naked and open,' and appear at the supreme tribunal in their due characters, ' and can no more be varnished over with fraudulent colouring.' "*

Others apprehend, the apostle here alludes to some grand procession, in which pageants or emblematical figures pass along the crowded streets. The staring crowd wait their appearance with eager eyes, and place themselves in the most convenient posture of observation: they gape at

* Dunlop's Sermons, Vol. I. pp. 212–215.

the passing show, they follow it with a wondering gaze;—
and now it is past, and now it begins to look dim to the
sight, and now it disappears.   Just such is this transitory
world.   Thus it begins to attract the eager gaze of mankind; thus it marches by in swift procession from our eyes
to meet the eyes of others; and thus it soon vanishes and
disappears.*

And shall we always be stupidly staring upon this empty
parade, and forget that world of substantial realities to
which we are hastening?   No; let us live and act as the
expectants of that world, and as having nothing to do with
this world, but only as a school, a state of discipline, to
educate and prepare us for another.

Oh! that I could successfully impress this exhortation
upon all your hearts!   Oh! that I could prevail upon you
all this day to break off your over-fond attachment to earth,
and to make ready for immortality!   Could I carry this
point, it would be a greater advantage than all the dead
could receive from any funeral panegyrics from me.   I
speak for the advantage of the living upon such occasions,
and not to celebrate the virtues of those who have passed
the trial, and received their sentence from the supreme
Judge.   And I am well satisfied the mourning relatives of
our deceased friend, who best knew and esteemed his
worth, would be rather offended than pleased, if I should
prostitute the present hour to so mean a purpose.   Indeed,

---

* Thus Dr. Doddridge understands the text, *Family Expositor*, in loc., and
thus he beautifully describes it in his Hyms:

> " The empty pageant rolls along ;
> The giddy inexperienc'd throng
> Pursue it with enchanted eyes ;
> It passeth in swift march away,
> Still more and more its charms decay,
> Till the last gaudy colours dies."—See HYMN 268.

Lucian has the best illustration of this passage, in this view, that I have
seen.   Dialogue XXXII., Murphy's Edit.

many a character less worthy of praise, often makes a shining figure in funeral sermons. Many that have not been such tender husbands, such affectionate fathers, such kind masters, such sincere, upright friends, so honest and punctual in trade, such zealous lovers of religion and good men, have had their putrefying remains perfumed with public praise from a place so solemn as the pulpit; but you can witness for me, it is not my usual foible to run to this extreme. My business is with you, who are as yet alive to hear me. To you I call, as with the voice of your deceased friend and neighbour,—Prepare! prepare for eternity! Oh! if the spirits that you once knew, while clothed in flesh, should take my place, would not this be their united voice, " Prepare, prepare for eternity! ye frail short-lived mortals! ye near neighbours of the world of spirits! ye borderers upon heaven or hell, make ready, loosen your hearts from earth, and all that it contains: weigh anchor, and prepare to launch away into the boundless ocean of eternity, which methinks is now within your ken, and roars within hearing!" And remember, " this I say, brethren," with great confidence, " the time is short: it remaineth therefore," for the future—" that they that have wives, be as if they had none; and they that weep, as if they wept not; and they that rejoice, as if they rejoiced not; and they that buy, as if they possessed not; and they that use this world, as not abusing it; for the fashion of this world," all its schemes of affairs, all the vain parade, all the idle farce of life, " passeth away." And away let it pass, if we may at last obtain a better country; that is, a heavenly : which may God grant for Jesus' sake! Amen.

SERMON XXIV.

THE PREACHING OF CHRIST CRUCIFIED THE MEAN OF SALVATION.

Cor. i. 22–24.—*For the Jews require a sign, and the Greeks seek after wisdom; but we preach Christ crucified, unto the Jews a stumbling-block, and unto the Greeks foolishness; but unto them which are called, both Jews and Greeks, Christ the power of God, and the wisdom of God.*

If we should consider Christianity only as an improvement of natural religion, containing a complete system of morality, and prescribing a pure plan of worship, it is a matter of the utmost importance, and worthy of universal acceptance. In the one view, it is necessary to inform the world in matters of sin and duty, and reform their vicious practices; and in the other, to put an end to that foolish and barbarous superstition which had over-run the earth, under the notion of religious worship. And these ends the Christian religion fully answers. Never was there such a finished system of morality, or such a spiritual and divine model of worship invented or revealed, as by the despised Galilean, and the twelve fishermen that received their instructions from him.

But this is not the principal excellency of the gospel; and did it carry its discoveries no farther, alas! it would be far from revealing a suitable religion for sinners. A religion for sinners must reveal a method of salvation for the lost, of pardon for the guilty, and of sanctifying grace for the weak and wicked. And, blessed be God! the gospel answers this end; and it is its peculiar excellency that it does so. It is its peculiar excellency that it publishes a crucified Christ as an all-sufficient Saviour to a guilty, perishing world. It is its glorious peculiarity that it reveals a method of salvation every way honourable to God and his government, and every way suitable to our necessities; and that is, by the sufferings of Christ, the Founder of this religion. This is the ground, the substance, and marrow of the gospel; and it is this, above all other things, that its ministers ought to preach and inculcate. It should have the same place in their sermons which it has in that gospel which it is their business to preach; that is, it should be the foundation, the substance, the centre, the drift of all.

This was the practice of the most successful preacher of the gospel that ever bore that commission: I mean St. Paul. And in this he was not singular; his fellow apostles heartily concurred with him, *We preach Christ crucified.* The sufferings of Christ, which had a dreadful consummation, in his crucifixion, their necessity, design, and consequences, and the way of salvation thereby opened for a guilty world, these are the principal materials of our preaching; to instruct mankind in these is the great object of our ministry, and the unwearied labour of our lives. We might easily choose subjects more pleasing and popular, more fit to display our learning and abilities, and set off the strong reasoner, or the fine orator; but our commission, as ministers of a crucified Jesus, binds us to the subject; and the necessity of the world peculiarly requires it. Further, this was not the apostle's occasional practice, or a hasty wavering purpose; but he was determined upon it. " I determined," says he, " not to know any thing among you,

save Jesus Christ, and him crucified:"* 1 Cor. ii. 2.   This
theme, as it were, engrossed all his thoughts; he dwelt so
much upon it, as if he had known nothing else: and as if
nothing else had been worth knowing.   Indeed, he openly
avows such a neglect and contempt of all other knowledge,
in comparison of this: " I count all things but loss, for the
excellency of the knowledge of Christ Jesus, my Lord:"
Phil. iii. 8.   The crucifixion of Christ, which was the most
ignominious circumstance in the whole course of his abasement, was an object in which he gloried; and he is struck
with horror at the thought of glorying in any thing else.
"God forbid," says he, "that I should glory, save in the
cross of our Lord Jesus Christ!" Gal. vi. 14.   In short,
he looked upon it as the perfection of his character as a
Christian and an apostle, to be a constant student, and a
zealous, indefatigable preacher of the Cross of Christ.

But though a crucified Jesus was of so much importance
in a religion for sinners; though this doctrine was the substance of the gospel, and the principal object of the apostle's ministry; yet, as it was not the invention of human
reason, so neither was it agreeable to the proud reasonings, or corrupt taste of the world.   *The preaching of the
cross is, to them that perish, foolishness.*   However, there
were some that had the same sentiment of it with St.
Paul; even as many as were in the way of salvation.
Unto us that are saved, it is the power of God, ver. 18.
To such, that weak and contemptible thing, the cross, was
the brightest display of divine power to be found in the
universe.

Mankind had had time enough to try what expedients

---

* Or *Jesus Christ, even that crucified one.* So Dr. Doddridge renders—'Ιησοῦν
Χριστὸν καὶ τοῦτον ἐσαυρώμενον.   Christ Jesus, and that under the most ignominious circumstances possible, viz., as crucified, was the principal object of
his study, and the substance of his preaching.

their reason could find out for the reformation and salvation of a degenerate and perishing world. The sages and
philosophers of the heathen world had had a clear stage
for many hundreds of years; and they might have done
their utmost without control. But, alas! did any of them,
amid all their boasted improvements, succeed in the experiment? Or could they so much as find out a method
in which sinners might be reconciled to their God? No;
in this most interesting point, they were either stupidly
thoughtless, or all their searches issued in perplexity, or
in the most absurd and impious contrivances. "Where is
the wise? where is the scribe? where is the disputer of
this world?" Let them appear and produce their schemes
upon this head. But *hath not God made foolish the wisdom of this world?* ver. 20. Yes, indeed, he has, by proposing a method most perfectly adapted to this end, which
they not only never would have once thought of, but
which, when revealed, their wisdom cannot relish. Their
wisdom appears but folly, in that when they had the world
to themselves about four thousand years, they could not,
in all that time, find out any successful expedient to amend
and save it. And now, if any thing be done at all, it is
time for God to do it; and how strange, how unexpected,
how mysterious was his expedient! and yet how glorious
and effectual! "For after that, in the wisdom of God,
the world by wisdom knew not God, it pleased God, by
the foolishness of preaching, to save them that believe;"
ver. 21. This was the contrivance for effecting what all
the wisdom and learning of the world could never effect;
the plain unadorned preaching of Christ crucified; which,
both for the matter and manner of it, was counted foolishness.

But how did the world bear this mortification of their
intellectual pride? And what reception did this bounteous

divine scheme meet with when revealed? Alas! I am sorry to tell you: The prejudices of their education were different: but they were unitedly set againt the gospel. The Jews had been educated in a religion established by a series of miracles; and therefore they were extravagant in their demands of this sort of evidence. Notwithstanding all the miracles Christ was working daily before their eyes, they were perpetually asking him, *What sign showest thou?* Those that are resolved not to be convinced, will be always complaining of the want of proof, and demanding more, to vindicate their infidelity. As for the Greeks, their prejudices were of another kind; it was even a proverb among them, that " miracles were for fools;"* and therefore they did not desire that sort of evidence. But *they seek after wisdom.* They had been accustomed to fine orations, strong reasoning, and a parade of learning; and these were the evidences they desired to recommend a doctrine to them. And finding the doctrine of Christ crucified had none of these embellishments, they despised and rejected it as foolishness and nonsense.

The method of salvation by the crucifixion of a supposed malefactor, was so extremely opposite to the reasoning, pride, and prejudices of Jews and Gentiles, that they could not bear it. The Jews expected the Messiah would appear as a victorious temporal prince, who instead of falling a prey to his enemies, would subdue them all with an irresistible power, and advance the family of David to universal empire. And of all other deaths, that of crucifixion was the most odious and abominable to them, because, according to the custom of the Romans, it was the punishment only of slaves; and by their own law it was pronounced accursed; *for it is written, cursed is every·one that hangeth on a tree.* Gal. iii. 13. Deut. xxi. 23.

* Θαύματα μωροις.

Hence, by way of contempt, the Jews called the blessed Jesus *the hanged man*. Nay, this was a shock to the faith of the apostles themselves, until their Jewish prejudices were removed by better information. Finding that, instead of setting up a glorious kingdom, their Master was apprehended by his enemies, and hung upon a cross, they had nothing to say, but, *We trusted that it had been he which should have delivered Israel:* we simply thought so; but alas! now we see our mistake. Luke xxiv. 21. No wonder the cross of Christ should be a stumbling-block to such as had imbibed such notions of the Messiah. When, instead of the power of signs and miracles which they were extravagantly demanding, they saw him crucified in weakness, they could not admit the thought that this was that illustrious character of an universal king. They were so dazzled with worldly glory, and so insensible of their spiritual wants, that they had notions of a spiritual Saviour, and a kingdom of grace; nor could they see how such prophecies were accomplished in one that only professed to deliver from the slavery of sin and Satan, and the wrath to come. Hence they stumbled at the cross, as an obstacle which they could not get over. When Christ called Lazarus from the dead, he had crowds of followers, who attended his triumphant procession into Jerusalem as a mighty conqueror; and when he had fed so many thousands with a few loaves, they were about forcibly to make him king; for they knew that one who could raise his soldiers to life after they had been killed, and support an army with so little provisions, could easily conquer the world, and rescue them from the power of the Romans. But when they saw him seized by his enemies, without making resistance, or working a miracle for his own defence, they immediately abandoned him; and the hosannas of the multitude were turned into another kind of cry, *Crucify him,*

Crucify him. And when they saw him hanging helpless and dying upon the cross, it was demonstrated to them that he was an impostor. It was this that rendered the preaching of Christ by his apostles so unpopular among the Jews: it seemed to them like a panegyric upon an infamous malefactor; and they thought it an insult to their nation to have such a one proposed to them as their Messiah. Thus Christ crucified was to the Jews a stumbling-block.

As to the Greeks, who were a learned philosophical people, it seemed to them the wildest folly to worship one as a God who had been crucified as a malefactor; and to trust in one for salvation who had not saved himself. Their Jupiter had his thunder, and according to their tradition, had crushed the formidable rebellion of the giants against heaven: their Bacchus had avenged himself upon the despisers of his worship; and the whole rabble of their deities had done some god-like exploit, if the fables of their poets were true; and would they abandon such gods, and receive in their stead a despised Nazarene, who had been executed as the vilest criminal by his own nation? Would they give up all their boasted wisdom and learning, and become the humble disciples of the cross, and receive for their teachers a company of illiterate fishermen, and a tent-maker from the despised nation of the Jews, whom they held in the utmost contempt from their ignorance, bigotry, and superstition? No, the pride of their understandings could not bear such a mortification. If their curiosity led them to be St. Paul's hearers, they expected to be entertained with a flourish of words, and fine philosophic reasoning; and when they found themselves disappointed, they pronounced him a babbler, (Acts xvii. 18,) and his preaching foolishness. Corinth, to which this epistle was sent by St. Paul, was a noted city among the

Greeks, and therefore, what he says upon this head was peculiarly pertinent and well applied.

The prejudices of the Jews and Greeks in this respect outlived the apostolic age, as we learn from the writings of the primitive fathers of the Christian church, who lived among them, and were conversant with them. Trypho, the Jew, in a dialogue with Justin Martyr, about a hundred years after St. Paul wrote this epistle, charges it upon the Christians as the greatest absurdity and impiety, that they placed their hopes in a crucified man. Justin, after long reasoning, constrains him at length to make sundry concessions, as, that the prophecies which he had mentioned did really refer to the Messiah; and that, according to these prophecies, the Messiah was to suffer. "But, (says the Jew,) that Christ should be so ignominiously crucified; that he should die a death which the law pronounces accursed, this we cannot but doubt; this I yet find a very hard thing to believe, and therefore if you have any further evidence upon this head, would willingly hear it." Here you see the cross was a stumbling-block, which the Jews could not get over in a hundred years; nay, they have not got over it to this day. Lactantius, about three hundred years after Christ's birth, observes, that the sufferings of Christ were wont to be cast upon Christians as a reproach; it was thought a strange and scandalous thing that they should worship a man; a man that had been crucified, and put to the most infamous and tormenting death by men.*
A heathen, in Minutius Felix, is introduced as saying, "He who represents a man punished for his crime with the severest punishment, and the savage wood of the cross, as the object of their worship, and a ceremony of their

---

* Passionnem quæ velut opprobrium nobis objectari solet: quod et hominem, et ab hominibus insigni supplicio affectum et excruciatum colamus. De ver. Sap. L. IV. c. 16.

religion, ascribes a very proper altar to such abandoned
and wicked creatures, that they may worship that which
they deserve to hang upon."*   And referring to the many
barbarous persecutions they then groaned under, he jeers
them!   "See here," says he, "are threatenings for you,
punishments, tortures, and crosses, not to be adored, but
endured."†   "The calumniating Greek," says Athanasius,
"ridicule us and set up a broad laugh at us, because we
regard nothing so much as the cross of Christ."

Thus you see, the doctrine of the cross was, of all
other things, the most unpopular among Jews and Gentiles, and the most disagreeable to their taste.   A man
could not expect to shine, or cut a figure as a man of
sense and learning, by making this the subject of his
discourses.   But will Paul give it up, and display his
talents upon some more acceptable theme?   This, as a
fine scholar, he was very capable of; but he abhors the
thought.

"Let the Jews and Greeks desire what they please;
we," says he, "will not humour them, nor gratify their
taste; however they take it, we will preach Christ crucified; though to the Jews he should prove a stumbling-
block, and to the Greeks foolishnesss."   And there are
some that relish this humble doctrine.   To them that
believe, both Jews and Greeks, whether learned or un-
learned, whether educated in the Jewish or Pagan religion,
however different their prejudices, or their natural tastes,
to all that believe, notwithstanding these differences, Christ,
that is, *Christ crucified, is the power of God, and the
wisdom of God.*   The wisdom and power of God are not

---

* Qui hominem summo supplicio pro facinore punitum, et crucis ligna
feralia eorum Ceremonias fabulatur, congruentia perditis sceleratisque tribuit
altaria, ut id colant quod merentur. P. 9.

† Ecce vobis minæ, supplicia, tormenta, etiam non adorandæ sed subeundæ
cruces. P. 11.

the only perfections that shine in this method of salvation by the cross; but the apostle particularly mentions these, as directly answering to the respective demands of Jews and Greeks. If the Jew desire the sign of power in working miracles, the believer sees in Christ crucified a power superior to all the powers of miracles. If the Greeks seek after wisdom, here, in a crucified Christ, the wisdom of God shines in the highest perfection. Whatever sign or wisdom the Jew or Greek desires and seeks after, the believer finds more than an equivalent in the cross. This is the greatest miracle of power, the greatest mystery of wisdom in all the world.

The prejudices of the Jews and Gentiles were not only confined to the early ages of Christianity; the same depraved taste, the same contempt of the humble doctrines of the cross may be found among us, though professed Christians; some resemble the Jews, who were perpetually demanding signs; they affect visions and impulses, and all the reveries of enthusiasm, instead of the preaching of Christ crucified. Others, like the Greeks, through an affectation of florid harangues, moral discourses, and a parade of learning and philosophy, nauseate this sort of preaching, and count it foolishness. It is therefore high time for the ministers of the gospel to stand up as advocates for the cross, and with a pious obstinacy to adhere to this subject, whatever contempt and ridicule it may expose them to. For my part, I know not what I have to do, as a minister of the gospel, but to preach Christ crucified. I would make him the substance, the centre, the end of all my ministrations. *And if we*, or an angel from heaven, *preach unto you any other gospel*—you know his doom—*let him be accursed.* Gal. i. 9.

We are to consider the apostles as sent out into the world to reform and save the corrupt and perishing sons of men, and the preaching of Christ crucified as the mean they used for this important end.   This is the formal view the apostle had of preaching Christ in this place, viz., as a mean found out by the wisdom of God to save them that believe, after that all the wisdom of the world had tried in vain to find out a method for this end.   This is evident from verse 21.   *After that the world by all its wisdom knew not God, it pleased God, by the foolishness of preaching;* that is, by the preaching a crucified Saviour, which the world counts foolishness, *to save them that believe.*   This is the excellency of this preaching, this is the reason why the apostle could not be prevailed upon by any motive to desert it, that it is the only mean of salvation; and it is in this view I now intend to consider it.   And if your everlasting salvation be of any importance to you, certainly this subject demands your most serious attention.

I have been the longer explaining the context, because it is so closely connected with the subject I have in view, and reflects light upon it.   And I shall only add, that preaching Christ crucified is the same thing as preaching salvation through the sufferings of Christ.   His sufferings were of long continuance, even from his conception to his resurrection; and they were of various kinds, poverty, weariness and labour, hunger and thirst, contempt and reproach, buffeting, scourging, and a thorny crown.   But there are two words, which by a synecdoche are often used in Scripture to signify all his sufferings of every kind, from first to last; viz., his blood and his cross.   And the reason is, the shedding of his blood, and the death of the cross, were the worst kind and highest degree of his sufferings.   In his crucifixion all his other sufferings were united and centred; this was a complete summary and consummation of them all; and therefore, they are fre-

quently included under this. In this latitude I shall use
the word in this discourse; which I hope you will take
notice of, that no part of the meaning may escape you.

Our inquiry shall be,

What are the reasons that the preaching of Christ crucified is, above all others, the best, and the only effectual
mean for the salvation of sinners?

These reasons may be reduced under two general
heads, namely, That through the crucifixion of Christ,
and through that only, a way is really opened for the salvation of sinners; and that the preaching of Christ crucified makes such a discovery of things, as has the most
direct tendency to bring them to repentance, and produce
in them that temper which is necessary to salvation. Or
in other words, in this way salvation is provided, and sinners are made fit to enjoy it; both which are absolutely
necessary. Our world is deeply and universally sunk in
sin. Men have cast contempt upon the divine government, broken the divine law, and so incurred its penalty;
they have forfeited the favour of God, and rendered themselves liable to his displeasure. Had mankind continued
innocent, there would have been no difficulty in their case.
It would be very plain what would be fit for the divine
government to do with dutiful subjects. But, alas! rebellion against God has made its entrance into our world,
and all its inhabitants are up in arms against Heaven.
This has thrown all into confusion, and rendered it a perplexing case what to do with them. In one view, indeed,
the case is plain, viz., that proper punishments should be
executed upon them. This would appear evidently just
to the whole universe, and no objection could be made
against it, though the criminals themselves, who are parties,
and therefore not fit judges, might murmur against it as
unmerciful and severe. But the difficulty is, how such

rebels may not only be delivered from the punishments
they deserve, but made happy for ever.   If they cannot
be saved in a way that displays the perfections of God,
and does honour to his government; a way in which sin
will meet with no encouragement, but, on the other hand,
an effectual warning will be given against it; a way in
which depraved creatures may be sanctified and made fit
for the pure bliss of heaven; I say, if they cannot be
saved in such a way as this, they cannot be saved at all;
their salvation is quite impossible : for each of these particulars is of such importance, that it cannot be dispensed
with.   God is the best and most glorious being in himself;
and it is fit he should do justice to his own perfections,
and exhibit them in the most God-like and glorious manner
to his creatures; to do otherwise would be to wrong himself, to obscure the brightest glory, and dishonour the
highest excellency.   This therefore cannot be done; men
and angels must be happy, in a way consistent with his
glory, otherwise they must perish; for the display of his
glory is a greater good, and a matter of more importance,
than the happiness of the whole creation.   God is also
the moral Governor of the world.   And his government
over our world is a government over a country of rebels;
and that is a tender point, and requires a judicious management.   An error in government, in such a case, may
have the most fatal consequences, both as to the ruler and
his subjects in all parts of his dominions.   A private person
may, if he pleases, give up his rights, may pardon offenders,
and conceal his justice, and other qualities for government; but a ruler is not at liberty in this case.   He must
maintain his character, make known his capacity for
government, and support the dignity of the law : otherwise, all might rush into confusion and lawless violence.
If the ruler of a small kingdom on our little globe should

fail to discover his justice; if he should pardon criminals, and admit them into favour, and into posts of honour and profit, without giving proper expressions of his displeasure against their conduct, and a striking warning against all disobedience, hòw fatal would be the consequences? how soon would such a ruler fall into contempt, and his government be unhinged? and how soon would his kingdom become a scene of confusion and violence? Criminals might like such an administration; but I appeal to yourselves, would you choose to live under it? Now, how much more terrible and extensively mischievous would be the consequences, if the universal Ruler of men and angels, and of more worlds than we have heard the fame of, should exercise such a government over our rebellious world? It would be reproachful to himself; and it would be most injurious to his subjects; in short, it might throw heaven and earth, and unknown regions of the universe, into confusion.* He must, therefore, display his own rectoral virtues; he must maintain the honour of his government, he must show his displeasure against disobedience, and deter his subjects from it; I say, he must do these things in saving the sinners of Adam's race, or he cannot save them at all. Should he save them upon other terms, it would reflect dishonour upon himself and administration; and it would be injurious to the good of the whole, which is always the end of a wise ruler; for the favour thus injudiciously shown to a part of the creation in our world, might occasion a more extensive mischief in other more important worlds; and so it would be promoting a private interest to the detriment of the public, which is always the character of a weak or wicked ruler. Again,

* Pardoning sin, receiving into favour, and bestowing happiness, are not to be considered, in this case, as private favours; but they are acts of government.

sinners cannot be saved until their dispositions be changed, so that they can relish and delight in the fruition and employments of the heavenly state. Provision, therefore, must be made for this; otherwise, their salvation is impossible.

Now, the way of salvation, through Christ crucified, most completely answers these ends in the most illustrious manner.

1. The salvation of sinners, in this way, gives the brightest display of the perfections of God, and particularly of those that belong to him, as the Supreme Ruler of the rational world, and maintains the honour of his government.

Justice and clemency, duly tempered, and exercised with wisdom, is a summary of those virtues that belong to a good ruler. Now these are most illustriously displayed in a happy conjunction in Christ crucified. Justice shines brighter than if every sin had been punished upon offenders, without any mercy ; and mercy and clemency shine brighter than if every sin had been pardoned, and every sinner made happy, without any execution of justice. Mercy appears in turning the divine mind with such a strong propensity upon the salvation of sinners; and justice appears in that when the heart of God was so much set upon it, yet he would not save them without a complete satisfaction to his justice. Mercy appears in providing such a Saviour; and justice, in inflicting the punishment due to sin upon him, without abatement, though he loved him more than the whole universe of creatures. Mercy, in transferring the guilt from the sinner upon the Surety, and accepting a vicarious satisfaction : justice in exacting the satisfaction, and not passing by sin, when it was but imputed to the darling Son of God. Mercy, in pardoning and saving guilty sinners : justice in punishing their sin.

Mercy, in justifying them, though destitute of all personal merit and righteousness : justice in justifying them only and entirely on account of the merit and righteousness of Christ. Thus the righteousness or justice of God is declared not only in the punishment, but in the remission of sins, Rom. iii. 26, and we are justified freely through his grace, and in the meantime by the redemption that is in Jesus Christ, (verse 24.) Mercy appears in providing a Saviour of such infinite dignity : justice, in refusing satisfaction from an inferior person. Mercy, in forgiving sin : justice, in not forgiving so much as one sin without a sufficient atonement. Mercy, rich, free mercy towards the sinner : justice, strict, inexorable justice towards the Surety. In short, mercy and justice, as it were, walk hand in hand through every step of this amazing scheme. They are not only glorious each of them apart, but they mingle their beams, and reflect a glory upon each other. By this scheme of salvation, by the Cross of Christ, also, the honour of the divine government is secured and advanced. The clemency and compassion of God towards his rebellious subjects, are most illustriously displayed; but, in the meantime, he takes care to secure the sacred rights of his government. Though innumerable multitudes of rebels are pardoned, yet not one of them is pardoned until their rebellion is punished according to its demerit in the person of the Surety. The precept of the law, which they had broken, was perfectly obeyed; the penalty which they had incurred, was fully endured, not by themselves indeed, but by one that presented himself in their place ; and it is only on this footing they are received into favour. So that the law is magnified, and made honourable, and the rights of government are preserved sacred and inviolable, and yet the prisoners of justice are set free, and advanced to the highest honours and blessedness.

2. In this way of salvation, God's hatred to sin is discovered in the most striking light; the evil of sin is exposed
in the most dreadful colours; and so an effectual warning
is given to all worlds to deter them from it. Now it appears, that such is the divine hatred against all sin, that
God can by no means connive at it, or suffer it to pass
without punishment; and that all the infinite benevolence
of his nature towards his creatures cannot prevail upon
him to pardon the least sin without an adequate satisfaction.
Nay, now it appears that when so malignant and abominable a thing is but imputed to his dear Son, his co-equal,
his darling, his favourite, even he could not escape unpunished, but was made a monument of vindictive justice to
all worlds. And what can more strongly expose the evil
of sin ? It is such an intolerably malignant and abominable thing, that even a God of infinite mercy and grace cannot let the least instance of it pass unpunished. It was
not a small thing that could arm his justice against the Son
of his love. But when he was but made sin for us, and
was perfectly innocent in himself, God spared not his own
Son, but delivered him up unto death, the shameful, tormenting, and accursed death of the cross. Go, ye fools,
that make a mock at sin, go and learn its malignity and
demerit at the cross of Jesus. Who is it that hangs there
writhing in the agonies of death, his hands and feet pierced
with nails, his side with a spear, his face bruised with
blows, and drenched with tears and blood, his heart melting like wax, his whole frame racked and disjointed; forsaken by his friends, and even by his Father; tempted by
devils, and insulted by men ? Who is this amazing specta-
cle of woe and torture ? It is Jesus, the eternal Word of
God; the man that is his fellow; his Elect, in whom his
soul delighteth; his beloved Son, in whom he is well
pleased. And what has he done ? He did no wicked-

ness; he knew no sin; but was holy, harmless, undefiled, and separate from sinners. And whence then all these dreadful sufferings from heaven, earth, and hell? Why, he only stood in the law-place of sinners; he only received their sin by imputation. And you see what it has brought upon him! you see how low it has reduced him! and what a horrid evil must that be, which has tremendous consequences, even upon the Darling of heaven! Oh! what still more dreadful havoc would it have made, if it had been punished upon the sinner himself in his own person! Surely all the various miseries which have been inflicted upon our guilty world in all ages, and even all the punishments of hell, do not so loudly proclaim the terrible desert and malignity of sin as the cross of Christ; and hence it follows, that in this way of salvation, the most effectual warning is given to the whole universe, to deter them from disobedience. Rebels are pardoned and made happy, without making a bad precedent, or giving any encouragement to others to repeat the transgression. And this was the tender and critical point. If rebels can be pardoned without reflecting dishonour upon the government, and doing injury to the society, it is well; but how this shall be done is the difficulty. But by the strange expedient of a crucified Saviour, all the difficulty is removed. Sinners can no more presume upon sin, with a pretence that the Supreme Ruler has no great indignation against it, or that there is no great evil in it; for, as I observed, his hatred to sin, and the infinite malignity of it, appear nowhere in so striking and awful a light as in the cross of Christ. Let a reasonable creature take but one serious view of that, and sure he must ever after tremble at the thought of the least sin. Again, though sinners are pardoned in this way, yet no encouragement is given to the various territories of the divine dominions to flatter themselves that they also will be forgiven in case they should imitate the race of man in their rebellion. There is but one instance that we know of in the whole universe of the forgiveness of sin, and the restoration of rebels into favour ; and we are so happy as to find that only instance in our guilty world. But what a strange revolution has been brought about! what amazing miracles have been wrought in order to prepare the way for it! The eternal Son of God must become a man, and die the death of a criminal and slave upon the cross. The very first effort of pardoning grace went thus far; and is it possible it should go any farther; or is there reason to hope that such a miracle should often be repeated?—that the Son of God should hang upon a cross as often as any race of creatures may fall into sin? Such hopes receive a damp from the case of the apostate angels, for whom he refused to die and assume the office of a Saviour. Or is there any other being that can perform that task for some other kingdom of rebels which Christ has discharged for the sons of men? No: he only is equal to it; and none else has sufficient dignity, power, or love. This, therefore, must strike a terror into all worlds at the thought of sin, and leave them no umbrage to presume they shall escape punishment, when they observe that the redeemed from among men could not be saved but at so prodigious an expense, and that the fallen angels are suffered to perish without any salvation provided for them at all.

3. In this way, provision is made for the sanctification of sinners, that they may be fit for the fruitions and employments of the heavenly state. Their taste is so vitiated, that they have no relish for that pure bliss, and therefore can no more be happy there than a sick man can relish the entertainments of a feast. And they are so far gone with the deadly disease of sin, that they are not able to re-

cover themselves; nay, they are not so much as disposed to use means for that end. They are estranged from God, and engaged in rebellion against him; and they love to continue so. They will not submit, nor return to their duty and allegiance. Hence, there is need of a superior power to subdue their stubborn hearts, and sweetly constrain them to subjection; to inspire them with the love of God, and an implacable detestation of all sin. And for this purpose, the Holy Spirit of God is sent into the world: for this purpose he is at work, from age to age, upon the hearts of men. And though he be most ungratefully resisted, grieved, and despitefully treated, and he gives up many to the lusts of their own hearts, yet numerous and glorious are the conquests he has gained over rebellious sinners. Many a stubborn will has he sweetly subdued; many a heart of stone has he softened, and dissolved into ingenuous repentance, like snow before the sun; many a depraved soul has he purified, and at length brought to the heavenly state in all the beauties of perfect holiness. And hence it is, that there is any such thing as true religion to be found upon earth, and that any of the sons of men are recovered to obedience and happiness. But for this inestimable blessing we are indebted to a crucified Christ. It is the dear purchase of his blood, and had it not been so purchased, it would never have been communicated to our guilty world; and consequently never would one rebel have submitted, never would one heart have felt the love of God, among all the sons of men.

Thus, my brethren, you see a way is really opened for the salvation of sinners through the crucifixion of Christ. And oh! what an amazing, unexpected, mysterious way! how far beyond the reach of human wisdom! and how brilliant a display of the divine! To display the perfections of God by occasion of sin more illustriously than if sin had never entered into the world, and thus bring the greatest good out of the greatest evil—to pardon and save the sinner, and yet condemn and punish his sin!—to give the brightest display of justice in the freest exercise of mercy; and the richest discovery of mercy in the most rigorous execution of justice—to dismiss rebels from punishment, and advance them to the highest honours, and yet secure and even advance the honour of the government against which they had rebelled—to give the most effectual warning against sin, even in rewarding the sinner; and to let it pass unpunished, without making a bad precedent, or giving any encouragement to it—to magnify the law in justifying those that had broken it—to discover the utmost hatred against sin, in showing the highest love to the sinner—what an astonishing God-like scheme is this! What a stupendous display of the infinite wisdom of God! Could the Socrateses, the Platos, and other oracles of the heathen world, ever have found out an expedient to answer this end, and reconcile these seeming contradictions! No; this would have nonplussed men and angels; for in what a strange, unthought-of way is it brought about! that the Son of God should become the Son of man; the Head of the universe appear in the form of a servant; the Author of life die upon a cross; the Lawgiver become the subject of his own law, and suffer its penalty, though perfectly innocent! Who would ever have thought of such strange events as these? This is to accomplish astonishing things in an astonishing way. You may as well set a human understanding to draw the plan of a world, as to form such a scheme as this. Oh! it is all divine; it is the wonder of angels; and the greatest miracle in the universe.

Thus, you see, there are very good reasons, reducible to this head, why the Cross of Christ should be the grand weapon to destroy the kingdom of darkness, and rescue sinners and bring them into a state of liberty and glory.

And there are reasons, equally important, that fall under the other head, viz.: That the preaching of Christ crucified makes such a discovery of things, as has the most direct tendency to bring sinners to repentance, and produce in them that temper which is necessary to their salvation.

If a representation of the most moving, the most alluring, and most alarming matters, can affect the mind of man, certainly the preaching of the cross cannot be without effect; for,

1. The preaching of a crucified Saviour gives the strongest assurance to the guilty sons of men, that their offended God is reconcilable to them, and willing to receive them into favour again, upon their penitent return to him. The provision he has made for this end, and particularly his appointing his Son to be their Saviour, and delivering him up to the death of the cross for them, leaves no room for doubt upon this head. It is full demonstration that he is not only willing, but that his heart is earnestly set upon reconciliation; otherwise he would not have been at such infinite pains and expense to remove obstructions, and clear the way for it. Now this is an assurance that the light of nature could never give. It leaves us dreadfully in the dark. And indeed, nothing but an express declaration from God himself can inform us what he intends to do with criminals that lie entirely at mercy, and that he may do what he pleases with. The heathen world were either stupidly thoughtless about this point, or full of anxiety; and their philosophers, amid all their boasted knowledge could only offer plausible conjectures. And yet this assurance is necessary to keep up religion in the world, and encourage rebellious sinners to return to obedience; for with

what heart can they serve that God, as to whom they fear
he will accept of no service at their hands, or return to
him, when they have no encouragement that he will receive them? The hope of acceptance is the spring of repentance and all attempts for reformation; and when once
the sinner concludes there is no hope, he lies down inactive and sullen in despair, or confirms himself in hardened
impenitence, and gives the full rein to his lusts. This the
Psalmist observed long ago: "There is forgiveness with
thee, that thou mayest be feared." Ps. cxxx. 4. The
fear of God is often used in Scripture for the whole of religion; and so it seems taken here. As much as to say,
"There is forgiveness with thee; and thou hast assured us
of it, that religion might be preserved in the world, that
mankind may not abandon thy service as wholly in vain:
or give up themselves to sin, as despairing of acceptance
upon their repentance." Oh! what an acceptable assurance must this be to a guilty, trembling sinner! And how
suitable a remedy to such sinners is the preaching of the
cross of Christ, which alone gives them this welcome assurance!

2. The preaching of a crucified Saviour gives the most
moving display of the love of God; and love is a strong
attractive to repentance and obedience. There cannot be
so strong an expression of love as the sufferings of Christ.
For God to give us life, and breath, and all things—what
is this, in comparison to the gift of his Son, and those immortal blessings which he has purchased with his blood?
To create such a world as this for our residence, to furnish it with such a rich variety of blessings for our accommodation, and to exercise a tender providence over us
every moment of our lives, this is amazing love and goodness. But what is this in comparison of his dying love!
To speak an all-creating word, and to hang, and agonize,

and expire upon the cross! to give us the blessings of the
earth, and to give the blood of his heart; these are very
different things; they will not hold in comparison.

My brethren, let me make an experiment upon you
with the cross of Christ, and try with that weapon to slay
your sins, and break your hearts. Can you view such
agonies and question the love that endured them? Or
can you place yourselves under the warm beams of that
love, and yet feel no love kindled in your hearts in return?
What! not the love of a worm for the dying love of a
God! The apostle John reasons very naturally, when he
says, *We love him, because he first loved us*, 1 John iv. 19.
Love for love is but a reasonable retaliation; especially
the love of a redeemed sinner for the love of a crucified
Saviour. St. Paul felt the energy of this love irresistible :
The love of Christ constraineth us, 2 Cor. v. 14; or according to the emphasis of the original word,* it carries us
away like a resistless torrent. And it appeared to him so
shocking, that he could not mention it without weeping,
that any should be enemies to the cross of Christ: Phil.
iii. 18. Hear what expectations he had from the energy
of his cross who himself hung upon it. "I," says he, "if
I be lifted up from the earth, will draw all men unto me."
John xii. 32. This the evangelist teaches us to understand of the manner of his death, viz., his being raised up
from the earth, and suspended on the cross. There, sinners, he hung to attract your love : and can you resist the
force of this attraction, this almighty magnet? Jesus, if I
may so speak, expects that this will carry all before it :
that every sinner who sees him hanging there will immediately melt into repentance, and be drawn to him by the
cords of love. And oh! can you find in your hearts to
resist! Where, then, is the gratitude? Is that generous

* συνέχει. So Dr. Doddridge translates it.

principle quite dead within you? I must honestly tell you, if the love of a crucified Saviour does not attract your love, nothing else will: you will continue his enemies, and perish as such. This is the most powerful inducement that can be proposed to you: all the reasonings of the ablest philosophers, all the persuasions of the ministers of the gospel, all the goodness of God in creation and providence, will never prevail upon you, if your hearts are proof against the attraction of the cross. But, blessed be his name who died upon it, many an obstinate and reluctant heart has this cross allured and subdued: and oh! that we may all feel its sweet constraints!

3. The preaching of Christ crucified gives such a representation of the evil of sin, and the dreadful punishment due to it, as naturally tends to turn sinners from it, and bring them to repentance. In the Cross of Christ the sinner may see what malignity there is in sin, when it brought such heavy vengeance on the head of the Surety. There the sinner may see how God hates it, when he punished it so severely in his beloved Son. If the almighty Redeemer sunk under the load, how shall the feeble sinner bear up under it? If God spared not his own Son, who was but a surety, how can the sinner escape, who was the original debtor! Oh sinners! never call it cruel that God should punish you for your sins; so he dealt with Jesus, his favourite; and how can you hope for more favour? Read the nature of sin as written in characters of blood on the cross of Christ, and surely you can make light of it no more. You must tremble at the very thought of it; and immediately reform and repent of it. All the harangues of moralists upon the intrinsic deformity, the unreasonableness, the incongruity of vice, never can represent it in such a shocking light as you view it in the sufferings of Christ. And can you look upon your sins

piercing him, stretching him upon the cross, and slaughtering him, and yet not mourn over them? Oh! can you indulge the murderous things that shed his blood? Then you practically pronounce him an impostor, and join the cry of the Jewish rabble, *Crucify him, crucify him!*

4. The preaching of Christ crucified presents us with such a perfect pattern of obedience, as has at once the force of an example, and an inducement to holiness. We need no longer view the law in theory: we see it reduced into an uniform practice, and presented to the life, in the whole of our Lord's conduct towards God and man. We see one in our nature, upon our guilty globe, in our circumstances, behaving exactly agreeable to the divine law, and leaving us an example that we might follow his steps. And shall we not delight to imitate our best friend, and the most perfect pattern that ever was exhibited? Oh! how sweet to walk as he walked in the world, and to trace the steps of his lovely feet! Until the doctrine of the cross was introduced, the world was sadly at a loss about a rule of duty. All the admired writings of pagan antiquity cannot furnish out one complete system even of morality; but here we have a perfect law, and a perfect example, which has the force of a law. Therefore, let us be followers of this incarnate God as dear children.

FOR AN APPLICATION:

1. Hence we may learn our great happiness in enjoying the preaching of Christ crucified. It is but a very small part of the world that has heard this joyful sound; and the time has been, when none of the sons of men enjoyed it in that full evidence which we are favoured with. Now, since it pleases God by this foolishness of preaching, to save them that believe, since this is the most effectual

mean for our recovery from sin and ruin—how great, how distinguishing, how peculiar is our privilege! It becomes us, my brethren, to know our happiness that we may be thankful. How few among the sons of men enjoy this privilege! How does the whole world lie in wickedness! Alas! they are fatally unconcerned, or fruitlessly anxious about a way of reconciliation with God. Their priests and philosophers can afford them no relief in this case; but either mislead them or increase their perplexity. But we have the strongest assurance that God is reconcilable to us; and the clearest discovery of the way. We have the most powerful inducements to repentance, and the most effectual restraints from sin. And what gratitude does this call for from us, to our divine Benefactor! and how solicitous should we be to make a proper improvement of our peculiar advantages!

2. Hence we may learn the shocking guilt and danger of our modern infidels, the Deists, who, like the Greeks, count the preaching of Christ crucified foolishness, and deny the Lord that bought them. This is to reject the best, the last, the only remedy. Now, let them consult their feeble reason; let them go to the oracles of wisdom in the heathen world, and ask of them how guilty offenders may be restored into favour, in consistency with the honour of the divine perfections and government! Alas, they can find no satisfactory answer! Now also they have lost the strongest motive to love and obedience, when they have turned away their eyes from the cross. They have lost the most full and amiable view of the divine nature and perfections that ever was exhibited to the world. Should they shut their eyes against the light of the sun, and abhor all the beauties of nature, it would not be such an astonishing instance of infatuation. St. Paul represents it as the most amazing folly, nay, a kind

of witchcraft and incantation, that any should desert
the truth, that had ever had the least view of Christ crucified. " Oh foolish Galatians! who hath bewitched you,
that ye should not obey the truth, before whose eyes
Jesus Christ hath been evidently set forth, crucified among
you ?" Gal. iii. 1. What wickedness, what madness, what
an unnatural conspiracy against their own lives must it be
for men to reject the only expedient found out by infinite
wisdom and goodness for their salvation! What base ingratitude thus to requite the dying love of Jesus! Can
such monsters expect salvation from his hands? No; they
wilfully cut themselves off from all hope, and bring upon
themselves swift destruction. If the cross of Christ does
not break their hearts, it is impossible to bring them to repentance; the last and most powerful remedy has proved
ineffectual; the last and strongest effort of divine grace
has been used with them in vain. Since they obstinately
reject the sacrifice of Christ, there remains no other sacrifice for their sin, and nothing awaits them but a fearful expectation of wrath and fiery indignation, which shall devour them as adversaries.

3. Hence we should inquire what effect the preaching
of Christ crucified has had upon us. Since this is the
grand mean Divine Wisdom has found out for the recovery
of our wicked world, when all other means had been in
vain, it is of the utmost importance to us, that we should
inquire, whether it is likely to answer this end upon us.
It pleases God by this foolishness of preaching, to save
them that believe. Observe the limitation—*them that believe.* They, and only they, can be saved by it. As for
unbelievers, they cannot be saved in this or any other
way. Let us then abandon every other concern for
a while, and seriously examine ourselves in this point.
Faith comes by hearing; and have we been brought to

believe by hearing the preaching of the cross? Do we relish this humble, despised doctrine with peculiar pleasure? Is it the life and nourishment of our souls, and the ground of all our hopes? Or do we secretly wonder what there can be in it, that some should be so much affected with it? "To them that perish," says the apostle, and to them only, "the preaching of the cross is foolishness." And is that our dreadful characteristic? Or does a crucified Christ appear to us as the wisdom of God, and the power of God, as he does to all them that believe, however different their natural tastes, and the prejudices of their education, and their outward circumstances? Do we suspend all our hopes upon the cross of Christ? Do we glory in it above all other things, whatever contempt the world may pour upon it? Do we feel our necessity of a Mediator in all our transactions with God, and depend entirely upon the merit of his death for acceptance, sensible that we have no merit of our own to procure one smile from God? Have we ever had our hearts enlightened to behold the glory of God in the face of Jesus Christ? Have we admired the scheme of salvation through a crucified Jesus, as illustrating the perfections of God, and securing the honour of the divine government, while it secures our salvation? And do we delight in it upon that account? Or are we quite indifferent about the glory of God, if we may be but saved? Alas! hereby we show we are entirely under the government of selfish principles, and have no regard for God at all. Do our thoughts frequently hover and cluster about the cross with the tenderest affections? And has the view of it melted our hearts into the most ingenuous lamentings for sin, and given us such a hatred against it, that we can never indulge it more? My brethren, put such questions as these home to your hearts, and then endeavour to come to some just conclusion with regard to yourselves. And if the conclusion be against you, then,

4. Consider your guilt and danger—consider your ingratitude in rejecting all the love of God, and a crucified Saviour—your hardness of heart, that has not been broken by such a moving representation—the aversion of your souls to God, that have not been allured to him by the powerful attraction of the cross—and oh! consider your danger: the last remedy has been tried upon you in vain; Christ's grand expedient for the salvation of sinners has had no effect upon you. Had the religion of the Jews, or of the heathen world, failed to bring you to repentance, there might be still some hope that the preaching of Christ crucified might prevail. But, alas! when that fails, how discouraging is your case! Therefore, I pray you, take the alarm, and labour to get your hearts affected with this representation. Oh yield to the attraction of the cross! let him draw you to himself whom you see lifted up on it; and do not attempt such an exploit of wickedness as to resist the allurements of such love. And oh! cry to God for his enlightening Spirit. Alas! it is your blindness that renders you unaffected with this moving object. Did you but know the Lord of glory, who was crucified; did you but see the glory of the plan of salvation through his sufferings, you would immediately become the captive of his cross, conquered by the power of his love. And such, believe me, such you must be, before you can be saved. But if the result of your examination turn out in your favour, then,

5. You may entertain the joyful hope of salvation; of salvation through one that was insulted as not able to save himself; of crowns of glory, through him that wore the crown of thorns; of fulness of joy through the man of sorrows; of immortal life through one that died upon a

cross; I say, you may entertain a joyful hope of all this; for in this way of salvation there is no hinderance, no objection. God will be glorified in glorifying you, the law magnified in justifying you. In short, the honour of God and his government concur with your interest; and, therefore, if you heartily embrace this plan of salvation, you may be as sure that God will save you, as that he will take care of his own glory, for they are inseparably connected. And do not your hearts, dead as they are, spring within you at the thought? Do you not long to see your Saviour on the throne, to whose cross you are indebted for all your hopes? And oh! will you not praise his name while you live, and continue the song through all eternity? Are you not ready to anticipate the anthem of heaven, *Worthy is the Lamb that was slain, to receive power, and riches, and wisdom, and strength, and honour, and glory, and blessing: for thou hast redeemed us to God by thy blood?* Rev. v. 9, 12.

Finally, let me congratulate* my reverend brethren, on their being made ministers of the New Testament, which reveals that glorious and delightful subject, *Christ cruci-fied*, in full light, and diffuses it through all their studies and discourses. The Lamb that was slain is the theme that animates the songs of angels and saints above, and even our unhallowed lips are allowed to touch it without profanation. Let us, therefore, my dear brethren, delight to dwell upon it. Let us do justice to the refined morality of the gospel; let us often explain and enforce the pre-cepts, the graces, and the virtues of Christianity; and teach men to live righteously, soberly, and godly in the world. But let us do this in an evangelical strain, as

---

* The author, towards the end of the discourse, writes, "At a Presbytery in Augusta, April 25, 1759;" which accounts for this particular address to ministers.

ministers of the crucified Jesus, and not as the scholars of Epictetus or Seneca. Let us labour to bring men to a hearty compliance with the method of salvation through Christ; and then we shall find it comparatively an easy matter, a thing of course, to make them good moralists. Then a short hint of their duty to God and man will be more forcible than whole volumes of ethics, while their spirits are not cast in the gospel-mould. Thus may we be enabled to go on, till our great Master shall take our charge off our hands, and call us to give an account of our stewardship!

SERMON XXV.

INGRATITUDE TO GOD AN HEINOUS BUT GENERAL INIQUITY.

2 CHRON. xxxii. 25.—*But Hezekiah rendered not again according to the benefit done unto him.*

AMONG the many vices that are at once universally decried, and universally practised in the world, there is none more base or more common than ingratitude; ingratitude towards the supreme Benefactor. Ingratitude is the sin of individuals, of families, of churches, of kingdoms, and even of all mankind. The guilt of ingratitude lies heavy upon the whole race of men, though, alas! but few of them feel and lament it. I have felt it of late with unusual weight; and it is the weight of it that now extorts a discourse from me upon this subject. If the plague of an ungrateful heart must cleave to us while in this world of sin and imperfection, let us at least lament it; let us bear witness against it; let us condemn ourselves for it; and let us do all we can to suppress it in ourselves. I feel myself, as it were, exasperated, and full of indignation against it, and against myself, as guilty of it. And in the bitterness of my spirit, I shall endeavour to expose it to your view in its proper infernal colours, as an object of horror and indignation.

None of us can flatter ourselves that we are in little or no danger of this sin, when even so good and great a man as Hezekiah did not escape the infection. In the memoirs of his life, which are illustrious for piety, zeal for reformation, victory over his enemies, glory and importance at home and abroad, this, alas! is recorded of him, "That he *rendered not again* to his divine Benefactor *according to the benefit done unto him;* for his heart was lifted up, therefore there was wrath upon him, and upon Judah and Jerusalem."

Many had been the blessings and deliverances of this good man's life. I shall only particularize two, recorded in this chapter. The Assyrians had overrun a great part of the country, and intended to lay siege to Jerusalem. Their haughty monarch who had carried all before him, and was grown insolent with success, sent Hezekiah a blasphemous letter, to intimidate him and his people. He profanely bullies and defies Hezekiah and his God together; and Rabshakeh, his messenger, comments upon his master's letter in the same style of impiety and insolence. But here observe the signal efficacy of prayer! Hezekiah, Isaiah, and no doubt many other pious people among the Jews, made their prayer to the God of Israel; and, as it were, complained to him of the threatenings and profane blasphemy of the Assyrian monarch. Jehovah hears, and works a miraculous deliverance for them. He sends out an angel (one was sufficient), who destroyed in one night, as we are elsewhere told, (2 Kings xix. 35,) no less than a hundred fourscore and five thousand men; which extensive slaughter, a Jewish tradition tells us, was made by means of lightning, a very supposable and sufficient cause. Sennacherib, with the thin remains of his army, fled home inglorious; and his two sons assassinated him at an idolatrous altar. Thus Jerusalem was freed from danger, and the country rescued from slavery and the ravages of war. Nay, we find from profane history, that this dreadful blow proved fatal in the issue to the Assyrian monarchy, which had oppressed the world so long; for upon this the Medes, and afterwards other nations, threw off their submission; and the empire fell to pieces. Certainly so illustrious a deliverance as this, wrought immediately by the divine hand, was a sufficient reason for ardent gratitude.

Another deliverance followed upon this. Hezekiah was sick unto death; that is, his sickness was in its own nature mortal, and would have been unto death, had it not been for the miraculous interposition of Providence. But, upon his prayer to God, he was recovered, and fifteen years added to his life. This also was great cause of gratitude. And we find it had this effect upon him, while the sense of his deliverance was fresh upon his mind; for in his eucharistic song upon his recovery, we find these grateful strains: *The living, the living, he shall praise thee, as I do this day : the father to the children shall make known thy truth. The* Lord *was ready to save me : therefore we will sing my songs to the stringed instruments all the days of our life in the house of the* Lord. But, alas! those grateful impressions wore off in some time; and pride, that uncreaturely temper, began to rise. He began to think himself the favourite of heaven, in some degree, on account of his own personal goodness. He indulged his vanity in ostentatiously exposing his treasures to the Babylonian messengers; which was the instance of selfish pride and ingratitude that seems here particularly referred to.

This pride and ingratitude passed not without evidences of the divine indignation; for we are told, *therefore there was wrath upon him, and upon Judah and Jerusalem.* As the crime was not peculiar to him, so neither is the punishment. Nations and individuals have suffered in this manner from age to age; and under the guilt of it we and our country are now languishing.

In order to make you the more sensible of your ingratitude towards your divine Benefactor, I shall give you a brief view of his mercies towards you, and expose the aggravated baseness of ingratitude under the reception of so many mercies.

Mercy has poured in upon you upon all sides, and followed you from the first commencement of your existence; rich, various, free, repeated, uninterrupted mercy. The blessings of a body wonderfully and fearfully made, complete in all its parts, and not monstrous in any: the blessings of a rational, immortal soul, preserved in the exercise of sound reason for so many years, amid all those accidents that have shattered it in others, and capable of the exalted pleasure of religion, and the everlasting enjoyment of the blessed God, the Supreme Good: the blessing of a large and spacious world, prepared and furnished for our accommodation; illuminated with an illustrious sun, and the many luminaries of the sky: the earth enriched and adorned with trees, vegetables, various sorts of grain, and animals, for our support or convenience; and the sea, a medium of extensive trade, and an inexhaustible store of fishes: the blessing of the early care of parents and friends, to provide for us in the helpless days of infancy, and direct or restrain us in the giddy, precipitant years of youth: the blessing of being born in the adult age of the world, when the improvements of art are carried to so high a degree of perfection; of being born, not among savages in a wilderness, but in a humanized, civilized country; not on the burning, sandy deserts of the torrid zone, nor under the frozen sky of Lapland or Iceland, but in a temperate climate, as favourable to the comfort and continuance of life as most countries upon earth; not in a barren soil, scarcely affording provision of the coarsest sort for its inhabitants, but in a land of unusual plenty, that has never felt the severities of famine: the blessing of not being a race of slaves under the tyranny of an arbitrary government, but free-born Britons and Virginians in a land of liberty : these birthright blessings are almost peculiar to us and our nation.   Let me enumerate also the blessing of a good education; good, at least, when compared to the many savage nations of the earth; the blessing of health for months and years; the blessing of raiment suited to the various seasons of the year; the blessing of rain from heaven, and fruitful seasons, of summer and winter, of seed-time and harvest; the agreeable vicissitude of night and day; the refreshing repose of sleep, and the activity and enjoyment of our waking hours, the numerous and refined blessings of society, and the most endearing relations; the blessings included in the tender names of friend, husband or wife, parent or child, brother or sister; the blessings of peace; peace in the midst of a peaceful country, which has been our happy lot till of late years: or peace in the midst of a ravaged, bleeding country, which is a more distinguished and singular blessing, and which we now enjoy, while many of our fellow-subjects feel a terrible reverse; blessings in every age of life; in infancy, in youth, in adult age, and in the decays of old age; blessings by sea and land, and in every country where we have resided; in short, blessings as numerous as our moments, as long con-tinued as our lives; blessings personal and relative, public and private; for while we have the air to breathe in, the earth to tread upon, or a drop of water to quench our thirst, we must own we are not left destitute of blessings from God.   From God, I say, all these blessings originally flow: and to him we are principally obliged for them. Indeed, they are conveyed to us by means of our fellow-creatures; or they seem to be the spontaneous productions of natural causes, acting according to the established laws of nature.   But then it was God, the Fountain of being and of all good, that gave our fellow-creatures the disposition, the ability, and the opportunity of conveying these blessings to us; and it is the great God who is the Author of those causes which spontaneously produce so many blessings for our enjoyment, and of those laws of nature, according to which they act. These are but channels, channels cut by his hand; and he is the source, the ocean of blessings. Creatures are but the hands that distribute his charity through a needy world; but his is the store from which they derive their supplies. On this account, therefore, we should receive all these blessings as gifts from God, and feel ourselves obliged to him, as the supreme, original Benefactor. Besides, it is very probable to me, that in order to bestow some of these blessings upon us by means of natural causes, God may give these causes a touch to turn them in our favour more than they would be according to the established course of nature; a touch so efficacious as to answer the kind design: though so gentle and agreeable to the established laws of nature, as not to be perceivable, or to cast the system of nature into disorder. The blessings conveyed in this way are not only the gifts of his hand, but the gifts of his immediate hand.

Therefore let God be acknowledged the supreme, the original Benefactor of the world, and the proper Author of all our blessings; and let all his creatures, in the height of their benevolence and usefulness, own that they are but the distributers of his alms, or the instruments of conveying the gifts of his hand. Let us acknowledge the light of yonder sun, the breath that now heaves our lungs, and fans the vital flame, the growing plenty that is now bursting its way through the clods of earth, the water that bubbles up in springs, that flows in streams and rivers, or rolls at large in the ocean; let us own, I say, that all these are the bounties of his hand, who supplies with good the various ranks

of being, as high as the most exalted angel, and as
low as the young ravens, and the grass of the field.
Let him stand as the acknowledged Benefactor of the
universe to inflame the gratitude of all to him, or to
array in the crimson colours of aggravated guilt the ingratitude of those sordid, stupid wretches, who still continue
unthankful.

The positive blessings I have briefly enumerated, have
some of them been interrupted at times; but even the interruption seemed only intended to make way for some
deliverance; a deliverance that reinstated us in the possession of our former blessings with a new and stronger relish,
and taught us, or at least was adapted to teach us, some
useful lessons, which we were not likely to learn, had not
our enjoyment been a while suspended. This very hour
let us turn our eyes backward, and take a review of a
length of ten, twenty, forty, or sixty years; and what a
series of deliverances rise upon us! Deliverances from
the many dangers of childhood, by which many have lost
their limbs, and many their lives; deliverances from many
threatening and fatal accidents; deliverances from exquisite
pains, and from dangerous diseases; deliverances from the
gates of death, and the mouth of the grave; and deliverances for yourselves, and for your dear families and friends!
When sickness, like a destroying angel, has entered your
neighbourhood, and made extensive havoc and desolation
around you, you and yours have escaped the infection,
while you were every day in anxious expectation of the
dreadful visit, and trembling at the dubious fate of some
dear relative or your own ; or if it has entered your houses,
like a messenger of death, it has not committed its usual
ravages in them. Or if it has torn from your hearts one
or more members of your family, still you have some left,
or perhaps some new members added to make up the loss.

When you have been in deep distress, and covered with the most tremendous glooms, deliverance has dawned in the most seasonable hour, and light and joy have succeeded to nights of darkness and melancholy. In short, your deliverances have been endless and innumerable. You appear this day so many monuments of delivering goodness. You have also shared in the deliverances wrought for your country and nation in former and latter times: deliverances from the open violences and clandestine plots and insurrections of enemies abroad, and traitors and rebels at home: deliverances from the united efforts of both, to subvert the British Constitution. and to enslave free-born Britons to civil or ecclesiastical tyranny, or a medley of both; and deliverances from drought, and the threatening appearances of famine, which we have so lately experienced in these parts; and yet they are long enough past to be generally forgotten!

In these instances of deliverances, as well as in the former, of positive blessings, let the great God be acknowledged the original efficient, whatever creatures he is pleased to make use of as his instruments. Fortuitous accidents are under his direction; and necessary causes are subject to his control. Diseases are his servants, his soldiers; and he sends them out, or recalls them according to his pleasure.

And now mention the benefactor if you can, to whom you are a thousandth part so much obliged as to this Benefactor. What a profusion of blessings and deliverances has the Almighty made you a subject of! And oh! what obligations of gratitude do such favours lay upon you! What ardent love, what sincere thanksgiving, what affectionate duty do they require of you! These are the cords of love, the bonds of a man, wherewith he would draw you to obedience.

Dare you now make the inquiry, What returns has this divine Benefactor received from you for all this goodness? Alas! the discovery which this inquiry will make, may convict, shock, confound, and mortify us all; for we are all, in a prodigious degree, though some much more than others, guilty in this respect, guilty of the vilest ingratitude. Alas! are there not many of you that do not return to God the gratitude of a dog to his master? That brute animal who receives but crumbs and blows from you, will welcome you home with a thousand fond and obliging motions. The very dull ox you fodder, knows his owner. But oh! the more than brutal ingratitude of reasonable creatures! Some of you, perhaps, do not so much as acknowledge the agency of Providence in these enjoyments; but, affecting a very unphilosophical infidelity under the name of philosophy, you make natural causes the authors of all good to you, without the agency of the first Mover of all the springs of nature. Others of you, who may be orthodox in your faith as to this point, yet are practical infidels, the most absurd and inconsistent sort in the world; that is, while you certainly acknowledge, and speculatively believe the agency of Providence in these things, yet you live as if there were no such thing: you live thoughtless of the divine Benefactor, and disobedient to him for days and years together. The very mercies he bestows upon you, you abuse to his dishonour, by making them occasions of sin. Do not your consciences now convict you of that monster sin, ingratitude, the most base, unnatural, and yet indulged ingratitude? How do you resent it, if one whom you have deeply obliged should prove ungrateful, and use you ill? But it is impossible any one of your fellow-creatures should be guilty of such enormous ingratitude towards you as you are guilty of towards God; because it is impossible any one of them should be so strongly obliged to you as you are to him.

Ye children of God, his peculiar favourites, whose hearts are capable of, and do actually feel some generous sensations of gratitude, what do you think of your conduct towards such a Benefactor? I speak particularly to you, because you are most likely to feel what I say. Have you rendered again to your God according to the benefits done you? Oh! are you not mortified, and shocked to reflect upon your ingratitude, your sordid, monstrous ingratitude? Do you not abhor yourselves because you were capable of such base conduct? From you I expect such a generous resentment. But, as to others, they are dead in trespasses and sins, dead toward God, and therefore it is no wonder if they are dead to all penitential ingenuous relentings for their ingratitude.

But if all this does not suffice to make you sensible of your enormous guilt in this particular, let me lay before you an inventory of still richer blessings. At the head of this stands Jesus Christ, the unspeakable gift of God. "God so loved the world, (hear it, men and angels, with grateful wonder!) that he gave his only begotten Son, that whosoever believeth in him should not perish, but have everlasting life." John iii. 16. "God sent not his Son into the world to condemn the world, but that the world through him, might be saved." John iii. 17. The comforts of this life alone would be a very inadequate provision for creatures who are to exist for ever in another; for what are sixty or seventy years in the long duration of an immortal being! But in the unsearchable riches of Christ are contained the most ample provisions for your immortal state. Jesus Christ is such a gift as draws all other gifts after it; for so the apostle argues, "He that spared not his own Son, but delivered him up for us all,

how shall he not with him also freely give us all things."
Rom. viii. 32. And the purposes for which he gave this
gift, render it the more astonishing. He gave him not
only to rule us by his power, but to purchase us with the
blood of his heart. He gave him up to death, even the
death of the cross. In consequence of which an economy
of grace, a ministry of reconciliation, is set up in our
guilty world. Various means are appointed, and various
endeavours are used to save you, perishing sinners. For
your salvation Jesus now intercedes in his native heaven,
at the right hand of God. For your salvation the Holy
Spirit strives with you; conscience admonishes you; Providence draws you by blessings, and drives you by chastisements; angels minister to you; Bibles are put into
your hands; ministers persuade you; friends advise you;
and thousands of saints pray for you. For this end,
prayer, preaching, baptism, and the Lord's supper, and a
great variety of means of grace, are instituted. For this
end, heaven is prepared and furnished with many mansions; the pearly gates open, and dart their splendours
from afar to attract our eyes; and things which the eye,
which has seen so many things, had never seen; which
the ear, that has had still more extensive intelligence, had
never heard; nor the heart of man, which is even unbounded in its conceptions, had never conceived, are
brought to light by the gospel. Nay, for this purpose,
your salvation, Sinai thunders, hell roars and throws its
devouring flames, even to warn a stupid world not to
plunge themselves into that place of torment. In short,
the kind designs of redeeming love run through the whole
economy of Providence towards our world. Heaven and
earth, and, in the sense mentioned, hell itself, are trying to
save you. The strongholds of sin and Satan, in which
you are held prisoners, are attacked in kindness to you

from all quarters. What beneficent efforts, what heroic exploits of divine goodness are these! And, blessed be God, these efforts are not in vain.

The celestial regions are fast peopling, though, alas! not so fast as the land of darkness, with numerous colonies from our guilty globe. Even in these dregs of time, when iniquity abounds, and the love of many waxes cold, Jesus is gaining many hearts and saving many souls, in the various apartments of his church. Though you and thousands more should be left, and continue to neglect, yet such excellencies shall not want admirers, such a Physician shall not want employ in our dying world. No, "he shall see of the travail of his soul, and shall be satisfied; and the pleasure of the Lord shall prosper in his hand." Isa. liii. 11. And I doubt not but there are some among you who are the trophies of his victorious love—of his victorious love, I say; for it is by the force of love he sweetly conquers.

Now you, my brethren, are the subjects of this administration of grace; with you, these means are used for your salvation; to you Jesus is offered as a Saviour; and heaven and earth are striving to lodge you safe in his arms. You should not rejoice in the wants of others; but certainly it may make you the more sensible of your peculiar obligations, to reflect that your lot, in this respect, is singular. It is but a very small part of mankind that enjoy these great advantages for a happy immortality. You live under the gospel, whilst the most of the nations of the earth are sunk in heathen idolatry, groaning under Popish tyranny, seduced by Mahometan imposture, or hardened in Jewish infidelity.

And what peculiar obligations of gratitude result from such peculiar, distinguishing favours? Men have obliged you, and you feel the obligation. But can men, can angels, can the whole created universe bestow such gifts upon you, and make such provisions for you, as those which have been mentioned? Gifts of infinite value, dear to the Giver; provisions for an everlasting state; an ever-lasting state of as complete happiness as your nature, in its highest improvements, is capable of. These are favours worthy of God; favours that bespeak him God. And must he not, then, be the object of your supreme gratitude? Can any thing in the world be more reasonable?

And yet—hear, oh earth, with horror; be astonished, O ye heavens, at this: be ye horribly afraid! how little gratitude does God receive from our world after all! How little gratitude from you, on whom these favours are showered down with distinguished profusion! Do not many of you neglect the unspeakable gift of God, Jesus Christ, as well as that salvation which he bought with his blood? Do you not ungratefully neglect the means of your salvation, and resist the generous efforts that are used, from all quarters, to save you! Oh! the mountainous load of ingratitude that lies upon you! enough to sink the whole world into the depth of hell.

But I must now address such of you, who are still more deeply obliged to your divine Benefactor, and whose in-gratitude therefore is black and horrid; I mean such of you who have not only shared in the blessings and de-liverances of life, and lived under the advantages of a dis-pensation of grace, but have experimentally known the love of God to your souls in a manner peculiar to your-selves, and are actually entitled to all the unknown bless-ings prepared for those that love him. If I am so happy as to belong to your number, I am sure I am so unhappy as to share deeply with you in the guilt, the black guilt of ingratitude. When you were dead in trespasses and sins, God quickened you, out of his great love wherewith he loved you. When you were rushing on towards destruction, in the enchanting paths of sin, he checked your mad career, and turned your faces heavenward. When you were sunk into sorrows, borne down with a sense of guilt, and trembling every moment with the fears of immediate execution, he relieved you, led you to Jesus, and, as it were, lodged you safe in his arms. When dismal glooms have again gathered upon your minds, and overwhelming fears rushed again upon you like a deluge, he has relieved you again by leading you to the same almighty and ever-constant Saviour. When your graces and virtues have withered in the absence of the Sun of righteousness, he has again risen upon you with healing in his wings, and revived your languishing souls. He has shed abroad his love in your hearts, which has made this wretched wilderness a paradise to you. He has, at times, afforded you, as you humbly hoped, joy and peace in believing; yea, even caused you to rejoice with *joy unspeakable, and full of glory*. He has met you in your retirements, and allowed you to converse with him in his ordinances, with the heart of a friend. He has, as it were, unlocked his peculiar treasures to enrich you, and given you an unshaken title to the most glorious inheritance of the saints in light. He has made you his own, his own in a peculiar sense: his people, his friends, his children. You are indeed his favourites: you were even so, long before time began. He loved you with an everlasting love, therefore with loving kindness has he drawn you; and having loved you once, he will love you always, and he will continue in his love to all eternity. Neither life, nor death, things present, nor things to come, shall ever be able to separate you from his love. Rom. viii. 38, 39. His love to you is an unbounded ocean, that spreads over eternity, and makes it, as it were, the channel of the ocean of your happiness.

In you he intends to show to all worlds what glorious creatures he can form of the dust, and of the polluted fragments of degenerate human nature.   What is all the profession of kings to their favourites, what are all the benefactions of creatures, nay, what are all the bounties of the divine hand itself within, the compass of time, when compared to these astonishing, unparalleled, immortal, infinite, God-like favours?   They all dwindle into obscurity, like the stars of night in the blaze of noon.

And now I am almost afraid to turn your thoughts to inquire, what return you have made for all these favours, lest you should not be able to bear the shock.   You know you have a thousand times repeated Hezekiah's offence. I need not be particular.   Your conscience accuses you, and points out the particulars; and I shall only join the cry of conscience against you.   Oh! the ingratitude! Oh! the base, vile, unnatural, horrid, unprecedented ingratitude!   From you your God might have expected better things; from you, whom he has so peculiarly, so infinitely obliged, and whose hearts he has made capable of generous sensations.   But oh! the shocking, horrid ingratitude!   Let our hearts burst into a flood of sorrows at the thought.   They may be justly too full to allow us to speak much upon it; but, oh! they can never be too full of shame, confusion, and tender relentings for the crime.   Methinks the thought must break the hardest heart among us.

Let me now add a consideration, that gives an astonishing emphasis to all that has been said.   All this profusion of mercy, personal and relative, temporal and spiritual, is bestowed upon creatures that deserve not the least mercy; creatures that deserve to be stripped naked of every mercy; nay, that deserve to be made miserable in time and eternity; creatures that deserve not to breathe this vital air, to tread the ground, or drink the stream that runs waste through the wilderness, much less to enjoy all the blessings which the infinite merit of Jesus could purchase, or the infinite goodness of God can bestow; creatures that are so far from deserving to be delivered from the calamities of life, that they deserve to have them all heightened and multiplied, till they convey them to the more intolerable punishments of hell; creatures that are so far from making adequate returns, that they are perpetually offending their God to his face; and every day receiving blessings from him, and every day sinning against him. Oh! astonishing! most astonishing! This wonder is pointed out by Jesus Christ himself, who best knows what is truly marvellous. The Most High, says he, "is kind to the unthankful and to the evil." Luke vi. 35. "Your heavenly Father maketh his sun to rise on the evil and on the good, and sendeth rain on the just and on the unjust." Matt. v. 45.

It need afford you no surprise, if my subject so overwhelms me, as to disable me from making a formal application of it. I leave you to your own thoughts upon it. And I am apt to think they will constrain you to cry out in a consternation with me, "Oh! the amazing, horrid, base, unprecedented ingratitude of man! and oh! the amazing, free, rich, overflowing, infinite, unprecedented goodness of God! Let these two miracles be the wonder of the whole universe!"

One prayer, and I have done. May our divine Benefactor, among his other blessings, bestow upon us that of a thankful heart, and enable us to give sincere, fervent, and perpetual praise to his name, through Jesus Christ, his unspeakable gift! Amen.

END OF VOL. I.